MW00387408

CODING THEORY AND CRYPTOGRAPHY

THE ESSENTIALS

PURE AND APPLIED MATHEMATICS

A Program of Monographs, Textbooks, and Lecture Notes

EXECUTIVE EDITORS

Earl J. Taft
Rutgers University
New Brunswick, New Jersey

Zuhair Nashed
University of Delaware
Newark, Delaware

EDITORIAL BOARD

M. S. Baouendi
University of California, San Diego

Jane Cronin
Rutgers University

Jack K. Hale
Georgia Institute of Technology

S. Kobayashi
University of California, Berkeley

Marvin Marcus
University of California, Santa Barbara

W. S. Massey
Yale University

Anil Nerode
Cornell University

Donald Passman
University of Wisconsin, Madison

Fred S. Roberts
Rutgers University

David L. Russell
Virginia Polytechnic Institute and State University

Walter Schempp
Universität Siegen

Mark Teply
University of Wisconsin, Milwaukee

MONOGRAPHS AND TEXTBOOKS IN PURE AND APPLIED MATHEMATICS

1. *K. Yano,* Integral Formulas in Riemannian Geometry (1970)
2. *S. Kobayashi,* Hyperbolic Manifolds and Holomorphic Mappings (1970)
3. *V. S. Vladimirov,* Equations of Mathematical Physics (A. Jeffrey, ed.; A. Littlewood, trans.) (1970)
4. *B. N. Pshenichnyi,* Necessary Conditions for an Extremum (L. Neustadt, translation ed.; K. Makowski, trans.) (1971)
5. *L. Narici et al.,* Functional Analysis and Valuation Theory (1971)
6. *S. S. Passman,* Infinite Group Rings (1971)
7. *L. Dornhoff,* Group Representation Theory. Part A: Ordinary Representation Theory. Part B: Modular Representation Theory (1971, 1972)
8. *W. Boothby and G. L. Weiss, eds.,* Symmetric Spaces (1972)
9. *Y. Matsushima,* Differentiable Manifolds (E. T. Kobayashi, trans.) (1972)
10. *L. E. Ward, Jr.,* Topology (1972)
11. *A. Babakhanian,* Cohomological Methods in Group Theory (1972)
12. *R. Gilmer,* Multiplicative Ideal Theory (1972)
13. *J. Yeh,* Stochastic Processes and the Wiener Integral (1973)
14. *J. Barros-Neto,* Introduction to the Theory of Distributions (1973)
15. *R. Larsen,* Functional Analysis (1973)
16. *K. Yano and S. Ishihara,* Tangent and Cotangent Bundles (1973)
17. *C. Procesi,* Rings with Polynomial Identities (1973)
18. *R. Hermann,* Geometry, Physics, and Systems (1973)
19. *N. R. Wallach,* Harmonic Analysis on Homogeneous Spaces (1973)
20. *J. Dieudonné,* Introduction to the Theory of Formal Groups (1973)
21. *I. Vaisman,* Cohomology and Differential Forms (1973)
22. *B.-Y. Chen,* Geometry of Submanifolds (1973)
23. *M. Marcus,* Finite Dimensional Multilinear Algebra (in two parts) (1973, 1975)
24. *R. Larsen,* Banach Algebras (1973)
25. *R. O. Kujala and A. L. Vitter, eds.,* Value Distribution Theory: Part A; Part B: Deficit and Bezout Estimates by Wilhelm Stoll (1973)
26. *K. B. Stolarsky,* Algebraic Numbers and Diophantine Approximation (1974)
27. *A. R. Magid,* The Separable Galois Theory of Commutative Rings (1974)
28. *B. R. McDonald,* Finite Rings with Identity (1974)
29. *J. Satake,* Linear Algebra (S. Koh et al., trans.) (1975)
30. *J. S. Golan,* Localization of Noncommutative Rings (1975)
31. *G. Klambauer,* Mathematical Analysis (1975)
32. *M. K. Agoston,* Algebraic Topology (1976)
33. *K. R. Goodearl,* Ring Theory (1976)
34. *L. E. Mansfield,* Linear Algebra with Geometric Applications (1976)
35. *N. J. Pullman,* Matrix Theory and Its Applications (1976)
36. *B. R. McDonald,* Geometric Algebra Over Local Rings (1976)
37. *C. W. Groetsch,* Generalized Inverses of Linear Operators (1977)
38. *J. E. Kuczkowski and J. L. Gersting,* Abstract Algebra (1977)
39. *C. O. Christenson and W. L. Voxman,* Aspects of Topology (1977)
40. *M. Nagata,* Field Theory (1977)
41. *R. L. Long,* Algebraic Number Theory (1977)
42. *W. F. Pfeffer,* Integrals and Measures (1977)
43. *R. L. Wheeden and A. Zygmund,* Measure and Integral (1977)
44. *J. H. Curtiss,* Introduction to Functions of a Complex Variable (1978)
45. *K. Hrbacek and T. Jech,* Introduction to Set Theory (1978)
46. *W. S. Massey,* Homology and Cohomology Theory (1978)
47. *M. Marcus,* Introduction to Modern Algebra (1978)
48. *E. C. Young,* Vector and Tensor Analysis (1978)
49. *S. B. Nadler, Jr.,* Hyperspaces of Sets (1978)
50. *S. K. Segal,* Topics in Group Kings (1978)
51. *A. C. M. van Rooij,* Non-Archimedean Functional Analysis (1978)
52. *L. Corwin and R. Szczarba,* Calculus in Vector Spaces (1979)
53. *C. Sadosky,* Interpolation of Operators and Singular Integrals (1979)
54. *J. Cronin,* Differential Equations (1980)
55. *C. W. Groetsch,* Elements of Applicable Functional Analysis (1980)

56. *I. Vaisman,* Foundations of Three-Dimensional Euclidean Geometry (1980)
57. *H. I. Freedan,* Deterministic Mathematical Models in Population Ecology (1980)
58. *S. B. Chae,* Lebesgue Integration (1980)
59. *C. S. Rees et al.,* Theory and Applications of Fourier Analysis (1981)
60. *L. Nachbin,* Introduction to Functional Analysis (R. M. Aron, trans.) (1981)
61. *G. Orzech and M. Orzech,* Plane Algebraic Curves (1981)
62. *R. Johnsonbaugh and W. E. Pfaffenberger,* Foundations of Mathematical Analysis (1981)
63. *W. L. Voxman and R. H. Goetschel,* Advanced Calculus (1981)
64. *L. J. Corwin and R. H. Szczarba,* Multivariable Calculus (1982)
65. *V. I. Istrăţescu,* Introduction to Linear Operator Theory (1981)
66. *R. D. Järvinen,* Finite and Infinite Dimensional Linear Spaces (1981)
67. *J. K. Beem and P. E. Ehrlich,* Global Lorentzian Geometry (1981)
68. *D. L. Armacost,* The Structure of Locally Compact Abelian Groups (1981)
69. *J. W. Brewer and M. K. Smith, eds.,* Emmy Noether: A Tribute (1981)
70. *K. H. Kim,* Boolean Matrix Theory and Applications (1982)
71. *T. W. Wieting,* The Mathematical Theory of Chromatic Plane Ornaments (1982)
72. *D. B. Gauld,* Differential Topology (1982)
73. *R. L. Faber,* Foundations of Euclidean and Non-Euclidean Geometry (1983)
74. *M. Carmeli,* Statistical Theory and Random Matrices (1983)
75. *J. H. Carruth et al.,* The Theory of Topological Semigroups (1983)
76. *R. L. Faber,* Differential Geometry and Relativity Theory (1983)
77. *S. Barnett,* Polynomials and Linear Control Systems (1983)
78. *G. Karpilovsky,* Commutative Group Algebras (1983)
79. *F. Van Oystaeyen and A. Verschoren,* Relative Invariants of Rings (1983)
80. *I. Vaisman,* A First Course in Differential Geometry (1984)
81. *G. W. Swan,* Applications of Optimal Control Theory in Biomedicine (1984)
82. *T. Petrie and J. D. Randall,* Transformation Groups on Manifolds (1984)
83. *K. Goebel and S. Reich,* Uniform Convexity, Hyperbolic Geometry, and Nonexpansive Mappings (1984)
84. *T. Albu and C. Năstăsescu,* Relative Finiteness in Module Theory (1984)
85. *K. Hrbacek and T. Jech,* Introduction to Set Theory: Second Edition (1984)
86. *F. Van Oystaeyen and A. Verschoren,* Relative Invariants of Rings (1984)
87. *B. R. McDonald,* Linear Algebra Over Commutative Rings (1984)
88. *M. Namba,* Geometry of Projective Algebraic Curves (1984)
89. *G. F. Webb,* Theory of Nonlinear Age-Dependent Population Dynamics (1985)
90. *M. R. Bremner et al.,* Tables of Dominant Weight Multiplicities for Representations of Simple Lie Algebras (1985)
91. *A. E. Fekete,* Real Linear Algebra (1985)
92. *S. B. Chae,* Holomorphy and Calculus in Normed Spaces (1985)
93. *A. J. Jerri,* Introduction to Integral Equations with Applications (1985)
94. *G. Karpilovsky,* Projective Representations of Finite Groups (1985)
95. *L. Narici and E. Beckenstein,* Topological Vector Spaces (1985)
96. *J. Weeks,* The Shape of Space (1985)
97. *P. R. Gribik and K. O. Kortanek,* Extremal Methods of Operations Research (1985)
98. *J.-A. Chao and W. A. Woyczynski, eds.,* Probability Theory and Harmonic Analysis (1986)
99. *G. D. Crown et al.,* Abstract Algebra (1986)
100. *J. H. Carruth et al.,* The Theory of Topological Semigroups, Volume 2 (1986)
101. *R. S. Doran and V. A. Belfi,* Characterizations of C*-Algebras (1986)
102. *M. W. Jeter,* Mathematical Programming (1986)
103. *M. Altman,* A Unified Theory of Nonlinear Operator and Evolution Equations with Applications (1986)
104. *A. Verschoren,* Relative Invariants of Sheaves (1987)
105. *R. A. Usmani,* Applied Linear Algebra (1987)
106. *P. Blass and J. Lang,* Zariski Surfaces and Differential Equations in Characteristic $p > 0$ (1987)
107. *J. A. Reneke et al.,* Structured Hereditary Systems (1987)
108. *H. Busemann and B. B. Phadke,* Spaces with Distinguished Geodesics (1987)
109. *R. Harte,* Invertibility and Singularity for Bounded Linear Operators (1988)
110. *G. S. Ladde et al.,* Oscillation Theory of Differential Equations with Deviating Arguments (1987)
111. *L. Dudkin et al.,* Iterative Aggregation Theory (1987)
112. *T. Okubo,* Differential Geometry (1987)

113. *D. L. Stancl and M. L. Stancl,* Real Analysis with Point-Set Topology (1987)
114. *T. C. Gard,* Introduction to Stochastic Differential Equations (1988)
115. *S. S. Abhyankar,* Enumerative Combinatorics of Young Tableaux (1988)
116. *H. Strade and R. Farnsteiner,* Modular Lie Algebras and Their Representations (1988)
117. *J. A. Huckaba,* Commutative Rings with Zero Divisors (1988)
118. *W. D. Wallis,* Combinatorial Designs (1988)
119. *W. Więsław,* Topological Fields (1988)
120. *G. Karpilovsky,* Field Theory (1988)
121. *S. Caenepeel and F. Van Oystaeyen,* Brauer Groups and the Cohomology of Graded Rings (1989)
122. *W. Kozlowski,* Modular Function Spaces (1988)
123. *E. Lowen-Colebunders,* Function Classes of Cauchy Continuous Maps (1989)
124. *M. Pavel,* Fundamentals of Pattern Recognition (1989)
125. *V. Lakshmikantham et al.,* Stability Analysis of Nonlinear Systems (1989)
126. *R. Sivaramakrishnan,* The Classical Theory of Arithmetic Functions (1989)
127. *N. A. Watson,* Parabolic Equations on an Infinite Strip (1989)
128. *K. J. Hastings,* Introduction to the Mathematics of Operations Research (1989)
129. *B. Fine,* Algebraic Theory of the Bianchi Groups (1989)
130. *D. N. Dikranjan et al.,* Topological Groups (1989)
131. *J. C. Morgan II,* Point Set Theory (1990)
132. *P. Biler and A. Witkowski,* Problems in Mathematical Analysis (1990)
133. *H. J. Sussmann,* Nonlinear Controllability and Optimal Control (1990)
134. *J.-P. Florens et al.,* Elements of Bayesian Statistics (1990)
135. *N. Shell,* Topological Fields and Near Valuations (1990)
136. *B. F. Doolin and C. F. Martin,* Introduction to Differential Geometry for Engineers (1990)
137. *S. S. Holland, Jr.,* Applied Analysis by the Hilbert Space Method (1990)
138. *J. Okniński,* Semigroup Algebras (1990)
139. *K. Zhu,* Operator Theory in Function Spaces (1990)
140. *G. B. Price,* An Introduction to Multicomplex Spaces and Functions (1991)
141. *R. B. Darst,* Introduction to Linear Programming (1991)
142. *P. L. Sachdev,* Nonlinear Ordinary Differential Equations and Their Applications (1991)
143. *T. Husain,* Orthogonal Schauder Bases (1991)
144. *J. Foran,* Fundamentals of Real Analysis (1991)
145. *W. C. Brown,* Matrices and Vector Spaces (1991)
146. *M. M. Rao and Z. D. Ren,* Theory of Orlicz Spaces (1991)
147. *J. S. Golan and T. Head,* Modules and the Structures of Rings (1991)
148. *C. Small,* Arithmetic of Finite Fields (1991)
149. *K. Yang,* Complex Algebraic Geometry (1991)
150. *D. G. Hoffman et al.,* Coding Theory (1991)
151. *M. O. González,* Classical Complex Analysis (1992)
152. *M. O. González,* Complex Analysis (1992)
153. *L. W. Baggett,* Functional Analysis (1992)
154. *M. Sniedovich,* Dynamic Programming (1992)
155. *R. P. Agarwal,* Difference Equations and Inequalities (1992)
156. *C. Brezinski,* Biorthogonality and Its Applications to Numerical Analysis (1992)
157. *C. Swartz,* An Introduction to Functional Analysis (1992)
158. *S. B. Nadler, Jr.,* Continuum Theory (1992)
159. *M. A. Al-Gwaiz,* Theory of Distributions (1992)
160. *E. Perry,* Geometry: Axiomatic Developments with Problem Solving (1992)
161. *E. Castillo and M. R. Ruiz-Cobo,* Functional Equations and Modelling in Science and Engineering (1992)
162. *A. J. Jerri,* Integral and Discrete Transforms with Applications and Error Analysis (1992)
163. *A. Charlier et al.,* Tensors and the Clifford Algebra (1992)
164. *P. Biler and T. Nadzieja,* Problems and Examples in Differential Equations (1992)
165. *E. Hansen,* Global Optimization Using Interval Analysis (1992)
166. *S. Guerre-Delabrière,* Classical Sequences in Banach Spaces (1992)
167. *Y. C. Wong,* Introductory Theory of Topological Vector Spaces (1992)
168. *S. H. Kulkarni and B. V. Limaye,* Real Function Algebras (1992)
169. *W. C. Brown,* Matrices Over Commutative Rings (1993)
170. *J. Loustau and M. Dillon,* Linear Geometry with Computer Graphics (1993)
171. *W. V. Petryshyn,* Approximation-Solvability of Nonlinear Functional and Differential Equations (1993)

172. *E. C. Young*, Vector and Tensor Analysis: Second Edition (1993)
173. *T. A. Bick*, Elementary Boundary Value Problems (1993)
174. *M. Pavel*, Fundamentals of Pattern Recognition: Second Edition (1993)
175. *S. A. Albeverio et al.*, Noncommutative Distributions (1993)
176. *W. Fulks*, Complex Variables (1993)
177. *M. M. Rao*, Conditional Measures and Applications (1993)
178. *A. Janicki and A. Weron*, Simulation and Chaotic Behavior of α-Stable Stochastic Processes (1994)
179. *P. Neittaanmäki and D. Tiba*, Optimal Control of Nonlinear Parabolic Systems (1994)
180. *J. Cronin*, Differential Equations: Introduction and Qualitative Theory, Second Edition (1994)
181. *S. Heikkilä and V. Lakshmikantham*, Monotone Iterative Techniques for Discontinuous Nonlinear Differential Equations (1994)
182. *X. Mao*, Exponential Stability of Stochastic Differential Equations (1994)
183. *B. S. Thomson*, Symmetric Properties of Real Functions (1994)
184. *J. E. Rubio*, Optimization and Nonstandard Analysis (1994)
185. *J. L. Bueso et al.*, Compatibility, Stability, and Sheaves (1995)
186. *A. N. Michel and K. Wang*, Qualitative Theory of Dynamical Systems (1995)
187. *M. R. Darnel*, Theory of Lattice-Ordered Groups (1995)
188. *Z. Naniewicz and P. D. Panagiotopoulos*, Mathematical Theory of Hemivariational Inequalities and Applications (1995)
189. *L. J. Corwin and R. H. Szczarba*, Calculus in Vector Spaces: Second Edition (1995)
190. *L. H. Erbe et al.*, Oscillation Theory for Functional Differential Equations (1995)
191. *S. Agaian et al.*, Binary Polynomial Transforms and Nonlinear Digital Filters (1995)
192. *M. I. Gil'*, Norm Estimations for Operation-Valued Functions and Applications (1995)
193. *P. A. Grillet*, Semigroups: An Introduction to the Structure Theory (1995)
194. *S. Kichenassamy*, Nonlinear Wave Equations (1996)
195. *V. F. Krotov*, Global Methods in Optimal Control Theory (1996)
196. *K. I. Beidar et al.*, Rings with Generalized Identities (1996)
197. *V. I. Arnautov et al.*, Introduction to the Theory of Topological Rings and Modules (1996)
198. *G. Sierksma*, Linear and Integer Programming (1996)
199. *R. Lasser*, Introduction to Fourier Series (1996)
200. *V. Sima*, Algorithms for Linear-Quadratic Optimization (1996)
201. *D. Redmond*, Number Theory (1996)
202. *J. K. Beem et al.*, Global Lorentzian Geometry: Second Edition (1996)
203. *M. Fontana et al.*, Prüfer Domains (1997)
204. *H. Tanabe*, Functional Analytic Methods for Partial Differential Equations (1997)
205. *C. Q. Zhang*, Integer Flows and Cycle Covers of Graphs (1997)
206. *E. Spiegel and C. J. O'Donnell*, Incidence Algebras (1997)
207. *B. Jakubczyk and W. Respondek*, Geometry of Feedback and Optimal Control (1998)
208. *T. W. Haynes et al.*, Fundamentals of Domination in Graphs (1998)
209. *T. W. Haynes et al.*, Domination in Graphs: Advanced Topics (1998)
210. *L. A. D'Alotto et al.*, A Unified Signal Algebra Approach to Two-Dimensional Parallel Digital Signal Processing (1998)
211. *F. Halter-Koch*, Ideal Systems (1998)
212. *N. K. Govil et al.*, Approximation Theory (1998)
213. *R. Cross*, Multivalued Linear Operators (1998)
214. *A. A. Martynyuk*, Stability by Liapunov's Matrix Function Method with Applications (1998)
215. *A. Favini and A. Yagi*, Degenerate Differential Equations in Banach Spaces (1999)
216. *A. Illanes and S. Nadler, Jr.*, Hyperspaces: Fundamentals and Recent Advances (1999)
217. *G. Kato and D. Struppa*, Fundamentals of Algebraic Microlocal Analysis (1999)
218. *G. X.-Z. Yuan*, KKM Theory and Applications in Nonlinear Analysis (1999)
219. *D. Motreanu and N. H. Pavel*, Tangency, Flow Invariance for Differential Equations, and Optimization Problems (1999)
220. *K. Hrbacek and T. Jech*, Introduction to Set Theory, Third Edition (1999)
221. *G. E. Kolosov*, Optimal Design of Control Systems (1999)
222. *N. L. Johnson*, Subplane Covered Nets (2000)
223. *B. Fine and G. Rosenberger*, Algebraic Generalizations of Discrete Groups (1999)
224. *M. Väth*, Volterra and Integral Equations of Vector Functions (2000)
225. *S. S. Miller and P. T. Mocanu*, Differential Subordinations (2000)

226. *R. Li et al.*, Generalized Difference Methods for Differential Equations: Numerical Analysis of Finite Volume Methods (2000)
227. *H. Li and F. Van Oystaeyen*, A Primer of Algebraic Geometry (2000)
228. *R. P. Agarwal*, Difference Equations and Inequalities: Theory, Methods, and Applications, Second Edition (2000)
229. *A. B. Kharazishvili*, Strange Functions in Real Analysis (2000)
230. *J. M. Appell et al.*, Partial Integral Operators and Integro-Differential Equations (2000)
231. *A. I. Prilepko et al.*, Methods for Solving Inverse Problems in Mathematical Physics (2000)
232. *F. Van Oystaeyen,* Algebraic Geometry for Associative Algebras (2000)
233. *D. Jagerman*, Difference Equations with Applications to Queues (2000)
234. *D.R. Hankerson, D. G. Hoffman, D. A. Leonard, C.C. Lindner, K.T. Phelps, C. A. Rodger, J. R. Wall* Coding Theory and Cryptography: The Essentials, Second Edition, Revised and Expanded (2000)
235. *S. Dascalescu et al.* Hopf Algebras: An Introduction (2000)
236. *Hagen et al.* C^*-Algebras and Numerical Analysis (2000)
237. *Y. Talpaert*, Differential Geometry: With Applications to Mechanics and Physics (2000)

Additional Volumes in Preparation

A. Samarskii, The Theory of Difference Schemes

CODING THEORY AND CRYPTOGRAPHY

THE ESSENTIALS

Second Edition, Revised and Expanded

D. R. Hankerson
D. G. Hoffman
D. A. Leonard
C. C. Lindner
K. T. Phelps
C. A. Rodger
J. R. Wall

Auburn University
Auburn, Alabama

MARCEL DEKKER, INC. NEW YORK • BASEL

First edition: D. G. Hoffman, D. A. Leonard, C. C. Lindner, K. T. Phelps, C. A. Rodger, J. R. Wall, *Coding Theory: The Essentials*. New York: Marcel Dekker, 1991.

ISBN: 0-8247-0465-7

This book is printed on acid-free paper.

Headquarters
Marcel Dekker, Inc.
270 Madison Avenue, New York, NY 10016
tel: 212-696-9000; fax: 212-685-4540

Eastern Hemisphere Distribution
Marcel Dekker AG
Hutgasse 4, Postfach 812, CH-4001 Basel, Switzerland
tel: 41-61-261-8482; fax: 41-61-261-8896

World Wide Web
http://www.dekker.com

The publisher offers discounts on this book when ordered in bulk quantities. For more information, write to Special Sales/Professional Marketing at the headquarters address above.

Copyright © 2000 by Marcel Dekker, Inc. All Rights Reserved.

Neither this book nor any part may be reproduced or transmitted in any form or by any means, electronic or mechanical, including photocopying, microfilming, and recording, or by any information storage and retrieval system, without permission in writing from the publisher.

Current printing (last digit):
10 9 8 7 6 5 4 3

PRINTED IN THE UNITED STATES OF AMERICA

To our wonderful spouses

Cindy, Gail, Jane, Ann, Janet, and Sue

Our children

Noel, Ian, Tim, Curt, Jimmy, Andrew, Meghan, Katrina, and Rebecca

And our parents

Eileen and Richard, Vally and Gale, Marjorie and Lewis, Mary and Charles
Ethel and Richard, Iris and Ian, and Beulah and Walter

Preface

This book, revised and updated from the first edition, is designed to teach coding theory and cryptography in a mathematically sound manner to students in engineering, computer science, and mathematics. It differs from most other texts on the subject in two important ways: the "just in time philosophy," and unnecessary mathematical generalizations are omitted.

The "just in time" philosophy consists of introducing the necessary mathematics just in time to be applied; i.e., juxtaposed, with the applications. We don't have 200 pages of mathematics (most of which is irrelevant) followed by 200 pages of coding theory and cryptography. So the format is roughly: mathematics, applications, mathematics, applications, etc. Avoiding unnecessary generalizations means that we don't find it necessary, for example, to describe a cyclic code as a principal ideal. In other words, we have for the most part omitted the mathematical generalizations and terminology that would normally be used in teaching a course to a class consisting entirely of advanced mathematics majors.

Part I (Chapters 1–9) of this text has been used to teach a two-semester sequence in coding theory at Auburn University. The minimal prerequisite for students taking this course is a rather elementary knowledge of linear algebra. However, the more linear algebra, as well as general modern algebra, students bring to the course the better. Students with more mathematical background and maturity will be able to move rather quickly through the early material.

The coding theory portion deals exclusively with binary codes and codes over fields of characteristic 2, stressing the construction, encoding and decoding of several important families of codes. Primarily, we have chosen families of codes that are of interest in engineering and computer science, such as Reed-Solomon codes and convolutional codes, which have been used in deep space communications and consumer electronics (to name but two areas of application). This choice of codes also reflects a broad range of algorithms for encoding and decoding.

Part II (Chapters 10–12) has its origins in an introductory semester-length course on cryptography taught at Auburn University. The course attracts a diverse audience of graduate and undergraduate students from computer science, engineering, education, and mathematics, some of whom will have had only an introductory course in algebra or number theory at the sophomore level. Fortunately, this level of sophistication is sufficient to develop a respectable course in cryptography—indeed, most of the material here requires only a review (included in Chapter 11) of basic results concerning the integers modulo n. The intent has been to write a concise and self-contained introduction to modern cryptography, with an emphasis on public-key methods. In Chapter 12 especially, the main points are covered in relatively short sections, with additional topics outlined (usually in some detail and with references) in the exercises.

In a broad sense, coding theory and cryptography are both concerned with the electronic transfer of information—one with reliability, the other with security. We recognize that not every degree program has the luxury of including courses devoted to each topic, so this text has been written to accommodate several course designs. In a single semester, one could choose to investigate coding theory in depth, covering Chapters 1 to 4 and then either Chapters 5 and 6 or Chapters 7 and 8. One could also delve into cryptography by covering just Chapters 10–12. It is also possible to gain some knowledge in each of the two areas in one semester, in which case we recommend that Chapters 1–3, 10, and 12 be covered, with topics selected from Chapter 11 as needed.

The authors would very much appreciate any comments that users of this text care to pass along. Our email address is rodgec1@auburn.edu.

Acknowledgments

We are deeply indebted to Alfred Menezes for providing detailed suggestions and reviews of several drafts of Chapters 10–12. Without his advice, the material would have contained more errors and would have been more poorly organized. We also wish to acknowledge and thank Selda Küçükçifçi for her reviews, suggestions, and corrections.

Rosie Torbert did exceptional work in creating the sources for the first edition of this book. Her never failing good cheer in enduring the slings and arrows of constant revisions places her in the saint category. We'd like to thank Heather Conner for doing such a great job in preparing this second edition. We especially appreciate the cover designs of Cindy Otterson and thank her for her work with us on several projects.

D. Hankerson, D.G. Hoffman, D.A. Leonard
C.C. Lindner, K.T. Phelps
C.A. Rodger, J.R. Wall

Contents

Chapter 1

Introduction to Coding Theory

1.1 Introduction

Coding theory is the study of methods for efficient and accurate transfer of information from one place to another. The theory has been developed for such diverse applications as the minimization of noise from compact disc recordings, the transmission of financial information across telephone lines, data transfer from one computer to another or from memory to the central processor, and information transmission from a distant source such as a weather or communications satellite or the Voyager spacecraft which sent pictures of Jupiter and Saturn to Earth.

The physical medium through which the information is transmitted is called a *channel*. Telephone lines and the atmosphere are examples of channels. Undesirable disturbances, called *noise*, may cause the information received to differ from what was transmitted. Noise may be caused by sunspots, lightning, folds in a magnetic tape, meteor showers, competing telephone messages, random radio disturbance, poor typing, poor hearing, poor speech, or many other things.

Coding theory deals with the problem of detecting and correcting transmission errors caused by noise on the channel. The following diagram provides a rough idea of a general information transmission system.

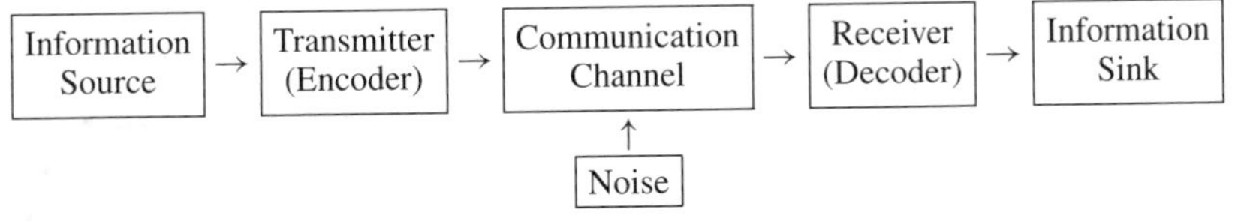

The most important part of the diagram, as far as we are concerned, is the noise, for without it there would be no need for the theory.

In practice, the control we have over this noise is the choice of a good channel to use for transmission and the use of various noise filters to combat certain types of interference which may be encountered. These are engineering problems. Once we have settled on the best mechanical system for solving these problems, we can focus our attention on the construction of the encoder and the decoder. Our desire is to construct these in such a way as to effect:

1. fast encoding of information,
2. easy transmission of encoded messages,
3. fast decoding of received messages,
4. correction of errors introduced in the channel, and
5. maximum transfer of information per unit time.

The primary goal is the fourth of these. The problem is that it is not generally compatible with the fifth, and also may not be especially compatible with the other three. So any solution is necessarily a trade-off among the five objectives.

In our everyday communications among one another we standardly use words, spoken or written, made from a limited alphabet. We have information to communicate; we encode it into strings of words which we then speak or write. These are then sent across a channel, the channel normally being the space from mouth to ear or from pen to paper to eye. The noise might be caused by poor speech, bad hearing, incorrect grammar, a loud stereo, competing speech, misspelling, misreading, or a faulty typewriter. The decoder is our reading (or hearing) and understanding of the received messages.

We have built-in error-correcting devices that that we don't even think about. Suppose we receive the message "Apt natural. I have a gub." which is a hold-up note in Woody Allen's "Take the Money and Run." Since our language does not use all possible words of any given length, we hopefully recognize that "gub" is not a word. We may safely assume that the transmitted word was close to "gub" in some sense. So it was more likely to have been "gut" or "gun" or "tub" than say "firetruck" or "rat." It is only the context of the message though that lets us choose "gun" as the most likely word. "Apt" is a perfectly good word, but again from the context we are led to correct it to "act." And if we happen to be literate, we will also correct "natural" to "naturally," even though this was probably an error attributed to the source and not to the noise on the channel.

Of these types of errors, we can probably only deal with the first: that is choosing the most likely word transmitted. The standard method for combating errors is through redundancy. Many businesses these days commonly add check digits to identification numbers; these are extra digits that are used to check the correctness of data or of account numbers. This is probably the most commonly recognized method of coding in real life. We shall deal with more sophisticated but similar ideas.

1.2 Basic assumptions

We state some fundamental definitions and assumptions which will apply throughout the text.

In many cases, the information to be sent is transmitted by a sequence of zeros and ones. We call a 0 or a 1 a *digit*. A *word* is a sequence of digits. The *length* of a word is the number of digits in the word. Thus 0110101 is a word of length seven. A word is transmitted by sending its digits, one after the other, across a *binary channel*. The term "binary" refers to the fact that only two digits, 0 and 1, are used. Each digit is transmitted mechanically, electrically, magnetically, or otherwise by one of two types of easily differentiated pulses.

A *binary code* is a set C of words. The code consisting of all words of length two is

$$C = \{00, 10, 01, 11\}.$$

A *block code* is a code having all its words of the same length; this number is called the *length* of a code. We will consider only block codes. So, for us, the term *code* will always mean a binary block code. The words that belong to a given code C_0, will be called *codewords*. We shall denote the number of codewords in a code C by $|C|$.

Exercises

1.2.1 List all words of length 3; of length 4; of length 5.

1.2.2 Find a formula for the total number of words of length n.

1.2.3 Let C be the code consisting of all words of length 6 having an even number of ones. List the codewords in C.

We also need to make certain basic assumptions about the channel. These assumptions will necessarily shape the theory that we formulate.

The first assumption is that a codeword of length n consisting of 0's and 1's is received as a word of length n consisting of 0's and 1's, although not necessarily the same as the word that was sent.

The second is that there is no difficulty identifying the beginning of the first word transmitted. Thus, if we are using codewords of length 3 and receive 011011001, we know that the words received are, in order, 011, 011, 001. This assumption means, again using length 3, that the channel cannot deliver 01101 to the receiver, because a digit has been lost here.

The final assumption is that the noise is scattered randomly as opposed to being in clumps called *bursts*. That is, the probability of any one digit being affected in transmission is the same as that of any other digit and is not influenced by errors made in neighboring digits. This is not a very realistic assumption for many types of noise such as lightning or scratches on compact discs. We shall eventually consider this type of noise.

In a *perfect*, or noiseless, channel, the digit sent, 0 or 1, is always the digit received. If all channels were perfect, there would be no need for coding theory. But fortunately (or unfortunately, perhaps) no channel is perfect; every channel is noisy. Some channels are less noisy, or more reliable, than others.

A binary channel is *symmetric* if 0 and 1 are transmitted with equal accuracy; that is the probability of receiving the correct digit is independent of which digit, 0 or 1, is being transmitted. The *reliability* of a binary symmetric channel (BSC) is a real number p, $0 \leq p \leq 1$, where p is the probability that the digit sent is the digit received.

If p is the probability that the digit received is the same as the digit sent, then $1-p$ is the probability that the digit received is *not* the digit sent. The following diagram may clarify how a BSC operates:

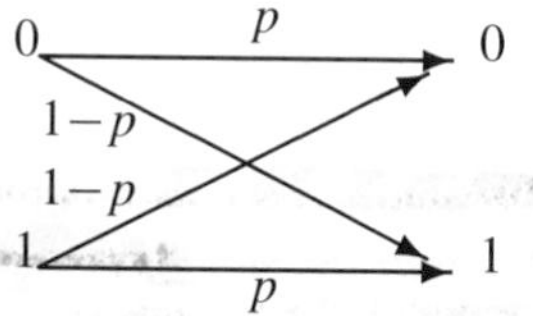

In most cases it may be hard to estimate the actual value of p for a given channel. However the actual value of p does not influence significantly the form of the theory.

We will call one channel more reliable than another if its reliability is higher. Note that if $p = 1$, then there is no chance of a digit being altered in transmission. Hence the channel is perfect and of no interest to us. Nor is a channel with $p = 0$ of any interest. Any channel with $0 < p \leq 1/2$ can be easily converted into a channel with $1/2 \leq p < 1$. *Henceforth we will always assume that we are using a BSC with probability p satisfying* $1/2 < p < 1$. (The case where $p = 1/2$ is raised in Exercise 1.2.6.)

Exercises

1.2.4 Explain why a channel with $p = 0$ is uninteresting.

1.2.5 Explain how to convert a channel with $0 < p \leq 1/2$ into a channel with $1/2 \leq p < 1$.

1.2.6 What can be said about a channel with $p = 1/2$?

1.3 Correcting and detecting error patterns

We consider now the possibilities of correcting and detecting errors. In this section we intend to develop an intuitive understanding of the concepts involved in correcting and detecting errors, while a formal approach is adopted in later sections.

Suppose a word is received that is not a codeword. Clearly some error has occurred during the transmission process, so we have *detected* that an error (perhaps several errors) has occurred. If however a codeword is received, then perhaps no errors occurred during transmission, so we cannot detect any error.

The concept of correcting an error is more involved. As in the introduction when we were inclined to correct 'gub' to 'gun' rather than to 'rat', we appeal to intuition to suggest that any received word should be *corrected* to a codeword that requires as few changes as possible. (In a later section we show that the probability that such a codeword was sent is at least as great as the probability that any other codeword was sent.) To consolidate these ideas, we shall discuss some particular codes. Notice that our assumption that no digits are lost or created in transmission precludes decoding 'gub' to 'firetruck'.

Example 1.3.1 Let $C_1 = \{00, 01, 10, 11\}$. Every received word is a codeword and so C_1 cannot detect any errors. Also C_1 corrects no errors since every received word requires no changes to become a codeword.

Example 1.3.2 Modify C_1 by repeating each codeword three times. The new code is

$$C_2 = \{000000, 010101, 101010, 111111\}.$$

This is an example of a *repetition code*. Suppose that 110101 is received. Since this is not a codeword we can detect that at least one error has occurred. The codeword 010101 can be formed by changing one digit, but all other codewords are formed by changing more than one digit. Therefore we expect that 010101 was the most likely codeword transmitted, so we correct 110101 to 010101. (A codeword that can be formed from a word w with the least number of digits being changed is called a *closest* codeword; this idea is formalized later.) In fact if any of the codewords, $c \in C_2$, is transmitted and one error occurs during transmission, then the unique closest codeword to the received word is c; so any single error results in a word that we correct to the codeword that was transmitted.

Example 1.3.3 Modify C_1 by adding a third digit to each codeword so that the number of 1's in each codeword is even. The resulting code is

$$C_3 = \{000, 011, 101, 110\}.$$

The added digit is called a *parity-check* digit. Suppose 010 is received, then since 010 is not a codeword we can detect that an error has occurred. Each of the codewords 110, 000 and 011 can be formed by changing one digit in the received word. In later sections we distinguish between how we treat received words that are closest to a unique codeword (and so is the single most likely codeword sent) as was the case in Example 1.3.2, and received words that are closest to several codewords as in this example. It suffices at this stage to observe that it seems more sensible to correct 010 to one of 110, 000 or 011 rather than to 101.

Exercises

1.3.4 Let C be the code of all words of length 3. Determine which codeword was most likely sent if 001 is received.

1.3.5 Add a parity check digit to the codewords in the code in Exercise 1.3.4, and use the resulting code C to answer the following questions.

(a) If 1101 is received can we detect an error?

(b) If 1101 is received what codewords were most likely to have been transmitted?

(c) Is any word of length 4 that is not in the code, closest to a unique codeword?

1.3.6 Repeat each codeword in the code C defined in Exercise 1.3.4 three times to form a repetition code of length 9. Find the closest codewords to the following received words:

(a) 001000001 (b) 011001011

(c) 101000101 (d) 100000010

1.3.7 Find the maximum number of codewords of length $n = 4$ in a code in which any single error can be detected.

1.3.8 Repeat Exercise 1.3.7 for $n = 5$, $n = 6$, and for general n.

1.4 Information rate

After the last section it is apparent that the addition of digits to codewords may improve the error correction and detection capabilities of the code. However, clearly the longer the codewords, the longer it takes to transmit each message. The *information rate* (or just *rate*) of a code is a number that is designed to measure the proportion of each codeword that is carrying the message. The information rate of a code C of length n is defined to be (for binary codes)

$$\frac{1}{n}\log_2|C|.$$

Since we may assume that $1 \leq |C| \leq 2^n$, it is clear that the information rate ranges between 0 and 1; it is 1 if every word is a codeword and 0 if $|C| = 1$.

For example, the information rates of the codes C_1, C_2 and C_3 in the previous section are 1, 1/3 and 2/3 respectively. Each of these information rates seems sensibly related to their respective codes, since the first 2 digits of the 6 in each codeword in C_2 can be considered to carry the message, as can the first 2 digits of the 3 in each codeword in C_3.

Exercises

1.4.1 Find the information rate for each of the codes in Exercises 1.3.4, 1.3.5 and 1.3.6.

1.5 The effects of error correction and detection

To exemplify the dramatic effect that the addition of a parity-check digit to a code can have in recognizing when error occur, we consider the following codes.

Suppose that all 2^{11} words of length 11 are codewords; then no error is detected. Let the reliability of the channel be $p = 1 - 10^{-8}$ and suppose that digits are transmitted at the rate of 10^7 digits per second. Then the probability that a word is transmitted incorrectly is approximately $11p^{10}(1-p)$, which is about $11/10^8$. So about

$$\frac{11}{10^8} \cdot \frac{10^7}{11} = .1 \text{ words per second}$$

are transmitted incorrectly without being detected. That is one wrong word every 10 seconds, 6 a minute, 360 an hour, or 8640 a day! Not too good.

Now suppose that a parity-check digit is added to each codeword, so the number of 1's in each of the 2048 codewords is even. Then any single error is always detected, so at least 2 errors must occur if a word is to be transmitted incorrectly without our knowledge. The probability of at least 2 errors occurring is $1 - p^{12} - 12p^{11}(1-p)$ which can be approximated by $\binom{12}{2}p^{10}(1-p)^2$ which for $p = 1 - 10^{-8}$ is about $\frac{66}{10^{16}}$. Now approximately $\frac{66}{10^{16}} \cdot \frac{10^7}{12} = 5.5 \times 10^{-9}$ words per second are transmitted incorrectly without being detected. That is about one error every 2000 days!

So if we are willing to reduce the information rate by lengthening the code from 11 to 12 we are very likely to know when errors occur. To decide where these errors have actually occurred, we may need to request the retransmission of the message. Physically this means that either transmission must be held up until confirmation is received or messages must be stored temporarily until retransmission is requested; both alternatives may be very costly in time or in storage space. It may also be that retransmission is impractical, such as with the Voyager mission and when using compact discs. Therefore, at the expense of further increase in wordlength, it may well be worth incorporating error-correction capabilities into the code. Introducing such capabilities may also make encoding and decoding more difficult, but will help to avoid the hidden costs in time or space mentioned above.

One simple scheme to introduce error-correction is to form a repetition code where each codeword is transmitted three times in succession. Then if at most one error is made per 33 digit codeword, at least two of the three transmissions will be correct. Since the comparisons of the three 11 digit words is relatively simple, the only real trade-off for being able to correct one error is an information rate of 1/3 instead of 1.

Still 1/3 is only 1/3. Perhaps we could do better. We will see later that it is possible to add only 4 extra digits to each 11 digit codeword and still be able to correct any single error. This produces a code with information rate 11/15, a valuable improvement provided that the extra encoding and decoding costs are not prohibitive.

It is our task, then, to design codes with reasonable information rates, low encoding and decoding costs and some error-correcting or error-detecting capabilities that make the need for retransmission unlikely.

1.6 Finding the most likely codeword transmitted

Suppose that we have an overall view of the transmission process, knowing both the codeword v that is transmitted and the word w that is received. For any given v and w, let $\phi_p(v,w)$ be the probability that if the codeword v is sent over a BSC with reliability p then the word w is received. Since we are assuming that noise is distributed randomly, we can treat the transmission of each digit as an independent event. So if v and w disagree in d positions, then we have $n-d$ digits correctly transmitted and d incorrectly transmitted and thus,

$$\phi_p(v,w) = p^{n-d}(1-p)^d.$$

Example 1.6.1 Let C be a code of length 5. Then for any v in C, the probability that v is received correctly is

$$\phi_p(v,v) = p^5.$$

Let 10101 be in C. Then

$$\phi_p(10101, 01101) = p^3(1-p)^2$$

and if $p = .9$ then

$$\phi_{.9}(10101, 01101) = (.9)^3(.1)^2 = .00729.$$

Exercises

1.6.2 Calculate $\phi_{.97}(v,w)$ for each of the following pairs of v and w:

(a) $v = 01101101, w = 10001110$

(b) $v = 1110101, w = 1110101$

(c) $v = 00101, w = 11010$

(d) $v = 00000, w = 00000$

(e) $v = 1011010, w = 0000010$

(f) $v = 10110, w = 01001$

(g) $v = 111101, w = 000010.$

In practice we know w, the word received but we do not know the actual codeword v that was sent. However each codeword v determines an assignment of probabilities $\phi_p(v,w)$ to words, w. Each such assignment is a mathematical model and we choose the model (that is, the codeword v) which agrees most with

Too Bad Getting In Isn't This Easy!
www.GradSchools.com

~~1.1.3 a)~~
~~1.1.5~~
~~1.1.10 c)~~
~~1.1.12 a)~~
~~1.1.17~~
~~1.2.3~~
1.2.5
1.2.6
1.3.4
1.3.5
1.3.6
1.9.6
1.9.7 a) b)
1.10.4
1.10.5 a) c)
1.11.3 a)
1.11.5
1.11.10 c)
1.11.12 a)
1.11.17
1.11.20
1.12.5
1.12.15

2.1.2
2.2.7
2.3.4 a)
2.5.3 a) b)
2.5.10 a) b)
2.6.4
2.6.5 a)
2.6.6 a)
2.6.10 a)
2.7.4 c)
2.7.9 b)
2.8.10 a)
2.9.4 a)
2.10.6 b)
2.10.8 a)
2.11.8
2.11.19 a)

GRADSCHOOLS.COM®

observation—in this case, which makes the word received most likely. That is, assume v is sent when w is received if

$$\phi_p(v, w) = \max\{\phi_p(u, w) : u \in C\}.$$

The following theorem provides a criterion for finding such a codeword v.

Theorem 1.6.3 *Suppose we have a BSC with $1/2 < p < 1$. Let v_1 and v_2 be codewords and w a word, each of length n. Suppose that v_1 and w disagree in d_1 positions and v_2 and w disagree in d_2 positions. Then*

$$\phi_p(v_1, w) \leq \phi_p(v_2, w) \textit{ if and only if } d_1 \geq d_2.$$

Proof: We have already established that $\phi_p(v_1, w) \leq \phi_p(v_2, w)$ iff $p^{n-d_1}(1-p)^{d_1} \leq p^{n-d_2}(1-p)^{d_2}$ iff $(\frac{p}{1-p})^{d_2-d_1} \leq 1$ iff $d_2 \leq d_1$ (since $\frac{p}{1-p} > 1$). □

This formally establishes the procedure for correcting words which until now we had adopted as being an intuitively sensible procedure: correct w to a codeword which disagrees with w in as few positions as possible, since such a codeword is the most likely to have been sent, given that w was received.

Example 1.6.4 If $w = 00110$ is received over a BSC with $p = .98$, which of the codewords 01101, 01001, 10100, 10101 was the most likely one sent?

v	d (number of disagreements with w)
01101	3
01001	4
10100	2 ← smallest d
10101	3

Using the above table, Theorem 1.6.3 says that 10100 was the most likely codeword sent. Note that we don't need to know the precise value of p in order to apply Theorem 1.6.3; we only need to know that $p > 1/2$.

Exercises

1.6.5 Suppose that $w = 0010110$ is received over a BSC with reliability $p = .90$. Which of the following codewords is most likely to have been sent?

$$1001011, 1111100, 0001110, 0011001, 1101001.$$

1.6.6 Which of the 8 codewords in the code of Exercise 1.3.6 is most likely to have been sent if $w = 101000101$ is received?

1.6.7 If $C = \{01000, 01001, 00011, 11001\}$ and a word $w = 10110$ is received, which codeword is most likely to have been sent?

1.6.8 Repeat Exercise 1.6.7 after replacing C with $\{010101, 110110, 101101, 100110, 011001\}$ and w with 101010.

1.6.9 Which of the codewords 110110, 110101, 000111, 100111, 101000 is most likely to have been sent if $w = 011001$ is received.

1.6.10 In Theorem 1.6.3 we assume that $1/2 < p < 1$. What would change in the statement of Theorem 1.6.3 if we replace this assumption with

(a) $0 < p < 1/2$, (b) $p = 1/2$?

1.7 Some basic algebra

A problem that we shall need to address is that of finding an efficient way of finding the closest codeword to any received word. If the code has many codewords then it is impractical to compare each received word w to each codeword in turn to find which codeword disagrees with w in as few positions as possible. For example, if the code contains 2^{12} codewords (as was used for the Voyager mission) then such a decoding procedure could never hope to keep up with the incoming transmission. To overcome this problem, we need to introduce some structure into our codes.

Let $K = \{0, 1\}$ and let K^n be the set of all binary words of length n. Define addition and multiplication of the elements of K as follows:

$$0+0=0, 0+1=1, 1+0=1, 1+1=0$$
$$0\cdot 0=0, 1\cdot 0=0, 0\cdot 1=0, 1\cdot 1=1.$$

Define addition for the elements of K^n componentwise, using the addition defined on K to add each component. For example, let

$$v = 01101 \text{ and } w = 11001 \text{ then } v + w = 10100.$$

Clearly the addition of two binary words of length n results in a binary word of length n, so K^n is closed under addition.

Using linear algebra terminology, we refer to an element of K as scalar. Then scalar multiplication of K^n is defined componentwise. Since the only scalars are 0 and 1, the only scalar multiples of a word w are $0 \cdot w$, which is the element of K^n with 0 in every component, and $1 \cdot w$, which is w. We refer to the element of K^n with 0 in all components as the *zero word*. Clearly K^n is closed under scalar multiplication.

With these definitions of addition and scalar multiplication, it can be shown that K^n is a vector space. That is, for any words of length n, u, v and w and for any scalars a and b:

1. $v + w \in K^n$
2. $(u + v) + w = u + (v + w)$
3. $v + 0 = 0 + v = v$, where 0 is the zero word

4. for some $v' \in K^n, v + v' = v' + v = 0$
5. $v + w = w + v$
6. $av \in K^n$
7. $a(v + w) = av + aw$
8. $(a + b)v = av + bv$
9. $(ab)v = a(bv)$
10. $1v = v$.

Exercises

1.7.1 Show that if v is a word in K^n then $v + v = 0$.

1.7.2 Show that if v and w are words in K^n and $v + w = 0$ then $v = w$.

1.7.3 Show that if u, v and w are words in K^n and $u + v = w$ then $u + w = v$.

Notice that if v is sent over a BSC and w is received then 0 occurs in a component of $v + w$ if the corresponding component of v was correctly transmitted and a 1 occurs if the component was incorrectly transmitted. $v + w$ is called the *error pattern*, or the *error*. For example if $v = 10101$ is transmitted and $w = 01100$ is received then errors occurred in the 1st, 2nd and 5th components. The error pattern is $v + w = 11001$.

1.8 Weight and distance

We introduce two important terms. Let v be a word of length n. The *Hamming weight*, or simply the *weight*, of v is the number of times the digit 1 occurs in v. We denote the weight of v by $\text{wt}(v)$. For example, $\text{wt}(110101) = 4$ and $\text{wt}(00000) = 0$.

Let v and w be words of length n. The *Hamming distance*, or simply *distance*, between v and w is the number of positions in which v and w disagree. We denote the distance between v and w by $d(v, w)$. For example, $d(01011, 00111) = 2$ and $d(10110, 10110) = 0$.

Note that the distance between v and w is the same as the weight of the error pattern $u = v + w$:

$$d(v, w) = \text{wt}(v + w).$$

For example, if $v = 11010$ and $w = 01101$, we have $d(v, w) = d(11010, 01101) = 4$, and $\text{wt}(v + w) = \text{wt}(11010 + 01101) = \text{wt}(10111) = 4$. Thus the probability formula in Section 1.6 can be re-expressed as

$$\phi_p(v, w) = p^{n-\text{wt}(u)}(1 - p)^{\text{wt}(u)},$$

where u is the error pattern $u = v + w$. We refer to $\phi_p(v, w)$ as the *probability of the error pattern* $u = v + w$.

Exercises

1.8.1 Compute the weight of each of the following words, and the distance between each pair of them: $v_1 = 1001010$, $v_2 = 0110101$, $v_3 = 0011110$, and $v_4 = v_2 + v_3$.

1.8.2 Let $u = 01011$, $v = 11010$, $w = 01100$. Compare each of the following pairs of quantities:

(a) $\mathrm{wt}(v+w)$ and $\mathrm{wt}(v)+\mathrm{wt}(w)$,

(b) $d(v,w)$ and $d(v,u)+d(u,w)$.

We now list a number of facts concerning weight and distance. Here u, v, and w are words of length n and a is a digit.

1. $0 \leq \mathrm{wt}(v) \leq n$.
2. $\mathrm{wt}(v) = 0$ if and only if $v = 0$.
3. $0 \leq d(v,w) \leq n$.
4. $d(v,w) = 0$ if and only if $v = w$.
5. $d(v,w) = d(w,v)$.
6. $\mathrm{wt}(v+w) \leq \mathrm{wt}(v)+\mathrm{wt}(w)$.
7. $d(v,w) \leq d(v,u)+d(u,w)$.
8. $\mathrm{wt}(av) = a \cdot \mathrm{wt}(v)$.
9. $d(av,aw) = a \cdot d(v,w)$.

Most of these facts are immediately clear from the definitions of weight and distance. In Exercise 1.8.2, the reader constructed examples of facts 6 and 7. To construct proofs, try using the basic relation $d(v,w) = \mathrm{wt}(v+w)$ and Exercises 1.7.1, 1.7.2, and 1.7.3 as necessary.

Exercises

1.8.3 Construct an example in K^5 of each of the nine rules above.

1.8.4 Prove each of the nine rules above.

These facts will be used as needed and without comment in the following sections.

1.9 Maximum likelihood decoding

We are now ready to give more precise formulations of two basic problems of coding theory. Let us assume we are at the receiving end of a BSC and we want to receive a message from the transmitter at the other end. The transmitter is, of course, one we have ourselves previously designed. In fact, the design of the transmitter is one of the basic problems.

There are two quantities over which we have no control. One is the probability p that our BSC will transmit a digit correctly. The second is the number of possible messages that might be transmitted. The actual messages are not nearly as important as the number of possible messages. For example, only two messages were necessary before Paul Revere set off on his famous midnight ride.

Recall that for any set S, we denote by $|S|$ the *number of elements* in S. Thus $|K^n| = 2^n$ from Exercise 1.2.2.

The two basic problems of coding then are:

1.9.1 Encoding We have to determine a code to use for sending our messages. We must make some choices. First we select a positive integer k, the length of each binary word corresponding to a message. Since each message must be assigned a different binary word of length k, k must be chosen so that $|M| \leq |K^k| = 2^k$. Next we decide how many digits we need to add to each word of length k to ensure that as many errors can be corrected or detected as we require; this is the choice of the codewords and the length of the code, n. To transmit a particular message, the transmitter finds the word of length k assigned to that message, then transmits the codeword of length n corresponding to that word of length k.

1.9.2 Decoding A word w in K^n is received. We now describe a procedure, called *maximum likelihood decoding*, or *MLD*, for deciding which word v in C was sent. There are actually two kinds of MLD.

1. *Complete Maximum Likelihood Decoding*, or *CMLD*. If there is one and only one word v in C closer to w than any other word in C, we decode w as v. That is, if $d(v, w) < d(v_1, w)$ for all v_1 in $C, v_1 \neq v$, then decode w as v. If there are several words in C closest to w, i.e., at the same distance from w, then we select arbitrarily one of them and conclude that it was the codeword sent.
2. *Incomplete Maximum Likelihood Decoding*, or *IMLD*. Again, if there is a unique word v in C closest to w, then we decode w as v. But if there are several words in C at the same distance from w, then we request a retransmission. In some cases we might even ask for a retransmission if the received word w is too far away from any word in the code.

We will use IMLD for the examples and exercises in this section, and throughout most of the rest of the text. We emphasize that MLD does not always work; in particular, if too many errors were made in transmitting across the BSC, then MLD fails.

The codeword v in C closest to the received word w is the v for which the distance $d(v, w)$ is least and hence, by Theorem 1.6.3, has the greatest associated probability $\phi_p(v, w)$ among all codewords, so is the most likely codeword sent. Example 1.6.4 demonstrates this. Since $d(v, w) = \text{wt}(v + w)$, the weight of the error pattern $u = v + w$, Theorem 1.6.3 may be restated as follows:

$$\phi_p(v_1, w) \leq \phi_p(v_2, w) \text{ iff } \mathrm{wt}(v_1 + w) \geq \mathrm{wt}(v_2 + w);$$

that is, *the most likely codeword sent is the one with the error pattern of smallest weight.*

Thus the strategy in IMLD is to examine the error patterns $v + w$ for all codewords v, and pick the v which yields the error pattern of smallest weight.

Example 1.9.3 Suppose $|M| = 2$, and we select $n = 3$ and $C = \{000, 111\}$. If $v = 000$ is transmitted, when will IMLD conclude this correctly, and when will IMLD incorrectly conclude that 111 was sent? We construct Table 1.1 as follows.

Received	Error Pattern		Decode
w	000 + w	111+ w	v
000	000*	111	000
100	100*	011	000
010	010*	101	000
001	001*	110	000
110	110	001*	111
101	101	010*	111
011	011	100*	111
111	111	000*	111

Table 1.1: *IMLD table for Example 1.9.3.*

The first column of Table 1.1 lists all possible words which might be received. This is all of K^3. The second and third columns list the error patterns $v + w$ for each word v in the code C. Since IMLD will select the error pattern of smallest weight, we have put an asterisk beside the entry in column two or three of least weight. In the last column we record the word v in the code C corresponding to the column in which the asterisk was placed. This is the word v which IMLD will conclude was sent for each possible word received. Thus IMLD will conclude correctly that 000 was sent if 000, 100, 010, or 001 is received (first four rows of Table 1.1). And IMLD will conclude incorrectly that 111 was sent if 110, 101, 011, or 111 was received (last four rows of Table 1.1).

Example 1.9.4 Suppose $|M| = 3$, and we select $C = \{0000, 1010, 0111\}$ with $n = 4$. We construct the IMLD Table 1.2, just as in Example 1.9.3 above, except that if two or more entries in the error pattern columns have the same smallest weight, then we do not place an asterisk in that row and record nothing (indicated by –) in the decoding column for v. This means, for IMLD, that we request a retransmission whenever there is a tie for smallest error pattern weight.

Received	Error Pattern			Decode
w	$0000 + w$	$1010 + w$	$0111 + w$	v
0000	0000*	1010	0111	0000
1000	1000	0010	1111	—
0100	0100*	1110	0011	0000
0010	0010	1000	0101	—
0001	0001*	1011	0110	0000
1100	1100	0110	1011	—
1010	1010	0000*	1101	1010
1001	1001	0011	1110	—
0110	0110	1100	0001*	0111
0101	0101	1111	0010*	0111
0011	0011	1001	0100*	0111
1110	1110	0100*	1001	1010
1101	1101	0111	1010*	0111
1011	1011	0001*	1100	1010
0111	0111	1101	0000*	0111
1111	1111	0101	1000*	0111

Table 1.2: *IMLD table for Example 1.9.4.*

Exercises

1.9.5 Let $|M| = 2$, $n = 3$, and $C = \{001, 101\}$. If $v = 001$ is sent, when will IMLD conclude this correctly, and when will IMLD incorrectly conclude that 101 was sent?

1.9.6 Let $|M| = 3$ and $n = 3$. For each word w in K^3 that could be received, find the word v in the code $C = \{000, 001, 110\}$ which IMLD will conclude was sent.

1.9.7 Construct the IMLD table for each of the following codes.

(a) $C = \{101, 111, 011\}$ (b) $C = \{000, 001, 010, 011\}$

(c) $C = \{0000, 0001, 1110\}$ (d) $C = \{0000, 1001, 0110, 1111\}$

(e) $C = \{00000, 11111\}$ (f) $C = \{00000, 11100, 00111, 11011\}$

(g) $C = \{00000, 11110, 01111, 10001\}$

(h) $C = \{000000, 101010, 010101, 111111\}$

Recall that we have to choose n and C (1.9.1). Some choices are better than others. We list three important criteria for measuring good choices:

1. Longer words take more time to transmit and decode, so n should not be too large; that is, the information rate should be as close to 1 as possible.
2. With many messages being received per second, if $|C|$ is large, say a few thousand or so, the procedure for IMLD described in this section would be too time consuming to implement. Fortunately, certain clever choices of C admit much slicker and faster methods for IMLD.

3. If many errors are made in transmission, MLD will not work. That is, the word MLD will conclude was sent will not be the same as the actual word sent. So C should be chosen so that the probability that MLD will work is very high. (We will consider this probability in the next section.)

Thus we claim that *the main goal of coding theory is to find sets C of words which are adequate when judged by the criteria above.* Most of the rest of our efforts will be devoted to this goal.

1.10 Reliability of MLD

Suppose n and C have been chosen. We now give a procedure for determining the probability $\theta_p(C, v)$ that if v is sent over a BSC of probability p then IMLD correctly concludes that v was sent.

Find the set $L(v)$ of all words in K^n which are closer to v than to any other word in C. Then $\theta_p(C, v)$ is the sum of all the probabilities $\phi_p(v, w)$ as w ranges over $L(v)$. That is,

$$\theta_p(C, v) = \sum_{w \in L(v)} \phi_p(v, w).$$

Note that $L(v)$ is precisely the set of words in K^n for which, if received, IMLD will correctly conclude that v was sent. We can find $L(v)$ from the IMLD table constructed as in the last section. In each row of the table where v is decoded in the last column, the word w in the first column of that row is in $L(v)$. And these are all the words in $L(v)$.

Also observe that $\theta_p(C, v)$ is the sum over the words w in $L(v)$ of the probabilities of the error patterns $v + w$ occuring during transmission.

θ_p can be used to compare two codes, judging them by the third criterion in the previous section. However, it should be noted that $\theta_p(C, v)$ as defined ignores the possibility of retransmission, when the received word is equidistant from two codewords. This does lead to some anomalies (such as $\theta_p(K^n, v) > \theta_p(C, u)$, for any v in K^n and u in C, where C is the parity check code formed from K^n), but is a reasonable first approximation for a measure of reliability. Certainly $\theta_p(C, v)$ is a lower bound for the probability that v is decoded correctly.

Example 1.10.1 Suppose $p = .90$, $|M| = 2$, $n = 3$, and $C = \{000, 111\}$, as in Example 1.9.3. If the word $v = 000$ is sent, we compute the probability that IMLD will correctly conclude this after one transmission. From Table 1.1, $v = 000$ is decoded in the first four rows, so the set $L(000)$ (words in K^3 closer to $v = 000$ than to 111) is

$$L(000) = \{000, 100, 010, 001\}.$$

Thus,

$$\begin{aligned}\theta_p(C,000) &= \phi_p(000,000)+\phi_p(000,100)+\phi_p(000,010)+\phi_p(000,001)\\ &= p^3+p^2(1-p)+p^2(1-p)+p^2(1-p)\\ &= p^3+3p^2(1-p)\\ &= .972 \text{ (assuming } p=.9).\end{aligned}$$

If $v = 111$ is transmitted, we compute the probability that IMLD correctly concludes this after one transmission. First,

$$L(111) = \{110, 101, 011, 111\},$$

so

$$\begin{aligned}\theta_p(C,111) &= \phi_p(111,110)+\phi_p(111,101)+\phi_p(111,011)+\phi_p(111,111)\\ &= p^2(1-p)+p^2(1-p)+p^2(1-p)+p^3\\ &= 3p^2(1-p)+p^3\\ &= .972 \text{ (assuming } p=.9).\end{aligned}$$

Exercises

1.10.2 Suppose $p = .90, |M| = 2, n = 3$, and $C = \{001, 101\}$, as in Exercise 1.9.5.

(a) If $v = 001$ is sent, find the probability that IMLD will correctly conclude this after one transmission.

(b) Repeat part (a) for $v = 101$.

Both answers in Exercise 1.10.2 are $\theta_p(C, v) = .900$. Comparing this to the results in Example 1.10.1, we conclude that since $.900 < .972$, the code $C = \{000, 111\}$ is better than the code $C = \{001, 101\}$, at least when judged by the third criterion in the last section. Our method provides a procedure, (although somewhat inefficient when n is large) for determining when the probability that IMLD works is high. Fortunately, most of the codes we design later on are structured so that the calculation of this probability is much easier.

Example 1.10.3 Suppose $p = .90, |M| = 3, n = 4$, and $C = \{0000, 1010, 0111\}$, as in Example 1.9.4. For each v in C, we compute $\theta_p(C, v)$.

(a)

$$\begin{aligned}v &= 0000\\ L(0000) &= \{0000, 0100, 0001\}, \text{ (from Table 1.2)}\\ \theta_p(C,v) &= \phi_p(0000,0000)+\phi_p(0000,0100)+\phi_p(0000,0001)\\ &= p^4+p^3(1-p)+p^3(1-p)\\ &= p^4+2p^3(1-p) = .8019\end{aligned}$$

(b)

$$\begin{aligned}
v &= 1010\\
L(1010) &= \{1010, 1110, 1011\}\\
\theta_p(C, v) &= \phi_p(1010, 1010) + \phi_p(1010, 1110) + \phi_p(1010, 1011)\\
&= p^4 + p^3(1-p) + p^3(1-p)\\
&= p^4 + 2p^3(1-p) = .8019
\end{aligned}$$

(c)

$$\begin{aligned}
v &= 0111\\
L(0111) &= \{0110, 0101, 0011, 1101, 0111, 1111\}\\
\theta_p(C, v) &= \phi_p(0111, 0110) + \phi_p(0111, 0101) + \phi_p(0111, 0011)\\
&\quad + \phi_p(0111, 1101) + \phi_p(0111, 0111) + \phi_p(0111, 1111)\\
&= p^3(1-p) + p^3(1-p) + p^3(1-p) + p^2(1-p)^2 + p^4 + p^3(1-p)\\
&= p^4 + 4p^3(1-p) + p^2(1-p)^2 = .9558.
\end{aligned}$$

Examining the three probabilities, we see that the probability that IMLD will conclude correctly that 0111 was sent is not too bad. However the probability that IMLD will conclude correctly that either 0000 or 1010 was sent is horrible. Thus, at least by the third criterion in the last section, $C = \{0000, 1010, 0111\}$ is not an especially good choice for a code.

Exercises

1.10.4 Suppose $p = .90$ and $C = \{000, 001, 110\}$, as in Exercise 1.9.6. If $v = 110$ is sent, find the probability that IMLD will correctly conclude this, and the probability that IMLD will incorrectly conclude that 000 was sent.

1.10.5 For each of the following codes C calculate $\theta_p(C, v)$ for each v in C using $p = .90$. (The IMLD tables for these codes were constructed in Exercise 1.9.7.)

(a) $C = \{101, 111, 011\}$
(b) $C = \{000, 001, 010, 011\}$
(c) $C = \{0000, 0001, 1110\}$
(d) $C = \{0000, 1001, 0110, 1111\}$
(e) $C = \{00000, 11111\}$
(f) $C = \{00000, 11100, 00111, 11011\}$
(g) $C = \{00000, 11110, 01111, 10001\}$
(h) $C = \{000000, 101010, 010101, 111111\}$

1.11 Error-detecting codes

We now make precise the notion of when a code C will detect errors. Recall that if v in C is sent and w in K^n is received, then $u = v + w$ is the error pattern. Any word u in K^n can occur as an error pattern, and we wish to know which error patterns C will detect.

We say that code C *detects* the error pattern u if and only if $v+u$ is not a codeword, for every v in C. In other words, u is detected if for any transmitted codeword v, the decoder, upon receiving $v+u$ can recognize that it is not a codeword and hence that some error has occurred.

Example 1.11.1 Let $C = \{001, 101, 110\}$. For the error pattern $u = 010$, we calculate $v + 010$ for all v in C:

$$001 + 010 = 011, 101 + 010 = 111, 110 + 010 = 100.$$

None of the three words 011, 111, or 100 is in C, so C detects the error pattern 010. On the other hand, for the error pattern $u = 100$ we find

$$001 + 100 = 101, 101 + 100 = 001, 110 + 100 = 010.$$

Since at least one of these sums is in C, C does not detect the error pattern 100.

Exercises

1.11.2 Let $C = \{001, 101, 110\}$. Determine whether C will detect the error patterns (a) 011, (b) 001, and (c) 000.

1.11.3 For each of the following codes C determine whether or not C detects u:

(a) $C = \{00000, 10101, 00111, 11100\}$

(i) $u = 10101$ (ii) $u = 01010$ (iii) $u = 11011$

(b) $C = \{1101, 0110, 1100\}$

(i) $u = 0010$ (ii) $u = 0011$ (iii) $u = 1010$

(c) $C = \{1000, 0100, 0010, 0001\}$

(i) $u = 1001$ (ii) $u = 1110$ (iii) $u = 0110$

1.11.4 Which error patterns will the code $C = K^n$ detect?

1.11.5 (a) Let C be a code which contains the zero word as a codeword. Prove that if the error pattern u is a codeword, then C will not detect u.

(b) Prove that no code will detect the zero error pattern $u = 0$.

The table constructed for IMLD can be used to determine which error patterns a code C will detect. The first column lists every word in K^n. Hence the first column can be reinterpreted as all possible error patterns, in which case the "error pattern" columns in the IMLD table then contain the sums $v + u$, for all v in C. If in any particular row none of these sums are codewords in C, then C detects the error pattern in the first column of that row.

Example 1.11.6 Consider the code $C = \{000, 111\}$ with IMLD Table 1.1. All possible error patterns u are in the first column. For a given u, all sums $v+u$ as v ranges over C are in the second and third columns of the row labeled by u. If none of these entries are in C (that is, neither is 000 or 111), then C detects u. Thus C detects the error patterns 100, 010, 001, 110, 101, and 011, as can be seen by inspecting rows 2 through 7 of the table, but not the error patterns 000 or 111.

Exercises

1.11.7 Determine the error patterns detected by each code in Exercise 1.9.7 by using the IMLD tables constructed there.

An alternative and much faster method for finding the error patterns that code C can detect is to first find all error patterns that C does not detect; then all remaining error patterns can be detected by C. Clearly, for any pair of codewords v and w, if $e = v + w$ then e cannot be detected, since $v + e = w$, which is a codeword. So the set of all error patterns that cannot be detected by C is the set of all words that can be written as the sum of 2 codewords.

Example 1.11.8 Consider the code $\{000, 111\}$. Since

$$000+000=000, 000+111=111 \text{ and } 111+111=000,$$

the set of error patterns that cannot be detected is $\{000, 111\}$. Therefore all error patterns in $K^3\backslash\{000, 111\}$ can be detected.

Example 1.11.9 Let $C = \{1000, 0100, 1111\}$. Since $1000+1000=0000$, $1000+0100=1100$, $1000+1111=0111$ and $0100+1111=1011$, the set of error patterns that cannot be detected by C is $\{0000, 1100, 0111, 1011\}$. Therefore all error patterns in $K^4\backslash\{0000, 1100, 0111, 1011\}$ can be detected.

Exercises

1.11.10 Find the error patterns detected by each of the following codes and compare your answers with those Exercises 1.11.7.

(a) $C = \{101, 111, 011\}$
(b) $C = \{000, 001, 010, 011\}$
(c) $C = \{0000, 0001, 1110\}$
(d) $C = \{0000, 1001, 0110, 1111\}$
(e) $C = \{00000, 11111\}$
(f) $C = \{00000, 11100, 00111, 11011\}$
(g) $C = \{00000, 11110, 01111, 10001\}$
(h) $C = \{000000, 101010, 010101, 111111\}$

There is also a way of determining some error patterns that code C will detect without any manual checking. First we have to introduce another number associated with C.

For a code C containing at least two words the *distance* of the code C is the smallest of the numbers $d(v, w)$ as v and w range over all pairs of different codewords in C. Note that since $d(v, w) = \text{wt}(v + w)$, the distance of the code is the smallest value of $\text{wt}(v + w)$ as v and $w, v \neq w$ range over all possible codewords.

The distance of a code has many of the properties of Euclidean distance; this correspondence may be useful to assist in understanding the concept of the distance of a code.

Example 1.11.11 Let $C = \{0000, 1010, 0111\}$. Then $d(0000, 1010) = 2, d(0000, 0111) = 3$, and $d(1010, 0111) = 3$. Thus the distance of C is 2.

Exercises

1.11.12 Find the distance of each of the following codes.

(a) $C = \{101, 111, 011\}$
(b) $C = \{000, 001, 010, 011\}$
(c) $C = \{0000, 0001, 1110\}$
(d) $C = \{0000, 1001, 0110, 1111\}$
(e) $C = \{00000, 11111\}$
(f) $C = \{00000, 11100, 00111, 11011\}$
(g) $C = \{00000, 11110, 01111, 10001\}$
(h) $C = \{000000, 101010, 010101, 111111\}$

1.11.13 Find the distance of the code formed by adding a parity check digit to K^n.

Now we can state a theorem which helps to identify many of the error patterns a code will detect.

Theorem 1.11.14 *A code C of distance d will at least detect all non-zero error patterns of weight less than or equal to $d - 1$. Moreover, there is at least one error pattern of weight d which C will not detect.*

Notice that C may detect some error patterns of weight d or more, but does not detect all error patterns of weight d.

Proof: Let u be a nonzero error pattern with $\text{wt}(u) \leq d - 1$, and let v be in C. Then

$$d(v, v + u) = \text{wt}(v + v + u) = \text{wt}(u) < d.$$

Since C has distance d, $v + u$ is not in C. Therefore C detects u. From the definition of d, there are codewords v and w in C with $d(v, w) = d$. Consider the error pattern $u = v + w$. Now $w = v + u$ is in C, so C will not detect the error pattern u of weight d. □

A code is an t *error-detecting* code if it detects all error patterns of weight at most t and does not detect at least one error pattern of weight $t + 1$. So, in view of Theorem 1.11.14, if a code has distance d then it is a $d - 1$ error-detecting code.

Example 1.11.15 The code $C = \{000, 111\}$ has distance $d = 3$. By Theorem 1.11.14, C detects all error patterns of weight 1 or 2, and C does not detect the only error pattern of weight 3, 111. The only error pattern not covered by Theorem 1.11.14 is 000. But by Exercise 1.11.5 we know that 000 is not detected.

Theorem 1.11.14 does not prevent a code C from detecting error patterns of weight d or greater. Indeed, C usually will detect some such error patterns.

Example 1.11.16 The code $C = \{001, 101, 110\}$ has distance $d = 1$. Since $d - 1 = 0$, Theorem 1.11.14 does not help us determine which error patterns C will detect. But it does tell us that there is at least one error pattern of weight $d = 1$ which C will not detect. As we saw in Example 1.11.1, such an error pattern is 100. Note, however, that C does detect the error pattern 010 of weight $d = 1$.

Exercises

1.11.17 The code $C = \{0000, 1010, 0111\}$ has distance $d = 2$. Using Exercise 1.11.5, show that the error pattern 1010 is not detected. Show that this is the only error pattern of weight 2 that C does not detect. Find all error patterns that C detects.

1.11.18 Find all error patterns which the code C_3 of Example 1.3.3 will detect. Note that C_3 is a single error-detecting code.

1.11.19 For each code C in Exercise 1.11.12 find the error patterns which Theorem 1.11.14 guarantees C will detect.

1.11.20 Let C be the code consisting of all words of length 4 which have even weight. Find the error patterns C detects.

1.12 Error-correcting codes

If a word v in a code C is transmitted over a BSC and if w is received resulting in the error pattern $u = v + w$, then IMLD correctly concludes that v was sent provided w is closer to v than to any other codeword. If this occurs every times the error pattern u occurs, regardless of which codeword is transmitted, then we say that C *corrects* the error pattern u. That is, *a code C corrects the error pattern u if, for all v in C, $v + u$ is closer to v than to any other word in C*. Also, a code is said to be an t *error-correcting code* if it corrects all error patterns of weight at most t and does not correct at least one error pattern of weight $t + 1$.

Example 1.12.1 Let $C = \{000, 111\}$.

(a) Take the error pattern $u = 010$. For $v = 000$,

$$d(000, v+u) = d(000, 010) = 1 \text{ and}$$
$$d(111, v+u) = d(111, 010) = 2.$$

And for $v = 111$,

$$d(000, v+u) = d(000, 101) = 2$$
$$d(111, v+u) = d(111, 101) = 1.$$

Thus C corrects the error pattern 010.

(b) Now take the error pattern $u = 110$. For $v = 000$,

$$d(000, v+u) = d(000, 110) = 2 \text{ and}$$
$$d(111, v+u) = d(111, 110) = 1.$$

Since $v+u$ is not closer to $v = 000$ than to 111, C does not correct the error pattern 110.

The IMLD table can be used to determine which error patterns a code C will correct. In each error pattern column of the table, all possible error patterns (which means each word in K^n) occurs once and only once (for if the error pattern u occurs twice in a column for some codeword v, then u occurs in rows corresponding to distinct received words, say w_1 and w_2; thus $u = v + w_1 = v + w_2$, which is impossible for $w_1 \neq w_2$). Also, an asterisk is placed beside the error pattern u in the column corresponding to a codeword v in the IMLD table precisely when $v+u$ is closer to v than it is to any other codeword. Therefore an error pattern u is corrected if an asterisk is placed beside u in *every* column of the IMLD table.

Example 1.12.2 For the code $C = \{000, 111\}$, the IMLD table is in Table 1.1. In every row of the table where the error pattern 010 occurs (rows 3 and 6), IMLD correctly concludes which word v was sent. Also, in at least one row (row 4) where the error pattern 110 occurs, if 111 is sent and 001 is received, IMLD incorrectly concludes that 000 was sent. Note that this code corrects the error patterns 000, 100, 010, and 001 which receive an asterisk each time they occur. So C is a 1 error correcting code.

Example 1.12.3 Let $C = \{0000, 1010, 0111\}$. The IMLD table for C is Table 1.2. The code C will not correct the error pattern $u = 1010$. This error pattern occurs in the rows where $w = 0000$, 1010, and 1101. In only one case, where $w = 1101$, does IMLD correctly conclude which word v was sent. Note that the error pattern $u = 1010$ receives an asterisk only in the column for $v = 0111$ and not in the other two columns. C does correct the error patterns 0000, 0100 and 0001.

Example 1.12.4 Let $C = \{001, 101, 110\}$. Does C correct the error pattern $u = 100$? We construct only the three rows of the IMLD table where 100 appears. Since $u = v + w$ and we know u and v, we can find the received words from $w = u + v$. Notice that $u = 100$ does not receive an asterisk in every column in the following table, so C does not correct 100.

Received	Error Pattern			Decode
w	001+ w	101 + w	110 + w	v
101	100	000*	011	101
001	000*	100	111	001
010	011	111	100*	110

Exercises

1.12.5 Let $C = \{001, 101, 110\}$. Does C correct the error pattern $u = 100$? What about $u = 000$?

1.12.6 Prove that the same error pattern cannot occur more than once in a given row of an IMLD table.

1.12.7 Prove that the zero error pattern is always corrected.

1.12.8 Which error patterns will the code $C = K^n$ correct?

The distance of a code can be used to devise a test for error-correcting which avoids at least some of the manual checking from the IMLD table. The next theorem gives the test. Recall that the symbol $\lfloor x \rfloor$ denotes the greatest integer less than or equal to the real number x. For example, $\lfloor 5/2 \rfloor = 2$, $\lfloor 3 \rfloor = 3$, and $\lfloor 1/2 \rfloor = 0$.

Theorem 1.12.9 *A code of distance d will correct all error patterns of weight less than or equal to $\lfloor (d-1)/2 \rfloor$. Moreover, there is at least one error pattern of weight $1 + \lfloor (d-1)/2 \rfloor$ which C will not correct.*

Proof: Let u be an error pattern of weight $\text{wt}(u) \le (d-1)/2$. Let v and w be codewords in C with $w \ne v$. We want to show that $d(v, v+u) < d(w, v+u)$.

$$\begin{aligned} d(w, v+u) + d(v+u, v) &\ge d(w, v) \\ &\ge d \\ d(w, v+u) + \text{wt}(u) &\ge 2\,\text{wt}(u) + 1 \\ d(w, v+u) &\ge \text{wt}(u) + 1 \\ &\ge d(v, v+u) + 1 \end{aligned}$$

since $\text{wt}(u) = d(v+u, v)$, and $2\,\text{wt}(u) + 1 \le d$.

Therefore C corrects u. Now let v and w be codewords with $d(v, w) = d$. Form an error pattern u by changing $d - 1 - \lfloor (d-1)/2 \rfloor$ of the d 1's in $v + w$ to 0's. Then

$$\begin{aligned} d(v, v+u) &= \text{wt}(u) = 1 + \lfloor (d-1)/2 \rfloor, \text{ and} \\ d(w, v+u) &= \text{wt}(w+v+u) = d(v+w, u) \\ &= d - (1 + \lfloor (d-1)/2 \rfloor). \end{aligned}$$

If d is odd, say $d = 2t+1$, then

$$d(v, v+u) = \text{wt}(u) = 1 + (2t)/2 = 1 + t, \text{ and}$$
$$d(w, v+u) = 2t + 1 - (1+t) = t,$$

so $d(v, v+u) > d(w, v+u)$. And if d is even, say $d = 2t$, then

$$d(v, v+u) = 1 + \lfloor t - 1/2 \rfloor = t, \text{ and}$$
$$d(w, v+u) = 2t - t = t.$$

In either case, $d(v, v+u) \geq d(w, v+u)$, so $v+u$ is not closer to v than to the codeword w. Thus C does not correct the error pattern u. □

In view of this theorem it is clear that any code of distance d is a $\lfloor (d-1)/2 \rfloor$ error-correcting code.

Example 1.12.10 The code $C = \{000, 111\}$ has distance $d = 3$. Since $\lfloor (d-1)/2 \rfloor = 1$, Theorem 1.12.9 ensures that C corrects all error patterns of weight 0 or 1. As we observed in Example 1.12.1, C does correct error patterns 000, 100, 010, and 001. The error pattern 110 has weight $1 + \lfloor (d-1)/2 \rfloor = 2$, and we saw that C does not correct 110.

Theorem 1.12.9 does not prevent a code C of distance d from correcting error patterns of weight greater than $\lfloor (d-1)/2 \rfloor$.

Example 1.12.11 Let $C = \{001, 101\}$. Then $d = 1$. The error pattern $u = 011$ has weight 2, which is greater than $1 + \lfloor (d-1)/2 \rfloor = 1$. As the following piece of the IMLD table shows, C does correct $u = 011$.

w	001+ w	101+ w	v
010	011*	111	001
110	111	011*	101

Exercises

1.12.12 For each of the following codes C: (i) determine the error patterns that C will correct (the IMLD tables for these codes were constructed in Exercise 1.9.7), and (ii) find the error patterns that Theorem 1.12.9 guarantees that C corrects.

(a) $C = \{101, 111, 011\}$
(b) $C = \{000, 001, 010, 011\}$
(c) $C = \{0000, 0001, 1110\}$
(d) $C = \{0000, 1001, 0110, 1111\}$
(e) $C = \{00000, 11111\}$
(f) $C = \{00000, 11100, 00111, 11011\}$
(g) $C = \{00000, 11110, 01111, 10001\}$
(h) $C = \{000000, 101010, 010101, 111111\}$

1.12.13 Use the technique described in Example 1.12.11 to decide whether or not the following error patterns are corrected by the accompanying code.

(a) $C = \{000000, 100101, 010110, 001111, 110011, 101010, 011001, 111100\}$

(i) $u = 001000$ (ii) $u = 000010$ (iii) $u = 100100$

(b) $C = \{1001011, 0110101, 1110010, 1111111\}$

(i) $u = 0100000$ (ii) $u = 0101000$ (iii) $u = 1100000$

1.12.14 For each code in Exercise 1.12.12, find an error pattern of weight $\lfloor (d-1)/2 \rfloor + 1$ that C does not correct.

1.12.15 Let C be the code consisting of all words of length 4 having even weight. Determine the error patterns that C will correct.

1.12.16 Let u_1 and u_2 be error patterns of length n, and assume that u_1 and u_2 agree at least in the positions where a 1 occurs in u_1. Prove that if a code C will correct u_2, then C will also correct u_1.

As we have observed, error patterns of small weight are more likely to occur than error patterns of large weight (Theorem 1.6.3). Therefore, in designing codes, we should concentrate on being able to correct, or at least to detect, error patterns of small weight.

Chapter 2

Linear Codes

2.1 Linear codes

In this section we introduce a broad class of codes. In fact, virtually every code we consider will belong to this class. We will be able to bring into play some powerful mathematical tools which will enable us to resolve some of the previously discussed problems of coding theory when applied to codes in this class.

A code C is called a *linear code* if $v+w$ is a word in C whenever v and w are in C. That is, a linear code is a code which is closed under addition of words. For example $C = \{000, 111\}$ is a linear code, since all four of the sums

$$000+000=000 \qquad 111+000=111$$
$$000+111=111 \qquad 111+111=000$$

are in C. But $C_1 = \{000, 001, 101\}$ is not a linear code, since 001 and 101 are in C_1 but $001+101$ is not in C_1.

A linear code C must contain the zero word. For if C is to be linear, then the sum $v+v=0$ must be in C by closure under addition. However, as the code C_1 above demonstrates, the zero word being in a code does not guarantee that the code is linear.

Exercises

2.1.1 Determine which of the following codes are linear.

(a) $C = \{101, 111, 011\}$ (b) $C = \{000, 001, 010, 011\}$

(c) $C = \{0000, 0001, 1110\}$ (d) $C = \{0000, 1001, 0110, 1111\}$

(e) $C = \{00000, 11111\}$ (f) $C = \{00000, 11100, 00111, 11011\}$

(g) $C = \{00000, 11110, 01111, 10001\}$

(h) $C = \{000000, 101010, 010101, 111111\}$

One advantage a linear code has over a nonlinear code is that its distance is easier to find. *The distance of a linear code is equal to the minimum weight of any nonzero codeword.* Exercise 2.1.4 below requests the easy proof.

Exercises

2.1.2 Show that $C = \{0000, 1100, 0011, 1111\}$ is a linear code and that its distance is $d = 2$.

2.1.3 Find the distance of each linear code in Exercise 2.1.1. Check answers with Exercise 1.11.12.

2.1.4 Prove that the distance of a linear code is the weight of the nonzero codeword of least weight.

As we will see in the following sections, linear codes are rather highly structured and have many other advantages over the arbitrary codes discussed so far. Here are some problems, tedious to settle in general, but relatively easy for linear codes:

1. For a linear code, there is a procedure for MLD that is simpler and faster to use than the one described earlier (certain linear codes with even more structure have very simple decoding algorithms).
2. Encoding a linear code is faster and requires less storage space than for arbitrary non-linear codes.
3. The probabilities $\theta_p(C, v)$ are straightforward to calculate for a linear code.
4. It is easy to describe the set of error patterns that a linear code will detect.
5. It is much easier to describe the set of error patterns a linear code will correct than it is for arbitrary non-linear codes.

The most important tools and techniques for studying linear codes come from linear algebra. In this and the next several sections we will review some basic facts from linear algebra and attempt to show their relevance to coding theory. Most proofs not depending on scalar products in K^n are exact replicas of the proofs in R^n, and hence are omitted.

Recall that we defined a vector space (over K), as consisting of scalars (K) and a set of vectors, or words, K^n, together with the operations of vector addition and scalar multiplication, which satisfy the ten properties listed in Section 1.7. A nonempty subset U of a vector space V is a *subspace* of V if U is closed under vector addition and scalar multiplication; that is, if v and w are in U, then $v + w$ and av are in U for any scalar a. In particular, since the only scalars in K are 0 and 1, U is a subspace of K^n if and only if U is closed under addition. Therefore C is a linear code if and only if C is a subspace of K^n. Over the next few sections we shall use the knowledge of subspaces to dramatically improve our techniques for encoding and decoding.

2.2 Two important subspaces

We consider two subspaces of the vector space K^n which will provide two interesting examples of linear codes and will be vital in future developments. Definitions and results will be stated for an arbitrary vector space, then interpreted for K^n.

The vector w is said to be a *linear combination* of vectors $v_1, v_2, \ldots, v_k$ if there are scalars $a_1, a_2, \ldots, a_k$ such that

$$w = a_1 v_1 + a_2 v_2 + \cdots + a_k v_k.$$

The set of all linear combinations of the vectors in a given set $S = \{v_1, v_2, \ldots, v_k\}$ is called the *linear span* of S, and is denoted by $\langle S \rangle$. If S is empty, we define $\langle S \rangle = \{0\}$.

In linear algebra it is shown that for any subset S of a vector space V, the linear span $\langle S \rangle$ is a subspace of V, called the subspace *spanned* or *generated* by S. For the vector space K^n, we have a very simple description of $\langle S \rangle$ which is stated in the next theorem. Since $\langle S \rangle$ is a subspace, in K^n we call $\langle S \rangle$ the linear code generated by S.

Theorem 2.2.1 *For any subset S of K^n, the code $C = \langle S \rangle$ generated by S consists precisely of the following words: the zero word, all words in S, and all sums of two or more words in S.*

Example 2.2.2 Let $S = \{0100, 0011, 1100\}$. Then the code $C = \langle S \rangle$ generated by S consists of

$$\begin{array}{llll} 0000, & 0100, & 0100+0011 = 0111, & 0100+0011+1100 = 1011, \\ 1100, & 0011, & 0100+1100 = 1000, & 0011+1100 = 1111; \end{array}$$

that is, $C = \langle S \rangle = \{0000, 0100, 0011, 1100, 0111, 1000, 1111, 1011\}$.

Exercises

2.2.3 For each of the following sets S, list the elements of the linear code $\langle S \rangle$.

(a) $S = \{010, 011, 111\}$
(b) $S = \{1010, 0101, 1111\}$
(c) $S = \{0101, 1010, 1100\}$
(d) $S = \{1000, 0100, 0010, 0001\}$
(e) $S = \{11000, 01111, 11110, 01010\}$
(f) $S = \{10101, 01010, 11111, 00011, 10110\}$

If $v = (a_1, a_2, \ldots, a_n)$ and $w = (b_1, b_2, \ldots, b_n)$ are vectors in K^n, we define the *scalar product* or *dot product* $v \cdot w$ of v and w as

$$v \cdot w = a_1 b_1 + a_2 b_2 + \cdots + a_n b_n.$$

Note that $v \cdot w$ is a scalar, not a vector. For instance, in K^5,

$$\begin{aligned} 11001 \cdot 01101 &= 1 \cdot 0 + 1 \cdot 1 + 0 \cdot 1 + 0 \cdot 0 + 1 \cdot 1 \\ &= 0 + 1 + 0 + 0 + 1 \\ &= 0. \end{aligned}$$

Exercises

2.2.4 Construct examples in K^5 of each of the following rules

(a) $u \cdot (v+w) = u \cdot v + u \cdot w$

(b) $a(v \cdot w) = (av) \cdot w = v \cdot (aw)$.

2.2.5 Prove that the two rules in Exercise 2.2.4 hold in K^n.

Vectors v and w are *orthogonal* if $v \cdot w = 0$. The example above shows that $v = 11001$ and $w = 01101$ are orthogonal in K^5. For a given set S of vectors in K^n, we say a vector v is *orthogonal to the set* S if $v \cdot w = 0$ for all w in S; that is, v is orthogonal to every vector in S. The set of all vectors orthogonal to S is denoted by $S^\perp$ and is called the *orthogonal complement* of S.

In linear algebra it is shown that for any subset S of a vector space V, the orthogonal complement $S^\perp$ is a subspace of V. For the vector space K^n, if $C = \langle S \rangle$, then we write $C^\perp = S^\perp$ and call $C^\perp$ the *dual code* of C.

Example 2.2.6 For $S = \{0100, 0101\}$, we compute the dual code $C^\perp = S^\perp$. We must find all words $v = (x, y, z, w)$ in K^4 such that both the equations

$$v \cdot 0100 = 0$$
$$v \cdot 0101 = 0$$

hold. Computing the scalar product we have

$$y = 0 \text{ and } y + w = 0.$$

Thus $y = w = 0$ but x and z can be either 0 or 1. Writing down all such choices for v we get

$$C^\perp = S^\perp = \{0000, 0010, 1000, 1010\}.$$

Exercises

2.2.7 Find the dual code $C^\perp$ for each of the codes $C = \langle S \rangle$ in Exercise 2.2.3.

2.2.8 Find an example of a nonzero word v such that $v \cdot v = 0$. What can you say about the weight of such a word?

2.2.9 For any subset S of a vector space V, $(S^\perp)^\perp = \langle S \rangle$. Use the example above to construct an example of this fact in K^4.

2.2.10 Prove that $\langle S \rangle \subseteq (S^\perp)^\perp$. (In fact $(S^\perp)^\perp = \langle S \rangle$; for a linear code C, this means $(C^\perp)^\perp = C$.)

2.3 Independence, basis, dimension

We review several important concepts from linear algebra and illustrate how to apply these concepts to linear codes. The main objective is to find an efficient way to describe a linear code without having to list all the codewords.

A set $S = \{v_1, v_2, \ldots, v_k\}$ of vectors is *linearly dependent* if there are scalars $a_1, a_2, \ldots, a_k$ not all zero such that

$$a_1 v_1 + a_2 v_2 + \cdots + a_k v_k = 0.$$

Otherwise the set S is *linearly independent.*

The test for linear independence, then, is to form the vector equation above using arbitrary scalars. If this question forces *all* the scalars $a_1, a_2, \ldots, a_k$ to be 0, then the set S is linearly independent. If *at least one* a_i can be chosen to be nonzero then S is linearly dependent.

Example 2.3.1 We test $S = \{1001, 1101, 1011\}$ for linear independence. Let a, b, and c be scalars (digits) such that

$$a(1001) + b(1101) + c(1011) = 0000.$$

Equating components on both sides yields the scalar equations

$$a+b+c=0, \ b=0, \ c=0, \ a+b+c=0.$$

These equations force $a = b = c = 0$. Therefore S is a linearly independent set of words in K^4.

Example 2.3.2 We test $S = \{110, 011, 101, 111\}$ for linear independence. Consider

$$a(110) + b(011) + c(101) + d(111) = 000.$$

This yields the system of scalar equations

$$\begin{aligned} a+c+d &= 0 \\ a+b+d &= 0 \\ b+c+d &= 0. \end{aligned}$$

Adding these three equations gives $d = 0$. Now we have $a + c = 0$, $a + b = 0$, $b + c = 0$. Thus we can choose $a = b = c = 1$. Therefore S is a linearly dependent set.

In linear algebra it is shown that *any set of vectors $S \neq \{0\}$ contains a largest linearly independent subset.* The next example shows how such a subset may be found.

Example 2.3.3 Let $S = \{110, 011, 101, 111\}$. The last example shows that S is linearly dependent. In fact, we found that

$$1(110) + 1(011) + 1(101) + 0(111) = 000,$$

so we can solve for 101 as a linear combination of the other words in S:

$$101 = 1(110) + 1(011) + 0(111).$$

In the dependent set S, if we take the words in the order given, we come to 101 as the first word which is dependent on, that is, is a linear combination of, the preceding words 110 and 011 in S. Discarding this word, we obtain a new set $S' = \{110, 011, 111\}$. Now S' can be tested for linear independence. If S' is linearly dependent, we discard the first word which is a linear combination of the preceding words, thus obtaining a new set S''. This process may be repeated until we find a new set which is linearly independent; such a set is always a largest linearly independent subset of the given set S. In the present example, this set is S'.

Exercises

2.3.4 Test each of the following sets for linear independence. If the set is linearly dependent, extract from S a largest linearly independent subset.

(a) $S = \{1101, 1110, 1011\}$ (b) $S = \{101, 011, 110, 010\}$
(c) $S = \{1101, 0111, 1100, 0011\}$ (d) $S = \{1000, 0100, 0010, 0001\}$
(e) $S = \{1000, 1100, 1110, 1111\}$ (f) $S = \{1100, 1010, 1001, 0101\}$
(g) $S = \{0110, 1010, 1100, 0011, 1111\}$
(h) $S = \{111000, 000111, 101010, 010101\}$
(i) $S = \{00000000, 10101010, 01010101, 11111111\}$

In Exercise 2.3.4(i) S is found to be a linearly dependent set. Note that S contains the zero word. It is always true that *any set of vectors containing the zero vector is linearly dependent.*

A nonempty subset B of vectors from a vector space V is a *basis* for V if both:

1. B spans V (that is, $\langle B \rangle = V$), and
2. B is a linearly independent set.

Note that *any linearly independent set B is automatically a basis for $\langle B \rangle$*. Also since any linearly dependent set S of vectors that contains a non-zero word always contains a largest independent subset B, we can extract from S a basis B for $\langle S \rangle$. If $S = \{0\}$ then we say that the basis of S is the empty set, $\emptyset$.

Example 2.3.5 Let $S = \{1001, 1101, 1011\}$. In Example 2.3.1 we found that S is linearly independent. Therefore S is a basis for the code $C = \langle S \rangle = \{0000, 1001, 1101, 1011, 0100, 0010, 0110, 1111\}$ which is a subspace of K^4.

Example 2.3.6 Let $S = \{110, 011, 101, 111\}$. In Example 2.3.2 we found that S is linearly dependent. But in Example 2.3.3 we extracted a maximal linearly independent subset $B = S' = \{110, 011, 111\}$ of S. Hence B is a basis for the code $C = \langle S \rangle$.

These examples illustrate how to obtain a basis for the code $C = \langle S \rangle$ generated by a nonempty subset S of K^n. To find a basis for the dual code $C^\perp$, extract a largest linearly independent subset from $C^\perp$ following the procedure in Example 2.3.3

Exercises

2.3.7 For each set in Exercise 2.2.3 find a basis B for the code $C = \langle S \rangle$ and a basis $B^\perp$ for the dual code $C^\perp$.

The set $B = \{110, 011, 111\}$ is not the only largest linearly independent subset of $S = \{110, 011, 101, 111\}$ (see Example 2.3.6). The set $B_1 = \{110, 101, 111\}$ is also such a subset of S. Thus B_1 is also a basis for the code $C = \langle S \rangle$.

In general a vector space usually has many bases. However, *all bases for a vector space contain the same number of elements.* The number of elements in any basis for a vector space is called the *dimension* of the space.

The dimension of K^n is n, since the set of all words of length n and weight one is a basis for K^n. At the other extreme, the basis of the subspace $\{0\}$ is $\emptyset$ and so has dimension 0.

Exercises

2.3.8 Find the dimensions of each code $C = \langle S \rangle$ and its dual $C^\perp$ in Exercise 2.2.3 (see also Exercise 2.2.7).

A basis provides an efficient way to describe a linear code. For any vector space V, if $\{v_1, v_2, \ldots, v_k\}$ *is a basis for* V, *then every vector* w *in* V *can be expressed as a unique linear combination of the basis vectors* $v_1, v_2, \ldots, v_k$; that is, there exist unique scalars $a_1, a_2, \ldots, a_k$ such that $w = a_1v_1 + a_2v_2 + \cdots + a_kv_k$.

Example 2.3.9 We write $w = 011$ as a unique linear combination of the words in the basis $\{110, 001, 100\}$ for K^3. We seek digits a, b, c such that

$$a(110) + b(001) + c(100) = 011.$$

This yields the scalar equations

$$a + c = 0,\ a = 1,\ b = 1,$$

which have the unique solution $a = b = c = 1$. Thus $011 = 1(110) + 1(001) + 1(100)$.

Exercises

2.3.10 Write each of the following words in K^4 as a unique linear combination of the words in the basis $\{1000, 1100, 1110, 1111\}$:

(a) 0011 (b) 1010 (c) 0111 (d) 0001 (e) 0000.

Another important fact about vector spaces is that *any linearly independent subset of a vector space is contained in a basis for the space.* The next example shows how this works.

Example 2.3.11 The set $S = \{110, 001\}$ is a linearly independent subset of K^3. We extend S to a basis for K^3. First we adjoin to S any known basis: $\{100, 010, 001\}$ is a convenient basis to adjoint for K^3. The resulting list of words

$$110, 001, 100, 010, 001$$

is then reduced to a basis for K^3 according to the procedure in Example 2.3.3, solving for 100, 010 or 001.

Exercises

2.3.12 (a) Find a basis for K^4 which contains $\{1001, 1111\}$. (b) Extend $\{101010, 010101\}$ to a basis for K^6.

We now come to two important theorems concerning dimension of linear codes. If a linear code C has dimension k and if $\{v_1, v_2, \ldots, v_k\}$ is a basis for C, then a word w in C can be written as

$$w = a_1 v_1 + a_2 v_2 + \cdots + a_k v_k$$

for a unique choice of digits $a_1, a_2, \ldots, a_k$. Since each a_1 is either 0 or 1, there are 2^k choices for $a_1, a_2, \ldots, a_k$, and hence 2^k words in C.

Theorem 2.3.13 *A linear code of dimension k contains precisely 2^k codewords.*

The next theorem can be proved using elementary results from the theory of systems of linear equations.

Theorem 2.3.14 *Let $C = \langle S \rangle$ be the linear code generated by a subset S of K^n. Then (dimension of C) + (dimension of $C^\perp$) $= n$.*

Exercises

2.3.15 Check your answers in Exercise 2.3.8 with the equation in Theorem 2.3.14.

2.3.16 Let S be a subset of K^7, let $C = \langle S \rangle$ and assume $C^\perp$ has dimension 3.

(a) Find the dimension of $C = \langle S \rangle$.

(b) Find the number of words in C.

2.3.17 Let S be a subset of K^8 and assume that $\{11110000, 00001111, 10000001\}$ is a basis for $C^\perp$. Find the number of words in $C = \langle S \rangle$.

2.3.18 Theorem 2.3.14 also holds in R^n. In R^n every vector can be written uniquely as the sum of a vector in $\langle S \rangle$ and a vector in $S^\perp$, and the zero vector is the only vector $\langle S \rangle$ and S have in common. (For example, in R^3 take $\langle S \rangle$ to be the xy-plane and $S^\perp$ the z-axis.) Use $S = \{000, 101\}$ in K^3 to show that this is not the case in general in K^n.

The last result in this section deals with the question of how many different bases a linear code can have. In R^n a subspace has infinitely many bases, but this is not so in K^n.

Theorem 2.3.19 *A linear code of dimension k has precisely $\frac{1}{k!}\prod_{i=0}^{k-1}(2^k - 2^i)$ different bases.*

Example 2.3.20 The linear code K^4 has dimension $k = 4$ and hence

$$\frac{1}{4!}\prod_{i=0}^{3}(2^4 - 2^i) = \frac{1}{4!}(2^4 - 1)(2^4 - 2)(2^4 - 2^2)(2^4 - 2^3) = 840$$

different bases. Any linear code contained in K^n, for $n \geq 4$, which has dimension 4 also has 840 different bases.

Exercises

2.3.21 Let b_n be the number of different bases for K^n. Verify the entries in the following table:

n	1	2	3	4	5	6
b_n	1	3	28	840	83,328	27,998,208

2.3.22 List all the bases for K^2 and for K^3.

2.3.23 Find the number of different bases for each code $C = \langle S \rangle$ for

(a) $S = \{010, 011, 111\}$, (b) $S = \{1010, 0101, 1111\}$,

(c) $S = \{0101, 1010, 1100\}$, (d) $S = \{1000, 0100, 0010, 0001\}$,

(e) $S = \{11000, 01111, 11110, 01010\}$,

(f) $S = \{10101, 01010, 11111, 00011, 10110\}$.

2.4 Matrices

An $m \times n$ *matrix* is a rectangular array of scalars with m rows and n columns. We assume the reader is familiar with the algebra of matrices over the real numbers. In this section we review the necessary parts of elementary matrix theory needed for coding theory.

If A is an $m \times n$ matrix and B is an $n \times p$ matrix, then the *product* AB is the $m \times p$ matrix which has for its (i, j)th entry (that is, the entry in row i and column j) the dot product of row i of A and column j of B. For example

$$\begin{bmatrix} 1011 \\ 0101 \end{bmatrix} \begin{bmatrix} 101 \\ 011 \\ 101 \\ 100 \end{bmatrix} = \begin{bmatrix} 100 \\ 111 \end{bmatrix}$$

Note that the number of columns of the first matrix must equal the number of rows of the second matrix in order for the product to be defined.

Exercises

2.4.1 Find the product of each pair of the following matrices whenever the product is defined.

$$A = \begin{bmatrix} 11011 \\ 00101 \\ 11011 \end{bmatrix} \quad B = \begin{bmatrix} 0101 \\ 1001 \\ 1100 \end{bmatrix} \quad C = \begin{bmatrix} 110110 \\ 011011 \\ 101101 \\ 101011 \end{bmatrix} \quad D = \begin{bmatrix} 1111 \\ 0101 \\ 1010 \\ 1101 \end{bmatrix}$$

The usual algebraic rules for matrices over the reals also hold for matrices over K. The $m \times n$ *zero matrix* is the $m \times n$ matrix with each entry equal to 0. The $n \times n$ (square) matrix I in which the (i, j)th entry is 1 if $i = j$ and is 0 otherwise is the $n \times n$ *identity matrix*. For any matrix A, $AI = A$ and $IA = A$. The next three exercises point out three algebraic rules which fail for matrices over K.

Exercises

2.4.2 Find 2×2 matrices A and B over K such that $AB \neq BA$.

2.4.3 Find 2×2 matrices A and B over K, both different from the zero matrix 0, such that $AB = 0$.

2.4.4 Find 2×2 matrices A, B, and C over K such that $AB = AC$ but $B \neq C$.

There are two types of *elementary row operations* which may be performed on a matrix over K. They are:

1. interchanging two rows, and
2. replacing a row by itself plus another row.

Two matrices are *row equivalent* if one can be obtained from the other by a sequence of elementary row operators.

A 1 in a matrix M (over K) is called a *leading* 1 if there are no 1s to its left in the same row, and a column of M is called a *leading column* if it contains a leading 1. M is in *row echelon form* (REF) if the zero rows of M (if any) are all at the bottom, and each leading 1 is to the right of the leading 1s in the rows above. If further, each leading column contains exactly one 1, M is in *reduced row echelon form* (RREF).

Any matrix over K can be put in REF or RREF by a sequence of elementary row operations. In other words, a matrix is row equivalent to a matrix in REF or in RREF. For a given matrix, its RREF is unique, but it may have many REFs.

Example 2.4.5 We find the RREF for the matrix M below using elementary row operations

$$M = \begin{bmatrix} 1011 \\ 1010 \\ 1101 \end{bmatrix} \to \begin{bmatrix} 1011 \\ 0001 \\ 0110 \end{bmatrix} \quad \text{(add row 1 to row 2 and to row 3)}$$

$$\to \begin{bmatrix} 1011 \\ 0110 \\ 0001 \end{bmatrix} \quad \text{(interchange rows 2 and 3)}$$

$$\to \begin{bmatrix} 1010 \\ 0110 \\ 0001 \end{bmatrix} \quad \text{(add row 3 to row 1)}$$

Exercises

2.4.6 Find the RREF for each of the four matrices in Exercise 2.4.1.

The *transpose* of an $m \times n$ matrix A is the $n \times m$ matrix A^T which has column i of A as its i-th row. For example,

$$\text{if } A = \begin{bmatrix} 1011 \\ 0000 \\ 0110 \end{bmatrix}, \text{ then } A^T = \begin{bmatrix} 100 \\ 001 \\ 101 \\ 100 \end{bmatrix}.$$

We will need two facts about the transpose of matrices A and B: $(A^T)^T = A$ and $(AB)^T = B^T A^T$.

2.5 Bases for $C = \langle S \rangle$ and $C^{\perp}$

We develop algorithms for finding bases for a linear code and its dual. These methods will be of great assistance in our study of linear codes.

Let S be a nonempty subset of K^n. The first two algorithms provide a basis for $C = \langle S \rangle$, the linear code generated by S.

Algorithm 2.5.1 Form the matrix A whose rows are the words in S. Use elementary row operations to find a REF of A. Then the nonzero rows of the REF form a basis for $C = \langle S \rangle$.

The algorithm works because the rows of A generate C and elementary row operations simply interchange words or replace one word (row) with another in C giving a new set of codewords which still generates C. Clearly the nonzero rows of a matrix in REF are linearly independent.

Example 2.5.2 We find a basis for the linear code $C = \langle S \rangle$ for $S = \{11101, 10110, 01011, 11010\}$.

$$A = \begin{bmatrix} 11101 \\ 10110 \\ 01011 \\ 11010 \end{bmatrix} \to \begin{bmatrix} 11101 \\ 01011 \\ 01011 \\ 00111 \end{bmatrix} \to \begin{bmatrix} 11101 \\ 01011 \\ 00111 \\ 00000 \end{bmatrix}.$$

The last matrix is a REF of A. By Algorithm 2.5.1, $\{11101, 01011, 00111\}$ is a basis for $C = \langle S \rangle$. Another REF of A is

$$\begin{bmatrix} 11101 \\ 01100 \\ 00111 \\ 00000 \end{bmatrix}$$

so $\{11101, 01100, 00111\}$ is also a basis for $C = \langle S \rangle$. Note that Algorithm 2.5.1 does not produce a unique basis for $\langle S \rangle$, nor are the words in the basis necessarily in the given set S.

Exercises

2.5.3 Use Algorithm 2.5.1 to find a basis for $C = \langle S \rangle$ for each of the following sets S.

(a) $S = \{010, 011, 111\}$ (b) $S = \{1010, 0101, 1111\}$
(c) $S = \{0101, 1010, 1100\}$ (d) $S = \{1000, 0100, 0010, 0001\}$
(e) $S = \{11000, 01111, 11110, 01010\}$
(f) $S = \{10101, 01010, 11111, 00011, 10110\}$
(g) $S = \{0110, 1010, 1100, 0011, 1111\}$
(h) $S = \{111000, 000111, 101010, 010101\}$
(i) $S = \{00000000, 10101010, 01010101, 11111111\}$

Algorithm 2.5.4 (finding a basis for C) Form the matrix A whose columns are the words in S. Use elementary row operations to place A in REF and locate the leading columns in the REF. Then the original columns of A corresponding to these leading columns form a basis for $C = \langle S \rangle$.

It is shown in elementary linear algebra that a linearly independent set of columns of a matrix is still linearly independent after applying a sequence of elementary row operations to the matrix. It is easy to see that the leading columns of a matrix in REF form a linearly independent set.

Example 2.5.5 We use Algorithm 2.5.4 to find a basis for $C = \langle S \rangle$ for the set S of Example 2.5.2.

$$A = \begin{bmatrix} 1101 \\ 1011 \\ 1100 \\ 0111 \\ 1010 \end{bmatrix} \to \begin{bmatrix} 1101 \\ 0110 \\ 0001 \\ 0111 \\ 0111 \end{bmatrix} \to \begin{bmatrix} 1101 \\ 0110 \\ 0001 \\ 0000 \\ 0000 \end{bmatrix}, \text{ which is in REF.}$$

Since columns 1, 2, and 4 of the REF are the leading columns, Algorithm 2.5.4 says that columns 1, 2, and 4 of A form a basis for $C = \langle S \rangle$. This basis {11101, 10110, 11010}. Note that Algorithm 2.5.4 has the property of producing a basis for $C = \langle S \rangle$, all of whose elements are words in the given set S.

Exercises

2.5.6 Use Algorithm 2.5.4 to find a basis for $C = \langle S \rangle$ for each set S in Exercise 2.5.3 and compare answers.

Now we give an algorithm for finding a basis for the dual code $C^\perp$. It will be a very useful algorithm in our subsequent work. Also, notice that this algorithm provides a basis for C (since it includes Algorithm 2.5.1).

Algorithm 2.5.7 (finding a basis for $C^\perp$) Form the matrix A whose rows are the words in S. Use elementary row operations to place A in RREF. Let G be the $k \times n$ matrix consisting of all the nonzero rows of the RREF. Let X be the $k \times (n-k)$ matrix obtained from G by deleting the leading columns of G. Form an $n \times (n-k)$ matrix H as follows:

(i) in the rows of H corresponding to the leading columns of G, place, in order, the rows of X;

(ii) in the remaining $n-k$ rows of H, place, in order, the rows of the $(n-k) \times (n-k)$ identity matrix I.

Then the columns of H form a basis for $C^\perp$.

The algorithm works because the $n-k$ columns of H are linearly independent, $\dim C^\perp = n - \dim C = n - k$, and to within a permutation of the columns of G and the rows of H, $GH = X + X = 0$.

The following description of Algorithm 2.5.7 may help in remembering it. The matrix G contains k leading columns. Permute the columns of G so that these columns come first. The other columns form the matrix X. Call this matrix G'. Then Algorithm 2.5.7 begins thus (each entry in O is 0):

$$A \to \begin{bmatrix} G \\ O \end{bmatrix} \text{ (RREF)}$$

Permute the columns of G to form $G' = [I_k, X]$. Form a matrix H' as follows:

$$H' = \begin{bmatrix} X \\ I_{n-k} \end{bmatrix}.$$

Apply the inverse of the permutation applied to the columns of G to the rows of H' to form H.

Example 2.5.8 We use Algorithm 2.5.7 to find a basis for $C^{\perp}$ for the set S of Example 2.5.2.

$$A = \begin{bmatrix} 11101 \\ 10110 \\ 01011 \\ 11010 \end{bmatrix} \rightarrow \begin{bmatrix} 11101 \\ 01011 \\ 00111 \\ 00000 \end{bmatrix} \rightarrow \begin{bmatrix} 11010 \\ 01011 \\ 00111 \\ 00000 \end{bmatrix} \rightarrow \begin{bmatrix} 10001 \\ 01011 \\ 00111 \\ 00000 \end{bmatrix},$$

which is in RREF. Now $G = \left[\begin{array}{c|c} 100 & 01 \\ 010 & 11 \\ 001 & 11 \end{array}\right]$, $k = 3$, and $X = \begin{bmatrix} 01 \\ 11 \\ 11 \end{bmatrix}$. The leading columns of G are columns 1, 2, and 3, so the rows of X are placed in rows 1, 2, and 3 respectively, of the $5 \times (5-3)$ matrix H. The remaining rows of H are filled with the 2×2 identity matrix. Thus

$$H = \left[\begin{array}{c} 01 \\ 11 \\ 11 \\ \hline 10 \\ 01 \end{array}\right].$$

By Algorithm 2.5.7, the columns of H form a basis for $C^{\perp}$. Note that, by Algorithm 2.5.1, the rows of G form a basis for $C = \langle S \rangle$.

Example 2.5.9 Suppose $n = 10$ and we have a set S of words in K^{10}. Suppose the RREF of the matrix A in Algorithm 2.5.7 has nonzero rows

$$G = \begin{bmatrix} 1\,0\,1\,0\,0\,1\,0\,1\,0\,1 \\ 0\,0\,0\,1\,0\,1\,0\,0\,0\,1 \\ 0\,0\,0\,0\,1\,0\,0\,1\,0\,0 \\ 0\,0\,0\,0\,0\,0\,1\,0\,0\,1 \\ 0\,0\,0\,0\,0\,0\,0\,0\,1\,1 \end{bmatrix}$$

The leading columns of G are columns 1, 4, 5, 7, and 9. We permute the columns of G into the order 1, 4, 5, 7, 9, 2, 3, 6, 8, 10 (so the leading columns are first) to form the matrix

$$G' = \left[\begin{array}{c|c} 1\,0\,0\,0\,0 & 0\,1\,1\,1\,1 \\ 0\,1\,0\,0\,0 & 0\,0\,1\,0\,1 \\ 0\,0\,1\,0\,0 & 0\,0\,0\,1\,0 \\ 0\,0\,0\,1\,0 & 0\,0\,0\,0\,1 \\ 0\,0\,0\,0\,1 & 0\,0\,0\,0\,1 \end{array}\right]$$

Then we form the matrix H' and finally rearrange the rows of H into their natural order to form the matrix H'.

$$H' = \begin{bmatrix} X \\ I \end{bmatrix} = \begin{bmatrix} 01111 \\ 00101 \\ 00010 \\ 00001 \\ 00001 \\ 10000 \\ 01000 \\ 00100 \\ 00010 \\ 00001 \end{bmatrix} \begin{matrix} 1 \\ 4 \\ 5 \\ 7 \\ 9 \\ 2 \\ 3 \\ 6 \\ 8 \\ 10 \end{matrix}; \quad H = \begin{bmatrix} 01111 \\ 10000 \\ 01000 \\ 00101 \\ 00010 \\ 00100 \\ 00001 \\ 00010 \\ 00001 \\ 00001 \end{bmatrix} \begin{matrix} 1 \\ 2 \\ 3 \\ 4 \\ 5 \\ 6 \\ 7 \\ 8 \\ 9 \\ 10 \end{matrix}$$

By Algorithm 2.5.7, the columns of H form a basis for $C^{\perp}$.

Exercises

2.5.10 Use Algorithm 2.5.7 to find a basis for $C^{\perp}$ for each of the codes $C = \langle S \rangle$ where

(a) $S = \{010, 011, 111\}$ (b) $S = \{1010, 0101, 1111\}$
(c) $S = \{0101, 1010, 1100\}$ (d) $S = \{1000, 0100, 0010, 0001\}$
(e) $S = \{11000, 01111, 11110, 01010\}$
(f) $S = \{10101, 01010, 11111, 00011, 10110\}$
(g) $S = \{0110, 1010, 1100, 0011, 1111\}$
(h) $S = \{111000, 000111, 101010, 010101\}$
(i) $S = \{00000000, 10101010, 01010101, 11111111\}$.

2.5.11 With the notation of Algorithm 2.5.7, explain why it is expected that $GH = 0$.

2.5.12 For each of the following sets S, use Algorithm 2.5.7 to produce a basis B for the code $C = \langle S \rangle$ and a basis $B^{\perp}$ for the dual code $C^{\perp}$.

(a) $S = \{000000, 111000, 000111, 111111\}$
(b) $S = \{1101000, 0110100, 0011010, 0001101, 1000110, 0100011, 1010001\}$
(c) $S = \{1111000, 0111100, 0011110, 0001111, 1000111, 1100011, 1110001\}$
(d) $S = \{101101110, 011011101, 110110010, 011011110, 111111101\}$
(e) $S = \{100100100, 010010010, 111111111, 000000000\}$
(f) $S = \{001101, 001000, 001111, 000101, 000001\}$

2.6 Generating matrices and encoding

We put the material of the last several sections to work to find an important matrix for a linear code and to see how this matrix is used to transmit messages.

First a few preliminary notes. The *rank* of a matrix over K is the number of nonzero rows in any REF of the matrix. The *dimension k of the code C* is the dimension of C, as a subspace of K^n. If C also has length n and distance d, then we refer to C as an (n,k,d) linear code. These three *parameters*, length, dimension and distance, provide vital information about C.

If C is a linear code of length n and dimension k, then any matrix whose rows form a basis for C is called a *generator matrix* for C. Note that a generator matrix for C must have k rows and n columns, and it must have rank k.

Theorem 2.6.1 *A matrix G is a generator matrix for some linear code C if and only if the rows of G are linearly independent; that is, if and only if the rank of G is equal to the number of rows of G.*

Because row equivalent matrices have the same rank, we have the following theorem.

Theorem 2.6.2 *If G is a generator matrix for a linear code C, then any matrix row equivalent to G is also a generator matrix for C. In particular, any linear code has a generator matrix in RREF.*

To find a generator matrix for a linear code C, form the matrix whose rows are the words in C. Since $C = \langle C \rangle$, either Algorithm 2.5.1 or Algorithm 2.5.7 can be used to produce a basis for C. The matrix whose rows are these basis vectors is a generator matrix for C.

Example 2.6.3 We find a generator matrix for the code $C = \{0000, 1110, 0111, 1001\}$. Using Algorithm 2.5.1,

$$A = \begin{bmatrix} 0000 \\ 1110 \\ 0111 \\ 1001 \end{bmatrix} \to \begin{bmatrix} 1110 \\ 0111 \\ 1001 \\ 0000 \end{bmatrix} \to \begin{bmatrix} 1110 \\ 0111 \\ 0111 \\ 0000 \end{bmatrix} \to \begin{bmatrix} 1110 \\ 0111 \\ 0000 \\ 0000 \end{bmatrix},$$

so $G = \begin{bmatrix} 1110 \\ 0111 \end{bmatrix}$ is a generator matrix for C. By Algorithm 2.5.7, since the RREF of A is $\begin{bmatrix} 1001 \\ 0111 \\ 0000 \\ 0000 \end{bmatrix}$, $G_1 = \begin{bmatrix} 1001 \\ 0111 \end{bmatrix}$ is also a generator matrix for C.

Exercises

2.6.4 Determine whether each of the following is a generator matrix for some linear code.

$$A = \begin{bmatrix} 0\,1\,0\,0\,1\,1\,1\,0\,1 \\ 1\,0\,0\,1\,0\,1\,1\,0\,1 \\ 1\,0\,1\,1\,0\,0\,1\,1\,0 \\ 1\,0\,1\,1\,0\,1\,1\,0\,1 \end{bmatrix} \qquad B = \begin{bmatrix} 1\,0\,0\,1\,1\,0\,1\,0\,0\,1 \\ 1\,1\,0\,1\,0\,0\,0\,1\,0\,1 \\ 0\,1\,1\,1\,0\,0\,1\,0\,1\,1 \\ 1\,0\,0\,0\,0\,1\,0\,1\,1\,1 \\ 1\,0\,1\,0\,0\,0\,1\,1\,1\,0 \end{bmatrix}$$

2.6.5 Find a generator matrix in RREF for each of the following codes.

(a) $C = \{000, 001, 010, 011\}$ (b) $C = \{0000, 1001, 0110, 1111\}$

(c) $C = \{00000, 11111\}$ (d) $C = \{00000, 11100, 00111, 11011\}$

(e) $C = \{00000, 11110, 01111, 10001\}$

(f) $C = \{000000, 101010, 010101, 111111\}$

2.6.6 Find a generator matrix for each of the following codes. Give the dimension of the code.

(a) $C = \{000000, 001011, 010101, 011110, 100110, 101101, 110011, 111000\}$

(b) $C = \{00000000, 01101111, 11011000, 11111101, 10010010, 00100101, 01001010, 10110111\}$

(c) $C = \{0000000000, 1111100000, 0000011111, 1111111111\}$

2.6.7 Find a generator matrix for the linear code generated by each of the following sets. Give the parameters (n, k, d) for each code.

(a) $S = \{11111111, 11110000, 11001100, 10101010\}$

(b) $S = \{11111100, 11110011, 11001111, 00111111\}$

(c) $S = \{100100100, 010010010, 001001001, 111111111\}$

(d) $S = \{10101, 01010, 11111, 00011, 10110\}$

(e) $S = \{1010, 0101, 1111\}$

(f) $S = \{101101, 011010, 110111, 000111, 110000\}$

(g) $S = \{1001011, 0101010, 1001100, 0011001, 0000111\}$

Let C be a linear code of length n and dimension k. If G is a generator matrix for C and if u is a word of length k written as a row vector, then $v = uG$ is a word in C, since v is a linear combination of the rows of G, which form a basis for C. Indeed, if $u = (a_1, a_2, \ldots, a_k)$ and if

$$G = \begin{bmatrix} g_1 \\ g_2 \\ \vdots \\ g_k \end{bmatrix},$$

where $g_1, g_2, \ldots, g_k$ are the rows of G, then $v = uG = a_1g_1 + a_2g_2 + \cdots + a_kg_k$. On the other hand, since every word v in C is a linear combination of basis words (rows of G), then $v = uG$ for some u in K^k. Moreover, if $u_1G = u_2G$, then $u_1 = u_2$ since each word in C is a *unique* linear combination of the words in a basis. Thus no word $v = uG$ is produced by more than one u in K^k.

Theorem 2.6.8 *If G is a generator matrix for a linear code C of length n and dimension k, then $v = uG$ ranges over all 2^k words in C as u ranges over all 2^k words of length k. Thus C is the set of all words uG, u in K^k. Moreover, $u_1G = u_2G$ if and only if $u_1 = u_2$.*

Note that Theorem 2.6.8 says that the messages that can be encoded by a linear (n, k, d) code are exactly all messages u in K^k. The message u is encoded as $v = uG$, so only k digits in any codeword are used to carry the message. Notice that the information rate of an (n, k, d) code is $\log_2(2^k)/n = k/n$.

Example 2.6.9 Let C be the (5, 3, d) linear code with generator matrix shown below. The information rate of C is $k/n = 3/5$. All messages u in K^3 may be encoded. For example the message $u = 101$ is encoded as

$$v = uG = [101]\begin{bmatrix} 1\,0\,1\,1\,0 \\ 0\,1\,0\,1\,1 \\ 0\,0\,1\,0\,1 \end{bmatrix} = 10011.$$

Exercises

2.6.10 For each of the following generating matrices, encode the given messages.

(a) $G = \begin{bmatrix} 1\,0\,0\,1\,1 \\ 0\,1\,0\,1\,0 \\ 0\,0\,1\,0\,1 \end{bmatrix}$

(i) $u = 100$ (ii) $u = 010$ (iii) $u = 111$

(b) $G = \begin{bmatrix} 1\,0\,0\,0\,1\,1\,1 \\ 0\,1\,0\,0\,1\,0\,1 \\ 0\,0\,1\,0\,0\,1\,1 \end{bmatrix}$

(i) $u = 000$ (ii) $u = 100$ (iii) $u = 111$

(c) $G = \begin{bmatrix} 1\,1\,0\,1\,0\,0\,1 \\ 0\,0\,1\,0\,1\,1\,1 \\ 0\,1\,0\,1\,0\,1\,0 \\ 1\,1\,1\,1\,1\,1\,1 \end{bmatrix}$

(i) $u = 1000$ (ii) $u = 1010$ (iii) $u = 0011$ (iv) $u = 1011$

2.6.11 Assign messages to the words in K^3 as follows:

000	100	010	001	110	101	011	111
A	B	E	H	M	R	T	W

Using the generator matrix in Example 2.6.9, encode the message BE THERE (ignore the space).

2.6.12 Let C be the code with generator matrix

$$G = \begin{bmatrix} 1\,0\,0\,0\,1\,1\,1 \\ 0\,1\,0\,0\,1\,1\,0 \\ 0\,0\,1\,0\,1\,0\,1 \\ 0\,0\,0\,1\,0\,1\,1 \end{bmatrix}.$$

Assign messages to the words in K^4 as follows:

0000	1000	0100	0010	0001	1100	1010	1001
A	B	C	D	E	F	G	H
0110	0101	0011	1110	1101	1011	0111	1111
I	J	K	L	M	N	O	P

(a) Encode the message HELP.

(b) Transmit the message HELP assuming that during transmission the first word receives an error in the first position, the second word receives no errors, the third an error in the seventh position, and the fourth an error in the fifth and sixth positions.

(c) Encode the message CALL HOME BAMA (ignore the spaces).

2.6.13 Find the number of messages which can be sent, and the information rate r, for each of the linear codes in Exercises 2.6.6 and 2.6.7.

2.7 Parity-check matrices

We develop another matrix associated with a linear code and closely connected with the generator matrix. This new matrix will be of great value in designing decoding schemes.

A matrix H is called a *parity-check matrix* for a linear code C if the columns of H form a basis for the dual code $C^\perp$. If C has length n and dimension k, then, since the sum of the dimensions of C and $C^\perp$ is n, any parity-check matrix for C must have n rows, $n-k$ columns and rank $n-k$. Compare the following theorem to Theorem 2.6.1.

Theorem 2.7.1 *A matrix H is a parity-check matrix for some linear code C if and only if the columns of H are linearly independent.*

The next theorem describes a linear code in terms of its parity-check matrix.

Theorem 2.7.2 *If H is a parity-check matrix for a linear code C of length n, then C consists precisely of all words v in K^n such that $vH = 0$.*

If we are given a generator matrix for a linear code C, then we can find a parity-check matrix for C using Algorithm 2.5.7. The parity-check matrix is the matrix H constructed in Algorithm 2.5.7, since the columns of H form a basis for $C^\perp$.

Example 2.7.3 We find a parity-check matrix for the code $C = \{0000, 1110, 0111, 1001\}$ of Example 2.6.3. There we found that

$$G_1 = \begin{bmatrix} 10 & 01 \\ 01 & 11 \end{bmatrix} = [I\ X]$$

is a generator matrix for C which is in RREF. By Algorithm 2.5.7, we construct H:

$$H = \begin{bmatrix} X \\ I \end{bmatrix} = \begin{bmatrix} 01 \\ 11 \\ 10 \\ 01 \end{bmatrix}$$

is a parity-check matrix for C. Note that $vH = 00$ for all words v in C.

Exercises

2.7.4 Find a parity-check matrix from each of the following codes.

(a) $C = \{000, 001, 010, 011\}$
(b) $C = \{0000, 1001, 0110, 1111\}$
(c) $C = \{00000, 11111\}$
(d) $C = \{00000, 11100, 00111, 11011\}$
(e) $C = \{00000, 11110, 01111, 10001\}$
(f) $C = \{000000, 101010, 010101, 111111\}$

2.7.5 Find a parity-check matrix for each of the following codes (the generating matrices were constructed in Exercises 2.6.6 and 2.6.7).

(a) $C = \{000000, 001011, 010101, 011110, 100110, 101101, 110011, 111000\}$
(b) $C = \{00000000, 01101111, 11011000, 11111101, 10010010, 00100101, 01001010, 10110111\}$
(c) $C = \{0000000000, 1111100000, 0000011111, 1111111111\}$
(d) $C = \langle S\rangle$, $S = \{11111111, 11110000, 11001100, 10101010\}$
(e) $C = \langle S\rangle$, $S = \{11111100, 11110011, 11001111, 00111111\}$
(f) $C = \langle S\rangle$, $S = \{100100100, 010010010, 001001001, 111111111\}$
(g) $C = \langle S\rangle$, $S = \{10101, 01010, 11111, 00011, 10110\}$
(h) $C = \langle S\rangle$, $S = \{1010, 0101, 1111\}$
(i) $C = \langle S\rangle$, $S = \{101101, 011010, 110111, 000111, 110000\}$
(j) $C = \langle S\rangle$, $S = \{1001011, 0101010, 1001100, 0011001, 0000111\}$

We now characterize the relationship between a generator matrix and parity check matrix for a linear code, and the relationship between these matrices for a linear code and its dual code.

Theorem 2.7.6 *Matrices G and H are generating and parity-check matrices, respectively, for some linear code C if and only if*

(i) *the rows of G are linearly independent,*

(ii) *the columns of H are linearly independent,*

(iii) *the number of rows of G plus the number of columns of H equals the number of columns of G which equals the number of rows of H, and*

(iv) $GH = 0$.

Theorem 2.7.7 *H is a parity-check matrix of C if and only if H^T is a generator matrix for $C^\perp$.*

Theorem 2.7.7 follows from Theorem 2.7.6 and the fact that

$$H^T G^T = (GH)^T = 0.$$

Given any one of the generating or parity-check matrices of C or of $C^\perp$, Algorithm 2.5.7 and Theorem 2.7.7 can be used to form the other three matrices. The following diagram indicates how this is done.

$$\begin{array}{ccc} H_{C^\perp} & \xleftarrow{\text{Algorithm 2.5.7}} & G_{C^\perp} \\ \text{Transpose} \downarrow & & \uparrow \text{Transpose} \\ G_C & \xrightarrow{\text{Algorithm 2.5.7}} & H_C \end{array}$$

Example 2.7.8 Let C be a linear code with parity-check matrix

$$H = \begin{bmatrix} 11 \\ 11 \\ 01 \\ 10 \\ 01 \end{bmatrix} = \begin{bmatrix} X \\ I \end{bmatrix}.$$

(a) Then a generator matrix for $C^\perp$ is

$$H^T = \begin{bmatrix} 11010 \\ 11101 \end{bmatrix}.$$

(b) The RREF of H^T is $\begin{bmatrix} 11010 \\ 00011 \end{bmatrix}$, so, by Algorithm 2.5.7, a parity-check matrix for $C^\perp$ is

$$\begin{bmatrix} 110 \\ 100 \\ 011 \\ 010 \\ 001 \end{bmatrix}.$$

(c) From the form of H, we have that

$$G = \begin{bmatrix} 100 & 11 \\ 010 & 11 \\ 001 & 01 \end{bmatrix} = [I, X]$$

is a generator matrix for C. This is seen by using Algorithm 2.5.7 backwards. Thus, by Theorem 2.7.7 G^T is also a parity-check matrix for $C^{\perp}$.

$$G^T = \begin{bmatrix} 1\,0\,0 \\ 0\,1\,0 \\ 0\,0\,1 \\ 1\,1\,0 \\ 1\,1\,1 \end{bmatrix}$$

Exercises

2.7.9 In each part, a parity-check matrix for a linear code C is given. Find (i) a generator matrix for $C^{\perp}$; (ii) a generator matrix for C.

(a) $H = \begin{bmatrix} 1\,0\,0 \\ 1\,0\,0 \\ 0\,1\,0 \\ 0\,0\,1 \\ 0\,1\,0 \\ 0\,0\,1 \end{bmatrix}$ (b) $H = \begin{bmatrix} 0\,1 \\ 1\,0 \\ 0\,1 \\ 1\,0 \\ 0\,1 \end{bmatrix}$ (c) $H = \begin{bmatrix} 1\,1\,1 \\ 1\,1\,0 \\ 1\,0\,1 \\ 0\,1\,1 \\ 1\,0\,0 \\ 0\,1\,0 \\ 0\,0\,1 \end{bmatrix}$

2.7.10 List all the words in the dual code $C^{\perp}$ for the code C = {00000, 11111}. Then find generating and parity-check matrices for $C^{\perp}$

2.7.11 For each code C described below, find the dimension of C, the dimension of $C^{\perp}$, the size of generating and parity-check matrices for C and for $C^{\perp}$, the number of words in C and in $C^{\perp}$, and the information rates r of C and $C^{\perp}$.

(a) C has length $n = 2^t - 1$ and dimension t.

(b) C has length $n = 23$ and dimension 11.

(c) C has length $n = 15$ and dimension 8.

2.8 Equivalent codes

Any $k \times n$ matrix G with $k < n$ whose first k columns form the $k \times k$ identity matrix I_k, so

$$G = [I_k, X],$$

automatically has linearly independent rows and is in RREF. Thus G is a generator matrix for some linear code of length n and dimension k. Such a generator matrix is said to be in *standard form*, and the code C generated by G is called a *systematic code*.

Not all linear codes have a generator matrix in standard form. For example, the code defined by the generator matrix in the exercise below has five other generating matrices; none of them are in standard form, and neither is G.

Exercises

2.8.1 Find the other five generator matrices for the code generated by

$$G = \begin{bmatrix} 1\,0\,0 \\ 0\,0\,1 \end{bmatrix}.$$

It is desirable, however, to use codes having generating matrices in standard form. One reason for this is that if a linear code C has generator matrix G in standard form, $G = [I, X]$, then Algorithm 2.5.7 yields at once that

$$H = \begin{bmatrix} X \\ I \end{bmatrix}$$

is a parity-check matrix for C.

By Theorem 2.6.8 each codeword v in a linear code C of length n and dimension k is equal to uG for one and only word u in K^k, where G is a generator matrix for C. We think of the word u of length k as the message to be sent. But rather than transmitting u, we of course transmit the codeword $v = uG$. If MLD manages to conclude correctly that $v = uG$ was sent, then the recipient of the transmission must recover somehow the original message u from uG. If G is in standard form, then it is trivial to recover u from uG. For in this case

$$v = uG = u[I\ X] = [uI\ uX] = [u\ uX].$$

So we obtain the following theorem, which points out an important advantage of having a generator matrix in standard form.

Theorem 2.8.2 *If C is a linear code of length n and dimension k with generator matrix G in standard form, then the first k digits in the codeword $v = uG$ form the word u in K^k.*

Example 2.8.3 If

$$G = \left[\begin{array}{c|c} 1\,0\,0\,0 & 1\,0\,1 \\ 0\,1\,0\,0 & 1\,0\,0 \\ 0\,0\,1\,0 & 1\,1\,0 \\ 0\,0\,0\,1 & 0\,1\,1 \end{array}\right] = [I_4\ X]$$

and if the message is $u = 0111$, then $uG = 0111001 = [u001]$. And if $u = 1011$, then $uG = 1011000$.

Exercises

2.8.4 Let C be the generator matrix in Example 2.8.3. Encode each of the following messages u, and observe that the first 4 digits in the resulting codeword form the message u.

(a) $u = 1111$ (b) $u = 1011$ (c) $u = 0000$

2.8.5 Explain a method for recovering u from uG if G is not in standard form.

2.8.6 If a linear code C has generator matrix

$$G = \begin{bmatrix} 1100101 \\ 0110101 \\ 1011011 \\ 1100110 \\ 0110000 \end{bmatrix},$$

recover u from $v = uG = 0000101$.

Under the hypotheses of Theorem 2.8.2 the first k digits of the codeword $v = uG$ are called the *information digits*, since they actually contain the message u, while the last $n-k$ digits of $v = uG$ are called the *redundancy* or *parity-check digits*.

With all these advantages of having a linear code with generator matrix in standard form, what can be done if we are stuck with a code C having no generator matrix in standard form? Consider the code C with generator matrix G from Exercise 2.8.1 (see below). As indicated in Exercise 2.8.1, C has no generator matrix in standard form. Suppose, in this example, we decide to rearrange the digits in all codewords and transmit the digits in the order "first, third, second," rather than "first, second, third." The four words in C have been transformed, then, into the four words in the new code C' as indicated in the following chart:

$$C = \{000, 100, 001, 101\}$$
$$C' = \{000, 100, 010, 110\}$$

Note that C', although a different code from C, shares many properties with C. For example, both C and C' are linear; both have length 3, dimension 2 and distance 1. But C' has an advantage over C, namely C' has a generator matrix in standard form. Observe that G' is obtained from G by switching the second and third columns, just as C' is obtained from C by consistently switching the second and third digits.

$$G = \begin{bmatrix} 100 \\ 001 \end{bmatrix}$$
$$G' = \begin{bmatrix} 100 \\ 010 \end{bmatrix}$$

If C is any block code of length n, we can always obtain a new block code C' of length n by choosing a particular permutation of the n digits and then consistently rearranging every word in C in the chosen way. The resulting code C' is said to be *equivalent* to C.

Example 2.8.7 If $n = 5$ and we choose to rearrange the digits in the order 2, 1, 4, 5, 3, then the code

$$C = \{11111, 01111, 00111, 00011, 00001\}$$

is equivalent to the code

$$C' = \{11111, 10111, 00111, 00110, 00010\}.$$

(Note that C and C' are *not* linear.)

Theorem 2.8.8 *Any linear code C is equivalent to a linear code C' having a generator matrix in standard form.*

Proof: If G is a generator matrix for C, place G in RREF. Rearrange the columns of the RREF so that the leading columns come first and form an identity matrix. The result is a matrix G' in standard form which is a generator matrix for a code C' equivalent to C. □

Example 2.8.9 The matrix

$$G = \begin{bmatrix} 0\,1\,1\,0\,0\,0\,0\,1\,0 \\ 0\,0\,0\,1\,0\,0\,1\,1\,0 \\ 0\,0\,0\,0\,1\,0\,0\,1\,0 \\ 0\,0\,0\,0\,0\,1\,1\,0\,0 \\ 0\,0\,0\,0\,0\,0\,0\,0\,1 \end{bmatrix}$$

is a generator matrix in RREF with columns 2, 4, 5, 6, and 9 as leading columns. Rearranging the columns in the order 2, 4, 5, 6, 9, 1, 3, 7, 8 yields the matrix

$$G' = \begin{bmatrix} 1\,0\,0\,0\,0 & 0\,1\,0\,1 \\ 0\,1\,0\,0\,0 & 0\,0\,1\,1 \\ 0\,0\,1\,0\,0 & 0\,0\,0\,1 \\ 0\,0\,0\,1\,0 & 0\,0\,1\,0 \\ 0\,0\,0\,0\,1 & 0\,0\,0\,0 \end{bmatrix} = [I\;X],$$

which is a generator matrix in standard form for a code equivalent to the code generated by G.

Exercises

2.8.10 Find a systematic code C' equivalent to the given code C. Check that C and C' have the same length, dimension, and distance.

(a) $C = \{00000, 10110, 10101, 00011\}$
(b) $C = \{00000, 11100, 00111, 11011\}$.

2.8.11 Find a generator matrix G in standard form for a code equivalent to the code with given generator matrix G.

(a) $G = \begin{bmatrix} 101010 \\ 011000 \\ 110100 \\ 101011 \end{bmatrix}$ (b) $G = \begin{bmatrix} 111000000 \\ 000111000 \\ 000111111 \end{bmatrix}$

2.8.12 Find a generator matrix G' in standard form for a code C' equivalent to the code C with given parity-check matrix H.

(a) $H = \begin{bmatrix} 110 \\ 100 \\ 011 \\ 010 \\ 001 \end{bmatrix}$ (b) $H = \begin{bmatrix} 100 \\ 111 \\ 010 \\ 110 \\ 101 \\ 001 \\ 011 \end{bmatrix}$

2.8.13 Prove that equivalent linear codes always have the same length, dimension, and distance.

2.8.14 Determine whether each of the following pairs of matrices G_1 and G_2 generate equivalent codes.

(a)

$$G_1 = \begin{bmatrix} 1100 \\ 0110 \\ 0011 \end{bmatrix}, \quad G_2 = \begin{bmatrix} 1001 \\ 0101 \\ 0011 \end{bmatrix}$$

(b)

$$G_1 = \begin{bmatrix} 110000 \\ 001100 \\ 000011 \end{bmatrix}, \quad G_2 = \begin{bmatrix} 111111 \\ 011011 \\ 001001 \end{bmatrix}$$

(c)

$$G_1 = \begin{bmatrix} 1000111 \\ 0100110 \\ 0010101 \\ 0001011 \end{bmatrix}, \quad G_2 = \begin{bmatrix} 1011000 \\ 0101100 \\ 0010110 \\ 0001011 \end{bmatrix}.$$

2.9 Distance of a linear code

We observed that the distance of a linear code is the minimum weight of any nonzero codeword. The distance of a linear code can also be determined from a parity-check matrix for the code.

Theorem 2.9.1 *Let H be a parity-check matrix for a linear code C. Then C has distance d if and only if any set of $d-1$ rows of H is linearly independent, and at least one set of d rows of H is linearly dependent.*

The idea is that if v is a word, then vH is a linear combination of exactly $\mathrm{wt}(v)$ rows of H. So if v is in C and $\mathrm{wt}(v) = d$, then since $vH = 0$, some d rows of H are linearly dependent. And if $vH = 0$ then v is a codeword so $\mathrm{wt}(v) \geq d$.

Example 2.9.2 Let C be the linear code with parity-check matrix

$$H = \begin{bmatrix} 110 \\ 011 \\ 100 \\ 010 \\ 001 \end{bmatrix}.$$

By inspection it is seen that no two rows of H sum to 000, so any two rows of H are linearly independent, but rows 1, 3, and 4, for instance sum to 000, and hence are linearly dependent. Therefore $d - 1 = 2$, so the distance of C is $d = 3$.

Exercises

2.9.3 Find the code C in the Example 2.9.2. Compute the weight of each codeword and verify that C has distance 3.

2.9.4 Find the distance of the linear code C with each of the given parity-check matrices. Use Theorem 2.9.1 and then check your answer by finding $\mathrm{wt}(v)$ for each v in C.

$$\text{(a)}\ H = \begin{bmatrix} 0111 \\ 1110 \\ 1000 \\ 0100 \\ 0010 \\ 0001 \end{bmatrix} \qquad \text{(b)}\ H = \begin{bmatrix} 1110 \\ 1101 \\ 1011 \\ 0111 \\ 1000 \\ 0100 \\ 0010 \\ 0001 \end{bmatrix} \qquad \text{(c)}\ H = \begin{bmatrix} 1101 \\ 1011 \\ 1110 \\ 1000 \\ 0100 \\ 0010 \\ 0001 \end{bmatrix}$$

2.9.5 Find, by Theorem 2.9.1, the distance of the linear code with the given generator matrix.

$$\text{(a)}\ G = \begin{bmatrix} 111000000 \\ 000111000 \\ 111111111 \end{bmatrix} \qquad \text{(b)}\ G = \begin{bmatrix} 1000111 \\ 0100110 \\ 0010101 \\ 0001011 \end{bmatrix}$$

2.10 Cosets

In this section we consider a topic which will be useful in decoding a linear code, to which we will turn in the next section.

If C is a linear code of length n, and if u is any word of length n, we define the *coset of C determined by u* to be the set of all words of the form $v+u$ as v ranges over all the words in C. We denote this coset by $C+u$. Thus

$$C+u=\{v+u \mid v \in C\}.$$

Example 2.10.1 Let C = {000, 111}, and let $u = 101$. Then

$$C+101=\{000+101, 111+101\}=\{101,010\}.$$

Note that also

$$C+111=\{000+111, 111+111\}=\{111,000\}=C$$

and

$$C+010=\{000+010, 111+010\}=\{010, 101\}=C+101.$$

Exercises

2.10.2 List the rest of the cosets of $C=\{000, 111\}$. Notice that there are eight possibilities for the cosets of C, one for each word in K^3, but only four of these cosets are distinct.

If C is a linear code of length n, then you might think that there are as many as 2^n different cosets $C+u$ of C, one for each of the 2^n different words u of length n. As Example 2.10.1 and Exercise 2.10.2 show, this is almost never so. It is quite possible for $C+u_1$ to be identical with $C+u_2$, but yet $u_1 \neq u_2$.

The following theorem contains several important and useful facts about cosets. A careful study of the examples following the theorem should help in understanding these facts. The proofs are technical, set-theoretic arguments, and hence relegated to the exercises.

Theorem 2.10.3 *Let C be a linear code of length n. Let u and v be words of length of n.*

1. *If u is in the coset $C+v$, then $C+u=C+v$; that is, each word in a coset determines that coset.*
2. *The word u is in the coset $C+u$.*
3. *If $u+v$ is in C, then u and v are in the same coset.*
4. *If $u+v$ is not in C, then u and v are in different cosets.*
5. *Every word in K^n is contained in one and only one coset of C; that is, either $C+u=C+v$, or $C+u$ and $C+v$ have no words in common.*
6. *$|C+u|=|C|$; that is, the number of words in a coset of C is equal to the number of words in the code C.*

7. *If C has dimension k, then there are exactly 2^{n-k} different cosets of C, and each coset contains exactly 2^k words.*
8. *The code C itself is one of its cosets.*

Example 2.10.4 We list the cosets of the code

$$C = \{0000, 1011, 0101, 1110\}.$$

First of all, C itself is a coset by (8) of Theorem 2.10.3. (Numbers in parentheses suggest that the reader refer to the parts of Theorem 2.10.3.) Every word in C will determine the coset C (by (1) and (5)), so we pick a word u in K^4 not in C. For later use in decoding, it will help to pick u of smallest weight possible. So let's take $u = 1000$. Then we get the coset

$$C + 1000 = \{1000, 0011, 1101, 0110\}$$

by adding 1000 to each word in C. Note that $u = 1000$ is in the coset $C + u = C + 1000$. Now pick another word, of small weight, in K^4 but not in C or $C + 1000$, say 0100. Form another coset

$$C + 0100 = \{0100, 1111, 0001, 1010\}.$$

Repeating the process with 0010 yields the coset

$$C + 0010 = \{0010, 1001, 0111, 1100\}.$$

The code C has dimension $k = 2$. We have listed $2^{n-k} = 2^{4-2} = 2^2 = 4$ cosets, each with $2^k = 2^2 = 4$ words, and every word in K^4 is accounted for by appearing in exactly one coset. Also observe that $0001 + 1010 = 1011$ is in C, thus 0001 and 1010 are in the same coset, namely $C + 0100$ (see (3)). On the other hand, $0100 + 0010 = 0110$ is not in C, and 0100 and 0010 are in different cosets (see (4)).

Example 2.10.5 We list the cosets of the linear code C with the generator matrix

$$G = \begin{bmatrix} 100110 \\ 010011 \\ 001111 \end{bmatrix}.$$

000000	100000	010000	001000
100110	000110	110110	101110
010011	110011	000011	011011
001111	101111	011111	000111
110101	010101	100101	111101
101001	001001	111001	100001
011100	111100	001100	010100
111010	011010	101010	110010

000100	000010	000001	000101
100010	100100	100111	100011
010111	010001	010011	010110
001011	001101	001110	001010
110001	110111	110100	110000
101101	101011	101000	101100
011000	011110	011101	011001
111110	111000	111000	111111

The eight cosets are listed. The first is the code C itself. The word u used to form $C+u$ is the top word in each coset, since $u=0+u$, and was chosen as in Example 2.10.4.

Exercises

2.10.6 List the cosets of each of the following linear codes.

(a) $C=\{0000, 1001, 0101, 1100\}$
(b) $C=\{0000, 1010, 1101, 0111\}$
(c) $C=\{00000, 10100, 01011, 11111\}$
(d) $C=\{0000\}$.

2.10.7 List the cosets of each of the linear codes having the given generator matrix.

(a) $G=\begin{bmatrix}111000\\001110\\100011\end{bmatrix}$ (b) $G=\begin{bmatrix}101010\\010101\end{bmatrix}$

(c) $G=\begin{bmatrix}1000111\\0100110\\0010101\\0001011\end{bmatrix}$ (d) $G=\begin{bmatrix}10001\\01001\\00101\\00011\end{bmatrix}$

(e) $G=\begin{bmatrix}1000\\0100\\0010\\0001\end{bmatrix}$ (f) $G=[1111]$.

2.10.8 List the cosets of the code having the given parity-check matrix.

(a) $H=\begin{bmatrix}10\\11\\10\\01\end{bmatrix}$ (b) $H=\begin{bmatrix}111\\110\\101\\011\\100\\010\\001\end{bmatrix}$ (c) $H=\begin{bmatrix}100\\010\\010\\001\\001\\001\end{bmatrix}$

2.10.9 Prove Theorem 2.10.3.

2.11 MLD for linear codes

One of our goals is to design codes which permit easy and rapid decoding of a received word. Linear codes do in fact admit a more efficient method for implementing MLD than using an IMLD table. We will describe a procedure for either CMLD or IMLD for a linear code. The parity-check matrix and the cosets of the code play fundamental roles in the decoding process.

Let C be a linear code. Assume the codeword v in C is transmitted and the word w is received, resulting in the error pattern $u = v + w$. Then $w + u = v$ is in C, so *the error pattern u and the received word w are in the same coset of C* by (3) of Theorem 2.10.3.

Since error patterns of small weight are the most likely to occur, here is how MLD works for a linear code C. Upon receiving the word w, we choose a word u of least weight in the coset $C + w$ (which must contain w) and conclude that $v = w + u$ was the word sent.

Example 2.11.1 Let $C = \{0000, 1011, 0101, 1110\}$. The cosets of C (Example 2.10.4) are

0000	1000	0100	0010
1011	0011	1111	1001
0101	1101	0001	0111
1110	0110	1010	1100

Suppose $w = 1101$ is received. The coset $C + w = C + 1101$ containing w is the second one listed. The word of least weight in this coset is $u = 1000$, which we choose as the error pattern. We conclude that $v = w + u = 1101 + 1000 = 0101$ was the most likely codeword sent. Now suppose $w = 1111$ is received. In the coset $C + w$ containing 1111 there are two words of smallest weight, 0100 and 0001. Since we are doing CMLD, we arbitrarily select one of these, say $u = 0100$, for the error pattern, and conclude that $v = w + u = 1111 + 0100 = 1011$ was a most likely codeword sent.

Exercises

2.11.2 Let C be the code of Example 2.10.5. Use the procedure for CMLD just outlined to decode each of the following received words.

(a) 000011 (b) 001001 (c) 001101

(d) 010110 (e) 110101 (f) 001010

The hardest parts of the above procedure are searching to find the coset containing the received word w and then finding a word of least weight in that coset. We can use a parity-check matrix to develop a slick procedure for easing these burdens.

Let C be a linear code of length n and dimension k. Let H be a parity check matrix for C. For any word w in K^n, the *syndrome* of w is the word wH in K^{n-k}.

Example 2.11.3 For the code C of Example 2.11.1 above, the matrix H below is a parity-check matrix. If $w = 1101$, then the syndrome of w is

$$wH = 1101 \begin{bmatrix} 11 \\ 01 \\ 10 \\ 01 \end{bmatrix} = 11.$$

Notice that the word of least weight in the coset $C + w$ is $u = 1000$ (see Example 2.11.1), and the syndrome of u is

$$uH = 1000 \begin{bmatrix} 11 \\ 01 \\ 10 \\ 01 \end{bmatrix} = 11 = wH.$$

Furthermore, if $w = 1101$ is received, CMLD concludes $v = w + u = 1101 + 1000 = 0101$ was sent, so there was an error in the first digit. Notice also that for the error pattern u, the syndrome uH picks up the row of H, the first, corresponding to the location of the most likely error.

The following theorem contains some basic and useful facts about the syndrome. Proofs may be constructed using the definitions of the concepts involved and the properties of cosets from Theorem 2.10.3.

Theorem 2.11.4 *Let C be a linear code of length n. Let H be a parity-check matrix for C. Let w and u be words in K^n.*

1. *$wH = 0$ if and only if w is a codeword in C.*
2. *$wH = uH$ if and only if w and u lie in the same coset of C.*
3. *If u is the error pattern in a received word w, then uH is the sum of the rows of H that correspond to the positions in which errors occurred in transmission.*

Note that if no errors occur in transmission and w is received, then $wH = 0$. But $wH = 0$ does not imply that no errors occurred, since the codeword w need not be the codeword that was sent.

Since words in the same coset have the same syndromes, while words in different cosets have different syndromes, we can identify a coset by its syndrome; the syndrome of a coset is the syndrome of any word in the coset. Thus if the code has length n and dimension k then the 2^{n-k} words of length $n-k$ each occurs as the syndrome of exactly one of the 2^{n-k} cosets.

Example 2.11.5 The code C of Example 2.11.1 has length $n = 4$ and dimension $k = 2$. The cosets of C (listed in Example 2.11.1) contain all $2^n = 2^4 = 16$ words of length $n = 4$. There are $2^{n-k} = 2^{4-2} = 2^2 = 4$ words of length $n-k = 2$; each one is the syndrome of exactly one of the $2^{n-k} = 4$ cosets of C.

To calculate the syndrome of a particular coset, we can choose any word w in that coset. Then wH will be the syndrome of that coset. For MLD, we want a word of least weight in the coset to use as the error pattern. In the examples in the last section, we carefully arranged the cosets so that a word of least weight was on top, or listed first. Any word of least weight in a coset is called a *coset leader*. If there was more than one candidate for coset leader, we selected one arbitrarily when doing CMLD.

Example 2.11.6 Again let C be the code of Example 2.11.1. For each coset, we calculate the syndrome, using the coset leader, and display the results in the following table.

Coset leader u	Syndrome uH
0000	00
1000	11
0100	01
0010	10

Note again that each word of length 2 occurs once and only once as a syndrome.

The table in the Example 2.11.6, which matches each syndrome with its coset leader, is called a *standard decoding array*, or *SDA*. To construct an SDA, first list all the cosets for the code, and choose from each coset a word of least weight as coset leader u. Then find a parity check matrix for the code and, for each coset leader u, calculate its syndrome uH. A quicker way to construct an SDA, given the parity check matrix H and distance d for the code C would be to generate all error patterns e with $\text{wt}(e) \leq \lfloor (d-1)/2 \rfloor$ and compute the syndrome $s = eH$ for each one.

Example 2.11.7 We construct an SDA for the code C of Example 2.10.5 (where the cosets of C have already been listed). For each of the first seven cosets we had no choice for coset leader—the top word is the only word of least weight in its coset. But in the last coset, the smallest weight of a word is 2, and that coset contains three words of weight 2, 000101, 001010, and 110000. Using CMLD we could arbitrarily select 000101 as our presumed error pattern. Using IMLD, we would ask for retransmission and place a "$*$" in that entry of the SDA to so indicate. We can construct the following parity-check matrix for C:

$$H = \begin{bmatrix} 110 \\ 011 \\ 111 \\ 100 \\ 010 \\ 001 \end{bmatrix}.$$

Then we can obtain the following SDA for C assuming CMLD is being used:

Error pattern	Syndrome uH
000000	000
100000	110
010000	011
001000	111
000100	100
000010	010
000001	001
000101	101

Note that the syndromes are precisely all words in K^3. The coset C always has the zero word as its coset leader and always has syndrome 0. The chosen coset leader for the last coset, $u = 000101$, gives us syndrome $uH = 101$, which is the sum of rows 4 and 6 of H, the positions with 1's in the error pattern u. Using IMLD, this entry would instead be "$*$".

Exercises

2.11.8 Construct an SDA assuming IMLD for each of the codes in Exercise 2.10.6.

2.11.9 Construct an SDA assuming IMLD for each of the codes in Exercise 2.10.7.

2.11.10 Construct an SDA assuming IMLD for each of the codes in Exercise 2.10.8.

2.11.11 Prove Theorem 2.11.4.

Finally we can do some decoding. Once we suffer the tedious construction of an SDA, it is easy to use MLD. When we receive a word w, we first calculate the syndrome wH. Then we find the coset leader u next to the syndrome $wH = uH$ in the SDA. We conclude that $v = w + u$ was the most likely codeword sent.

Example 2.11.12 Let C be the code of Example 2.11.1. An SDA appears in Example 2.11.6. The parity-check matrix H is in Example 2.11.3. Assume that $w = 1101$ is received. Then the syndrome is $wH = 11$, directing us to the second row of the SDA, where the coset leader is $u = 1000$. We conclude that $v = w+u = 0101$ was sent. If $w = 1111$ is received, then $wH = 01 = uH$ for $u = 0100$ from the SDA. We decode w as $v = w+u = 1011$. These results are the same as found in Example 2.11.1.

For $w = 1101$ received, we decoded $v = 0101$ as the word sent. The calculations

$$d(0000, 1101) = 3 \qquad d(0101, 1101) = 1$$
$$d(1011, 1101) = 2 \qquad d(1110, 1101) = 2$$

give the distances between w and each codeword in C, and show that indeed $v = 0101$ is the closest word in C to w.

For $w = 1111$ received, however, the same calculations

$$d(0000,1111) = 4 \qquad d(0101,1111) = 2$$
$$d(1011,1111) = 1 \qquad d(1110,1111) = 1$$

reveal a tie for the closest word in C to w. This is not surprising, since there was a choice for a coset leader in the coset containing w. We are doing CMLD, so we arbitrarily choose a coset leader, which in effect arbitrarily selected one word in C closest to w.

Example 2.11.13 Let C be the code of Example 2.10.5. An SDA was constructed in Example 2.11.7. We do some decoding using this SDA. Suppose we receive $w = 110111$. Then $wH = 010$, which directs us to the sixth row of the SDA. The coset leader in that row is $u = 000010$. Thus CMLD concludes that $v = w + u = 110111 + 000010 = 110101$ was the codeword sent. Now suppose $w = 110000$ is received. The syndrome $wH = 101$ directs us to the last row of the SDA where the coset leader is $u = 000101$. We decode w as $v = w + u = 110000 + 000101 = 110101$. Had we chosen the word $u' = 001010$ as the coset leader for the last coset, then we would instead decode w as $w + u' = 110000 + 001010 = 111010$.

Exercises

2.11.14 Continuing the last example with $w = 110000$ received. Decode assuming that $u'' = 110000$ had been chosen as the coset leader for the last coset.

2.11.15 Refer to Example 2.11.13 with $w = 110111$ received. Check that in fact $v = 110101$ is the closest codeword in C to w.

2.11.16 Again refer to Example 2.11.13 with $w = 110000$ received. Find all the codewords in C closest to w.

2.11.17 Repeat the decoding in Exercise 2.11.2 using the SDA in Example 2.11.7.

2.11.18 For the code in Example 2.11.13 above, decode the following received words w.

(a) 011101 (b) 110101 (c) 111111 (d) 000000

2.11.19 For each of the following codes, use the SDA to decode the given received words. (The SDA's for these codes were constructed in Exercises 2.11.8 and 2.11.9.)

(a) $C = \{0000, 1001, 0101, 1100\}$

(i) $w = 1110$ (ii) $w = 1001$ (iii) $w = 0101$

(b) $C = \{00000, 10100, 01011, 11111\}$

(i) $w = 10101$ (ii) $w = 01110$ (iii) $w = 10001$

(c) $C = \langle 111000, 001110, 100011 \rangle$

(i) $w = 101010$ (ii) $w = 011110$ (iii) $w = 011$

2.11.20 Let C be the code with the parity-check matrix

$$H = \begin{bmatrix} 011 \\ 101 \\ 110 \\ 100 \\ 010 \\ 001 \end{bmatrix}.$$

Decode (a) 110100, (b) 111111, (c) 101010, and (d) 000110.

2.11.21 Let C be the code of length 7 which has as a parity-check matrix the 7×3 matrix H whose rows are all nonzero words of length 3.

(a) Construct an SDA for C.

(b) Decode 1010101.

If we want to construct an SDA when using IMLD, we can proceed as follows. If a word w is received, then the number of words in the code C closest to w is the same as the number of error patterns in the coset $C + w$ of least weight. If in some coset of C there is more than one word of smallest weight, then this coset and its syndrome are omitted from the SDA when using IMLD. Furthermore, the weight of a coset leader is the number of errors corrected by MLD when a word in that coset is received. If this weight is excessively high, then we may decide to eliminate this coset and its syndrome from the SDA in IMLD even though there is only one word of least weight in that coset. To use the shortened SDA for IMLD, if the received word has a syndrome which does not occur in the SDA, then we request a retransmission.

In practice, it may not be unusual to have on the order of 2^{50}, about 1.126×10^{15} coset leaders and syndromes, which makes the SDA for an arbitrary linear code an unmanageable list. Thus, in practice, we have not solved the problem of decoding using MLD. As we will see later, however, MLD is computationally effective if the linear code is constructed to certain specifications. Indeed, one goal of coding theory is to construct codes which are easy to decode using MLD.

2.12 Reliability of IMLD for linear codes

Let C be a linear code of length n and dimension k. Recall that $\theta_p(C, v)$ is the probability that if v in C is sent over a BSC of probability p, then IMLD will correctly conclude that v was sent.

For each unique coset leader u and for each codeword v in C, $v+u$ is closer to v than to any other codeword. Also, if $w \neq v+u$ for some codeword v and some unique coset leader u then w is at least as close to some other codeword as it is to v. So for a linear code, the set $L(v)$ of words that are closer to v than to any other codeword is

$$L(v) = \{w \mid w = v + u \text{ where } u \text{ is a unique coset leader}\}.$$

If $w = v + u$ then $\theta_p(v, w)$ depends only on $\mathrm{wt}(u)$; therefore, for a linear code $C, \theta_p(C, v)$ does not depend on v. We denote this common value by $\theta_p(C)$, and so

$$\theta_p(C) = \sum_{u \in L(0)} p^{n-\mathrm{wt}(u)}(1-p)^{\mathrm{wt}(u)}.$$

Thus, to find the reliability of a linear code, we need be concerned only with the unique coset leaders. Simply calculate the probability of each unique coset leader occurring as an error pattern, then sum these probabilities to get $\theta_p(C)$.

Notice that we have also shown that for a linear code, the set of error patterns that can be corrected using IMLD is equal to the set of unique coset leaders.

Example 2.12.1 Let C be the code of Example 2.10.5. Using IMLD there is one coset leader of weight 0 and six of weight 1. Thus

$$\theta_p(C) = p^6 + 6p^5(1-p).$$

Exercises

2.12.2 Calculate $\theta_p(C)$ for each of the codes in Exercises 2.10.6, 2.10.7, 2.10.8.

Chapter 3

Perfect and Related Codes

3.1 Some bounds for codes

We now turn our attention to the problem of determining how many words a linear code of given length n and distance d can have. This problem is far from solved in general, though it has been settled for certain values of n and d. We can, however, find some bounds on the size of a code with these given parameters.

Recall that if t and n are integers, $0 \leq t \leq n$, then the symbol

$$\binom{n}{t} = \frac{n!}{t!(n-t)!},$$

is just the number of ways that an unordered collection of t objects can be chosen from a set of n objects. *Thus* $\binom{n}{t}$ *is the number of words of length* n *and weight* t.

Theorem 3.1.1 *If* $0 \leq t \leq n$ *and if* v *is a word of length* n*, then the number of words of length* n *of distance at most* t *from* v *is precisely*

$$\binom{n}{0} + \binom{n}{1} + \binom{n}{2} + \cdots + \binom{n}{t}.$$

Since there are 2^n words of length n, setting $t = n$ in Theorem 3.1.1 yields

$$\binom{n}{0} + \binom{n}{1} + \binom{n}{2} + \cdots + \binom{n}{n} = 2^n.$$

Exercises

3.1.2 Illustrate Theorem 3.1.1 for $v = 10110$ and $t = 3$ by listing all words in K^5 of distance at most 3 from v, and then check that Theorem 3.1.1 does give the correct number of such words.

To find all words of a given distance t from a fixed word v, we simply add to v, all words of weight t. There are $\binom{n}{t}$ such words. If C is a code of length

n and distance $d = 2t + 1$, then there is no word w at distance at most t from two different codewords v_1 and v_2. Indeed, if $d(w, v_1) \le t$ and $d(w, v_2) \le t$ with $v_1 \ne v_2$, then

$$d(v_1, v_2) \le d(v_1, w) + d(w, v_2) \le 2t < d = 2t + 1,$$

which is impossible since C has minimum distance d. Thus, if C has length n and distance $2t + 1$, the list of words in K^n at a distance at most t from a codeword v_1 has no codewords in common with the list of words a distance at most t from a codeword v_2, $v_1 \ne v_2$. This establishes the following result.

Theorem 3.1.3 (*Hamming bound*) *If C is a code of length n and distance $d = 2t + 1$ or $2t + 2$ then*

$$|C|\left(\binom{n}{0} + \binom{n}{1} + \cdots + \binom{n}{t}\right) \le 2^n,$$

or

$$|C| \le \frac{2^n}{\binom{n}{0} + \binom{n}{1} + \cdots + \binom{n}{t}}.$$

The Hamming bound is an upper bound for the number of words in a code (linear or not) of length n and distance $d = 2t + 1$. Note that $t = \lfloor (d-1)/2 \rfloor$, so, by Theorem 1.12.9, such a code will correct all error patterns of weight less than or equal to t.

Example 3.1.4 We compute an upper bound for the size or dimension k of a linear code C of length $n = 6$ and distance $d = 3$. From $d = 3 = 2t + 1$ we get $t = 1$. The Hamming bound gives

$$|C| \le \frac{2^6}{\binom{6}{0} + \binom{6}{1}} = \frac{64}{1+6} = \frac{64}{7}.$$

But $|C|$ must be a power of 2, so $|C| \le 8$, and thus $k \le 3$.

Exercises

3.1.5 Find an upper bound for the size or dimension of a linear code with the given values of n and d.

(a) $n = 8, d = 3$ (b) $n = 7, d = 3$ (c) $n = 10, d = 5$
(d) $n = 15, d = 3$ (e) $n = 15, d = 5$ (f) $n = 23, d = 7$

3.1.6 Verify the Hamming bound for the linear code C with the given generator matrix.

(a) $G = \begin{bmatrix} 111110000000000 \\ 000001111100000 \\ 000001111111111 \end{bmatrix}$ (b) $G = \begin{bmatrix} 100111 \\ 010101 \\ 001011 \end{bmatrix}$ (c) $G = \begin{bmatrix} 1000111 \\ 0100110 \\ 0010101 \\ 0001011 \end{bmatrix}$

Recall that from Section 2.7 and Theorem 2.9.1 we know that the parity check matrix H of an (n,k,d) linear code is an n by $n-k$ matrix such that every $d-1$ rows of H are independent. Since the rows have length $n-k$, you can never have more than $n-k$ independent row vectors. Hence $d-1 \leq n-k$ or equivalently $k \leq n-d+1$. This establishes the following result, which is known as the Singleton bound.

Theorem 3.1.7 (*Singleton bound*) *For any (n,k,d) linear code, $d-1 \leq n-k$.*

The Singleton bound in one sense is much weaker than the Hamming bound. For example, if $n=15$ and $d=5$ then Theorem 3.1.7 implies that $k \leq 11$, whereas Theorem 3.1.3 (Hamming bound) implies that $k \leq 8$. However some codes do attain equality in the Singleton bound, so the Singleton bound is used to define an important and useful class of codes called maximum distance separable codes.

A linear (n,k,d) code is said to be a *maximum distance separable* (or MDS) code if $d=n-k+1$ (or $k=n-d+1$). There are several equivalent characterizations of MDS codes.

Theorem 3.1.8 *For a (n,k,d) linear code C, the following are equivalent:*

(1) $d=n-k+1$,

(2) every $n-k$ rows of the parity check matrix are linearly independent,

(3) every k columns of the generator matrix are linearly independent, and

(4) C is MDS.

Proof: Theorem 3.1.7 states that $d \leq n-k+1$; but $d \geq n-k+1$ iff every $n-k$ rows of the parity check matrix are independent. Thus (1) and (2) are equivalent. For (3), note that if $d=n-k+1$, no nonzero codeword can have more than $k-1$ zeros in it. However, k columns of the $k \times n$ generator matrix are linearly dependent iff some nonzero codeword has k zeros in those coordinate positions. The last statement is relatively easy to see and is left to the exercises. □

Corollary 3.1.9 *The dual of an $(n,k,n-k+1)$ MDS code is an $(n,n-k,k+1)$ MDS code.*

We will encounter MDS codes later when we study Reed-Solomon codes.

Exercises

3.1.10 Columns 2, 3, and 5 of the generator matrix

$$G = \begin{bmatrix} 11001 \\ 01110 \\ 00101 \end{bmatrix}$$

are linearly dependent. Find a codeword which has zeros in positions 2, 3, and 5

3.1.11 Show that if a $k \times n$ generator matrix has k linearly dependent columns then there is a nonzero codeword with zeros in those k positions.

We still would like to construct codes for given parameters n, k and d. Upper bounds rule out some parameter values for example the Hamming bound says that a code of length $n = 15$ and distance $d = 5$ can not have dimension $k = 10$. However, this bound does not rule out the possibility of a $(15, 8, 5)$ code existing.

How would we go about finding a $(15, 8, 5)$ code? In general this is a very difficult problem. One approach is to find the parity check matrix for such a code. That is, assuming $r = n - k$, we must find n vectors of length r to form the rows of H such that every set of $d - 1$ of these vectors is linearly independent.

Example 3.1.12 Let $n = 15$, $k = 6$, and $d = 5$. Then $r = 15 - 6 = 9$. So we wish to find 15 nonzero vectors of length 9 with the property that any 4 of these are linearly independent. Finding the first 9 rows is easy: take the 9×9 identity matrix I_9.

Suppose we have some how found 3 more vectors for a total of 12 rows and so we have,

$$H = \begin{bmatrix} I_9 \\ 111100000 \\ 100011100 \\ 101000011 \\ ? \end{bmatrix}$$

Before searching for the next vector we notice that the following counting argument tells us that one must exist. Among all 2^9 vectors, we cannot select the zero vector nor any of the 12 choosen so far. This rules out $1 + 12$ vectors. We also rule out any vector which can be written as the sum of 2 or 3 of these vectors, as this would create a dependent set of 3 or 4 vectors respectively. This rules out at most $\binom{12}{2} + \binom{12}{3}$ additional vectors. However, any remaining vector can be selected.

Since

$$1 + \binom{12}{1} + \binom{12}{2} + \binom{12}{3} < 2^9$$

we know that we can find yet another vector. For example one could choose the vector 010101010 to be the next row of H. The chore of finding the remaining rows of H is left to Exercise 3.1.21.

Example 3.1.12 (and the related exercises) show that a $(15, 6, 5)$ code exists. This establishes a *lower bound* on the maximum size (or dimension) of a linear code with $n = 15$ and $d = 5$, i.e., $6 \leq k \leq 8$.

The next result formalizes the approach of Example 3.1.12 to constructing linear codes (and thus establishing lower bounds). The proofs are left to Exercise 3.1.22.

Theorem 3.1.13 (*Gilbert-Varshamov bound*) *There exists a linear code of length n, dimension k, and distance d if*

$$\binom{n-1}{0}+\binom{n-1}{1}+\cdots+\binom{n-1}{d-2}<2^{n-k}.$$

Corollary 3.1.14 *If $n \neq 1$ and $d \neq 1$, then there exists a linear code C of length n and distance at least d with*

$$|C| \geq \frac{2^{n-1}}{\binom{n-1}{0}+\binom{n-1}{1}+\cdots+\binom{n-1}{d-2}}.$$

Example 3.1.15 Does there exist a linear code of length $n=9$, dimension $k=2$, and distance $d=5$?

To determine if such a code exists, we use the Gilbert-Varshamov bound:

$$\begin{aligned}\binom{n-1}{0}+\cdots+\binom{n-1}{d-2} &= \binom{8}{0}+\binom{8}{1}+\binom{8}{2}+\binom{8}{3}\\ &= 93\end{aligned}$$

and $2^{n-k}=2^{9-2}=2^7=128$. Since $93<128$, such a code exists.

Example 3.1.16 What is a lower and an upper bound on the size or the dimension, k, of a linear code with $n=9$ and $d=5$?

To find a lower bound for the most number of codewords such a code C could have, we use Corollary 3.1.14:

$$|C| \geq \frac{2^{n-1}}{\binom{n-1}{0}+\cdots+\binom{n-1}{d-2}} = \frac{2^{9-1}}{\binom{8}{0}+\binom{8}{1}+\binom{8}{2}+\binom{8}{3}} = \frac{2^8}{93} = \frac{256}{93} = 2.75.$$

Since $|C|$ is linear, it is a power of 2, and thus $|C| \geq 4$.

To find an upper bound for $|C|$, we use the Hamming bound:

$$|C| \leq \frac{2^9}{\binom{9}{0}+\binom{9}{1}+\binom{9}{2}} = \frac{512}{1+9+36} = \frac{512}{46} = 11.13.$$

Since $|C|$ is linear, it is a power of 2, and thus $|C| \leq 8$.

Combining the bounds, a linear code with parameters $(9,k,5)$ with 4 codewords exists, but no $(9,k,5)$ linear code with more than 8 codewords exists.

Example 3.1.17 Does there exist a $(15,7,5)$ linear code? Again we can try to use the Gilbert-Varshamov bound to answer this question.

$$\begin{aligned}\binom{n-1}{0}+\cdots+\binom{n-1}{d-2} &= \binom{14}{0}+\binom{14}{1}+\binom{14}{2}+\binom{14}{3}\\ &= 1+14+91+364\\ &= 470,\end{aligned}$$

and $2^{n-k} = 2^{15-7} = 256$. In this case the inequality is not satisfied, so the Gilbert-Varshamov bound does not tell use whether or not such a code exists. In fact, as we shall see later, these are the parameters of the 2 error-correcting BCH code, so such a code does exist.

Exercises

3.1.18 For each part of Exercise 3.1.5, let $k = 2d$ and decide, if possible, whether or not a linear code with the given parameters exists. Find a lower and upper bound for the maximum number of codewords such a code can have, assuming that k is unrestricted.

3.1.19 Find a lower and an upper bound for the maximum number of codewords in a linear code of length n and distance d where

(a) $n = 15, d = 5$ (b) $n = 15, d = 3$ (c) $n = 11, d = 3$
(d) $n = 12, d = 3$ (e) $n = 12, d = 4$ (f) $n = 12, d = 5$.

3.1.20 Is it possible to have a linear code with parameters (8, 3, 5)?

3.1.21 Find a (15, 6, 5) code by constructing the parity check matrix. (See Example 3.1.12, each of the 3 missing vectors must have weight at least 4. Why?)

3.1.22 Let H_i be any $i \times (n-k)$ matrix with no $d-1$ rows linearly dependent.

(a) Prove that there are at most

$$N_i = \binom{i}{0} + \binom{i}{1} + \cdots + \binom{i}{d-2}$$

words in K^{n-k} which are linear combinations of at most $d-2$ rows of H_i.

(b) Prove that if $N_i < 2^{n-k}$, then a row can be added in such a way that no $d-1$ rows of the resulting matrix are linearly dependent.

(c) Prove the Gilbert-Varshamov bound.

(d) Prove Corollary 3.1.14.

3.2 Perfect codes

A code C of length n and odd distance $d = 2t+1$ is called a *perfect code* if C attains the Hamming bound of Theorem 3.1.3; that is, if

$$|C| = \frac{2^n}{\binom{n}{0} + \binom{n}{1} + \cdots + \binom{n}{t}}.$$

Unfortunately, there are not many linear perfect codes, but the ones that do exist are quite useful. The main problem in finding linear perfect codes is that the number $\binom{n}{0} + \binom{n}{1} + \cdots + \binom{n}{t}$ must be a power of 2 (since $|C|$ is a power of 2).

Example 3.2.1 Let $t = 0$. Then $\binom{n}{0} = 1 = 2^0$, so $|C| = 2^n/\binom{n}{0} = 2^n$. The only code with 2^n codewords of length n is $C = K^n$. K^n is a perfect code.

Example 3.2.2 Let $n = 2t + 1$. Then

$$\binom{n}{n-i} = \frac{n!}{(n-i)!(n-(n-i))!} = \frac{n!}{(n-i)!i!} = \binom{n}{i}.$$

Thus

$$\binom{n}{0} = \binom{n}{n}, \binom{n}{1} = \binom{n}{n-1}, \binom{n}{2} = \binom{n}{n-2}, \ldots,$$

and, from $n = 2t + 1$,

$$\binom{n}{t} = \binom{n}{n-t} = \binom{n}{t+1}.$$

Therefore

$$\binom{n}{0} + \cdots + \binom{n}{t} = \frac{1}{2}\left(\binom{n}{0} + \cdots + \binom{n}{n}\right) = \frac{1}{2} \cdot 2^n = 2^{n-1}.$$

Hence

$$|C| = \frac{2^n}{\binom{n}{0} + \cdots + \binom{n}{t}} = \frac{2^n}{2^{n-1}} = 2.$$

Thus any perfect code of length and distance $2t + 1$ has exactly 2 codewords. Among linear codes there is only one such code, the repetition code consisting of the zero word and the word in which each digit is 1, and indeed this code is perfect.

The codes in Examples 3.2.1 and 3.2.2, while perfect, are not very interesting. They are called the *trivial* perfect codes.

Example 3.2.3 Let $n = 7$ and $d = 3$. Then $t = 1$ and

$$|C| = \frac{2^7}{\binom{7}{0} + \binom{7}{1}} = \frac{128}{8} = 16 = 2^4.$$

Thus, there may exist a linear perfect code with $n = 7$ and $d = 3$. In the next section we shall see that there is such a code, the Hamming code.

Example 3.2.4 Let $n = 23$ and $d = 7$. Then $t = 3$, and

$$|C| = \frac{2^{23}}{\binom{23}{0} + \binom{23}{1} + \binom{23}{2} + \binom{23}{3}} = \frac{2^{23}}{1 + 23 + 253 + 1771}$$

$$= \frac{2^{23}}{2048} = \frac{2^{23}}{2^{11}} = 2^{12} = 4096.$$

This shows that a linear perfect code with $n = 23$ and $d = 7$ may exist. In a later section, we shall see that such a code does exist, namely the Golay code.

Exercises

3.2.5 Show that for $n = 2^r - 1$, $\binom{n}{0} + \binom{n}{1} = 2^r$.

3.2.6 Can there exist perfect codes for the following values of n and d?

(a) $n = 15, d = 3$ (b) $n = 31, d = 3$ (c) $n = 15, d = 5$

The possible lengths and distances for a perfect code were determined by Tietäväiren and van Lint in 1973. The proof of their result is beyond the scope of these notes.

Theorem 3.2.7 *If C is a non-trivial perfect code of length n and distance $d = 2t+1$, then either $n = 23$ and $d = 7$, or $n = 2^r - 1$ for some $r \geq 2$ and $d = 3$.*

If a linear code of length n has distance $d = 2t+1$, then, by Theorem 1.12.9, C will correct all error patterns of weight less than or equal to $t = (d-1)/2$. Thus every word of length n and weight less than or equal to t is a coset leader. There are precisely $\binom{n}{0} + \binom{n}{1} + \cdots + \binom{n}{t}$ such words. But this is precisely the number of cosets if the code is perfect. We have proved another theorem.

Theorem 3.2.8 *If C is a perfect code of length n and distance $d = 2t+1$, then C will correct all error patterns of weight less than or equal to t, and no other error patterns.*

We can interpret Theorem 3.2.8 as saying that each of the 2^n words in K^n lies within distance t of exactly one codeword. This property enables us, for example, to count the number of codewords of minimum non-zero weight in a perfect code.

A perfect code which corrects all error patterns of weight less than or equal to t is called a *perfect t-error correcting code*. From Theorem 3.2.7 the only possible values for t here are $t = 1$ and $t = 3$. We examine the case $t = 1$ in the next section.

3.3 Hamming codes

Finally it's time to design a code. We consider an important family of codes which are easy to encode and decode, and which correct all single errors.

A code of length $n = 2^r - 1$, $r \geq 2$, having parity check matrix H whose rows consist of all nonzero vectors of length r is called a *Hamming code* of length $2^r - 1$.

Example 3.3.1 One possiblity for a parity check matrix for a Hamming code of length 7 ($r = 3$) is

$$H = \begin{bmatrix} 111 \\ 110 \\ 101 \\ 011 \\ 100 \\ 010 \\ 001 \end{bmatrix}.$$

From Algorithm 2.5.7, a generator matrix for Hamming code of length 7 is, therefore,

$$G = \begin{bmatrix} 1000111 \\ 0100110 \\ 0010101 \\ 0001011 \end{bmatrix}.$$

Thus the code has dimension 4 and contains $2^4 = 16$ codewords. Theorem 2.9.1 can be used to find the distance of the code, which is 3. The information rate is 4/7. In Exercise 2.6.12, we encoded some messages using this code. There are other possibilities for a parity check matrix for a Hamming code of length 7, but all yield equivalent codes.

Since the parity check matrix H for a Hamming code C contains all r rows of weight one, the r columns of H are linearly independent. Thus *a Hamming code has dimension* $2^r - 1 - r$ *and contains* 2^{2^r-1-r} *codewords.*

No row of H is the zero word, so no single row of H is linearly dependent. Thus C has distance at least 2. No two rows of H are equal, so no two rows of H are linearly dependent. Thus C has distance at least 3. But H contains the rows $100\ldots0, 010\ldots0$, and $110\ldots0$, which form a linearly dependent set. Therefore, by Theorem 2.9.1, *a Hamming code has distance* $d = 3$.

Now for $n = 2^r - 1$ and $d = 2t + 1 = 3$ (so $t = 1$),

$$\frac{2^n}{\binom{n}{0} + \cdots + \binom{n}{t}} = \frac{2^n}{\binom{n}{0} + \binom{n}{1}} = \frac{2^{2^r-1}}{1+n} = \frac{2^{2^r-1}}{1+2^r-1} = 2^{2^r-1-r},$$

so Hamming codes are perfect codes. By Theorem 3.2.8, *Hamming codes are perfect single error-correcting codes.*

It is trivial to construct an SDA for a Hamming code. All single errors are corrected so all words of length $2^r - 1$ and weight one are error patterns that are corrected, and hence must must be coset leaders. Since if e is an error pattern then eH sums the rows of the parity check matrix H corresponding to positions where errors occurred, and since H has $2^r - 1$ rows, we have the following as an SDA for a Hamming code:

coset leader	syndrome
$000\ldots0$	$00\ldots0$
I_{2^r-1}	H

Example 3.3.2 For the Hamming code in Example 3.3.1, decode $w = 1101001$. The syndrome is $wH = 011$, which is the fourth row of H. Thus the coset leader u is the fourth row of I_7: $u = 0001000$. We decode w as $w + u = 1100001$.

Exercises

3.3.3 Find a generator matrix in standard form for a Hamming code of length 15, then encode the message 11111100000.

3.3.4 Construct an SDA for a Hamming code of length 7, and use it to decode the following words:

(a) 1101011 (c) 0011010 (e) 0100011
(b) 1111111 (d) 0101011 (f) 0001011

3.3.5 Construct an SDA for a Hamming code of length 15, and use it to decode the following words:

(a) 01010 01010 01000 (b) 11110 00101 10110
(c) 11100 01110 00111 (d) 11100 10110 00000
(e) 00011 10100 00110 (f) 11001 11001 11000

3.3.6 Show that each of the following is a parity check matrix for a Hamming code of length 7, and that the codes are both equivalent to the one in Example 3.3.1.

$$H' = \begin{bmatrix} 001 \\ 010 \\ 011 \\ 100 \\ 101 \\ 110 \\ 111 \end{bmatrix} \qquad H'' = \begin{bmatrix} 100 \\ 110 \\ 111 \\ 011 \\ 101 \\ 010 \\ 001 \end{bmatrix}.$$

3.3.7 Prove that all Hamming codes of a given length are equivalent.

3.3.8 Is the following matrix the transpose of a parity check matrix for a Hamming code of length 15?

$$H^T = \begin{bmatrix} 10001 & 10111 & 01000 \\ 11100 & 10001 & 11110 \\ 01011 & 00101 & 11101 \\ 10001 & 01011 & 00111 \end{bmatrix}$$

3.3.9 Show that the Hamming code of length $2^r - 1$ for $r = 2$ is a trivial code.

3.3.10 Use the Hamming code of length 7 in Example 3.3.1 and the message assignment in Exercise 2.6.12. Decode the following message received:

$$1010111, 0110111, 1000010, 0010101, 1001011, 0010000, 1111100.$$

3.4 Extended codes

Sometimes increasing the length of a code by one digit, or perhaps a few digits, result in a new code with improved error detection or error correction capabilities which are worth the price of a lower information rate. We consider one simple possibility in this section.

Let C be a linear code of length n. The code C^* of length $n+1$ obtained from C by adding one extra digit to each codeword in order to make each word in the new code have even weight is called the *extended code* of C.

In Example 1.3.3 we constructed the extended code of K^2, and the reader did the same for K^3 in Exercise 1.3.5.

If the original code C has a $k \times n$ generator matrix G, then the extended code C^* has $k \times (n+1)$ generator matrix

$$G^* = [G, b],$$

where the last column b of G^* is appended so that each row of G^* has even weight.

A parity check matrix for C^* can be constructed from G^* using Algorithm 2.5.7. But there is an easier way if we are given a parity check matrix H for the original code C. In this case, the extended code C^* has a parity check matrix

$$H^* = \begin{bmatrix} H & j \\ 0 & 1 \end{bmatrix},$$

where j is the $n \times 1$ column of all ones. Note that H^* is an $(n+1) \times (n+1-k)$ matrix. Since H has rank $n-k$, the last row of H^* ensures that H^* has rank $n-k+1$. Moreover,

$$G^*H^* = [G, b]\begin{bmatrix} H & j \\ 0 & 1 \end{bmatrix} = [GH, Gj+b].$$

Now $GH = 0$ and Gj sums the ones in each row of G. From the definition of b, it follows that $Gj + b = 0$. Therefore $G^*H^* = 0$. By Theorem 2.7.6, G^* and H^* are indeed generating and parity check matrices respectively for the linear code C^*.

Example 3.4.1 Let C be the linear code with generator matrix

$$G = \begin{bmatrix} 10010 \\ 01001 \\ 00111 \end{bmatrix}.$$

Then

$$H = \begin{bmatrix} 10 \\ 01 \\ 11 \\ 10 \\ 01 \end{bmatrix}$$

is a parity check matrix for C by Algorithm 2.5.7. So we obtain the following generating and parity check matrices for the extended code:

$$G^* = \left[\begin{array}{c|c} 10010 & 0 \\ 01001 & 0 \\ 00111 & 1 \end{array}\right] \text{ and } H^* = \left[\begin{array}{c|c} 10 & 1 \\ 01 & 1 \\ 11 & 1 \\ 10 & 1 \\ 01 & 1 \\ \hline 00 & 1 \end{array}\right].$$

If v is a word in the original code C and if v^* is the corresponding word in the extended code C^* then

$$\text{wt}(v^*) = \begin{cases} \text{wt}(v) & \text{if wt}(v) \text{ is even} \\ \text{wt}(v)+1 & \text{if wt}(v) \text{ is odd.} \end{cases}$$

Therefore if the distance d of C is odd then the distance of C^* is $d+1$, but if d is even then the distance of C^* is d. So an extended code is of use only when d is odd, in which case it corrects no more errors than C but will detect one more error. Notice then that there is no point in extending a code twice.

Example 3.4.2 Assume C has distance $d = 5$. Then C^* has distance $d^* = 6$. By Theorem 1.11.14, C detects all nonzero error patterns of weight less than or equal to $d-1=4$, and C^* detects all nonzero error patterns of weight less than or equal to $d^*-1=5$. By Theorem 1.12.9, C corrects all error patterns of weight less than or equal to $\lfloor (d-1)/2 \rfloor = \lfloor 4/2 \rfloor = 2$, and C^* corrects all error patterns of weight less than or equal to $\lfloor (d^*-1)/2 \rfloor = \lfloor 5/2 \rfloor = 2$.

Exercises

3.4.3 Find generating and parity check matrices for an extended Hamming code of length 8.

3.4.4 Construct an SDA for an extended Hamming code of length 8, and use it to decode the following words.

(a) 10101010 (b) 11010110 (c) 11111111

3.4.5 Show that an extended Hamming code of length 8 is a self-dual code (that is, show $C = C^\perp$).

3.4.6 Find a formula for the distance d^* of the extended code C^* in terms of the distance of the original code C.

3.4.7 Let C be a Hamming code of length 15. Find the number of error patterns that Theorem 1.11.14 guarantees the extended code C^* will detect, and the number of error patterns Theorem 1.12.9 guarantees C^* will correct. How may error patterns does C^* correct?

3.5 The extended Golay code

In this and the next two sections we construct and decode two codes which will correct three or fewer errors. The extended Golay code, discussed in this and the next section, was in fact used in the Voyager spacecraft program which, in the early 1980's, brought us those marvelous close-up photographs of Jupiter and Saturn.

Let B be the 12×12 matrix

$$B = \begin{bmatrix} 1&1&0&1&1&1&0&0&0&1&0&1\\ 1&0&1&1&1&0&0&0&1&0&1&1\\ 0&1&1&1&0&0&0&1&0&1&1&1\\ 1&1&1&0&0&0&1&0&1&1&0&1\\ 1&1&0&0&0&1&0&1&1&0&1&1\\ 1&0&0&0&1&0&1&1&0&1&1&1\\ 0&0&0&1&0&1&1&0&1&1&1&1\\ 0&0&1&0&1&1&0&1&1&1&0&1\\ 0&1&0&1&1&0&1&1&1&0&0&1\\ 1&0&1&1&0&1&1&1&0&0&0&1\\ 0&1&1&0&1&1&1&0&0&0&1&1\\ 1&1&1&1&1&1&1&1&1&1&1&0 \end{bmatrix}.$$

Let G be the 12×24 matrix $G = [I, B]$, where I is the 12×12 identity matrix. The linear code C with generator matrix G is called the *extended Golay code* and will be denoted by C_{24}.

As an aid to remembering B, note that the 11×11 matrix B_1 obtained from B by deleting the last row and column has a cyclic structure. The first row of B_1 is 11011100010. The second row is obtained from the first by shifting each digit one position to the left and moving the first digit to the end. The third row is obtained from the second row in the same way, and so on for the remaining rows. Thus B may be remembered as the matrix

$$B = \begin{bmatrix} B_1 & j^T \\ j & 0 \end{bmatrix},$$

where j is the word of all ones of length 11. By inspection, we see that $B^T = B$; that is, B is a symmetric matrix.

We now list seven important facts about the extended Golay code C_{24} with generator matrix $G = [I, B]$:

(1) C_{24} has length $n = 24$, dimension $k = 12$ and $2^{12} = 4096$ codewords. This is clear upon inspection of G.

(2) A parity check matrix for C_{24} is the 24×12 matrix

$$\begin{bmatrix} B \\ I \end{bmatrix}$$

Algorithm 2.5.7 yields this fact.

(3) Another parity check matrix for C_{24} is the 24×12 matrix

$$H = \begin{bmatrix} I \\ B \end{bmatrix}.$$

To see this, note first that each row of B has odd weight (7 or 11). The scalar (dot) product of any row with itself is therefore 1. Next, a manual check shows that the scalar product of the first row of B with any other row is 0. From the cyclic structure of B_1 it follows that the scalar product of any two different rows of B is 0. Thus $BB^T = I$. But $B^T = B$, so $B^2 = BB^T$ and,

$$GH = [I, B]\begin{bmatrix} I \\ B \end{bmatrix} = I^2 + B^2 = I + BB^T = I + I = 0.$$

We shall use both parity check matrices to decode C_{24}.

(4) Another generator matrix for C_{24} is the 12×24 matrix $[B, I]$.

(5) C_{24} is self-dual; that is, $C_{24} = C_{24}^{\perp}$.

(6) The distance of C is 8.

(7) C_{24} is a three-error-correcting code.

The proofs of facts (4) and (5) are requested in exercises. We will give a proof of fact (6) which, in the bargain, contains further useful information about the code C_{24}. The proof is divided into three stages:

Stage I The weight of any word in C_{24} is a multiple of 4. To see this, note first that the rows of G have weight 8 or 12. Let v be a word in C_{24} which is the sum $v = r_i + r_j$ of two different rows of G. The rows of B are orthogonal; hence the rows of G are orthogonal. Therefore r_i and r_j have an even number, say $2x$, of ones in common. Thus

$$\mathrm{wt}(v) = \mathrm{wt}(r_i) + \mathrm{wt}(r_j) - 2(2x)$$

is a multiple of 4.

Now suppose the word v in C_{24} is the sum $v = r_i + r_j + r_k$ of three different rows of G. Let $v_1 = r_i + r_j$. Since C_{24} is self-dual, v_1 and r_k have scalar product 0, and hence an even number, say $2y$, of ones in common. Thus

$$\mathrm{wt}(v) = \mathrm{wt}(v_1) + \mathrm{wt}(r_k) - 2(2y)$$

is a multiple of 4. Continuing in this vein (formally, by induction) we see that if v in C_{24} is a linear combination of rows of G, then $\mathrm{wt}(v)$ must be a multiple of 4.

Stage II The first eleven rows of G are codewords in C_{24} of weight 8, so the distance of C_{24} must be either 4 or 8.

Stage III We rule out words of weight 4 being codewords in C_{24}. Let v be a nonzero codeword in C_{24}, and suppose $\text{wt}(v) = 4$. Then $v = u_1[I, B]$ and $v = u_2[B, I]$ for some u_1 and u_2 (since both $[I, B]$ and $[B, I]$ generate C_{24}) and $\text{wt}(u_1) \leq 2$ or $\text{wt}(u_2) \leq 2$ (since one half of v must contain at most two 1's). However no sum of one or two row of B has weight at most 3, so $\text{wt}(v) = \text{wt}(u_i) + \text{wt}(u_i B) > 4$. Therefore v does not have weight 4. □

Exercises

3.5.1 Show that the word of all ones is in C_{24}. Deduce that C_{24} contains no words of weight 20.

3.5.2 Prove fact (4) about C_{24}.

3.5.3 Prove fact (5) about C_{24}.

3.5.4 Use Theorem 2.9.1 to verify that C_{24} has distance 8.

3.6 Decoding the extended Golay code

We shall now find an algorithm for IMLD for the code C_{24}. Throughout this section, w denotes the word received, v the closest codeword to w and u the error pattern $v + w$. For C_{24} we want to correct all error patterns of weight at most 3, so we assume that $\text{wt}(u) \leq 3$. A comma will be placed between the first 12 and the last 12 digits of words in K^{24}. The error pattern u will be denoted by $[u_1, u_2]$, where u_1 and u_2 each have length 12. Our aim is to determine the coset leader, u of the coset containing w without having to refer to the SDA of C_{24}

Since we are assuming that $\text{wt}(u) \leq 3$, either $\text{wt}(u_1) \leq 1$ or $\text{wt}(u_2) \leq 1$. Let s_1 be the syndrome of $w = v + u$ using the parity check matrix

$$H = \begin{bmatrix} I \\ B \end{bmatrix}.$$

Then $s_1 = wH = [u_1, u_2]H = u_1 + u_2 B$. So if $\text{wt}(u_2) \leq 1$ then s_1 consists of either a word of weight at most 3 (if $\text{wt}(u_2) = 0$) or a row of B with at most 2 of its digits changed (if $\text{wt}(u_2) = 1$). Similary, if $\text{wt}(u_1) \leq 1$ then the syndrome

$$s_2 = w \begin{bmatrix} B \\ I \end{bmatrix} = u_1 B + u_2$$

consists of either a word of weight at most 3 or a row of B with at most 2 of its digits changed.

In any case, if u has weight at most 3 then it is easily identified, since at most 3 rows of one of the two parity check matrices can be found to add to the corresponding syndrome. Using this observation we obtain the following decoding algorithm. We shall make use of the fact that $B^2 = I$ and

$$\begin{aligned} s_1 &= u_1 + u_2 B = wH \\ s_2 &= u_1 B + u_2 \\ &= (u_1 + u_2 B)B = s_1 B. \end{aligned}$$

To avoid incorporating both of the parity check matrices into the algorithm, only $H = \begin{bmatrix} I \\ B \end{bmatrix}$ is used. Of course once u has been determined, w is decoded to the codeword $v = w + u$. e_i is the word of length 12 with a 1 in the ith position and 0s elsewhere, and b_i is the ith row of B.

Algorithm 3.6.1 (decoding the extended Golay code)

1. Compute the syndrome $s = wH$.
2. If $\text{wt}(s) \leq 3$ then $u = [s, 0]$.
3. If $\text{wt}(s + b_i) \leq 2$ for some row b_i of B then $u = [s + b_i, e_i]$.
4. Compute the second syndrome sB.
5. If $\text{wt}(sB) \leq 3$ then $u = [0, sB]$.
6. If $\text{wt}(sB + b_i) \leq 2$ for some row b_i of B then $u = [e_i, sB + b_i]$.
7. If u is not yet determined then request retransmission.

The above algorithm requires at most 26 weight calculations in the decoding procedure. (Of course, once u has been determined then no further steps in the algorithm need to be done.)

Example 3.6.2 Decode $w = 101111101111, 010010010010$. The syndrome is

$$\begin{aligned} s = wH &= 101111101111 + 001111101110 \\ &= 100000000001, \end{aligned}$$

which has weight 2. Since $\text{wt}(s) \leq 3$, we find that

$$u = [s, 0] = 100000000001, 000000000000$$

and conclude that

$$v = w + u = 001111101110, 010010010010$$

was the codeword sent.

Because $G = [I, B]$ is in standard form and any word in K^{12} can be encoded as a message (C_{24} has dimension 12), the message sent appears in the first 12 digits of the decoded word v. In Example 3.6.2 the message 001111101110 was sent.

Example 3.6.3 Decode $w = 001001001101, 101000101000$. The syndrome is

$$s = wH = 001001001101 + 111000000100 = 110001001001,$$

which has weight 5. Proceeding to step 3 of the Algorithm 3.6.1 we compute

$$\begin{aligned} s + b_1 &= 000110001100 \\ s + b_2 &= 011111000010 \\ s + b_3 &= 101101011110 \\ s + b_4 &= 001001100100 \\ s + b_5 &= 000000010010. \end{aligned}$$

Since $\mathrm{wt}(s + b_5) \leq 2$, we find that

$$u = [s + b_5, e_5] = 000000010010, 000010000000$$

and conclude that

$$v = w + u = 001001011111, 101010101000$$

was the codeword sent.

Example 3.6.4 Decode $w = 000111000111, 011011010000$. The syndrome is

$$\begin{aligned} s = wH &= u_1 + u_2 B \\ &= 000111000111 + 101010101101 \\ &= 101101101010, \end{aligned}$$

which has weight 7. Proceeding to step 3, we find $\mathrm{wt}(s + b_i) \geq 3$ for each row b_i of B. We continue to step 4; the second syndrome is

$$sB = 111001111101,$$

which has weight 9. Forging ahead to step 5 we compute

$$\begin{aligned} sB + b_1 &= 001110111000 \\ sB + b_2 &= 010111110110 \\ sB + b_3 &= 100101101010 \\ sB + b_4 &= 000001010000. \end{aligned}$$

Since $\mathrm{wt}(sB + b_4) \leq 2$, we find that

$$u = [e_4, sB + b_4] = 000100000000, 000001010000$$

and conclude that

$$v = w + u = 000011000111, 011010000000$$

was the codeword sent.

Exercises

3.6.5 The code is C_{24}. Find the most likely error pattern if possible, for each of the following received words w.

(a) 111 000 000 000, 011 011 011 011
(b) 111 111 000 000, 100 011 100 111
(c) 111 111 000 000, 101 011 100 111
(d) 111 111 000 000, 111 000 111 000
(e) 111 000 000 000, 110 111 001 101
(f) 110 111 001 101, 111 000 000 000
(g) 000 111 000 111, 101 000 101 101
(h) 110 000 000 000, 101 100 100 000
(i) 110 101 011 101, 111 000 000 000.

3.6.6 Find the most likely error pattern for any word with the given syndromes.

(a) $s_1 = 010010000000, s_2 = 011111010000$
(b) $s_1 = 010010100101, s_2 = 001000110000$
(c) $s_1 = 111111000101, s_2 = 111100010111$
(d) $s_1 = 111111111011, s_2 = 010010001110$
(e) $s_1 = 001101110110, s_2 = 111110101101$
(f) $s_1 = 010111111001, s_2 = 100010111111$

3.6.7 Show that if s or sB has weight 4 then IMLD requires that the word be retransmitted.

3.7 The Golay code

Another interesting three-error-correcting code can be obtained by *puncturing* C_{24}, that is, by removing a digit from every word in C_{24}. The same digit must be removed from each word. We shall remove the last digit.

Let $\hat{B}$ be the 12×11 matrix obtained from the matrix B by deleting the last column. Let G be the 12×23 matrix $G = [I_{12}, \hat{B}]$. The linear code with generator matrix G is called the Golay code and is denoted by C_{23}. The Golay code has length $n = 23$, dimension $k = 12$, and contains $2^{12} = 4096$ codewords. Note that the extended code C_{23}^* is indeed C_{24}. C_{23} has distance 7. This is most easily seen from the fact that $C_{23}^* = C_{24}$ (see Exercise 3.4.6), but can be shown using Theorem 3.2.8 or by modifying the proof that C_{24} has distance 8.

The Golay code C_{23} is a perfect code (Example 3.2.4) *and will correct all error patterns of weight* 3 *or less, and no others* (Theorem 3.2.8). Therefore every received word w is at most distance 3 from exactly one codeword. So if we append the digit 0 or 1 to w forming $w0$ or $w1$ respectively so that the resulting word has odd weight, then the resulting word is distance at most 3 from a codeword c in C_{24} (see Exercise 3.7.10). Decoding to c using Algorithm 3.6.1 and removing the last digit from c then gives the closest codeword to w in C_{23}.

Algorithm 3.7.1 (decoding the Golay code)

1. Form $w0$ or $w1$, whichever has odd weight.
2. Decode wi (i is 0 or 1) using Algorithm 3.6.1 to a codeword c in C_{24}.
3. Remove the last digit from c.

In practice, the received word w is normally a codeword, however wi formed in step 1 is never a codeword (Why?). If w is a codeword then the syndrome of wi is the last row of H (Why?) so this can easily be checked before implementing Algorithm 3.6.1.

Example 3.7.2 Decode $w = 001001001001, 11111110000$. Since w has odd weight, form $w0 = 001001001001, 111111100000$. Then $s_1 = 100010111110$. Since $s_1 = b_6 + e_9 + e_{12}$, $w0$ is decoded to $001001000000, 111110100000$ and so w is decoded to $001001000000, 11111010000$.

Exercises

3.7.3 Decode each of the following received words that were encoded using C_{23}.

(a) 101011100000, 10101011011
(b) 101010000001, 11011100010
(c) 100101011000, 11100010000
(d) 011001001001, 01101101111.

3.7.4 Prove that C_{23} has distance $d = 7$.

3.7.5 Find the reliability of C_{23} transmitted over a BSC of probability p.

3.7.6 Determine whether C_{23} or C_{24} has the greater reliability. Use the same BSC for both.

3.7.7 Use the fact that every word of weight 4 is distance 3 from exactly one codeword (why?) to count the number of codewords of weight 7 in the Golay code. (Hint: for any codeword c, the number of words that have weight 4 and are distance 3 from c is $\binom{7}{3}$.)

3.7.8 Use Exercise 3.7.7 to show that C_{24} contains precisely 759 codewords of weight 8. (Hint: each word of weight 5 is at distance at most 3 from exactly one codeword.)

3.7.9 Use Exercises 3.5.1 and 3.7.8 to verify the following weight distribution table for C_{24}:

weight	0	4	8	12	16	20	24
number of words	1	0	759	2576	759	0	1

3.7.10 Let w be a received word that was encoded using C_{23}. Append a digit i to w to form a word wi of odd weight. Show that wi is within distance 3 of a codeword in C_{24}. (Hint: all words in C_{24} have even weight.)

3.8 Reed-Muller codes

In this section we briefly consider another important class of codes which includes the extended Hamming code discussed earlier (see also Chapter 9). The rth order Reed-Muller code of length 2^m will be denoted by $RM(r,m)$, $0 \le r \le m$. We present a recursive definition of these codes:

(1) $RM(0,m) = \{00\ldots0, 11\ldots1\}$, $RM(m,m) = K^{2^m}$

(2) $RM(r,m) = \{(x, x+y) \mid x \in RM(r,m-1),\ y \in RM(r-1,m-1)\}, 0 < r < m$.

So $RM(m,m)$ is all words of length 2^m and $RM(0,m)$ is just the all ones word (and the zero word).

Example 3.8.1

$$\begin{array}{ll} RM(0,0) = \{0,1\} & \\ RM(0,1) = \{00,11\}, & RM(1,1) = K^2 = \{00,01,10,11\} \\ RM(0,2) = \{0000,1111\}, & RM(2,2) = K^4 \\ RM(1,2) = \{(x,x+y) \mid x \in \{00,01,10,11\},\ y \in \{00,11\}\} & \end{array}$$

Rather than use this description of the code, we will give a recursive construction for the generator matrix of $RM(r,m)$, which we will denote by $G(r,m)$. For $0 < r < m$, define $G(r,m)$ by

$$G(r,m) = \begin{bmatrix} G(r,m-1) & G(r,m-1) \\ 0 & G(r-1,m-1) \end{bmatrix}$$

For $r = 0$ define

$$G(0,m) = [11\ldots1]$$

and for $r = m$, define

$$G(m,m) = \begin{bmatrix} G(m-1,m) \\ 0\ldots01 \end{bmatrix}$$

Example 3.8.2 The generator matrices for $RM(0,1)$ and $RM(1,1)$ are

$$G(0,1) = [1\ 1] \text{ and } G(1,1) = \begin{bmatrix} 1 & 1 \\ 0 & 1 \end{bmatrix}$$

Example 3.8.3 Let $m = 2$, then the length is $4 = 2^2$ and for $r = 1, 2$ we have

$$G(1,2) = \begin{bmatrix} G(1,1) & G(1,1) \\ 0 & G(0,1) \end{bmatrix}, \quad G(2,2) = \begin{bmatrix} G(1,2) \\ 0001 \end{bmatrix}.$$

Using Example 3.8.2 we have,

$$G(1,2) = \begin{bmatrix} 11 & 11 \\ 01 & 01 \\ 00 & 11 \end{bmatrix}, \quad G(2,2) = \begin{bmatrix} 1111 \\ 0101 \\ 0011 \\ 0001 \end{bmatrix}$$

Example 3.8.4 For $m = 3, n = 2^3 = 8$, we have

$$G(0,3) = (11111111), \quad G(3,3) = \begin{bmatrix} G(2,3) \\ 00000001 \end{bmatrix}$$

$$G(1,3) = \begin{bmatrix} G(1,2) & G(1,2) \\ 0 & G(0,2) \end{bmatrix}, \quad G(2,3) = \begin{bmatrix} G(2,2) & G(2,2) \\ 0 & G(1,2) \end{bmatrix}.$$

Thus using Example 3.8.3

$$G(1,3) = \begin{bmatrix} 1111 & 1111 \\ 0101 & 0101 \\ 0011 & 0011 \\ 0000 & 1111 \end{bmatrix}.$$

Exercises

3.8.5 Find the generator matrix $G(2,3)$.

3.8.6 Find generator matrix $G(r,4)$, for the codes $RM(r,4)$ for $r = 0,1,2$.

With this recursive definition it is a simple matter to prove via induction the basic properties of a Reed-Muller code.

Theorem 3.8.7 *The rth order Reed-Muller code $RM(r,m)$ defined above has the following properties:*

(1) length $n = 2^m$

(2) distance $d = 2^{m-r}$

(3) dimension $k = \sum_{i=0}^{r} \binom{m}{i}$

(4) $RM(r-1,m)$ is contained in $RM(r,m), r > 0$

(5) dual code $RM(m-1-r,m), r < m$.

Proof: The proofs of these claims all use induction. We leave it as an exercise to show that this theorem holds for all $RM(r,m)$ codes for $m = 1,2,3,4$. Also, we note that these claims are obviously true for $r = 0$ and $r = m$.

First we want to show that $RM(r-1,m) \subseteq RM(r,m)$. We start with

$$G(1,m) = \begin{bmatrix} G(1,m-1) & G(1,m-1) \\ 0 & G(0,m-1) \end{bmatrix}.$$

Since **1** is the top row of $G(1, m-1)$ then the all ones vector $(\mathbf{1}, \mathbf{1})$ is the top row vector in $(G(1, m-1), G(1, m-1))$. Thus $RM(0, m) = \{\mathbf{0}, \mathbf{1}\}$ is contained in $RM(1, m)$.

In general since $G(r-1, m-1)$ is a submatrix of $G(r, m-1)$ and $G(r-2, m-1)$ is a submatrix of $G(r-1, m-1)$ we have obviously

$$G(r-1, m) = \begin{bmatrix} G(r-1, m-1) & G(r-1, m-1) \\ 0 & G(r-2, m-1) \end{bmatrix}$$

is a submatrix of $G(r, m)$ and thus $RM(r-1, m)$ is a subcode of $RM(r, m)$.

Next we establish the distance $d = 2^{m-r}$ for $RM(r, m)$, using induction on r.

Since $RM(r, m) = \{(x, x+y) \mid x \in RM(r, m-1), y \in RM(r-1, m-1)\}$ and $RM(r-1, m-1) \subseteq RM(r, m-1)$ then $x + y \in RM(r, m-1)$ and so if $x \neq y$, then, by our inductive hypothesis, $\text{wt}(x+y) \geq 2^{m-1-r}$. Also $\text{wt}(x) \geq 2^{m-1-r}$. Hence $\text{wt}(x, x+y) = \text{wt}(x+y) + \text{wt}(x) \geq 2 \cdot 2^{m-1-r} = 2^{m-r}$. If $x = y$, then $(x, x+y) = (y, 0)$ but $y \in RM(r-1, m-1)$ and thus $\text{wt}(y, 0) = \text{wt}(y) \geq 2^{m-1-(r-1)} = 2^{m-r}$.

From the definition of $G(r, m)$, we have

$$\begin{aligned} \dim RM(r, m) &= \dim RM(r, m-1) + \dim RM(r-1, m-1) \\ &= \sum_{i=0}^{r} \binom{m-1}{i} + \sum_{i=0}^{r-1} \binom{m-1}{i} \\ &= \sum_{i=1}^{r} \left(\binom{m-1}{i} + \binom{m-1}{i-1} \right) + \binom{m-1}{0}. \end{aligned}$$

Since $\binom{m}{i} = \binom{m-1}{i} + \binom{m-1}{i-1}$ and $\binom{m-1}{0} = 1 = \binom{m}{0}$ we have,

$$\dim RM(r, m) = \sum_{i=0}^{r} \binom{m}{i}.$$

Finally let

$$RM(r, m) = \{(x, x+y) \mid x \in RM(r, m-1), y \in RM(r-1, m-1)\}$$

and let

$$\begin{aligned} RM(m-r-1, m) = \{(x', x'+y') \mid\ & x' \in RM(m-r-1, m-1), \\ & y' \in RM(m-r-2, m-1)\}. \end{aligned}$$

By induction the dual of $RM(r, m-1)$ is $RM(m-r-2, m-1)$ and the dual of $RM(r-1, m-1)$ is $RM(m-r-1, m-1)$ thus $x \cdot y' = 0$, and $x' \cdot y = 0$. Also since $RM(r-1,m-1) \subseteq RM(r,m-1)$, $y \cdot y' = 0$. Hence

$$\begin{aligned}(x,x+y)\cdot(x',x'+y') &= (x+y)\cdot(x'+y') + x\cdot x' \\ &= 2(x\cdot x') + x\cdot y' + y\cdot x' + y\cdot y' \\ &= 0.\end{aligned}$$

We see that every vector in $RM(r,m)$ is orthogonal to every vector in $RM(m-r-1,m)$. Since

$$\begin{aligned}\dim RM(r,m) + \dim RM(m-r-1,m) &= \sum_{i=0}^{r}\binom{m}{i} + \sum_{i=0}^{m-r-1}\binom{m}{i} \\ &= \sum_{i=0}^{r}\binom{m}{m-i} + \sum_{j=0}^{m-r-1}\binom{m}{j} \\ &= \sum_{j=0}^{m}\binom{m}{j} = 2^m\end{aligned}$$

the $RM(m-r-1,m)$ code is the dual of the $RM(r,m)$ code. □

Exercises

3.8.8 Show that Theorem 3.8.7 holds for the codes $RM(r,m)$, $1 \le m \le 4$, constructed in Examples 3.8.1, 3.8.3, 3.8.4 and Exercises 3.8.5, 3.8.6.

We consider the first order Reed-Muller code $RM(1,m)$. Notice that $RM(m-2,m)$ has dimension $2^m - m - 1$ and has distance 4, length 2^m and therefore is an extended Hamming code. By Theorem 3.8.7, $RM(1,m)$ is the dual of this extended Hamming code. We present a decoding algorithm for this code which is quite efficient. We postpone a discussion of a decoding algorithm for general $RM(r,m)$ codes until Chapter 9.

Note that the $RM(1,m)$ code is a small code with a large minimum distance, so a good decoding algorithm is in fact the most elementary: for each received word w, find the codeword in $RM(1,m)$ closest to w. This can be done very efficiently.

Example 3.8.9 Let $m=3$, consider the $RM(1,3)$ code which has length $8 = 2^3$, and $16 = 2^{3+1}$ codewords. The minimum distance is 4. Let

$$G(1,3) = \begin{bmatrix} 1111 & 1111 \\ 0101 & 0101 \\ 0011 & 0011 \\ 0000 & 1111 \end{bmatrix}$$

Note that if w is received and $d(w,c) < 2$ then we decode w to c but if $d(w,c) > 6$, then $d(w,\mathbf{1}+c) < 2$ and we decode w to $\mathbf{1}+c$. (Recall $\mathbf{1}$ is a codeword.) For example, if $w = 1000\,1111$ is received then $c = 0000\,1111$ is the nearest codeword.

If $w = (10101011)$ is received and we find $c = (01010101)$ with $d(w,c) > 6$, then $c + \mathbf{1} = 10101010$ is the nearest codeword. Thus we have to examine at most half of the codewords in $RM(1,m)$.

In fact, there are very efficient matrix methods to compute these distances which we will present in the next section.

Exercises

3.8.10 Let $G(1,3)$ be the generator for the $RM(1,3)$ code, decode the following received words

(a) 0101 1110 (b) 0110 0111
(c) 0001 0100 (d) 1100 1110

3.8.11 Let $G(1,4)$ be the generator for the $RM(1,4)$ code, decode the following received words

(a) 1011 0110 0110 1001
(b) 1111 0000 0101 1111

3.9 Fast decoding for $RM(1,m)$

In this section we present briefly and without justification a very efficient decoding method for $RM(1,m)$ codes. It utilizes the Fast Hadamard Transform to find the nearest codeword. First we need to introduce the Kronecker product of matrices.

Define $A \times B = [a_{ij}B]$; that is, entry a_{ij} in A is replaced by the matrix $a_{ij}B$.

Example 3.9.1 Let $H = \begin{bmatrix} 1 & 1 \\ 1 & -1 \end{bmatrix} I_2 = \begin{bmatrix} 1 & 0 \\ 0 & 1 \end{bmatrix}$. Then

$$I_2 \times H = \begin{bmatrix} 1 & 1 & 0 & 0 \\ 1 & -1 & 0 & 0 \\ 0 & 0 & 1 & 1 \\ 0 & 0 & 1 & -1 \end{bmatrix} \quad \text{and} \quad H \times I_2 = \begin{bmatrix} 1 & 0 & 1 & 0 \\ 0 & 1 & 0 & 1 \\ 1 & 0 & -1 & 0 \\ 0 & 1 & 0 & -1 \end{bmatrix}.$$

Now we consider a series of matrices defined as:

$$H_m^i = I_{2^{m-i}} \times H \times I_{2^{i-1}}$$

for $i = 1, 2, \ldots, m$, where H is as in Example 3.9.1.

Example 3.9.2 Let $m = 2$. Then

$$H_2^1 = I_2 \times H \times I_1 = I_2 \times H$$
$$H_2^2 = I_1 \times H \times I_2 = H \times I_2$$

(see Example 3.9.1).

Example 3.9.3 Let $m = 3$ then

$$H_3^1 = I_4 \times H \times I_1 = \begin{bmatrix} 1 & 1 & 0 & 0 & 0 & 0 & 0 & 0 \\ 1 & -1 & 0 & 0 & 0 & 0 & 0 & 0 \\ & & & & & & & \\ 0 & 0 & 1 & 1 & 0 & 0 & 0 & 0 \\ 0 & 0 & 1 & -1 & 0 & 0 & 0 & 0 \\ & & & & & & & \\ 0 & 0 & 0 & 0 & 1 & 1 & 0 & 0 \\ 0 & 0 & 0 & 0 & 1 & -1 & 0 & 0 \\ & & & & & & & \\ 0 & 0 & 0 & 0 & 0 & 0 & 1 & 1 \\ 0 & 0 & 0 & 0 & 0 & 0 & 1 & -1 \end{bmatrix}$$

$$H_3^2 = I_2 \times H \times I_2 = \begin{bmatrix} 1 & 0 & 1 & 0 & 0 & 0 & 0 & 0 \\ 0 & 1 & 0 & 1 & 0 & 0 & 0 & 0 \\ 1 & 0 & -1 & 0 & 0 & 0 & 0 & 0 \\ 0 & 1 & 0 & -1 & 0 & 0 & 0 & 0 \\ 0 & 0 & 0 & 0 & 1 & 0 & 1 & 0 \\ 0 & 0 & 0 & 0 & 0 & 1 & 0 & 1 \\ 0 & 0 & 0 & 0 & 1 & 0 & -1 & 0 \\ 0 & 0 & 0 & 0 & 0 & 1 & 0 & -1 \end{bmatrix}$$

$$H_3^3 = H \times I_4 = \begin{bmatrix} 1 & 0 & 0 & 0 & 1 & 0 & 0 & 0 \\ 0 & 1 & 0 & 0 & 0 & 1 & 0 & 0 \\ 0 & 0 & 1 & 0 & 0 & 0 & 1 & 0 \\ 0 & 0 & 0 & 1 & 0 & 0 & 0 & 1 \\ & & & & & & & \\ 1 & 0 & 0 & 0 & -1 & 0 & 0 & 0 \\ 0 & 1 & 0 & 0 & 0 & -1 & 0 & 0 \\ 0 & 0 & 1 & 0 & 0 & 0 & -1 & 0 \\ 0 & 0 & 0 & 1 & 0 & 0 & 0 & -1 \end{bmatrix}$$

The recursive nature of the construction of $RM(1,m)$ codes suggests that there is a recursive approach to decoding as well. This is the intuitive basis for the following decoding algorithm for $RM(1,m)$.

Algorithm 3.9.4 (decoding the $RM(1,m)$ code) Suppose w is received and $G(1,m)$ is the generator matrix for $RM(1,m)$ code.

1. Replace 0 by -1 in w forming $\overline{w}$.
2. Compute $w_1 = \overline{w} H_m^1$ and $w_i = w_{i-1} H_m^i$ for $i = 2, 3, \ldots, m$.
3. Find the position j of the largest component (in absolute value) of w_m.

Let $v(j) \in K^m$ be the binary representation of j (low order digits first). Then if the jth component of w_m is positive, the presumed message is $(1, v(j))$, and if it is negative the presumed message is $(0, v(j))$.

Example 3.9.5 Let $m = 3$, and $G(1, 3)$ be the generator matrix for $RM(1, 3)$ (see Example 3.8.9). If $w = 10101011$ is received, convert w to $\overline{w} = (1, -1, 1, -1, 1, -1, 1, 1)$. Compute:

$$w_1 = \overline{w}H_3^1 = (0, 2, 0, 2, 0, 2, 2, 0)$$
$$w_2 = w_1 H_3^2 = (0, 4, 0, 0, 2, 2, -2, 2)$$
$$w_3 = w_2 H_3^3 = (2, 6, -2, 2, -2, 2, 2, -2)$$

(see Example 3.9.2 for H_3^1, H_3^2, H_3^3). The largest component of w_3 is 6 occurring in position 1. Since $v(1) = 100$ and $6 > 0$, then the presumed message is $m = (1100)$.

Suppose $w = (10001111)$. Then $\overline{w} = (1, -1, -1, -1, 1, 1, 1, 1)$ and

$$w_1 = \overline{w}H_3^1 = (0, 2, -2, 0, 2, 0, 2, 0)$$
$$w_2 = w_1 H_3^2 = (-2, 2, 2, 2, 4, 0, 0, 0)$$
$$w_3 = w_2 H_3^3 = (2, 2, 2, 2, -6, 2, 2, 2).$$

The largest component of w_3 is -6 occurring in position 4. Since $v(4) = 001$ and $-6 < 0$ the presumed message is (0001).

Exercises

3.9.6 Decode the received words in Exercise 3.8.10 using Algorithm 3.9.4 (and Example 3.9.2).

3.9.7 Compute H_4^i for $i = 1, 2, 3, 4$.

3.9.8 Decode the received words in Exercise 3.8.11 using Algorithm 3.9.4 (and Exercise 3.9.6).

	Binary	v(j) low order 1st
0	000	000
1	001	100
2	010	010
3	011	110
4	100	001
5	101	101
6	110	011
7	111	111

m tells # of digits v(j) is

If m=2 cutoff first digit in binary column

Chapter 4

Cyclic Linear Codes

4.1 Polynomials and words

We will find it convenient to represent cyclic codes in terms of polynomials. For this reason we review some needed facts about polynomials (of one variable).

A *polynomial of degree n over K* is a polynomial $a_0 + a_1x + \cdots + a_nx^n$ where the coefficients $a_0, \ldots, a_n$ are elements of K. The set of all polynomials over K is denoted by $K[x]$. Elements of $K[x]$ will be denoted by $f(x), g(x), p(x)$ and so forth, and the degree of $f(x)$ is denoted by $\deg(f(x))$.

Polynomials over K are added and multiplied in the usual fashion except that since $1+1=0$, we have that $x^k + x^k = 0$. This means that the degree of $f(x) + g(x)$ need not be $\max\{\deg(f(x)), \deg(g(x))\}$.

Example 4.1.1 Let $f(x) = 1 + x + x^3 + x^4$, $g(x) = x + x^2 + x^3$ and $h(x) = 1 + x^2 + x^4$. Then:

(a) $f(x) + g(x) = 1 + x^2 + x^4$;

(b) $f(x) + h(x) = x + x^2 + x^3$;

(c) $f(x)g(x) = (x + x^2 + x^3) + x(x + x^2 + x^3) + x^3(x + x^2 + x^3) + x^4(x + x^2 + x^3) = x + x^7$.

Exercises

4.1.2 Find the sum and the product of each of the following pairs of polynomials over K:

(a) $f(x) = x^5 + x^6 + x^7$, $h(x) = 1 + x^2 + x^3 + x^4$;

(b) $f(x) = 1 + x^2 + x^3 + x^8 + x^{13}$, $h(x) = 1 + x^3 + x^9$,

(c) $f(x) = 1 + x$, $h(x) = 1 + x + x^2 + x^3 + x^4$.

4.1.3 Let $f(x) = 1 + x$. Find:

(a) $(f(x))^2$ (b) $(f(x))^3$ (c) $(f(x))^4$.

4.1.4 Repeat Exercise 4.1.3 for $f(x) = 1 + x + x^2$.

4.1.5 List all polynomials over K of degree n, for $n = 0$, $n = 2$, $n = 3$, and $n = 4$.

4.1.6 Find the number of polynomials over K of degree at most 10.

4.1.7 As you may have noticed in Exercises 4.1.3 (a) and 4.1.4 (a), for any polynomials $f(x)$ and $g(x)$ in $K[x]$,

$$(f(x) + g(x))^2 = (f(x))^2 + (g(x))^2$$

since $x^k + x^k = 0$. Is there also a special rule in $K[x]$ for

(a) $(f(x) + g(x))^4$,
(b) $(f(x) + g(x))^3$,
(c) $(f(x) + g(x))^n$, for any positive integer n?

The usual long division process works for polynomials over K just as it does for polynomials over the rational numbers.

Algorithm 4.1.8 (Division algorithm) Let $f(x)$ and $h(x)$ be in $K[x]$ with $h(x) \neq 0$. Then there exist unique polynomials $q(x)$ and $r(x)$ in $K[x]$ such that

$$f(x) = q(x)h(x) + r(x),$$

with $r(x) = 0$ or $\deg(r(x)) < \deg(h(x))$.

The polynomial $q(x)$ is called the *quotient*, and $r(x)$ is called the *remainder*. The procedure for finding the quotient and the remainder when $h(x)$ is divided into $f(x)$ is the familiar long division process, but with the arithmetic in K among the coefficients.

Example 4.1.9 Let $f(x) = x + x^2 + x^6 + x^7 + x^8$ and $h(x) = 1 + x + x^2 + x^4$. Then

$$\begin{array}{r|l}
 & x^4 + x^3 \\
\hline
x^4 + x^2 + x + 1 & x^8 + x^7 + x^6 + x^2 + x \\
 & x^8 + x^6 + x^5 + x^4 \\
\cline{2-2}
 & \quad x^7 + x^5 + x^4 + x^2 + x \\
 & \quad x^7 + x^5 + x^4 + x^3 \\
\cline{2-2}
 & \qquad\qquad x^3 + x^2 + x
\end{array}$$

Thus the quotient is $q(x) = x^3 + x^4$ and the remainder is $r(x) = x + x^2 + x^3$. We may write $f(x) = h(x)(x^3 + x^4) + (x + x^2 + x^3)$. Note that $\deg(r(x)) < \deg(h(x)) = 4$.

Exercises

4.1.10 Find the quotient and remainder when $h(x)$ is divided into $f(x)$ for each of the pairs of polynomials over K in Exercise 4.1.2.

4.1.11 Find the quotient and remainder in each part when $h(x)$ is divided into $f(x)$.

(a) $f(x) = x^2 + x^3 + x^4 + x^8$, $h(x) = 1 + x^5$.
(b) $f(x) = 1 + x^{10}$, $h(x) = 1 + x^5$
(c) $f(x) = 1 + x^7$, $h(x) = 1 + x + x^3$
(d) $f(x) = 1 + x^{15}$, $h(x) = 1 + x^4 + x^6 + x^7 + x^8$.

The polynomial $f(x) = a_0 + a_1x + a_2x^2 + \cdots + a_{n-1}x^{n-1}$ of degree at most $n-1$ over K may be regarded as the word $v = a_0a_1a_2 \ldots a_{n-1}$ of length n in K^n. For example if $n = 7$,

polynomial	word
$1+x+x^2+x^4$	1110100
$1+x^4+x^5+x^6$	1000111
$1+x+x^3$	1101000

Thus *a code C of length n can be represented as a set of polynomials over K of degree at most $n-1$.*

Note that it may be convenient for purposes of representing words by polynomials to number the digits of a word of length n from 0 to $n-1$, rather than from 1 to n. The word $a_0a_1a_2a_3$ of length 4 is represented by the polynomial $a_0 + a_1x + a_2x^2 + a_3x^3$ of degree 3, for instance.

Example 4.1.12 The code C in the left column of the array is represented by the polynomials in the right column.

codeword c	polynomial $c(x)$
0000	0
1010	$1+x^2$
0101	$x+x^3$
1111	$1+x+x^2+x^3$

Exercises

4.1.13 Represent each codeword C in the following codes with polynomials.

(a) $C = \{000, 001, 010, 011\}$
(b) $C = \{00000, 11111\}$
(c) $C = \{0000, 0001, 1110\}$
(d) $C = \{0000, 1001, 0110, 1111\}$
(e) $C = \{00000, 11100, 00111, 11011\}$

4.1.14 Write out the Hamming code of length 7 generated by the matrix G and then represent this code by polynomials.

$$G = \begin{bmatrix} 1000111 \\ 0100110 \\ 0010101 \\ 0001011 \end{bmatrix}$$

In Exercise 4.1.11(a), the reader computed the remainder $r(x)$ when $f(x) = x^2+x^3+x^4+x^8$ was divided by $h(x) = 1+x^5$. The result was $r(x) = x^2+x^4$. By the Division Algorithm, $r(x)$ is unique. Also $r(x)$ has degree less than the degree of the divisor $h(x)$.

We say that $f(x)$ *modulo* $h(x)$ is $r(x)$ if $r(x)$ is the remainder when $f(x)$ is divided by $h(x)$; we shall write $r(x) = f(x) \bmod h(x)$. Furthermore, we say that two functions $f(x)$ and $p(x)$ are *equivalent modulo* $h(x)$ if and only if they have the same remainder when divided by $h(x)$; that is if

$$f(x) \bmod h(x) = r(x) = p(x) \bmod h(x).$$

We denote this by

$$f(x) \equiv p(x) \pmod{h(x)}.$$

Example 4.1.15 Let $h(x) = 1+x^5$ and $f(x) = 1+x^4+x^9+x^{11}$. Then dividing $f(x)$ by $h(x)$ gives a remainder of $r(x) = 1+x$. We say that $r(x) = f(x) \bmod h(x)$.

Similarly, if $p(x) = 1+x^6$, then $1+x = 1+x^6 \bmod (1+x^5)$ and thus we say $p(x) \equiv f(x) \pmod{h(x)}$.

Example 4.1.16 Let $h(x) = 1+x^2+x^5$. Computing $f(x) \bmod h(x)$, with $f(x) = 1+x^2+x^6+x^9+x^{11}$ we find that the remainder $r(x) = x+x^4$ and hence $x+x^4 = f(x) \bmod h(x)$. Note that if $p(x) = x^2+x^8$ then $p(x) \bmod h(x) = 1+x^3$ and $p(x)$ and $f(x)$ are not equivalent mod $h(x)$.

Addition and multiplication of polynomials "respects" the equivalence of polynomials defined above. That is to say:

Lemma 4.1.17 *If $f(x) \equiv g(x) \pmod{h(x)}$, then*

$$f(x)+p(x) \equiv g(x)+p(x) \pmod{h(x)}$$

and

$$f(x)p(x) \equiv g(x)p(x) \pmod{h(x)}.$$

Proof: Suppose $r(x) = f(x) \bmod h(x)$ and $r(x) = g(x) \bmod h(x)$ and $s(x) = p(x) \bmod h(x)$ then we have

$$\begin{aligned} f(x)+p(x) &= q_1(x)h(x)+r(x)+q_2(x)h(x)+s(x) \\ &= (q_1(x)+q_2(x))h(x)+r(x)+s(x). \end{aligned}$$

Equivalently $r(x)+s(x) = (f(x)+p(x)) \bmod h(x)$ since $\deg(r(x)+s(x)) < \deg(h(x))$. (Why?) Similar arguments show that $r(x)+s(x) = (g(x)+p(x)) \bmod h(x)$. We leave the remaining arguments to Exercise 4.1.22. □

Example 4.1.18 Let $h(x)=1+x^5$, $f(x)=1+x+x^7$, $g(x)=1+x+x^2$ and $p(x)=1+x^6$; so $f(x)\equiv g(x) \pmod{h(x)}$. Then

$$f(x)+p(x)=x+x^6+x^7$$

and

$$g(x)+p(x)=x+x^2+x^6$$

but

$$(x+x^6+x^7) \bmod h(x)=x^2=(x+x^2+x^6) \bmod h(x).$$

Similarly

$$(1+x+x^7)(1+x^6) \bmod h(x)=1+x^3=(1+x+x^2)(1+x^6) \bmod h(x).$$

Note that $1+x=(1+x^6) \bmod h(x)$. Thus we have

$$\begin{aligned}(1+x+x^7)(1+x^6) &\equiv (1+x+x^2)(1+x^6)\\ &\equiv (1+x+x^2)(1+x)\equiv 1+x^3 \pmod{h(x)}.\end{aligned}$$

Exercises

4.1.19 Let $h(x)=1+x^3+x^5$. Compute $f(x) \bmod h(x)$ and its corresponding word:

(a) $f(x)=1+x+x^6$
(b) $f(x)=x+x^4+x^7+x^8$
(c) $f(x)=1+x^{10}$

4.1.20 Let $h(x)=1+x^7$. Compute $f(x) \bmod h(x)$ and $p(x) \bmod h(x)$, and decide whether $f(x)\equiv p(x) \pmod{h(x)}$:

(a) $f(x)=1+x^3+x^8$, $p(x)=x+x^3+x^7$
(b) $f(x)=x+x^5+x^9$, $p(x)=x+x^5+x^6+x^{13}$
(c) $f(x)=1+x$, $p(x)=x+x^7$

4.1.21 Let $h(x)=1+x^7$ compute $(f(x)+g(x)) \bmod h(x)$ and $(f(x)g(x)) \bmod h(x)$, where

(a) $f(x)=1+x^6+x^8$, $g(x)=1+x$
(b) $f(x)=1+x^5+x^9$, $g(x)=x+x^2+x^7$
(c) $f(x)=1+x^4+x^5$, $g(x)=1+x+x^2$

4.1.22 Prove that if $f(x)\equiv g(x)$ (mod $(h(x))$ then $f(x)p(x)\equiv g(x)p(x)$ (mod $h(x)$).

4.2 Introduction to cyclic codes

We now begin the study of a class of codes, called cyclic codes. Eventually we will be able to use our knowledge of cyclic codes to construct a generating matrix for the two error correcting BCH codes, as well as some other codes. In fact we shall also see that the Hamming and Golay codes are cyclic codes or are equivalent to cyclic codes.

Let v be a word of length n. The *cyclic shift* $\pi(v)$ of v is the word of length n obtained from v by taking the last digit of v and moving it to the beginning, all other digits moving one position to the right. For example:

v	10110	111000	0000	1011
$\pi(v)$	01011	011100	0000	1101

A code C is said to be a *cyclic code* if the cyclic shift of each codeword is also a codeword.

Example 4.2.1 The code $C = \{000, 110, 101, 011\}$ is a linear cyclic code. First C is linear. Next we compute $\pi(v)$ for all v in C.

$$\pi(000) = 000,\ \pi(110) = 011,\ \pi(101) = 110,\ \pi(011) = 101.$$

Since $\pi(v)$ is also in C, for each v in C, C is cyclic.

Example 4.2.2 The code $C = \{000, 100, 011, 111\}$ is not cyclic. The cyclic shift of $v = 100$ is $\pi(100) = 010$ which is not in C.

Note that the cyclic shift π is a linear transformation; that is,

Lemma 4.2.3 $\pi(v+w) = \pi(v)+\pi(w)$ *and* $\pi(av) = a\pi(v), a \in K = \{0, 1\}$. *Thus to show that a linear code C is cyclic it is enough to show that $\pi(v) \in C$ for each word v in a* basis *for C.*

Proof: Let $v = (v_0 v_1 \dots v_{n-1})$, $w = (w_0 w_1 \dots w_{n-1})$ then $v+w = (v_0+w_0, v_1+w_1, \dots, v_{n-1}+w_{n-1})$ and $\pi(v+w) = (v_{n-1}+w_{n-1}, v_0+w_0, \dots, v_{n-2}+w_{n-2}) = \pi(v)+\pi(w)$. □

Example 4.2.4 In Example 4.2.1, $\{110, 101\}$ is a basis for C. Since $\pi(110) = 011$ and $\pi(101) = 110$ are in C, C is a linear cyclic code.

If we wish to construct a cyclic linear code then we can pick a word, v, form a set S consisting of v and all of its cyclic shifts, $S = \{v, \pi(v), \pi^2(v), \dots, \pi^{n-1}(v)\}$ and define C to be the linear span of S; that is $C = \langle S \rangle$. (We use the notation $\pi^2(v) = \pi(\pi(v))$, $\pi^3(v) = \pi(\pi(\pi(v)))$, etc.) Since S contains a basis for C, C must be cyclic by Lemma 4.2.3.

Example 4.2.5 Let $n = 3$ and $v = 100$. Then $S = \{v, \pi(v), \pi^2(v)\} = \{100, 010, 001\}$ and $\langle S \rangle = K^3$. Note that if $w = a_0 v + a_1 \pi(v) + a_2 \pi^2(v)$ then $\pi(w) = a_0\pi(v) + a_1\pi^2(v) + a_2\pi^3(v) = a_2 v + a_0\pi(v) + a_1\pi^2(v)$.

Example 4.2.6 Let $n = 4$ and $v = 0101$. Then $\pi(v) = 1010$ and $\pi^2(v) = 0101 = v$. Thus $S = \{0101, 1010\}$ and $C = \langle S \rangle$ is the cyclic code, $C = \{0000, 0101, 1010, 1111\}$.

If a word v and its cyclic shifts form a set $S = \{v, \pi(v), \ldots, \pi^{n-1}(v)\}$ which spans the code C (so $C = \langle S \rangle$), then we say v is a *generator* of the linear cyclic code C. Since every linear cyclic code which contains v must contain S as well, we say that C is the smallest linear cyclic code containing v. It is worth noting that a linear cyclic code can have many generators.

Exercises

4.2.7 Find a basis for the smallest linear cyclic code of length n, containing v:

(a) $v = 1101000, n = 7$
(b) $v = 010101, n = 6$
(c) $v = 11011000, n = 8$

4.2.8 Find all words v of length n, such that $\pi(v) = v$.

4.2.9 Find all words v of length 6 such that

(a) $\pi^2(v) = v$
(b) $\pi^3(v) = v$.

Cyclic codes have a slick representation in terms of polynomials. This is based on the simple observation that if the word v corresponds to the polynomial $v(x)$ then the cyclic shift of $v, \pi(v)$ corresponds to the polynomial $xv(x) \bmod 1 + x^n$. Note that in general $1 \equiv x^n \pmod{1 + x^n}$.

Example 4.2.10 Let $v = 100$ then $v(x) = 1$ and $\pi(v) = 010$ corresponds to $xv(x) = x$. Similarly if $v = 1101$ then $v(x) = 1 + x + x^3$ and $\pi(v) = 1110$ corresponds to $xv(x) \bmod 1 + x^4 = 1 + x + x^2$.

For cyclic codes we refer to the elements of the code both as codewords and polynomials. We can now restate the previous discussion of cyclic codes in terms of polynomials. Given a word v of length n, let the polynomial corresponding to it be $v(x)$; then the cyclic shifts of v correspond to the polynomials $x^i v(x) \bmod 1 + x^n$ for $i = 0, 1, \ldots, n-1$.

Example 4.2.11 Let $v = 1101000$ and $n = 7$. Then $v(x) = 1 + x + x^3$ and we calculate $x^i v(x)$ for $1 \le i \le 6$ in Table 4.1.

Clearly if $c(x) \in \langle\{v(x), xv(x), \ldots, x^{n-1}v(x)\}\rangle$ (reducing each product mod $1 + x^n$), then that means that

$$\begin{aligned}
c(x) &= (a_0 v(x) + a_1 x v(x) + \cdots + a_{n-1} x^{n-1} v(x)) \bmod 1 + x^n \\
&= (a_0 + a_1 x + a_2 x^2 + \cdots + a_{n-1} x^{n-1}) v(x) \bmod 1 + x^n \\
&= a(x) v(x) \bmod 1 + x^n
\end{aligned}$$

word	polynomial (mod $1+x^7$)
0110100	$xv(x) = x + x^2 + x^4$
0011010	$x^2v(x) = x^2 + x^3 + x^5$
0001101	$x^3v(x) = x^3 + x^4 + x^6$
1000110	$x^4v(x) = x^4 + x^5 + x^7 \equiv 1 + x^4 + x^5 \pmod{1+x^7}$
0100011	$x^5v(x) = x^5 + x^6 + x^8 \equiv x + x^5 + x^6 \pmod{1+x^7}$
1010001	$x^6v(x) = x^6 + x^7 + x^9 \equiv 1 + x^2 + x^6 \pmod{1+x^7}$

Table 4.1: *Polynomial representation of cyclic shifts.*

Therefore we obtain the following result.

Lemma 4.2.12 *Let C be a cyclic code and let $v \in C$. Then for any polynomial $a(x)$, $c(x) = a(x)v(x) \bmod (1+x^n)$ is a codeword in C.*

Among all non-zero codewords in a linear cyclic code C, there is a unique word $g \in C$, such $g(x)$ has minimum degree, as the following argument indicates. Certainly there is at least one word or polynomial of smallest degree in C. If two non-zero words g and g' correspond to polynomials $g(x)$ and $g'(x)$ of minimum degree k then $g(x) + g'(x) = c(x) \in C$ since C is linear and degree $(c(x)) < k$ (since $x^k + x^k = 0$). Since g is a non-zero word of smallest degree, degree $(c(x)) < k$ means that $c(x) = 0$, so $g(x) = g'(x)$ and so $g(x)$ is unique.

We define *the generator polynomial* of a linear cyclic code C to be the unique non-zero polynomial of minimum degree in C. From the above discussion we know it is unique, but is it a generator?

To see that it is, we must show that for any codeword $c(x) \in C$, there exists $a(x)$ such that, $c(x) = a(x)g(x) \bmod 1+x^n$; in fact we shall show that $c(x) = a(x)g(x)$. Since $\deg(c(x)) \geq \deg(g(x))$ we have by the Division Algorithm,

$$c(x) = q(x)g(x) + r(x)$$

or

$$r(x) = q(x)g(x) + c(x).$$

However both $c(x)$ and $q(x)g(x)$ are codewords of C by Lemma 4.2.12 and thus so is $r(x)$. But by the Division Algorithm either $r(x) = 0$ or $\deg(r(x)) < \deg(g(x))$. Since the latter is impossible unless $r = 0$, we conclude that $r(x) = 0$ and thus $g(x)$ is a divisor of every codeword $c(x)$ in C.

Theorem 4.2.13 *Let C be a cyclic code of length n and let $g(x)$ be the generator polynomial. If $n - k =$ degree $(g(x))$ then*

1. *C has dimension k,*
2. *the codewords corresponding to $g(x), xg(x), \ldots, x^{k-1}g(x)$ are a basis for C, and*

3. *$c(x) \in C$ if and only if $c(x) = a(x)g(x)$ for some polynomial $a(x)$ with degree $(a(x)) < k$ (that is, $g(x)$ is a divisor of every codeword $c(x)$).*

Proof: The discussion before Theorem 4.2.13 proves (3). If $g(x)$ has degree $n-k$ then $g(x), xg(x), \ldots, x^{k-1}g(x)$ must be linearly independent. (Why?) Since $g(x)$ divides every codeword there is a unique polynomial $a(x) = a_0 + a_1x + \cdots + a_{k-1}x^{k-1}$ such that $c(x) = a(x)g(x) = a_0g(x) + a_1xg(x) + \cdots + a_{k-1}x^{k-1}g(x)$. Therefore $c(x)$ is in $\langle\{g(x), xg(x), \ldots, x^{k-1}g(x)\}\rangle$ and thus $\{g(x), xg(x), \ldots, x^{k-1}g(x)\}$ is a basis for C. □

Example 4.2.14 Let $n = 7, g(x) = 1 + x + x^3$ be the generator for the cyclic code C. A basis for C is

$$\begin{aligned} g(x) &= 1 + x + x^3 \leftrightarrow 1101000 \\ xg(x) &= x + x^2 + x^4 \leftrightarrow 0110100 \\ x^2g(x) &= x^2 + x^3 + x^5 \leftrightarrow 0011010 \\ x^3g(x) &= x^3 + x^4 + x^6 \leftrightarrow 0001101 \end{aligned}$$

Note $x^4g(x) \bmod 1 + x^7 = 1 + x^4 + x^5$ is a codeword since $1 + x^4 + x^5 = (1 + x + x^2)(1 + x + x^3) = (1 + x + x^2)g(x)$.

Example 4.2.15 Let C be the cyclic code $C = \{0000, 1010, 0101, 1111\}$; the corresponding polynomials are $\{0, 1 + x^2, x + x^3, 1 + x + x^2 + x^3\}$. Note, $1 + x^2 \leftrightarrow 1010$ is the generator polynomial for C, since C contains only one polynomial of degree 2 and none of degree 1. Also, every word (polynomial) in C is a multiple of the generator polynomial:

$$\begin{aligned} 0 &= 0(1 + x^2) & x + x^3 &= x(1 + x^2) \\ 1 + x^2 &= 1(1 + x^2) & 1 + x + x^2 + x^3 &= (1 + x)(1 + x^2). \end{aligned}$$

Example 4.2.16 The smallest linear cyclic code C of length 6 containing $g(x) = 1 + x^3 \leftrightarrow 100100$ is

$$= \{000000, 100100, 010010, 001001, 110110, 101101, 011011, 111111\}.$$

This can be verified by the techniques described earlier in this section. The polynomial of smallest degree representing a word in C is seen by inspection to be $g(x) = 1 + x^3$, and C contains no other polynomial of degree 3. Thus $g(x) = 1 + x^3$ is the generator polynomial for C. We represent each word in C as a multiple of $g(x)$ (see Table 4.2).

We can generate cyclic codes easily enough by picking a word v and setting $C = \langle\{v(x), xv(x), \ldots, x^{n-1}v(x)\}\rangle$ (modulo $1 + x^n$). However we need to find the generator polynomial for such a code and listing all codewords is not a reasonable approach. The generator polynomial for a cyclic code has one important property:

word	polynomial $f(x)$	factorization $h(x)g(x)$ of $f(x)$
000000	0	$0(1+x^3)$
100100	$1+x^3$	$1(1+x^3)$
010010	$x+x^4$	$x(1+x^3)$
001001	x^2+x^5	$x^2(1+x^3)$
110110	$1+x+x^3+x^4$	$(1+x)(1+x^3)$
101101	$1+x^2+x^3+x^5$	$(1+x^2)(1+x^3)$
011011	$x+x^2+x^4+x^5$	$(x+x^2)(1+x^3)$
111111	$1+x+x^2+x^3+x^4+x^5$	$(1+x+x^2)(1+x^3)$

Table 4.2: *Codewords are multiples of the generator polynomial.*

Theorem 4.2.17 *$g(x)$ is the generator polynomial for a linear cyclic code of length n if and only if $g(x)$ divides $1+x^n$ (so $1+x^n = h(x)g(x)$).*

Proof: By Lemma 4.2.12, $c(x) = h(x)g(x) \pmod{1+x^n} = h(x)g(x)+q(x)(1+x^n)$, is a codeword for any $h(x)$. By the Division Algorithm, $g(x)$ will divide every codeword $c(x)$ if and only if it divides $1+x^n$. Hence by Theorem 4.2.13 $g(x)$ is the generator for a cyclic code of length n if and only if $g(x)$ divides $1+x^n$. □

Corollary 4.2.18 *The generator polynomial $g(x)$ for the smallest cyclic code of length n containing the word v (polynomial $v(x)$) is the greatest common divisor of $v(x)$ and $1+x^n$ (that is, $g(x) = \gcd(v(x), 1+x^n)$).*

Proof: If $g(x)$ is the generator polynomial then $g(x)$ divides both $v(x)$ and $1+x^n$. But $g(x)$ is in $\langle\{v(x), xv(x), \ldots, x^{n-1}v(x)\}\rangle$, thus we have

$$g(x) = a(x)v(x) \bmod 1+x^n$$

or equivalently by the Division Algorithm:

$$g(x) = a(x)v(x) + b(x)(1+x^n).$$

Thus any common divisor of $v(x)$ and $1+x^n$ must divide $g(x)$ and thus $g(x)$ is the greatest common divisor. □

Example 4.2.19 Let $n = 8$ and $v = 11011000$, i.e., $v(x) = 1+x+x^3+x^4$. The gcd of $v(x)$ and $1+x^8$ is $1+x^2$. Thus $g(x) = 1+x^2$ and the smallest linear cyclic code containing $v(x)$ has dimension of 6 and $g(x)$ as the generator polynomial.

The Euclidean Algorithm for computing the gcd of two polynomials is discussed in the Appendix A. An alternate approach to finding the generator polynomial for a cyclic code of length n and dimension $n-k$ involves simple row reduction. If one takes a basis (or generator matrix) and puts it into RREF with the last k columns as the "leading columns" then the row (codeword) of minimum degree will be the generator polynomial.

Exercises

4.2.20 For each of the words below, find the generator polynomial for the smallest linear cyclic code containing that word.

(a) 010101
(b) 010010
(c) 01100110
(d) 0101100
(e) 001000101110000
(f) 000010010000000
(g) 010111010000000

4.2.21 Find the generator polynomial of the smallest linear cycle code containing each of the following words.

(a) 101010
(b) 1100
(c) 10001000
(d) 011011
(e) 10101
(f) 111111.

4.2.22 For each of the codes $C = \langle S \rangle$ with S defined below, find the generator polynomial $g(x)$ and then represent each word in the code as a multiple of $g(x)$.

(a) $S = \{010, 011, 111\}$
(b) $S = \{1010, 0101, 1111\}$
(c) $S = \{0101, 1010, 1100\}$
(d) $S = \{1000, 0100, 0010, 0001\}$
(e) $S = \{11000, 01111, 11110, 01010\}$

4.3 Generating and parity check matrices for cyclic codes

One can find various generator matrices for linear cyclic codes; the simplest is the matrix in which the rows are the codewords corresponding to the generator polynomial and its first $k-1$ cyclic shifts (see Theorem 4.2.13):

$$G = \begin{bmatrix} g(x) \\ xg(x) \\ \vdots \\ x^{k-1}g(x) \end{bmatrix}.$$

Example 4.3.1 Let $C = \{0000, 1010, 0101, 1111\}$ be a linear cyclic code. The generator polynomial for C is $g(x) = 1 + x^2$. Here $n = 4$ and $k = 2$, so a basis for C consists of

$$g(x) = 1 + x^2 \leftrightarrow 1010, \; xg(x) = x + x^3 \leftrightarrow 0101,$$

as can be easily verified. A generating matrix for C is

$$G = \begin{bmatrix} g(x) \\ xg(x) \end{bmatrix} = \begin{bmatrix} 1010 \\ 0101 \end{bmatrix}$$

Example 4.3.2 Let C be the linear cyclic code of length $n = 7$ with generator polynomial $g(x) = 1+x+x^3$ of degree $n-k = 3$. Then $k = 4$, so a basis for C is

$$\begin{aligned} g(x) &= 1+x+x^3 \\ xg(x) &= x+x^2+x^4 \\ x^2g(x) &= x^2+x^3+x^5 \\ x^3g(x) &= x^3+x^4+x^6 \end{aligned}$$

and a generating matrix for C is

$$G = \begin{bmatrix} 1101000 \\ 0110100 \\ 0011010 \\ 0001101 \end{bmatrix}.$$

Let C be a linear cyclic code of length n and dimension k (so the generator polynomial $g(x)$ has degree $n-k$). The k information digits $(a_0, a_1, \ldots, a_{k-1})$ to be encoded can be represented by the polynomial $a(x) = a_0 + a_1x + \cdots + a_{k-1}x^{k-1}$ called the *information* or *message polynomial*. Encoding consists simply of polynomial multiplication; that is, $a(x)$ is encoded as $a(x)g(x) = c(x)$. So instead of storing the entire $k \times n$ generator matrix one only has to store the generator polynomial, which is a significant improvement in terms of the complexity of encoding.

The inverse operation to polynomial multiplication is polynomial division. Hence finding the message corresponding to the closest codeword $c(x)$ to the received word consists of dividing $c(x)$ by $g(x)$, thus recovering the message polynomial $a(x)$.

Example 4.3.3 Let $g(x) = 1+x+x^3$ and $n = 7$. Then $k = 7-3 = 4$. Let $a(x) = 1+x^2$ be the message polynomial corresponding to the word $a = 1010$. The message $a(x)$ is encoded as $c(x) = a(x)g(x)$, so

$$c(x) = (1+x^2)(1+x+x^3) = 1+x+x^2+x^5$$

with $c = 1110010$ as the corresponding codeword.

If $c(x) = 1+x+x^4+x^6$ then the corresponding message polynomial is $c(x)/g(x) = a(x) = 1+x^3$ corresponding to the message $a = 1001$.

Exercises

4.3.4 Let $g(x) = 1+x^2+x^3$ be the generator polynomial of a linear cyclic code of length 7.

(a) Encode the following message polynomials: $1+x^3$, x, $x+x^2+x^3$.

(b) Find the message polynomial corresponding to the codewords $c(x)$: $x^2 + x^4 + x^5$, $1 + x + x^2 + x^4$, $x^2 + x^3 + x^4 + x^6$.

4.3.5 Find a basis and generating matrix for the linear cyclic code of length n with generator polynomial $g(x)$.

(a) $n = 7$, $g(x) = 1 + x^2 + x^3$
(b) $n = 9$, $g(x) = 1 + x^3 + x^6$
(c) $n = 15$, $g(x) = 1 + x + x^4$
(d) $n = 15$, $g(x) = 1 + x^4 + x^6 + x^7 + x^8$
(e) $n = 15$, $g(x) = 1 + x + x^2 + x^4 + x^5 + x^8 + x^{10}$.

4.3.6 Show that the linear code with given generator matrix is cyclic and find the generator polynomial.

(a) $G = \begin{bmatrix} 110110 \\ 001001 \\ 101101 \end{bmatrix}$ (b) $G = \begin{bmatrix} 010101 \\ 111111 \end{bmatrix}$

Having found an effective generating matrix for a linear cyclic code described in terms of its generator polynomial, we next turn our attention to finding a parity check matrix for such codes. To do so, we find a matrix H such that $wH = 0$ if and only if w is a codeword. So we begin by writing $w(x) = c(x) + e(x)$, thinking of $c(x)$ as a codeword and $e(x)$ as the error polynomial.

The *syndrome polynomial*, $s(x)$, is defined by $s(x) = w(x) \bmod g(x)$. Assuming $g(x)$ has degree $n-k$, then $s(x)$ will have degree less than $n-k$ and will correspond to a binary word s, of length $n-k$. Since $w(x) = c(x) + e(x)$ and $c(x) = a(x)g(x)$ for some polynomial $a(x)$, we have that $s(x) = e(x) \bmod g(x)$. That is, the syndrome polynomial is dependent only on the error.

We can define a matrix H in which the ith row r_i is the word of length $n-k$ corresponding to $r_i(x) = x^i \bmod g(x)$. It turns out that this matrix is a parity check matrix for the code. For, if w is a received word then $w(x) = c(x) + e(x)$, so

$$\begin{aligned} wH &= (c+e)H \\ &= \textstyle\sum_{i=0}^{n-1}(c_i + e_i)r_i \\ &\leftrightarrow \textstyle\sum_{i=0}^{n-1}(c_i + e_i)r_i(x) \\ &= (\textstyle\sum_{i=0}^{n-1} c_i x^i) \bmod g(x) + (\textstyle\sum_{i=0}^{n-1} e_i x^i) \bmod g(x) \\ &= c(x) \bmod g(x) + e(x) \bmod g(x) \\ &= 0 + e(x) \bmod g(x) \\ &= s(x). \end{aligned}$$

Then $s(x) = 0$ if and only if $w(x)$ is a codeword, so H is a parity check matrix. Also, if $wH = s$ then s corresponds to $s(x) = w(x) \bmod g(x)$. It is now clear why we refer to $s(x)$ as the syndrome polynomial. We will use this representation of the syndrome when we consider the correction of bursts of errors in Chapter 7.

Example 4.3.7 Let $n = 7$, and $g(x) = 1 + x + x^3$. Then $n - k = 3$. We produce H as follows.

$$\begin{array}{llll}
r_0(x) = 1 & \bmod g(x) = 1 & \leftrightarrow & 100 \\
r_1(x) = x & \bmod g(x) = x & \leftrightarrow & 010 \\
r_2(x) = x^2 & \bmod g(x) = x^2 & \leftrightarrow & 001 \\
r_3(x) = x^3 & \bmod g(x) = 1 + x & \leftrightarrow & 110 \\
r_4(x) = x^4 & \bmod g(x) = x + x^2 & \leftrightarrow & 011 \\
r_5(x) = x^5 & \bmod g(x) = 1 + x + x^2 & \leftrightarrow & 111 \\
r_6(x) = x^6 & \bmod g(x) = 1 + x^2 & \leftrightarrow & 101
\end{array}$$

$$\text{so } H = \begin{bmatrix} 100 \\ 010 \\ 001 \\ 110 \\ 011 \\ 111 \\ 101 \end{bmatrix}.$$

If $w(x) = 1 + x^5 + x^6$ is received, $w = 1000011$, then $wH = s = 110$ and $s(x) = 1 + x = 1 + x^5 + x^6 \bmod (1 + x + x^3) = w(x) \bmod g(x)$.

Exercises

4.3.8 Find a parity check matrix for the linear cyclic code of length 7 with generator $g(x) = 1 + x + x^2 + x^4$.

4.3.9 Find a parity check matrix for a cyclic code of length n and with generator $g(x)$:

(a) $n = 6$, $g(x) = 1 + x^2$

(b) $n = 6$, $g(x) = 1 + x^3$

(c) $n = 8$, $g(x) = 1 + x^2$

(d) $n = 9$, $g(x) = 1 + x^3 + x^6$

(e) $n = 15$, $g(x) = 1 + x + x^4$ (this generates a Hamming code)

(f) $n = 23$, $g(x) = 1 + x + x^5 + x^6 + x^7 + x^9 + x^{11}$ (this generates a Golay code)

(g) $n = 15$, $g(x) = 1 + x^4 + x^6 + x^7 + x^8$ (this generates a 2-error correcting BCH code, constructed in Chapter 5).

4.4 Finding cyclic codes

To construct a linear cyclic code of length n and dimension k, one must find a factor of $1 + x^n$ having degree $n - k$. Of course there maybe several choices or none for given n and k. There is also the question of minimum distance for cyclic codes which we have not considered, a question which is not settled in general. We will put this issue off until later.

To reiterate, the fact that every generator must divide $1+x^n$ enables us to find all linear cyclic codes of a given length n. All we have to do is find all factors of $1+x^n$, which means first finding all irreducible factors.

A polynomial $f(x)$ in $K[x]$ of degree at least one is *irreducible* if it is not the product of two polynomials in $K[x]$, both of which have degree at least one. Finding the irreducible factors (which essentially gives all the factors of $1+x^n$) is not all that easy. The factorization of $1+x^n$ for $n \leq 31$ into irreducible polynomials is in Appendix B, and a method to factor $1+x^n$ is discussed below (see 4.4.14).

The factor 1 of $1+x^n$ has degree 0 and hence generates a cyclic code of dimension n; this code must be K^n, which proves that K^n is cyclic. We can also, as a special case, define the code $\{0\}$ consisting of only the zero word of length n to be cyclic with "generator" $g(x) = 0 = 1+x^n \bmod 1+x^n$.

We will call these linear cyclic codes K^n and $\{0\}$, *improper cyclic codes*. Otherwise, the code is a *proper cyclic code*.

Example 4.4.1 For $n = 3$, $1+x^3 = (1+x)(1+x+x^2)$ is the factorization of $1+x^3$ into irreducible factors. Thus there are two proper cyclic codes of length 3. One has generator $g(x) = 1+x$ and generating matrix

$$G = \begin{bmatrix} 110 \\ 011 \end{bmatrix}.$$

The code is $C = \{000, 110, 011, 101\}$. The other code has generator $g(x) = 1+x+x^2$ and generating matrix $G = [111]$, so is the code $C = \{000, 111\}$.

Example 4.4.2 For $n = 6$, we factor $1+x^6$ into irreducible factors.

$$1+x^6 = (1+x^3)^2 = (1+x)^2(1+x+x^2)^2.$$

Then to find the generators of proper linear cyclic codes of length 6, we form all possible products of these factors except for 1 and $1+x^6$. Each such product is the generator for a proper cyclic linear code of length 6. These products and the dimension of the cyclic linear code of length 6 that each product generates are given in the following table.

generator	dimension
$1+x$	5
$(1+x)^2 = 1+x^2$	4
$1+x+x^2$	4
$(1+x+x^2)^2 = 1+x^2+x^4$	2
$(1+x)(1+x+x^2) = 1+x^3$	3
$(1+x)^2(1+x+x^2) = 1+x+x^3+x^4$	2
$(1+x)(1+x+x^2)^2 = 1+x+x^2+x^3+x^4+x^5$	1

Theorem 4.4.3 *If $n = 2^r s$ then $1 + x^n = (1 + x^s)^{2^r}$.*

Proof: If $n = 2s$, then $(1+x^s)^2 = 1 + x^s + x^s + x^{2s} = 1 + x^{2s}$. We then proceed by induction on r. □

Corollary 4.4.4 *Let $n = 2^r s$, where s is odd and let $1 + x^s$ be the product of z irreducible polynomials. Then there are $(2^r + 1)^z$ linear cyclic codes of length n and $(2^r + 1)^z - 2$ proper linear cyclic codes of length n.*

Example 4.4.5 In Example 4.4.1 it is shown that $1 + x^3$ is the product of two irreducible polynomials, namely $1 + x$ and $1 + x + x^2$. By applying Corollary 4.4.4 with $r = 0, s = 3$ and $z = 2$ we find that there are $(2^0 + 1)^2 = 4$ linear cyclic codes of length 3, 2 of which are proper (as shown in Example 4.4.1). Also, for $1 + x^6$, we have $n = 6 = 2^1 3$ so $r = 1, z$ is still 2 thus there are $(2 + 1)^2 = 9$ linear cyclic codes of length 6, 7 of which are proper (as was shown in Example 4.4.2).

Exercises

4.4.6 Find the number of proper linear cyclic codes of length n, where

(a) $n = 4$,
(b) $n = 5$,
(c) $n = 7$,
(d) $n = 14$,
(e) $n = 56$,
(f) $n = 15$,
(g) $n = 120$,
(h) $n = 1024$.

4.4.7 Find the generator polynomial for all proper linear cyclic codes of length n, where (a) $n = 4$ and (b) $n = 5$.

4.4.8 Find two generators of degree 4 for a linear cyclic code of length 7.

4.4.9 Find a generator and a generating matrix for a linear code of length n and dimension k where

(a) $n = 12, k = 5$
(b) $n = 12, k = 7$
(c) $n = 14, k = 5$
(d) $n = 14, k = 6$
(e) $n = 14, k = 8$.

4.4.10 Show that the Golay Code C_{23} is equivalent to a linear cyclic code.

One can find all cyclic codes or equivalently factor $1 + x^n$, by a relatively simple procedure. Throughout our discussion we will assume that n is odd.

The first step involves generating all polynomials $I(x)$ (mod $1 + x^n$) such that $I(x) = I(x)^2$ (mod $1 + x^n$). These polynomials are called *idempotent* polynomials. It is easy to see that if $u(x)$ and $v(x)$ are idempotent, so is their sum $u(x) + v(x)$ and product $u(x)v(x)$ (mod $1 + x^n$). Thus we need to construct only a "basic" set of idempotent polynomials. To do this we need to partition $Z_n = \{0, 1, \ldots, n-1\}$ into "classes."

Let $C_i = \{s = 2^j \cdot i \pmod{n} \mid j = 0, 1, \ldots, r\}$ where $1 = 2^r \bmod n$.

Example 4.4.11 For $n = 7$ we have

$$C_0 = \{0\},\ C_1 = \{1,2,4\} = C_2 = C_4,\ \text{and } C_3 = \{3,5,6\} = C_5 = C_7.$$

For $n = 9$ we have

$$C_0 = \{0\},\ C_1 = \{1,2,4,8,7,5\},\ \text{and } C_3 = \{3,6\}.$$

Next for each different class C_i we form a polynomial

$$c_i(x) = \sum_{j \in C_i} x^j.$$

We will show that $c_i(x)$ is an idempotent, and note in passing that any idempotent $I(x)$ (mod $1 + x^n$) is

$$I(x) = \sum_{i=0}^{k} a_i c_i(x),\ a_i \in \{0,1\}.$$

To see that $c_i(x)$ is an idempotent,

$$c_i(x)^2 = c_i(x^2) = \sum_{j \in C_i} x^{2j} = \sum_{k \in C_i} x^k \pmod{1 + x^n},$$

since if $j \in C_i$ then so is $2j$ (mod n).

Example 4.4.12 For $n = 7$ we have,

$$\begin{aligned} C_0 &= \{0\}, && \text{so} \quad c_0(x) = x^0 = 1, \\ C_1 &= \{1,2,4\}, && \text{so} \quad c_1(x) = x^1 + x^2 + x^4, \text{ and} \\ C_3 &= \{3,5,6\}, && \text{so} \quad c_3(x) = x^3 + x^6 + x^5. \end{aligned}$$

Then any idempotent polynomial (mod $1 + x^7$) can be expressed as

$$I(x) = a_0c_0(x) + a_1c_1(x) + a_3c_3(x),\ a_i \in \{0,1\}.$$

Thus we have $2^3 - 1$ different idempotents (mod $1 + x^7$). (We ignore $I(x) = 0$ which is trivially idempotent.)

The connection between idempotents and cyclic codes is the following:

Theorem 4.4.13 *Every cyclic code contains a unique idempotent polynomial which generates the code.*

Proof: Let $g(x)$ be the generator of a cyclic code of length n and let $g(x)h(x) = 1+x^n$ (n is odd). Then $\gcd(h(x), g(x)) = 1$ and by the Euclidean Algorithm (Appendix A) there exists polynomials $t(x), s(x)$ such that

$$1 = t(x)g(x) + s(x)h(x).$$

Multiplying both sides by $t(x)g(x)$ gives,

$$t(x)g(x) = (t(x)g(x))^2 + t(x)s(x)(1+x^n)$$

or

$$t(x)g(x) = (t(x)g(x))^2 \bmod 1+x^n.$$

Thus $t(x)g(x)$ is an idempotent and

$$g(x) = \gcd(t(x)g(x), 1+x^n).$$ □

Example 4.4.14 To find all cyclic codes of length 9, we simply find all idempotent polynomials and find the corresponding generator polynomial. Since

$$C_0 = \{0\},\ C_1 = \{1,2,4,8,7,5\},\ C_3 = \{3,6\}$$

we have

$$c_0(x) = 1,\ c_1(x) = x + x^2 + x^4 + x^5 + x^7 + x^8,\ c_3(x) = x^3 + x^6,$$

and

$$I(x) = a_0c_0(x) + a_1c_1(x) + a_3c_3(x).$$

Idempotent polynomial $I(x)$	The generator polynomial $g(x) = \gcd(I(x), 1+x^9)$
1	1
$x+x^2+x^4+x^5+x^7+x^8$	$1+x+x^3+x^4+x^6+x^7$
x^3+x^6	$1+x^3$
$1+x+x^2+x^4+x^5+x^7+x^8$	$1+x+x^2$
$1+x^3+x^6$	$1+x^3+x^6$
$x+x^2+x^3+x^4+x^5+x^6+x^7+x^8$	$1+x$
$1+x+x^2+x^3+x^5+x^6+x^7+x^8$	$1+x+x^2+x^3+x^5+x^6+x^7+x^8$

Exercises

4.4.15 Find all idempotents polynomials mod $1+x^n$, and the corresponding generator polynomials for,

(a) $n = 5$ (b) $n = 7$ (c) $n = 11$
(d) $n = 15$ (e) $n = 31$

4.5 Dual cyclic codes

Another fact about cyclic codes which is useful, is that the dual codes are also cyclic. We will in fact give a procedure for constructing the generator polynomial of the dual code.

It is a simple matter to see that the dual of a cyclic code is cyclic. This follows directly from the fact that if $a \cdot b = 0$ then $\pi(a) \cdot \pi(b) = 0$ where π is the cyclic shift, as the following argument shows. (Note that $a \cdot b = a_0 b_0 + a_1 b_1 + \cdots + a_n b_n$ and $\pi(a) \cdot \pi(b) = a_1 b_1 + a_2 b_2 + \cdots + a_n b_n + a_0 b_0 = a \cdot b = 0$.) Consider the cyclic code which is generated by the word v; so $C = \langle\{v, \pi(v), \ldots, \pi^{n-1}(v)\}\rangle$. If $u \in C^\perp$ then $\pi^i(v) \cdot u = 0$ for $i = 0, 1, \ldots, n-1$. However this means that $\pi^{i+1}(v) \cdot \pi(u) = 0$ and thus $\pi(u)$ is orthogonal to $\langle\{\pi(v), \pi^2(v), \ldots, \pi^n(v)\}\rangle = C$ because $\pi^n(v) = v$. Since $u \in C^\perp$ implies $\pi(u) \in C^\perp$ we conclude that $C^\perp$ is cyclic.

To find the generator of the dual we need to relate the product of polynomials and the dot product of vectors.

Lemma 4.5.1 *Let $a \leftrightarrow a(x)$, $b \leftrightarrow b(x)$ and $b' \leftrightarrow b'(x) = x^n b(x^{-1}) \bmod 1 + x^n$, then $a(x)b(x) \bmod 1 + x^n = 0$ if and only if $\pi^k(a) \cdot b' = 0$ for $k = 0, 1, \ldots, n-1$.*

Proof: Let $c(x) = a(x)b(x) \bmod 1 + x^n$. Then the coefficient of x^k in $c(x)$ is

$$c_k = a_k b_0 + a_{k+1} b_{n-1} + \cdots + a_{n-1} b_{k+1} + a_0 b_k + \cdots + a_{k-1} b_1$$

since $x^k \equiv x^{n+k} \pmod{1 + x^n}$. Note that if $a = (a_0, a_1, \ldots, a_{n-1})$ and $b = (b_0, b_1, \ldots, b_{n-1})$ then $b' = (b_0, b_{n-1}, b_{n-2} \ldots, b_1)$ and so $c_k = \pi^k(a) \cdot b'$. Thus $c_k = 0$ for $k = 0, 1, \ldots, n-1$ if and only if $c(x) = 0 = a(x)b(x) \bmod 1 + x^n$. □

Again let C be a cyclic linear code of length n and $g(x)$ be the generator polynomial for C. We know that $g(x)$ divides $1 + x^n$ and thus there is a unique polynomial $h(x)$, such that $1 + x^n = g(x)h(x)$. By Lemma 4.5.1 we know that $x^n h(x^{-1})$ is in $C^\perp$, but we want to find the generator for $C^\perp$.

Theorem 4.5.2 *If C is a linear cyclic code of length n and dimension k with generator $g(x)$ and if $1 + x^n = g(x)h(x)$ then $C^\perp$ is a cyclic code of dimension $n - k$ with generator $x^k h(x^{-1})$.*

Proof: Since C has dimension k, $g(x)$ has degree $n - k$ and thus $h(x)$ has degree k. Since

$$g(x)h(x) = 1 + x^n$$

we have

$$g(x^{-1})h(x^{-1}) = 1 + (x^{-1})^n$$

and

$$x^n g(x^{-1})h(x^{-1}) = x^n(1 + x^{-n})$$
$$x^{n-k} g(x^{-1}) x^k h(x^{-1}) = 1 + x^n.$$

Thus $x^k h(x^{-1})$ is a factor of $1+x^n$, having degree k and hence the generator polynomial for the linear cyclic code, $C^{\perp}$ of dimension $n-k$ containing $x^n h(x^{-1})$. □

Example 4.5.3 $g(x) = 1+x+x^3$ is the generator of a cyclic code of length 7 and dimension $k = 7-3 = 4$. Since $g(x)$ is a factor of $1+x^7$ we can find $h(x)$ where $1+x^7 = g(x)h(x)$ by long division. In this case $h(x) = 1+x+x^2+x^4$. The generator for $C^{\perp}$ is $g^{\perp}(x) = x^4 h(x^{-1}) = x^4(1+x^{-1}+x^{-2}+x^{-4}) = 1+x^2+x^3+x^4$ which corresponds to $1011100 = w$. Clearly $g \cdot w = (11010000) \cdot (1011100) = 0$ and $\pi^k(g) \cdot w = 0$ as well. Note that $g^{\perp}(x) \neq h(x)$.

Example 4.5.4 Let $g(x) = 1+x+x^2$ be the generator for a linear cyclic code of length 6. We find $h(x) = 1+x+x^3+x^4$ satisfies $g(x)h(x) = 1+x^6$. Therefore $g^{\perp}(x) = x^4 h(x^{-1}) = x^4(1+x^{-1}+x^{-3}+x^{-4}) = x^4+x^3+x+1$ is the generator for the dual code. Note in this example $g^{\perp}(x) = h(x)$.

Exercises

4.5.5 Find the generator polynomial for the dual code of the cyclic code of length n having generator polynomial $g(x)$ where:

(a) $n = 6$, $g(x) = 1+x^2$
(b) $n = 6$, $g(x) = 1+x^3$
(c) $n = 8$, $g(x) = 1+x^2$
(d) $n = 9$, $g(x) = 1+x^3+x^6$
(e) $n = 15$, $g(x) = 1+x+x^4$
(f) $n = 15$, $g(x) = 1+x^4+x^6+x^7+x^8$
(g) $n = 23$, $g(x) = 1+x+x^5+x^6+x^7+x^9+x^{11}$
(h) $n = 7$, $g(x) = 1+x+x^2+x^4$

Chapter 5

BCH Codes

5.1 Finite fields

In this chapter we consider a special class of cyclic codes and a different approach to decoding them, one which utilizes Galois fields $GF(2^r)$.

Recall that a polynomial $d(x)$ is a divisor or factor of $f(x)$ if $f(x) = g(x)d(x)$. Of course 1 and $f(x)$ are always divisors of $f(x)$ but these are trivial. Any other divisor is said to be a nontrivial or *proper* divisor of $f(x)$. A polynomial $f(x) \in K[x]$ is said to be *irreducible* over K if it has no proper divisors in $K[x]$; otherwise it is said to be *reducible* (or factorable) over K.

Example 5.1.1 Polynomials x and $1+x$ are irreducible by definition; $1+x+x^2$ has neither x nor $1+x$ as a divisor so it too is irreducible. However, $x^2, 1+x^2$, and $x+x^2$ are not irreducible: x^2 and $x+x^2$ both have x as a divisor; $1+x^2$ has $1+x$ as a divisor.

In general $1+x$ is a divisor or factor of $f(x)$ if and only if 1 is a root of $f(x)$; that is, if and only if $f(1) = 0$. Note that $1+x$ is a factor of $f(x) = 1+x^2$ and $f(1) = 1+1 = 0$. Similarly x is a factor of $g(x)$ if and only if $g(0) = 0$. However finding other irreducible factors of a polynomial is more difficult and at this point is simply a matter of trial and error.

Example 5.1.2 If $f(x) = 1+x+x^2+x^3$, then $f(1) = 1+1+1+1 = 0$, and so $1+x$ is a factor of $f(x)$. By long division $f(x) = (1+x)(1+x^2) = (1+x)^3$. On the other hand, if $g(x) = 1+x+x^3$, then $g(0) = 1 \neq 0$ and $g(1) = 1 \neq 0$, so $g(x)$ has no linear factor. Therefore $g(x)$ is irreducible over K, since if a cubic polynomial is reducible then it must have a linear factor.

Example 5.1.3 Let $f(x) = 1+x+x^4$. Since $f(0) \neq 0$ and $f(1) \neq 0$, $f(x)$ has no linear factors. So, if $f(x)$ is reducible, then $f(x)$ must have an irreducible quadratic factor. The only irreducible quadratic over K is $g(x) = 1+x+x^2$. After dividing $g(x)$ into $f(x)$, we find a non-zero remainder. So $1+x+x^2$ is not a factor of $f(x)$. Therefore $f(x)$ is irreducible over K.

Exercises

5.1.4 Determine whether each of the following polynomials is irreducible over K.

(a) $f(x)=1+x^2+x^4$
(b) $f(x)=1+x^8$
(c) $f(x)=1+x^2+x^3+x^5$
(d) $f(x)=1+x^2+x^6$
(e) $f(x)=1+x^4+x^5$
(f) $f(x)=1+x+x^3+x^7$

5.1.5 Find all irreducible polynomials of degree 3 and 4 over K.

5.1.6 Find all irreducible polynomials of degree 5 over K.

An irreducible polynomial over K of degree $n>1$ is said to be *primitive* if it is not a divisor of $1+x^m$ for any $m<2^n-1$. We will see that an irreducible polynomial of degree n always divides $1+x^m$ when $m=2^n-1$.

Example 5.1.7 Since $1+x+x^2$ is not a factor of $1+x^m$ for $m<3=2^2-1$, it is primitive. Similarly $1+x+x^3$ is not a factor of $1+x^m$ for any $m<7=2^3-1$ and thus it too is primitive.

However $1+x^5=(1+x)(1+x+x^2+x^3+x^4)$ and $1+x+x^2+x^3+x^4$ is irreducible (see Exercise 5.1.5) but $5<15=2^4-1$ and thus $1+x+x^2+x^3+x^4$ is not primitive.

Recall that we can define addition and multiplication of polynomials modulo a polynomial $h(x)$ of degree n. Let $K^n[x]$ denotes the set of all polynomials in $K[x]$ having degree less than n. Of course each word in K^n corresponds to a polynomial in $K^n[x]$ so we can in effect define addition and multiplication of words in K^n.

In this chapter we introduce the additional structure of finite fields to assist in constructing and decoding codes. We already have a definition of addition and multiplication of words in K^n, but for this to form a field we need to be careful in our choice of $h(x)$. For example, in a field it must be the case that if $ab=0$ then either $a=0$ or $b=0$.

Example 5.1.8 We try using multiplication of polynomials modulo $1+x^4$ to define multiplication of words in K^4. However,

$$\begin{aligned}(0101)(0101) &\leftrightarrow (x+x^3)(x+x^3)\\ &= x^2+x^6\\ &= (x^2+x^2) \pmod{1+x^4}\\ &= 0\\ &\leftrightarrow 0000,\end{aligned}$$

so $(0101)(0101)=0000$, but $0101\neq 0000$ in K^4. Thus K^4 cannot be a field under this definition of multiplication.

The difficulty in the last example arises because $1+x^4$ is not irreducible over K. The way to define multiplication in K^n in order to make K^n into a field is to *define multiplication in K^n modulo an irreducible polynomial of degree n*. We leave the proof that this is the field $GF(2^n)$ to a course in modern algebra.

Example 5.1.9 Define multiplication in K^4 using the irreducible polynomial $h(x) = 1+x+x^4$. To find the product $(1101)(0101)$ note that

$$(1101)(0101) \leftrightarrow (1+x+x^3)(x+x^3).$$

But $(1+x+x^3)(x+x^3) = x+x^2+x^3+x^6$ and

$$x = x+x^2+x^3+x^6 \bmod (1+x+x^4).$$

Thus $(1101)(0101) = 0100 \leftrightarrow x$.

Exercises

5.1.10 Define multiplication in K^4 modulo $h(x) = 1+x+x^4$. Calculate the following products.

(a) $(0011)(1011)$
(b) $(1110)(1001)$
(c) $(1010)(0110)$
(d) $(0100)(0010)$
(e) $(1100)(0111)$
(f) $(1111)(0001)$

5.1.11 Find all products of elements in K^2 using $1+x+x^2$ to define multiplication (that is, make a multiplication table).

Example 5.1.12 Let us consider the construction of $GF(2^3)$ using the primitive polynomial $h(x) = 1+x+x^3$ to define multiplication. We do this by computing x^i mod $h(x)$:

word	$\leftrightarrow$	x^i mod $h(x)$
100		1
010		x
001		x^2
110		$x^3 \equiv 1+x$
011		$x^4 \equiv x+x^2$
111		$x^5 \equiv 1+x+x^2$
101		$x^6 \equiv 1+x^2$

To compute $(110)(001) \leftrightarrow (1+x)x^2$ note that from the above table $1+x = x^3$ mod $h(x)$ so

$$\begin{aligned}(x^2)(1+x) &\equiv x^2 \cdot x^3 \\ &\equiv x^5 \\ &\equiv 1+x+x^2 \quad (\text{mod } h(x))\end{aligned}$$

thus $(110)(001) = 111$.

Using a primitive polynomial to construct $GF(2^r)$ makes computing in the field much easier than using a non-primitive irreducible polynomial. To see this, let $\beta \in K^n$ represent the word corresponding to $x \bmod h(x)$, where $h(x)$ is a primitive polynomial of degree n. Then $\beta^i \leftrightarrow x^i \bmod h(x)$. Note that $1 = x^m \bmod h(x)$ means that $0 = 1 + x^m \bmod h(x)$ and thus that $h(x)$ divides $1 + x^m$. Since $h(x)$ is primitive we know that $h(x)$ does not divide $1 + x^m$ for $m < 2^n - 1$ and thus $\beta^m \neq 1$ for $m < 2^n - 1$. Since $\beta^j = \beta^i$ for $j \neq i$ if and only if $\beta^i = \beta^{j-i}\beta^i$ which implies $\beta^{j-i} = 1$, we conclude that

$$K^n \backslash \{0\} = \{\beta^i \mid i = 0, 1, \ldots, 2^n - 2\}.$$

That is, every non-zero word in K^n can be represented by some power of β. This is the property that makes multiplication in the field easy.

word	polynomial in x (modulo $h(x)$)	power of β
0000	0	—
1000	1	$\beta^0 = 1$
0100	x	β
0010	x^2	β^2
0001	x^3	β^3
1100	$1 + x \equiv x^4$	β^4
0110	$x + x^2 \equiv x^5$	β^5
0011	$x^2 + x^3 \equiv x^6$	β^6
1101	$1 + x + x^3 \equiv x^7$	β^7
1010	$1 + x^2 \equiv x^8$	β^8
0101	$x + x^3 \equiv x^9$	β^9
1110	$1 + x + x^2 \equiv x^{10}$	β^{10}
0111	$x + x^2 + x^3 \equiv x^{11}$	β^{11}
1111	$1 + x + x^2 + x^3 \equiv x^{12}$	β^{12}
1011	$1 + x^2 + x^3 \equiv x^{13}$	β^{13}
1001	$1 + x^3 \equiv x^{14}$	β^{14}

Table 5.1: *Construction of* $GF(2^4)$ *using* $h(x) = 1 + x + x^4$.

An element $\alpha \in GF(2^r)$ is *primitive* if $\alpha^m \neq 1$ for $1 \leq m < 2^r - 1$. Equivalently, α is *primitive* if every non-zero word in $GF(2^r)$ can be expressed as a power of α. From the above discussion we see that if a primitive polynomial is used to construct $GF(2^r)$, with β being the word defined above, then β is a primitive element.

Example 5.1.13 Construct $GF(2^4)$ using the primitive polynomial $h(x) = 1 + x + x^4$. Write every vector as a power of $\beta \leftrightarrow x \bmod h(x)$ (see Table 5.1). Note that $\beta^{15} = 1$.

To compute $(0110)(1101) = \beta^5 \cdot \beta^7 = \beta^{12} = 1111$ since $(x + x^2)(1 + x + x^3) \equiv x^5 \cdot x^7 \equiv x^{12} \pmod{h(x)}$.

Exercises

5.1.14 Use $GF(2^4)$ constructed in Table 5.1 to compute the products in K^4 in Exercise 5.1.10.

5.1.15 Construct the following fields as in Example 5.1.13 (Table 5.1).

(a) Construct $GF(2^2)$.

(b) Construct $GF(2^3)$ using $h(x) = 1 + x^2 + x^3$.

(c) Construct $GF(2^4)$ using $h(x) = 1 + x^3 + x^4$.

(d) Construct $GF(2^5)$ using $h(x) = 1 + x^2 + x^5$.

5.1.16 Show that if $h(x) \in K[x]$ is an irreducible polynomial of degree n, then $h(x)$ divides $1 + x^m$ for some $m \leq 2^n - 1$.

5.1.17 Find all primitive elements in $GF(2^4)$ (see Table 5.1).

5.1.18 Show that $\beta^i \in GF(2^r)$ is primitive iff $\gcd(i, 2^r - 1) = 1$.

5.2 Minimal polynomials

Recall that α, an element in a field $F = GF(2^r)$ is said to be a root of a polynomial $p(x) \in F[x]$ if and only if $p(\alpha) = 0$. That is, if $p(x) = a_0 + a_1x + \cdots + a_kx^k$ then

$$p(\alpha) = a_0 + a_1\alpha + \cdots + a_k\alpha^k = 0.$$

Example 5.2.1 Let $p(x) = 1 + x^3 + x^4$, and let β be the primitive element in $GF(2^4)$ constructed using $h(x) = 1 + x + x^4$ (see Table 5.1).

$$\begin{aligned} p(\beta) = 1 + \beta^3 + \beta^4 &= 1000 + 0001 + 1100 \\ &= 0101 \\ &= \beta^9. \end{aligned}$$

So β is not a root of $p(x)$. However

$$\begin{aligned} p(\beta^7) &= 1 + (\beta^7)^3 + (\beta^7)^4 \\ &= 1 + \beta^{21} + \beta^{28} \\ &= 1 + \beta^6 + \beta^{13} \text{ (since } \beta^{15} = 1) \\ &= 1000 + 0011 + 1011 = 0000 \\ &= 0. \end{aligned}$$

Since $p(\beta^7) = 0, \beta^7$ is a root of $p(x)$. Note that we used the convention that $1 \leftrightarrow 1000$ and $0 \leftrightarrow 0000$ as well as the fact that $\beta^{15} = 1$. Thus $\beta^{21} = \beta^{15}\beta^6 = 1 \cdot \beta^6 = \beta^6$ and $\beta^{28} = \beta^{15}\beta^{13} = 1 \cdot \beta^{13} = \beta^{13}$.

In general the *order* of non-zero element α in $GF(2^r)$ is the smallest positive integer m such that $\alpha^m = 1$. We know that for any non-zero α in $GF(2^r), \alpha$ has order $m \leq 2^r - 1$. In particular, α in $GF(2^r)$ is a primitive element if it has order $2^r - 1$.

For any element α in $GF(2^r)$, we define the *minimal polynomial* of α as the polynomial in $K[x]$ of smallest degree having α as a root. Let $m_\alpha(x)$ denote the minimal polynomial of α. Note that if α has order m (that is, $\alpha^m = 1$) then α is a root of $1 + x^m$, so every element in $GF(2^r)$ is a root of some polynomial in $K[x]$.

To find the minimal polynomial of an element of $GF(2^r)$, it will help to have some facts concerning minimal polynomials.

Theorem 5.2.2 *Let $\alpha \neq 0$ be an element of $GF(2^r)$. Let $m_\alpha(x)$ be the minimal polynomial of α. Then*

(a) $m_\alpha(x)$ is irreducible over K,

(b) if $f(x)$ is any polynomial over K such that $f(\alpha) = 0$, then $m_\alpha(x)$ is a factor of $f(x)$,

(c) the minimal polynomial is unique, and

(d) the minimal polynomial $m_\alpha(x)$ is a factor of $1 + x^{2^r - 1}$.

Proof: (a) If $m_\alpha(x) = g(x)h(x)$, then $m_\alpha(\alpha) = 0$ implies $g(\alpha)h(\alpha) = 0$. Thus either $g(\alpha) = 0$ or $h(\alpha) = 0$. Since $m_\alpha(x)$ is the polynomial of smallest degree such that $m_\alpha(x) = 0$, then either $g(x) = 1$ or $h(x) = 1$. Therefore $m_\alpha(x)$ is irreducible over K.

(b) By the Division Algorithm,

$$f(x) = m_\alpha(x)g(x) + r(x),$$

where $r(x) = 0$ or $\deg r(x) < \deg m_\alpha(x)$. Now $f(\alpha) = 0$, so since

$$f(\alpha) = m_\alpha(\alpha)g(\alpha) + r(\alpha) = 0 \cdot g(\alpha) + r(\alpha) = r(\alpha)$$

we have that $r(\alpha) = 0$. By the minimality of the degree of $m_\alpha(x), r(x) = 0$. Therefore $f(x) = m_\alpha(x)q(x)$, and $m_\alpha(x)$ is a factor of $f(x)$.

(c) If $m'(x)$ is also a polynomial of smallest degree such that $m'(\alpha) = 0$, then, by part (b), $m_\alpha(x)$ is a factor of $m'(x)$ and $m'(x)$ is a factor of $m_\alpha(x)$. Therefore $m_\alpha(x) = m'(x)$, so the minimal polynomial is unique.

(d) Let β be a primitive element in $GF(2^r)$ and $\alpha = \beta^i$. Then $\alpha^{2^r - 1} = (\beta^i)^{2^r - 1} = (\beta^{2^r - 1})^i = 1^i = 1$. Thus α is a root of $1 + x^{2^r - 1}$ and by (b) $m_\alpha(x)$ is a factor of $1 + x^{2^r - 1}$. □

Finding the minimal polynomial of $\alpha, \alpha \in GF(2^r)$, reduces to finding a linear combination of the vectors $\{1, \alpha, \alpha^2, \ldots, \alpha^r\}$ which sums to 0. Since any set of $r + 1$ vectors in K^r is dependent we know such a combination does exist.

Once we have constructed $GF(2^r)$ using a primitive polynomial, it is naturally convenient to represent $m_\alpha(x)$ by $m_i(x)$ where $\alpha = \beta^i$. We introduce this notation in the following example.

Example 5.2.3 Find the minimal polynomial of $\alpha = \beta^3$, $\alpha \in GF(2^4)$ constructed using $h(x) = 1+x+x^4$ (see Table 5.1). Let $m_\alpha(x) = m_3(x) = a_0 + a_1x + a_2x^2 + a_3x^3 + a_4x^4$ then we must find the values for $a_0, a_1, \dots, a_4 \in \{0,1\}$. Note,

$$\begin{aligned} m_\alpha(\alpha) = 0 &= a_0 1 + a_1\alpha + a_2\alpha^2 + a_3\alpha^3 + a_4\alpha^4 \\ &= a_0\beta^0 + a_1\beta^3 + a_2\beta^6 + a_3\beta^9 + a_4\beta^{12} \\ \text{so } 0000 &= a_0(1000) + a_1(0001) + a_2(0011) + a_3(0101) + a_4(1111) \end{aligned}$$

Solving for a_0, a_1, a_2, a_3, a_4 we find that

$$a_0 = a_1 = a_2 = a_3 = a_4 = 1 \text{ and}$$
$$m_\alpha(x) = 1 + x + x^2 + x^3 + x^4.$$

The roots of $m_\alpha(x)$ are $\{\alpha, \alpha^2, \alpha^4, \alpha^8\} = \{\beta^3, \beta^6, \beta^{12}, \beta^9\}$, and thus $m_3(x) = m_6(x) = m_9(x) = m_{12}(x)$ (where $m_i(x)$ denotes the minimal polynomial of β^i).

If the minimal polynomials for all elements in $GF(2^r)$ are being sought then we have other useful facts. Recall that $f(x)^2 = f(x^2)$, so

$$\left(\sum_{i=0}^{n} a_i x^i\right)^2 = \sum_{i=0}^{n} a_i^2 (x^i)^2 = \sum_{i=0}^{n} a_i (x^2)^i.$$

This follows from the fact that $(a+b)^2 = a^2 + b^2$ and the fact that $a_i^2 = a_i$ since $a_i \in \{0,1\}$.

Thus if $f(\alpha) = 0$ then $f(\alpha^2) = (f(\alpha))^2 = 0$ and so α^2 is also a root of $f(x)$. Similarly $f(\alpha^4) = (f(\alpha^2))^2 = 0$, etc. and so we have that if α is a root of $f(x)$ so are $\alpha, \alpha^2, \alpha^4, \dots, \alpha^{2^i}, \dots$, etc. With some more effort one can prove:

Theorem 5.2.4 *Let α be an element in $GF(2^r)$ with minimal polynomial $m_\alpha(x)$, then $\{\alpha, \alpha^2, \alpha^4, \dots, \alpha^{2^{r-1}}\}$ is the set of all the roots of $m_\alpha(x)$. In particular, the degree of $m_\alpha(x)$ is $|\{\alpha, \alpha^2, \dots, \alpha^{2^r-1}\}|$.*

Example 5.2.5 Let $m_5(x)$ be the minimal polynomial of $\alpha = \beta^5$, $\beta^5 \in GF(2^4)$ (see Table 5.1). Since $\{\alpha, \alpha^2, \alpha^4, \alpha^8\} = \{\beta^5, \beta^{10}\}$ by Theorem 5.2.3 the roots of $m_5(x)$ are β^5 and β^{10} which means that degree $(m_5(x)) = 2$ (from Theorem 5.2.4). Thus $m_5(x) = a_0 + a_1x + a_2x^2$, hence

$$\begin{aligned} 0 &= a_0 + a_1\beta^5 + a_2\beta^{10} \\ &= a_0(1000) + a_1(0110) + a_2(1110). \end{aligned}$$

Thus $a_0 = a_1 = a_2 = 1$ and $m_5(x) = 1 + x + x^2$.

Similarly we can find the minimal polynomials of the rest of the field elements in $GF(2^4)$ constructed using $1+x+x^4$. The results are summarized in Table 5.2.

element of $GF(2^4)$	minimal polynomial
0	x
1	$1+x$
$\beta, \beta^2, \beta^4, \beta^8$	$1+x+x^4$
$\beta^3, \beta^6, \beta^9, \beta^{12}$	$1+x+x^2+x^3+x^4$
β^5, β^{10}	$1+x+x^2$
$\beta^7, \beta^{11}, \beta^{13}, \beta^{14}$	$1+x^3+x^4$

Table 5.2: *Minimal polynomials in $GF(2^4)$.*

Exercises

5.2.6 Verify the entries in Table 5.2, for $GF(2^4)$.

5.2.7 Find the minimal polynomial of each element of $GF(2^3)$ constructed using $p(x) = 1+x+x^3$ (see Exercise 5.1.15).

5.2.8 Find the minimal polynomial of each element of $GF(2^4)$ constructed using $p(x) = 1+x^3+x^4$ (see Exercise 5.1.15).

5.2.9 Find the minimal polynomial of each element of $GF(2^5)$ constructed using $p(x) = 1+x^2+x^5$ (see Exercise 5.1.15).

5.2.10 Show that $1+x+x^2 = (\beta^5+x)(\beta^{10}+x)$ (use Table 5.1).

5.2.11 Show that $m_\alpha(x)$ is a primitive polynomial if and only if α is a primitive element.

5.3 Cyclic Hamming codes

We already know that Hamming codes have the important advantages of being perfect single-error-correcting codes and of admitting a very simple decoding scheme. In this section we show that there is a cyclic Hamming code of length $n = 2^r - 1$, for each $r \geq 2$. This code has the added advantage common to all cyclic codes of easy encoding.

The parity check matrix of a Hamming code of length $n = 2^r - 1$ has as its rows all $2^r - 1$ nonzero words of length r. If β is a primitive element of $GF(2^r)$, then by definition the powers of β are all distinct. Therefore we can construct a Hamming code of length $n = 2^r - 1$ which has

$$H = \begin{bmatrix} 1 \\ \beta \\ \beta^2 \\ \vdots \\ \beta^{2^r-2} \end{bmatrix}$$

as its parity check matrix. Note H is a $(2^r - 1) \times r$ matrix. Next, notice that for any received word $w = w_0 w_1 \ldots w_{n-1}$, $wH = w_0\beta^0 + w_1\beta + \cdots + w_{n-1}\beta^{n-1} \leftrightarrow w(\beta)$, so w is a codeword if and only if β is a root of $w(x)$. Therefore, by Theorem 5.2.2 (b), $m_\beta(x)$ divides every codeword and clearly is a codeword itself, so this code is cyclic and $m_\beta(x)$ is its generator polynomial. So we have the following result.

Theorem 5.3.1 *A primitive polynomial of degree r is the generator polynomial of a cyclic Hamming code of length $2^r - 1$.*

Example 5.3.2 Let $r = 3$, so $n = 2^3 - 1 = 7$. Use $p(x) = 1 + x + x^3$ to construct $GF(2^3)$, and $\beta \leftrightarrow 010$ as the primitive element. Recall that $\beta^i \leftrightarrow x^i \bmod p(x)$. Therefore a parity check matrix for a Hamming code of length 7 is

$$\begin{bmatrix} 1 \\ \beta \\ \beta^2 \\ \beta^3 \\ \beta^4 \\ \beta^5 \\ \beta^6 \end{bmatrix} \leftrightarrow \begin{bmatrix} 100 \\ 010 \\ 001 \\ 110 \\ 011 \\ 111 \\ 101 \end{bmatrix} = H$$

which is the same as the parity check matrix of the cyclic code with a generator polynomial $p(x) = m_\beta(x)$.

Decoding the cyclic Hamming code is easy. If the generator is the primitive polynomial $m_\alpha(x)$, and $w(x)$ is received, then $w(x) = c(x) + e(x)$, where $c(x)$ is a codeword, and $w(\alpha) = e(\alpha)$. But since e has weight 1, we know that $e(\alpha) = \alpha^j$ (where j is the position of the 1 in e, labeling the positions of e with $0, 1, \ldots, n-1$). Therefore, the most likely error polynomial is $e(x) = x^j$ and so $c(x) = w(x) + x^j$.

Example 5.3.3 Suppose $GF(2^3)$ was constructed using $1 + x + x^3$. Then $m_1(x) = 1 + x + x^3$ is the generator for a cyclic Hamming code of length 7. Suppose $w(x) = 1 + x + x^3 + x^6$ is received. Then

$$\begin{aligned} w(\beta) &= 1 + \beta^2 + \beta^3 + \beta^6 \\ &= 100 + 001 + 110 + 101 \\ &= 110 \\ &= \beta^3. \end{aligned}$$

Thus $e(x) = x^3$ and $c(x) = w(x) + x^3 = 1 + x^2 + x^6$.

Exercises

5.3.4 Find a parity check matrix for a cyclic Hamming code of length 7 using $GF(2^3)$ constructed with $1+x+x^3$, where the generator polynomial is $m_3(x)$. If $w(x)=x+x^2+x^4$ is received find the most likely codeword $c(x)$.

5.3.5 Repeat Exercise 5.3.4 using $GF(2^3)$ constructed with $p(x)=1+x^2+x^3$ and generator polynomial $m_1(x)$.

5.3.6 Repeat Exercise 5.3.4 using $GF(2^3)$ constructed with $p(x)=1+x^2+x^3$ and where the generator polynomial is $m_3(x)$.

5.3.7 Construct a parity check matrix for a cyclic Hamming code of length 15.

5.3.8 Find the generator polynomial for a cyclic code of length 15 having roots $1, \beta^7, \beta^5 \in GF(2^4)$ (constructed using $1+x+x^4$). Construct a parity check matrix for this code. Show that $c(x) \in C$ iff $wt(c)$ is even.

5.3.9 Show that every codeword of a cyclic code has even weight iff $1+x$ is a factor of the generator polynomial.

It is probably worth stating here that more general results follow from the observations discussed in this section. Let C be a cyclic code of length n with generator polynomial $g(x)$. Suppose $\alpha \in GF(2^r)$ is a root of $g(x)$. Then for all $c(x) \in C, c(\alpha)=0$ and so by Theorem 5.2.2(b) $m_\alpha(x)$ is a divisor of $c(x)$. We can always write $g(x)$ as a product of minimal polynomials of elements in $GF(2^r)$. We can use this to construct a parity check matrix and to find a decoding algorithm for C. The case where $g(x)=m_\beta(x)m_{\beta^3}(x)$ is discussed in Section 5.4.

5.4 BCH codes

An important class of multiple-error-correcting codes is the class of *Bose-Chaudhuri-Hocquengham codes*, or *BCH codes*. The construction and decoding procedure for general BCH codes will be developed later. First we shall construct and decode an important example of the class, namely the family of two-error-correcting BCH codes.

BCH codes are important for two reasons. First, they admit a relatively easy decoding scheme and secondly the class of BCH codes is quite extensive. Indeed, for any positive integers r and t with $t \leq 2^{r-1}-1$, there is a BCH code of length $n=2^r-1$ which is t-error correcting and has dimension $k \geq n-rt$.

The 2 error-correcting BCH code of length 2^r-1 is the cyclic linear code that is generated by $g(x)=m_\beta(x)m_{\beta^3}(x)$, where β is a primitive element in $GF(2^r)$ and $r \geq 4$. Since $n=2^r-1$ and $g(x)$ divides $1+x^n$ (by Theorem 5.2.2(c)) $g(x)$ is the generator polynomial for a cyclic code.

Example 5.4.1 β is a primitive element in $GF(2^4)$ constructed with $p(x)=1+x+x^4$ (see Table 5.1). We have that $m_1(x)=1+x+x^4$ and $m_3(x)=1+x+$

$x^2+x^3+x^4$. Therefore

$$g(x) = m_1(x)m_3(x) = 1+x^4+x^6+x^7+x^8$$

is the generator for a 2 error-correcting BCH code of length 15.

Exercises

5.4.2 2 error-correcting BCH codes are defined for $r \geq 4$. What code does $g(x) = m_1(x)m_3(x)$ generate when $r = 3$?

5.4.3 β is a primitive element of $GF(2^4)$ constructed using the irreducible polynomial $p(x) = 1+x^3+x^4$. Find the generator polynomial $g(x)$ the 2-error-correcting BCH code of length 15 using this representation of $GF(2^4)$; that is, find $g(x) = m_1(x)m_3(x)$. (See Exercise 5.1.15)

5.4.4 Find a generator polynomial for a 2 error-correcting BCH code of length 31 constructing $GF(2^5)$ with the irreducible polynomial $1+x^2+x^5$ (see Exercise 5.1.15).

Lemma 5.4.5 *The following matrix H is a parity-check matrix for the 2 error-correcting BCH code of length $2^r - 1$, where β is a primitive element in $GF(2^r)$, and the generator polynomial is $g(x) = m_1(x)m_3(x)$*

$$H = \begin{bmatrix} \beta^0 & \beta^0 \\ \beta & \beta^3 \\ \beta^2 & \beta^6 \\ \vdots & \vdots \\ \beta^i & \beta^{3i} \\ \vdots & \vdots \\ \beta^{2^r-2} & \beta^{3(2^r-2)} \end{bmatrix}$$

Since β^i is an element of $GF(2^r)$, it represents a word of length r, so H is a $(2^r - 1) \times (2r)$ matrix. Also, since $\deg(m_1(x)) = r = \deg(m_3(x))$, the degree of $g(x) = m_1(x)m_3(x)$ is $2r$ and thus the code has dimension $n - 2r = 2^r - 1 - 2r$. (We leave the proof that $m_3(x)$ has degree r to Exercises 5.4.9).

For example, we use $GF(2^4)$ constructed in Table 5.1 with the primitive polynomial $p(x) = 1+x+x^4$ to construct a 2 error-correcting BCH code C_{15}. We define C_{15} to be the linear code with the 15×8 parity check matrix H, and generator polynomial $m_1(x)m_3(x)$ (see Table 5.3).

Theorem 5.4.6 *For any integer $r \geq 4$ there is a 2 error-correcting BCH code of length $n = 2^r - 1$, dimension $k = 2^r - 2r - 1$ and distance $d = 5$ having generator polynomial $m_1(x)m_3(x)$.*

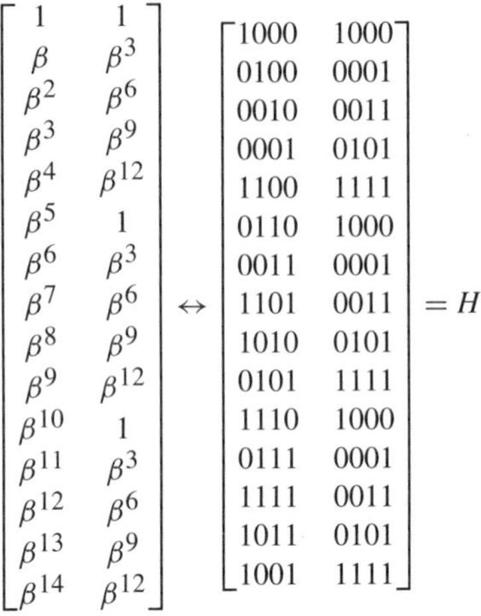

$$\begin{bmatrix} 1 & 1 \\ \beta & \beta^3 \\ \beta^2 & \beta^6 \\ \beta^3 & \beta^9 \\ \beta^4 & \beta^{12} \\ \beta^5 & 1 \\ \beta^6 & \beta^3 \\ \beta^7 & \beta^6 \\ \beta^8 & \beta^9 \\ \beta^9 & \beta^{12} \\ \beta^{10} & 1 \\ \beta^{11} & \beta^3 \\ \beta^{12} & \beta^6 \\ \beta^{13} & \beta^9 \\ \beta^{14} & \beta^{12} \end{bmatrix} \leftrightarrow \begin{bmatrix} 1000 & 1000 \\ 0100 & 0001 \\ 0010 & 0011 \\ 0001 & 0101 \\ 1100 & 1111 \\ 0110 & 1000 \\ 0011 & 0001 \\ 1101 & 0011 \\ 1010 & 0101 \\ 0101 & 1111 \\ 1110 & 1000 \\ 0111 & 0001 \\ 1111 & 0011 \\ 1011 & 0101 \\ 1001 & 1111 \end{bmatrix} = H$$

Table 5.3: *The parity check matrix of C_{15}.*

For the proof that the distance is 5, we will show that it can correct 2 errors and thus has distance at least 5. From the definition of the parity check matrix it is clear that $n = 2^r - 1$, and since $m_1(x)$ and $m_3(x)$ each have degree r, degree $(g(x)) = n - k = 2r$ and so $k = 2^r - 2r - 1$.

Exercises

5.4.7 Show that the columns of the parity check matrix of C_{15} in Table 5.3 are linearly independent and hence that C_{15} has dimension $k = 7$.

5.4.8 Show that $d = 5$ for C_{15} by using the parity check matrix.

5.4.9 Show that if β is a primitive element of $GF(2^r)$, $r > 2$ then $|\{\beta^{2^i} \mid 0 \le i \le r-1\}| = r$ and $|\{(\beta^3)^{2^i} \mid 0 \le i \le r-1\}| = r$. Therefore $m_1(x)$ and $m_3(x)$ both have degree r.

5.4.10 Determine whether each of the following words of length 15 is a codeword in C_{15}, where $g(x) = 1 + x^4 + x^6 + x^7 + x^8$.

(a) 011001011000010 (b) 000111010000110

(c) 011100000010001 (d) 111111111111111

5.5 Decoding 2 error-correcting BCH code

We describe a decoding scheme for the 2 error-correcting BCH codes constructed in the last section. Throughout this section, we shall identify a binary word of length r with the corresponding power of β.

A parity check matrix for the $(2^r-1, 2^r-2r-1, 5)$ 2 error-correcting BCH code with generator $g(x) = m_1(x)m_3(x)$ is H as defined in Lemma 5.4.5.

Assume the word w is received, and $w \leftrightarrow w(x)$. Then the syndrome of w is

$$wH = [w(\beta), w(\beta^3)] = [s_1, s_3]$$

where s_1 and s_3 each are words of length r.

If no errors occurred in transmission, then the syndrome is $wH = 0$, so $s_1 = s_3 = 0$. If just one error occurred in transmission, then, the error polynomial is $e(x) = x^i$ thus $wH = eH = [e(\beta), e(\beta^3)] = [\beta^i, \beta^{3i}] = [s_1, s_3]$. Therefore $s_1^3 = s_3$.

If two errors occurred in transmission, say in positions i and j, $i \neq j$, then $e(x) = x^i + x^j$ and $wH = eH = [e(\beta), e(\beta^3)] = [s_1, s_3]$. Thus the syndrome wH is given by

$$wH = [s_1, s_3] = [\beta^i + \beta^j, \beta^{3i} + \beta^{3j}].$$

We consider the resulting system of equations

$$\begin{aligned} \beta^i + \beta^j &= s_1 \\ \beta^{3i} + \beta^{3j} &= s_3. \end{aligned}$$

Now we have the factorization

$$(\beta^i + \beta^j)(\beta^{2i} + \beta^{i+j} + \beta^{2j}) = \beta^{3i} + \beta^{3j},$$

and

$$s_1^2 = (\beta^i + \beta^j)^2 = \beta^{2i} + \beta^{2j}.$$

Therefore

$$\begin{aligned} s_3 &= \beta^{3i} + \beta^{3j} \\ &= (\beta^i + \beta^j)(\beta^{2i} + \beta^{2j} + \beta^{i+j}) \\ &= s_1(s_1^2 + \beta^{i+j}). \end{aligned}$$

Thus

$$\frac{s_3}{s_1} + s_1^2 = \beta^{i+j}.$$

Now β^i and β^j are roots of the quadratic equation

$$x^2 + (\beta^i + \beta^j)x + \beta^{i+j} = 0$$

and hence roots of

$$x^2 + s_1 x + (\frac{s_3}{s_1} + s_1^2) = 0.$$

Therefore we can find the positions of the errors by finding the solutions of this equation. The polynomial on the left side of this equation is called the *error locator polynomial*.

Example 5.5.1 Let $w \leftrightarrow w(x)$ be a received word with syndromes $s_1 = 0111 = w(\beta)$ and $s_3 = 1010 = w(\beta^3)$, where w was encoded using C_{15}. From Table 5.1 we have that $s_1 \leftrightarrow \beta^{11}$ and $s_3 \leftrightarrow \beta^8$. Then

$$\begin{aligned}\frac{s_3}{s_1} + s_1^2 &= \beta^8\beta^{-11} + \beta^{22}\\ &= \beta^{12} + \beta^7\\ &= \beta^2.\end{aligned}$$

We form the polynomial $x^2 + \beta^{11}x + \beta^2$ and find that it has roots β^4 and β^{13}. Therefore we can decide that the most likely errors occurred in positions 4 and 13 (that is, $e(x) = x^4 + x^{13}$), so the most likely error pattern is

$$000010000000010.$$

Exercises

5.5.2 Verify by substitution that β^4 and β^{13} are indeed solutions of the quadratic equation $x^2 + \beta^{11}x + \beta^2 = 0$. Also check that the sum of the 4th and 13th rows of H in Table 5.3 is $[s_1, s_3]$.

5.5.3 Find the roots in $GF(2^4)$ of the following polynomials, if possible (use Table 5.1).

(a) $x^2 + \beta^4x + \beta^{13}$ (b) $x^2 + \beta^7x + \beta^2$

(c) $x^2 + \beta^2x + \beta^5$ (d) $x^2 + \beta^6$

(e) $x^2 + \beta^2x$ (f) $x^2 + x + \beta^8$.

We have arrived at a scheme for incomplete maximum likelihood decoding for the 2 error-correcting BCH codes. Let w be a received word. Clearly once an error pattern is determined then the algorithm is terminated.

Algorithm 5.5.4 (decoding 2 error-correcting BCH codes) Suppose the generator polynomial is $m_1(x)m_3(x)$.

1. Calculate the syndrome $wH = [s_1, s_3] = [w(\beta), w(\beta^3)]$.
2. If $s_1 = s_3 = 0$, conclude that no errors occurred. Decode $c = w$ as the codeword sent.
3. If $s_1 = 0$ and $s_3 \neq 0$ then ask for retransmission.
4. If $s_1^3 = s_3$ then correct a single error at position i, where $s_1 = \beta^i$.
5. Form the quadratic equation

$$x^2 + s_1x + \frac{s_3}{s_1} + s_1^2 = 0. \qquad (*)$$

6. If equation $(*)$ has two *distinct* roots β^i and β^j, correct errors at positions i and j.

7. If equation (∗) does not have two distinct roots in $GF(2^r)$, conclude that at least three errors occurred in transmission, and ask for a retransmission.

All examples and exercises that follow use C_{15} whose parity check matrix is listed in Table 5.3 and generator polynomial $g(x)$ listed in example 5.4.1.

Example 5.5.5 Assume w is received and the syndrome is $wH = 01111010 \leftrightarrow [\beta^{11}, \beta^8]$. Now

$$s_1^3 = (\beta^{11})^3 = \beta^{33} = \beta^3 \neq \beta^8 = s_3.$$

In this case equation (∗) is $x^2 + \beta^{11}x + \beta^2 = 0$, as is shown in Example 5.5.1. This equation has roots β^4 and β^{13}. So we correct errors in positions $i = 4$ and $j = 13$; in other words, the most likely error pattern is $u = 000010000000010$, and $e(x) = x^4 + x^{13}$ is the presumed error polynomial.

Example 5.5.6 Assume the syndrome is $wH = [w(\beta), w(\beta^3)] = [\beta^3, \beta^9]$. Then $s_1^3 = (\beta^3)^3 = \beta^9 = s_3$. Therefore it is most likely that a single error occurred at position $i = 3$. The most likely error pattern is $u = 000100000000000$, and $e(x) = x^3$ is the error polynomial.

Example 5.5.7 Assume $w = 110111101011000$ is received. The syndrome is

$$wH = 01110110 \leftrightarrow [\beta^{11}, \beta^5] = [s_1, s_3].$$

Now $s_1^3 = (\beta^{11})^3 = \beta^{33} = \beta^3 \neq s_3 = \beta^5$. To form the quadratic equation (∗), we first calculate

$$\begin{aligned} \frac{s_3}{s_1} + s_1^2 &= \beta^5\beta^{-11} + (\beta^{11})^2 \\ &= \beta^9 + \beta^7 \\ &\leftrightarrow 0101 + 1101 \\ &= 1000 \\ &\leftrightarrow \beta^0. \end{aligned}$$

So in this case, (∗) becomes

$$x^2 + \beta^{11}x + \beta^0 = 0.$$

Trying the elements of $GF(2^4)$ in turn as possible roots, we come to $x = \beta^7$ and find

$$\begin{aligned} (\beta^7)^2 + \beta^{11}\beta^7 + \beta^0 &= \beta^{14} + \beta^3 + \beta^0 \\ &\leftrightarrow 1001 + 0001 + 1000 \\ &= 0000. \end{aligned}$$

Now $\beta^7\beta^j = 1 = \beta^{15}$, so $\beta^j = \beta^8$ is the other root. Therefore we correct errors at positions $i = 7$ and $j = 8$; that is $u = 000000011000000$ is the most likely error pattern. We decode $v = w + u = 110111110011000$ as the word sent.

Example 5.5.8 Assume a codeword in C_{15} is sent, and errors occur in positions 2, 6, and 12. Then the syndrome wH is the sum of rows 2, 6, and 12 of H, where w is the word received. Thus

$$\begin{aligned} wH &= 00100011 + 00110001 + 11110011 \\ &= 11100001 \leftrightarrow [\beta^{10}, \beta^3] = [s_1, s_3]. \end{aligned}$$

Now $s_1^3 = (\beta^{10})^3 = \beta^{30} = 1 \neq \beta^3 = s^3$. We calculate

$$\begin{aligned} \frac{s_3}{s_1} + s_1^2 &= \beta^3\beta^{-10} + \beta^{20} = \beta^8 + \beta^5 \\ &\leftrightarrow 1010 + 0110 = 1100 \leftrightarrow \beta^4 \end{aligned}$$

and then form the quadratic equation

$$x^2 + \beta^{10}x + \beta^4 = 0.$$

By trying each of the elements of $GF(2^4)$, we see that this equation has no roots in $GF(2^4)$. Therefore IMLD for C_{15} concludes correctly, that at least three errors occurred, and we request a retransmission.

Exercises

5.5.9 Messages are encoded using C_{15}. Determine, if possible the locations of the errors if w is received and the syndrome wH is a given in each part.

(a) 0100 0101
(b) 1110 1000
(c) 1100 1101
(d) 0100 0000
(e) 0000 0100
(f) 1010 0100
(g) 0011 1101
(h) 0000 0000

5.5.10 The code is C_{15}. Decode, if possible, each of the following received words w.

(a) 11000 00000 00000
(b) 00001 00001 00001
(c) 01000 10101 00000
(d) 11001 11001 11000
(e) 11001 11001 00000
(f) 11100 00000 00001
(g) 10111 00000 00000
(h) 10101 00101 10001
(i) 01000 01000 0000
(j) 01010 10010 11000
(k) 11011 10111 01100
(l) 10111 00000 01000
(m) 11100 10110 00000
(n) 00011 10100 00110

Chapter 6

Reed-Solomon Codes

6.1 Codes over $GF(2^r)$

We now turn to one of the most practical codes known, namely the Reed-Solomon codes. They are currently being used by both NASA and the European Space Agency; the codes chosen for use in compact discs also come from this family.

In the previous few sections we have extensively studied the 2-error correcting binary BCH codes. In fact, the Reed-Solomon codes are also BCH codes, but the digits in each codeword are no longer binary digits. This may seem strange as we have just finished praising the practical uses of these codes, and transmissions are always across binary channels. As will be shown, these codes do have a binary representation, but that is not how we shall first see the codes.

Before continuing, we develop some notation. Let $GF(2^r)[x]$ denote the set of all polynomials with coefficients from $GF(2^r)$. This set contains $K[x]$, $K = GF(2) = \{0, 1\}$, the set of all polynomials with binary coefficients. As before we can identify codewords $c \in C, C$ a linear code over $GF(2^r)$ of length n, with polynomials $c(x) \in GF(2^r)[x]$ having degree $c(x) < n$.

Recall we defined cyclic codes of length n in terms of roots of the corresponding polynomials. For instance, the (binary) 2-error correcting BCH code of length $n = 2^r - 1$, can be described by $c(x) \in C_K$ if and only if $\beta^1, \beta^2, \beta^3, \beta^4$ are all roots of $c(x)$ where $c(x) \in K[x]$, degree $(c(x)) < n$ and β is a primitive element in the field $GF(2^r)$. In this case $g_K(x) = m_1(x)m_3(x)$ is the generator polynomial for this cyclic code and $c(x) \in C_K$ if and only if $c(x) = a(x)g_K(x)$.

We can generalize this to codes over $GF(2^r)$ by choosing $c(x) \in GF(2^r)[x]$, instead. Again $c(x) \in C$ if and only if $\{\beta^1, \beta^2, \beta^3, \beta^4\}$ are all roots of $c(x)$. Now however polynomials $x + \beta, x + \beta^2, x + \beta^3$, and $x + \beta^4$ are in $GF(2^r)[x]$ and thus $c(x) \in C$ if and only if $g(x) = (x + \beta)(x + \beta^2)(x + \beta^3)(x + \beta^4)$ divides $c(x)$.

The binary code C_K defined above is a BCH code. The code C over $GF(2^r)$, just defined, contains C_K as a subcode and is an example of a Reed-Solomon code. In general, the code C_K is said to be a *subfield subcode* of C_K because $C_K \subseteq C$ and all words in C_K have all their digits in the subfield K of $GF(2^r)$; that is $C_K = C \cap K^n$.

Both of these codes C_K and C are cyclic since $c(x) \in C$ implies $c(x) = xc(x) \bmod (1+x^n)$ is in C. This follows from the division algorithm and the fact that β^i is a root of $1+x^n$ and $xc(x)$. In fact, it is not hard to show that if $g(x)$ generates a linear cyclic code of length $2^r - 1$ over $GF(2^r)$, then the generator of the binary subfield subcode is the polynomial $g_K(x)$ with the set of roots being the smallest set R that satisfies:

(a) if α is a root of $g(x)$ then $\alpha \in R$, and

(b) if $\alpha \in R$ then $\alpha^2 \in R$.

Putting these observations together gives us the following result:

Theorem 6.1.1 *Let $\alpha_1, \alpha_2, \ldots, \alpha_t$ be distinct non-zero elements of $GF(2^r)$. Then $g(x) = (\alpha_1 + x)(\alpha_2 + x)\cdots(\alpha_t + x)$ generates a linear cyclic code of length $2^r - 1$ over $GF(2^r)$.*

Example 6.1.2 Let $F = GF(2^4)$ constructed using $1+x+x^4$ (see Table 5.1). $g(x) = (\beta+x)(\beta^2+x) = \beta^3 + \beta^5 x + x^2$ generates a linear cyclic code over F of length 15. The codeword corresponding to $g(x)$ is of course $\beta^3\beta^5 1000000000000$.

Also $g_K(x) = 1+x+x^4 \leftrightarrow 110010000000000$ is in this code and in fact generates the cyclic binary subfield subcode. To see this, using the notation above, we find R: from (a) $\beta, \beta^2 \in R$, and from (b) $(\beta^2)^2 = \beta^4 \in R$ and $(\beta^4)^2 = \beta^8 \in R$; so $R = \{\beta, \beta^2, \beta^4, \beta^8\}$ and thus $g_K(x) = (\beta^4 + x)(\beta^8 + x)g(x)$.

We summarize some basic results about cyclic codes over $GF(2^r)$:

Theorem 6.1.3 *Let C be a linear cyclic code of length n over $GF(2^r)$. Then every codeword $c(x)$ can be written uniquely as $m(x)g(x)$ for some $m(x)$ in $GF(2^r)[x]$ of degree less than $n - \deg(g(x))$. Also, $g(x)$ divides $f(x)$ if and only if $f(x)$ is a codeword, and $g(x)$ divides $1+x^n$.*

Corollary 6.1.4 *Let $g(x)$ have degree $n-k$. If $g(x)$ generates a linear cyclic code C over $GF(2^r)$ of length $n = 2^r - 1$, and dimension k then*

$$G = \begin{bmatrix} g(x) \\ xg(x) \\ \vdots \\ x^{k-1}g(x) \end{bmatrix}$$

is a generating matrix for C, and the number of codewords in C is $(2^r)^k$.

Remark The fact that $|C| = 2^{rk}$ follows from Theorem 6.1.3, since all of the polynomials $m(x)$ in $GF(2^r)[x]$ of degree less than k give different codewords $m(x)g(x)$; but there are 2^{rk} such polynomials $m(x)$ since each of the k coefficients in $m(x)$ can be any one of the 2^r field elements.

Example 6.1.5 Construct $GF(2^3)$ using $1+x+x^3$ with β as the primitive element. Let $g(x) = (\beta + x)(\beta^2 + x) = \beta^3 + \beta^4 x + x^2$. Then $g(x)$ generates a linear cyclic code C over $GF(2^3)$ of length 7. A generating matrix for C is

$$G = \begin{bmatrix} \beta^3 & \beta^4 & 1 & 0 & 0 & 0 & 0 \\ 0 & \beta^3 & \beta^4 & 1 & 0 & 0 & 0 \\ 0 & 0 & \beta^3 & \beta^4 & 1 & 0 & 0 \\ 0 & 0 & 0 & \beta^3 & \beta^4 & 1 & 0 \\ 0 & 0 & 0 & 0 & \beta^3 & \beta^4 & 1 \end{bmatrix}.$$

C has 8^5 codewords. The codeword corresponding to $m(x) = 1 + \beta x + \beta^3 x^4 \leftrightarrow 1\beta 00\beta^3 = m$, for example, is $m(x)g(x) \leftrightarrow mG = \beta^3 0 \beta^4 \beta\beta^6 1 \beta^3$.

Exercises

6.1.6 Construct $GF(2^3)$ using $1+x+x^3$. Let $g(x) = (1+x)(\beta+x)$ generate a code C of length 7 over $GF(2^3)$.

(a) How many codewords does C have?

(b) Construct a generating matrix G for C using Corollary 6.1.4.

(c) Encode the following messages using G:

(i) $m(x) = 1 + \beta^6 x$

(ii) $m(x) = \beta^4 x^4$

(iii) $m(x) = 1 + x + x^2$

(d) Find the generating polynomial of the cyclic binary subfield subcode.

6.1.7 Construct $GF(2^4)$ using $1+x+x^4$. Let $g(x) = (\beta+x)(\beta^2+x)(\beta^3+x)(\beta^4+x)$ generate a linear cyclic code C over $GF(2^4)$.

(a) How many codewords does C have?

(b) Construct a generating matrix G for C using Corollary 6.1.4.

(c) Encode the following messages using G:

(i) $m(x) = 1 + \beta^7 x^{10}$

(ii) $m(x) = \beta^2 x + x^2$

(iii) $m(x) = 1 + x + x^2$

(d) Find the generator polynomial $g_K(x)$ of the binary subfield subcode. Find $m(x)$ such that $g_K(x) = m(x)g(x)$.

6.2 Reed-Solomon codes

In Section 6.1, generators for linear cyclic codes over $GF(2^r)$ were introduced, but no idea of the error correction capabilities of these codes was given. Here we shall address that question and then define the Reed-Solomon codes. We consider only Reed-Solomon codes, but most of the results about these codes apply directly to BCH codes, which are just subfield subcodes. We begin with a technical lemma.

Lemma 6.2.1 *Let $\alpha_1, \alpha_2, \ldots, \alpha_t$ be non-zero elements of $GF(2^r)$. Then*

$$\det \begin{bmatrix} 1 & \alpha_1 & \alpha_1^2 & \cdots & \alpha_1^{t-1} \\ 1 & \alpha_2 & \alpha_2^2 & \cdots & \alpha_2^{t-1} \\ \vdots & \vdots & \vdots & & \vdots \\ 1 & \alpha_t & \alpha_t^2 & \cdots & \alpha_t^{t-1} \end{bmatrix} = \prod_{1 \le j < i \le t} (\alpha_i + \alpha_j).$$

Proof: If $\alpha_i = \alpha_j$ for some $i \neq j$ then two rows of the matrix are identical, so the determinant is zero. Therefore for $t \geq i > j \geq 1, (\alpha_i + \alpha_j)$ is a factor of the determinant, so $\prod_{t \geq i > j \geq 1} (\alpha_i + \alpha_j)$ divides the determinant. Using the fact that both sides are both polynomials in $\alpha_1, \ldots, \alpha_t$ of the same degree, we have shown that they differ by at most a common factor. This common factor must be 1 as can be seen by comparing the coefficients of $\prod_{i=1}^{t} \alpha_i^{i-1}$ on both sides. □

Example 6.2.2 Using Lemma 6.2.1 and $GF(2^4)$ constructed using $1+x+x^4$ (see Table 5.1) we find that

$$\begin{aligned} \det \begin{bmatrix} 1 & \beta^2 & \beta^4 \\ 1 & \beta^7 & \beta^{14} \\ 1 & \beta^{10} & \beta^5 \end{bmatrix} &= (\beta^7 + \beta^2)(\beta^{10} + \beta^2)(\beta^{10} + \beta^7) \\ &= \beta^{12} \cdot \beta^4 \cdot \beta^6 \\ &= \beta^7 \end{aligned}$$

Exercises

6.2.3 Find the following determinants using Lemma 6.2.1. Assume β is the primitive elements in $GF(2^4)$ constructed using $1+x+x^4$ (Table 5.1).

(a) $\det \begin{bmatrix} 1 & \beta & \beta^2 \\ 1 & \beta^4 & \beta^8 \\ 1 & \beta^7 & \beta^{14} \end{bmatrix}$ (b) $\det \begin{bmatrix} 1 & \beta^2 & \beta^4 & \beta^6 \\ 1 & \beta^3 & \beta^6 & \beta^9 \\ 1 & \beta^5 & \beta^{10} & 1 \\ 1 & \beta^8 & \beta^1 & \beta^9 \end{bmatrix}$ (c) $\det \begin{bmatrix} 1 & \beta^3 \\ 1 & \beta^7 \end{bmatrix}$

We are now ready to present the main theorem concerning general BCH codes. The result is not presented in its more general form, but is sufficient when considering Reed-Solomon codes.

Theorem 6.2.4 *Let $g(x) = (\beta^{m+1} + x)(\beta^{m+2} + x) \cdots (\beta^{m+\delta-1} + x)$ be the generator of a linear cyclic code C over $GF(2^r)$ of length $n = 2^r - 1$, where β is a primitive element in $GF(2^r)$ and m is some integer. Then $d(C) \geq \delta$.*

Proof: For $1 \le i \le \delta - 1$, β^{m+i} is a root of $g(x)$, and thus the columns of

$$H = \begin{bmatrix} 1 & 1 & \cdots & 1 \\ \beta^{m+1} & \beta^{m+2} & \cdots & \beta^{m+\delta-1} \\ (\beta^{m+1})^2 & (\beta^{m+2})^2 & \cdots & (\beta^{m+\delta-1})^2 \\ \vdots & \vdots & & \vdots \\ (\beta^{m+1})^{n-1} & (\beta^{m+2})^{n-1} & \cdots & (\beta^{m+\delta-1})^{n-1} \end{bmatrix}$$

span $C^{\perp}$. No linear combination of $\delta - 1$ rows of this matrix is zero, as can be seen by evaluating the determinant of any $\delta - 1$ rows, say

$$\det \begin{bmatrix} (\beta^{m+1})^{j_1} & \cdots & (\beta^{m+\delta-1})^{j_1} \\ (\beta^{m+1})^{j_2} & \cdots & (\beta^{m+\delta-1})^{j_2} \\ \vdots & & \vdots \\ (\beta^{m+1})^{j_{\delta-1}} & \cdots & (\beta^{m+\delta-1})^{j_{\delta-1}} \end{bmatrix}$$

$$= \beta^{(m+1)(j_1+j_2+\cdots+j_{\delta-1})} \begin{bmatrix} 1 & \beta^{j_1} & \cdots & (\beta^{j_1})^{\delta-2} \\ 1 & \beta^{j_2} & \cdots & (\beta^{j_2})^{\delta-2} \\ \vdots & \vdots & & \vdots \\ 1 & \beta^{j_{\delta-1}} & \cdots & (\beta^{j_{\delta-1}})^{\delta-2} \end{bmatrix}$$

$$= \beta^{(m+1)(j_1+j_2+\cdots+j_{\delta-1})} \prod_{1 \le y \le x \le \delta-1} (\beta^{j_x} + \beta^{j_y})$$

which is not zero since β is of order $n = 2^r - 1$ and $1 \le j_1 < j_2 \cdots < j_{\delta-1} \le n-1$. Therefore no linear combination of $\delta - 1$ or fewer rows of the matrix is zero and so by Theorem 2.9.1 $d(C) \ge \delta$. Note, the columns of the H are linearly independent and thus H is a parity check matrix for C. □

Remark The proof of this theorem applies to any cyclic binary linear code of length $2^r - 1$ with a generator containing $\beta^{m+1}, \ldots, \beta^{m+\delta-1}$ among its roots. These binary codes are called *primitive* BCH codes and δ is called the *designed distance* of the code. Since they are binary subfield subcodes, $C_K \subset C$, of Reed Solomon codes C we must have $d(C_K) \ge \delta$ for these codes as well.

A binary *Reed-Solomon code* $RS(2^r, \delta)$ is a cyclic linear code over $GF(2^r)$ with generator $g(x) = (\beta^{m+1} + x)(\beta^{m+2} + x) \cdots (\beta^{m+\delta-1} + x)$ for some integer m and some primitive element β of $GF(2^r)$.

So for example, the code constructed in Example 6.1.5 is an $RS(8, 3)$, and the code constructed in Exercise 6.1.7 is an $RS(16, 5)$.

Theorem 6.2.5 *If C is an $RS(2^r, \delta)$ then*

(a) $n = 2^r - 1$,

(b) $k = 2^r - \delta$,

(c) $d = \delta$, *and*

(d) $|C| = 2^{rk}$.

Proof: (a) follows from Theorem 6.1.1, and (b) and (d) follow from Corollary 6.1.4. (Notice that a linear code over $GF(2^r)$ of dimension k has 2^{rk} codewords, which is consistent with the result that a binary linear code (that is, a linear code over $GF(2)$) of dimension k has 2^k codewords.) The fact that $d \geq \delta$ follows from Theorem 6.2.4 and that $d \leq \delta$ follows from the Singleton bound (see Theorem 3.1.7). □

Remark Notice that since $d = n - k + 1$, Reed-Solomon codes are MDS (maximum distance separable) codes (see Theorem 3.1.8).

Before we do another example, notice that any $RS(2^r, \delta)$ code C, can be represented as a binary code simply by replacing each digit in each codeword by the binary word of length r given by an index table of $GF(2^r)$. This code has length $r(2^r - 1)$ whereas the binary subfield subcode has length $2^r - 1$.

Let $\hat{c}$ denote the binary representation of $c \in C$ formed in this way and $\hat{C}$ denote the binary code formed from C, by this method. One of the reasons that $\hat{C}$ is so useful is that it performs well as a burst error correcting code (see Theorem 7.1.15).

Example 6.2.6 Let C be the $RS(4, 2)$ with $g(x) = \beta + x$ and where $GF(2^2)$ is constructed using $1 + x + x^2$. From Theorem 6.2.5, C has $n = 3, k = 2, d = 2$, and $|C| = 16$. From Corollary 6.1.4, a generating matrix for C is

$$G = \begin{bmatrix} \beta & 1 & 0 \\ 0 & \beta & 1 \end{bmatrix}$$

From $GF(2^2)$ we have that $0, 1, \beta, \beta^2$ correspond to the vectors $00, 10, 01$ and 11 respectively. The 16 messages u with their binary representation $\hat{u}$ along with the corresponding codewords $c = uG$ of C and their binary representations $\hat{c}$ are:

$\hat{u}$	u	$c = uG$	$\hat{c}$	$\hat{u}$	u	$c = uG$	$\hat{u}$
0000	$0\,0$	$0\,0\,0$	000000	0001	$0\,\beta$	$0\,\beta^2\beta$	001101
1000	$1\,0$	$\beta\,1\,0$	011000	1001	$1\,\beta$	$\beta\beta\beta$	010101
0100	$\beta\,0$	$\beta^2\beta\,0$	110100	0101	$\beta\beta$	$\beta^2 1\beta$	111001
1100	$\beta^2\,0$	$1\,\beta^2 0$	101100	1101	$\beta^2\beta$	$1\,0\,\beta$	100001
0010	$0\,1$	$0\,\beta\,1$	000110	0011	$0\,\beta^2$	$0\,1\,\beta^2$	001011
1010	$1\,1$	$\beta\beta^2 1$	011110	1011	$1\,\beta^2$	$\beta 0\beta^2$	010011
0110	$\beta 1$	$\beta^2 01$	110010	0111	$\beta\beta^2$	$\beta^2\beta^2\beta^2$	111111
1110	$\beta^2 1$	$1\,1\,1$	101010	1111	$\beta^2\beta^2$	$1\,\beta\beta^2$	100111

Exercises

6.2.7 Let C be the $RS(4,3)$ with generator $g(x) = (1+x)(\beta+x)$.

(a) Find n, k, d and $|C|$ for this code.

(b) Construct a generating matrix G for C using Corollary 6.1.4.

(c) Find all the codewords in C, their corresponding binary codewords in $\hat{C}$ and the corresponding messages (of course, encode the messages using G from (b)).

6.2.8 Let C be the $RS(8,5)$ with generator $g(x) = (1+x)(\beta+x)(\beta^2+x)(\beta^3+x)$ using $GF(2^3)$ constructed with $1+x+x^3$.

(a) Find n, k, d, and $|C|$ for this code.

(b) Find a generating matrix G for C using Corollary 6.1.4.

(c) Encode the following message using G to a codeword in C and then to a codeword in $\hat{C}$:

(i) $10\beta^2$ (ii) 111 (iii) $\beta^2\beta^4\beta^6$

6.2.9 Using the fields constructed in Exercise 5.1.15, find generator polynomials for the $RS(2^r, \delta)$ code with the following values of r, δ and m:

(a) $r = 2, \delta = 3, m = 2$ (b) $r = 3, \delta = 3, m = 2$

(c) $r = 3, \delta = 5, m = 0$ (d) $r = 4, \delta = 5, m = 0$

(e) $r = 5, \delta = 7, m = 0$

6.2.10 For each of the codes in Exercise 6.2.9, find the values of n, k, d and $|C|$.

From Theorem 6.2.5 we have that if C is an $RS(2^r, \delta)$ then $n = 2^r - 1$. Often one needs to have codes of lengths other than $2^r - 1$, but such codes can easily be formed from an $RS(2^r, \delta)$ code. For any integer s with $1 \leq s < 2^r - \delta$, and for any $RS(2^r, \delta)$ code C, form the *shortened* $RS(2^r, \delta)$ code $C(s)$ from C by taking all the codewords in C that have 0's in the last s positions and then deleting the last s positions.

Example 6.2.11 Let C be the $RS(4,2)$ code of Example 6.2.6. The *shortened* $RS(4,2)$ code $C(1)$ (so $s = 1$) is formed by taking all codewords that have 0's in the last $s = 1$ position, namely

$$000,\ \beta 10,\ \beta^2\beta 0 \text{ and } 1\beta^2 0,$$

then deleting the last s positions. So

$$C(1) = \{00, \beta 1, \beta^2\beta, 1\beta^2\}.$$

Alternatively, using the polynomial representation for an $RS(2^r, \delta)$ code C, the shortened code $C(s)$ is formed by the set of polynomials in C of degree less than

$n - s = 2^r - 1 - s$. So, if $g(x)$ is the generator polynomial of C, then $C(s)$ is the set of polynomials $c(x) = a(x)g(x)$, where $\deg(a(x)) < k - s = 2^r - \delta - s$ (since $\deg(g(x)) = \delta$). Therefore, a generating matrix $G(s)$ for the code $C(s)$ is given by

$$G(s) = \begin{bmatrix} g(x) \\ xg(x) \\ \vdots \\ x^{k-s-1}g(x) \end{bmatrix}.$$

Comparing this to the generating matrix G of C given by Corollary 6.1.4, $G(s)$ is the first $k - s$ rows of G with the last s columns deleted.

So if C is an $RS(2^r, \delta)$ code with parameters n, k and d then clearly we have that $C(s)$ has length $n(s) = n - s = 2^r - 1 - s$ and dimension $k(s) = k - s = 2^r - \delta - s$.

To find the distance $d(s)$ of $C(s)$, notice that if c_1 and c_2 are codewords in $C(s)$ then the distance between c_1 and c_2 is the same as the distance between the corresponding codewords $c_1 00\ldots0$ and $c_2 00\ldots0$ in C. Therefore $d(C(s)) \geq d(C) = \delta$. Also, from the Singleton bound in Theorem 3.1.7,

$$\begin{aligned} d(s) &\leq n(s) - k(s) + 1 \\ &= 2^r - 1 - s(2^r - \delta - s) + 1 \\ &= \delta \end{aligned}$$

So we have that $d(s) = \delta$, and from Theorem 3.1.8 we have that $C(s)$ is also an MDS code. Therefore we have the following result.

Theorem 6.2.12 *Let C be an $RS(2^r, \delta)$ code and let $C(s)$ be the shortened $RS(2^r, \delta)$ code with parameters $n(s)$, $k(s)$, and $d(s)$. Then*

$$\begin{aligned} n(s) &= 2^r - 1 - s, \\ k(s) &= 2^r - \delta - s, \\ d(s) &= \delta, \end{aligned}$$

and $C(s)$ is an MDS code (see Theorem 3.1.8).

Remark Other shortened $RS(2^r, \delta)$ codes can be formed by deleting any set of s coordinates, instead of the last s coordinates as was presented here. Because $RS(2^r, \delta)$ codes are MDS codes, any shortened $RS(2^r, \delta)$ code will also have the properties described in Theorem 6.2.12.

Example 6.2.13 In Example 6.1.5 we constructed an $RS(2^3, 3)$ code C with generator polynomial $g(x) = \beta^3 + \beta^4 x + x^2$. The shortened $RS(2^3, 3)$ code $C(2)$ has generating matrix

$$G(2) \leftrightarrow \begin{bmatrix} \beta^3\beta^4100 \\ 0\beta^3\beta^410 \\ 00\beta^3\beta^41 \end{bmatrix}$$

and has parameters $n(2) = 5$, $k(2) = 3$ and $d(2) = 3$. Notice that $G(2)$ is formed by deleting the last $s = 2$ rows columns of the generating matrix G in Example 6.1.5.

6.3 Decoding Reed-Solomon codes

Since digits in $RS(2^r, \delta)$ codes are elements from $GF(2^r)$, correcting a received word involves not only finding the locations of errors, but also the "magnitudes" of those errors since the digits of a most likely error pattern come from $GF(2^r)$. With this in mind, we make the following definitions. The *error locations* of a received word are the coordinates in which the (most likely) error pattern is non-zero. The error locations are referred to by an *error location number*: if the jth coordinate of the received word is an error location then its error location number is β^j (as with 2 error-correcting BCH codes, the coordinates are labeled $0, 1, \ldots, n-1$). For example, steps 4 and 6 of Algorithm 5.5.4 find the error location numbers of the most likely error pattern when using the 2 error-correcting BCH code. The *error magnitude* of an error location i is the element of $GF(2^r)$ that occurs in coordinate i of the (most likely) error pattern. Since the 2 error-correcting BCH code defined in Chapter 5 is a code over $GF(2)$, all error magnitudes must be 1 (the only non-zero element of $GF(2)$) and so are completely determined by the error locations. This is not the case for codes over $GF(2^r)$, $r \geq 2$, so to decode the Reed-Solomon codes we need to find the error locations and their corresponding error magnitudes.

Example 6.3.1 Using $RS(8, 3)$ constructed in Example 6.1.5, if $c = \beta^3\beta^4\beta^00000$ is transmitted and $w = \beta^3\beta^4\beta^50000$ is received then the most likely error pattern is $c + w = e = 00\beta^40000$. So the error location number is β^2 and the corresponding error magnitude is β^4.

We shall now develop an algorithm for decoding the $RS(2^r, \delta)$ code (and the corresponding BCH subfield subcode) with generator $g(x) = (\beta^{m+1} + x)(\beta^{m+2} + x) \cdots (\beta^{m+\delta-1} + x)$ where β is a primitive element of $GF(2^r)$. Let $t = \lfloor (\delta - 1)/2 \rfloor$ as usual, and let $a_1, \ldots, a_e$ and $b_1, \ldots, b_e$ be the error location numbers and their corresponding error magnitudes respectively, where $e \leq t$. (So in Example 6.3.1, $t = 1$ and since one error occurred in the second position, $a_1 = \beta^2$ and $b_1 = \beta^4$.) If $e < t$ then it will be convenient to define $a_i = 0$ for $e + 1 \leq i \leq t$, even though no such error locations exist. Then we can calculate $\delta - 1$ syndromes $s_{m+1}, \ldots, s_{m+\delta-1}$ which are defined by:

$$s_j = w(\beta^j) \text{ for } m + 1 \leq j \leq m + \delta - 1.$$

(Notice that this is the same definition of s_1 and s_3 used for the 2 error-correcting BCH code.) For $m+1 \le j \le m+\delta-1$, β^j is a root of $g(x)$ and therefore is a root of all codewords, so

$$s_j = w(\beta^j) = c(\beta^j) + e(\beta^j) = e(\beta^j) = \sum_{i=1}^{t} b_i a_i^j. \tag{6.1}$$

So the decoding problem is to find an effective way of solving $2e$ of the $\delta - 1$ equations given by (6.1) for the $2e$ unknowns $a_1, \ldots, a_e$ and $b_1, \ldots, b_e$. (Notice that $2e \le 2t \le \delta - 1$.) The difficulty in doing this lies in the non-linearity of the equations resulting from a_i being raised to the jth power. However we shall now show how to easily find a polynomial whose roots are $a_1, \ldots, a_e$, just as we did in step 6 of Algorithm 5.5.4 when decoding the 2 error-correcting binary BCH code.

Let $A = \{a_1, \ldots, a_e\}$ and define the *error locator polynomial* $\sigma_A(x)$ to be the polynomial whose roots are precisely $a_1, \ldots, a_e$. So

$$\sigma_A(x) = (a_1 + x)(a_2 + x) \cdots (a_e + x). \tag{6.2}$$

Now define σ_j to be coefficient of x^j in $\sigma_A(x)$. Then after expanding the above product of $\sigma_A(x)$ we get

$$\sigma_A(x) = \sigma_0 + \sigma_1 x + \cdots + \sigma_{e-1} x^{e-1} + x^e. \tag{6.3}$$

For any i with $1 \le i \le e$, we can multiply both sides of (6.3) by $b_i a_i^j$, then substitute $x = a_i$ and sum both sides over i from 1 to t; then from (6.2) we have that $\sigma_A(a_i) = 0$, and so we get

$$\begin{aligned} 0 &= \Big(\sum_{i=1}^{t} b_i a_i^j\Big)\sigma_0 + \Big(\sum_{i=1}^{t} b_i a_i^{j+1}\Big)\sigma_1 + \cdots + \sum_{i=1}^{t} b_i a_i^{j+e} \\ &= s_j \sigma_0 + s_{j+1}\sigma_1 + \cdots + s_{j+e} \end{aligned} \tag{6.4}$$

which may be rewritten as

$$s_{j+e} = s_j \sigma_0 + s_{j+1}\sigma_1 + \cdots + \sigma_{e-1} s_{j+e-1}. \tag{6.5}$$

But fortunately we know the values of $s_{m+1}, s_{m+2}, \ldots, s_{m+2e}$, so we can substitute $j = m+1, \ldots, m+e$ in turn to obtain e linear equations in the unknowns $\sigma_0, \ldots, \sigma_{e-1}$. These equations can most neatly be written in matrix form (where the ith row represents (6.5) with $j = m+i$) as follows:

$$\begin{bmatrix} s_{m+1} & s_{m+2} & \cdots & s_{m+e} \\ s_{m+2} & s_{m+3} & \cdots & s_{m+e+1} \\ \vdots & \vdots & & \vdots \\ s_{m+e} & s_{m+e+1} & \cdots & s_{m+2e-1} \end{bmatrix} \begin{bmatrix} \sigma_0 \\ \sigma_1 \\ \vdots \\ \sigma_{e-1} \end{bmatrix} = \begin{bmatrix} s_{m+e+1} \\ s_{m+e+2} \\ \vdots \\ s_{m+2e} \end{bmatrix} \tag{6.6}$$

It is important to know that this linear system always has a non-trivial solution. Let the $e \times e$ matrix in (6.6) be called M. Then indeed M does have full rank. This can be seen by writing

$$M = \begin{bmatrix} 1 & \cdots & 1 \\ a_1 & \cdots & a_e \\ \vdots & & \vdots \\ a_1^{e-1} & \cdots & a_e^{e-1} \end{bmatrix} \begin{bmatrix} b_1 a_1^{m+1} & & 0 \\ & \ddots & \\ 0 & & b_e a_e^{m+1} \end{bmatrix} \begin{bmatrix} 1 & a_1 & \cdots & a_1^{e-1} \\ \vdots & \vdots & & \vdots \\ 1 & a_e & \cdots & a_e^{e-1} \end{bmatrix}.$$

Each of the 3 matrices has full rank by Lemma 6.2.1, since $a_1, \ldots, a_e$ are distinct and $a_1, \ldots, a_e, b_1, \ldots, b_e$ are all non-zero. Therefore (6.6) can always be solved for $\sigma_0, \ldots, \sigma_{e-1}$. Notice also that if the decoder begins by assuming that $e = t$ (of course the value of e is, at first, unknown to the decoder) then M is a $t \times (t+1)$ matrix but will have rank e. This follows also by splitting M into the 3 matrices above and using the fact that we defined $a_i = 0$ for $e+1 \leq i \leq t$. Therefore the decoder now knows the value of e.

Now we can find $a_1, \ldots, a_e$ by substituting the field elements into $\sigma_A(x) = \sigma_0 + \alpha_1 x + \cdots + x^e$ (which is now known), since the roots of $\sigma_A(x)$ are precisely $a_1, \ldots, a_e$.

Now that $a_1, \ldots, a_e$ are known, equations (6.1) form a linear system in the variables $b_1, \ldots, b_e$ which can now be solved. Again these equations can most easily be represented in matrix form as follows:

$$\begin{bmatrix} a_1^{m+1} & a_2^{m+1} & \cdots & a_e^{m+1} \\ a_1^{m+2} & a_2^{m+2} & \cdots & a_e^{m+2} \\ \vdots & \vdots & & \vdots \\ a_1^{m+e} & a_2^{m+e} & \cdots & a_e^{m+e} \end{bmatrix} \begin{bmatrix} b_1 \\ b_2 \\ \vdots \\ b_e \end{bmatrix} = \begin{bmatrix} s_{m+1} \\ s_{m+2} \\ \vdots \\ s_{m+e} \end{bmatrix} \tag{6.7}$$

(Again, by Lemma 6.2.1 and since $a_1, \ldots, a_e$ are distinct and non-zero, this matrix has full rank, so the linear system can always be solved for $b_1, \ldots, b_e$.)

Therefore we have the following decoding algorithm for Reed-Solomon codes. In this algorithm, we define M' be the extended matrix formed from M by adding a column $e+1$ to M which is simply the right hand side of (6.6); that is,

$$M' = \begin{bmatrix} s_{m+1} & s_{m+2} & \cdots & s_{m+e+1} \\ s_{m+2} & s_{m+3} & \cdots & s_{m+e+2} \\ \vdots & \vdots & & \vdots \\ s_{m+e} & s_{m+e+1} & \cdots & s_{m+2e} \end{bmatrix}$$

Algorithm 6.3.2 (decoding $RS(2^r, \delta)$) Suppose that a codeword in an $RS(2^r, \delta)$ code C with generator $g(x) = (\beta^{m+1} + x) \cdots (\beta^{m+\delta-1} + x)$ is transmitted and w is received. Let $t = \lfloor (\delta - 1)/2 \rfloor$. Find the closest codeword in C to w as follows:

1. Calculate $s_j = w(\beta^j)$ for $m+1 \le j \le m+2t$.
2. Setting $e = t$, find the rank of the extended matrix M'.
3. Now let e be the rank of M' and solve the linear system (6.6) for $\sigma_0, \ldots, \sigma_{e-1}$.
4. Find the roots of $\sigma_A(x) = \sigma_0 + \sigma_1 x + \cdots + x^e$; these roots are the error location numbers $a_1, \ldots, a_e$.
5. Solve the linear system (6.7) for $b_1, \ldots, b_e$; these are the error magnitudes corresponding to $a_1, \ldots a_e$, so the most likely error pattern is completely determined.

Notice that no further row reduction of a matrix is required in Step 3 of Algorithm 6.3.2 since the matrix here is a submatrix of the one that is put into echelon form in Step 2. The following example makes this clear.

Example 6.3.3 Let

$$g(x) = (1+x)(\beta+x)(\beta^2+x)(\beta^3+x) = \beta^6 + \beta^5 x + \beta^5 x^2 + \beta^2 x^3 + x^4$$

be the generator of an $RS(2^3, 5)$ code (so $m = -1$ and $t = 2$), where $GF(2^3)$ is constructed using $1 + x + x^3$. Suppose that the received word is

$$w = \beta^6 \beta \beta^5 \beta^2 1 0 \beta^2.$$

We shall now decode w using Algorithm 6.3.2.

1. Since $m = -1$ and $\delta = 5$, we calculate the 4 syndromes s_0, s_1, s_2, and s_3 (in other words, calculate s_i if β^i is a root of $g(x)$).

$$\begin{aligned} s_0 &= w(\beta^0) = \beta^6 + \beta + \beta^5 + \beta^2 + 1 + 0 + \beta^2 = 1, \\ s_1 &= w(\beta) = \beta^6 + \beta^2 + \beta^7 + \beta^5 + \beta^4 + 0 + \beta^8 = \beta^3, \\ s_2 &= w(\beta^2) = \beta^6 + \beta^3 + \beta^9 + \beta^8 + \beta^8 + 0 + \beta^{14} = \beta^3, \text{ and} \\ s_3 &= w(\beta^3) = \beta^6 + \beta^4 + \beta^{11} + \beta^{11} + \beta^{12} + 0 + \beta^{20} = 1. \end{aligned}$$

2. Setting $e = t = 2$, the extended matrix M' is

$$M' = \begin{bmatrix} 1 & \beta^3 & \beta^3 \\ \beta^3 & \beta^3 & 1 \end{bmatrix}.$$

Row reducing M' yields the matrix

$$\begin{bmatrix} 1 & \beta^3 & \beta^3 \\ 0 & \beta^4 & \beta^2 \end{bmatrix}$$

which has rank 2.

3. Since M' has full rank, $e = 2$ and so we now solve the linear system

$$M \begin{bmatrix} \sigma_0 \\ \sigma_1 \end{bmatrix} = \begin{bmatrix} s_2 \\ s_3 \end{bmatrix}.$$

However, as observed above, we have already row reduced M in Step 2, so we have to solve

$$\begin{bmatrix} 1 & \beta^3 \\ 0 & \beta^4 \end{bmatrix} \begin{bmatrix} \sigma_0 \\ \sigma_1 \end{bmatrix} = \begin{bmatrix} \beta^3 \\ \beta^2 \end{bmatrix}.$$

Then $\beta^4\sigma_1 + \beta^2 = 0$ so $\sigma_1 = \beta^5$, and $\sigma_0 + \beta^3\beta^5 + \beta^3 = 0$ so $\sigma_0 = 1$.

4. We now know the error locator polynomial $\sigma_A(x) = \sigma_0 + \sigma_1 x + x^2 = 1 + \beta^5 x + x^2$. On substituting field elements into $\sigma_A(x)$, we find that $\sigma_A(\beta) = 0$ and $\sigma_A(\beta^6) = 0$. Therefore

$$\sigma_A(x) = 1 + \beta^5 x + x^2 = (\beta + x)(\beta^6 + x).$$

So the error location numbers are $a_1 = \beta$ and $a_2 = \beta^6$.

5. Now we solve the following linear system:

$$\begin{bmatrix} 1 & 1 \\ \beta & \beta^6 \end{bmatrix} \begin{bmatrix} b_1 \\ b_2 \end{bmatrix} = \begin{bmatrix} 1 \\ \beta^3 \end{bmatrix}$$

or

$$\begin{bmatrix} 1 & 1 \\ 0 & \beta^5 \end{bmatrix} \begin{bmatrix} b_1 \\ b_2 \end{bmatrix} = \begin{bmatrix} 1 \\ 1 \end{bmatrix}.$$

Then $\beta^5 b_2 = 1$ so $b_2 = \beta^2$, and $b_1 + b_2 = 1$ so $b_1 = \beta^6$. Therefore the most likely error pattern is

$$e = 0\beta^6 0000\beta^2$$

and the most likely codeword is

$$c = w + e = \beta^6\beta^5\beta^5\beta^2 100.$$

Example 6.3.4 Let

$$\begin{aligned} g(x) &= (1+x)(\beta+x)(\beta^2+x)(\beta^3+x)(\beta^4+x)(\beta^5+x) \\ &= 1 + \beta^4 x + \beta^2 x^2 + \beta x^3 + \beta^{12} x^4 + \beta^9 x^5 + x^6 \end{aligned}$$

be the generator of an $RS(2^4, 7)$ code (so $m = -1$ and $t = 3$), where $GF(2^4)$ is constructed using $1 + x + x^4$ (see Table 5.1). Suppose that the received word is

$$w(x) = 1 + \beta^4 x + \beta x^3 + \beta^9 x^5 + x^6.$$

1.

$$\begin{aligned}
s_0 &= w(\beta^0) = 1+\beta^4+\beta+\beta^9+1 = \beta^7,\\
s_1 &= w(\beta) = 1+\beta^5+\beta^4+\beta^{14}+\beta^6 = 1,\\
s_2 &= w(\beta^2) = 1+\beta^6+\beta^7+\beta^{19}+\beta^{12} = \beta^9,\\
s_3 &= w(\beta^3) = 1+\beta^7+\beta^{10}+\beta^{24}+\beta^{18} = \beta^{12},\\
s_4 &= w(\beta^4) = 1+\beta^8+\beta^{13}+\beta^{29}+\beta^{24} = \beta^9, \text{ and}\\
s_5 &= w(\beta^5) = 1+\beta^9+\beta^{16}+\beta^{34}d+\beta^{30} = \beta^7.
\end{aligned}$$

2.

$$M' = \begin{bmatrix} \beta^7 & 1 & \beta^9 & \beta^{12} \\ 1 & \beta^9 & \beta^{12} & \beta^9 \\ \beta^9 & \beta^{12} & \beta^9 & \beta^7 \end{bmatrix} \leftrightarrow \begin{bmatrix} \beta^7 & 1 & \beta^9 & \beta^{12} \\ 0 & \beta^{12} & \beta^7 & \beta^6 \\ 0 & \beta^7 & \beta^2 & \beta \end{bmatrix}$$

$$\leftrightarrow \begin{bmatrix} \beta^7 & 1 & \beta^9 & \beta^{12} \\ 0 & \beta^{12} & \beta^7 & \beta^6 \\ 0 & 0 & 0 & 0 \end{bmatrix}.$$

So M has rank 2 and therefore the most likely error pattern has weight $e = 2$.

3. With $e = 2$, the linear system (6.7) becomes

$$\begin{bmatrix} \beta^7 & 1 \\ 1 & \beta^9 \end{bmatrix} \begin{bmatrix} \sigma_0 \\ \sigma_1 \end{bmatrix} = \begin{bmatrix} \beta^9 \\ \beta^{12} \end{bmatrix},$$

but in Step 2 we row reduced this matrix:

$$\begin{bmatrix} \beta^7 & 1 \\ 0 & \beta^{12} \end{bmatrix} \begin{bmatrix} \sigma_0 \\ \sigma_1 \end{bmatrix} = \begin{bmatrix} \beta^9 \\ \beta^7 \end{bmatrix}.$$

Then $\beta^{12}\sigma_1 + \beta^7 = 0$, so $\sigma_1 = \beta^{10}$, and $\beta^7\sigma_0 + \sigma_1 + \beta^9 = 0$ so $\sigma_0 = \beta^6$.

4. $\sigma_A(x) = \beta^6 + \beta^{10}x + x^2 = (\beta^2 + x)(\beta^4 + x)$. Therefore $a_1 = \beta^2$ and $a_2 = \beta^4$.

5.

$$\begin{bmatrix} 1 & 1 \\ \beta^2 & \beta^4 \end{bmatrix} \begin{bmatrix} b_1 \\ b_2 \end{bmatrix} = \begin{bmatrix} \beta^7 \\ 1 \end{bmatrix},$$

so

$$\begin{bmatrix} 1 & 1 \\ 0 & \beta^{10} \end{bmatrix} \begin{bmatrix} b_1 \\ b_2 \end{bmatrix} = \begin{bmatrix} \beta^7 \\ \beta^7 \end{bmatrix}.$$

Therefore $b_2 = \beta^{12}$ and $b_1 = \beta^2$. So the most likely error pattern is $e = 00\beta^2 0\beta^{12}0\ldots0$ and the most likely codeword sent is

$$c = w + e = 1\beta^4\beta^2\beta\beta^{12}\beta^9 100\ldots0.$$

Note that this decoding scheme is independent of the cyclic nature of the code, and thus will work for shortened $RS(2^r, \delta)$ codes of length n as well.

Exercises

6.3.5 Let C be the $RS(2^4,7)$ code with generator $g(x)=(1+x)(\beta+x)(\beta^2+x)(\beta^3+x)(\beta^4+x)(\beta^5+x)$ where $GF(2^4)$ is constructed using $1+x+x^4$ (see Table 5.1). Decode the following received words which were encoded using C.

(a) $0\beta^3\beta\beta^5\beta^3\beta^2\beta^6\beta^{10}\beta000000$
(b) $1\beta^4\beta^2\beta0010\beta\beta^5\beta^3\beta^2 0\beta^{10}\beta$
(c) $\beta0\beta^7 0\beta^{12}\beta^3\beta^3 10000000$

6.3.6 Let C be the $RS(2^4,5)$ code with generator $g(x)=(\beta+x)(\beta^2+x)(\beta^3+x)(\beta^4+x)$ where $GF(2^4)$ is constructed using $1+x+x^4$ (see Table 5.1; notice here that $m=0$). Decode the following received words that were encoded using C.

(a) $001\beta^8 00\beta^5 00000000$
(b) $0\beta^{10}0\beta^6\beta^{13}0\beta^8\beta^{11}\beta^3\beta^5 00000$
(c) $\beta^4 0100\beta^2\beta^5\beta^{12}\beta^{14}000000$

6.3.7 Take the $RS(2^4,5)$ code in exercise 6.3.6 and form the shortened code $C(4)$ of length $n=11$ (and dimension $k=7$). Decode the following received words, that were encoded using C.

(a) $001\beta^8 00\beta^5 0000$
(b) $0\beta^{10}0\beta^6\beta^{13}0\beta^8\beta^{11}\beta^3\beta^5 0$
(c) $\beta^4 0100\beta^2\beta^5\beta^{12}\beta^{14}00$

6.3.8 Let C be the $RS(2^4,9)$ with generator $g(x)=(1+x)(\beta+x)\cdots(\beta^7+x)$ and with $GF(2^4)$ constructed using $1+x+x^4$ (see Table 5.1). Find the most likely error pattern for received words that were encoded using C and have the following syndromes.

(a) $s_0=\beta^2, s_1=\beta^3, s_2=\beta^4, s_3=\beta^5, s_4=\beta^6, s_5=\beta^7, s_6=\beta^8$ and $s_7=\beta^9$.
(b) $s_0=\beta^9, s_1=\beta^{13}, s_2=\beta^7, s_3=\beta^4, s_4=\beta^{12}, s_5=\beta^4, s_6=\beta^8$ and $s_7=\beta^2$.
(c) $s_0=1, s_1=1, s_2=1, s_3=1, s_4=1, s_5=1, s_6=1$ and $s_7=1$.
(d) $s_0=\beta^{10}, s_1=\beta^3, s_2=\beta^{13}, s_3=\beta^3, s_4=\beta^{12}, s_5=\beta^5, s_6=\beta^{13}$ and $s_7=\beta^3$.
(e) $s_0=\beta^{12}, s_1=\beta^8, s_2=0, s_3=\beta^7, s_4=\beta^{13}, s_5=\beta^4, s_6=\beta^{13}$ and $s_7=1$.
(f) $s_0=\beta^2, s_1=0, s_2=0, s_3=\beta^2, s_4=0, s_5=0, s_6=\beta^2$ and $s_7=0$.

6.4 Transform approach to Reed-Solomon codes

There is an alternate approach to the construction and decoding of Reed-Solomon codes which is sometimes referred to as the *transform* approach. It is based on an alternate representation of vectors in K^n. Rather than think of a vector as representing the coefficients of a polynomial, we consider a vector as representing a function from a set S to a field $F=GF(2^r)$.

We first develop this approach and show that it gives a different generator matrix for Reed-Solomon codes.

Example 6.4.1 Let $S = GF(2^3)$, constructed using $1+x+x^3$ with primitive element β. First consider $f : S \to \{0,1\}$ where $f(0) = 0$, $f(1) = 0$, $f(\beta) = f(\beta^2) = f(\beta^4) = 1$, $f(\beta^6) = f(\beta^3) = f(\beta^5) = 0$. Then $f(x)$ can be prescribed by the vector $v_f = (f(0), f(1), f(\beta), \ldots, f(\beta^6)) = (0,0,1,1,0,1,0,0)$.

Example 6.4.2 Let $S = GF(2^3)$. Consider a function $g : S \to S$, defined by

$$\begin{aligned} v_g &= (g(0), g(1), g(\beta), \ldots, g(\beta^6)) \\ &= (\beta^4, 0, 1, \beta^2, 1, \beta, 0, 0). \end{aligned}$$

In this case, we can also represent $g(x)$ as a polynomial,

$$g(x) = \beta^4 + \beta^2 x + \beta^3 x^2 + x^3$$

Two polynomials $p(x)$ and $q(x)$ represent the same function from S to $GF(2^r)$, $S \subseteq GF(2^r)$, if and only if $p(\alpha) = q(\alpha)$ for all $\alpha \in S$. If we consider all polynomials of degree $\leq k-1$ with coefficients from $GF(2^r)$, or equivalently the *vector form* of these polynomials as functions from $S \subseteq GF(2^r)$ to $GF(2^r)$, we see that they form a vector space and the basis is the set of polynomials $\{1, x, x^2, \ldots, x^{k-1}\}$. We will refer to such a vector space as a *function space* on S.

Theorem 6.4.3 *The set of all functions from S to $F = GF(2^r)$ represented by polynomials of degree $\leq k-1$ form a function space of dimension k with basis $\{1, x, x^2, \ldots, x^{k-1}\}$.*

Proof: Certainly every polynomial of degree $\leq k-1$ is in the span of $\{1, x, x^2, \ldots, x^{k-1}\}$. All we need to prove is that each function has a unique representation. Suppose that $p(x)$ and $q(x)$ are equal as functions on S. Then $p(\alpha) = q(\alpha)$ for all $\alpha \in S$. But then $p(\alpha) - q(\alpha) = 0$ and $p(x) - q(x)$ is a polynomial of degree $< k$ with n roots $n \geq k$, which is impossible unless $p(x) - q(x) = 0$ and thus $p(x)$ and $q(x)$ are equal as polynomials. □

Example 6.4.4 Let $F = GF(2^3)$, constructed using $1+x+x^3$ and consider all polynomials of degree ≤ 2. A basis for this function space is $\{1, x, x^2\}$ with the corresponding vector forms,

$$\begin{array}{ccc} 1 & \leftrightarrow & (1,1,1,1,1,1,1,1) \\ x & \leftrightarrow & (0,1,\beta,\beta^2,\beta^3,\beta^4,\beta^5,\beta^6) \\ x^2 & \leftrightarrow & (0,1,\beta^2,\beta^4,\beta^6,\beta,\beta^3,\beta^5). \end{array}$$

Clearly any polynomial $p(x) = a_0 + a_1 x + a_2 x^2$ considered as a function can be represented in vector form by a matrix product:

$$v_p = [a_0, a_1, a_2] \begin{bmatrix} 1 & 1 & 1 & 1 & 1 & 1 & 1 & 1 \\ 0 & 1 & \beta & \beta^2 & \beta^3 & \beta^4 & \beta^5 & \beta^6 \\ 0 & 1 & \beta^2 & \beta^4 & \beta^6 & \beta & \beta^3 & \beta^5 \end{bmatrix}$$

Recall that a Maximum Distance Separable code (MDS-code) is a linear code (n,k,d) with the distance $d = n-k+1$.

Theorem 6.4.5 *The function space on $S \subseteq GF(2^r)$ of all polynomials of degree $\leq k-1$ with coefficients from $GF(2^r)$ form a linear $(n,k,n-k+1)$ MDS code, where $n = |S| \leq 2^r$.*

Proof: We choose a subset $S \subseteq GF(2^r)$, $|S| = n$ and consider the function space of all polynomials $p : S \to GF(2^r)$ of degree $\leq k-1$. Clearly the length of each vector form (and hence of the code) is n and the dimension from Theorem 6.4.3 is $k, k \leq n$. To establish the minimum distance, note that any polynomial $p(x)$ of degree $\leq k-1$ has at most $k-1$ different roots; hence the vector form of $p(x)$ has at most $k-1$ zeros and thus has weight at least $n-k+1$. By the Singleton bound (Theorem 3.1.7), $d \leq n-k+1$ for any linear code, so therefore $d = n-k+1$. □

The subset $S = \{\alpha \in F \mid \alpha^n = 1\}$, is said to be the set of nth *roots of unity* in $F = GF(2^r)$. Then n is necessarily a divisor of $2^r - 1$ (but n need not equal 2^r-1), and so n is odd. S consists of all roots of $1+x^n$ in F. An element $\beta \in S$ is said to be a primitive nth root of unity (in $GF(2^r)$) if $S = \{1, \beta, \beta^2, \ldots, \beta^{n-1}\}$. This generalizes the idea of a primitive element of a field and will allow for the construction of cyclic Reed-Solomon codes of lengths n that divide, but are not necessarily equal to $2^r - 1$. In fact everything done previously in this chapter for codes of length $2^r - 1 = n$ where β is a primitive element remains true when β is just a primitive nth root of unity.

Example 6.4.6 Let $F = GF(2^4)$ constructed using $1+x+x^4$, with primitive element β. Then the 5th roots of unity are $\{1, \beta^3, \beta^6, \beta^9, \beta^{12}\}$, and the set of 3rd roots of unity are $\{1, \beta^5, \beta^{10}\}$. In this case β^3 is a primitive 5th root of unity, and β^5 is a primitive 3rd root of unity.

We wish to construct cyclic Reed-Solomon codes, but first we need to establish that two polynomials will represent the same function on S if and only if they are equivalent (mod $1+x^n$).

Theorem 6.4.7 *Let $p(x), q(x) \in GF(2^r)[x]$, and $S \subseteq GF(2^r)$ be the set of nth roots of unity. Then $p(x)$ and $q(x)$ represent the same function $f : S \to GF(2^r)$ (i.e., $p(\beta^i) = q(\beta^i)$, for all $\beta^i \in S$) if and only if $p(x) \equiv q(x) \pmod{1+x^n}$.*

Proof: Let $q(x) = h(x)(1+x^n) + p(x)$, where degree $(p(x)) < n$. Then $q(\beta^i) = h(\beta^i)(\beta^{in}+1) + p(\beta^i) = p(\beta^i)$ because β^i is a root of $(1+x^n)$. Conversely if $q(\beta^i) = p(\beta^i)$, $\beta^i \in S$ then β^i is a root of $p(x) - q(x)$. Hence

$$p(x) - q(x) = h(x)\prod_{i=0}^{n-1}(x+\beta^i) = h(x)(1+x^n).$$ □

Theorem 6.4.8 *Let S be the set of nth roots of unity in $GF(2^r)$. The function space of all polynomials in $GF(2^r)[x]$ of degree $\le k-1$ on S forms a cyclic $(n, k, n-k+1)$ code over $GF(2^r)$.*

Proof: In order for the code C to be cyclic, if $v_p = (p(1), p(\beta), \ldots, p(\beta^{n-1})) \in C$, we must have that $(p(\beta), p(\beta^2), \ldots, p(\beta^{n-1}), p(1))$ is also in C. But, note that $p(\beta x)$ is still a polynomial of degree $\le k-1$ and so $p'(x) = p(\beta x) \in C$. But $(p'(1), p'(\beta), \ldots, p'(\beta^{n-1})) = (p(\beta), p(\beta^2), \ldots, p(\beta^{n-1}), p(1))$. □

Example 6.4.9 Consider $GF(2^3)$ constructed using $1+x+x^3$. Let $p(x) = \beta^4 + \beta^2 x + \beta^3 x^2 + x^3$ with vector form $(0, 1, \beta^2, 1, \beta, 0, 0)$. Then the shift of this vector $(1, \beta^2, 1, \beta, 0, 0, 0)$ corresponds to the function $p(\beta x) = \beta^4 + \beta^3 x + \beta^5 x^2 + \beta^3 x^3 = (\beta^4 + x)(\beta^5 + x)(\beta^6 + x)\beta^3$.

If we have a polynomial $V(x) = V_0 + V_1 x + \cdots + V_{n-1}x^{n-1}$ we say that $v(x) = v_0 + v_1 x + \cdots + v_{n-1}x^{n-1}$ is the *transform* of $V(x)$ if $V(\beta^j) = \sum V_i \beta^{ji} = v_j$ for $j = 0, 1, \ldots, n-1$. In terms of matrix notation this is equivalent to $(V_0, V_1, \ldots, V_{n-1})A = (v_0, v_1, \ldots v_{n-1})$ where $A = (a_{ij})$ and $a_{ij} = \beta^{ij}$; β a primitive nth root of unity in $GF(2^r)$. The matrix A is usually referred to as the *finite Fourier transform* (or finite field transform). It has an inverse A^{-1}. Thus we have

$$(V_0, V_1, \ldots, V_n) = (v_0, v_1, \ldots, v_n)A^{-1}$$

or

$$V_i = \sum_{j=0}^{n-1} v_j \beta^{-ij} = v(\beta^{-i})$$

We saw earlier in Lemma 6.2.1 that A was invertible but we produce an alternate proof of this, by showing that A^{-1} transforms v back to V.

Theorem 6.4.10 *Let β be a primitive nth root of unity. If $v_j = V(\beta^j)$ for $V(x) = V_0 + V_1 x + \cdots + V_{n-1}x^{n-1}$ then $V_i = v(\beta^{-i})$, where $v(x) = v_0 + v_1 x + \cdots + v_{n-1}x^{n-1}$.*

Proof: $v(\beta^{-i}) = \sum_j v_j \beta^{-ij} = \sum_j (\sum_k V_k \beta^{kj})\beta^{-ij} = \sum_k V_k (\sum_j \beta^{(k-i)j}) = V_i$ because

$$\sum_{j=0}^{n-1} \beta^{(k-i)j} = \begin{cases} n \bmod 2, & \text{if } k-i=0, \\ 0, & \text{if } k-i \ne 0. \end{cases}$$

Note that $(1+x^n) = (1+x)(1+x+\cdots+x^{n-2}+x^{n-1})$ so if $\beta^{k-i} \ne 1$ then it is a root of $1+x+\cdots+x^{n-2}+x^{n-1}$. Also, recall that n divides $2^r - 1$, so is odd. □

As we see, given a vector of values $(v_0, v_1, \ldots, v_{n-1})$ we can recover the coefficients of the polynomial $V(x) = V_0 + V_1x + \cdots + V_{n-1}x^{n-1}$. This is essentially what the decoding algorithm presented in Section 6.3 is trying to do.

Theorem 6.4.11 *Let S be the set of nth roots of unity in $GF(2^r)$. The function space of all polynomials of degree $< n - \delta + 1$ on S is a cyclic MDS code with generator polynomial $g(x) = (\beta + x)(\beta^2 + x)\cdots(\beta^{\delta-1} + x)$, where β is a primitive nth root of unity.*

Proof: The polynomial function $C(x)$ whose vector form corresponds to $c(x) = a(x)g(x)$ is $C(x) = \sum_{i=0}^{n-1} c(\beta^{n-i})x$. Since $c(\beta^{n-i}) = 0$ for $i = n - \delta + 1, n - \delta + 2, \ldots, n - 1$ the coefficient of x^i is zero in $C(x)$ and thus $C(x)$ has degree $< n - \delta + 1$. □

In summary, we have produced an alternate method of constructing a $RS(2^r, \delta)$ code when $n = 2^r - 1$, one which results in a different generator matrix (and a different view of the information digits).

Example 6.4.12 Let β be a primitive element in $GF(2^3)$ constructed using $1 + x + x^3$. Consider a $RS(2^3, 5)$ code (Exercise 6.2.8) with generator polynomial $g(x) = (1 + x)(\beta + x)(\beta^2 + x)(\beta^3 + x) = \beta^6 + \beta^5 x + \beta^5 x^2 + \beta^2 x^3 + x^4$ which corresponds to $(\beta^6, \beta^5, \beta^5, \beta^2, 1, 0, 0)$. The transform of $g(x)$ is the polynomial $G(x) = \sum_{k=0}^{6} g(\beta^{7-k})x^k$.

Since $(g(\beta^0), g(\beta^1), \ldots, g(\beta^6)) = (0, 0, 0, 0, 1, \beta, \beta^4)$ then $G(x) = g(\beta^{7-1})x + g(\beta^{7-2})x^2 + g(\beta^{7-3})x^3 = \beta^4 x + \beta x^2 + x^3 = x(\beta^4 + \beta x + x^2)$.

It is easy to check that $G(x)$ represents a function with vector form

$$(G(\beta^0), G(\beta^1), \ldots, G(\beta^6)) = (\beta^6, \beta^5, \beta^5, \beta^2, 1, 0, 0).$$

In this case we think of this $RS(2^3, 5)$ code as the function space of all polynomials with degrees of all terms between 1 and 3. Clearly the basis for these polynomials is $\{x, x^2, x^3\}$ and the corresponding generator matrix for this function space is:

$$\begin{pmatrix} 1 & \beta & \beta^2 & \beta^3 & \beta^4 & \beta^5 & \beta^6 \\ 1 & \beta^2 & \beta^4 & \beta^6 & \beta^1 & \beta^3 & \beta^5 \\ 1 & \beta^3 & \beta^6 & \beta^2 & \beta^5 & \beta^1 & \beta^4 \end{pmatrix}$$

Thus $G(x) = \beta^4 x + \beta x^2 + x^3$ if and only if its vector form is

$$(\beta^4, \beta, 1) \begin{pmatrix} 1 & \beta & \beta^2 & \beta^3 & \beta^4 & \beta^5 & \beta^6 \\ 1 & \beta^2 & \beta^4 & \beta^6 & \beta^1 & \beta^3 & \beta^5 \\ 1 & \beta^3 & \beta^6 & \beta^2 & \beta^5 & \beta^1 & \beta^4 \end{pmatrix} = (\beta^6, \beta^5, \beta^5, \beta^2, 1, 0, 0).$$

Now we consider how this approach can help with the decoding of Reed-Solomon codes. Recall that if $g(x)$ is the generator polynomial for an RS code and $w(x)$ is the received word then $w(x) = c(x) + e(x)$, where $c(x) = a(x)g(x)$

and $e(x)$ is the error polynomial. Let $W(x)$, $C(x)$, and $E(x)$ be the transforms of $w(x)$, $c(x)$, and $e(x)$, respectively. The transform is a linear mapping. So

$$\begin{aligned} W(x) = \sum_k w(\beta^{n-k})x^k &= \sum_k c(\beta^{n-k})x^k + \sum_k e(\beta^{n-k})x^k \\ &= C(x) + E(x). \end{aligned}$$

Since $g(x)$ has $\delta - 1$ consecutive roots β^k, $k = m+1, m+2, \ldots, m+\delta-1$, we have $c(\beta^k) = 0$, and thus the syndromes s_{n-k} are $w(\beta^{n-k}) = e(\beta^{n-k}) = E_k$ for these values of k. That is, the syndromes give us $\delta - 1$ of the coefficients of the transform of $e(x)$. What we want to do is find the remaining coefficients. For this we need the error locator polynomial!

$\sigma(x)$ was defined so that $\sigma(\beta^k) = 0$ if and only if $e_k \neq 0$ (recall that $\sigma(\beta^k) = 0$ if and only if β^k is an error location number, which happens if and only if $e(x)$ is non-zero in the kth position). Since $E(\beta^k) = e_k$, we have that $\sigma(\beta^k)E(\beta^k) = 0$ for all k and thus

$$\sigma(x)E(x) \equiv 0 \pmod{1 + x^n}$$

and

$$\sigma(x)E(x) \equiv \sum_{i=0}^{t} \sigma_i x^i \sum_{\ell} E_\ell x^\ell \pmod{1 + x^n}$$

(since $\sigma(x)$ is a polynomial of degree at most $t = \lfloor(\delta - 1)/2\rfloor$), thus equating coefficients of the x^{t+k} we have

$$0 = \sigma_t E_k + \sigma_{t-1} E_{k+1} + \sigma_{t-2} E_{k+2} + \cdots + \sigma_0 E_{k+t}.$$

Since we know $\delta - 1$ consecutive values E_k (that is, the syndromes s_{n-k}), we can compute the coefficients σ_i and use this to generate all values of E_k.

Example 6.4.13 Let $\sigma(x) = \sigma_0 + \sigma_1 x + x^2$ and $E(x) = E_0 + E_1 x + \cdots + E_6 x^6$. Then $\sigma(x)E(x) \equiv 0 \pmod{1 + x^7}$ if and only if

$$E_k = \sigma_1 E_{k+1} + \sigma_0 E_{k+2}, \quad k = 0, 1, \ldots, 6$$

Example 6.4.14 Consider Example 6.3.3. Suppose $w = (\beta^6, \beta, \beta^5, \beta^2, 1, 0, \beta^2)$. Since $d = 5$, $t \leq 2$ and $E_0 = w(\beta^0) = 1$, $E_6 = w(\beta) = \beta^3$, $E_5 = w(\beta^2) = \beta^3$, $E_4 = w(\beta^3) = 1$ and $\sigma(x) = x^2 + \sigma_1 x + \sigma_0$. We solve for σ_1, σ_0 as in Example 6.3.3, and find $\sigma_1 = \beta^5$, $\sigma_0 = 1$. Thus, $E_k = \beta^5 E_{k+1} + E_{k+2}$.

Since $(E_0, E_6, E_5, E_4) = (1, \beta^3, \beta^3, 1)$, we see that

$$\begin{aligned} E_3 &= \beta^5 E_4 + E_5 = \beta^5 + \beta^3 = \beta^2 \\ E_2 &= \beta^5 E_3 + E_4 = \beta^5 + \beta^2 + 1 = 0 \\ E_1 &= \beta^5 E_2 + E_3 = 0 + \beta^2 = \beta^2 \end{aligned}$$

Now we know that the transform of $e(x)$ is $E(x) = \sum E_k x^k$ where

$$(E_0, E_1, \ldots, E_6) = (1, \beta^2, 0, \beta^2, 1, \beta^3, \beta^3).$$

At this point our decoding algorithm will depend on the encoding procedure. Since $E(x) = 1 + \beta^2 x + \beta^2 x^3 + x^4 + \beta^3 x^5 + \beta^3 x^6$, we know that the most likely error vector is $e = (E(\beta^0), E(\beta^1), \ldots, E(\beta^6)) = (0, \beta^6, 0, 0, 0, 0, \beta^2)$ and thus the most likely codeword is $c = w + e = (\beta^6, \beta^5, \beta^5, \beta^2, 1, 0, 0)$.

On the other hand if we used the generator matrix of Example 6.4.12 we would not need to find the error vector, but simply compute all values of $w(\beta^k), k = 0, \ldots, 6$ to obtain the most likely message directly. That is, find the transform of $w(x)$ and add it to the transform of $e(x)$.

$$(w_0, w_1, \ldots, w_6) = (w(\beta^0), w(\beta^6), w(\beta^5), \ldots, w(\beta^1)) = (1, \beta, \beta, \beta^6, 1, \beta^3, \beta^3),$$
$$(E_0, E_1, \ldots, E_6) = (1, \beta^2, 0, \beta^2, 1, \beta^3, \beta^3),$$

and thus

$$\begin{aligned}(C_0, C_1, \ldots C_6) &= (W_0, W_1, \ldots, W_6) + (E_0, E_1, \ldots, E_6)\\ &= (0, \beta^4, \beta, 1, 0, 0, 0),\end{aligned}$$

So $C(x) = \beta^4 x + \beta x^2 + x^3$. Hence our information digits are $(\beta^4, \beta, 1)$. We leave it as an exercise to show that $c = (\beta^6, \beta^5, \beta^5, \beta^2, 1, 0, 0)$ is the vector form of $C(x)$.

Exercises

6.4.15 Show that $C(x) = \beta^4 x + \beta x^2 + x^3$ has vector form $(\beta^6, \beta^5, \beta^5, \beta^2, 1, 0, 0)$, β the primitive element in $GF(2^3)$ constructed using $1 + x + x^3$.

6.4.16 Given $GF(2^3)$ constructed using $1 + x + x^3$, find the generator matrix for the MDS code of length 7 for the function space of all polynomials defined on $S = GF(2^3)\backslash\{0\}$ with basis

(a) $\{x, x^2, x^3\}$
(b) $\{1, x, x^2, x^3, x^4\}$
(c) $\{x, x^3, x^6\}$

6.4.17 Show that all codes in the previous exercise are cyclic. Find the generator polynomial for each code.

6.4.18 Given $GF(2^3)$ constructed using $1 + x + x^3$, for each $G(x)$ find the corresponding vector form v_g in the function space.

(a) $G(x) = x + \beta x^3$
(b) $G(x) = 1 + x^2 + x^4$

6.4.19 Given $GF(2^3)$ constructing using $1+x+x^3$ with primitive element β, find the coefficients of the polynomial $G(x)$ given the values v_g.

(a) $v_g = (\beta^3, \beta, \beta^4, 0, \beta^6, \beta^5, \beta^2)$
(b) $v_g = (\beta^4, \beta^2, \beta, \beta^3, 0, \beta^6, 1)$

6.4.20 For Exercises 6.3.5, 6.3.6, and 6.3.8, use the transform approach to compute the most likely error pattern and decode.

6.5 Berlekamp-Massey algorithm

The following algorithm for finding the error locator polynomial is faster than solving the linear system (6.6). The algorithm is essentially the algorithm of Berlekamp and Massey for calculating the error locator polynomial $\sigma(x)$ given the syndromes $s_j = w(\beta^j)$ for $m+1 \le j \le m+2t$.

Let $\sigma_R(x) = 1 + \sigma_{t-1}x + \sigma_{t-2}x^2 + \cdots + \sigma_0 x^t$; that is, $\sigma_R(x)$ is the "reverse" of the error locator polynomial $\sigma(x)$. Let $s(x) = 1 + s_{m+1}x + s_{m+2}x^2 + \cdots + s_{m+2t}x^{2t}$ be the *syndrome polynomial*. Using the division algorithm, we can write

$$\sigma_R(x)s(x) = q(x)x^{2t+1} + r(x)$$

with $\deg(r(x)) \le 2t$. But, since the coefficients of $x^{t+1}, \ldots, x^{2t}$ in $\sigma_R(x)s(x)$ are all zero from (6.4), in fact $\deg(r(x)) \le t$.

The version of the Berlekamp-Massey algorithm below produces a polynomial $P_{2t}(x)$ satisfying $P_{2t}(x)s(x) = q_{2t}(x)x^{2t+1} + r_{2t}(x)$ with $\deg(P_{2t}(x)) \le t$, $\deg(r_{2t}(x)) \le t$ and $P_{2t}(0) = 1$ (if such exists). This is clearly enough to show that $P_{2t}(x) = \sigma_R(x)$.

(The algorithm actually produces a sequence of polynomials $P_i(x)$ and integers D_i such that if $P_i(x)s(x) = q_i(x)x^{i+1} + r_i(x)$ with $\deg(r_i(x)) \le i$, then $\deg(P_i(x)) \le i - \lfloor D_i/2 \rfloor$ and $\deg(r_i(x)) \le i - \lfloor (1+D_i)/2 \rfloor$. Moreover $P_i(x)$ is a combination of $P_{i-1}(x)$ and some specific previous polynomial $P_{z_{i-1}}(x)$.)

Let $q_i(x) = q_{i,0} + q_{i,1}x + \cdots + q_{i,2t-1-i}x^{2t-1-i}$ and let $p_i(x) = x^{2t+1-i}P_i(x) = p_{i,0} + p_{i,1}x + \cdots + p_{i,\ell}x^\ell$. At step i, the algorithm calculates $q_i(x)$, $p_i(x)$, the integers D_i, and the subscripts z_i (which are used to determine which other polynomial $P_{z_i}(x)$ besides $P_i(x)$ is needed for the next calculation). The proof that this version of the algorithm works is straightforward, so is left for the exercises. We now give the algorithm precisely.

Algorithm 6.5.1 (Berlekamp-Massey; to find the error locator polynomial) Let w be a received word that was encoded using a generator $g(x)$ having as roots the consecutive powers $\beta^{m+1}, \ldots, \beta^{m+2t}$ of β. Decode w as follows.

1. Calculate $s_j := w(\beta^j)$ for $m+1 \le j \le m+2t$.

2. Define

$$\begin{aligned} q_{-1}(x) &:= 1 + s_{m+1}x + s_{m+2}x^2 + \cdots + s_{m+2t}x^{2t}, \\ q_0(x) &:= s_{m+1} + s_{m+2}x + \cdots + s_{m+2t}x^{2t-1}, \\ p_{-1}(x) &:= x^{2t+1}, \text{ and} \\ p_0(x) &:= x^{2t}. \end{aligned}$$

Let $D_{-1} := -1$ and $D_0 := 0$; and let $z_0 := -1$.

3. For $1 \le i \le 2t$, recursively define $q_i(x)$, $p_i(x)$, D_i, and z_i as follows.
   (a) If $q_{i-1,0} = 0$, then let

$$\begin{aligned} q_i(x) &:= q_{i-1}(x)/x \\ p_i(x) &:= p_{i-1}(x)/x \\ D_i &:= 2 + D_{i-1}, \text{ and} \\ z_i &:= z_{i-1}. \end{aligned}$$

   (b) If $q_{i,0} \neq 0$, then let

$$q_i(x) := \Big(q_{i-1}(x) - \frac{q_{i-1,0}}{q_{z_{i-1},0}} q_{z_{i-1}}(x)\Big)/x,$$

   which can be truncated to have degree at most $2t - 1 - i$; and let

$$\begin{aligned} p_i(x) &:= \Big(p_{i-1}(x) - \frac{q_{i-1,0}}{q_{z_{i-1},0}} p_{z_{i-1}}(x)\Big)/x \\ D_i &:= 2 + \min\{D_{i-1}, D_{z_{i-1}}\} \\ z_i &:= \begin{cases} i-1, & \text{if } D_{i-1} \ge D_{z_{i-1}}, \\ z_{i-1}, & \text{otherwise.} \end{cases} \end{aligned}$$

If $e \le t$ errors have occurred during transmission then $p_{2t}(x) = \sigma_R(x)$ has degree e; the error locator polynomial is $\sigma(x) = p_{2t,e} + p_{2t,e-1}x + \cdots + p_{2t,1}x^{e-1} + x^e$, which has e distinct roots.

Although we did not actually calculate the remainder polynomials $r_i(x)$ in this algorithm, they certainly are part of the theory involved. In fact $r_{2t}(x) := p_{2t}(x)q_{-1}(x) \bmod x^{2t+1}$ has a further use in decoding. Either $r(x) := r_{2t}(x)$ or $\rho(x) := r_{2t}(x) - p_{2t}(x)$ is called the *error evaluator polynomial* because, together with $\sigma'_R(x)$, it can be used to calculate the error magnitudes b_j, given the error locations a_j.

The following is a quick derivation for a formula for b_j in terms of ($\rho(x)$ or) $r(x)$ and $\sigma'_R(x)$. Let

$$S(x) := \sum_{i=0}^{\infty} s_{i+m+1}x^i.$$

Then

$$S(x) = \sum_{i=0}^{\infty}\left(\sum_{j=1}^{t} b_j a_j^{i+m+1}\right)x^i = \sum_{j=1}^{t} b_j a_j^{m+1}\sum_{i=0}^{\infty} a_j^i x^i = \sum_{j=1}^{t}\frac{b_j a_j^{m+1}}{1-a_j x}.$$

Since $\sigma_R(x) := \prod_{k=1}^{t}(1-a_k x)$, let $\sigma_j(x) := \sigma_R(x)/(1-a_j x)$ to get

$$\rho(x) := \sigma_R(x)S(x) = \sum_{j=1}^{t} b_j a_j^{m+1}\sigma_j(x)$$

a polynomial in x with degree clearly less than the degree of $\sigma(x)$. Then

$$\rho(a_k^{-1}) = \sigma_R(a_k^{-1})S(a_k^{-1}) = \sum_{j=1}^{t} b_j a_j^{m+1}\sigma_j(a_k^{-1}).$$

But $\sigma_j(a_k^{-1}) = 0$ unless $j = k$, so $\rho(a_k^{-1}) = b_k a_k^{m+1}\sigma_k(a_k^{-1})$. Note also that

$$\sigma'_R(a_k^{-1}) = -a_k \prod_{j=1, j\neq k}^{t}(1-a_j a_k^{-1}) = -a_k\sigma_k(a_k^{-1})$$

so that

$$b_k = -\frac{\rho(a_k^{-1})}{a_k^m \sigma'_R(a_k^{-1})}.$$

Since $\sigma_R(a_k^{-1}) = 0$, the numerator can be viewed as $a_k r(a_k^{-1})$ instead of $\rho(a_k^{-1})$, to get

$$b_k = -\frac{r(a_k^{-1})}{a_k^{m-1}\sigma'_R(a_k^{-1})}.$$

Example 6.5.2 Consider Example 6.3.4 with the syndromes $s_0 = \beta^7$, $s_1 = \beta^0$, $s_2 = \beta^9$, $s_3 = \beta^{12}$, $s_4 = \beta^9$, $s_5 = \beta^7$. Working step by step through Algorithm 6.5.1, we obtain the following. We begin by setting

$$\begin{aligned}
q_{-1}(x) &= 1+\beta^7 x + x^2 + \beta^9 x^3 + \beta^{12}x^4 + \beta^9 x^5 + \beta^7 x^6,\\
q_0(x) &= \beta^7 + x + \beta^9 x^2 + \beta^{12}x^3 + \beta^9 x^4 + \beta^7 x^5\\
p_{-1}(x) &= x^7,\\
p_0(x) &= x^6,\\
D_{-1} &= -1, D_0 = 0 \text{ and } z_0 = -1.
\end{aligned}$$

Let $i = 1$. Since $q_{0,0} = \beta^7 \neq 0$, we use step 3(b):

$$(q_0(x) + \beta^7 q_{-1}(x))/x = \beta^3 + x + \beta^{13}x^2 + \beta^{14}x^3 + \beta^{14}x^4 + \beta^{14}x^5$$

which is truncated to degree $2t - i - 1 = 4$ to give

$$\begin{aligned} q_1(x) &= \beta^3 + x + \beta^{13}x^2 + \beta^{14}x^3 + \beta^{14}x^4. \\ p_1(x) &= 1 + \beta^7 x, \\ D_1 &= 2 + \min\{D_{-1}, D_0\} = 0, \end{aligned}$$

and since $D_0 \geq D_{-1}, z_i = i - 1 = 0$.

Before proceeding, we shall adopt a more concise format by representing the polynomials by their corresponding words. Then the information we have found so far is represented by the following table.

i				q_i			—		p_i	D_i	z_i
-1	β^0	β^7	β^0	β^9	β^{12}	β^9	β^7	—	β^0	-1	
0	β^7	β^0	β^9	β^{12}	β^9	β^7	—	β^0		0	-1
1	β^3	β^0	β^{13}	β^{14}	β^{14}	—	β^0	β^7		1	0

Proceeding from $i = 2$ to $i = 2t = 6$ we obtain the following table.

i				q_i			—		p_i	D_i	z_i
-1	β^0	β^7	β^0	β^9	β^{12}	β^9	β^7	—	β^0	-1	
0	β^7	β^0	β^9	β^{12}	β^9	β^7	—	β^0		0	-1
1	β^3	β^0	β^{13}	β^{14}	β^{14}	—	β^0	β^7		1	0
2	β^{12}	β^7	β^6	β^{12}	—	β^0	β^8			2	1
3	β^0	β^{10}	β^9	—	β^0	β^{12}	β^1			3	2
4	0	0	—	β^0	β^{10}	β^6				4	3
5	0	—	β^0	β^{10}	β^6					6	3
6	—	β^0	β^{10}	β^6						8	3

So finally we obtain $\sigma(x)$ by reading $p_{2t}(x) = p_6(x)$ backwards:

$$\sigma(x) = \beta^6 + \beta^{10}x + x^2.$$

Example 6.5.3 Let C be the $RS(2^4, 9)$ code with generator $g(x) = (1 + x)(\beta + x) \cdots (\beta^7 + x)$ and with $GF(2^4)$ constructed using $1 + x + x^4$ (Table 5.1). Suppose that w is the received word and the syndromes of w are:

$$s_0 = \beta^{12}, s_1 = \beta^9, s_2 = \beta^6, s_3 = \beta^3, s_4 = \beta^5, s_5 = \beta^{12}, s_6 = \beta^6, s_7 = \beta^6.$$

Using Algorithm 6.5.1 and the notation described in Example 6.5.2, we obtain the error locator polynomial as follows.

i	q_i								—		p_i	D_i	z_i
−1	β^0	β^{12}	β^9	β^6	β^3	β^5	β^{12}	β^6	β^6	–	β^0	−1	
0	β^{12}	β^9	β^6	β^3	β^5	β^{12}	β^6	β^6	–	β^0		0	−1
1	0	0	0	β^{10}	β^7	β^5	β^2	–	β^0	β^{12}		1	0
2	0	0	β^{10}	β^7	β^5	β^2	–	β^0	β^{12}			3	0
3	0	β^{10}	β^7	β^5	β^2	–	β^0	β^{12}				5	0
4	β^{10}	β^7	β^5	β^2	–	β^0	β^{12}					7	0
5	0	β^8	β^5	–	β^0	β^{12}	0	0	β^{13}			2	4
6	β^8	β^5	–	β^0	β^{12}	0	0	β^{13}				4	4
7	0	–	β^0	β^{12}	β^{13}	β^{10}	β^{13}					6	4
8	–	β^0	β^{12}	β^{13}	β^{10}	β^{13}						8	4

Therefore the error locator polynomial is

$$\sigma(x) = \beta^{13} + \beta^{10}x + \beta^{13}x^2 + \beta^{12}x^3 + x^4.$$

Remark Notice that in Algorithm 6.5.1, at every step z_i is either $i-1$ or z_{i-1}. Therefore at each step we need only store q_{i-1}, p_{i-1}, D_{i-1}, z_{i-1}, $q_{z_{i-1}}$, and $p_{z_{i-1}}$, and not everything calculated so far, as is suggested by the tables of Examples 6.5.2 and 6.5.3. Clearly this is an important practical consideration, but to describe the algorithm it is convenient to display all the calculations in one table.

Exercises

6.5.4 Let C be the $RS(2^4, 9)$ with generator $g(x) = (1+x)(\beta+x)\cdots(\beta^7+x)$ and with $GF(2^4)$ constructed using $1+x+x^4$ (Table 5.1). Use Algorithm 6.5.1 to find the error locator polynomial for received words that were encoded using C and have the following syndromes. (See also Exercise 6.3.8 which has the same syndromes.)

(a) $s_0 = \beta^2$, $s_1 = \beta^3$, $s_2 = \beta^4$, $s_3 = \beta^5$, $s_4 = \beta^6$, $s_5 = \beta^7$, $s_6 = \beta^8$, and $s_7 = \beta^9$.

(b) $s_0 = \beta^9$, $s_1 = \beta^{13}$, $s_2 = \beta^7$, $s_3 = \beta^4$, $s_4 = \beta^{12}$, $s_5 = \beta^4$, $s_6 = \beta^8$, and $s_7 = \beta^2$.

(c) $s_0 = 1$, $s_1 = 1$, $s_2 = 1$, $s_3 = 1$, $s_4 = 1$, $s_5 = 1$, $s_6 = 1$, and $s_7 = 1$.

(d) $s_0 = \beta^{10}$, $s_1 = \beta^3$, $s_2 = \beta^{13}$, $s_3 = \beta^3$, $s_4 = \beta^{12}$, $s_5 = \beta^5$, $s_6 = \beta^{13}$, and $s_7 = \beta^3$.

(e) $s_0 = \beta^{12}$, $s_1 = \beta^8$, $s_2 = 0$, $s_3 = \beta^7$, $s_4 = \beta^{13}$, $s_5 = \beta^4$, $s_6 = \beta^{13}$, and $s_7 = 1$.

(f) $s_0 = \beta^2$, $s_1 = 0$, $s_2 = 0$, $s_3 = \beta^2$, $s_4 = 0$, $s_5 = 0$, $s_6 = \beta^2$, and $s_7 = 0$.

6.5.5 (proof of Berlekamp-Massey)

(a) Prove recursively that $\deg(P_i(x)) \le i - \lfloor D_i/2 \rfloor$ (noting that $P_i(0) = 1$).

(b) Prove recursively that $\deg(R_i(x)) \le i - \lfloor (1+D_i)/2 \rfloor$, after first showing that the choice of $q_i(0)$ forces the coefficient of x^i in $P_i(x)q_{-1}(x)$ to be zero.

(c) Prove that since all the D_j are distinct, that at least one of the D_j, $j \le i$, must be at least i; and hence that either $D_i \ge i$ or $D_{z_i} \ge i$.

(d) When $D_{2t} \geq 2t$, show that $\deg(P_{2t}(x)) \leq t$, and that since $\deg(R_{2t}(x)) \leq t$, note that at least t consecutive coefficients of $P_{2t}(x)q_{-1}(x)$ are zero (meaning that at least t consecutive Newton's identities are satisfied).

6.6 Erasures

An *erasure* is an error for which the error location number is known but the error magnitude is not known. An *erasure location number* is the location number of an erasure. Knowledge of the error location number may come from the physical reading of the signal being received (the received digit not looking like a zero or a one), but can also come from the structure of the code. For example, suppose that C is an $RS(2^r, \delta)$ code and $\hat{C}$ is the binary representation of C. Define $\hat{C}'$ to be the binary code formed from C by adding a parity check digit to the binary representation of each digit in each codeword of C.

Example 6.6.1 Let C be the $RS(4,2)$ defined in Example 6.2.6. To form $\hat{C}'$ the digits $0, 1, \beta$ and β^2 of codewords in C are replaced by $000, 101, 011$ and 110 respectively (the third digit in each of these words is a parity check digit). So the codeword in $\hat{C}'$ that corresponds to the codeword $\beta\ 1\ 0$ in C is 011101000.

Exercises

6.6.2 Let C be the $RS(4,3)$ with generator $g(x) = (1+x)(\beta+x)$ (see Exercise 6.2.7). Find all of the codewords in $\hat{C}'$.

Since each digit in a codeword c from an $RS(2^r, \delta)$ code C is represented by a binary word of length $r+1$ in the corresponding codeword $\hat{c}'$ in $\hat{C}'$, has length $(2^r-1)(r+1)$. Also, since each non-zero digit in c is replaced by a word of even weight in $\hat{c}'$, $\hat{c}'$ consists of 2^r-1 words of length $r+1$, each of which should have even weight. Therefore if one of these 2^r-1 groups has odd weight in a received word $\hat{w}'$ then we know an error has occurred among these $r+1$ digits. We could try decoding $\hat{w}'$ by decoding w, the word having digits in $GF(2^r)$ that corresponds $\hat{w}'$, to the closest codeword in C. Knowing that errors occurred in a group of $r+1$ digits corresponds to knowing one error location number of w, which therefore is an erasure.

Example 6.6.3 Using the code $\hat{C}'$ defined in Example 6.2.6, suppose that 011 100 000 is received. Then we know errors occurred among the second group of 3 digits (since this group of 3 digits has odd weight), so β^1 is an erasure location number. Since this position of w is an erasure, we may as well replace it with 0 (to make it easier to find the syndromes), so we now try to decode $w = \beta\ 0\ 0$ to the closest codeword in C, knowing that one error location number is $a_1 = \beta$.

Theorem 6.6.4 *Let C be an $RS(2^r, \delta)$ which is used to transmit messages and let w be a received word containing ϵ erasures and e errors which are not erasures. Then w can be decoded correctly if*

$$2e + \epsilon \leq \delta - 1.$$

Proof: Let B be the set of erasure locations and let A be the set of error locations; so $A - B$ is the set of error locations which are not erasure locations. Define

$$\sigma_B(x) = \prod_{i \in B} (\beta^i + x)$$

to be the *erasure locator polynomial*. Then we can express the error locator polynomial as

$$\sigma_A(x) = \sigma_B(x)\sigma_{A-B}(x).$$

Finding the unknown error locations requires finding the roots of $\sigma_{A-B}(x)$. Providing we can remove the effect of the erasures on the syndromes, finding the roots of $\sigma_{A-B}(x)$ can simply be done with Algorithm 6.3.2 (or Algorithm 6.5.1) using "modified" syndromes.

To see what the modified syndromes should be, we slightly alter the development of Algorithm 6.3.2. Write

$$\sigma_B(x) = B_0 + B_1 x + \cdots + B_{\epsilon-1} x^{\epsilon-1} + x^{\epsilon}$$

and

$$\sigma_{A-B}(x) = A_0 + A_1 x + \cdots + A_{e-1} x^{e-1} + x^e.$$

In the same way as (6.4) was obtained, multiply both sides of $\sigma_B(x)\sigma_{A-B}(x) = \sigma_A(x)$ by $b_i a_i^j$ (where $m + 1 \leq j \leq m + \delta - 1$, and $a_1, \ldots, a_{e+\epsilon}$ are the error location numbers) and substitute $x = a_i$, then sum both sides from $i = 1$ to $e + \epsilon$ to obtain

$$\begin{aligned}(B_0 s_j + B_1 s_{j+1} + \cdots + B_{\epsilon-1} s_{j+\epsilon-1} + s_{j+\epsilon}) A_0 \\ + (B_0 s_{j+1} + B_1 s_{j+2} + \cdots + B_{\epsilon-1} s_{j+\epsilon} + s_{j+\epsilon+1}) A_1 \\ + \cdots + (B_0 s_{j+e} + B_1 s_{j+e+1} + \cdots + s_{j+e+\epsilon}) = 0. \quad (6.8)\end{aligned}$$

So we form the *modified syndromes* by defining

$$s_j^* = B_0 s_j + B_1 s_{j+1} + \cdots + B_{\epsilon-1} s_{j+\epsilon-1} + s_{j+\epsilon}.$$

Since we know the values of s_j for $m + 1 \leq j \leq m + \delta - 1$ and since $B_0, \ldots, B_{\epsilon-1}$ are known, s_j^* is known for $m + 1 \leq j \leq \delta - 1 - \epsilon$. But since $2e + \epsilon \leq \delta - 1$,

$2e \leq \delta - 1 - \epsilon$ so as when writing (6.6), we can solve the linear system formed from (6.8):

$$\begin{bmatrix} s^*_{m+1} & s^*_{m+2} & \cdots & s^*_{m+e} \\ \vdots & \vdots & & \vdots \\ s^*_{m+e} & s^*_{m+e+1} & \cdots & s^*_{m+2e-1} \end{bmatrix} \begin{bmatrix} A_0 \\ A_1 \\ \vdots \\ A_{e-1} \end{bmatrix} = \begin{bmatrix} s^*_{m+e+1} \\ \vdots \\ s^*_{m+2e} \end{bmatrix} \tag{6.9}$$

for the e unknown values $A_0, A_1, \ldots, A_{e-1}$. □

We can now decode Reed-Solomon codes with erasures by modifying Algorithm 6.3.2 in the obvious manner suggested by the proof of Theorem 6.6.4.

Algorithm 6.6.5 (decoding erasures in $RS(2^r, \delta)$) Suppose that c is a codeword in an $RS(2^r, \delta)$ code C with generator $g(x) = (\beta^{m+1} + x) \cdots (\beta^{m+\delta-1} + x)$ that is transmitted and w is received containing ϵ erasures with erasure location numbers being the elements of $B = \{a_1, \ldots, a_\epsilon\}$. Let $\sigma_B(x) = (a_1 + x) \cdots (a_\epsilon + x) = B_0 + B_1 x + \cdots + B_{\epsilon-1} x^{\epsilon-1} + x^\epsilon$ be the erasure locator polynomial. The error locator polynomial $\sigma_A(x) = \sigma_{A-B}(x)\sigma_B(x)$ can be found by finding $\sigma_{A-B}(x) = A_0 + A_1 x + \cdots + A_{e-1} x^{e-1} + x^e$ as follows:

1. Calculate $s_j = w(\beta^j)$ for $m + 1 \leq j \leq m + \delta - 1$.
2. Calculate $s^*_j = B_0 s_j + B_1 s_{j+1} + \cdots + B_{\epsilon-1} s_{j+\epsilon-1} + s_{j+\epsilon}$ for $m + 1 \leq j \leq m + \delta - 1 - \epsilon$.
3. Solve the linear system (6.9) for $A_0, A_1, \ldots, A_{e-1}$.

Then decoding w can be completed using steps 4 and 5 of Algorithm 6.3.2.

As would now be expected, the modified syndromes of Algorithm 6.6.5 can be used to adapt Algorithm 6.5.1 for finding the error locator polynomial when erasures are included.

Algorithm 6.6.6 (Berlekamp-Massey decoding with erasures) Suppose C is an $RS(2^r, \delta)$ code with generator $g(x) = (\beta^{m+1} + x) \cdots (\beta^{m+\delta-1} + x)$ and let w be a received word. Let $\sigma_B(x) = B_0 + B_1 x + \cdots + x^\epsilon$ be the erasure locator polynomial of w. Modify Algorithm 6.5.1 for finding the error locator polynomial of w as follows:

1. Calculate $s_j = w(\beta^j)$ for $m + 1 \leq j \leq m + \delta - 1$.
2. Calculate $s^*_j = B_0 s_j + B_1 s_{j+1} + \cdots + B_{\epsilon-1} s_{j+\epsilon-1} + s_{j+\epsilon}$ for $m + 1 \leq j \leq m + \delta - 1 - \epsilon$.
3. Define

$$q_{-1}(x) = 1 + s^*_{m+1} x + s^*_{m+2} x^2 + \cdots + s^*_{m+\delta-1-\epsilon} x^{m+\delta-1-\epsilon},$$
$$q_0(x) = s^*_{m+1} + s^*_{m+2} x + \cdots + s^*_{m+\delta-2-\epsilon} x^{m+\delta-2-\epsilon},$$

and define $p_{-1}(x)$, $p_0(x)$, D_{-1}, D_0, and z_0 as in step 2 of Algorithm 6.5.1.

4. Repeat step 3 of Algorithm 6.5.1, except that i is now restricted to $1 \leq i \leq \delta - 1 - \epsilon$, to produce $\sigma_{A-B}(x)$. Then the error locator polynomial is $\sigma(x) = \sigma_B(x)\sigma_{A-B}(x)$.

Remark To complete the decoding, $b_1, b_2, \ldots, b_{\epsilon+e}$ can be found using step 5 of Algorithm 6.3.2 using the original syndromes; of course (6.7) is now a system of $\epsilon + e$ linear equations.

In the following examples we will use the code $\hat{C}'$ to transmit messages. Then from the structure of the code, some erasures can be recognized.

Example 6.6.7 Messages are encoded using $\hat{C}'$ where C is the $RS(2^4, 6)$ code with generator $g(x) = (1+x)(\beta+x)\cdots(\beta^4+x)$, where $GF(2^4)$ is constructed using $1+x+x^4$. Decode the received word

$$\hat{w}' = 11101\ 11001\ 00101\ 00000\ 00110\ 10010\ 0\ldots0.$$

The only erasure location number is β^1, and so

$$\sigma_B(x) = \beta + x.$$

We can now use Algorithm 6.6.6 to find the error locator polynomial for

$$w = \beta^{10}0\beta^2 0\beta^6\beta^{14}0\ldots0.$$

where we have set the digit in the position corresponding to the erasure equal to zero (this makes calculating the syndromes easier). Since $w(x) = \beta^{10} + \beta^2x^2 + \beta^6x^4 + \beta^{14}x^5$, we find that $s_0 = \beta^5$, $s_1 = 0$, $s_2 = \beta^3$, $s_3 = \beta^4$, and $s_4 = \beta^3$. Since $B_0 = \beta$ and $\epsilon = 1$, we find (from Step 2) that $s_0^* = \beta^6$, $s_1^* = \beta^3$, $s_2^* = 0$, and $s_3^* = \beta^{11}$. Proceeding as in Algorithm 6.5.1, but now using the modified syndromes, we obtain:

i			p_i					q_i			D_i	z_i
-1	1	β^6	β^3	0	β^{11}					1	-1	
0	β^6	β^3	0	β^{11}					1		0	-1
1	β^{10}	β^9	β^{11}					1	β^6		1	0
2	β^0	β^{11}					1	β^{12}			2	1
3	β^{10}					1	β^{14}	β^{11}			3	2
4					1	β^{11}	β^8				4	3

So $\sigma_{A-B}(x) = \beta^8 + \beta^{11}x + x^2$. Hence

$$\begin{aligned}\sigma_A(x) &= \sigma_B(x)\sigma_{A-B}(x)\\ &= (\beta+x)(\beta^8+\beta^{11}x+x^2)\\ &= (\beta+x)(\beta^3+x)(\beta^5+x).\end{aligned}$$

Therefore the error location numbers are $a_1 = \beta$, $a_2 = \beta^3$, and $a_3 = \beta^5$.

Of course we can then complete the decoding by finding b_1, b_2, and b_3: we use step 5 of Algorithm 6.3.2, the original syndromes and (6.7):

$$\begin{bmatrix} 1 & 1 & 1 \\ \beta & \beta^3 & \beta^5 \\ \beta^2 & \beta^6 & \beta^{10} \end{bmatrix} \begin{bmatrix} b_1 \\ b_2 \\ b_3 \end{bmatrix} = \begin{bmatrix} \beta^5 \\ 0 \\ \beta^3 \end{bmatrix},$$

or

$$\begin{bmatrix} 1 & 1 & 1 \\ 0 & \beta^9 & \beta^2 \\ 0 & 0 & 1 \end{bmatrix} \begin{bmatrix} b_1 \\ b_2 \\ b_3 \end{bmatrix} \begin{bmatrix} \beta^5 \\ \beta^6 \\ \beta^3 \end{bmatrix},$$

which gives $b_1 = \beta^{12}$, $b_2 = 1$ and $b_3 = \beta^3$. So $w(x)$ is decoded to

$$\begin{aligned} c(x) = w(x) + e(x) &= (\beta^{10} + \beta^2x^2 + \beta^6x^4 + \beta^{14}x^5) + (\beta^{12}x + x^3 + \beta^3x^5), \\ c(x) &\leftrightarrow \beta^{10}\beta^{12}\beta^2 1 \beta^6 10\ldots0, \end{aligned}$$

and $\hat{w}'$ is decoded to

$$11101\ 11110\ 00101\ 10001\ 00110\ 10001\ 0\ldots0.$$

Example 6.6.8 Messages are encoded using the code $\hat{C}'$ as defined in Example 6.6.7. Decode

$$\overline{f}(w) = 11101\ 11001\ 00101\ 00100\ 00110\ 10010\ 0\ldots0.$$

The erasure locator polynomial is

$$\sigma_B(x) = (\beta + x)(\beta^3 + x) = \beta^4 + \beta^9 x + x^2.$$

We decode

$$w = \beta^{10}0\beta^2 0\beta^6\beta^{14}0\ldots0$$

to a codeword in C (again, the digits in w occurring in positions corresponding to erasures have been set equal to 0). Since $w(x) = \beta^{10} + \beta^2x^2 + \beta^6x^4 + \beta^{14}x^5$, $s_0 = \beta^5$, $s_1 = 0$, $s_2 = \beta^3$, $s_3 = \beta^4$ and $s_4 = \beta^3$. Therefore, from Step 2 of Algorithm 6.6.6, $s_0^* = \beta$, $s_1^* = \beta^6$ and $s_2^* = \beta^{11}$.

i	p_i					q_i			D_i	z_i
-1	1	β^1	β^6	β^{11}				1	-1	
0	β^1	β^6	β^{11}				1		0	-1
1	β^3	β^8				1	β		1	1
2	0				1	β^5			2	2
3				1	β^5				4	3

So $\sigma_{A-B}(x) = \beta^5 + x$, so $\sigma_A(x) = (\beta + x)(\beta^3 + x)(\beta^5 + x)$ and the error magnitudes can be calculated as in Example 6.6.7.

When introducing the code $\hat{C}'$ with C an $RS(2^r, \delta)$ code, we noted that $\hat{C}'$ has minimum distance at least 2δ and so can correct all binary error patterns of weight at most $\delta - 1$. Using Algorithm 6.6.6 will find the closest codeword to a received word if at most $\delta - 1$ binary errors occur during transmission of $\hat{c}'$ as the following argument shows. Suppose that u is the most likely binary error pattern, that $\mathrm{wt}(u) \leq \delta - 1$, and that u causes ϵ erasures and e error which are not erasures. Then since at least 2 errors must be made in $\hat{w}'$ to cause an error which is not an erasure in w, we have that $2e + \epsilon \leq \delta - 1$. Then by Theorem 6.6.4, w (and so therefore $\hat{w}'$) will be decoded correctly.

However, if Algorithm 6.6.6 decodes $\hat{w}'$ to a codeword $\hat{c}$ that is further than $\delta - 1$ from $\hat{w}'$ then the reader should be critical of the answer as we have no guarantee that $\hat{c}'$ is the closest codeword to $\hat{w}'$.

Exercises

6.6.9 Let C be the $RS(2^3, 5)$ with generator $g(x) = (1 + x)(\beta + x)(\beta^2 + x)(\beta^3 + x)$ where $GF(2^3)$ is constructed using $1 + x + x^3$. Decode the following received words that were encoded with $\hat{C}'$ by using Algorithm 6.6.6:

(a) 1011 1010 1111 0011 1001 0000 0000

(b) 1011 0000 1000 0011 1010 0011 1001

(c) 0101 1000 0000 1100 1100 1100 0101

(d) 0000 1010 1011 1101 0111 1001 0000

6.6.10 Use the code $\hat{C}'$ defined in Example 6.6.7 and use Algorithm 6.6.6 to decode the following received words:

(a) 11101 11110 11010 00111 11110 10100 10110 10100 0 ... 0

(b) 11000 00000 01010 11111 11011 00000 10001 00101 0 ... 0

(c) 00000 10000 10000 10000 00101 10100 11101 0 ... 0

6.6.11 Let C be the $RS(2^4, 7)$ with generator $g(x) = (\beta + x) \cdots (\beta^6 + x)$ where $GF(2^4)$ is constructed using $1 + x + x^4$. Decode the following received word which was encoded using $\hat{C}'$:

01011 11011 10001 11011 01001 11101 11110 10000 0...0.

Chapter 7

Burst Error-Correcting Codes

7.1 Introduction

Until now we have only been interested in designing codes that correct randomly distributed errors. However there exist channels in which errors are likely to occur very close to each other. For example, a possible source of noise in a compact disc is a scratch across the disc: all digits occurring at the scratch may be either altered or erased causing a group of errors to occur close together. Also, sunspots are a factor in disrupting messages sent from satellites to earth, so once such activity starts in the sun we can expect several errors to occur close together. We call many errors occurring together in this fashion a *burst* of errors.

Suppose the polynomial $e(x)$ corresponding to the word e can be factored as $e(x) = x^k e'(x)$, where $e'(0) = 1$, then we say the *burst length* of e is $\deg(e'(x)) + 1$. So the burst length is the number of digits from the first 1 in e to the last 1 in e.

A related concept is the cyclic burst length of a word e. The word $e \in K^n$ is said to have *cyclic burst length* ℓ, if the minimum degree of $x^k e(x) \bmod (1+x^n)$ for $k = 0, 1, \ldots, n-1$ is $\ell - 1$.

Example 7.1.1 Let $n = 7$, and $e = 0101100$. Then $e(x) = x + x^3 + x^4 = x(1 + x^2 + x^3)$ and e therefore has burst length 4. If we consider $x^k e(x) \bmod (1+x^7)$, that is all cyclic shifts of e, we see that $x^6 e(x) \bmod (1+x^7)$ has the smallest degree, 3, and thus the cyclic burst length is also 4.

On the other hand $e = 1000100 \leftrightarrow 1 + x^4$ has burst length 5 but $1 + x^3 = x^3(1+x^4) \bmod (1+x^7)$ and thus e has cyclic burst length 4.

Up until now we have always assumed that the most likely error pattern is the error pattern that has least weight. This is based on the fundamental assumption that errors occur independently. In various actual situations this assumption is not valid and thus our error correction strategy must change.

Recall that in MLD for a linear code, we take as coset representatives the words of least *weight* in the cosets, and say that such a code is t error-correcting precisely when all the words of weight at most t are in different cosets of the code.

In the correction of burst error patterns, we take as coset representatives the error patterns with burst of least *length* in each coset. So a linear code is an ℓ *burst error-correcting code* if all the words of burst length at most ℓ are in different cosets of the code. In general, if C is t error-correcting and ℓ burst error-correcting, then $t \leq \ell$ (Why?) and this inequality may be strict (see Exercises 7.1.5, 7.1.6, and 7.1.7).

Similarly, a linear code is an *ℓ-cyclic burst error correcting code* if all error patterns of cyclic burst length at most ℓ are in different cosets.

Example 7.1.2 Consider all non-zero cyclic burst error patterns of length at most 3 in K^{15}. Each such non-zero error pattern is $e(x) = x^k e'(x)$, $k = 0, 1, \ldots, 14$ for $e'(x) \in \{1, 1+x, 1+x^2, 1+x+x^2\}$. Thus there are $4 \cdot 15 = 60$ such error patterns.

Example 7.1.3 Let $g(x) = 1+x+x^2+x^3+x^6$ be a generator for a cyclic linear code of length 15 and dimension 9. Clearly this code is not a 3 error-correcting code since there are 576 error patterns of weight 3 or less but there are only 64 cosets. However there are only 61 error patterns of cyclic burst length 3 or less (see Example 7.1.2) so this code may be, and in fact is, a 3 cyclic burst error-correcting code (see Exercise 7.1.4). This can be checked by calculating the syndromes of $x^k e'(x) \bmod g(x)$, $k = 0, 1, \ldots, 14$, and $e'(x) \in \{1, 1+x, 1+x^2, 1+x+x^2\}$.

Exercises

7.1.4 Verify that the cyclic burst error patterns of length 3 in K^{15} occur in different cosets for the code in Example 7.1.3.

7.1.5 Show that $g(x) = 1+x^2+x^4+x^5$ generates a 2 cyclic burst error-correcting linear code C of length 15. Is C a 2 error-correcting code?

7.1.6 Show that $g(x) = 1+x^3+x^4+x^5+x^6$ generates a 3 cyclic burst error-correcting linear cyclic codes of length 15. Is C a 3 error-correcting code? (Hint: Use the Hamming bound.)

7.1.7 Show that $g(x) = 1+x^4+x^6+x^7+x^8$ generates a 2 error-correcting, 4 cyclic burst error-correcting linear cyclic code of length 15.

As we have noticed, if C is a t error-correcting, ℓ burst error-correcting code then $\ell \geq t$. The following result gives an upper bound for the value ℓ. A better upper bound can be obtained (see Exercise 7.1.10) but this result will be sufficient for our purpose.

Theorem 7.1.8 *If C is an ℓ burst error-correcting linear code of length n and dimension k then $\ell \leq n-k$.*

Proof: Let C be an ℓ burst error-correcting linear (n, k) code. Then no two error patterns, each with burst of length at most ℓ occur together in the same coset. Therefore no two words in which all the 1's occur in the first ℓ positions can occur in the same coset. As there are 2^ℓ such words, there must be at least 2^ℓ cosets, and so $n-k \geq \ell$. □

Exercises

7.1.9 Verify that each of the codes in Exercises 7.1.5, 7.1.6 and 7.1.7 satisfy the bound of Theorem 7.1.8.

7.1.10 Show that if C is an ℓ burst error-correcting linear code of length n and dimension k then $\ell \leq (n-k)/2$. (Hint: show that any error pattern with burst of length 2ℓ can be written as the sum of two error patterns with bursts e_1 and e_2 respectively, each burst of which has length at most ℓ. Then show that $e_1 + e_2$ is not a codeword.)

It turns out that there is an excellent decoding algorithm for correcting cyclic burst error patterns if we use a linear cyclic code. Suppose that C is an ℓ burst error-correcting linear cyclic code with generator polynomial $g(x)$ of degree $n-k$. Recall from the discussion before Example 4.3.7 that

$$H = \begin{bmatrix} r_0 \\ r_1 \\ \vdots \\ r_{n-1} \end{bmatrix} = \begin{bmatrix} I_{n-k} \\ \text{---} \\ r_{n-k} \\ r_{n-k+1} \\ \vdots \\ r_{n-1} \end{bmatrix}$$

is a parity check matrix for C, where, for $1 \leq i \leq n-1$, r_i is the word of length $n-k$ that corresponds to the polynomial $r_i(x) = x^i \bmod g(x)$. By using H, if $w(x) = c(x) + e(x)$ is the received word, then it was shown that $w \leftrightarrow w(x)$ has syndrome $wH = s \leftrightarrow s(x) = w(x) \bmod g(x)$. There are two important facts that make C and H useful for decoding cyclic burst error patterns.

1. If $e \leftrightarrow e(x)$ is an error pattern with burst of length at most ℓ, then $\ell \leq n-k$ by Theorem 7.1.8. Therefore for some i with $0 \leq i \leq n-1$, the ith cyclic shift e_i of e has all its 1s in the first ℓ positions (that is, $x^i e(x) \bmod 1 + x^n \leftrightarrow e_i$ has degree less than ℓ).
2. It is easy to calculate the syndrome of w_i, the ith cyclic shift of w, since

$$\begin{aligned} s_i &= w_i H \\ &\leftrightarrow (x^i w(x) \bmod 1 + x^n) \bmod g(x) \\ &= x^i w(x) \bmod g(x) \quad (\text{since } g(x) \text{ divides } 1 + x^n) \\ &= x^i s(x) \bmod g(x). \end{aligned}$$

So to correct $w = c + e$ we can proceed as follows. For each i with $0 \leq i \leq n-1$ in turn we calculate the syndrome $s_i \leftrightarrow x^i s(x) \bmod g(x)$ (by fact 2) of w_i until we find one, say s_j, such that $\deg(s_j(x)) < \ell$. So to correct $w = c + e$ we can proceed as follows. For each i with $0 \le i \le n-1$ in turn we calculate the syndrome $s_i \leftrightarrow x^i s(x) \bmod g(x)$ (by fact 2) of w_i until we find one, say s_j, such that $\deg(s_j(x)) < \ell$. At this point, since the first $n-k$ rows of H form an identity matrix, we know that $e_j = s_j 00\ldots0$, formed by appending k 0s to the end of s_j, has syndrome $e_j H = s_j$. Since C is cyclic, we therefore know that $w_j = c_j + e_j$, where c_j is the codeword formed by the jth cyclic shift of c. Thus, we can shift e_j back through j cyclic shifts to find $e = e_0$, the most likely cyclic burst error pattern. This gives the following algorithm.

Algorithm 7.1.11 (decoding cyclic burst error patterns) Suppose w is a received word that was encoded using an ℓ-cyclic burst error correcting cyclic linear code with generator polynomial $g(x)$.

1. Calculate the syndrome polynomial $s(x) = w(x) \bmod g(x)$.
2. For each $i \ge 0$, calculate $s_i(x) = x^i s(x) \bmod g(x)$ until a syndrome polynomial $s_j(x)$ is found with $\deg(s_j(x)) \le \ell - 1$. Then the most likely cyclic burst error pattern is $e(x) = x^{n-j} s_j(x) \bmod (1+x^n)$.

Example 7.1.12 $g(x) = 1+x+x^2+x^3+x^6$ generates a 3-cyclic burst error-correcting linear cyclic code of length 15. Use Algorithm 7.1.11 to decode the received word 111100100001010, assuming that cyclic burst error patterns are most likely to occur.

1. $$\begin{aligned} s(x) &= 1+x+x^2+x^3+x^6+x^{11}+x^{13} \bmod g(x) \\ &= 1+x^3+x^4+x^5 \end{aligned}$$
2. $$\begin{aligned} s_1(x) &= xs(x) \bmod g(x) = 1+x^2+x^3+x^4+x^5, \\ s_2(x) &= x^2 s(x) \bmod g(x) = 1+x^2+x^4+x^5, \\ s_3(x) &= x^3 s(x) \bmod g(x) = 1+x^2+x^5, \\ s_4(x) &= x^4 s(x) \bmod g(x) = 1+x^2, \end{aligned}$$

and $\deg(s_4(x)) = 2 \le \ell - 1$. Therefore the most likely error pattern is

$$\begin{aligned} e(x) &= x^{15-4} s_4(x) \bmod (1+x^{15}) \\ &= x^{11}+x^{13}. \end{aligned}$$

So the most likely codeword sent is

$$\begin{aligned} c(x) = w(x)+e(x) &= 1+x+x^2+x^3+x^6 \\ &\leftrightarrow 111100100000000. \end{aligned}$$

Exercises

7.1.13 $g(x) = 1+x+x^2+x^3+x^6$ generates a 3 cyclic burst error correcting linear cyclic code C of length 15. Decode the following received words that were encoded using C.

(a) 101101110001000 (b) 001101100010101
(c) 100110101010011 (d) 101101000010111
(e) 000000111110000.

7.1.14 $g(x) = 1 + x^2 + x^4 + x^5$ generates a 2 cyclic burst error-correcting linear cyclic code C of length 15. Decode the following received words that were encoded using C.

(a) 010101000010010 (b) 011010010010100
(c) 001101000000100 (d) 000100010100101
(e) 000000011111001.

Reed-Solomon codes also have good burst error correction capability. Recall that if C is an $RS(2^r, \delta)$ code then $\hat{C}$ is the binary representation of C (see Example 6.2.6).

Theorem 7.1.15 *Let C be an $RS(2^r, 2t+1)$ code. Then $\hat{C}$ is an ℓ burst error correcting code, where $\ell \geq r(t-1)+1$.*

Proof: Any burst error pattern e of length at most $r(t-1)+1$ produces a word $\hat{w} = \hat{c} + e$, where $d(w, c) \leq t$. So w is decoded to the codeword c in the $RS(2^r, 2t+1)$ code and therefore $\hat{c}$ is the closest codeword in $\hat{C}$ to $\hat{w}$. □

Two places where Reed-Solomon codes are used are in compact discs, where scratches on the disc cause bursts of errors, and in space communications by NASA and the ESA, where sunspots cause bursts of errors in the transmissions which are in the form of electromagnetic waves. Under such circumstances, assuming that errors occur in bursts is a better model than the assumption of random errors.

Example 7.1.16 The $RS(8, 5)$ code of Exercise 6.2.8 will correct all burst error patterns of length at most $r(t-1)+1 = 4$.

7.2 Interleaving

One method for improving the burst error correcting capability of a code is to make use of interleaving. This technique rearranges the order in which code digits are transmitted. Until now, messages $m_1, m_2, \ldots$ have been encoded to corresponding codewords $c_1, c_2, \ldots$ and these codewords are transmitted in turn. Suppose now that the first s codewords are selected, then the first digit from each of these s codewords is transmitted, followed by the second digits, third digits, and so on. Once all ns digits in the first s codewords have been transmitted in this order, the same process is applied to the second set of s codewords to be sent, then the third set, and so on. This rearrangement of the order in which codeword digits are transmitted is called *interleaving to depth s*. More formally, interleaving

$c_1, c_2, \ldots$ to depth s requires that for $i = 0, 1, 2\ldots$ in turn the codeword digits are transmitted in the order:

$$c_{is+1,1}, c_{is+2,1}, \ldots, c_{is+s,1}, c_{is+1,2}, c_{is+2,2}, \ldots, c_{is+s,2}, \ldots, c_{is+1,n}, \ldots, c_{is+s,n}.$$

It is probably simpler to see this ordering by listing each of the codewords c_{is+1}, $\ldots, c_{is+s}$ row by row (see Table 7.1), then transmitting these digits column by column.

$$\begin{array}{ccccc} c_{is+1,1} & c_{is+1,2} & c_{is+1,3} & \cdots & c_{is+1,n} \\ c_{is+2,1} & c_{is+2,2} & c_{is+2,3} & \cdots & c_{is+2,n} \\ \vdots & \vdots & \vdots & & \vdots \\ c_{is+s,1} & c_{is+s,2} & c_{is+s,3} & \cdots & c_{is+s,n} \end{array}$$

Table 7.1: *Interleaving to depth s.*

Example 7.2.1 Let C be the linear code with generating matrix

$$G = \begin{bmatrix} 1 & 0 & 0 & 1 & 1 & 0 \\ 0 & 1 & 0 & 1 & 0 & 1 \\ 0 & 0 & 1 & 0 & 1 & 1 \end{bmatrix}.$$

With no interleaving, the codewords

$$\begin{aligned} c_1 &= 100110, & c_4 &= 010101, \\ c_2 &= 010101, & c_5 &= 100110, \text{ and} \\ c_3 &= 111000, & c_6 &= 111000 \end{aligned}$$

would be sent one after the other, so the code digits would be sent in the following order:

$$100110\;010101\;111000\;010101\;100110\;111000.$$

If these codewords are interleaved to depth 3, then the first digits of c_1, c_2 and c_3, namely $1, 0$ and 1 are transmitted first, followed by their second digits 0, 1 and 1, and so on. So the digits in c_1, c_2 and c_3 are transmitted in the following order:

$$101\;011\;001\;110\;100\;010.$$

Notice that in this string, the digits in c_1 appear in positions $3i+1$, for $0 \leq i \leq 5$. Notice also that with c_1, c_2 and c_3 written in rows as in Table 7.1, the digits are simply transmitted column by column. After these 21 digits have been transmitted, a similar rearrangement of the digits in c_4, c_5 and c_6 is used and so those digits are transmitted in the order:

$$011\;101\;001\;110\;010\;100.$$

What is the effect of interleaving to depth s on the burst error correcting capabilities of a code C? Notice that if the first digit of a codeword c is the ith digit transmitted, then the remaining digits occur in positions $i+s, i+2s, \ldots, i+(n-1)s$. Suppose that C is an ℓ burst error correcting code. If C is interleaved to depth s then any burst of errors of length at most $s\ell$ during transmission will produce a burst error pattern of length at most ℓ in c, so c will be decoded correctly, providing that this is the only burst error pattern that affects c. Therefore we have the following result.

Theorem 7.2.2 *Let C be an ℓ burst error correcting code. If C is interleaved to depth s then all bursts of length at most $s\ell$ will be corrected, providing that each codeword is affected by at most one burst of errors.*

Remark The provision that each codeword is affected by at most one burst of errors essentially requires that bursts of errors are separated by periods of error free transmission which are sufficiently long to avoid two bursts of errors affecting one block of s codewords. So choosing s to be large increases the burst length that Theorem 7.2.2 guarantees can be corrected, but also increases the length of error free transmission surrounding the burst required by Theorem 7.2.2.

Example 7.2.3 The code C in Example 7.2.1 is a 1 error-correcting code. When interleaved to depth 3 it corrects all bursts of length 3.

Exercises

7.2.4 Encode the messages $m_1 = 1000, m_2 = 0110, m_3 = 1110, m_4 = 0011, m_5 = 0110, m_6 = 0001$, then find the string of digits transmitted if the code is interleaved to depth s, where

$$G = \begin{bmatrix} 1000110 \\ 0100101 \\ 0010011 \\ 0001111 \end{bmatrix}.$$

(a) $s = 1$ (b) $s = 2$ (c) $s = 3$

7.2.5 In Example 7.1.3, it was stated that $g(x) = 1 + x + x^2 + x^3 + x^6$ is the generator for a linear cyclic code C of length 15 that is a 3 cyclic burst error correcting code. Use the generating matrix

$$G = \begin{bmatrix} 1\,1\,1\,1\,0\,0\,1\,0\,0\,0\,0\,0\,0\,0\,0 \\ 0\,1\,1\,1\,1\,0\,0\,1\,0\,0\,0\,0\,0\,0\,0 \\ \vdots \\ 0\,0\,0\,0\,0\,0\,0\,0\,1\,1\,1\,1\,0\,0\,1 \end{bmatrix}$$

for C to encode the messages $m_1(x) = 1$, $m_2(x) = x^2$, $m_3(x) = 1 + x$, $m_4(x) = 1 + x^2$, $m_5(x) = x^3$, and $m_6(x) = 1$. Find the string of digits transmitted if C is interleaved to depth s, where

(a) $s = 1$ (b) $s = 2$ (c) $s = 3$.

In each case, what does Theorem 7.2.2 say about the burst error correcting capability of the code?

In practice, interleaving to depth s has the disadvantage that s codewords must be encoded before any of them are transmitted. This drawback can be overcome by using *s-frame delayed interleaving*, which lists the digits in each codeword as in Table 7.2 (compare this with Table 7.1) and again transmits the digits column by column. The array in Table 7.2 has n rows. Each codeword c_i has exactly one digit $c_{i,j}$ in row j (for $1 \leq i \leq n$) and $c_{i,j+1}$ is one row below and s columns across from $c_{i,j}$ (for $1 \leq j \leq n-1$).

$$\begin{array}{llllllll}
c_{1,1}\ c_{2,1}\ \cdots & c_{s+1,1} & c_{s+2,1}\ \cdots & c_{2s+1,1} & c_{2s+2,1} & \cdots & c_{(n-1)s+1,1} & \cdots \\
 & c_{1,2} & c_{2,2}\ \cdots & c_{s+1,2} & c_{s+2,2} & \cdots & c_{(n-2)s+1,2} & \cdots \\
 & & & c_{1,3} & c_{2,3} & \cdots & c_{(n-3)s+1,3} & \cdots \\
 & & & & & & \vdots & \\
 & & & & & & c_{1,n} & \cdots
\end{array}$$

Table 7.2: *s-frame delayed interleaving.*

Clearly there is some initialization process that must take place when using s-frame delayed interleaving, since for example if $s \geq 1$ then the only entry defined in the first column of Table 7.2 is $c_{1,1}$. To ensure that each column of Table 7.2 contains n digits we place a 0 in any position that contains no codeword digits. The following example makes this clear, though the 0's introduced in this initialization process have been replaced by $*$ to distinguish them from the 0 codeword digits.

Example 7.2.6 Consider again the six codewords $c_1, \ldots, c_6$ of Example 7.2.1. If we use 1-frame delayed interleaving, the Table 7.2 becomes

$$\begin{array}{cccccccccccc}
1 & 0 & 1 & 0 & 1 & 1 & \cdots & & & & & \\
* & 0 & 1 & 1 & 1 & 0 & 1 & \cdots & & & & \\
* & * & 0 & 0 & 1 & 0 & 0 & 1 & \cdots & & & \\
* & * & * & 1 & 1 & 0 & 1 & 1 & 0 & \cdots & & \\
* & * & * & * & 1 & 0 & 0 & 0 & 1 & 0 & \cdots & \\
* & * & * & * & * & 0 & 1 & 0 & 1 & 0 & 0 & \cdots
\end{array}$$

where we have placed $*$ in the positions where the initialization process defines the entry 0. The string of digits transmitted is

$$1 * * * * * 0 0 * * * * 1 1 0 * * * 0 1 0 1 * * \ldots.$$

If we use 2-frame delayed interleaving, then Table 7.2 becomes

$$\begin{array}{ccccccccccccccccc}
1 & 0 & 1 & 0 & 1 & 1 & \ldots & & & & & & & & & & \\
* & * & 0 & 1 & 1 & 1 & 0 & 1 & \ldots & & & & & & & & \\
* & * & * & * & 0 & 0 & 1 & 0 & 0 & 1 & \ldots & & & & & & \\
* & * & * & * & * & * & 1 & 1 & 0 & 1 & 1 & 0 & \ldots & & & & \\
* & * & * & * & * & * & * & * & 1 & 0 & 0 & 0 & 1 & 0 & \ldots & & \\
* & * & * & * & * & * & * & * & * & * & 0 & 1 & 0 & 1 & 0 & 0 & \ldots
\end{array}$$

and the string of digits transmitted is

$$1 * * * * * 0 * * * * * 1 0 * * * * 0 1 * * * * 1 1 0 * * * \ldots$$

It is easy to get the analogue of Theorem 7.2.2 for s-frame delayed interleaving.

Theorem 7.2.7 *Let C be an ℓ burst error correcting code. If C is s-frame delay interleaved then all bursts of length $\ell(sn+1)$ will be corrected, providing that each codeword is affected by at most one burst of errors.*

Exercises

7.2.8 Use s-frame delayed interleaving and the codewords found in Exercise 7.2.4 to find the string of digits transmitted when

(a) $s = 1$ (b) $s = 2$.

7.2.9 What string of digits is transmitted if 0-frame delayed interleaving is used?

7.2.10 Prove Theorem 7.2.7.

In practice, the encoding of a message often uses 2 codes. For example, 2 codes are used in the encoding of music on to compact discs (see Section 7.3) where both codes are Reed-Solomon codes, and 2 codes are used by NASA and the European Space Agency, where one code is a Reed-Solomon code, the other a convolutional code (see Section 8.2). Interleaving to depth s is an important technique in this 2 step encoding, as we shall now see.

Let C_1 be an (n_1, k_1, d_1) linear code and C_2 an (n_2, k_2, d_2) linear code. *Cross-interleaving* of C_1 *with* C_2 is done as follows. Messages are first encoded using C_1 and the resulting codewords are interleaved to depth k_2. The columns formed (as in Table 7.1) in this interleaving process are all of length k_2, so can now be regarded as messages and encoded using C_2. The codewords resulting from this second encoding can themselves be interleaved to any depth s, or s-frame delay interleaved.

The main advantage of this 2 step encoding is the following. C_2 can be used to detect $d_2 - 1$ errors, rather than to correct errors. If errors are detected in a codeword in C_2 then all digits in this codeword are flagged and treated as digits that may be incorrect. The codewords in C_1 are then considered. Notice that if we know that $n_1 - d_1 + 1$ digits in a codewords c in C_1 are correct then we can always find the remaining $d_1 - 1$ digits. (This is so because it is impossible for another codeword in C_1 to agree with c in the $n_1 - d_1 + 1$ correct digits since all codewords disagree in at least d_1 positions.) Therefore, if each codeword in C_1 contains at most $d_1 - 1$ flagged digits, and if we assume that all incorrect digits are flagged, then the codewords will be decoded correctly.

Example 7.2.11 Let C_1 and C_2 be the codes with generating matrices

$$G_1 = \begin{bmatrix} 10001110 \\ 01001101 \\ 00101011 \\ 00010111 \end{bmatrix} \text{ and } G_2 = \begin{bmatrix} 100110 \\ 010101 \\ 001011 \end{bmatrix}$$

respectively. Then, $(n_1, k_1, d_1) = (8, 4, 4)$ and $(n_2, k_2, d_2) = (6, 3, 3)$. We shall encode the messages $m_1 = 1000, m_2 = 1100$ and $m_3 = 1010$ by the cross interleaving of C_1 with C_2, C_2 being interleaved to depth $s = 3 = d_1 - 1$. Encoding m_1, m_2 and m_3 with C_1 gives:

$$\begin{aligned} c_1 &= m_1 G_1 = 10001110, \\ c_2 &= m_2 G_1 = 11000011, \text{ and} \\ c_3 &= m_3 G_1 = 10100101. \end{aligned}$$

The columns produced by interleaving these codewords to depth $k_2 = 3$ produces the messages

$$111,\ 010,\ 001,\ 000,\ 100,\ 101,\ 110,\ \text{and } 011.$$

These are encoded using C_2 to produce 8 codewords that are then to be interleaved to depth $s = 3$:

$$\begin{array}{lll} c'_1 = 111000 & c'_4 = 000000 & c'_7 = 110011 \\ c'_2 = 010101 & c'_5 = 100110 & c'_8 = 011110 \\ c'_3 = 001011 & c'_6 = 101101 & \end{array}$$

(c'_7 and c'_8 will be interleaved with the first codeword c'_9 produced from the next 3 messages m_4, m_5 and m_6.) So the string of digits transmitted begins

$$100\ 110\ 101\ 010\ 001\ 011\ 011\ 000\ 001\ 011\ 010\ 001\ \ldots.$$

To see how decoding proceeds, suppose the first 6 digits are transmitted incorrectly; so

$$011\ 001\ 101\ 010\ 001\ 011\ \ldots$$

is received. Removing the effect of the interleaving to depth $s = 3$ leaves the received words of length $n_2 = 6$:

$$0\,0\,1\,0\,0\,0,\ 1\,0\,0\,1\,0\,1 \text{ and } 1\,1\,1\,0\,1\,1$$

(notice that compared to c'_1, c'_2 and c'_3 respectively, each of these has errors in the first 2 positions). C_2 detects errors in all 3 codewords (show that the syndrome wH_2 of each of these received words w is not 0, where H_2 is a parity check matrix for C_2), so all 18 digits are flagged (we shall replace them with an $*$). Assuming that there are no more errors, after carrying out a similar process for the subsequent received digits, $c'_4, c'_5, \ldots, c'_8$ contain no flagged digits. Then, removing the effect of the interleaving of depth $k_2 = 3$ leaves three words of length $n_1 = 8$:

$$c_1 = * * * 0 1 1 1 0$$
$$c_2 = * * * 0 0 0 1 1$$
$$c_3 = * * * 0 0 1 0 1.$$

There is exactly one way to replace each flagged digit with a 0 or a 1 to produce codewords, and the codewords produced are c_1, c_2 and c_3. Notice that each of the above has only $3 = d_1 - 1$ flagged digits.

Exercises

7.2.12 Use the codes C_1 and C_2 to encode the following sets of messages by cross interleaving C_1 with C_2, with C_2 being interleaved to depth s.

(a) $m_1 = 0110, m_2 = 1011, m_3 = 1111, s = 2$

(b) $m_1 = 0110, m_2 = 1011, m_3 = 1111, s = 3$

(c) $m_1 = 0010, m_2 = 1111, m_3 = 1010, s = 3$

(d) $m_1 = 1000$, $m_2 = 0100$, $m_3 = 0010$, $m_4 = 0001$, $m_5 = 0011$, $m_6 = 0100$, $s = 3$

7.2.13 The following string of digits was originally encoded by cross interleaving the codes C_1 and C_2 of Example 7.2.11, C_2 being interleaved to depth 3. Decode the following strings by finding the most likely messages m_1, m_2, and m_3.

(a) 000001001110110001000111000111000111000000000000000000...

(b) 100011001111101010011001111010100110100100011101000100....

7.2.14 Let C_i be an (n_i, k_i, d_i) linear code for $1 \leq i \leq 2$. Suppose C_1 is cross-interleaved with C_2 to form codewords. Find how long a burst of errors the decoding algorithm described before Example 7.2.11 will correct if these codewords are

(a) interleaved to depth s, or

(b) s-frame delay interleaved

before they are transmitted.

7.3 Application to compact discs

The recording of music on compact discs has taken the music-loving world by storm. The high quality reproduction from compact disc players is due in large part to the error correcting codes that are used when storing the music. Each compact disc contains a spiral track in which pits (lower levels) have been made. A laser beam following the spiral track determines where changes in height in the spiral track occur by detecting changes in the intensity of the light reflected by the compact disc. In this way, a binary string of digits is produced, each change in height corresponding to the digit 1, an absence of a change in height being a 0 digit.

0 0 0 0 0 1 0 0 1 0 0 0 1 0 0 0 0 0 1 0 0

During the recording, the music is sampled 44, 100 times per second, the amplitude of the sound wave at each sample being assigned a binary word of length 16. So the range of amplitudes is divided into 2^{16} values. Recording in stereo requires 2 amplitude measurements to be taken 44, 100 times per second, one from the left and one from the right.

For encoding purposes, each binary word of length 16 corresponding to an amplitude measurement is represented by 2 field elements in $GF(2^8)$; we refer to each field element as a *byte*. So when recording in stereo, 4 bytes $m_{4t}, m_{4t+1}, m_{4t+2}$, and m_{4t+3} are produced at each "tick" t (calling $1/44, 100^{\text{th}}$ of a second a *tick*). Then measurements of the amplitude from 6 consecutive ticks $m_{24t}, m_{24t+1}, \ldots,$ m_{24t+23} are grouped together to form a message M_t of length 24, each byte being in $GF(2^8)$. Let C be an $RS(2^8, 5)$ code. Then M_t is encoded to the codeword c_t using the code $C_1 = C(227)$, the shortened Reed-Solomon code over $GF(2^8)$ with $(n_1, k_1, d_1) = (28, 24, 5)$ (see Example 6.2.11).

The codewords in C, thus produced are then 4-frame delay interleaved (see Table 7.2). Notice that each column in the array in Table 7.2 in this case has length $n_1 = 28$. Also, since the bytes of the codeword c_t occur in columns $t, t+4, t+8, \ldots, t+108$, it is natural to label the bytes in c_t with $c_{1,t}, c_{2,t+4}, c_{3,t+8}, \ldots, c_{28,t+108}$.

Column t of the array in Table 7.2 contains the bytes $c_{1,t}, c_{2,t}, \ldots, c_{28,t}$ (recall that $c_{i,j}$ is the ith byte in the codeword $c_{j-4(i-1)}$), and these are now used as messages of length 28 over $GF(2^8)$ that then are encoded using $C_2 = C(223)$, the shortened Reed-Solomon code over $GF(2^8)$ with $(n_2, k_2, d_2) = (32, 28, 5)$.

To each codeword in C_2, one further byte is added for control and display purposes, so codewords now have length 33.

Up until now, all bytes carry information or have been added for error correction and detection purposes. However, physical limitations of the laser tracking make it desirable that changes in height in the spiral track do not occur too close together nor too far apart. It was therefore determined that in the binary representation of each codeword, between any two 1's there should be at least two and at most ten 0's. The Reed-Solomon codewords do not have this property. However there are exactly 267 binary words of length 14 that do have this property. The 256 field elements are matched to 256 of these words using a table look up, 11 of the 267 words being discarded. This process is called *eight to fourteen modulation* (EFM). Then, to make sure that the property holds between the words of length 14, 3 further bits (0's or 1's) are added. So now, the binary representation of each codeword has length $33 \times 17 = 561$.

Finally, to each codeword, a binary word of length 27 is added for synchronization purposes, which also has the above property. Therefore in total, audio information from 6 consecutive ticks is initially stored as a binary vector of length $24 \times 8 = 196$, and after all the processes are complete, appear on the compact disc as a binary word of length 588.

It remains to discuss the decoding. First, all extra manipulation such as the EFM (see also the remark at the end of this section) is undone to leave "received" words which are hopefully codewords in C_1. C_2 is used to correct all single errors. However if more than one error is detected then all bytes in the received word are flagged (see Section 7.2 on cross-interleaving). The effect of the 4-frame delay interleaving is then removed. Finally C_1 is used to correct up to 4 erasures (recall C_1 has distance 5), treating all flagged bytes as erasures, and all unflagged bytes as being correct.

How good is this decoding? First, notice that the only way that the decoding using C_2 can go wrong is if the received word is within distance 1 of a C_2 codeword that is not the right codeword. There are very few error patterns that will do this! There are $(2^r)^k = (2^8)^{28} = 2^{224}$ codewords in C_2, one of which is the right codeword. Each of the remaining $2^{224} - 1$ codewords is within distance 1 of $1 + 32(2^8 - 1)$ words of length 32. So of all $(2^8)^{32}$ binary error patterns that might be added to a C_2 codeword, only $(2^{224} - 1)(1 + 32(2^8 - 1))$ of them result in a word within distance 1 of a different C_2 codeword; that is about 1 in 2^{19} of them. This correction of single error by C_2 is designed to cope with small random errors caused by inaccuracies in the coating and cutting of the compact discs.

Secondly, after the effect of the 4-frame delay interleaving is removed, a received word will be decoded to the correct codeword in C_1 if it contains at most 4 flagged digits (and assuming that C_2 detects all errors, which we just saw is very likely). But for a single burst to affect 5 digits of a C_1 codeword, it would have to affect 17 columns of the array in Table 7.2, or more precisely, at least $15 \times 32 + 2 + 2$ bytes (if 2 bytes are altered in the first or seventeenth columns, then all bytes in that column are flagged by C_2). Since each column of Table 7.2 is represented by a word of length 588 on the compact disc, all bursts of length $(15 \times 588) + (3 \times 17) = 8871$ (or if you prefer, all bursts affecting $(15 \times 24 \times 8) + (3 \times 8) = 2904$ audio bits) are decoded correctly. This burst length corresponds to approximately 2.5mm of track length on the compact disc.

Remark Here we have presented the most important aspects of the encoding process. In practice, several other interleaving operations are incorporated into the encoding.

For example, the bytes in the odd numbered positions in the codewords in C_2 are all moved along $n_2 = 32$ positions, so they are mixed with the bytes in the even numbered positions of the following codeword. This is done to improve the chances of correcting single errors with C_2, since now 2 consecutive errors affect different codewords.

Also, the bytes within codewords in C_1 are reorganized. Such a codeword contains information from 6 consecutive ticks from the left and right, say $L_1, \dots, L_6$ and $R_1, \dots, R_6$ as well as two parity symbols Q_1 and Q_2 added when encoding with C_1. These are arranged in the following order:

$$L_1\ L_3\ L_5\ R_1\ R_3\ R_5\ Q_1\ Q_2\ L_2\ L_4\ L_6\ R_2\ R_4\ R_6.$$

The point of this is that if several consecutive bytes are still flagged after the decoding process, they can be treated as unreliable information. In such a case, an unreliable value say L_i can be replaced by an amplitude found by interpolating the (hopefully) reliable values of L_{i-1} and L_{i+1}. For example, if the values L_3, L_5, R_1, R_3, R_5, Q_1 and Q_2 are all still flagged, L_3 can be found by "averaging" the amplitudes of the reliable values of L_2 and L_4, and so on.

Chapter 8

Convolutional Codes

8.1 Shift registers and polynomials

One reason cyclic codes are so useful is that polynomial encoding and decoding can be implemented easily and efficiently by hardware devices known as *shift registers*. Briefly, these devices consist of n registers (or delay elements) and a "clock" which controls the movement or shifting of the data contained in the registers. After each clock "tick," the new contents of the registers are combined (binary addition) to form the output. In Figure 8.1, the squares denote registers; arrows indicate the flow of data, and $\oplus$ means binary addition.

Example 8.1.1 In the shift register of Figure 8.1, we have four registers X_0, X_1, X_2, X_3 each containing binary digits. As the arrows indicate, the output at each clock tick is formed by adding the contents of the registers X_0, X_1, and X_3. Suppose registers X_0, X_1, X_2, and X_3 contain 1, 1, 0, and 1 respectively. If the next input digit is 0, then at the next clock tick, the input digit is "shifted" into X_0 and at the same time the contents of each register is shifted into the next. The new contents of X_0, X_1, X_2, X_3 will be $0, 1, 1, 0$, and the output digit will be $0+1+0=1$.

Suppose we have an input sequence $a_0, a_1, \ldots$, etc. then we can keep track of the input, output and contents of the registers at each clock tick by means of a table.

Example 8.1.2 Consider the 4-stage shift register in Figure 8.1. Assume the contents of the registers is initially $(0,0,0,0)$ and the input stream $a_0, a_1, a_2, \ldots a_6$ is

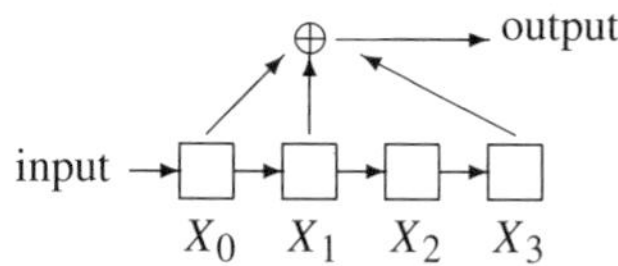

Figure 8.1: *A shift register.*

1010000. The contents of the registers and outputs are summarized in the following table.

time	input	$X_0X_1X_2X_3$	output $= X_0+X_1+X_3$
-1	—	0000	—
0	1	1000	1
1	0	0100	1
2	1	1010	1
3	0	0101	0
4	0	0010	0
5	0	0001	1
6	0	0000	0

Thus the shift register outputs 1110010 for input 1010000, where the initial state of the registers was 0000.

In general, an s-*stage* shift register is a shift register with s registers. The output of an s-stage shift register is a linear combination of the contents of the registers and can be described using coefficients $g_0, g_1, \ldots, g_{s-1}$, with $g_i \in K = \{0, 1\}$; that is, $c_t = g_0X_0(t) + \cdots + g_{s-1}X_{s-1}(t)$ where c_t is the output at time t and $X_i(t)$ is the value of the contents of register X_i at time t.

The action of these devices can be described in terms of polynomials. If $g_0, g_1, \ldots, g_{s-1}$ are the coefficients of the s-stage shift register then $g(x) = g_0 + g_1x + \cdots + g_{s-1}x^{n-1}$ is the polynomial corresponding to this shift register; this polynomial is the *generator* of the shift register. For instance $g(x) = 1 + x + x^3$ is the generator of the 4-stage shift register in Figure 8.1. If we represent the input and output sequences by polynomials $a(x)$ and $c(x)$, then we claim that for input sequences $a(x)$, the shift register with polynomial $g(x)$ will output $c(x) = a(x)g(x)$.

Example 8.1.3 Let $g(x) = 1 + x + x^3$, the polynomial corresponding to the shift register in Figure 8.1. The input sequence 1010000 corresponds to $a(x) = 1 + x^2$. Assuming the 4 registers all contain 0, then from Example 8.1.2 we know that the output sequence of the device will be 1110010, or $c(x) = 1 + x + x^2 + x^5$. But,

$$\begin{aligned} a(x)g(x) &= (1 + x^2)(1 + x + x^3) \\ &= 1 + x + x^2 + x^5 \\ &= c(x). \end{aligned}$$

Example 8.1.4 Let $g(x) = 1 + x + x^3$ be the polynomial associated with the shift register of Figure 8.1. The following table gives us the output sequence for the arbitrary input sequence $a_0, a_1, a_2, a_3, 0, 0, 0$.

time	input	X_0	X_1	X_2	X_3	output $= X_0 + X_1 + X_3$
-1	——	0	0	0	0	——
0	a_0	a_0	0	0	0	a_0
1	a_1	a_1	a_0	0	0	$a_1 + a_0$
2	a_2	a_2	a_1	a_0	0	$a_2 + a_1$
3	a_3	a_3	a_2	a_1	a_0	$a_3 + a_2 + a_0$
4	0	0	a_3	a_2	a_1	$a_3 + a_1$
5	0	0	0	a_3	a_2	a_2
6	0	0	0	0	a_3	a_3

Clearly,

$$\begin{aligned} a(x)g(x) &= (a_0 + a_1x + a_2x^2 + a_3x^3)(1 + x + x^3) \\ &= a_0 + (a_1 + a_0)x + (a_2 + a_1)x^2 \\ &\quad + (a_3 + a_2 + a_0)x^3 + (a_3 + a_1)x^4 + a_2x^5 + a_3x^6 \\ &= c(x) \end{aligned}$$

and the coefficients of $c(x)$ correspond to the output sequence of the device.

Given a fixed generator polynomial $g(x)$ of degree $n-k$ for a cyclic linear code one can build an $n-k+1$ stage shift register with generator $g(x)$ to implement polynomial encoding of information polynomials $a(x)$.

Exercises

8.1.5 Draw the diagrams for the shift registers corresponding to generator polynomials $g(x)$:

(a) $1 + x$ (b) $1 + x^2$

(c) $1 + x^2 + x^3$ (d) $1 + x^3 + x^4$

8.1.6 Use the shift registers constructed in Exercise 8.1.5 to compute $a(x)g(x) = c(x)$. Compute $a(x)g(x)$ directly and compare the results.

(a) $g(x) = 1 + x^2$, $a(x) = 1 + x$

(b) $g(x) = 1 + x^3 + x^4$, $a(x) = 1 + x^3 + x^6$

(c) $g(x) = 1 + x^2 + x^3$, $a(x) = x + x^2$

(d) $g(x) = 1 + x^3 + x^4$, $a(x) = x^2 + x^5 + x^6$

8.1.7 For the shift register in Figure 8.1, with $g(x) = 1 + x + x^3$, compute the output sequence $c_0, c_1, \ldots$ for each input sequence $a_0, a_1, \ldots$ below. Assume registers are all initially zero.

(a) $10101000\ldots$

(b) $0011000\ldots$

(c) $1010010000\ldots$

Now we show that, in general, shift registers accomplish polynomial multiplication. Let $a(x) = a_0 + a_1x + \cdots + a_{k-1}x^{k-1}$ and $g(x) = g_0 + g_1x + \cdots + g_{\ell-1}x^{\ell-1}$. First recall that $a(x)g(x) = c(x)$ means that c_t, the coefficient of x^t in $c(x)$, is

$$c_t = g_0a_t + g_1a_{t-1} + \cdots + a_0g_t \ \text{ if } t \leq \ell - 1$$

and

$$c_t = g_0a_t + g_1a_{t-1} + \cdots + a_{t-\ell+1}g_{\ell-1} \ \text{ if } t > \ell - 1.$$

For convenience we assume that $a_t = 0$ if $t > k - 1 = \deg(a(x))$.

Consider now the shift register with generator $g(x)$. The output at time t, is the linear combination of the $X_i(t)$:

$$c_t = g_0X_0(t) + \cdots + g_{\ell-1}X_{\ell-1}(t).$$

At time $t = 0$, $X_0(0) = a_0$, and $X_1(0) = \cdots = X_{n-1}(0) = 0$, so $c_0 = g_0a_0$.

More generally at time t, $t \leq \ell - 1$, $X_0(t) = a_t, X_1(t) = a_{t-1}, \ldots, X_t(t) = a_0$ and the remaining registers are all zero. Thus,

$$c_t = g_0a_t + g_1a_{t-1} + \cdots + g_ta_0, \ \text{ for } t \leq \ell - 1.$$

Finally at time $t > \ell - 1$, we have

$$X_0(t) = a_t, X_1(t) = a_{t-1}, \ldots, X_{\ell-1}(t) = a_{t-\ell+1}$$

and $c_t = g_0a_t + g_1a_{t-1} + \cdots + g_{\ell-1}a_{t-\ell+1}$, $t > \ell - 1$. (We note again that we use the convention that if $a_0, a_1, \ldots, a_{k-1}$ is the input sequence then $a_t = 0$, for $t \geq k$.)

Theorem 8.1.8 *A shift register with generator $g(x)$, given an input sequence $a_0, a_1, \ldots$ will output $c_0, c_1, \ldots,$ where $c(x) = a(x)g(x)$, with $c(x) = c_0 + c_1x + \cdots$, and $a(x) = a_0 + a_1x + \cdots$.*

We see that polynomial multiplication (and hence polynomial encoding for cyclic codes) can be implemented using shift registers: the generator $g(x)$ of the shift register is the generator polynomial of the linear cyclic code. We can also modify the shift registers to implement division of polynomials, which is of use when decoding linear cyclic codes. Polynomial division (and thus polynomial decoding for cyclic codes) can be implemented by hardware devices known as *feedback shift registers* (FSR). Basically an FSR is a shift register with the output fed back into the device.

(For those readers only interested in convolutional codes, the rest of this section may be omitted.)

First recall that in computing the parity check matrix H for the cyclic code with generator $g(x)$, the ith row of H is $r_i \leftrightarrow r_i(x)$, where

$$r_i(x) \equiv x^i \pmod{g(x)}.$$

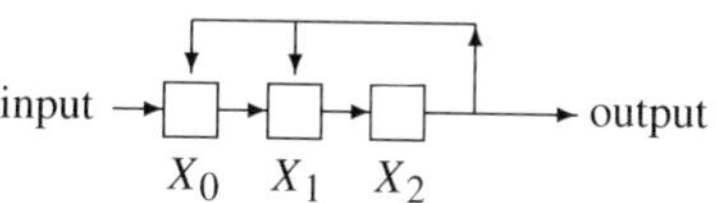

Figure 8.2: *A feedback shift register.*

In particular

$$r_i(x) = xr_{i-1}(x) \bmod g(x)$$

Example 8.1.9 Let $g(x) = 1 + x + x^3$ be the generator polynomial. In the parity matrix,

$$\begin{aligned} r_3 &= 110 \leftrightarrow 1 + x = x^3 \bmod g(x), \text{ and} \\ r_4 &= 011 \leftrightarrow x + x^2 = x^4 \bmod g(x). \end{aligned}$$

But $r_5 \leftrightarrow x^2 + x^3 \bmod g(x)$ or $r_5 = 001 + 110$. We consider the vector 110 to be the feedback vector which is added back in to the registers if the output digit is 1. The feedback shift register in Figure 8.2 performs this operation.

We use the convention that if more than one input comes into a register the contents will be the binary sum of their values. That is, the two diagrams below represent the same thing.

At each clock tick the input and contents of the registers are shifted and the output digit c_t, is added back into selected registers. Equivalently the (new) vector $c_t(1, 1, 0)$ is added to the contents of the registers.

time	input	$X_0 + c_t$	$X_1 + c_t$	X_2	$c_t =$ output
-1	—	0	0	0	—
0	1	1	0	0	0
1	0	0	1	0	0
2	0	0	0	1	0
3	0	$0+1$	$0+1$	0	1
4	0	0	1	1	0
5	0	$0+1$	$0+1$	1	1
6	0	$0+1$	$1+1$	1	1
7	0	1	0	0	1

In general, an s-*stage* FSR with feedback vector $(g_0, g_1, \ldots, g_{s-1})$ corresponds to a polynomial $g(x) = g_0 + g_1x + \cdots + g_{s-1}x^{s-1} + x^s$ of degree s. The contents of the registers at time $t = \deg(c(x))$ will be the remainder of $c(x)/g(x)$ and the output sequence will be the quotient $a(x)$. However, the received word must be fed in reverse order, high order digits first. (Notice that for an FSR, the associated polynomial has degree s, whereas the polynomial associated with a shift register has degree $s-1$; however in both cases we have s registers.)

Example 8.1.10 Let $x+x^2+x^4$ be the received polynomial and 0110100 be the corresponding word. Assume $g(x)=1+x+x^3$ and so the corresponding FSR be as in Figure 8.2.

time	input	X_0	X_1	X_2	output
−1	—	0	0	0	—
0	1	1	0	0	0
1	0	0	1	0	0
2	1	1	0	1	0
3	1	1+1	1+1	0	1
4	0	0	0	0	0

The remainder is 000 and the quotient $x \leftrightarrow 0100000$, corresponding to the output sequence in reverse order.

In general the contents of the registers at time $t=n$, will be the remainder of $c(x) \bmod g(x)$, where $c(x)$ represents the input sequence.

Theorem 8.1.11 *Feeding $c(x)=c_0+c_1x+\cdots+c_{n-1}x^{n-1}$ into a FSR corresponding to $g(x)=g_0+g_1x+\cdots+1\cdot x^s$ with high order coefficients fed in first (i.e., $c_{n-1}, c_{n-2}, \ldots, c_0$) is equivalent to dividing $c(x)$ by $g(x)$. The output after n clock ticks will be the quotient (high order coefficients first) and the registers will contain the remainder (high order digits to the right).*

Proof: Since the output of the sum of two input streams will be the sum of the corresponding output streams all we need to do is verify this theorem for $c(x)=x^\ell$. But it is clear that the FSR corresponds to our earlier algorithm for computing $x^\ell \bmod g(x)$ (see Example 4.3.7). Thus the registers will contain the remainder. It is less obvious but not too difficult to prove that the output will be the quotient on dividing $c(x)$ by $g(x)$. □

Exercises

8.1.12 Given the feedback shift register in Figure 8.2, with the registers initially set to zero, generate the output sequence for each of the following received words. Indicate the final state of the registers and quotient if the remainder is zero.

(a) 0011010 (b) 1010110 (c) 0010001

8.1.13 Given $g(x)=1+x+x^3$, compute the syndrome polynomials for each of the received words in Exercise 8.1.12. Compare the syndrome polynomial with the corresponding final state of the registers computed in 8.1.12.

8.1.14 For each generator polynomial $g(x)$ construct a corresponding feedback shift register. Compute the output sequence and find the final state of the registers for the given input sequence $c(x)$.

(a) $g(x) = 1 + x^2 + x^3$, $c = 0010110$
(b) $g(x) = 1 + x + x^2$, $c = 111$
(c) $g(x) = 1 + x + x^4$, $c = 010000000100000$

8.2 Encoding convolutional codes

Convolutional codes are extremely practical codes. They have been adopted by both NASA and the European Space Agency for ensuring that communications during space missions are reliable. In fact, they are used in conjunction with Reed-Solomon codes: each message is first encoded with a Reed-Solomon code, and the resulting codeword is then encoded with a convolutional code. In the following sections we consider the encoding and decoding of convolutional codes, then some problems that arise with these codes. We begin with a definition.

An $(n, k = 1, m)$ (binary) *convolutional code* with *generators* $g_1(x), \ldots, g_n(x)$, where $g_i(x) = g_{i,0} + g_{i,1}x + \cdots + g_{i,m}x^m$, $g_i \in K[x]$ is the code consisting of all codewords

$$c(x) = (c_1(x), c_2(x), \ldots, c_n(x))$$

where $c_i(x) = m(x)g_i(x)$, and $m(x) = m_0 + m_1x + m_2x^2 + \cdots \in K[x]$. (We will briefly discuss the parameter k, later, which for simplicity is set equal to one in this definition.) Of course, $m(x)$ is the message and is encoded to $c(x)$. Suppose that $c(x)$ and $c'(x)$ are codewords. Then

$$\begin{aligned} c(x) + c'(x) &= (c_1(x), \ldots, c_n(x)) + (c_1'(x), \ldots, c_n'(x)) \\ &= (m(x)g_1(x), \ldots, m(x)g_n(x)) + (m'(x)g_1(x), \ldots, m'(x)g_n(x)) \\ &= ((m(x) + m'(x))g_1(x), \ldots, (m(x) + m'(x))g_n(x)) \end{aligned}$$

which is just the codeword corresponding to the message $m(x) + m'(x)$. Therefore convolutional codes are linear codes.

Convolutional codes are different from the codes considered so far in that they are codes of infinite length, and the message also has infinite length.

Example 8.2.1 Let C_1 be the $(2, 1, 3)$ convolutional code with $g_1(x) = 1 + x + x^3$ and $g_2(x) = 1 + x^2 + x^3$. We use C_1 to encode the following messages.

(a) The message $m(x) = 1 + x^2$ is encoded to

$$\begin{aligned} c(x) &= ((1 + x^2)g_1(x), (1 + x^2)g_2(x)), \\ &= (1 + x + x^2 + x^5, 1 + x^3 + x^4 + x^5), \\ &\leftrightarrow (11100100\ldots, 10011100\ldots), \end{aligned}$$

(b) The message $m(x) = 1 + x + x^2 + x^3 + \cdots = \sum_{i=0}^{\infty} x^i$ is encoded to

$$\begin{aligned} c(x) &= (1 + x^3 + x^4 + x^5 + \ldots, 1 + x + x^3 + x^4 + x^5 + \ldots) \\ &= (1 + \textstyle\sum_{i=3}^{\infty} x^i, 1 + x + \sum_{i=3}^{\infty} x^i) \\ &\leftrightarrow (100111\ldots, 110111\ldots). \end{aligned}$$

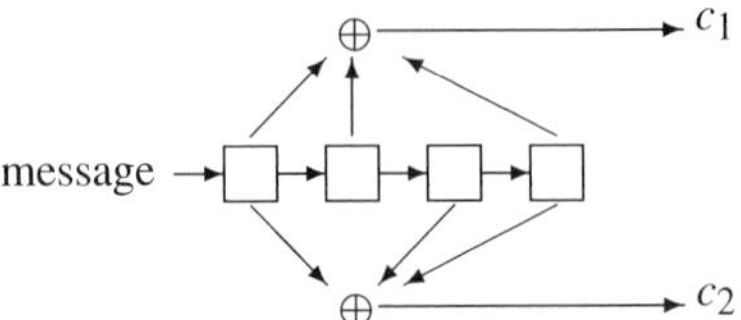

Figure 8.3: *Encoding the* $(2,1,3)$ *convolutional code* C_1.

Exercises

8.2.2 Encode the following messages using the $(3,1,3)$ convolutional code with generators $g_1(x)=1+x+x^3$, $g_2(x)=1+x+x^2+x^3$ and $g_3(x)=1+x^2+x^3$.

(a) $m(x)=1+x^3$

(b) $m(x)=1+x+x^3$

(c) $m(x)=1+x+x^2+\cdots=\sum_{i=0}^{\infty}x^i$

8.2.3 Encode the following messages using the $(2,1,4)$ convolutional code with generators $g_1(x)=1+x^3+x^4$ and $g_2(x)=1+x+x^2+x^4$.

(a) $m(x)=1+x+x^2$

(b) $m(x)=1+x+x^3$

(c) $m(x)=1+x^2+x^4+\cdots=\sum_{i=0}^{\infty}x^{2i}$

As can easily be seen from Theorem 8.1.8, an alternate description of convolutional codes can be given in terms of shift registers: $c_i(x)$ is the output from the shift register with generator $g_i(x)$ when $m(x)$ is the input.

Example 8.2.4 Let's consider the convolutional code C_1 in Example 8.2.1. We can describe the code with a shift register with the 2 generators $g_1(x)=1+x+x^3$ and $g_2(x)=1+x^2+x^3$ (see Figure 8.3).

Using this description, if we encode $m(x)=1+x^2\leftrightarrow 10100\ldots$ then it is clear that $c_1=11100100\ldots$ as was calculated in Example 8.1.2 (and this agrees with the calculation in Example 8.2.1), and similarly c_2 can be shown to be $10011100\ldots$.

Of course $c(x)$ can be made into a single stream of digits, instead of the n streams we have been describing, by interleaving $c_1(x),c_2(x),\ldots,c_n(x)$. For the rest of this chapter we will display $c(x)$ in this interleaved form, so the output consists of the coefficients of x^0 in $c_1(x),\ldots,c_n(x)$ followed by the coefficients of $x,x^2,\ldots$. When displaying the interleaved form of $c\leftrightarrow c(x)$, the n digits consisting of the coefficients of x^i, for $i\geq 0$, will be grouped together.

Example 8.2.5 The interleaved representation of $c(x)$ in Example 8.2.1(a) is

$$c=11\ 10\ 10\ 01\ 01\ 11\ 00\ 00\ldots,$$

and in Example 8.2.1(b) is

$$c = 11\,01\,00\,11\,11\,11\ldots.$$

Exercises

8.2.6 For the convolutional codes in Exercises 8.2.2 and 8.2.3, construct the relevant shift register which can be used to encode the code. Then check your answers to those exercises by using the shift registers to encode the given messages. Finally, represent each codeword in its interleaved form.

Considering an $(n, 1, m)$ convolutional code as being encoded with shift registers, when 1 message digit is moved into the shift register, n code digits are produced. Therefore each message digit in an $(n, k = 1, m)$ binary convolutional code in effect produces n code digits, one in each of $c_1(x), \ldots, c_n(x)$, so the *rate* of such a convolutional code is defined to be $1/n$ (recall that the rate of a code measures the fraction of information that each code digit carries). One might then ask if it is possible to design convolutional codes with rates other than $1/n$, and in particular rates higher than $1/2$.

The obvious way to do this is to move more than one, say k, message digits into the shift register before calculating the next code digits, thus producing a code of rate k/n. This is, in fact the definition of the parameter k for an (n, k, m) convolutional code. Notice that if we do this then each message digit will appear in the registers $X_i, X_{i+k}, X_{i+2k}, \ldots,$ for some i, $0 \leq i < k$. Therefore, rather than moving k message digits at a time into the shift register, we could equivalently divide the shift register into k shift registers $X_0 X_k X_{2k} \ldots, X_1 X_{k+1} X_{2k+1} \ldots,$ and so on. Correspondingly, the message is divided into k streams, each stream being fed into one of the k shift registers. The one complication is that now contents from registers in different shift registers may be combined in a single generator. This last description is the method of encoding that is used in practice. The following example makes all this clear.

Example 8.2.7 Use the $(3, 2, 3)$ convolutional code C with generators $g_1(x) = 1 + x^3$, $g_2(x) = 1 + x + x^3$ and $g_3(x) = x + x^2 + x^3$ to encode the message $m = 100101110000\cdots$.

The first interpretation of $k = 2$ is to encode m using the single shift register in Figure 8.4 and moving $k = 2$ message digits in to the shift register at each tick. Then the contents of the registers and the outputs are summarized in the following table.

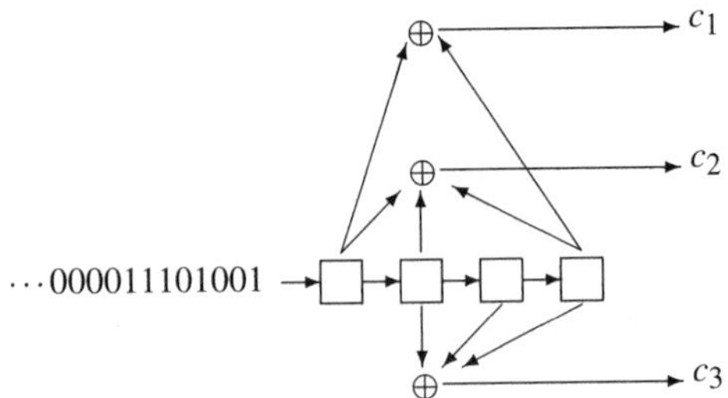

Figure 8.4: *Encoding a* $(3,2,3)$ *convolutional code.*

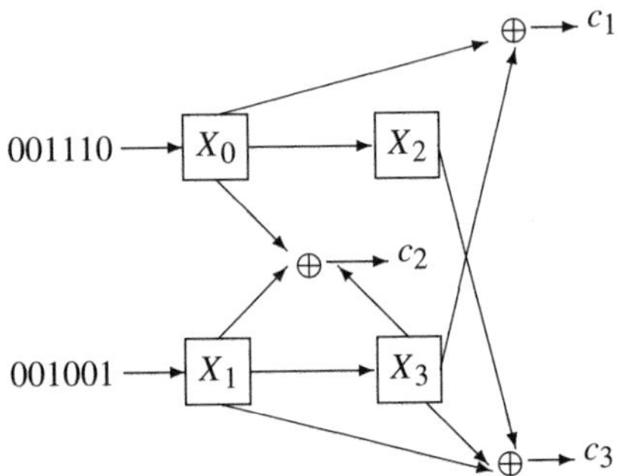

Figure 8.5: *Encoding a* $(3,2,3)$ *convolutional code.*

time	input	$X_0X_1X_2X_3$	output $c_1\ c_2\ c_3$
−1	–	0 0 0 0	–
0	01	0 1 0 0	0 1 1
1	10	1 0 0 1	0 0 1
2	10	1 0 1 0	1 1 1
3	11	1 1 1 0	1 0 0
4	00	0 0 1 1	1 1 0
5	00	0 0 0 0	0 0 0

So m is encoded to the codeword (in interleaved form)

$$c = 011\ 001\ 111\ 100\ 110\ 000\ \ldots$$

The second interpretation of $k = 2$ is to notice that the first, third, fifth, ... message digits fed into this shift register only ever appear in X_0 and X_2, and the second, fourth, sixth, ... message digits fed into the shift register only every appear in X_1 and X_3. Therefore we can split the message and the registers into $k = 2$ parts as Figure 8.5 suggests.

Exercises

8.2.8 Encode the following messages using the $(3,2,4)$ convolutional code with generators $g_1(x) = 1+x^3$, $g_2(x) = x+x^4$ and $g_3(x) = 1+x+x^2+x^3+x^4$. Use both techniques of encoding described above.

(a) $m(x) = 1+x+x^3+x^4+x^5$

(b) $m(x) = 1+x^3+x^5+x^7+x^8$

(c) $m(x) = 1+x+x^2+x^3$

The rest of the chapter mainly deals with rate $r = 1/2$, $(2,1,m)$ binary convolutional codes. The results and techniques presented can be generalized to (n,k,m) convolutional codes, but the main ideas can all be found in this notationally simpler setting. For those interested in convolutional codes with $k > 1$, we have included some exercises that indicate how to generalize the material presented for $k = 1$.

It is worth noting that NASA's Mars Global Surveyor uses a convolutional code with $r = 1/2$ and $m = 7$ when sending information to Earth from Mars, and the Mars Pathfinder can choose a convolutional code with $(r,m) = (1/2,7)$ or $(1/6,15)$. At the time of printing, photographs taken by these NASA missions were displayed on the internet at "http://www.msss.com".

Finally, there is another way of viewing the encoding of convolutional codes. Recall that a $(2,1,m)$ convolutional code can be encoded using a shift register containing $m+1$ registers. At each tick, the contents of the first m registers is called the *state* of the shift register. The *zero state* is the state when each of the first m registers contains 0. If the shift register is currently in state $s_0, s_1, \ldots, s_{m-1}$ then at the next tick, it will be either in state $0, s_0, s_1, \ldots, s_{m-2}$ or in state $1, s_0, s_1, \ldots, s_{m-2}$, depending on whether the message digit shifted in to register X_0 was a 0 or a 1 respectively. Also, if we know the current state $s_0, s_1, \ldots, s_{m-1}$ and the previous state $s_1, s_2, \ldots, s_m$, then we know the current contents of ALL of the registers; therefore we know the current output. This information is often presented graphically: the *state diagram* of a $(2,1,m)$ convolutional code is a directed graph in which the vertices, or *states*, are all binary words of length m, and for each state $s = s_1, s_2, \ldots, s_m$ there is an edge directed from s to state $0, s_1, s_2, \ldots, s_{m-1}$ that is labeled with the output when the registers $X_0, X_1, \ldots, X_m$ contain $0, s_1, \ldots, s_m$ respectively and there is an edge directed from s to state $1, s_1, s_2, \ldots, s_{m-1}$ that is labeled with the output when the registers $X_0, X_1, \ldots, X_m$ contain $1, s_1, \ldots, s_m$ respectively.

The information in the state diagram of a $(2,1,m)$ convolutional code can also be represented in *tabular form*. Each row of the table lists the current state (that is, the contents of registers $X_0, X_1, \ldots, X_{m-1}$) and the corresponding output, which of course depends on whether $X_m = 0$ or $X_m = 1$.

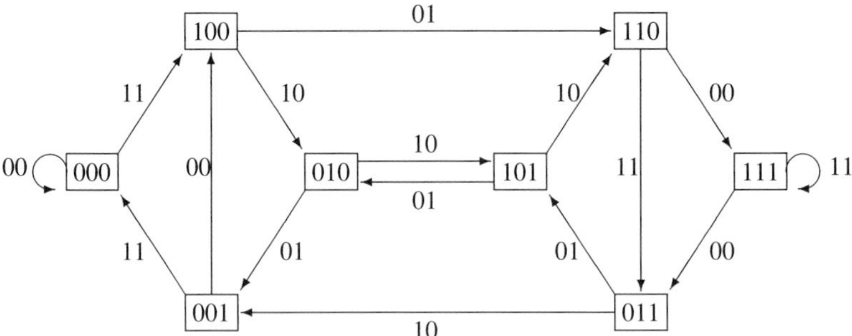

Figure 8.6: *The state diagram for C_1.*

Example 8.2.9 Let C_1 be the $(2,1,3)$ convolutional code with generators $g_1(x) = 1+x+x^3$ and $g_2(x) = 1+x^2+x^3$ (see Examples 8.2.1 and 8.2.4). The states are all binary words of length $m = 3 : 000, 100, 010, 001, 110, 101, 011, 111$. Considering the state $s = s_1s_2s_3 = 011$ for example, there is a directed edge from s to the state $0s_1s_2 = 001$, and a directed edge from s to $1s_1s_2 = 101$. The directed edge from 011 to 001 is labeled with the output when $X_0X_1X_2X_3 = 0011$, namely 10, and the edge directed from 011 to 101 is labeled with the output when $X_0X_1X_2X_3 = 1011$, namely 01. If we do this for every state then we obtain the state diagram in Figure 8.6.

This state diagram can also be represented by the following table.

State	Output	
$X_0X_1X_2$	$X_3 = 0$	$X_3 = 1$
000	00	11
100	11	00
010	10	01
110	01	10
001	01	10
101	10	01
011	11	00
111	00	11

Recall that initially the contents of each register is set equal to 0, so the initial state of the shift register is $X_0X_1 \dots X_{m-1} = 00\dots0$. As each message digit is fed into the shift register, the shift register moves to a different state and each generator outputs a code digit. In the state diagram, this obviously corresponds to moving from state to adjacent state following directed edges, the outputs being the labels on the directed edges. In this way, a codeword naturally corresponds to a (*directed*) *walk* in the state diagram that begins at the zero state and moves along directed edges to adjacent states. Notice that at each tick, the message digit being moved in to the shift register is the first digit in the state in the state diagram to which the shift register moves. Therefore it is also easy to recover the message corresponding to any codeword.

Example 8.2.10 Continuing Examples 8.2.1 and 8.2.9, the message $m(x) = 1 + x^2 \leftrightarrow 10100\ldots$ corresponds to the walk starting at state 000, then moving to states 100, 010, 101, 010, 001, 000, 000, ..., in turn. The labels on these directed edges are 11, 10, 10, 01, 01, 11, 00, ..., respectively, and this is precisely the codeword to which $m(x)$ is encoded (in interleaved form; see Example 8.2.5).

Also, given a codeword, we can easily recover the corresponding message. Consider the codeword

$$c = 00\ 11\ 01\ 11\ 01\ 01\ 01\ 11\ 00\ldots.$$

The walk in the state diagram that produces c proceeds through the states

$$000, 000, 100, 110, 011, 101, 010, 001, 000, 000\ldots$$

(of course, all codewords start at the zero state 000). Since, at each tick, the message digit is the first digit in the state to which the register moves, the message corresponding to c is produced by writing down the first digit in each of the states in the walk other than the initial state:

$$m = 0\ 1\ 1\ 0\ 1\ 0\ 0\ 0\ 0\ \ldots$$

Exercises

8.2.11 (a) Find the state diagram, and its representation in tabular form, for the $(2, 1, 2)$ convolutional code with generators $g_1(x) = 1 + x^2$ and $g_2(x) = 1 + x + x^2$.

(b) Use the state diagram to encode the following messages:

(i) $m(x) = 1 + x^2$
(ii) $m(x) = 1 + x + x^2$

(c) Use the state diagram to find the message corresponding to the following codewords:

(i) 11 01 00 01 11 00 ...
(ii) 00 11 10 01 01 10 00...

8.2.12 (a) Find the state diagram, and its representation in tabular form, for the $(2, 1, 3)$ convolutional code with generators $g_1(x) = 1 + x + x^2 + x^3$ and $g_2(x) = 1 + x^2 + x^3$.

(b) Use the state diagram to encode the following messages.

(i) $m(x) = 1 + x^3$
(ii) $m(x) = 1 + x + x^3$

(iii) $m(x) = 1 + x + x^2 + \cdots = \sum_{i=0}^{\infty} x^i$

(c) Use the state diagram to find the message corresponding to the following partial codewords.

(i) 11 10 00 01 00 10 10...
(ii) 00 11 01 10 01 10 00 ...

8.2.13 (a) Find the state diagram, and its representation in tabular form, for the $(2,1,4)$ convolutional code with generators $g_1(x) = 1 + x^3 + x^4$ and $g_2(x) = 1 + x + x^2 + x^4$.

(b) Use the state diagram to encode the following messages.

(i) $m(x) = 1 + x + x^2$
(ii) $m(x) = 1 + x + x^3$
(iii) $m(x) = 1 + x^2 + x^4 + \cdots = \sum_{i=0}^{\infty} x^{2i}$

Compare your answers to those of Exercise 8.2.3.

8.2.14 For $1 \leq k \leq m/2$, we can similarly define a state diagram for (n,k,m) convolutional codes. The states are all binary words of length $m+1-k$ and for each state $s = s_k, s_{k+1}, \ldots, s_m$ and for each binary word u of length k there is an edge directed from state s to state $u, s_k, s_{k+1}, \ldots, s_{m-k}$ that is labeled with the output when the registers $X_0, X_1, \ldots, X_m$ contain $u, s_k, s_{k+1}, \ldots, s_m$ (for $k > 1$, here we are using the encoding description of shifting k message digits into a single shift register at each tick).

Find the state diagram for the (n,k,m) convolutional codes with the following generators.

(a) $g_1(x) = 1 + x + x^3$, $g_2(x) = 1 + x + x^2 + x^3$, and $g_3(x) = 1 + x^2 + x^3$, with $k = 1$

(b) $g_1(x) = 1 + x^3$, $g_2(x) = 1 + x + x^3$, and $g_3(x) = x + x^2 + x^3$, with $k = 2$

(c) $g_1(x) = 1 + x^3$, $g_2(x) = x + x^4$, and $g_3(x) = 1 + x + x^2 + x^3 + x^4$, with $k = 2$

8.3 Decoding convolutional codes

Clearly, decoding convolutional codes is going to be somewhat different from the decoding of other codes because each codeword has infinite length. To avoid storage problems, decoding must begin before the entire codeword is received, so it is natural to consider how long we should wait before beginning to decode. For example, consider C_1, the $(2,1,3)$ convolutional code with generators $g_1(x) = 1 + x + x^3$ and $g_2(x) = 1 + x^2 + x^3$ (the state diagram for this code in Figure 8.6 will be useful in the following discussion). Suppose that the received word is $w(x) = 1 + x \leftrightarrow 11\ 00\ 00\ 00\ \cdots = w$. We know that codewords correspond to directed walks in the state diagram that start at state 000, but clearly there is no directed walk that would give an output of w. Therefore we are faced with finding a codeword that "most closely" fits w; that is, a directed walk in the state diagram with an output that is close to w.

If we know *all* of w, then the directed walk that never leaves state 000 produces the codeword $c_1 = 00\,00\,00\,\ldots$ that is distance 2 from w. It is not hard to check that every other walk produces an output that differs from w in more than 2 places, so c_1 is the "closest codeword." So we decode w to the message $m = 000\cdots$.

However, suppose that our storage capabilities are so limited that at each tick we have to decode a message digit. At the first tick, we start at state 000 and we see the digits 11 in w. Our best choice is to move to state 100, because 11 is the label on the directed edge from state 000 to state 100, so is an output that agrees with the received digits of w. Therefore we decode the first message digit as 1. At the second tick, we are in state 100, we see the digits 00 of w and so we are in a quandary: moving to adjacent state 010 or 110 produces an output of 10 or 01 respectively, both of which are distance 1 from the received digits. We are forced to make an arbitrary decision, knowing that errors have occurred during transmission that we have been unable to correct. So we have decoded w to either $c_2 = 11\,10\,\ldots$ or to $c_2' = 11\,01\ldots$, with the most likely message being $m = 1*\ldots$ (we write $*$ whenever we face an arbitrary decision between decoding a 0 or a 1). Notice that if we decode $*$, then the next current state must also be arbitrarily chosen from the two states adjacent to the current state.

Consider one further possibility, where we can store two ticks worth of information before decoding. So now we can begin by considering all walks of length 2 from the zero state and compare their labels with the first 2 ticks of w, namely 11 00, to obtain the information in Figure 8.7. Two of the walks are closest to 11

Walk	Output	Distance from 11 00
000, 000, 000	00 00	2
000, 000, 100	00 11	4
000, 100, 010	11 10	1
000, 100, 110	11 01	1

Figure 8.7: *Information for the first decoding decision.*

00, the part of w that we have seen so far. However this is not a problem, because both of these walks agree that we should first move to state 100. These two walks only disagree as to where to proceed after state 100, but that decision need not yet be made; we make that decision after receiving another two digits of w. Therefore we make the decoding decision to move to state 100 and decode the first message digit as 1. Now we use the second and third ticks of information of w, namely 00 00, to make the next decoding decision. We consider the distance from 00 00 to the output of each walk of length 2 from the current state 100 (see Figure 8.8). In this case there is a unique closest walk to the piece of w we are currently considering. That walk is 100, 110, 111, so we make the decoding decision to move

Walk	Output	Distance from 00 00
100, 010, 001	10 01	2
100, 010, 101	10 10	2
100, 110, 011	01 11	3
100, 110, 111	01 00	1

Figure 8.8: *Information for the second decoding decision.*

to state 110 and decode the second message digit to 1.

Exercises

8.3.1 Let C be the $(2,1,3)$ convolutional code with generators $g_1(x) = 1+x+x^2+x^3$ and $g_2(x) = 1+x^2+x^3$ (the state diagram for C is constructed in Exercise 8.2.12). By forming tables similar to those in Figures 8.7 and 8.8, decode the first 4 message digits of the received word $w = 11\ 00\ 00\ 00\ \cdots \leftrightarrow 1+x = w(x)$ by waiting for

(a) 2 ticks before decoding,
(b) 3 ticks before decoding,
(c) 4 ticks before decoding.

Decode the "message digit" $*$ if two closest walks disagree as to which state to move. If an $*$ is decoded, assume that the message digit 0 is decoded to determine the next current state.

Notice that if we decide to wait τ steps before decoding, then a decoding decision looks at all walks of length τ from the current state, compares each such walk to the τ ticks of information of the received word currently in our possession, then moves to the next state in all walks that most closely agree with w. Another tick of w is received before another step is taken. Also, if two closest walks to w disagree as to which state to move to (as was the case at the second tick when we chose $\tau = 1$), then we could arbitrarily select one of the states. Call this decoding algorithm the *exhaustive decoding algorithm* for convolutional codes (because *all* walks of length τ from the current state are considered for *each* message digit to be decoded), and call τ the *window size* (since τ is the amount of w we "see" when making each decoding decision).

Clearly the amount of time we wait before making a decoding decision is affecting our answer to what is the closest codeword. The problem now is to see if there is a happy medium, between making a decoding decision at every tick and decoding after all of the received word has been seen, that allows all error patterns of a certain type to be corrected. But this raises another question: which error patterns can be corrected? We will obtain several answers to this question, then in each case address the problem of how long to wait before decoding.

First, however, we need to consider yet another problem! Consider the $(2,1,3)$ convolutional code with generators $g_1(x) = 1 + x^3$ and $g_2(x) = 1 + x + x^2$. The state diagram for this code is in Figure 8.9. Suppose that the codeword transmit-

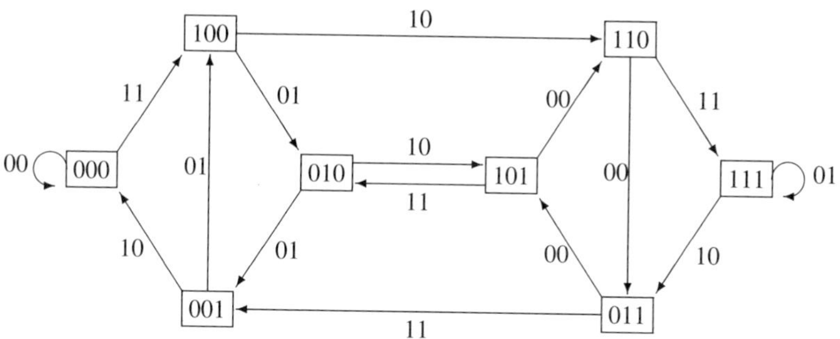

Figure 8.9: *The state diagram of a catastrophic convolutional code.*

ted is the zero codeword, with corresponding message $m = 000\ldots$, and that the received word is

$$w = 11\ 10\ 00\ 00\cdots \leftrightarrow 1 + x + x^2 = w(x).$$

Decoding w is simple because it *is* a codeword, as can be seen from the state diagram, following the walk through the states $000, 100, 110, 011, 101, 110, \ldots$. In this case we presume that no errors occurred during transmission, and so we assume that the most likely message is $m = 1\,1\,0\,1\,1\,0\cdots \leftrightarrow \sum_{i=0}^{\infty}(x^{3i} + x^{3i+1})$. This is a *disastrous* situation because in fact what happened was that the first three digits were transmitted incorrectly (we were assuming that $c = 00\,00\ldots$ was sent) and this led us to make infinitely many errors in decoding (because we decoded $m = 110110\ldots$ instead of $m = 000000\ldots$). Fortunately it is easy to see what the problem is: the state diagram has a cycle, other than the loop on the zero state, in which every directed edge is labeled with the zero output. Whenever such a cycle occurs, this problem of finitely many errors during transmission causing infinitely many decoding errors can occur. Define the *weight* of a walk (or cycle) in the state diagram to be the weight of the outputs on the directed edges in the walk. Then a convolutional code is called *catastrophic* if its state diagram contains a zero weight cycle different from the loop on the zero state. (The loop on the zero state in any convolutional code has weight 0. Why?) It is not hard to prove that a $(2,1,m)$ convolutional code is catastrophic precisely when the $\gcd(g_1(x), g_2(x)) \neq 1$. Notice that in the convolutional code we are considering, $g_1(x) = 1 + x^3 = (1+x)(1+x+x^2)$, so $\gcd(g_1(x), g_2(x)) = 1 + x + x^2 \neq 1$.

Exercises

8.3.2 Find the gcd$(g_1(x), g_2(x))$ for each of the following $(2,1,m)$ convolutional codes to decide if the code is catastrophic. If the gcd $\neq 1$ then find a zero weight cycle in the state diagram other than the loop on the zero state.

(a) $g_1(x) = 1+x$ and $g_2(x) = 1+x+x^2+x^3$
(b) $g_1(x) = 1+x+x^4$ and $g_2(x) = 1+x^2+x^4$
(c) $g_1(x) = 1+x+x^2$ and $g_2(x) = 1+x+x^3+x^4$

Throughout the rest of this chapter we shall assume that the codes are not catastrophic.

We now return to the questions of how long to wait before decoding and which error patterns can be corrected. Obviously we should begin by considering the minimum distance, d of a convolutional code (this is often called the *minimum free distance*). We observed earlier that convolutional codes are linear, so d is the weight of a non-zero codeword of least weight. Since we are only considering non-catastrophic convolutional codes, a non-zero, finite weight codeword corresponds to a walk that leaves the zero state (so that the weight of the codeword is non-zero) and at some time returns to the zero state and stays there forever more (so that the weight of the codeword is finite). Notice that for a non-catastrophic code, if ever a walk leaves the zero state it must accumulate some positive weight because there are no zero weight cycles other than the loop on the zero state. For example, in Figure 8.6, the walk through the states $000, 100, 010, 001, 000, 000\ldots$ has weight 6 (corresponding to the codeword 11 10 01 11 00 00... of weight 6), as does the walk through states $000, 100, 110, 111, 011, 001, 000, 000$ (corresponding to the codeword 11 01 00 00 10 11 00 00...), but all other walks have weight greater than 6. Therefore the minimum distance of the code C_1 is $d(C_1) = 6$. (An algorithmic procedure for calculating $d(C)$ will be presented in the next section.)

Exercises

8.3.3 Find the minimum distance for the convolutional codes with the following generators (the state diagrams for these codes were constructed in Exercises 8.2.11, 8.2.12 and 8.2.13).

(a) $g_1(x) = 1+x^2$ and $g_2(x) = 1+x+x^2$
(b) $g_1(x) = 1+x+x^2+x^3$ and $g_2(x) = 1+x^2+x^3$
(c) $g_1(x) = 1+x^3+x^4$ and $g_2(x) = 1+x+x^2+x^4$.

Having calculated the minimum distance, we should at least try to correct all error patterns of weight at most $\lfloor (d-1)/2 \rfloor$. But now the second question arises: how long should we wait before starting to decode? Recall that $d(C_1) = 6$, yet we found that if we use the exhaustive decoding algorithm with window size $\tau = 1$ then the received word $w = 11\,00\,00\ldots$ was not decoded to $00\,00\,00\ldots$, so this error pattern w of weight $2 < 3 = \lfloor (d(C_1) - 1)/2 \rfloor$ is not corrected. However w is corrected to 00 00... if we wait "forever."

Define the *length* of a walk to be the number of directed edges in the walk (count each directed edge as many times as it appears in the walk). If all error patterns of weight at most e are to be corrected then the time $\tau(e)$ that we must wait before decoding should be long enough so that all walks of length $\tau(e)$ from the zero state that immediately leave the zero state have weight greater than $2e$.

To see this, suppose that the zero codeword is sent and at most e errors occur during transmission (by the linearity of convolutional codes, there is no loss of generality in assuming that the zero codeword is sent). Using the exhaustive decoding algorithm with window size $\tau(e)$, after $\tau(e)$ ticks we compare the labels on all walks from the zero state that have length $\tau(e)$ to the first $\tau(e)$ ticks of the received word w, then select the closest walks to determine to which state we should move. Of course, to decode correctly we should decide to stay at the zero state since we are assuming that the zero codeword was sent. By the choice of $\tau(e)$, all walks that immediately leave the zero state have weight greater than $2e$ after $\tau(e)$ steps, so disagree with the first $\tau(e)$ ticks of w in more than e positions. On the other hand, the walk that never leaves the zero state has weight zero, so is distance $\mathrm{wt}(w) \leq e$ from the first $\tau(e)$ ticks of w. Therefore *none* of the walks that immediately leave the zero state are closest walks, and so *all* closest walks to w over the first $\tau(e)$ ticks agree that we should stay in the zero state. As we noted when considering the information in Figures 8.7 and 8.8, no further decoding step is made until we receive another tick of w. However, having received such new information, the same argument can be repeated, thus showing that indeed we decode w correctly. In fact, this argument proves that we can decode w correctly if at most e errors occur in *any* $\tau(e)$ consecutive ticks of the received word. So we can correct infinitely many errors, providing we never get more than e errors in some $\tau(e)$ consecutive ticks. (This is similar to the situation with block codes of finite length since for such codes, errors are corrected providing at most e errors occur in any codeword.)

Therefore we now know how long to wait. Given a non-catastrophic convolutional code C, for $1 \leq e \leq \lfloor (d-1)/2 \rfloor$ define $\tau(e)$ to be the least integer x such that all walks of length x in the state diagram that immediately leave the zero state have weight greater than $2e$.

Notice that the exhaustive decoding algorithm with window size $\tau(e)$ requires that we consider *all* walks of length $\tau(e)$ from the current state for *each* message digit to be decoded. Constructing all $2^{\tau(e)}$ such walks at each tick is very time consuming, so we will present a faster algorithm in Section 8.4. However, at least we now have the following result.

Theorem 8.3.4 *Let C be a non-catastrophic convolutional code. For any e, $1 \leq e \leq \lfloor (d-1)/2 \rfloor$, if any error pattern containing at most e errors in any $\tau(e)$ con-*

secutive steps occurs during transmission, then the exhaustive decoding algorithm using the window size $\tau(e)$ will decode the received word correctly.

Example 8.3.5 Consider again C_1, the convolutional code with generators $g_1(x) = 1+x+x^3$ and $g_2(x) = 1+x^2+x^3$ (Figure 8.6 is the state diagram of C_1). Since $d(C_1) = 6$, we consider both $e = 1$ and $e = 2$.

$\underline{e = 1}$ All walks of length 2 immediately leaving the zero state have weight more than $2e = 2$. At least one walk of length 1 immediately leaving the zero state has weight at most $2e$. Therefore $\tau(1) = 2$.

$\underline{e = 2}$ All walks of length 7 immediately leaving the zero state have weight more than $2e = 4$ (this takes some checking!). At least one walk of length 6 immediately leaving the zero state has weight at most $2e$: 000, 100, 110, 111, 011, 001, 100 is such a walk. Therefore $\tau(2) = 7$. (The faster decoding algorithm to be presented in Section 8.4 will also calculate $\tau(e)$ quickly.)

Theorem 8.3.4 says that if we use the exhaustive decoding algorithm with window size $\tau(1)$, then all error patterns with at most $e = 1$ errors in any $\tau(1) = 2$ consecutive ticks will be corrected. So for example, the error pattern

$$e_1 = 10\,00\,01\,00\,01\,00\,10\ldots$$

will be corrected. Also, if we use the exhaustive decoding algorithm with window size $\tau(2)$, then all error patterns with at most $e = 2$ errors in any $\tau(2) = 7$ consecutive ticks will be corrected. So for example, the error pattern

$$e_2 = 11\,00\,00\,00\,00\,00\,00\ \ldots$$

will be corrected. Notice though that Theorem 8.3.4 does not guarantee that e_2 will be corrected if we choose $e = 1$ (there are $2 > e$ errors in the first tick of e_2), nor that e_1 will be corrected if we choose $e = 2$ (there are $4 > e$ errors in the first $\tau(2) = 7$ consecutive ticks of e_1). So, unlike the situation with block codes (of finite length) where there was no reason to consider $e < \lfloor (d-1)/2 \rfloor$, for decoding convolutional codes we have to make such a decision, choosing e so that the "most likely" (in some sense) error patterns will be corrected.

Exercises

8.3.6 For each of the following codes C and for $1 \le e \le \lfloor (d(C)-1)/2 \rfloor$, find $\tau(e)$ ($d(C)$ is found in Exercise 8.3.3, the state diagrams were found in Exercise 8.2.11, 8.2.12, and 8.2.13).

(a) $g_1(x) = 1+x^2$ and $g_2(x) = 1+x+x^2$

(b) $g_1(x) = 1+x+x^2+x^3$ and $g_2(x) = 1+x^2+x^3$

(c) $g_2(x) = 1+x^3+x^4$ and $g_2(x) = 1+x+x^2+x^4$

8.3.7 What happens if you try to calculate $\tau(e)$ when $e > \lfloor (d-1)/2 \rfloor$?

8.4 Truncated Viterbi decoding

In this section we present a *truncated Viterbi decoding algorithm* for $(2, 1, m)$ binary convolutional codes. This algorithm only makes 2^m calculations and stores 2^m walks of length τ at each tick, compared to calculating and storing 2^τ walks of length τ that the exhaustive decoding algorithm requires. It's worth mentioning at this point that in practice the window size τ is chosen to be somewhere between $4m$ and $6m$ (a number which is often considerably more than $\tau(e)$); this choice is based on probabilistic arguments that show that with such a choice of the window size, "very few" error patterns will be decoded incorrectly. So storing 2^m walks instead of 2^τ walks is a considerable saving in both time and space.

The truncated Viterbi decoder is faster than the exhaustive decoding algorithm because, for each state s, at most one walk of length τ from the current state to s is stored. We briefly describe this decoder, then present the algorithm more formally. Let the received word be $w = w_0, w_1, \ldots$. Recall that for $i \geq 0$, w_i is an n-tuple since we are representing codewords and received words in interleaved form. Therefore, because we are considering the case $n = 2$, w_i consists of 2 digits (the 2 digits received at time i).

For the first m ticks the decoder is still storing all walks from the zero state. However at time m, there are 2^m walks, each ending in a different state, so $t = m$ is the first time at which we have exactly one walk ending in each state. As the decoder builds the 2^m walks, it calculates how far the output of such a walk is from the received word and stores that distance together with the walk.

Once $t > m$, for each state $s = s_0, s_1, \ldots, s_{m-1}$ there are two states from which there are directed edges to state s; these two states are of course $S_0 = s_1, s_2, \ldots, s_{m-1}, 0$ and $S_1 = s_1, s_2, \ldots, s_{m-1}, 1$. At $t = m$ the decoder stores walks W_0 and W_1 from the current state to S_0 and S_1 respectively, as well as the distances $d(S_0; t)$ and $d(S_1; t)$ of W_0 and W_1 respectively to the received word. For $t > m$, at tick t the distance between w_{t-1} and the outputs on the directed edges from S_0 and S_1 to s are added to $d(S_0, t-1)$ and $d(S_1, t-1)$ respectively; the smaller of these two sums becomes $d(s; t)$ along with the extension of the walk W_0 or W_1 (whichever gave the smaller distance) to state s.

The walks are stored as a sequence of message digits, rather than a sequence of states or a sequence of outputs on directed edges. Once $t \geq \tau$, a message digit is to be decoded at each tick. The states with the smallest distance function $d(s; t)$ are considered: if the walks stored in each such state agree on which state to move to (that is, the walks have the same oldest message digit), then this message digit is decoded; if not all walks agree then we will flag the decoded message digit by decoding to $*$ (we could just arbitrarily decode to 0 in these situations, but it helps to see where neither message digit is obviously best). Since we have now decided upon this message digit, it can be removed from all stored walks. So the length of the stored walks is now reduced to $\tau - 1$, but will be increased back to τ when these walks are extended at tick $t+1$.

Algorithm 8.4.1 (truncated Viterbi decoding of $(n, 1, m)$ convolutional codes with window size τ) Let $w_0 w_1 \ldots$ be the received word.

1. (Initialization) If $t = 0$ then define

$$W(s;t) = s{*}{*}\cdots{*} \text{ (of length } \tau), \text{ and}$$

$$d(s;t) = \begin{cases} 0, & \text{if } s \text{ is the zero state, and} \\ \infty, & \text{otherwise.} \end{cases}$$

2. (Distance calculation) For $t > 0$ and for each state $s = s_0, s_1, \ldots, s_{m-1}$, define

$$d(s;t) = \min\{d(s_1, s_2, \ldots, s_{m-1}, 0; t-1) + d_0(s), \\ d(s_1, s_2, \ldots, s_{m-1}, 1; t-1) + d_1(s)\}$$

where $d_i(s)$ is the distance between w_{t-1} and the output on the directed edge from $s_1, s_2, \ldots, s_{m-1}, i$ to s.

3. (Walk calculation)

   (a) If $d(s_1, \ldots, s_{m-1}, i; t-1) + d_i(s) < d(s_1, \ldots, s_{m-1}, j; t-1) + d_j(s)$, $\{i, j\} = \{0, 1\}$, then form $W(s;t)$ from $W(s_1, \ldots, s_{m-1}, i; t-1)$ by adding the leftmost digit of s to the left of $W(s_1, \ldots, s_{m-1}, i; t-1)$ and then deleting the rightmost digit.

   (b) If $d(s_1, \ldots, s_{m-1}, 0; t-1) + d_0(s) = d(s_1, \ldots, s_m, 1; t-1) + d_1(s)$ form $W(s, t)$ from $W(s_1, \ldots, s_{m-1}, 0; t-1)$ by adding the leftmost digit of s to the left of $W(s_1, \ldots, s_{m-1}, 0; t-1)$, replacing each digit that disagrees with $W(s_1, \ldots, s_{m-1}, 1; t-1)$ with $*$, and then deleting the rightmost digit.

4. (Decoding) For $t \geq \tau$, let $S(t) = \{s \mid d(s;t) \leq d(s';t) \text{ for all states } s'\}$. If the rightmost digit in $W(s;t)$ is the same, say i, for all $s \in S(t)$ then decode the message digit i; otherwise decode the message digit $*$.

Remark Notice that the leftmost m digits in $W(s;t)$ necessarily equal s, so do not need to be stored. In Exercise 8.4.6 a generalization of Algorithm 8.4.1 is presented that decodes (n, k, m) convolutional codes.

Example 8.4.2 Consider the code C_1 with $g_1(x) = 1 + x + x^3$ and $g_2(x) = 1 + x^2 + x^3$. Let $w = w_0 w_1 w_2 \cdots = 11\ 00\ 00 \cdots \leftrightarrow 1 + x$ be the received word. We considered this example in some detail in Section 8.3. Choose a window size of $\tau = \tau(2) = 7$ (see Example 8.3.5). Recall that the state diagram for C_1 is Figure 8.10.

$\underline{t = 0}$ Define $W(s;0) = s{*}{*}{*}{*}$ for all states s, define $d(000;0) = 0$ and $d(s';0) = \infty$ for all states s' other than the zero state.

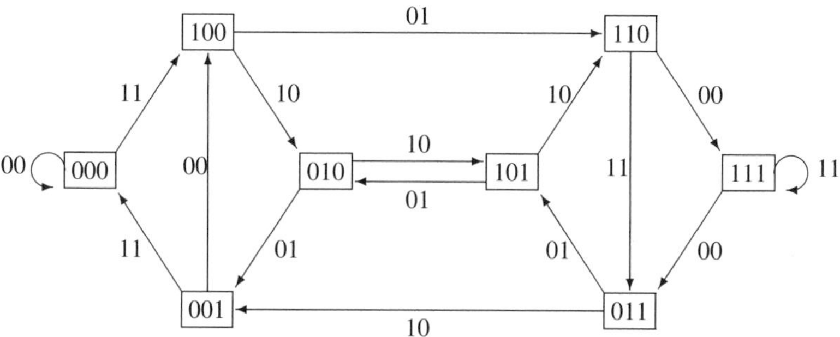

Figure 8.10: *The state diagram of C_1.*

$\underline{t=1}$ $w_{t-1} = w_0 = 11$. From step 2 of Algorithm 8.4.1 , we consider each state in turn.

$s = 000$:

$$\begin{aligned} d(000;1) &= \min\{d(000;0)+2, d(001;0)+0\} \\ &= \min\{2, \infty\} \\ &= 2. \end{aligned}$$

(The fact that $d_0(000) = 2$ follows from observing that the output on the directed edge from state 000 to 000 is 00, which differs from $w_0 = 11$ in 2 positions. Similarly $d_1(000) = 0$ since the output on the directed edge from state 001 to 000 is 11 which differs from w_0 in no positions.) Using the notation of step 3*a* of Algorithm 8.4.1, this minimum is achieved when $i = 0$, so we form $W(000;1)$ from $W(000,0)$ by adding the leftmost digit of state 000 to $W(000;0) = 000{*}{*}{*}{*}$ and then deleting the rightmost digit; therefore $W(000;1) = 0000{*}{*}{*}$.

$s = 100$:

$$\begin{aligned} d(100;1) &= \min\{d(000;0)+d_0(100), d(001;0)+d_1(100)\} \\ &= \min\{0+0, \infty+2\} \\ &= 0. \end{aligned}$$

Again the minimum is achieved when $i = 0$, so form $W(100;1)$ from $W(000;0)$ by adding the leftmost digit of $s = 100$ to $W(000;0)$ then deleting the rightmost digit; so $W(100;1) = 1000{*}{*}{*}$.

$s = 010$:

$$\begin{aligned} d(010;1) &= \min\{d(100;0)+d_0(010), d(101;0)+d_1(010)\} \\ &= \min\{\infty+1, \infty+1\} \\ &= \infty. \end{aligned}$$

In this case we use step 3*b*, since the minimum is achieved by both terms. We have

$$W(100;0) = 100{*}{*}{*}{*}, \text{ and}$$
$$W(101;0) = 101{*}{*}{*}{*}, \text{ so}$$
$$W(010;1) = 010{*}{*}{*}{*}.$$

The fourth "digit" of $W(010;1)$ is an $*$ because $W(100;0)$ and $W(101;0)$ disagree in this position.

Similarly, we can calculate $W(s;t)$ and $d(s;t)$ for the remaining states. Altogether we have calculated the following.

State s	$t=0$	$t=1$
000	$0, 000{*}{*}{*}{*}$	$2, 0000{*}{*}{*}$
100	$\infty, 100{*}{*}{*}{*}$	$0, 1000{*}{*}{*}$
010	$\infty, 010{*}{*}{*}{*}$	$\infty, 010{*}{*}{*}{*}$
110	$\infty, 110{*}{*}{*}{*}$	$\infty, 110{*}{*}{*}{*}$
001	$\infty, 001{*}{*}{*}{*}$	$\infty, 001{*}{*}{*}{*}$
101	$\infty, 101{*}{*}{*}{*}$	$\infty, 101{*}{*}{*}{*}$
011	$\infty, 011{*}{*}{*}{*}$	$\infty, 011{*}{*}{*}{*}$
111	$\infty, 111{*}{*}{*}{*}$	$\infty, 111{*}{*}{*}{*}$

(Each entry in the above table is: $d(s;t), W(s;t)$.)

Notice that the tabular representation of the state diagram lists beside each state s, the output on the edges directed in to s in the state diagram. These are precisely the outputs needed in the calculation of $d_0(s)$ and $d_1(s)$, so the tabular form is extremely useful here. We shall include it in the following tables.

Continuing the decoding process for $t=2$ and $t=3$, we obtain the following (notice now $w_1 = 00$ and $w_2 = 00$).

State	Output			
$s = X_0X_1X_2$	$X_3 = 0$	$X_3 = 1$	$t=2$	$t=3$
000	00	11	$2, 00000{*}{*}$	$2, 000000{*}$
100	11	00	$4, 10000{*}{*}$	$4, 100000{*}$
010	10	01	$1, 01000{*}{*}$	$5, 010000{*}$
110	01	10	$1, 11000{*}{*}$	$5, 110000{*}$
001	01	10	$\infty, 001{*}{*}{*}{*}$	$2, 001000{*}$
101	10	01	$\infty, 101{*}{*}{*}{*}$	$2, 101000{*}$
011	11	00	$\infty, 011{*}{*}{*}{*}$	$3, 011000{*}$
111	00	11	$\infty, 111{*}{*}{*}{*}$	$1, 111000{*}$

Notice that we have reached $t = 3 = m$. At this point $d(s;t) < \infty$ for all states s. This represents the fact that there is a walk of length m from the zero state to each other state. Until this point, when calculating the minimum value of the set in step 2 of Algorithm 8.4.1, one of the two values was ∞. For $t > m$, this is no longer the case.

$\underline{t=4}$ $w_3 = 00$. Consider each state in turn.
$s = 000$:

$$\begin{aligned} d(000;4) &= \min\{d(000;3)+d_0, d(001;3)+d_1\} \\ &= \min\{2+0, 2+2\} \\ &= 2 \end{aligned}$$

with the minimum being achieved when $i = 0$; so $W(000;4)$ is produced from $W(000;3)$. Therefore $W(000;4) = 0000000$.
$s = 100$:

$$\begin{aligned} d(100;4) &= \min\{d(000;3)+d_0, d(001;3)+d_1\} \\ &= \min\{2+2, 2+0\} \\ &= 2 \end{aligned}$$

with the minimum being achieved when $i = 1$; so $W(100;4)$ is produced from $W(001;3)$. Therefore $W(100;4) = 1001000$.
$s = 010$:

$$\begin{aligned} d(010;4) &= \min\{d(100;3)+d_0, d(101;3)+d_1\} \\ &= \min\{4+1, 2+1\} \\ &= 3 \end{aligned}$$

(where d_0 is the distance from w_3 to the output on the directed edge from state 100 to state 010, so $d_0 = 1$, and d_1 is the distance from w_3 to the output on the directed edge from 101 to 100, so $d_1 = 1$). Therefore $W(010;4)$ is produced from $W(101;3)$; so $W(0101;4) = 0101000$.

Proceeding similarly for each other state we get the following.

State	Output		
s	$X_3 = 0$	$X_3 = 1$	$t = 4$
000	00	11	2,0000000
100	11	00	2,1001000
010	10	01	3,0101000
110	01	10	3,1101000
001	01	10	4,0011000
101	10	01	4,1011000
011	11	00	1,0111000
111	00	11	3,1111000

$\underline{t=5}$ $w_4 = 00$. Consider each state in turn.
$s = 000$:

$$\begin{aligned} d(000;5) &= \min\{d(000;4)+d_0, d(001,4)+d_1\} \\ &= \min\{2+0, 4+2\} \\ &= 2, \end{aligned}$$

and $W(000;5) = 0000000$.

$s = 100$:

$$
\begin{aligned}
d(100;5) &= \min\{d(000;4)+d_0, d(001;4)+d_1\} \\
&= \min\{2+2, 4+0\} \\
&= 4.
\end{aligned}
$$

In this case, $d(000;4)+d_0 = d(001;4)+d_1$, so from step 3b, $W(100;5)$ is produced from both $W(000;4)$ and $W(001;4)$ by putting an $*$ whenever they disagree, adding the leftmost digit of 100 to the left and deleting the rightmost digit. Since $W(000;4) = 0000000$ and $W(001;4) = 0011000$, we get $W(100;5) = 100{*}{*}00$.

Proceeding similarly for the remaining states and then for $t = 6$ and 7 produces the following information.

State s	Output $X_3 = 0$	Output $X_3 = 1$	$t = 5$	$t = 6$	$t = 7$
000	00	11	2,0000000	2,0000000	2,0000000
100	11	00	4,100**00	2,1001110	4,100****
010	10	01	3,0100100	3,0101110	3,0100111
110	01	10	3,1100100	3,1101110	3,1100111
001	01	10	2,0011100	4,001**10	4,001*1*1
101	10	01	2,1011100	4,101**10	4,101*1*1
011	11	00	3,0111100	3,0111010	3,0111001
111	00	11	3,1110100	3,1110010	3,1110111

Finally we have reached $t = \tau$. We can now decode our first message digit using step 4 of Algorithm 8.4.1. In this case, $S(7) = \{000\}$ since $d(000;7) = 2 < d(s;7)$ for all states $s \neq 000$. Therefore the first message digit we decode is the rightmost digit in $W(000;7)$, namely 0. The rightmost digit in $W(s;7)$ is no longer used, so is discarded at $t = 8$ when constructing $W(s;8)$ (see step 3 of Algorithm 8.4.1).

The following table continues the decoding for several more ticks.

State s	$t = 8$	$t = 9$	$t = 10$	$t = 11$	$t = 12$
000	2,0000000	2,0000000	2,0000000	2,0000000	2,0000000
100	4,100****	4,100***0	4,100****	4,100***0	4,1000000
010	5,010****	5,010****	5,010****	5,010****	5,0100***
110	5,110****	5,110****	5,110****	5,110****	5,1100***
001	4,001****	4,0011101	4,0011100	6,001****	6,001****
101	4,101****	4,1011101	4,1011100	6,101****	6,101****
011	3,0111011	3,0111001	5,0111***	5,01110**	5,01110**
111	3,1110011	5,111****	5,1110***	5,1110***	5,1110***
Decode to:	0	0	0	0	0

Example 8.4.3 Again consider the code C_1 of Example 8.4.2 and let $w = 11\ 00\ 00\ 00\ 10\ 00 \cdots \leftrightarrow 1+x+x^8$ be the received word. Again we will apply Algorithm 8.4.1 using a window size of $\tau(2) = 7$ (see Example 8.3.5). The calculations are the same as in Example 8.4.2 until $t = 5$, at which point the x^8 term in $w(x)$ comes in to play.

State	Output					
s	$X_3 = 0$	$X_3 = 1$	$t = 4$	$t = 5$	$t = 6$	$t = 7$
000	00	11	2,0000000	3,0000000	3,000∗∗∗0	3,0000∗∗∗
100	11	00	2,1001000	3,1000000	1,1001110	3,1001001
010	10	01	3,0101000	2,0100100	4,010∗∗∗0	2,0100111
110	01	10	3,1101000	4,110∗100	4,110∗∗∗0	2,1100111
001	01	10	4,0011000	1,0011100	3,0010010	5,001∗∗∗∗
101	10	01	4,1011000	3,101∗100	3,1010010	5,101∗∗∗∗
011	11	00	1,0111000	4,011∗100	4,0111∗10	4,01110∗1
111	00	11	3,1111000	4,111∗100	4,1110∗10	4,1110∗∗∗
Decode to:						1

In this case, at $t = 7$ the message digit 1 is decoded. If we assume the zero word was sent, then the third error introduced in $w(x)$ has caused the decoder to decode incorrectly.

Exercises

8.4.4 Continue to decode $w(x)$ in Example 8.4.3 for $t = 8, 9, 10, 11$ and 12. Will the decoded message digit be 0 for $t \geq 12$?

8.4.5 Again using the convolutional code C_1 with $g_1(x) = 1+x+x^3$ and $g_2(x) = 1+x^2+x^3$, use Algorithm 8.4.1 with a window size of $\tau(2) = 7$ to decode the following received words. Continue decoding until $t = 9$.

(a) $w(x) = 1+x^3 \leftrightarrow 10\ 01\ 00\ 00\ldots$

(b) $w(x) = 1+x+x^2 \leftrightarrow 11\ 10\ 00\ 00\ldots$

(c) $w(x) = x^3+x^8+x^{12} \leftrightarrow 00\ 01\ 00\ 00\ 10\ 00\ 10\ 00\ldots$

8.4.6 Algorithm 8.4.1 can be generalized to decode (n, k, m) convolutional codes as follows. (The state diagrams for such codes are defined in Exercise 8.2.14.)

1. Same as Algorithm 8.4.1.
2. For all $t > 0$ and for each state $s_0, s_1, \ldots, s_{m-k}$ define

$$d(s;t) = \min_u\{d(s_k, \ldots, s_{m-k}, u; t-1) + d_u\}$$

where u ranges over all binary words of length k and where d_u is the distance between w_{t-1} and the output on the directed edge from state $s_k, \ldots, s_{m-k}, u$ to state s in the state diagram.

3. (a) If $d(s_k, \ldots, s_{m-k}, u; t-1) + d_u < d(s_k, \ldots, s_{m-k}, v; t-1) + d_v$ for all $v \neq u$ then form $W(s; t)$ from $W(s_k, \ldots, s_{m-k}, u; t-1)$ by deleting the rightmost k digits from it and adding the leftmost k digits of s to it.

   (b) If $d(s_k, \ldots, s_{m-k}, u; t-1)$ is not the smallest value for a unique choice of u, then we could form $W(s; t)$ by choosing any such u and proceeding as in 3(a). Alternatively, as in Algorithm 8.4.1, we can take a combination of all the walks $W(s_k, \ldots, s_{m-k}, u; t-1)$ for which $d(s_k, \ldots, s_{m-k}, u; t-1)$ is a minimum, placing an $*$ in any position where 2 such walks disagree.
4. For $t \geq \tau$, let $S(t) = \{s \mid d(s; t) \leq d(s'; t)$ for all states $s'\}$. Decode the message digits $m_{1,t}, m_{2,t} \ldots m_{k,t}$ where $m_{i,t}$ is the ith digit in the rightmost k digits of $W(s, t)$, for all $s \in S(t)$, unless two such walks disagree in the ith position in which case $m_{i,t} = *$.

Check that this is a generalization of Algorithm 8.4.1.

There are several comments that should be made concerning Algorithm 8.4.1. First, there are other ways to define the decoding step, step 4, of Algorithm 8.4.1. For example, it could be argued that decoding should not take place until the walks to each state agree on the rightmost digit (that is, the digit used for decoding). However in such an algorithm we might need to wait for many ticks before any decoding can be done, thus raising the problem of open ended storage requirements. Another variation of step 4 of Algorithm 8.4.1 would be to delete each walk in which the rightmost digit disagrees with the message digit currently being decoded (because such walks choose to move to a different state). This decoding technique poses theoretical problems in the analysis of the algorithm, as it is conceivable that such a decoding algorithm might itself impose infinitely many decoding errors after a finite burst of errors during transmission.

Second, we should ask if we can still prove a result as strong as Theorem 8.3.4 for the truncated Viterbi decoder of Algorithm 8.4.1. The answer is no, because this truncated Viterbi decoding algorithm takes some time to recover from errors imposed on the codeword during transmission. To see why there should be a difference between the two algorithms, consider tick $t = 2$ in Example 8.4.2. When using the truncated Viterbi decoding algorithm, the walk staying in state 000 "remembers" the 2 errors that occurred in w at tick $t = 1$ when $w_{t-1} = 11$. It remembers the errors because $d(000; 2) = 2$. In Example 8.4.7 we will see that the effect of these 2 errors lasts until $t = 12$. On the other hand, for the exhaustive decoding algorithm the 2 errors affected the decoding decision at tick $t = 1$, but had no effect for $t \geq 2$ (recall that for $t \geq 2$, the walks of length τ from state 000 were all compared to $w_{t-1}, w_t, \ldots, w_{t+\tau-2} = 00\ldots0$, a portion of the received word that agrees exactly with the walk staying in the zero state).

We shall now be more precise about how long errors during transmission will affect the decoding when using the truncated Viterbi decoder with window size $\tau(e)$ defined by Algorithm 8.4.1. We begin with some definitions. Let $w(s, s')$ be the weight of a least weight path from s to s' in the state diagram. Suppose that state $s(t)$ is the correct state at some tick t (that is, $s(t)$ is the state the codeword sent is in at tick t). Then the decoder is defined to be *e-ready* at tick t if the following conditions hold:

(1) $d(s';t) \geq d(s(t);t) + \min\{1+e, w(s(t),s')\}$ for all states $s' \neq s(t)$, and

(2) if $w(s(t),s') < 1+e$ then $W(s';t) = s'v$ (of length τ), where v is defined by $W(s(t);t) = s(t)v$.

Example 8.4.7 Consider Example 8.4.2. The correct state for all $t \geq 1$ is $s(t) = 000$, since we are assuming that the codeword sent was the zero word. Since in this case $m = 3$ is small, it is not hard to calculate $w(s(t),s') = w(000,s')$ for all states $s' \neq 000$ from the state diagram:

$$w(000,100) = 2, w(000,010) = 3, w(000,001) = 4, w(000,110) = 3,$$
$$w(000,101) = 4, w(000,011) = 3, w(000,111) = 3.$$

The first time that the decoder is 2-ready in Example 8.4.2 is at $t = 12$. To see this, notice the following observations.

At $t = 10, d(001;10) = 4 < 5 = d(000;10) + \min\{1+e, w(000,001)\}$, so (1) in the definition of e-ready is not satisfied.

At $t = 11$, all states satisfy (1) in the definition of e-ready, but $w(000,100) = 2 < 3 = 1+e$ and $W(100;11) = 100{*}{*}{*}{*} \neq 100v$ (since $W(000;11) = 0000000 = s(11)v$, so $v = 0000$).

At $t = 12$, all states satisfy (1). $s' = 100$ is the only state with $w(000,s') < 1+e$, and $W(100;12) = 1000000 = s'0000 = s'v$.

The following result demonstrates the value of being e-ready.

Theorem 8.4.8 *Let C be a non-catastrophic convolutional code which is decoded using the truncated Viterbi decoder of Algorithm 8.4.1. At tick t, if the decoder is e-ready, then correct decoding will occur if at most e errors are subsequently made during transmission.*

This result makes sense of the name e-ready. However, clearly this result is still much weaker than Theorem 8.3.4. A *guard space* is defined to be a time period of error-free transmission following a burst of errors. To obtain a result comparable to Theorem 8.3.4 would require knowing how long a guard space is required before the decoder is e-ready. For the exhaustive decoder, Theorem 8.3.4 says that the guard space required is 0 (if we think of e-ready as meaning that any subsequent error pattern of weight at most e will still result in a received word that is decoded correctly). It turns out that it can be proved that the guard space required for our truncated Viterbi decoder to become e-ready after a burst of errors is finite, and that the length of the guard space is known for some convolutional codes where m is small. The closest we can get to Theorem 8.3.4 is the following result.

Theorem 8.4.9 *Let C be a non-catastrophic convolutional code which is decoded using the truncated Viterbi decoder with window size $\tau(e)$ of Algorithm 8.4.1. If the error pattern can be partitioned into bursts of errors, each of weight at most e and each followed by a sufficiently long (finite) guard space, then the decoder will decode correctly.*

Exercises

8.4.10 (a) Apply Algorithm 8.4.1 using a window size of $\tau(2) = 6$ to decode the received word $w = 11\ 00\ 00 \cdots \leftrightarrow 1 + x = w(x)$ that was originally encoded using the $(2, 1, 2)$ convolutional code with generators $g_1(x) = 1 + x^2$ and $g_2(x) = 1 + x + x^2$. Continue decoding to show that the decoder is 2-ready at $t = 10$, assuming that the zero word is the codeword that was sent (so the correct state $s(t)$ is the zero state, for all t).

(b) At $t = 9$ the decoder is not 2-ready, so Theorem 8.4.8 does not guarantee that any subsequent error pattern of weight at most $e = 2$ will be decoded correctly. Show that if at $t = 10$ and at $t = 11$, the digits in the received word are each changed to 10, (so the received word is $w(x) = 1 + x + x^{18} + x^{20}$) then the decoder decodes an $*$ at $t = 12$.

8.4.11 For each of the received words in Exercise 8.4.5, find the smallest t such that at tick t the decoder is 2-ready.

Finally, we return to the calculation of $d(C)$ and $\tau(e)$. In both cases we have to find weights of walks from the zero state that immediately leave the zero state. To find $d(C)$ we want the weight of such a walk that has the smallest possible weight, to find $\tau(e)$ we want the length x such that all such walks of length at least x have weight more than $2e$. We can modify the truncated Viterbi decoder of Algorithm 8.4.1 to do both these tasks. First, by assuming that the zero word is sent, the distance function is simply measuring the weights of the walks, as we now require. Second, to force the walks to immediately leave the zero state, we simply define $d(00\ldots0; 1) = \infty$. This has the effect of removing the walk that stays at the zero state from consideration, since the only walk remaining with $d(s; 1)$ being finite is the walk to $s = 100\ldots0$ (that is, the walk that immediately leaves the zero state). Third, we need not store the walks $W(s; t)$ since they are of no concern in these calculations. Fourth, we need to recognize the answer! For any non-catastrophic code, every finite weight walk returns to the zero state and remains there. At each tick $t, d(s; t)$ is the weight of a least weight walk of length t that immediately leaves the zero state (in view of the second consideration) and ends in state s. Also, if at tick t $d(s; t) \geq d(00\ldots0; t)$ for all states s then $d(00\ldots0; t') = d(00\ldots0; t)$ for all $t' \geq t$ (because from Step 2 of Algorithm 8.4.1 it is clear that for any state

$s', d(s';t') \geq \min_s\{d(s;t'-1)\}$). Therefore $d(C) = d(00\ldots0;t)$. Similarly, once $d(s;t) > 2e$ for all states s, all walks of length t that immediately leave the zero state have weight more than $2e$. So $\tau(e)$ is the first tick t such that $d(s;t) > 2e$ for all states s. Therefore we have the following modification of Algorithm 8.4.1 to find $d(C)$ and $\tau(e)$.

Algorithm 8.4.12 (finding $d(C)$ and $\tau(e)$ for a non-catastrophic convolutional code) Let $\text{wt}(s;s')$ be the weight on the edge in the state diagram directed from s to s'.

1. If $t = 1$ then define

$$d(s;t) = \begin{cases} \text{wt}(00\ldots0;100\ldots0), & \text{if } s = 100\ldots0, \\ \infty, & \text{otherwise.} \end{cases}$$

2. For $t > 1$ and for each state $s = s_0,\ldots,s_{m-1}$, define

$$d(s;t) = \min\{d(s_1,\ldots,s_{m-1},0;t-1) + \text{wt}(s_1,\ldots,s_{m-1},0;s), \\ d(s_1,\ldots,s_{m-1}1;t-1) + \text{wt}(s_1,\ldots,s_{m-1},1;s)\}.$$

3. If $d(00\ldots0;t) \geq d(s;t)$ for all states s then $d(C) = d(00\ldots0;t)$.
4. If $d(s;t) > 2e$ for all states s and if $d(s';t-1) \leq 2e$ for some state s' then $\tau(e) = t$.

Remark If we assume that $w = 000\ldots$ is the received word, then Algorithm 8.4.12 is essentially Algorithm 8.4.1 except that $d(00\ldots0;1)$ is defined to be ∞ and $W(s;t)$ is never calculated.

Example 8.4.13 We find $d(C)$ and $\tau(e)$, $1 \leq e \leq \lfloor (d(C)-1)/2 \rfloor$ for the convolutional code C_1 with generators $g_1(x) = 1+x+x^3$ and $g_2(x) = 1+x^2+x^3$. (These were previously calculated in Example 8.3.6 and in the text before Exercise 8.3.5.) We follow the format used in Example 8.4.2 when applying Algorithm 8.4.1.

State	Output											
s	$X_3 = 0$	$X_3 = 1$	$t = 1$	2	3	4	5	6	7	8	9	10
000	00	11	∞	∞	∞	6	6	6	6	6	6	6
100	11	00	2	∞	∞	4	6	4	6	6	6	6
010	10	01	∞	3	∞	5	5	5	5	7	7	7
110	01	10	∞	3	∞	5	5	5	5	7	7	7
001	01	10	∞	∞	4	6	4	6	6	6	6	6
101	10	01	∞	∞	4	6	4	6	6	6	6	6
011	11	00	∞	∞	5	3	5	5	5	5	5	7
111	00	11	∞	∞	3	5	5	5	5	5	7	7

At $t = 10, d(000; 10) \geq d(s; 10)$ for all states s, so $d(C) = d(000; 10) = 6$ (by Step 3 of Algorithm 8.4.11).

Since $1 \leq e \leq \lfloor (d(C) - 1)/2 \rfloor$, we consider $e = 1$ and $e = 2$ in turn.

If $e = 1$ then $d(s; 2) > 2e$ for all states s and $d(100; 1) = 2 \leq 2e$. Therefore $\tau(1) = 2$ (by Step 4 of Algorithm 8.4.12).

If $e = 2$, then $d(s; 7) > 2e$ for all states s and $d(100; 6) = 4 \leq 2e$. Therefore $\tau(2) = 7$ (by Step 4 of Algorithm 8.4.12).

Exercises

8.4.14 For each of the convolutional codes C with the following generators, use Algorithm 8.4.12 to find $d(C)$ and $\tau(e)$ for $1 \leq e \leq \lfloor (d(C) - 1)/2 \rfloor$. Compare your answers to those of Exercises 8.3.3 and 8.3.6.

(a) $g_1(x) = 1 + x^2$ and $g_2(x) = 1 + x + x^2$

(b) $g_1(x) = 1 + x + x^2 + x^3$ and $g_2(x) = 1 + x^2 + x^3$

(c) $g_1(x) = 1 + x^3 + x^4$ and $g_2(x) = 1 + x + x^2 + x^4$.

Chapter 9

Reed-Muller and Preparata Codes

9.1 Reed-Muller codes

In Chapter 3, we gave a method of constructing Reed-Muller Codes, $RM(r, m)$ and established many basic properties. Recall that these are linear (n, k, d) codes with $n = 2^m$, $k = \sum_{i=0}^{r} \binom{m}{i}$, and $d = 2^{m-r}$. In this section we will give an alternate construction of these codes; one that is better suited to decoding.

As with Reed-Solomon and other codes we will label the coordinate positions of words of length $n = 2^m$, this time by vectors in K^m. As a matter of convenience and consistency we will label coordinate position i with vector $u_i \in K^m$, where u_i is the binary representation of the integer i, with digits in reverse order (low order digit first); call this the *standard ordering* of K^m.

Example 9.1.1 Standard ordering for

$$K^2 \text{ is } (00, 10, 01, 11), \text{ and for } K^3 \text{ is } (000, 100, 010, 110, 001, 101, 011, 111).$$

Any function, f, from K^m to $\{0, 1\}$ has a unique representation or *vector form* $v = (f(u_0), f(u_1), \ldots, f(u_{2^m-1})) \in K^n$ where $u_i \in K^m$, $n = 2^m$ and $u_0, u_1, \ldots,$ u_{2^m-1} is the standard ordering of vectors in K^m as described above.

We are interested in a certain class of basic functions. Given a subset $I \subseteq \{0, 1, \ldots, m-1\}$, define a function

$$f_I(x_0, x_1, \ldots, x_{m-1}) = \begin{cases} \prod_{i \in I}(x_i + 1), & \text{if } I \neq \emptyset, \\ 1, & \text{if } I = \emptyset. \end{cases}$$

(f_I is a function mapping K^m to $\{0, 1\}$.) Define v_I to be the corresponding vector form of f_I.

Example 9.1.2 Let $m = 3$, so $n = 2^3$.

(a) If $I = \{1, 2\}$ then $f_I(x_0, x_1, x_2) = (x_1 + 1)(x_2 + 1)$. The vector form of $f_{\{1,2\}}(x_0, x_1, x_2)$ is formed by taking each of the elements $x_0x_1x_2 \in K^3$ (using the standard ordering) and evaluating $f_{\{1,2\}}(x_0, x_1, x_2)$. So $f_{\{1,2\}}(0, 0, 0)$

$= 1$, $f_{\{1,2\}}(1,0,0) = 1$, $f_{\{1,2\}}(0,1,0) = 0$, $f_{\{1,2\}}(1,1,0) = 0$, $f_{\{1,2\}}(0,0,1) = 0$, $f_{\{1,2\}}(1,0,1) = 0$, $f_{\{1,2\}}(0,1,1) = 0$ and $f_{\{1,2\}}(1,1,1) = 0$. Therefore $v_I = 11000000$.

(b) If $I = \{0\}$ then $f_I(x_0, x_1, x_2) = (x_0 + 1)$ and $v_I = 10101010$.

(c) If $I = \emptyset$, then $f_\emptyset(x_0, x_1 x_2) = 1$ and $v_I = 11111111$.

There are two facts about the function f_I, which we will use later. First of all, $f_I(x_0, x_1, \ldots, x_{m-1}) = 1$ if and only if $x_i = 0$ for all $i \in I$. Thus in Example 9.1.2(a), $I = \{1,2\}$, $f_I(x_0, x_1, x_2) = (x_1+1)(x_2+1)$ and $f(x_0, 0, 0) = (0+1)(0+1) = 1$ for $x_0 \in \{0,1\}$. Second, for each $u_i \in K^m$ $f_I(u_i) f_J(u_i) = f_{I \cup J}(u_i)$ and thus

$$\begin{aligned} v_I \cdot v_J &= \sum_{i=0}^{2^m-1} f_I(u_i) f_J(u_i) \\ &= \sum_{i=0}^{2^m-1} f_{I \cup J}(u_i) \\ &= \mathrm{wt}(v_{I \cup J}) \pmod 2. \end{aligned}$$

We will use Z_m to denote the set of integers $\{0, 1, 2, \ldots, m-1\}$.

Exercises

9.1.3 Let $m = 4$, so $n = 2^4$. For each of the following choices of I, subsets of Z_4, find f_I and v_I:

(a) $I = \{0, 3\}$

(b) $I = \{0, 1, 3\}$

(c) $I = \{1\}$

(d) $I = \{2, 3\}$

(e) $I = \emptyset$

(f) $I = Z_4$

9.1.4 Let $m = 5$, so $n = 2^5$. For each of the following choices of I, subsets of Z_5, find f_I and v_I:

(a) $I = \{0, 2, 4\}$

(b) $I = \{0, 1, 3, 4\}$

(c) $I = \{1\}$

(d) $I = \{1, 2, 4\}$

(e) $I = \emptyset$

(f) $I = Z_5$.

9.1.5 Let I be a subset of Z_m. Use the first fact above to show that $\mathrm{wt}(v_I) = 2^{m-|I|}$.

9.1.6 If v is a linear combination of vectors of the form v_I, when will v have even weight?

9.1.7 Let $m = 4$, so $n = 2^4$. For $I = \{0, 1, 3\}$ and $J = \{2, 3\}$, compute $v_I \cdot v_J$.

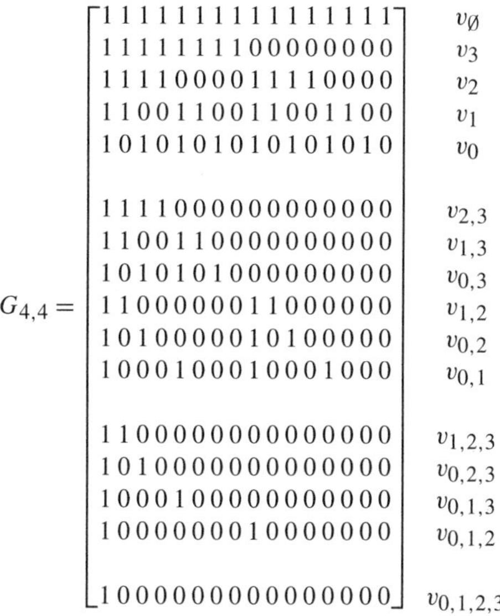

Figure 9.1: The generator matrix $G_{4,4}$.

The *Reed-Muller code* $RM(r,m)$ can be defined as the linear code $\langle\{v_I \mid I \subseteq Z_m, |I| \leq r\}\rangle$. We claim that $S = \{v_I \mid I \subseteq Z_m, |I| \leq r\}$ is a linearly independent set (see Exercise 9.1.10), and thus a basis for $RM(r,m)$. By counting the number of words v_I with $I \subseteq Z_m$ and $|I| \leq r$, we have that for $RM(r,m)$,

$$k = \binom{m}{0} + \binom{m}{1} + \cdots + \binom{m}{r},$$

and clearly $n = 2^m$. Of course the words v_I can be arranged in any order to form a generating matrix for $RM(r,m)$. We define the generating matrix $G_{r,m}$ of $RM(r,m)$ to be in *canonical form* if the rows are ordered so that v_I comes before v_J if $|I| < |J|$, or if $|I| = |J|$, $f_I(u_j) < f_J(u_j)$ and $f_I(u_i) = f_J(u_i)$ for $i > j$.

Example 9.1.8 The generator matrix for $R(4,4)$ in canonical form is $G_{4,4}$ given in Figure 9.1. For convenience, we have written $v_{\{3\}}$ as v_3 (and similarly for the other subscripts). This ordering follows from the definition as the following examples indicate. If $I = \{3\}$ and $J = \{2,3\}$, since $|I| < |J|, v_3 = v_I$ precedes $v_{2,3} = v_J$. If $I = \{2,3\}$ and $J = \{0,2\}$ then $f_I(u_i) = f_J(u_i)$ for $i > 10$ but $f_I(u_{10}) = 0 < 1 = f_J(u_{10})$ (of course, u_{10} in the standard ordering of K^4 is 0101). Therefore $v_{2,3} = v_I$ precedes $v_{0,2} = v_J$.

Now it is easy to see that $G_{0,4}$, $G_{1,4}$, $G_{2,4}$ and $G_{3,4}$ are simply the submatrices of $G_{4,4}$ formed by the first $\binom{4}{0} = 1$, $\binom{4}{0} + \binom{4}{1} = 5$, $\binom{4}{0} + \binom{4}{1} + \binom{4}{2} = 11$ and $\binom{4}{0} + \binom{4}{1} + \binom{4}{2} + \binom{4}{3} = 15$ rows respectively.

Exercises

9.1.9 Find (a) $G_{2,3}$ (b) $G_{2,4}$ (c) $G_{3,5}$ (d) $G_{0,10}$

9.1.10 Show that for all $r \leq m$, $\{v_I \mid |I| \leq r, I \subseteq Z_m\}$ is a linearly independent set. (Hint: Arrange the words in this set so that v_I comes before v_J if, for some j, $f_I(u_i) = f_J(u_i)$ for $j+1 \leq i \leq m$ and $f_I(u_j) > f_J(u_j)$. Or, more formally, use induction on m and r.)

Encoding is done, as for any linear code, by multiplying a message by $G_{r,m}$. Then any codeword c can be written as

$$c = \sum_{I \subseteq Z_m, |I| \leq r} m_I v_I,$$

(where the message digits are labeled m_I to correspond to the rows v_I of $G_{r,m}$).

Example 9.1.11 Encoding the following messages m using $G_{2,4}$ results in the corresponding codeword c.

(a) If $m = 1\ 0000\ 001000$ (so $m_\emptyset = 1$ and $m_{0,3} = 1$) then

$$c = v_\emptyset + v_{0,3} = 0101010111111111.$$

(b) If $m = 0\ 0101\ 001001$ (so $m_2 = m_0 = m_{0,3} = m_{0,1} = 1$) then

$$c = v_2 + v_0 + v_{0,3} + v_{0,1} = 0111100011010010.$$

Exercises

9.1.12 Encode the following messages using $G_{2,4}$.

(a) 0 0101 000000

(b) 0 0000 000001

(c) 0 0100 001000

9.2 Decoding Reed-Muller codes

We shall decode the Reed-Muller codes using an easily implementable process known as *majority logic decoding*. To understand this, we shall need some preliminary results. For any $I \subseteq Z_m$, define $I^c = Z_m \backslash I$ to be the *complement* of I in Z_m.

Let $H_I = \{u \in K^m \mid f_I(u) = 1\}$. Recall $f_I(x_0, \ldots, x_{m-1}) = \prod_{i \in I}(x_i + 1) = 1$ if and only if $x_i = 0$ for all $i \in I$. Clearly if $x, y \in H_I$, then $x_i = y_i = 0 = x_i + y_i$ for all $i \in I$, thus $x + y \in H_I$. Therefore H_I is a subspace of K^m.

For any $u = (x_0, x_1, \ldots, x_{m-1}) \in K^m$ and for any $t = (t_0, t_1, \ldots, t_{m-1}) \in K^m$, define another function $f_{I,t}(x_0, x_1, \ldots, x_{m-1}) = f_I(x_0 + t_0, \ldots, x_{m-1} + t_{m-1}) = f_I(x + t)$ and define $v_{I,t}$ to be the vector form of $f_{I,t}$.

We will be interested in finding $v_{I,s} \cdot v_{J^c,t}$, and so we need to count the number of words $u \in K^m$ for which $f_{I,s}(u)f_{J^c,t}(u) = 1$. By the definition of H_I, $f_{I,t}(u) = f_I(u+t) = 1$ if and only if $u+t = u' \in H_I$, or equivalently $u = u'+t \in H_I + t$, where $H_I + t$ is the coset of H_I determined by t. And the value of $f_{I,s}(u)f_{J^c,t}(u) = \prod_{i \in I}(x_i + s_i + 1)\prod_{j \in J^c}(x_j + t_j + 1)$ remains the same for all choices of $x_k \in \{0, 1\}, k \in Z_m \backslash (I \cup J^c)$. As there are $2^{m-|I \cup J^c|}$ such choices for u as u ranges over the elements of K^m, the number of times

$$f_{I,s}(u)f_{J^c,t}(u) = 1$$

is a multiple of $2^{m-|I \cup J^c|}$ and thus even unless $|I \cup J^c| = m$; that is, unless $I \cup J^c = Z_m$. However, if we assume that $|I| \leq |J|$ then $|J^c| \leq |I^c|$. So $|I \cup J^c| = |I| + |J^c| - |I \cap J^c| < m$ unless $I = J$. If $I = J$ then there is only one $u \in K^m$ for which $f_{I,s}(u)f_{I^c,t}(u) = 1$, namely the u for which $x_i = s_i$ for all $i \in I$ and $x_i = t_i$ for all $i \in I^c$.

Of course, finding the number of places where $f_{I,s}(u)f_{J^c,t}(u) = 1$ immediately gives $v_{I,s} \cdot v_{J^c,t}$, so we have the following result.

Lemma 9.2.1 *Let I and J be subsets of Z_m, with $|I| \leq |J|$. For any $s \in H_{I^c}$ and for any $t \in H_J$,*

$$v_{I,s} \cdot v_{J^c,t} = 1 \text{ if and only if } I = J.$$

Now we can easily obtain the following result which is the basis of the decoding scheme that we shall use.

Corollary 9.2.2 *If c is a codeword in $RM(r,m)$ and if $|J| = r$ then $m_J = c \cdot v_{J^c,t}$ for any $t \in H_J$.*

Proof: If $|J| = r$ then for any $t \in H_J$,

$$c \cdot v_{J^c,t} = \sum_{I \subseteq Z_m, |I| \leq r} m_I v_I \cdot v_{J^c,t} = m_J v_J \cdot v_{J^c,t} = m_J.$$

since by Lemma 9.2.1, the only dot product in the sum which is not zero is the one with $I = J$. □

Lemma 9.2.3 *Let $J \subseteq Z_m$. For any word e (of length 2^m), $e \cdot v_{J^c,t} = 1$ for at most $\mathrm{wt}(e)$ values of $t \in H_J$.*

Proof: Recall that for any subspace S of K^m, two words are in the same coset in the coset decomposition of S precisely when their sum is a word in S. Also, H_J is a subspace of K^m and the only word in both H_J and H_{J^c} is the zero word. It follows from these observations that no two words of H_J occur together in a coset of H_{J^c}. Therefore as t ranges over the elements of H_J, $H_{J^c} + t$ forms the coset decomposition of H_{J^c}.

The result now follows since if $t_1 \neq t_2$ are two different elements of H_J, we have just shown that $(H_{J^c} + t_1) \cap (H_{J^c} + t_2) = \emptyset$, so v_{J^c,t_1} and v_{J^c,t_2} have no positions in common where both the digits are 1. Therefore each of the wt(e) non-zero digits in e affects at most one of the values of $e \cdot v_{J^c,t}$ as t ranges over the elements of H_J. □

We can now obtain a decoding algorithm as follows. Let $w = c + e$ be a received word where c is a codeword in $RM(r,m)$; so $c = \sum_{I \subseteq Z_m} m_I v_I$, where $|I| \leq r$. Let $J \subseteq Z_m$ be a set of size r. Then by Lemma 9.2.3, $e \cdot v_{J^c,t} = 0$ for at least $|H_J| - \mathrm{wt}(e)$ values of t in H_J; for such values of t we have that

$$\begin{aligned} w \cdot v_{J^c,t} &= c \cdot v_{J^c,t} + e \cdot v_{J^c,t} \\ &= c \cdot v_{J^c,t} \\ &= m_J \text{ (by Corollary 9.2.2)} \end{aligned}$$

So if $2\,\mathrm{wt}(e) < |H_J|$, as t ranges over the elements of H_J, more than half of the $w \cdot v_{J^c,t}$ will be m_J.

Once m_J has been calculated in this way for all $J \subseteq I_m$ with $|J| = r$, let $w(r-1) = w + \sum_{|J|=r} m_J v_J$. Now $w(r-1)$ can be decoded by treating it as a received word that was encoded using $RM(r-1,m)$. This process can be continued until m_J has been found for all $J \subseteq I_m$ with $|J| \leq r$.

Before summarizing this algorithm we make note of the fact that this algorithm corrects all error patterns of weight less than $|H_J|/2$ where $|J| \leq r$. However by Exercise 9.1.5, $|H_J| = \mathrm{wt}(v_J) = 2^{m-|J|}$. So all error patterns of weight less than 2^{m-r-1} are corrected and therefore $RM(r,m)$ has minimum distance at least 2^{m-r}. However, if $I \subseteq Z_m$ and $|I| = r$ then v_I is a codeword in $RM(r,m)$ and has weight 2^{m-r}, so we have another proof of the following result:

Lemma 9.2.4 *The minimum distance of $RM(r,m)$ is 2^{m-r}.*

Algorithm 9.2.5 (majority logic decoding of $RM(r,m)$) To decode a received word, proceed as follows.

1. Let $i = r$ and let $w(r) = w$.
2. For each $J \subseteq Z_m$ with $|J| = i$, calculate $w(i) \cdot v_{J^c,t}$ for each $t \in H_J$ until either 0 or 1 occurs more than 2^{m-i-1} times and let m_J be 0 or 1 respectively; if both 0 and 1 occur more than $e = 2^{m-r-1} - 1$ times then ask for retransmission.
3. If $i > 0$ then let $w(i-1) = w(i) + \sum_{J \subseteq Z_m} m_J v_J$ where $|J| = i$. If $w(i-1)$ has weight at most $e = 2^{m-r-1} - 1$ then set $m_J = 0$ for all $J \subseteq Z_m$ with $|J| \leq r$ and stop. Otherwise replace i with $i-1$ and return to step 2. (If $i = 0$ then m_J has been calculated for all $J \subseteq Z_m$ with $|J| \leq r$, so the most likely message has been found.)

J	t	$v_{J^c,t}$	$w \cdot v_{J^c,t}$	m_J
$\{0, 1\}$	0000	1111 0000 0000 0000	0	
	0010	0000 1111 0000 0000	1	0
	0001	0000 0000 1111 0000	0	
	0011	0000 0000 0000 1111	0	
$\{0, 2\}$	0000	1100 1100 0000 0000	0	
	0100	0011 0011 0000 0000	1	1
	0001	0000 0000 1100 1100	1	
	0101	0000 0000 0011 0011	1	
$\{1, 2\}$	0000	1010 1010 0000 0000	1	
	1000	0101 0101 0000 0000	0	0
	0001	0000 0000 1010 1010	0	
	1001	0000 0000 0101 0101	0	
$\{0, 3\}$	0000	1100 0000 1100 0000	0	
	0100	0011 0000 0011 0000	0	0
	0010	0000 1100 0000 1100	1	
	0110	0000 0011 0000 0011	0	
$\{1, 3\}$	0000	1010 0000 1010 0000	0	
	1000	0101 0000 0101 0000	0	0
	0010	0000 1010 0000 1010	1	
	1010	0000 0101 0000 0101	0	
$\{2, 3\}$	0000	1000 1000 1000 1000	1	
	1000	0100 0100 0100 0100	0	0
	0100	0010 0010 0010 0010	0	
	1100	0001 0001 0001 0001	0	

Figure 9.2: *Majority logic decoding of* $RM(2,4)$*, Step 1 (see Example 9.2.6).*

Example 9.2.6 Use Algorithm 9.2.5 to decode the received word $w =$ 0101011110100000 that was originally encoded using $G_{2,4}$.

Begin with $i = r = 2$ and $w(2) = w$. From the computations of Figure 9.2 we see that $m_{2,3} = 0, m_{1,3} = 0, m_{0,3} = 0, m_{1,2} = 0, m_{0,2} = 1$, and $m_{0,1} = 0$. Then

$$w(1) = w(2) + v_{0,2} = 1111\,0111\,0000\,0000$$

and $i = 1$.

Again from the computations of Figure 9.3 we conclude that $m_3 = 1, m_2 = 0$, $m_1 = 0$, and $m_0 = 0$. Let $w(0) = w(1) - v_3 = 0000\,1000\,0000\,0000$ and let $i = 0$. Since $w(0)$ has weight at most $e = 1$, set $m_\emptyset = 0$ and stop.

So the most likely message is 0 1000 000010 (since messages were encoded using $G_{2,4}$).

Exercises

9.2.7 Messages are encoded using the generator matrix $G_{2,4}$. If possible decode the following received words:

J	t	$v_{J^c,t}$	$w_{(1)} \cdot v_{J^c,t}$	m_J
{0}	0000	1100 0000 0000 0000	0	
	0100	0011 0000 0000 0000	0	
	0010	0000 1100 0000 0000	1	0
	0110	0000 0011 0000 0000	0	
	0001	0000 0000 1100 0000	0	
	0101	0000 0000 0011 0000	0	
	0011	0000 0000 0000 1100		
	0111	0000 0000 0000 0011		
{1}	0000	1010 0000 0000 0000	0	
	1000	0101 0000 0000 0000	0	
	0010	0000 1010 0000 0000	1	0
	1010	0000 0101 0000 0000	0	
	0001	0000 0000 1010 0000	0	
	1001	0000 0000 0101 0000	0	
	0011	0000 0000 0000 1010		
	1011	0000 0000 0000 0101		
{2}	0000	1000 1000 0000 0000	1	
	1000	0100 0100 0000 0000	0	
	0100	0010 0010 0000 0000	0	0
	1100	0001 0001 0000 0000	0	
	0001	0000 0000 1000 1000	0	
	1001	0000 0000 0100 0100	0	
	0101	0000 0000 0010 0010		
	1101	0000 0000 0001 0001		
{3}	0000	1000 0000 1000 0000	1	
	1000	0100 0000 0100 0000	1	
	0100	0010 0000 0010 0000	1	1
	1100	0001 0000 0001 0000	1	
	0010	0000 1000 0000 1000	0	
	1010	0000 0100 0000 0100	1	
	0110	0000 0010 0000 0010		
	1110	0000 0001 0000 0001		

Figure 9.3: *Majority logic decoding of $RM(2,4)$, Step 2 (see Example 9.2.6).*

(a) $w = 0111\ 0101\ 1000\ 1000$
(b) $w = 0110\ 0110\ 0001\ 0000$
(c) $w = 0101\ 1010\ 0100\ 0101$
(d) $w = 1110\ 1000\ 1001\ 0001$
(e) $w = 0011\ 0000\ 0011\ 0100$
(f) $w = 1001\ 0110\ 0101\ 1010$
(g) $w = 1010\ 1000\ 1010\ 0000$
(h) $w = 0011\ 1100\ 0001\ 1100$
(i) $w = 1001\ 1101\ 0001\ 1101$

9.2.8 Messages are encoded using the generator matrix $G_{2,5}$. If possible decode the following received words:

(a) $w = 1100\ 1000\ 1110\ 0000\ 1100\ 0000\ 1100\ 0100$
(b) $w = 0101\ 0111\ 0101\ 1000\ 1000\ 1000\ 0111\ 1010$
(c) $w = 0011\ 0011\ 1111\ 0011\ 0011\ 0011\ 1111\ 1111$
(d) $w = 0100\ 0000\ 1111\ 1111\ 0000\ 1100\ 0000\ 1111$
(e) $w = 1001\ 0101\ 0110\ 1001\ 1001\ 0111\ 0110\ 1010$
(f) $w = 0011\ 1111\ 0011\ 0011\ 1100\ 1100\ 1100\ 0100$
(g) $w = 0100\ 0100\ 1111\ 1111\ 0000\ 1100\ 0000\ 1111$

9.3 Extended Preparata codes

In this section we shall refer to the coordinate positions of words of length 2^r by using the elements of $GF(2^r)$. This labeling of the positions was also used when considering BCH codes, although there the field element 0 was never used as a label. So for any subset U consisting of elements of $GF(2^r)$ let $\chi(U)$ be the word of length 2^r which is

$$\begin{array}{llll} 1 & \text{in position} & i & \text{if} \quad \beta^i \in U \text{ (for } 0 \le i \le 2^r - 2), \\ 1 & \text{in position} & 2^r - 1 & \text{if} \quad 0 \in U, \text{ and} \\ 0 & \text{otherwise} & & \end{array}$$

(where, as usual β is a primitive element of $GF(2^r)$).

Example 9.3.1 Let β be a primitive element of $GF(2^3)$. Then

$$\chi(\{0\}) = 000000001,$$
$$\chi(\{\beta^2, \beta^5, \beta^6\}) = 00100110, \text{ and}$$
$$\chi(\emptyset) = 00000000.$$

For any element α and any subset U of elements of $GF(2^r)$, let $U + \alpha = \{u + \alpha \mid u \in U\}$ and let $\alpha U = \{\alpha u \mid u \in U\}$. Also, for any two subsets U and V of elements of $GF(2^r)$, define the *symmetric difference* $U \triangle V$ of U and V to be $\{x \mid x \in U \text{ or } x \in V \text{ but } x \notin U \cap V\}$. Then it is easy to see that $\chi(U) + \chi(V) = \chi(U \triangle V)$.

Example 9.3.2 Let $GF(2^3)$ be constructed using $1+x+x^3$. Let $U=\{\beta^2,\beta^5,\beta^6\}$ and let $V=\{\beta^5,0\}$. Then

$$U+\beta^2=\{\beta^2+\beta^2,\beta^5+\beta^2,\beta^6+\beta^2\}=\{0,\beta^3,\beta^0\},$$

$\beta^2 U=\{\beta^2\beta^2,\beta^2\beta^5,\beta^2\beta^6\}=\{\beta^4,\beta^0,\beta\}$, and

$$\begin{aligned}\chi(U)+\chi(V)&=00100110+00000101\\&=00100011\\&=\chi(\beta^2,\beta^6,0\})\\&=\chi(U\triangle V).\end{aligned}$$

Definition 9.3.3 The *extended Preparata code* $P(r)$ is the set of codewords of the form $\chi(U)$ followed by $\chi(V)$ where U and V are subsets of elements of $GF(2^r)$ which satisfy

(i) $|U|$ and $|V|$ are even,

(ii) $\sum_{u\in U} u=\sum_{v\in V} v$,

(iii) $\sum_{u\in U} u^3+(\sum_{u\in U} u)^3=\sum_{v\in V} v^3$, and

(iv) r is odd.

We denote such codewords by $[\chi(U),\chi(V)]$. Since both $\chi(U)$ and $\chi(V)$ have length 2^r, $P(r)$ is a code of length 2^{r+1}.

Example 9.3.4 Construct $GF(2^3)$ using $1+x+x^3$. Let $U=\{\beta,\beta^2,\beta^5,0\}$ and let $V=\{\beta^0,\beta,\beta^2,\beta^3,\beta^6,0\}$. Clearly (i) and (iv) of Definition 9.3.3 are satisfied. Also

$$\sum_{u\in U} u=\beta+\beta^2+\beta^5+0=010+001+111+000=\beta^0,$$

$$\sum_{v\in V} v=\beta^0+\beta+\beta^2+\beta^3+\beta^6+0=100+010+001+110+101+000=\beta^0,$$

so (ii) is satisfied, and

$$\sum_{u\in U} u^3=\beta^3+\beta^6+\beta+0=110+101+010+000=\beta^2,$$

$$\sum_{v\in V} v^3=\beta^0+\beta^3+\beta^6+\beta^2+\beta^4+0=100+110+101+001+011+000=\beta^6,$$

so (iii) is satisfied since $\beta^2+(\beta^0)^3=\beta^6$. Therefore $[\chi(U),\chi(V)]=01100101$ 11110011 is a codeword in $P(3)$.

Notice that whether or not 0 is an element of U or of V does not affect any of the calculations in (ii), (iii) or (iv) of Definition 9.3.3. So 0 is only used in U or V to make $|U|$ or $|V|$ even. Therefore the digit in position 2^{r-1} of $\chi(U)$ is simply a parity check digit for $\chi(U)$, and similarly the digit in position $2^r - 1$ of $\chi(V)$ is a parity check digit for $\chi(V)$.

It turns out that $P(r)$ is not a linear code as the following result suggests (see Theorem 9.3.18). Therefore $P(r)$ does not have a dimension.

Lemma 9.3.5 *Suppose that* $[\chi(U), \chi(V)]$ *and* $[\chi(A), \chi(B)]$ *are codewords in* $P(r)$. *Let* $\alpha = \sum_{u\in U} u$. *Then* $[\chi(U \triangle A + \alpha), \chi(V \triangle B)]$ *is also a codeword in* $P(r)$.

Proof: We check that conditions (i), (ii), and (iii) of Definition 9.3.3 are satisfied by $[\chi(U \triangle A + \alpha), \chi(V \triangle B)]$.

(i) Since $|U|$, $|V|$, $|A|$, and $|B|$ are even,

$$\begin{aligned}|V \triangle B| &= |V| + |B| - 2|V \cap B| \text{ is even, and}\\ |U \triangle A + \alpha| &= |U \triangle A| \text{ (see Example 9.3.2)}\\ &= |U| + |A| - 2|U \cap A| \text{ is even.}\end{aligned}$$

(ii) First notice that for any subsets I and J of elements of $GF(2^r)$, $\sum_{x\in I\triangle J} x = \sum_{x\in I} x + \sum_{x\in J} x$ since any element β^i in both I and J is counted twice on the right hand side and not at all on the left, but $2\beta^i = 0$. Therefore

$$\begin{aligned}\sum_{x\in U\triangle A+\alpha} x = \sum_{y\in U\triangle A} (y+\alpha) &= \sum_{y\in U\triangle A} y + \alpha|U \triangle A|,\\ &= \sum_{y\in U} y + \sum_{y\in A} y + 0 \text{ (since } |U \triangle A| \text{ is even)}\\ &= \sum_{y\in V} y + \sum_{y\in B} y\\ &= \sum_{y\in V\triangle B} y.\end{aligned}$$

(iii)

$$\begin{aligned}&\sum_{x\in U\triangle A+\alpha} x^3 + \Big(\sum_{x\in U\triangle A+\alpha} x\Big)^3 = \sum_{y\in U\triangle A} (y+\alpha)^3 + \Big(\sum_{y\in V\triangle B} y\Big)^3\\ &= \sum_{y\in U} (y+\alpha)^3 + \sum_{y\in A} (y+\alpha)^3 + \Big(\sum_{y\in V} y + \sum_{y\in B} y\Big)^3\end{aligned}$$

$$= \sum_{y\in U} y^3 + \alpha \sum_{y\in U} y^2 + \alpha^2 \sum_{y\in U} y + \alpha^3 |U| + \sum_{y\in A} y^3 + \alpha \sum_{y\in A} y^2$$
$$+ \alpha^2 \sum_{y\in A} y + \alpha^3 |A| + \Big(\sum_{y\in V} y\Big)^3 + \Big(\sum_{y\in V} y\Big)^2 \Big(\sum_{y\in B} y\Big)$$
$$+ \Big(\sum_{y\in V} y\Big)\Big(\sum_{y\in B} y\Big)^2 + \Big(\sum_{y\in B} y\Big)^3.$$

But $\alpha = \sum_{y\in U} y$ and so $\sum_{y\in V} y = \sum_{y\in U} y = \alpha$. Also, $\left(\sum_{y\in V} y\right)^2 = \sum_{y\in V} y^2$ and again we use the fact that $|U|$ and $|A|$ are even. Therefore the above expression reduces to simply

$$\sum_{y\in V} y^3 + \sum_{y\in B} y^3 = \sum_{y\in V\triangle B} y^3. \qquad \square$$

Even though $P(r)$ is a non-linear code, it does have some properties in common with linear codes.

Definition 9.3.6 A code is *distance invariant* if for any pair of codewords c_1 and c_2, the number of codewords distance i from c_1 equals the number of codewords distance i from c_2 for $1 \le i \le n$.

So for any distance invariant code that contains the zero word, it follows immediately that the minimum distance is the weight of a non-zero codeword of smallest weight.

Corollary 9.3.7 *$P(r)$ is distance invariant.*

Proof: Let $[\chi(U), \chi(V)]$ and $[\chi(A), \chi(B)]$ be codewords in $P(r)$ that are distance i apart. By Lemma 9.3.5, $[\chi(U\triangle U+\alpha), \chi(V\triangle V)]$ and $[\chi(U\triangle A+\alpha), \chi(V\triangle B)]$ are both codewords, and it's not hard to see they must also be distance i apart. Since $U\triangle U = \emptyset$, $[\chi(U\triangle U+\alpha), \chi(V\triangle V)]$ is the zero word and so $[\chi(U\triangle A+\alpha), \chi(V\triangle B)]$ is a codeword of weight i. $\square$

The following lemma lists various properties of $P(r)$. These can be proved using the same ideas as were used in proving Lemma 9.3.5, and so are left as exercises.

Lemma 9.3.8 *Suppose that $[\chi(U), \chi(V)]$ is a codeword in $P(r)$. Then $P(r)$ also contains the following codewords:*

(i) $[\chi(V), \chi(U)]$,

(ii) $[\chi(U+\alpha), \chi(V+\alpha)]$ *for any* $\alpha \in GF(2^r)$ *and*

(iii) $[\chi(\alpha U), \chi(\alpha V)]$ *for any* $\alpha \in GF(2^r)$, $\alpha \neq 0$.

Example 9.3.9 From Example 9.3.4, $[\chi(U), \chi(V)]$ is a codeword in $P(3)$ where $U = \{\beta, \beta^2, \beta^5, 0\}$ and $V = \{\beta^0, \beta, \beta^2, \beta^3, \beta^6, 0\}$. By applying Lemma 9.3.8 with $\alpha = \beta^3$, we find that the following are also codewords:

(i) $[\chi(V), \chi(U)] = 11110011\,01100101$,

(ii)

$$[\chi(U+\alpha), \chi(V+\alpha)] = [\chi(\{\beta^0, \beta^5, \beta^2, \beta^3\}), \chi(\{\beta, \beta^0, \beta^5, 0, \beta^4, \beta^3\})]$$
$$= 10110100\,11011101,$$

(iii)

$$[\chi(\alpha U), \chi(\alpha V)] = [\chi(\{\beta^4, \beta^5, \beta, 0\}), \chi(\{\beta^3, \beta^4, \beta^5, \beta^6, \beta^2, 0\})]$$
$$= 01001101\,00111111.$$

Exercises

9.3.10 Apply Lemma 9.3.8 to the codeword $[\chi(U), \chi(V)]$ defined in Example 9.3.9 by using

(a) $\alpha = \beta^0$ (b) $\alpha = \beta$ (c) $\alpha = \beta^6$

9.3.11 Why is $[\chi(\alpha U), \chi(\alpha V)]$ not a codeword when $\alpha = 0$ (this possibility is excluded in Lemma 9.3.8)?

9.3.12 Show that the three words formed in Example 9.3.9 satisfy Definition 9.3.6.

We can use Lemma 9.3.8 to simplify the problem of finding the minimum distance of $P(r)$, but first we need one more lemma which indicates the reason that we require r to be odd.

Lemma 9.3.13 *If β is a primitive element of $GF(2^r)$ then β^3 is a primitive element if r is odd and is not primitive if r is even.*

Proof: We know that β^i is primitive if and only if the greatest common divisor of i and $2^r - 1$ is 1; that, is i and $2^r - 1$ are relatively prime (Exercise 5.1.18). If r is odd then $2^r - 1 \equiv 1 \pmod 3$ and if r is even then $2^r - 1 \equiv 0 \pmod 3$ (this is easy to prove, say by induction). So if r is even then we can write $2^r - 1 = 3x$ for some integer x and β^3 is not primitive. However if r is odd then write $2^r - 1 = 3x + 1$ and clearly β^3 is a primitive element. □

Corollary 9.3.14 *If r is odd then for each nonzero element x of $GF(2^r)$ there is a unique element y (called the cube root of x) such that $y^3 = x$.*

Theorem 9.3.15 *$P(r)$ has minimum distance 6.*

Proof: Since $P(r)$ is distance invariant, $P(r)$ contains a codeword of weight d, say $[\chi(U), \chi(V)]$. Then

$$d = \text{wt}(\chi(U)) + \text{wt}(\chi(V)) = |U| + |V|.$$

By (i) of Definition 9.3.3, d is even so we only need to show that $d \neq 2, d \neq 4$ and that there is a codeword of weight 6.

Suppose that $d = 2$. Then by using Lemma 9.3.8 (i) we can assume that $|U| = 2$ and $|V| = 0$. From (ii) of Lemma 9.3.8 we can assume that $U = \{0, x\}$ for some $x \in K; x \neq 0$. But then $\sum_{u \in U} u = 0 + x = x$ and since $V = \emptyset$, condition (ii) of Definition 9.3.3 does not hold.

Suppose that $d = 4$. Then again from Lemma 9.3.8 (i) we can assume that either $|U| = 4$ and $|V| = 0$ or $|U| = 2$ and $|V| = 2$. In the former case, by Lemma 9.3.8 (ii) we can assume that $U = \{0, x, y, z\}$ where x, y and z are distinct non-zero elements of K^r. Then condition (iii) of Definition 9.3.3 gives that

$$0^3 + x^3 + y^3 + z^3 + (0 + x + y + z)^3 = 0, \text{ so}$$
$$(x + y)(x + z)(y + z) = 0$$

which is impossible since x, y and z are distinct and non-zero. In the latter case, from Lemma 9.3.8 (ii) we can assume that $U = \{0, x\}$ and that $V = \{y, z\}, y \neq z$. Then from condition (iii) of Definition 9.3.3 we know that

$$0^3 + x^3 + (0 + x)^3 = y^3 + z^3.$$

But by Corollary 9.3.14 if $y^3 = z^3$ then $y = z$ which is a contradiction.

To find a codeword of weight 6, for any distinct non-zero elements x, y and z of K^r, let w be the unique (by Corollary 9.3.14) element of K^r for which $w^3 = x^3 + y^3 + z^3$. Also, define $u = w + x + y + z$. Then w is not equal to x, y or z (since if $w = x$ say, then $w^3 = x^3$, so $0 = y^3 + z^3$, so by Corollary 9.3.14 $y = z$) and $u \neq 0$ (for $w^3 + (x + y + z) = (x + y)(x + z)(y + z) \neq 0$, so by Corollary 9.3.14 $w \neq +x + y \neq z$). Now let $U = \{0, u\}$ and $V = \{w, x, y, z\}$. Since $u \neq 0$ and since w, x, y and z are distinct, $[\chi(U), \chi(V)]$ is a word of weight 6 and it is easy to check that it is also a codeword in $P(r)$. □

Example 9.3.16 Construct K^3 as in Example 9.3.14. Following the notation of Theorem 9.3.15, let x, y, and z be distinct non-zero field elements, say $x = \beta$, $y = \beta^3$, and $z = \beta^5$. Then define

$$\begin{aligned} w^3 = x^3 + y^3 + z^3 &= \beta^3 + \beta^9 + \beta^{15} \\ &= 110 + 001 + 100 \\ &= \beta^4 \\ &= \beta^{18} \text{ (since } \beta^7 = 1) \\ &= (\beta^6)^3 \end{aligned}$$

so $w = \beta^6$. Now define $u = w + x + y + z = \beta^6 + \beta + \beta^4 + \beta^5 = \beta^4$. Then with $U = \{0, u\} = \{0, \beta^4\}$ and $V = \{w, x, y, z\} = \{\beta^6, \beta, \beta^3, \beta^5\}$, we have that

$$[\chi(U), \chi(V)] = 00001001\ 01010110$$

is a codeword in $P(3)$ of weight 6.

Exercises

9.3.17 Construct K^3 with $1 + \beta + \beta^3 = 0$. For the following elements x, y and z of K^3 define w and u as in Theorem 9.3.15 to construct a codeword of weight 6 in $P(3)$.

(a) $x = \beta, y = \beta^2, z = \beta^3$

(b) $x = \beta, y = \beta^4, z = \beta^6$

(c) $x = \beta^0, y = \beta^3, z = \beta^6$

Theorem 9.3.18 *$P(r)$ is not a linear code.*

Proof: As was noted at the beginning of the section, $[\chi(U), \chi(V)] + [\chi(A), \chi(B)] = [\chi(U \triangle A), \chi(V \triangle B)]$. From the proof of Theorem 9.3.15, we can construct codewords $[\chi(U), \chi(V)]$ and $[\chi(A), \chi(B)]$ of $P(r)$ with $U = \{0, u_1\}$, $V = \{x, y_1, z_1, w_1\}$, $A = \{0, u_2\}$ and $B = \{x_2, y_2, z_2, w_2\}$. Then by Lemma 1.5, $c = [\chi(U \triangle A + u_1), \chi(V \triangle B)]$ is codeword in $P(r)$. Since $|U \triangle A + u_1| \leq 2$, since the distance between c and $[\chi(U \triangle A), \chi(V \triangle B)]$ is at most $2|U \triangle A + u_1| \leq 4$ and since $P(r)$ has minimum distance 6, $[\chi(U), \chi(V)] + [\chi(A), \chi(B)]$ is not a codeword in $P(r)$. Therefore $P(r)$ is a nonlinear code. □

Being nonlinear, $P(r)$ does not have a dimension, and we do not yet know the number of codewords in $P(r)$ but this number will be obtained as a consequence of the encoding scheme.

9.4 Encoding extended Preparata codes

In Section 5.4 we saw that $g(x) = m_\beta(x) m_{\beta^3}(x)$ is the generator of a 2 error-correcting BCH code with parity-check matrix

$$H = \begin{bmatrix} \beta^0 & \beta^0 \\ \beta^1 & \beta^3 \\ \beta^2 & \beta^6 \\ \vdots & \\ \beta^{2^m-2} & \beta^{3(2^m-2)} \end{bmatrix} \tag{9.1}$$

where β is a primitive element of $GF(2^r)$. Recall that $\deg(g(x)) = 2r$. Since $g(x)$ is the non-zero codeword of smallest degree, no linear combination of the first $2r$

rows of H in 9.1 can be zero. In fact, since $g(x)$ generates a cyclic code, it follows that each submatrix of H formed by $2r$ consecutive rows has full rank, and so has an inverse. Define A to be the submatrix of H formed by the last $2r$ rows, and let H' be formed by deleting the last $2r$ rows from H.

Example 9.4.1 Constructing K^3 using $1+x+x^3$, we have that

$$A = \begin{bmatrix} 010 & 110 \\ 001 & 101 \\ 110 & 001 \\ 011 & 111 \\ 111 & 010 \\ 101 & 011 \end{bmatrix} \leftrightarrow \begin{bmatrix} \beta & \beta^3 \\ \beta^2 & \beta^6 \\ \beta^3 & \beta^2 \\ \beta^6 & \beta^5 \\ \beta^5 & \beta^1 \\ \beta^6 & \beta^4 \end{bmatrix} \text{ and } A^{-1} = \begin{bmatrix} 001 & 011 \\ 111 & 010 \\ 011 & 101 \\ 110 & 100 \\ 101 & 110 \\ 111 & 001 \end{bmatrix}$$

Constructing $GF(2^5)$ using $1+x^2+x^5$ (see Exercise 5.1.15) we have that

$$A = \begin{bmatrix} 00011 & 01000 \\ 10101 & 00001 \\ 11110 & 00101 \\ 01111 & 10001 \\ 10011 & 00111 \\ 11101 & 11011 \\ 11010 & 01100 \\ 01101 & 10101 \\ 10010 & 10011 \\ 01001 & 01101 \end{bmatrix} \leftrightarrow \begin{bmatrix} \beta^{21} & \beta^{63} \\ \beta^{22} & \beta^{66} \\ \vdots & \vdots \\ \beta^{30} & \beta^{90} \end{bmatrix} \text{ and } A^{-1} = \begin{bmatrix} 00111 & 00010 \\ 00011 & 10001 \\ 10011 & 00011 \\ 11011 & 01010 \\ 01101 & 10101 \\ 10101 & 11001 \\ 00110 & 11111 \\ 11001 & 01110 \\ 11000 & 00111 \\ 10001 & 10100 \end{bmatrix}$$

Let $m = m_L, m_R$ be any binary word of length $2^{r+1} - 2r - 2$, where m_L is a binary word of length $2^r - 1$ and m_R is a binary word of length $2^r - 2r - 1$. Then by using polynomial notation for m_L and m_R, we have that

$$\begin{aligned} [m_L(\beta), m_L(\beta^3)] &\leftrightarrow m_L H, \text{ and} \\ [m_R(\beta), m_R(\beta^3)] &\leftrightarrow m_R H. \end{aligned}$$

Now define

$$v_R = [m_L(\beta) + m_R(\beta), m_L(\beta^3) + (m_L(\beta))^3 + m_R(\beta^3)]A^{-1}$$

Theorem 9.4.2 *Let r be odd. For any binary word m of length $2^{r+1} - 2r - 2$, if $\chi(U) = [m_L, p_L]$ and if $\chi(V) = [m_R, v_R, p_R]$, where p_L and p_R are parity-check digits for m_L and $[m_R, v_R]$ respectively, then $[\chi(U), \chi(V)]$ is a codeword in $P(r)$.*

Proof:

$$\begin{aligned} [m_R, v_R]H &= [m_R]H' + [v_R]A \\ &= [m_R(\beta), m_R(\beta^3)] + [m_L(\beta) + m_R(\beta), m_L(\beta^3) + (m_L(\beta))^3 + m_R(\beta^3)] \\ &= [m_L(\beta), m_L(\beta^3) + (m_L(\beta))^3]. \end{aligned}$$

But $[m_R, v_R]H = [\sum_{v \in V} v, \sum_{v \in V} v^3]$. Similarly, $m_L(\beta) = \sum_{u \in U} u$ and $m_L(\beta^3) + (m_L(\beta))^3 = \sum_{u \in U} u^3 + \left(\sum_{u \in U} u\right)^3$. Therefore conditions (ii) and (iii) of Definition 9.3.3 hold, and clearly conditions (i) and (iv) are satisfied. Therefore $[\chi(U), \chi(V)]$ is a codeword in $P(r)$. □

Corollary 9.4.3 *$P(r)$ has $2^{2^{r+1}-2r-2}$ codewords.*

Proof: In Theorem 9.4.2 there are $2^{2^{r+1}-2r-2}$ choices for m, each giving a different codeword, the remaining digits of the codeword containing m being completely determined by conditions (i), (ii), and (iii) of Definition 9.3.3. □

Algorithm 9.4.4 (encoding $P(r)$) Let m_L and m_R be words of length 2^{r-1} and $2^r - 2r - 1$ respectively. Let v_R be as defined in Theorem 9.4.2. Then $[m_L, p_L, m_R, v_R, p_R]$ is the codeword corresponding to the message $m = [m_L, m_R]$.

Example 9.4.5 Let $r = 3$, $m_L = 0110010$ and $m_R = 1$. Then

$$m_L(\beta) = \beta + \beta^2 + \beta^5 = \beta^0, \; m_R(\beta) = \beta^0,$$
$$m_L(\beta^3) = \beta^3 + \beta^6 + \beta^{15} = \beta^2 \text{ and } m_L(\beta^3) = \beta^0.$$

From (2.3)

$$\begin{aligned} v_R &= [\beta^0 + \beta^0, \beta^2 + \beta^2 + \beta^0 + \beta^0]A^{-1} \\ &= [000, 001]A^{-1} \\ &= 111001, \end{aligned}$$

where A^{-1} was constructed in Example 9.4.1. Then we encode $m = [0110010, 1]$ to $c = [m_L, p_L, m_R, v_R, p_R] = [0110010, 1, 1, 111001, 1]$. So in the notation used in Section 9.1, $c = [\chi(U), \chi(V)]$, where

$$\chi(U) = 01100101 \text{ and } \chi(V) = 11110011.$$

This is the codeword of $P(3)$ considered in Example 9.3.4.

Exercises

9.4.6 Construct K^3 using $1 + x + x^3$. A^{-1} was constructed in Example 9.4.1. Encode the following messages using $P(3)$.

(a) $m_L = 1010100$ and $m_R = 1$.
(b) $m_L = 1010100$ and $m_R = 0$.
(c) $m_L = 1111111$ and $m_R = 1$.
(d) $m_L = 1111111$ and $m_R = 0$.
(e) $m_L = 0000000$ and $m_R = 1$.

9.4.7 Construct K^5 using $1 + x^2 + x^5$ (see Exercise 5.1.5). A^{-1} was constructed in Example 9.4.1 Encode the following messages using $P(5)$.

(a) $m_L = 10100\ldots0$ and $m_R = 000001000100\ldots0$.
(b) $m_L = 10100\ldots0$ and $m_R = 00\ldots0$.
(c) $m_L = 10100\ldots0$ and $m_R = 11110\ldots0$.
(d) $m_L = 00\ldots0$ and $m_R = 100\ldots0$.

9.4.8 In Exercise 9.4.7, what is the length of
(a) m_L? (b) m_R?

9.5 Decoding extended Preparata codes

From Theorem 9.3.15, $P(r)$ has minimum distance 6 so we want an algorithm that corrects up to 2 errors. Let w be a received word and write $w = [w_L, p_L, w_R, p_R]$ where w_L and w_R are both words of length $2^r - 1$ and where p_L and p_R are the parity check digits. Then we can calculate $[w_L(\beta), w_L(\beta^3)] = w_L H$ and $[w_R(\beta), w_R(\beta^3)] \leftrightarrow w_R(H)$. We consider various cases depending on where the errors occur.

1. If errors are confined to the parity check digits then
$$w_L(\beta) = w_R(\beta), \text{ and}$$
$$w_L(\beta^3) + (w_L(\beta))^3 = w_R(\beta^3)$$
(by Definition 9.3.3 (ii) and (iii)), so this case is easily checked.

2. If there are no errors in w_L, one error in position i of w_R and at most one error in the parity check digits, then
$$w_L(\beta) = w_R(\beta) + \beta^i, \text{ and}$$
$$w_L(\beta^3) + (w_L(\beta))^3 = w_R(\beta^3) + \beta^{3i}, \text{ so}$$
$$(w_L(\beta) + w_R(\beta))^3 = w_L(\beta^3) + (w_L(\beta))^3 + w_R(\beta^3);$$
(by Definition 9.3.3 (ii) and (iii)). If this last equation holds then write $\beta^i = w_L(\beta) + w_R(\beta)$ and change the ith digit in w_R and at most one parity check digit.

3. If there are no errors in w_R, one error in position i of w_L and at most one error in the parity check digits, then using Lemma 9.3.8(i) we can repeat the steps in case 2 above to find that $(w_R(\beta) + w_L(\beta))^3 = w_R(\beta^3) + w_R(\beta))^3 + w_L(\beta^3)$; in this case write $\beta^i = w_R(\beta) + w_L(\beta)$, change the ith digit of w_L and at most one parity check digit.

4. If two errors occur in w_R, say in positions i and j, then again by Definition 9.3.3
$$w_L(\beta) = w_R(\beta) + \beta^i + \beta^j, \text{ and}$$
$$w_L(\beta^3) + (w_L(\beta))^3 = w_R(\beta^3) + \beta^{3i} + \beta^{3j},$$

so $\beta^i + \beta^j$ and $\beta^{3i} + \beta^{3j}$ are known; i and j can be found in the same manner as was used for the 2 error-correcting BCH code (see Section 5.5).

5. If two errors occur in w_L then, as in case 3, we can use Lemma 9.3.8(i) and the argument in case 4 to find the locations of the errors.

6. If there is one error in w_L and one error in w_R, say in positions i and j respectively, then again by Definition 9.3.3

$$w_L(\beta) + \beta^i = w_R(\beta) + \beta^j, \text{ and}$$
$$w_L(\beta^3) + \beta^{3i} + (w_L(\beta) + \beta^i)^3 = w_R(\beta^3) + \beta^{3j}.$$

We can solve these two equations for β^i and β^j as follows. From the first equation,

$$\beta^j = w_L(\beta) + \beta^i + w_R(\beta).$$

Substituting this into the second equation gives

$$\begin{aligned} w_L(\beta^3) + \beta^{3i} + (w_L(\beta) + \beta^i)^3 = w_R(\beta^3) &+ (w_L(\beta) + \beta^i)^3 \\ &+ (w_L(\beta) + \beta^i)^2 w_R(\beta) \\ &+ (w_L(\beta) + \beta^i) w_R(\beta)^2 + w_R(\beta)^3. \end{aligned}$$

Simplifying this gives

$$\begin{aligned} &\beta^{3i} + \beta^{2i} w_R(\beta) + \beta^i (w_R(\beta))^2 + (w_R(\beta))^3 \\ &\qquad = w_L(\beta^3) + w_R(\beta^3) + w_L(\beta)^2 w_R(\beta) + w_L(\beta) w_R(\beta)^2 \end{aligned}$$

so

$$\begin{aligned} (\beta^i + w_R(\beta))^3 &= (w_L(\beta^3) + w_R(\beta^3)) + (w_L(\beta) + w_R(\beta))^3 \\ &\quad + w_L(\beta)^3 + w_R(\beta)^3. \\ &= \Delta, \text{ say }. \end{aligned}$$

Therefore

$$\beta^i = w_R(\beta) + \Delta^{1/3}, \text{ and}$$
$$\beta^j = w_L(\beta) + \Delta^{1/3}.$$

So in all cases we can easily calculate the locations of the errors. The parity check conditions on each half of w make it easy to decide which of the above cases applies to w. Putting all of these observations together we get the following algorithm. The steps in the algorithm correspond to the cases just considered.

Algorithm 9.5.1 (decoding $P(r)$) Let $w = [w_L, P_L, w_R, p_R]$ be a received word.

0. Calculate $L_1 = w_L(\beta)$, $L_3 = w_L(\beta^3)$, $R_1 = w_R(\beta)$ and $R_3 = w_R(\beta^3)$.
1. If $L_1 + R_1 = 0$ and $L_3 + L_1^3 + R_3 = 0$ then the only errors occur in the parity check digits.
2. If $(L_1 + R_1)^3 + L_3 + L_1^3 + R_3 = 0$ then write $\beta^i = L_1 + R_1$. Correct position i of w_R and *at most one* parity check digit; ask for retransmission if both parity check digits need to be changed.
3. If $(L_1 + R_1)^3 + R_3 + R_1^3 + L_3 = 0$ then write $\beta^i = L_1 + R_1$. Correct position i of w_L and at most one parity check digit; ask for retransmission if both parity check digits need to be changed.
4. If both halves of w have even parity and
$$x^2 + (L_1 + R_1)x + \frac{L_3 + L_1^3 + R_3 + (L_1 + R_1)^3}{L_1 + R_1} = (x + \beta^i)(x + \beta^j)$$
for some i and j, then correct positions i and j of w_L.
5. If both halves of w have even parity and
$$x^2 + (L_1 + R_1)x + \frac{R_3 + R_1^3 + L_3 + (L_1 + R_1)^3}{L_1 + R_1} = (x + \beta^i)(x + \beta^j)$$
for some i and j then correct positions i and j of w_R.
6. If both halves of w have odd parity, then write $\beta^i = R_1 + (L_1^3 + R_1^3 + (L_1 + R_1)^3 + L_3 + R_3)^{1/3}$, and $\beta^j = L_1 + (L_1^3 + R_1^3 + (L_1 + R_1)^3 + L_3 + R_3)^{1/3}$. Correct position i of w_L and position j of w_R.
7. If no closest codewords has yet been found then conclude that at least three errors occurred during transmission, and ask for a retransmission.

Example 9.5.2 Decode the following received words which were encoded using $P(3)$, where $GF(2^3)$ is constructed using $1 + x + x^3$.

(a) 10010011 11100111

(b) 10100100 10001001

(c) 10001000 11101001

Decoding (a):

(0) $[L_1, L_3] = w_L H = [111, 110]$ and $[R_1, R_3] = w_R H = [101, 110]$.

(1) $L_1 + R_1 = 111 + 101 = \beta \neq 0$.

(2) $(L_1 + R_1)^3 + L_3 + L_1^3 + R_3 = \beta^3 + \beta^3 + \beta^{15} + \beta^3 = \beta^0 \neq 0$.

(3) $(L_1 + R_1)^3 + R_3 + R_1^3 + L_1 = \beta^3 + \beta^3 + \beta^{18} + \beta^3 = \beta^6 \neq 0$.

(4) $x^2+\beta x+(\beta^3+\beta^{15}+\beta^3+\beta^3+\beta^3)/\beta = x^2+\beta x+\beta^6 = (x+\beta^2)(x+\beta^4)$.

Decode w to 10010011 11001111.

Decoding (b):

(0) $[L_1, L_3] = w_L H = [010, 011]$ and $[R_1, R_3] = w_R H = [111, 011]$.

(1) $L_1 + R_1 = 010 + 111 = \beta^6 \neq 0$.

(2) $(L_1+R_1)^3 + L_3 + L_1^3 + R_3 = \beta^{18} + \beta^4 + \beta^3 + \beta^4 = \beta^6 \neq 0$.

(3) $(L_1+R_1)^3 + R_3 + R_1^3 + L_3 = \beta^{18} + \beta^4 + \beta^{15} + \beta^4 = \beta^2 \neq 0$.

(4) and (5) Both halves of w have odd parity.

(6)

$$\begin{aligned}\beta^i &= \beta^5 + (\beta^3+\beta^{15}+\beta^{18}+\beta^4+\beta^4)^{1/3}\\ &= \beta^5 + (\beta^5)^{1/3}\\ &= \beta^5 + (\beta^{12})^{1/3}\\ &= \beta^5 + \beta^4\\ &= \beta^0,\end{aligned}$$

so $i = 0$. Then we can immediately write

$$\begin{aligned}\beta^j &= \beta + \beta^4\\ &= \beta^2,\end{aligned}$$

so $j = 2$. Decode w to 00100100 10101001.

Decoding (c):

(0) $[L_1, L_3] = w_L H = [111, 011]$ and $[R_1, R_3] = w_R H = [100, 000]$.

(1) $L_1 + R_1 = 11 + 100 = \beta^4 \neq 0$.

(2) $(L_1+R_1)^3 + L_3 + L_1^3 + R_3 = \beta^{12} + \beta^4 + \beta^{15} + 0 = \beta^3 \neq 0$.

(3) $(L_1+R_1)^3 + R_3 + R_1^3 + L_3 = \beta^{12} + 0 + \beta^0 + \beta^4 = 0$.

Let $\beta^i = L_1 + R_1 = \beta^4$, so $i = 4$. However, changing position 4 of w_L requires both parity check digits to be changed, so we ask for retransmission (since we can find a codeword distance 3 from w).

Exercises

9.5.3 Decode the following received words that were encoded using $P(3)$, where $GF(2^3)$ is constructed using $1+x+x^3$.

(a) 10000001, 11101000 (b) 00011010, 01000010

(c) 00100101, 10100100 (d) 01010110, 00011110

(e) 11101000, 10001001 (f) 10011001, 01010101
(g) 01000111, 11001000 (h) 10101101, 11010000
(i) 11101110, 01010101 (j) 10111011, 01101010
(k) 01011101, 11101101 (l) 10011100, 10100100
(m) 01101101, 10011000 (n) 10101010, 10111011
(o) 10100101, 00010001

9.5.4 Decode the following received words that were encoded using $P(5)$, where $GF(2^5)$ is constructed using $1+x^2+x^5$ (see Exercise 5.1.15).

(a) 11000 11000 10000 00000 00000 10000 10,
00011 11000 00000 00000 00011 00100 00

(b) 10100 00000 10000 00000 00000 00000 00,
00000 10001 00000 00100 01010 10111 00

9.5.5 If w is a received word, the left half of which has odd parity and the right half has even parity, can w ever be decoded to a codeword distance at most 2 from w at Step 2 of Algorithm 9.5.1?

Chapter 10

Classical Cryptography

Cryptography is about communication in the presence of adversaries.[1] The best-known example is that of *confidentiality* or *privacy*—maintaining secrecy in communications over an unsecured channel. The cryptographic solution is *encryption*, which modifies the data in an attempt to render the communication unintelligible to all but the intended recipients. Cryptography can be regarded as the science of mathematical techniques for protecting data (from malicious or unauthorized actions) by transforming the data itself.

In addition to confidentiality, cryptography can be used to satisfy various information security objectives collectively known as *authentication*. *Data integrity* provides detection of data manipulation, including alteration, delay, and replay of messages. *Message* (or *data origin*) *authentication* provides proof of the source of the information. *Identification* corroborates the identity of an entity. *Non-repudiation* is a service which prevents entities from denying previous commitments. A digital analogue of the hand-written signature, specific to the message, is fundamental to many authentication schemes.

Cryptography is closely connected with *cryptanalysis*, the study of mathematical and other techniques for defeating information security objectives; together, these areas are known as *cryptology*. Cryptanalysis under various assumptions concerning the capabilities of the adversary is an essential part of applied cryptology, providing some measure of confidence in schemes for which mathematical proof of security is not available.

Section 10.1 establishes the basic framework used in Chapters 10–12. In classical cryptography, privacy of communications depends on a secret shared between the communicating parties; Section 10.2 examines a few such *symmetric-key* schemes. The one-time pad is of particular interest, as an example of a simple scheme that cannot be broken regardless of the computing power of the adversary. Unfortunately, the one-time pad is rather unwieldy in practice due to the amount of key material required. Section 10.3 discusses the Data Encryption Standard, the

[1] Ronald L. Rivest, from [71].

best-known symmetric-key scheme in history. Rather than the unconditional security of the one-time pad, DES was designed so that it would be "computationally infeasible" for an adversary to break the scheme.

A basic symmetric-key property is that the secret in the scheme must be shared with correspondents—the ability to create a secret message cannot be separated from the ability to interpret such a message. A landmark 1976 paper by Diffie and Hellman [27] introduced the concept of *public-key* cryptography; the separation of creation and interpretation capabilities is a consequence. Security relies on the apparent intractability of various computational problems. Chapter 11 contains an overview of several number-theoretic topics fundamental to public-key schemes. Chapter 12 discusses public-key concepts and methods.

10.1 Encryption schemes

The following framework will be used in the study of cryptographic tools or *primitives*.

- An *alphabet* $\mathcal{A}$ is a finite set.
- A *message space* $\mathcal{M}$ over $\mathcal{A}$ consists of strings of symbols from the alphabet. For example, if $\mathcal{A} = \{0,1\}$ then messages consist of strings of 0s and 1s; the set of messages of length n is denoted $\{0,1\}^n$, and the set $\{0,1\}^*$ consists of all messages of finite length.
- An *encryption scheme* or *cipher* consists of message spaces $\mathcal{M}$ and $\mathcal{C}$, a set $\mathcal{K}$ (known as the *key space*), and functions $E_k : \mathcal{M} \to \mathcal{C}$, $D_k : \mathcal{C} \to \mathcal{M}$ for $k \in \mathcal{K}$ with $D_k(E_k(m)) = m$ for all $m \in \mathcal{M}$. E_k is called an *encryption* function, and D_k is the corresponding *decryption* function. In this setting, elements of $\mathcal{M}$ are *plaintext*, $\mathcal{C}$ is called a *ciphertext space*, and elements of $\mathcal{C}$ are *ciphertext*.
- In some schemes, keys are written as ordered pairs $k = (e,d)$ where e is used for encryption and d is used for decryption. In this context, (e,d) is called a *key-pair*, and we will write $E_e = E_k$ and $D_d = D_k$.

Figure 10.1 is a schematic of the basic scenario where Alice wishes to pass a private message m to Bob in the presence of an adversary Eve. In traditional symmetric-key ciphers (see Section 10.2), the secure channel is required in order to pass the keys themselves, and may represent a trusted courier or other reliable method for maintaining privacy. In public-key schemes (see Chapter 12), the channel represents a method of verifying the authenticity of the public portion of a key.

Adversaries may be classified by capability. A *passive adversary* is limited to eavesdropping on the unsecured portion of the conversation between Alice and Bob. An *active adversary*, in addition to eavesdropping, may alter or inject messages, or perhaps even block transmission entirely. Cryptography can hope to pro-

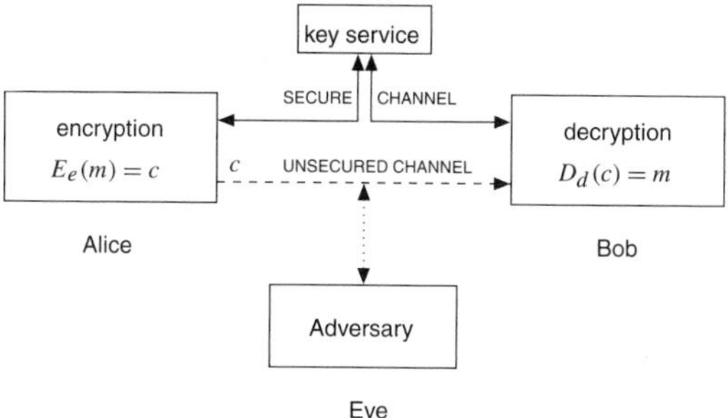

Figure 10.1: *Communication using encryption.*

vide secrecy, and detect altered or forged messages. Delivery of messages in the face of a sufficiently powerful adversary cannot be guaranteed, although encrypted messages may be sent periodically to discover communication disruptions.

Informally, an encryption system is considered *breakable* if an adversary can systematically recover plaintext from ciphertext (or even worse, the key can be computed). Three kinds of security are noted:

- The system is *unconditionally secure* if the adversary can gain no knowledge about plaintext (except possibly its length), regardless of the amount of ciphertext available and the computational resources available to the adversary.
- A system is *computationally secure* if breaking it is "computationally infeasible" under some prescribed level of available computing resources, and using the best known cryptanalytic techniques.
- If breaking is provably at least as difficult as solving a mathematical problem believed to be intractable, the system is said to be *provably secure*.

These intuitive notions of security will be made somewhat more precise in the following sections.

In 1883, Auguste Kerckhoffs published what Kahn calls the second great book in cryptology of the "outward-looking kind."[2] Several fundamental principles for selecting ciphers were listed: the system should be, if not theoretically unbreakable, unbreakable in practice; compromise of the system should not inconvenience the correspondents; the key should be rememberable without notes and should be easily changeable; the cryptograms should be transmissible by telegraph; the apparatus or documents should be portable and operable by a single person; the system should be easy, neither requiring knowledge of a long list of rules nor involving mental strain. The second of these is sometimes called *Kerckhoffs' prin-*

[2] Kahn [48] credits Naples-born Giovanni Battista Porta as "the first to delineate a coherent image of cryptology" in a 1563 work, but whose "views no longer sufficed after the invention of the telegraph."

ciple, and says that security of the cipher should rest with the keys alone; that is, security is maintained even in the face of an adversary in possession of the encryption scheme.

Attacks on the communication of Figure 10.1 typically have the objective of recovering plaintext from ciphertext, or even the key itself, although other more limited information (such as particular plaintext bits) may be targeted. Traffic analysis attempts to learn something about the messages by examination of the pattern of transmission. For example, a sudden flurry of exchanges may be notable even if the underlying messages cannot be discovered. We are mainly interested in attacks against the encryption scheme itself.

1. In a *ciphertext-only attack*, the adversary attempts to recover plaintext or the key by observing some amount of ciphertext. A scheme vulnerable to this kind of attack is considered completely insecure.
2. In a *known-plaintext attack*, the adversary is in possession of some quantity of plaintext and corresponding ciphertext. The typical case is that the plaintext and ciphertext pairs correspond to some (unknown) key, and the goal is to recover the key or decrypt some additional ciphertext which is believed to have been encrypted with the same key.
3. In a *chosen-plaintext attack*, ciphertext corresponding to plaintext selected by the adversary is available. A possible scenario is that the adversary has obtained temporary access to the equipment (but not the key) used for encryption. If the ciphertext may be chosen interactively based on previous results, the attack is called *adaptive*.
4. In a *chosen-ciphertext attack*, plaintext corresponding to ciphertext selected by the adversary is available.

Other possibilities include implementation-specific and tempest attacks which exploit device properties; timing of computations and power consumption, for example, have been used against certain systems [53, 52]. Bribery, blackmail, and other "give-me-the-key" attacks have been historically rather successful.

10.2 Symmetric-key encryption

Many classical ciphers have the property that a "secret" is shared between parties, and knowledge of this information allows both parties to encrypt and decrypt. More precisely, an encryption scheme is said to be *symmetric-key* if finding D_d from e and E_e from d require roughly the same resources.

A *simple substitution cipher* consists of 1–1 mappings k on the source alphabet. Encryption is performed by applying k to each symbol in the message; i.e., if $m = m_0 m_1 \cdots$, where m_i are symbols from the alphabet, then $E_k(m) = E_k(m_0 m_1 \cdots) = k(m_0)k(m_1)\cdots$.

Example 10.2.1 The *shift cipher* is a special case of the substitution cipher. The key k is a fixed shift $0 \le k < n$ on the symbols $\{a_0, \ldots, a_{n-1}\}$ of the alphabet, mapping $a_j \mapsto a_{(j+k) \bmod n}$.[3] The popular rot13 encryption function corresponds to $k = 13$ on the source alphabet $\{\mathtt{a}, \ldots, \mathtt{z}\}$, rotating by 13 positions; i.e., the letters are numbered 0–25, and rot13 adds 13 to each source letter, reducing the result modulo 26.[4] As a visual clue, lowercase letters will be used for plaintext, and uppercase for ciphertext. For example, since

$$\mathrm{rot13}(\mathtt{rotate}) = \mathrm{rot13}(17, 14, 19, 0, 19, 4) = (4, 1, 6, 13, 6, 17) = \mathtt{EBGNGR},$$

the plaintext 'rotate' is encrypted to ciphertext 'EBGNGR'. This particular shift also has the property that $\mathrm{rot13}(\mathrm{rot13}(m)) = m$; i.e., encryption and decryption are the same function. Julius Caesar is reputed to have used a shift cipher with $k = 3$.

The shift cipher is completely insecure against a chosen-plaintext attack. In fact, a ciphertext-only attack is easily mounted, since the 26 possible keys can be examined exhaustively.

A simple substitution cipher may resist exhaustive search of the keyspace, even if the source alphabet is small. However, frequency analysis may be effective if the underlying source text characteristics are known. For example, Figure 10.2 lists single-character frequencies obtained from a modest sampling of English-language newspapers and novels [3]. Ciphertext from simple substitution respects the frequency distribution of the source. If the source statistics are roughly according to Figure 10.2, for example, then the most common ciphertext symbol probably corresponds to 'e'. Similarly, the symbols {j, q, x, z} are significantly less frequent in this kind of source, and likely correspond to less frequent ciphertext symbols. Statistics from digrams (pairs of letters) and trigrams (triples of letters) can be used in a similar fashion.

Example 10.2.2 Consider the case that the alphabet is the 26 letters a–z, and the substitution cipher is a permutation on these letters, perhaps

$$k = \begin{pmatrix} \mathtt{a\ b\ c\ d\ e\ f\ g\ h\ i\ j\ k\ l\ m\ n\ o\ p\ q\ r\ s\ t\ u\ v\ w\ x\ y\ z} \\ \mathtt{T\ U\ V\ W\ X\ Y\ Z\ B\ I\ K\ E\ A\ C\ D\ F\ G\ H\ J\ L\ M\ N\ O\ P\ Q\ R\ S} \end{pmatrix}$$

where the source letters in the first row are mapped to the ciphertext letters in the second row; e.g., $E_k(\mathtt{trek}) = \mathtt{MJXE}$. This particular permutation is easy to remember, since it is constructed by placing the keyword 'BIKE' under the letter 'h' and then filling in the rest of the letters in order.

[3] The "mod" notation is reviewed in Chapter 11; here, "$(j + k) \bmod n$" adds integers j and k as usual, subtracting n if the result exceeds $n - 1$.

[4] The source documentation with the GNU Emacs editor notes that "Rot13 encryption is sometimes used on USENET...for material some might consider offensive."

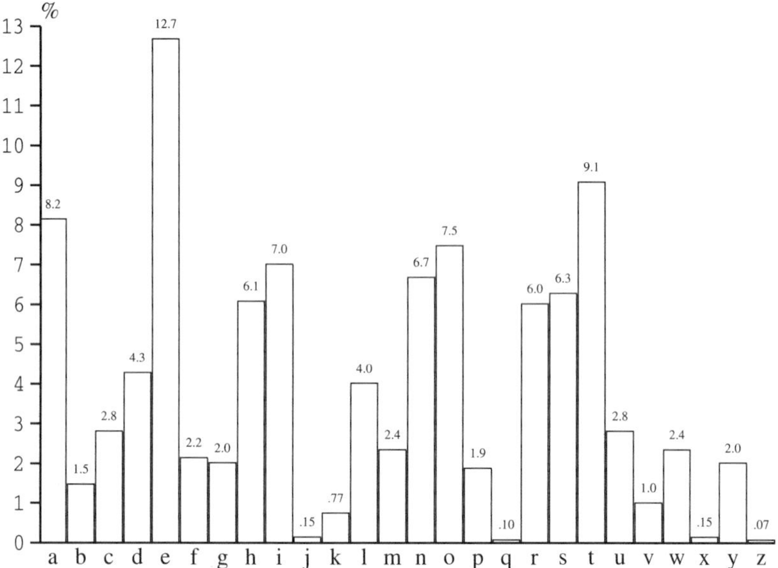

Figure 10.2: *Frequencies of single characters in English text.*

The scheme is completely insecure against a chosen-plaintext attack (since the key can be recovered by encrypting the message $m = \texttt{ab} \cdots \texttt{z}$). Having only ciphertext available makes things a little more difficult. Although the exhaustive attack of trying each possible key in turn may be infeasible (since the keyspace is of size $26! \approx 4 \cdot 10^{26}$), the scheme may be subject to frequency analysis.

A simple substitution cipher is sometimes called a *monoalphabetic substitution cipher*. Attacks based on frequency analysis become infeasible if the message space is over some large alphabet. Small alphabets, such as that in Example 10.2.2, can be expanded by combining several symbols and forming a message space over this much larger alphabet. The Data Encryption Standard (DES, to be discussed in Section 10.3.2) in its basic form is a substitution cipher over a source alphabet of size 2^{64}.

Polyalphabetic ciphers attempt to hide the original source frequencies by mapping each source symbol to one of several possible ciphertext symbols. The *Vigenère cipher* is a well-known example. Symbols from the source alphabet $\mathcal{A}$ are identified with integers in $[0, |\mathcal{A}|)$, and a keyword $k = k_0 \cdots k_{n-1}$ is selected for some $k_i \in \mathcal{A}$. Encryption is performed on n-character blocks of the source by character-wise addition modulo $|\mathcal{A}|$ with the keyword.

As an example, suppose $\mathcal{A}$ consists of the symbols `a`–`z` numbered 0–25. The following table illustrates the procedure on a short plaintext using key '`KEY`'

plaintext	she sells sea shells by the seashore
+ key	KEY KEYKE YKE YKEYKE YK EYK EYKEYKEY
ciphertext	CLC CIJVW QOE QRIJVW ZI XFO WCKWFYVC

where the addition is modulo 26. Decryption is performed by subtracting modulo 26 the keyword from the ciphertext.

The simple analysis based on source frequency characteristics is partially thwarted by the mapping of alphabet symbols to different ciphertext letters, depending on the position in the source; e.g., the source letter 'e' is mapped onto the set {C, I, O} in the above example. However, if the keylength ℓ can be discovered, then monoalphabetic frequency analysis can be used on the submessages formed from letters that are a multiple of ℓ apart in the ciphertext. In the above fragment, the submessage formed from the ciphertext in positions $0, 3, 6, \ldots$, for example, is obtained by adding (modulo 26) the first letter of the 3-letter key to plaintext letters from the corresponding positions.

In 1863, Friedrich Kasiski proposed a method (now known as a *Kasiski examination*) to recover the keylength via analysis of the distances separating identical fragments of ciphertext.[5] Occasionally, identical fragments of source text will align with the same portion of the key, resulting in identical portions of ciphertext. In the example, this occurs with the 4-character fragment 'ells'. Typically, there will also be "accidental" matches—identical fragments of ciphertext which did not result from identical fragments of plaintext—although these tend to be less likely with longer match lengths. In the case of a "true" match, the keylength divides the difference in positions. The possibility of accidental matches means that it may not be enough to look only at the greatest common divisor of the distances, and in general the larger and more common factors are examined first as keylength candidates.

Example 10.2.3 A Vigenère cipher has been used on "typical" English source text which was first processed to remove punctuation and blanks so that the source consists only of the 26 letters a–z. The following ciphertext was produced:

offset	ciphertext
0	UPVZB BVUPN KKFOL OGAKU FBTKF LFXUJ VIPZV KFZXO FIDLO ONLUP
50	KKFUZ OMQFQ MQXKU AFIUP VVVVK KFDFL DMFIU PVVFI ZVTMU XDBZY
100	FVVYF ZTHBA ZQHEY LTXVU JVXFM IDRSQ EJNCI PVZZQ HQEYJ BZQHB
150	YHTWL OUWND OLVUJ VREZA JHTWW VPTZW VLVDM TROPV XWIMN KJBVE
200	FITKV XRQEL FZOBY HSMND TVFOJ DZQHB YLOOZ QTQXK UISLS LNLUP
250	RESWB HOEZQ HERVC MRWJV XWIMR LSISR WMIHF TZQHN CXUBV UJVXF
300	JZTOJ VXGJA REMMU GPEEG PEEWP BYHXI KHS

The spaces in the ciphertext were added for readability, and are not represented in the offsets.

[5] Kahn [48] writes that Kasiski died in 1881 "almost certainly without realizing that he had wrought a revolution in cryptology."

The 3-character fragment ‘ZQH’ appears in several places, three of which are underlined. The corresponding offsets are 110, 138, and 226, respectively. It is likely that the keyword length ℓ divides the difference of any two of these offsets. The differences $138 - 110 = 28 = 2^2 7$ and $226 - 110 = 2^2 29$ suggest $\ell \mid (2^2 7, 2^2 29) = 2^2$. The case $\ell = 1$ corresponds to a simple shift.

At this stage, the cryptanalyst may examine the frequency distributions for each candidate keylength, looking for those which have the characteristics of the expected source language. The frequencies are tabulated corresponding to each position of the key; e.g., for the candidate keylength $\ell = 2$, the frequencies are tabulated for the submessage formed from the characters in the even offsets, then from the odd offsets. This gives, for example,

ℓ	submessage offsets	frequencies of letters in submessage (sorted)
2	$0, 2, 4, \ldots$	19 16 12 12 11 10 9 8 8 7 6 6 5 5 5 5 5 4 4 3 2 2 2 1 0 0
	$1, 3, 5, \ldots$	14 14 13 10 10 10 9 9 9 8 8 7 6 6 5 5 5 3 3 3 2 2 2 2 1 0
4	$0, 4, 8, \ldots$	12 10 10 7 6 6 6 5 5 4 2 2 2 1 1 1 1 1 1 1 0 0 0 0 0 0
	$1, 5, 9, \ldots$	10 9 8 7 5 5 5 5 5 5 4 3 3 2 2 2 1 1 1 0 0 0 0 0 0 0
	$2, 6, 10, \ldots$	12 11 8 8 7 5 5 5 4 4 2 2 2 2 2 1 1 1 1 0 0 0 0 0 0 0
	$3, 7, 11, \ldots$	9 9 8 8 7 5 5 5 4 3 3 3 3 3 2 2 2 1 1 0 0 0 0 0 0 0

For a given source distribution, we expect that each line for the correct keylength should reflect the source frequencies. In this example, the frequencies suggest that $\ell = 4$ is more likely than $\ell = 2$, although the limited amount of ciphertext hinders the analysis.

In short, the analysis so far suggests that $\ell = 4$ is a likely candidate. The frequency analysis of Figure 10.2 shows that ‘e’ is significantly more prevalent than any other letter in typical English text. We suspect that one of the higher-frequency ciphertext letters, in each of the $\ell = 4$ lines, corresponds to plaintext letter ‘e’. In this particular example, choosing 3 or 4 (or perhaps a few more) ciphertext letters from each of the lines in the $\ell = 4$ case appears likely to yield the mapping from plaintext letter ‘e’.

The following table lists the 4 most frequent ciphertext letters corresponding to the higher frequencies in each line of the $\ell = 4$ case, along with the appropriate key letters which map ‘e’ to each of these ciphertext letters:

common ciphertext letters for $\ell = 4$		corresponding key letters
F J U P	$\xrightarrow{(c - \text{‘e’}) \bmod 26}$	B F Q L
B V M I		X R I E
V Z R X		R V N T
K Q H L		G M D H

At this stage, an exhaustive search using keywords built from the likely key letters could be performed by machine. In the example, this requires $4^4 = 256$ decryptions (using keywords such as ‘BXRG’).

If the keyword was chosen from a dictionary, then it may be especially easy to locate. In the example, this restriction leads to words such as 'LEND' and 'BIRD', and the second of these yields:

ciphertext	UPVZB BVUPN KKFOL OGAKU FBTKF LFXUJ VIPZV KFZXO FIDLO ONLUP
− key	BIRDB IRDBI RDBIR DBIRD BIRDB IRDBI RDBIR DBIRD BIRDB IRDBI
plaintext	thewa terof thegu lfstr etche doutb efore hergl eamin gwith

which appears to be English text. The complete decryption, with punctuation and case restored, is:

> The water of the Gulf stretched out before her, gleaming with the million lights of the sun. The voice of the sea is seductive, never ceasing, whispering, clamoring, murmuring, inviting the soul to wander in abysses of solitude. All along the white beach, up and down, there was no living thing in sight. A bird with a broken wing was beating the air above, reeling, fluttering, circling disabled down, down to the water.[6]

The 'ZQH' ciphertext fragments used in the Kasiski test correspond to plaintext 'ing'. Longer repeated fragments, such as 'NLUP' (corresponding to 'with') and 'ZQHBY' (corresponding to 'ingth'), each appearing twice, could have been chosen. We conveniently avoided fragments such as 'PVZ' (appearing at positions 1 and 135) which are accidental matches and correspond to 'hew' and 'mur', respectively. These fragments suggest keylengths dividing 134, which would have been incorrect.

More challenging examples of cryptanalysis of a Vigenère cipher may be found in Kahn [48] and Stinson [86]. In particular, the indices of coincidence defined in [86] provide a more methodical approach to finding the keylength and the keyword candidates.

The simple substitution and Vigenère ciphers are examples of *block ciphers*, since they transform a message by applying a fixed mapping to blocks consisting of a fixed number of characters. They are *memoryless* in the sense that the mapping of a block does not depend on its position in the message. *Stream ciphers* allow the mapping to depend on the position within the message, and are sometimes called *state ciphers*.

Encryption schemes are typically defined for a binary alphabet $\mathcal{A} = \{0, 1\}$, and block (and stream) ciphers are defined on some fixed number of bits, called the *blocklength*. Messages over an alphabet $\mathcal{A} = \{a_0, \dots, a_{n-1}\}$ can be regarded as written over a binary alphabet by associating $a_j \leftrightarrow j$ and writing j as a binary number with $\lceil \log_2 n \rceil$ bits. In the case of a 26-letter alphabet as in Example 10.2.2, each letter is replaced by a 5-digit binary number, with 'g'$\leftrightarrow 6 = 00110$, for example. The encryption and decryption functions in these examples are then considered to operate on blocks of length 5.

---

[6] From *The Awakening* by Kate Chopin.

For messages m and m' over $\{0,1\}$ of the same length, bitwise addition modulo 2 will be written $m \oplus m'$; e.g., $1100 \oplus 1010 = 0110$. Programmers know this operation as "exclusive or," sometimes written XOR, and amounts to the schoolchild's paradise where addition is never complicated by carry.

Example 10.2.4 The *Vernam cipher* is a stream cipher on $\mathcal{A} = \{0,1\}$. Keys also consist of messages over $\mathcal{A}$, and encryption maps $m \mapsto c = m \oplus k$. By the usual properties of modular arithmetic, it is easy to see that the plaintext is recovered from c by $c \oplus k = m \oplus k \oplus k = m \oplus 0 = m$; i.e., decryption is the same as encryption.

If the key digits (known as the *keystream*) are the result of independent Bernoulli trials with probability $1/2$ (e.g., independent tosses of a fair coin) and are used only once, then the cipher is known as a *one-time pad*, and is unconditionally secure against a ciphertext-only attack. The intuitive idea is that every message (of the same length as the ciphertext) maps to the ciphertext for some key, and there is no reason to favor one key over another. Shannon's work in the 1940s [80] made these notions precise, showing that, roughly speaking, any unconditionally secure symmetric-key encryption scheme requires a key as long as the message. (A more precise statement on the requirements for keys can be given in terms of the entropy associated with the message space.)

In some early applications of the Vernam cipher, the key information was written on notepads and pages were discarded after a single use, leading to the name "one-time pad." Ciphertext obtained from the same key would enable an adversary to learn something about the underlying messages; e.g., if $c = m \oplus k$ and $c' = m' \oplus k$ then

$$c \oplus c' = (m \oplus k) \oplus (m' \oplus k) = m \oplus m'$$

which may allow cryptanalysis (in particular, $m = m'$ is immediately discovered).

The Codebreakers has a few amusing accounts of early attempts to manage the quantity of key material required, and the problem continues to limit the application of the one-time pad. According to Peter Wright of British Intelligence [101], the Russians ran short of key material during the early years of WWII, and duplicate sets of the pads were distributed to different embassies in the West. The "VENONA codebreak" exploited this misuse of the scheme, examining vast amounts of ciphertext for matches across several channels used by the Russian government.[7]

Widely-used ciphers such as DES sacrifice the unconditional security of the one-time pad for more manageable schemes that are hoped to be computationally

[7] As part of a series on the "Cold War Experience" in 1998, the Cable News Network (CNN) reported that "The VENONA project at the U.S. National Security Agency cracked many supposedly secure Soviet messages, including some that employed one-time pads. The project lasted from 1943 to 1980, and some of its records were declassified in 1995." Unfortunately, CNN neglected to note that the scheme failed the fundamental single-use requirement, and claimed that the one-time pad "can also be cracked by painstaking trial and error, trying all of the millions of possible combinations."

secure. The requirement of randomly-generated keys should also be noted. Common "random number generators" produce a sequence of numbers completely determined by an initial *seed* chosen from a finite set. Although they possess many of the features useful in simulations, they are not random in the sense of unpredictability required in cryptography.[8]

Exercises

10.2.5 The following ciphertext was obtained under a Vigenère cipher of the type discussed in Example 10.2.3:

offset	ciphertext
0	VHVVG NRWGA EGCLJ RVHVO GAUHT OWWJE FSROJ LVIFQ KNKKG IIDPG
50	VUJAM HLUJW CLCRY EUWJE DVGLM HUBFW JTFEG CFPGV LOPEI DDLVW
100	QOLUE ALVGM VVJAC OCTKD EKKKG MRVBE BHRLR QPEUW QMFUT ONLPD
150	RBNIX KVBLM

Recover the key word of the cipher, given that the underlined triple of letters represents a very common three-letter word, and that the overscored letters 'AE' represents the combination 'an' at the beginning of a three-letter word.

10.2.6 Write a program to implement a substitution cipher of the form in Example 10.2.2 (the authors used *awk*). The program should accept a keyword and alignment position as arguments. Encrypt a sample of at least 300 characters of English-language text, and then perform a cryptanalysis using frequency information and knowledge of the scheme used (but proceed as if the keyword itself is unknown).

10.2.7 This exercise follows the outline given in Example 10.2.3, providing sufficient information to recover the plaintext without the use of a computer. Readers with access to software tools may wish to develop a more realistic exercise.

The following intercepted ciphertext is known to have been produced by a Vigenère cipher:

offset	ciphertext
0	TUIRD SFOGK YLBVL OORXX RVDPL SHRSB POCBT TLQPG AOMHM SVONM
50	HDHDN TRTCX RYCJL NHGHT BRIIM HHQWB NHGTI ERDAX BHWCZ IQGEB
100	RHRQR TKSGX VRZJM IRBXG BXQWT RHGIU ELXXG GDIIA OUWIB EVAPR
150	DHQXW EWCTQ THBSF AUHXT LOOLN NWWAM HHOHB AQUPF EVGRA EGIAX
200	DICGL ESHTF BHFGX MRJXG GPOGM IDZAT WZCJE DESPL IJBPE AGWEE
250	OPOIL ALREX OSZTP OXZSM ANSXM TRATT NWVPM WKOIA ASDTG EGPTY
300	OUSRH UORHM AUHJI AJOXG IQOHM AWSRH UQQXE MHSIB NJCCP EGBTL
350	DDMBK LLRTY EQRTW BHWYB NJGJL ERTBB LLHPK YICGV EWCRK AFYSH
400	WQCCM HHGIN DHBIF OYSBX NWHWX CUIHA IQUDY TKSRH UQHTK RHJDE

[8] Goldberg and Wagner [39] discovered that random number generation in early versions of the Netscape web browser was significantly more predictable than advertised, compromising security of transactions. The episode was rather embarrassing for Netscape, which had refused to allow public scrutiny of its algorithms.

Repeated fragments of 'MHH' are located at positions 74, 179, and 404 (other choices are possible, including the longer fragment 'SRHU').

(a) If ℓ is the length of the (unknown) key, then we may suspect that $\ell \mid 179 - 74 = 3 \cdot 5 \cdot 7$ and $\ell \mid 404 - 179 = 3^2 5^2$. If these repeated fragments of ciphertext align with identical portions of plaintext, show that $\ell \in \{1, 3, 5, 15\}$.

(b) Suppose the candidate $\ell = 15$ is considered unlikely. The relative frequencies (from 830 total ciphertext letters) for the remaining candidates, along with corresponding ciphertext letters, are given by:

ℓ	offsets	frequencies of letters in submessage																									
1	0, 1, …	60	53	45	42	40	40	39	39	39	39	38	37	33	32	30	27	27	26	25	25	21	20	17	13	13	10
		H	T	R	E	O	W	B	D	G	I	S	A	X	L	Q	C	P	U	M	N	F	V	K	J	Y	Z
3	0, 3, …	22	19	18	18	16	14	13	13	13	13	13	11	11	9	9	9	8	8	8	8	6	5	5	4	3	1
		H	E	B	R	T	O	A	G	I	S	W	C	U	D	Q	X	F	L	N	P	M	K	V	Z	J	Y
	1, 4, …	22	17	16	15	15	14	14	13	13	11	11	10	10	10	9	9	9	9	8	8	8	7	6	6	4	3
		H	T	G	D	W	O	X	A	E	Q	R	I	K	S	B	C	N	V	L	P	U	M	J	Y	F	Z
	2, 5, …	20	16	16	16	16	15	15	12	12	12	12	11	11	10	10	10	10	9	8	7	7	6	6	4	3	2
		T	H	I	L	R	D	S	B	M	O	W	A	P	E	G	Q	X	F	N	C	U	V	Y	J	Z	K
5	0, 5, …	24	15	15	13	12	12	11	11	7	7	6	5	5	4	4	3	3	3	3	2	1	0	0	0	0	0
		E	A	N	T	O	R	I	S	B	D	U	H	L	C	G	M	P	W	Y	V	F	J	K	Q	X	Z
	1, 6, …	22	15	14	14	13	12	12	10	8	8	6	6	6	5	4	3	2	2	1	1	1	1	0	0	0	0
		H	Q	D	U	W	L	R	O	K	V	F	G	J	P	X	S	I	Y	B	E	N	Z	A	C	M	T
	2, 7, …	18	15	13	13	12	11	9	9	9	8	7	7	6	5	5	4	3	3	2	2	2	2	1	0	0	0
		S	O	H	W	Q	C	G	I	R	B	A	F	Z	D	V	M	T	U	J	P	X	Y	K	E	L	N
	3, 8, …	24	14	13	12	12	11	11	10	9	8	7	7	6	6	5	2	2	2	2	2	1	0	0	0	0	0
		T	P	I	C	X	D	H	G	A	E	R	W	B	S	J	L	N	Q	V	Y	U	F	K	M	O	Z
	4, 9, …	18	17	15	13	13	10	9	9	8	7	7	6	5	4	4	4	3	3	3	3	2	2	1	0	0	0
		M	B	X	L	T	G	E	H	K	F	N	A	R	I	W	Y	O	P	V	Z	D	U	Q	C	J	S

Explain why this summary suggests that $\ell = 5$ is more likely than the others, under the assumption that the original message has single-letter frequencies corresponding roughly to Figure 10.2.

(c) Find the corresponding key letter candidates for several of the popular ciphertext letters in the case $\ell = 5$, where the mapping is from the distinguished plaintext letter 'e'.

(d) It is suspected that the correspondents choose keywords from a dictionary. Find the keyword, and decrypt at least part of the ciphertext. It may be helpful to note that some of the submessages contain a distinguished (high-frequency) ciphertext letter.

10.2.8 Data compression removes some redundancy in the data. If compression is to be used in conjunction with encryption, does it make more sense to compress and then encrypt, or vice versa?

10.3 Feistel ciphers and DES

This section examines in brief a class of ciphers which includes DES, the best-known symmetric-key cipher. We're mainly interested in the "structural" features and vulnerabilities of these ciphers; readers interested in the details of DES should consult the references listed in Section 10.4.

Two ciphers are considered, the New Data Seal (NDS) and the Data Encryption Standard (DES), each built on a Feistel cipher. Feistel ciphers are block ciphers, although a larger framework (such as DES) is commonly used in *modes* in which the overall scheme is a stream cipher. Among typical design criteria for block ciphers, the most fundamental is the requirement that the keyspace be sufficiently large so that exhaustive search is infeasible. Similarly, the blocksize should be large enough to frustrate the building of a significant database from observed ciphertext. The goal of *confusion* is to complicate the relationship between key and ciphertext, and *diffusion* attempts to spread the structure present in the plaintext so that a ciphertext bit depends on many plaintext bits. Efficiency in terms of speed, memory, and other computer resources may be essential, and the scheme may need to be suitable for hardware implementation.

A Feistel cipher maps messages of length $2n$ bits to ciphertext of the same length, where $n \in \mathbb{N}$. The input to the scheme is the message itself and a key k. Encryption proceeds through a series of r *rounds*.

- A *key-scheduling algorithm* determines subkeys $k_1, \ldots, k_r$ from a specified key k. Each subkey determines a function

$$f_{k_i} : \{0,1\}^n \to \{0,1\}^n.$$

- A $2n$-bit message m is split into n-bit left and right halves, written $m = (m_0, m_1)$. The rounds can be written

$$\begin{array}{ll}
1: & (m_0, m_1) \mapsto (m_1, m_2 = m_0 \oplus f_{k_1}(m_1)) \\
2: & (m_1, m_2) \mapsto (m_2, m_3 = m_1 \oplus f_{k_2}(m_2)) \\
\vdots & \qquad\qquad\qquad \vdots \\
r: & (m_{r-1}, m_r) \mapsto (m_r, m_{r+1} = m_{r-1} \oplus f_{k_r}(m_r))
\end{array}$$

The output interchanges the left and right halves of the last round, giving $c = (m_{r+1}, m_r)$.

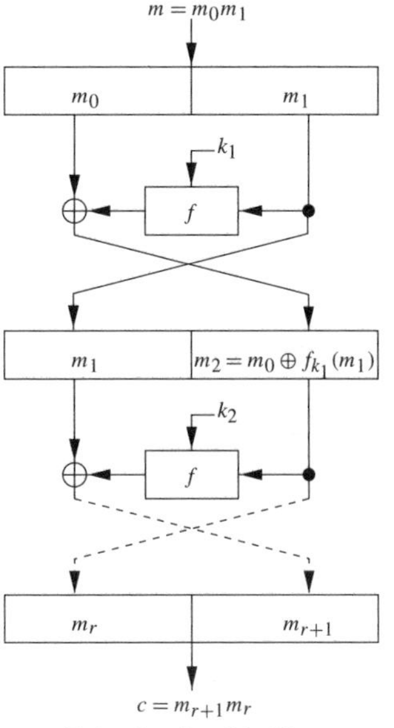

Feistel twisted ladder

- The interchange allows decryption to use the same form of the r rounds, but with the subkeys in reverse order. To see this, define $c_j = m_{r+1-j}$. Then $c = (c_0, c_1)$ and the assignment in round r is easily solved for m_{r-1}, giving

$$c_2 = m_{r-1} = m_{r+1} \oplus f_{k_r}(m_r) = c_0 \oplus f_{k_r}(c_1)$$

which is of the form found in round 1.

The use of rounds in this fashion is attractive, as it offers the possibility of using relatively simple (if not elegant) mappings at each stage, reducing resource requirements. Multiple rounds ($r = 16$ in DES) add confusion and diffusion. The keyspace, of course, must be sufficiently large to prevent exhaustive search under some specified level of computing ability granted to the adversary.

10.3.1 The New Data Seal

NDS is a relatively simple Feistel cipher, in part because the key schedule consists of a single key. Unfortunately, this turns out to be an Achilles' heel, leading to a chosen-plaintext attack considered in this section.

We consider the case that $n = 64$ (so that messages are $2n = 128$ bits in length) and $r = 16$ rounds. The key is a mapping $k : \{0, 1\}^8 \to \{0, 1\}^8$. The necessary (but not sufficient) requirement of a keyspace sufficiently large to prevent exhaustive search is clearly satisfied, as the number of such keys is $(2^8)^{2^8} = 2^{2048}$.

The system contains two fixed (non-secret) maps, $S_0, S_1 : \{0, 1\}^4 \to \{0, 1\}^4$, and the key schedule consists of the single key k, used on each round. To compute $f_k(m_i)$ for a 64-bit half-message m_i:

1. Break m_i into eight 8-bit bytes, and let m_i^* denote the byte formed from the first bit of each byte of m_i.
2. Break each byte of m_i into two 4-bit nibbles, applying S_0 to the left half and S_1 to the right half.
3. Interchange the nibbles of the jth byte of the S_0S_1-output in the case that the jth bit of $k(m_i^*)$ is 1.
4. A fixed (non-secret) permutation is applied to the 64 bits of output.

A schematic for the round appears in Figure 10.3. The final permutation prevents a reduction to eight independent smaller schemes.

Chosen-plaintext attack on NDS

The use of the same key in every round of NDS is a weakness which can be exploited in a chosen-plaintext attack. The key itself can be recovered, completely breaking the scheme.

Let $T = T_k$ be the transformation corresponding to a single round of NDS, i.e., $T(m_{i-1}, m_i) = T_k(m_{i-1}, m_i) = (m_i, m_{i-1} \oplus f_k(m_i))$, and let $F = T^{16}$ denote all 16 rounds. The essential observation is that F and T commute: $FT(m) = T^{16}T(m) = TT^{16}(m) = TF(m)$.

Under Kerckhoffs' principle, we assume that the adversary knows everything about the scheme except the key k. Fix $q \in \{0, 1\}^8$. The key is recovered if we can find $k(q)$ for each such q. The attack proceeds as follows.

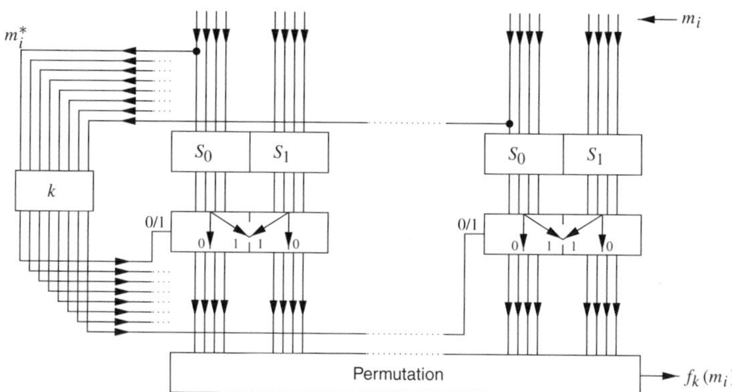

Figure 10.3: *The function f in one round of NDS.*

1. Embed q in a message $m = (m_0, m_1)$ so that $m_1^* = q$. The adversary obtains the ciphertext $(m_{16}, m_{17}) = F(m)$ corresponding to the chosen-text m.
2. Let $\tilde{k}$ denote one of the 2^8 8-bit possibilities for $k(q)$, and let $\tilde{T} = T_{\tilde{k}}(m)$ be the mapping of the message by one round under the candidate $\tilde{k}$.
3. If $\tilde{k} = k(q)$, then $\tilde{T} = T(m)$ and

$$F(\tilde{T}) = FT(m) = TF(m) = T(m_{16}, m_{17}) = (m_{17}, ?)$$

and hence the left-half of $F(\tilde{T})$ agrees with the right-half of $F(m)$. The adversary obtains ciphertext $F(\tilde{T})$ corresponding to the chosen-text $\tilde{T}$; if the right half of $F(m)$ agrees with the left half of $F(\tilde{T})$, then $\tilde{T}$ is considered a match for $T(m)$, and $\tilde{k}$ is accepted as a likely value of $k(q)$. At most $2^8 = 256$ values of $\tilde{k}$ must be checked in order to obtain a match.

The procedure is applied for each $q \in \{0, 1\}^8$, yielding a candidate for k using at most $2^8(2^8 + 1) = 65792$ chosen-plaintexts.

The candidate for the key k may be incorrect. In step 3, $\tilde{T}$ could be a "match" without actually having the value $T(m)$. However, if the cipher was designed to add confusion and diffusion, then we may assume that it is unlikely that more than one choice of $\tilde{k}$ leads to a match at this stage.

We'd also like $\tilde{k} = k(q)$ whenever $\tilde{T} = T(m)$ at step 3. The only unknown part of the single-round calculation $T(m)$ is the interchange condition $k(m_1^*)$ on the output of the S_0, S_1 transformations. If the output of S_0 and S_1 agree on one of the bytes of m_1, then the corresponding bit of $k(m_1^*)$ cannot be determined from an examination of $T(m)$. Hence, in addition to the requirement that $m_1^* = q$, m should be chosen so that output of S_0 and S_1 differ in each byte of m_1. (The inability to choose such an m may indicate a system vulnerable to simpler attacks.)

Toy example

Consider an NDS-like cipher with $n = 4$ and $r = 3$ rounds. Messages are $2n = 8$ bits, and the key is a mapping $k : \{0,1\}^2 \rightarrow \{0,1\}^2$. (Each of the 3 subkeys is k. The keyspace has size $(2^2)^{2^2} = 256$.) Let S_0 be the identity, and let S_1 perform bitwise complement. The permutation writes the bits in reverse order. A schematic similar to Figure 10.3 has two pairs of S_0, S_1 boxes, each box accepting 1-bit of the $n = 4$ bits of m_i.

Suppose the key k is defined by

$$k(00) = 10 \quad k(10) = 11$$
$$k(01) = 00 \quad k(11) = 10$$

and the message to be encrypted is $m = (m_0, m_1) = (0111, 1100)$. The value of $m_2 = m_0 \oplus f(m_1)$ is calculated as

$$m_1 = 1100 \xrightarrow{S_0S_1} 1001 \xrightarrow{k} 0110 \xrightarrow{\text{permute}} 0110 \xrightarrow{\oplus m_0} 0001 = m_2.$$

The other rounds are similar, giving

$$(m_0, m_1) = (0111, 1100) \mapsto (1100, 0001) \mapsto (0001, 1101)$$
$$\mapsto (1101, 0011) = (m_3, m_4) = F(m).$$

We illustrate the chosen-plaintext attack to recover $k(q)$ for $q = 10$.

1. We wish to choose $m = (m_0, m_1)$ so that $m_1^* = q$ and so that the output of S_0 and S_1 on halves of m_1 differ. We may select $m = (0111, 1100)$, obtaining $F(m) = (1101, \underline{0011})$.
2. Build a table of possible one-round encryptions $\tilde{T}$, one entry for each guess $\tilde{k}$ of $k(q)$. Then $F(\tilde{T})$ corresponding to each chosen-plaintext $\tilde{T}$ is obtained.

$\tilde{k}$	00	01	10	11
m_1	1100	1100	1100	1100
S_0S_1	1001	1001	1001	1001
apply $\tilde{k}$	1001	1010	0101	0110
permute	1001	0101	1010	0110
$\oplus m_0$	1110	0010	1101	0001
$\tilde{T}$	(1100, 1110)	(1100, 0010)	(1100, 1101)	(1100, 0001)
$F(\tilde{T})$	(0000, 1011)	(1100, 0100)	$(\underline{0011}, 1000)$	$(\underline{0011}, 1011)$

3. $\tilde{T}$ is considered a match whenever the left-half of $F(\tilde{T})$ agrees with the right-half of $F(m) = (1101, 0011)$. Unfortunately, two matches have been obtained, corresponding to underlined entries in the table. At this stage, the possibilities for $k(q)$ have been narrowed to $\tilde{k} = 10$ or $\tilde{k} = 11$.

The example illustrates that the proposed attack may fail to isolate the key value. Additional plaintexts could be tried; e.g., $m = (0101, 1100)$ determines $\tilde{k} = 11$ as the correct value of $k(10)$.

Exercises

10.3.1 Given that $c = (m_{r+1}, m_r) = (1111, 0100)$ is an output of the cipher in the toy example, find the corresponding message m.

10.3.2 Follow the procedure outlined in the toy NDS example to find $k(00)$.

10.3.3 Define two functions $f_0, f_1 : \{0,1\}^4 \to \{0,1\}^4$ by

$$f_0(x_1, x_2, x_3, x_4) = (x_2 \oplus x_4, 1, x_1 x_2, 1 \oplus x_3)$$
$$f_1(x_1, x_2, x_3, x_4) = (1, x_1 \oplus x_3, x_4, x_2).$$

Let F be the toy Feistel cipher defined as follows:

- $n = 4$ (so that messages are $2n = 8$ bits long), and there are $r = 2$ rounds;
- the key of F is a pair (k_1, k_2) of binary digits;
- in round $i \in \{1, 2\}$, the function f_{k_i} is used.

A message m is encrypted to ciphertext c under the key $(0, 1)$. If $c = m_{r+1} m_r = 10101011$, then find m.

10.3.2 The Data Encryption Standard

DES is the result of a 1973 solicitation for encryption standards by the National Bureau of Standards (NBS, now NIST). Developed at IBM and modified jointly with the US National Security Agency (NSA), the cipher is also known as the Data Encryption Algorithm. DES is based on a 16-round Feistel cipher, acting on 64-bit input. The key schedule produces a 48-bit subkey k_i for each of the rounds from a given 56-bit key k. There are eight fixed *S-box* mappings which are fundamental to the security of the system, shown in Figure 10.4.

The adoption of DES as a standard in 1977 was a milestone in the use of cryptography. DES would become the most widely-used symmetric-key scheme. The standard was controversial, in part because not all of the design principles were made public. The secrecy invited speculation that the scheme may contain a "trap door" which permits the NSA to decrypt messages.

The size of the keyspace has been criticized heavily. The description of the scheme would be known to everybody; security rested entirely with the key. The standard specifies a keylength of 64 bits, of which 8 are parity, giving an effective keylength of 56 bits. An exhaustive search of the keyspace by a determined adversary with specialized hardware was a concern.

In 1977, Diffie and Hellman [28] proposed a DES exhaustive search machine at an estimated cost of US$20 million, searching the entire keyspace in a day. In 1993, Michael Wiener presented a detailed design for a machine which could search the entire keyspace in 7 hours for $1 million [93]; a 1997 version of the $1 million machine would perform the search in a little over an hour [94].

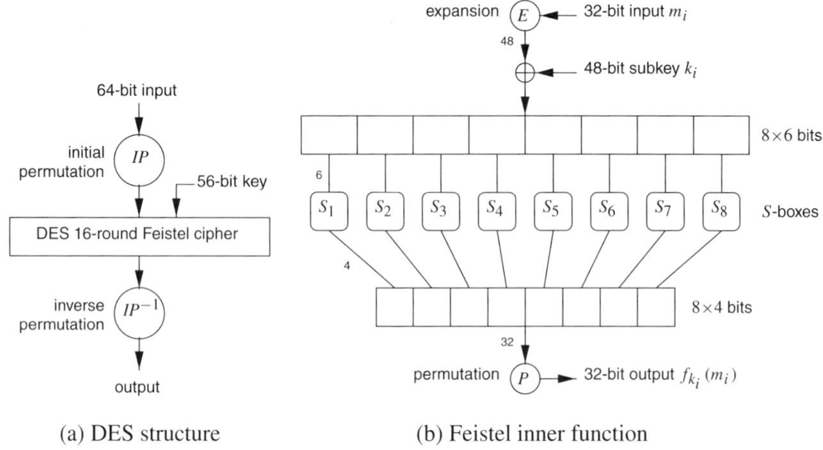

(a) DES structure (b) Feistel inner function

Figure 10.4: *Schematics for the Data Encryption Standard.*

In January 1997, RSA Laboratories launched the "DES Challenge," offering prizes for uncovering the DES key from three known-plaintext pairs. The DES-CHALL group claimed the prize in June 1997, using exhaustive search with a large-scale distributed network of computers connected by the internet. This was a volunteer effort, requiring 96 days with an estimated 70000 machines involved at some stage. Approximately 25% of the keyspace had been searched when the key was found. In 1998, a similar contest was solved in 40 days by distributed.net, searching 88% of the keyspace. Near the close of the contest, they recorded a peak rate of over $34 \cdot 10^9$ keys per second by nearly 1400 active teams.

In 1998, the Electronic Frontier Foundation (EFF) claimed a DES Challenge in 56 hours using a \$0.2 million custom-built machine. In January 1999, distributed.net and the EFF combined forces, claiming a Challenge in a little over 22 hours, testing $245 \cdot 10^9$ keys per second when the key was found. There had been concern that US Government officials deliberately overestimated the costs of such a machine and underestimated the applicability of known-plaintext attacks, in order to protect other interests. As Diffie noted, by publishing the complete software and hardware details for their relatively inexpensive cracker [34], it is no longer "a question of whether DES keys can be extracted by exhaustive search; it is a question of how cheaply they can be extracted and for what purposes." The DES Challenge permitted known-plaintext attacks, but effective exhaustive search is possible if partial information concerning structure or content-type of the plaintext is known.

Multiple encryption (discussed below) can be used with DES to defeat exhaustive search, although there is a speed penalty (see also Exercise 10.3.5). DES is entrenched, however. As Whitfield Diffie remarked in the forward to the EFF cracker [34], "The most convincing argument that DES is insecure would not outweigh the vast investment in DES equipment that has accumulated throughout the world. People will continue using DES whatever its shortcomings, convincing themselves that it is adequate for their needs."

A possible DES replacement, the Advanced Encryption Standard (AES; see Section 10.4) was in the process of selecting an algorithm in 2000. Apparently, it will address the fundamental weakness of DES, the ability to effectively mount an exhaustive search of the keyspace. In [9], a group of well-known cryptographers recommended a 75-bit key to protect 1996 data and a 90-bit key for 20-year security, noting that "the cost of very strong encryption is not significantly greater than that of weak encryption."

Multiple encryption

Block ciphers such as DES may be applied in succession, in an attempt to obtain a cipher with a larger keyspace. Double encryption with a single cipher, for example, takes the form $E(m) = E_{k_2} E_{k_1}(m)$ for given keys k_1, k_2. Multiple encryption need not enhance security—in fact, it need not even enlarge the effective keyspace. If an encryption scheme is closed under composition in the sense that given k_1, k_2 there exists $k_3 \in \mathcal{K}$ so that $E_{k_2} E_{k_1} = E_{k_3}$, then double encryption offers no additional security. As an example, the simple substitution cipher over all permutations k of some alphabet (as in Example 10.2.2) has $k_3 = k_2 \circ k_1$.

For key k, DES_k is a permutation on $\{0, 1\}^{64}$. The keyspace defines at most 2^{56} (out of a possible $2^{64}!$) such permutations. This collection of permutations is not closed under composition, and multiple encryption is often used with the hope of defeating exhaustive search of the keyspace.

In the case of double-DES, an unsophisticated exhaustive search tries all $(2^{56})^2 = 2^{112}$ keys. However, double encryption is vulnerable to a *meet-in-the-middle* attack which reduces the effort to 2^{57} DES operations at the cost of 2^{56} storage. If at least one known-plaintext pair (m, c) is available, where $c = \text{DES}_{k_2}\,\text{DES}_{k_1}(m)$ for unknown keys k_1, k_2, then the attack to recover the keys is:

1. Form a table of $(i, \text{DES}_i(m))$ for all keys i, sorted by the second entry.
2. For each possible key j, determine if $\text{DES}_j^{-1}(c)$ appears in the table; if so, then $\text{DES}_j^{-1}(c) = \text{DES}_i(m)$ for some i, and hence $c = \text{DES}_j\,\text{DES}_i(m)$ and (i, j) is a candidate for (k_1, k_2). Additional known-plaintext pairs (if available) are used at this stage to discard spurious matches.

If at least two known-plaintext pairs are available, the attack is expected to determine the keys.

In practice, triple-DES is used, having a keyspace of size $(2^{56})^3 = 2^{168}$. Given keys k_1, k_2, k_3, the encryption is $E(m) = E_{k_3} E_{k_2} E_{k_1}(m)$, where E_k denotes DES_k

or DES_k^{-1}. The *two-key triple-DES* variant uses $E_{k_2} = \text{DES}_{k_2}^{-1}$ and $k_3 = k_1$; choosing $k_2 = k_1$ gives DES. The meet-in-the-middle attack on triple-DES is no longer feasible, requiring on the order of 2^{112} DES operations. However, there are attacks on two-key triple-DES (requiring large numbers of either chosen-plaintext pairs or DES operations) showing it to be weaker than triple-DES [63].

Modes of operation

Block ciphers are often used in modes which process the plaintext in fragments (often the size of a block). Two such modes are considered in this section. DES will be used in the examples, but the ideas apply to any block cipher.

Let $m = m_1 m_2 \cdots$ be a message, where each m_i is a block (64 bits in DES). *Electronic codebook* (ECB) mode applies DES to each block, obtaining $c_i = \text{DES}_k(m_i)$. It has the advantage of simplicity, and bit errors in a ciphertext block affect decryption of that block only. A disadvantage is that identical messages (under the same key) map to the same ciphertext, possibly leaking information to an adversary.

Cipher-block chaining (CBC) chooses an initial block c_0 and encrypts as $c_i = \text{DES}_k(m_i \oplus c_{i-1})$ for $i \geq 1$. Decryption is performed by $m_i = \text{DES}_k^{-1}(c_i) \oplus c_{i-1}$. The first block of plaintext can be chosen at random to prevent identical plaintexts from always giving the same output. Unlike ECB mode, there are chaining dependencies causing c_j to depend on c_{j-1} (which depends on all preceding plaintext blocks).

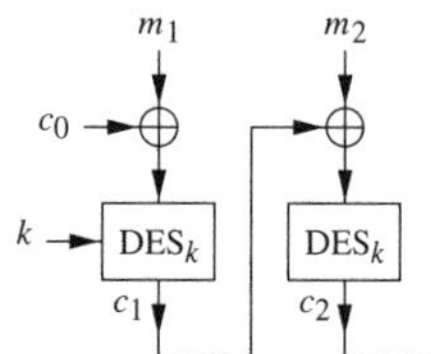

Cipher-block chaining

In ECB mode, errors introduced (outside of the encryption process) into ciphertext c affect only the decryption of the damaged blocks. The chaining in CBC propagates an error in c_j, affecting the recovery of both m_j and m_{j+1}. In fact, an adversary with the ability to modify c_j can force bit errors into the recovery of m_{j+1} by changing the corresponding bits of c_j (Exercise 10.3.4).

Applications to authentication

Symmetric-key systems can be used to provide authentication. We consider two specific examples, the first employing cipher-block chaining to provide message authentication, and the second providing identification (entity authentication) using a password scheme built from DES. The difference between entity and message authentication can be subtle, although the latter tends to involve an actual message rather than simply a claim of identity.

Message authentication Suppose Bob and Alice are exchanging messages (perhaps by email) over an unsecured channel. On receipt of a message purported to be from Alice, Bob should be able to convince himself that the message is genuine. At least two kinds of attacks are of concern: impersonation and forgery.

One possibility is to use a symmetric-key scheme such as DES. Alice and Bob share a secret key, and Alice encrypts the message m, sending $c = E_k(m)$. Bob decrypts c with the secret key, accepting the message if it "makes sense." To prevent replay attacks—messages resent by an adversary—Alice could add time or sequence information to m before calculating c. If the cipher is such that it is difficult to create meaningful messages without knowledge of the key, then some protection from forgery is provided; however, some ciphers may allow selective changes to go undetected. For example, if a block cipher is applied in ECB mode, then the adversary could re-order, substitute, or delete ciphertext blocks. The one-time pad allows an adversary to force bit changes by changing the corresponding bits in the ciphertext.

A more robust scheme can be developed using cipher-block chaining. A block cipher E is selected and the message is written $m = m_1 \cdots m_t$ where each m_i has bitlength matching the blocksize of the cipher (if $E = \text{DES}$, then the blocks are of length 64 bits). The block cipher is applied in CBC mode, giving $c_i = E_k(m_i \oplus c_{i-1})$, $1 \leq i \leq t$. Alice sends the message m along with c_t, known as a *message authentication code* (MAC). Bob computes the CBC-MAC (as Alice did), and accepts the message as genuine if this value agrees with the received MAC. To defeat exhaustive search of the keyspace, a second key k' may be selected and two-key triple-encryption performed on the last block (delivering $E_k E_{k'}^{-1}(c_t)$ rather than c_t as the MAC).

Identification Conventional password schemes rely on a secret shared between a user and the system; access to a system resource is granted when the user reveals the secret itself. We consider the traditional password mechanism used on many Unix computer systems: to gain access, a userid and password pair are presented to the system; access is granted if the system determines from its own stored information that the password corroborates the identity of the user.

A password of up to 8 characters is used in forming the key k for a modified DES encryption function. Each character provides 7 bits of the 56-bit key; zero bits are added if the password is less than 8 characters. An additional 12 bits (known as the *salt*) obtained from the system clock at the time of password creation is used to modify the expansion E in Figure 10.4, specifying one of $2^{12} = 4096$ variations. The system calculates $m_i = \text{DES}_k^*(m_{i-1})$, $1 \leq i \leq 25$, where DES* denotes the modified DES scheme and m_0 is the 64-bit zero value. The 12-bit salt and 64-bit m_{25} (known as the hashed password) are stored on the system, traditionally in /etc/passwd (a file). When subsequently presented with a userid and password, the system performs the same calculations, granting access if the result agrees with the stored value.

The calculation is known as the Unix *crypt* password algorithm. An adversary in possession of an entry from /etc/passwd can mount a known-plaintext attack, since the message input to the algorithm is known. Even if exhaustive search is infeasible, an attack using a dictionary of passwords which are known to be favored by users may be successful. The salt makes the dictionary attack more difficult, since 4096 variations of each password are possible. The salting procedure was also designed so that off-the-shelf DES hardware could not be used for password cracking.

Adversaries often obtain the /etc/passwd file itself (on many systems, all users could read this file), and perform various kinds of attacks, perhaps in the privacy of their own chambers. Recovery of some passwords is a significant threat, even by adversaries with relatively modest computing power.[9] Systems that rely on this mechanism have countered by forcing users to choose better passwords (in an attempt to defeat dictionary attacks), and have moved the hashed passwords to a separate file which requires special privileges to read.

The password scheme is an example of *weak authentication*. The user receives no explicit corroboration of the identity of the system; if the channel is unsecured, then an adversary may be able to impersonate the system in addition to simple eavesdropping. We will return to authentication in Chapter 12.

Exercises

10.3.4 (Errors in DES ciphertexts) Suppose that t plaintext blocks $m_1, \ldots, m_t$ are encrypted using DES producing ciphertexts $c_1, \ldots, c_t$, respectively.

(a) Suppose that one ciphertext, say c_j, is transmitted incorrectly. Explain briefly the procedure to determine the number and location of blocks which will be decrypted incorrectly in ECB mode and CBC mode.

(b) Suppose CBC mode has been used and an adversary interchanges the ciphertext blocks c_3 and c_6. When the ciphertext is received, how many plaintext blocks will be in error?

(c) In CBC mode, show how an adversary forces specific bit errors in m_{j+1} by adjusting c_j.

10.3.5 This problem concerns proposals to protect DES from exhaustive key search. The key is $k = (k_1, k_2)$ where $k_1 \in \{0,1\}^{56}$ and $k_2 \in \{0,1\}^{64}$. Let $m \in \{0,1\}^{64}$ be the plaintext message.

(a) Show that encryption defined by $E_k(m) = \text{DES}_{k_1}(m) \oplus k_2$ does not increase the work needed to break the encryption scheme using exhaustive search. That is, show how to break this scheme using on the order of 2^{56} DES operations. You may assume that you have a moderate number of pairs $(m_i, c_i = E_k(m_i))$.

[9] Feldmeier and Karn [32] report that their 1989 dictionary attacks typically recovered over 30% of the passwords on a given system. The authors present a fast crypt algorithm, used in password-cracking attacks where the hashed passwords have been obtained.

(b) Does encryption defined by $E_k(m) = \text{DES}_{k_1}(m \oplus k_2)$ make exhaustive search less feasible?

A "DESX" extension suggested by Rivest is discussed in the proceedings of CRYPTO '96 [49]. For key $k = (k_1, k_2, k_3)$, the encryption function is $E_k(m) = k_3 \oplus \text{DES}_{k_1}(m \oplus k_2)$. The inexpensive XOR pre- and post-processing may be used with existing DES machinery.

10.3.6 Suppose that Eve has obtained three pairs (m_1, c_1), (m_2, c_2), and (m_3, c_3) which were encrypted by Alice using triple-DES with $E(m) = \text{DES}_{k_3}\,\text{DES}_{k_2}\,\text{DES}_{k_1}(m)$. Devise a meet-in-the-middle attack that recovers Alice's key (k_1, k_2, k_3) in roughly 2^{112} operations.

10.3.7 (DES complementation property) Let $\overline{m}$ denote the bitwise complement of a bit string m. If $c = \text{DES}_k(m)$, then an examination of the description of DES establishes that $\overline{c} = \text{DES}_{\overline{k}}(\overline{m})$. Does it appear that this property can be used to improve the running time of exhaustive key search under a known-plaintext attack? Under a chosen-plaintext attack?

10.3.8 The CBC-MAC described provides data integrity but not confidentiality. Consider the following proposal to add secrecy. The MAC is appended to message $m = m_1 \cdots m_t$, giving $m' = mm_{t+1}$. Then m' itself is encrypted in CBC mode (using the same initial c_0 and key), giving $c_1 \cdots c_{t+1}$, where $c_i = E_k(m_i \oplus c_{i-1})$, $1 \le i \le t+1$; the first t of these calculations are identical to those performed in obtaining the MAC.

The method appears attractive, obtaining the ciphertext directly from the calculations for the MAC. Show that the scheme results in a final ciphertext block $c_{t+1} = E_k(m_{t+1} \oplus c_t)$ which is independent of the plaintext and the ciphertext. Explain why this means that the added encryption has compromised the authentication, and illustrate how an adversary may exploit this fundamental flaw.

10.4 Notes

The opening sentence of this chapter is from Rivest [71], an excellent introduction to cryptography. Simmons [81] contains contributions from several authors, including *The First Ten Years of Public Key Cryptography* by Diffie [26]. The *Handbook of Applied Cryptography* by Menezes, van Oorshot, and Vanstone [63] is recommended for its well-organized and comprehensive coverage.

Kahn's *The Codebreakers* is often cited for its complete (and lively) nontechnical history of cryptology up to 1967; a few notes on more recent developments appear in a revised 1996 edition [48]. Garfinkel [37] discusses some of the political, legal, privacy, and policy questions concerning cryptography, along with the history of the Pretty Good Privacy (PGP) application. The textbooks of Stinson [86] and Koblitz [50] are natural choices to extend the material introduced here.

Extensive material from the VENONA project at the National Security Agency is available via http://www.nsa.gov. The historical introduction begins with the following paragraph.

> On 1 February 1943, the U.S. Army's Signal Intelligence Service, a forerunner of the National Security Agency, began a small, very secret program, later codenamed VENONA. The object of the VENONA program was to examine and possibly exploit, encrypted Soviet diplomatic communications. These messages had been accumulated by the Signal Intelligence Service (later renamed the U.S. Army Signal Security Agency and commonly called "Arlington Hall" after the Virginia location of its headquarters) since 1939 but had not been studied previously. Miss Gene Grabeel, a young Signal Intelligence Service employee, who had been a school teacher only weeks earlier, started the project.

The description of the New Data Seal is from Beker and Piper [3]. Details of DES may be found in [63, 86, 3]. Early commentary on the "DES controversy" appears in a series of IEEE Spectrum articles beginning with [87]. Some design criteria for the S-boxes may be found in Coppersmith [23], Stinson [86], and Schneier [76]. RSA's DES Challenges are described on http://www.rsa.com. The non-profit Electronic Frontier Foundation maintains a web page on various civil liberties issues at http://www.eff.org; on-line versions of *Cracking DES* [34] are available.

Use of DES CBC has been standardized by the International Organization for Standards (ISO 9797) and the American National Standards Institute (ANSI X9.9) for authentication purposes [63]. ANSI X9.9 is widely used by banks in financial applications. Triple-DES was approved by ANSI in November 1998 as a standard (ANSI X9.52). In 1999, the National Institute of Standards and Technology (NIST) was in the process of considering triple-DES for a US Government Federal Information Processing Standard (FIPS 46-3; see http://csrc.nist.gov/cryptval). The draft announcement contained:

> Additionally, knowing that the DES' security life was nearing an end, NIST has been working with industry and the cryptographic community to develop an Advanced Encryption Standard (AES) for the 21st century. On January 2, 1997, NIST announced the initiation of an effort to develop the AES (62 FR 93). It is intended that the AES will specify an unclassified, publicly disclosed encryption algorithm capable of protecting sensitive government information well into the next century. Unfortunately, since it takes a substantial amount of time to gain confidence in a new encryption algorithm, the AES is not expected to be a fully developed FIPS for some time to come. Information on NIST's multi-year effort to develop the AES can be obtained at http://www.nist.gov/aes.
>
> Recently claims have been made of a special-purpose hardware based attack on the DES. In light of this most recent attack, NIST can no longer support

the use of the DES for many applications. As with other security tools, encryption must balance cost against risk. The recent brute force exhaustion attack by a "cracking machine" costing $250000 took 56 hours to crack a single message. With this special-purpose technology, the average time of cracking per message would be twice that, since only a quarter of all keys were tested. In some cases this kind of attack may not pose an immediate or significant threat—for example where short-term protection of perishable information is desired. However, advances in technology are likely to further reduce the average cracking time. Therefore, NIST recommends the following:

- For existing systems, develop a prudent transition strategy to move to Triple DES. This strategy should match the strength of the protective measures against the associated risk. Critical systems should receive priority.
- When building new systems, use Triple DES to protect sensitive, unclassified data.

These recommendations are reflected in the proposed draft FIPS 46-3...by recognizing Triple DES, as described in ANSI X9.52, as a FIPS approved algorithm.

Chapter 11

Topics in Algebra and Number Theory

Public-key cryptography relies for security on the (supposed) intractability of various number-theoretic problems. The integer factorization problem (FACTOR) and the discrete logarithm problem (DLP) are well-known examples:

FACTOR: Find the prime factorization of a given positive integer n.
DLP: Given prime p, generator α of $\mathbb{Z}_p^*$, and $\alpha^x \bmod p$, find x.

To be slightly more precise, public-key schemes require two (related) problems, one which is computationally feasible, and one which is intractable. In the case of integer factorization, for example, it is relatively easy to find the product $n = pq$; efficient recovery of p and q given n in the general case remains an open problem.

Four topics are considered in the following sections: quadratic residues, primality testing, integer factorization, and discrete logarithms. Clearly, the coverage will not be exhaustive, and the goal is to consider a respectable sampling of material from algebra and number theory (and algorithmic number theory) fundamental to public-key schemes.

11.1 Algorithms, complexity, and modular arithmetic

Several algorithms involving arithmetic operations on integers are presented in this section. One measure of efficiency is a count of the number of operations involving single-bit arithmetic. For example, if x and y are k-bit binary numbers, then $x + y$ may be done in at most k bit operations, and the usual approach to calculating xy requires at most k^2 bit operations (there are at most $k - 1$ additions, each requiring at most k bit operations). These are "worst-case" counts, over all integers with at most k bits. We can regard the number of bit operations as a measure of the *running time*, in terms of the "size" k of the input, required by an algorithm.

The running times in terms of the input size are often written using the following notation. Given sequences f and g defined on the positive integers, we say that f is "big-oh" of g, written $f = O(g)$, in case there exist numbers c and n_0 so that $|f(n)| \leq c|g(n)|$ for all $n \geq n_0$. For example, $f(n) = 3n^4 + 7n - 1 = O(n^4)$, $\log n = O(n^t)$ for any $t > 0$, and $f = O(1)$ means that $|f|$ is bounded above by a constant. In the examples of addition and multiplication of k-bit binary numbers, the bit complexity may be said to be $O(k)$ and $O(k^2)$, respectively. Note that big-oh notation is about asymptotic upper bounds; the statement $f(n) = O(2^n)$ does not preclude the possibility that $f(n) = O(n^2)$, a much slower-growing bound.

An algorithm for arithmetic on k-bit binary numbers x and y is said to be *polynomial-time* if the worst-case running time is bounded by a polynomial in the size k of the input; i.e., the running time is $O(k^t)$ for some integer t. Roughly speaking, such algorithms will be considered *efficient*, although it is important to note that it is possible for a polynomial-time algorithm to be slower than an exponential-time algorithm for all input values of interest.

If x and y are integers with $0 \leq x, y \leq n$, then the size of the input to the algorithm may be taken to be the number of bits $k = \lfloor \log_2 n \rfloor + 1$ in the binary representation of n. In the big-oh notation, we may use the simpler expression $k = \log_2 n$. In particular, the algorithm is efficient if the running time is $O(k^t)$ not $O(n^t)$.

The integers

Let $a, b \in \mathbb{Z}$, the set of integers $\{0, \pm 1, \pm 2, \ldots\}$. Then *a divides b*, written $a \mid b$, if there is an integer c such that $b = ac$. As examples, $-3 \mid 15$ since $15 = (-3)(-5)$, and every integer divides 0. If b has a divisor $a \notin \{\pm 1, \pm b\}$, then a is said to be *nontrivial*. An integer $a \geq 2$ is *prime* if it has no nontrivial divisors; otherwise, a is *composite*. The prime number theorem gives an asymptotic estimate on the number of primes $\pi(x)$ in the interval $[2, x]$ as $\pi(x) \sim x/\log x$. The estimate is in fact a lower bound; for example, with $x = 10^3$, $\pi(x) = 168 > x/\log x \approx 144.8$.

It is routine (Exercise 11.1.9) to verify the following properties: if $a \mid b$ and $b \mid c$ then $a \mid c$; if c is a *common divisor* of a and b in the sense that $c \mid a$ and $c \mid b$, then $c \mid ax + by$ for every $x, y \in \mathbb{Z}$; if p is prime and $p \mid ab$, then $p \mid a$ or $p \mid b$. A common divisor $d \geq 0$ of a and b is the *greatest common divisor*, written $d = \gcd(a, b)$ or more simply $d = (a, b)$, if $c \mid d$ for all common divisors c of a and b. The Euclidean algorithm discussed below shows that the greatest common divisor exists. The fundamental theorem of arithmetic (every integer $a \geq 2$ can be written uniquely, up to ordering, as a product of primes) can be used to find common divisors; for example, $36 = 2^2 \cdot 3^2$, $24 = 2^3 \cdot 3$, and $(36, 24) = 2^2 \cdot 3$.

Exhibiting the prime factorization of a given integer is believed to be a difficult problem; however, it is possible to find the greatest common divisor without factoring. First, recall the division algorithm: given integers a and $b \geq 1$, then long division may be used to write $a = qb + r$ with $0 \le r < b$. The integers q (the *quotient*) and r (the *remainder*, denoted $r = a \bmod b$) are unique. The Euclidean algorithm for finding the greatest common divisor uses the fact that $(a,b) = (b, a \bmod b)$ if $a > b > 0$.

Algorithm 11.1.1 (Euclidean algorithm for greatest common divisor) Input: integers $a \ge b \ge 0$. Output: the greatest common divisor (a,b) of a and b.

1. Set $r_0 = a$ and $r_1 = b$.
2. Determine the first $n \ge 0$ so that $r_{n+1} = 0$, where $r_{i+1} = r_{i-1} \bmod r_i$; i.e., r_{i+1} is defined by $r_{i-1} = q_{i+1}r_i + r_{i+1}$ obtained from the division algorithm.
3. Return (r_n).

It is clear that the process will terminate, since $0 \le r_{i+1} < r_i$ for $i > 0$. In fact, $r_{i+2} < r_i/2$, so that there are at most $1 + 2\log_2 a$ divisions. Each division takes $O(\log_2^2 a)$ bit operations, so the running time of the Euclidean algorithm is $O(\log_2^3 a)$ bit operations. A more careful analysis shows that the time is actually $O(\log_2^2 a)$; in any case, the Euclidean algorithm is efficient. (Exercise 11.1.11 verifies that the value returned is indeed (a,b).)

Example 11.1.2 We apply the algorithm to calculate $(299, 221)$. The long divisions may be written:

$$\begin{aligned} 299 &= 1 \cdot 221 + 78 && (q_2 = 1, r_2 = 78) \\ 221 &= 2 \cdot 78 + 65 && (q_3 = 2, r_3 = 65) \\ 78 &= 1 \cdot 65 + 13 && (q_4 = 1, r_4 = 13) \\ 65 &= 5 \cdot 13 + 0 && (q_5 = 5, r_5 = 0) \end{aligned}$$

and $(299, 221) = r_4 = 13$.

The Euclidean algorithm may be written somewhat more concisely; however, the present form is easily extended to provide integers x and y so that $ax + by = (a,b)$. The basic idea is to walk through the long divisions, beginning at the bottom (Appendix A presents this more formally). The first two steps are:

$$\begin{aligned} (a,b) = r_n &= r_{n-2} - q_n r_{n-1} \\ &= r_{n-2} - q_n(r_{n-3} - q_{n-1}r_{n-2}) \\ &= (1 + q_n q_{n-1})r_{n-2} - q_n r_{n-3} \end{aligned}$$

obtaining (a,b) as a linear combination of r_{n-2} and r_{n-3}. The process, known as the extended Euclidean algorithm, eventually obtains (a,b) as a linear combination of $r_0 = a$ and $r_1 = b$. In the example,

$$\begin{aligned} (299, 221) = 13 &= 78 - 65 \\ &= 78 - (221 - 2 \cdot 78) = 3 \cdot 78 - 221 \\ &= 3(299 - 1 \cdot 221) - 221 = 3 \cdot 299 - 4 \cdot 221 \end{aligned}$$

and $(a = 299, b = 221) = 13 = 3a - 4b$.

If $(a,b) = 1$, then a and b are said to be *relatively prime*. For $n \geq 1$, the number of integers in the interval $[1,n]$ which are relatively prime to n is denoted $\phi(n)$, known as the Euler phi function. For example, $\phi(6) = 2$ and $\phi(p^i) = p^{i-1}(p-1)$ if p is prime. The phi function is multiplicative in the sense that $\phi(ab) = \phi(a)\phi(b)$ if $(a,b) = 1$; in particular, $\phi(pq) = (p-1)(q-1)$ for primes $p \neq q$.

The integers modulo *n*

Let n be a positive integer. Then a is *congruent* to b modulo n, written $a \equiv b \pmod{n}$, if $n \mid a - b$. As examples, $14 \equiv 9 \pmod{5}$, $-11 \equiv 3 \pmod{7}$, and $-1 \equiv n-1 \pmod{n}$. Congruence is an equivalence relation on $\mathbb{Z}$; that is, congruence is reflexive ($a \equiv a \pmod{n}$), symmetric (if $a \equiv b \pmod{n}$ then $b \equiv a \pmod{n}$), and transitive (if $a \equiv b \pmod{n}$ and $b \equiv c \pmod{n}$ then $a \equiv c \pmod{n}$). If $a = qn + r$ with $0 \leq r < n$, then $a \equiv r \pmod{n}$. Hence every integer a is congruent to a unique integer in $[0, n-1]$, namely $r = a \bmod n$. An equivalence (or residue) class $[a]$ consists of all integers congruent to a modulo n; the set of equivalence classes modulo n is denoted $\mathbb{Z}_n$.

It can be shown that the operations of addition and multiplication on $\mathbb{Z}_n$ given by $[a] + [b] = [a+b]$ and $[a][b] = [ab]$, respectively, are well-defined; that is, if $a \equiv a' \pmod{n}$ and $b \equiv b' \pmod{n}$ then $a + b \equiv a' + b' \pmod{n}$ and $ab \equiv a'b' \pmod{n}$. Under these definitions of addition and multiplication, $(\mathbb{Z}_n, +, \cdot)$ is a *ring* (see Exercise 11.1.12). The class notation is commonly omitted, and the set of equivalence classes is written $\mathbb{Z}_n = \{0, \ldots, n-1\}$ with the understanding that an integer a is identified with its equivalence class $[a]$.

Given $a \in \mathbb{Z}_n$, if there exists $x \in \mathbb{Z}_n$ such that $ax \equiv 1 \pmod{n}$, then a is said to be *invertible* and its inverse x is denoted a^{-1}. For example, in $\mathbb{Z}_9$, $2^{-1} = 5$ since $2 \cdot 5 \equiv 1 \pmod{9}$; the elements in $\{0, 3, 6\}$ do not have inverses. If $a \in \mathbb{Z}_n$ is invertible, then $ax \equiv 1 \pmod{n}$ and $n \mid ax - 1$ so that $ax - ny = 1$ for some integer y, and (a,n) must be 1. Conversely, if $(a,n) = 1$, then x and y exist by the extended Euclidean algorithm. Hence, $a \in \mathbb{Z}_n$ is invertible if and only if $(a,n) = 1$, in which case the inverse may be found by the extended Euclidean algorithm.

Example 11.1.3 Let $a = 7$ and $n = 9$. The first column uses the Euclidean algorithm to show that $(7,9) = 1$, and hence a is invertible in $\mathbb{Z}_9$. The second column finds integers x and y so that $xa + yn = (a,n)$.

Euclidean algorithm to find (a,n)	extended Euclidean algorithm to write $(a,n) = xa + yn$
$9 = 1 \cdot 7 + 2$	$1 = 7 - 3 \cdot 2$
$7 = 3 \cdot 2 + 1$	$= 7 - 3(9 - 1 \cdot 7) = 4 \cdot 7 - 3 \cdot 9$
$2 = 2 \cdot 1 + 0$	

Hence, $7^{-1} = 4$, which can be verified by $7 \cdot 4 \equiv 28 \equiv 1 \pmod{9}$.

The set $\mathbb{Z}_n^* = \{a \in \mathbb{Z}_n \mid (a, n) = 1\}$ of invertible elements of $\mathbb{Z}_n$ forms a group under multiplication, containing $\phi(n)$ elements. For example, $\mathbb{Z}_{12}^* = \{1, 5, 7, 11\}$ and $\mathbb{Z}_p^* = \{1, \ldots, p-1\}$ if p is prime. For prime p and $a \in \mathbb{Z}_p^*$, Fermat's (little) theorem says $a^{p-1} \equiv 1 \pmod{p}$; a generalization due to Euler shows $a^{\phi(n)} \equiv 1 \pmod{n}$ for integer $n \geq 2$ and $a \in \mathbb{Z}_n^*$. In particular, we may define the *order* of $a \in \mathbb{Z}_n^*$, written $\mathrm{ord}(a)$, as the least positive integer t such that $a^t \equiv 1 \pmod{n}$. Exercise 11.1.21 establishes some elementary properties concerning $\mathbb{Z}_n^*$; in particular, $\mathrm{ord}(a) \mid \phi(n)$ for $a \in \mathbb{Z}_n^*$. If $a \in \mathbb{Z}_n^*$ has $\mathrm{ord}(a) = |\mathbb{Z}_n^*| = \phi(n)$, then a is said to be a *generator* of $\mathbb{Z}_n^*$; in this case, $\mathbb{Z}_n^* = \{a^i \mid 0 \leq i < \phi(n)\}$. It is known that $\mathbb{Z}_p^*$ for p prime has a generator; for example, it is easily verified that 2 is a generator of $\mathbb{Z}_{13}^*$.

Example 11.1.4 Consider $\mathbb{Z}_{15}^* = \{1, 2, 4, 7, 8, 11, 13, 14\}$, having $\phi(15) = \phi(3)\phi(5) = (3-1)(5-1) = 8$ elements. The orders of the elements are:

$a \in \mathbb{Z}_{15}^*$	1	2	4	7	8	11	13	14
$\mathrm{ord}(a)$	1	4	2	4	4	2	4	2

As promised, the order of every element divides $\phi(n) = 8$. Note that $\mathbb{Z}_{15}^*$ does not have a generator (since no element has order 8).

Theorem 11.1.5 (*Chinese remainder*) *If the integers $n_1, \ldots, n_k$ are pairwise relatively prime, then the system of congruences*

$$\begin{aligned} x &\equiv a_1 \pmod{n_1} \\ &\vdots \\ x &\equiv a_k \pmod{n_k} \end{aligned}$$

has a unique solution modulo $n = n_1 \cdots n_k$.

Consider the case $k = 2$ in the Chinese remainder theorem. Since $(n_1, n_2) = 1$, there exist integers s and t so that $sn_1 + tn_2 = 1$. The verification that $x = (sn_1 a_2 + tn_2 a_1) \bmod n$ is the solution to the system is Exercise 11.1.18. As a specific example, consider

$$\begin{aligned} x &\equiv 3 \pmod{7}, \\ x &\equiv 6 \pmod{13}. \end{aligned}$$

The extended Euclidean algorithm gives $(7, 13) = 1 = 2 \cdot 7 - 1 \cdot 13$, and then $x = 2 \cdot 7 \cdot 6 - 1 \cdot 13 \cdot 3 = 45$ is the unique solution (modulo $n = 7 \cdot 13 = 91$) to the pair of congruences. The generalization is Gauss' algorithm.

Algorithm 11.1.6 (Gauss) The solution x to the system in the Chinese remainder theorem may be computed as $x = \sum_{i=1}^{k} a_i N_i M_i \bmod n$, where $N_i = n/n_i$ and $M_i = N_i^{-1} \bmod n_i$. The computations can be performed in $O(\log_2^2 n)$ bit operations.

Table 11.1: *Bit complexity of basic operations in* $\mathbb{Z}_n$.

modular operation		bit complexity
addition	$(a+b) \bmod n$	$O(\log_2 n)$
multiplication	$ab \bmod n$	$O((\log_2 n)^2)$
inversion	$a^{-1} \bmod n$	$O((\log_2 n)^2)$
exponentiation	$a^k \bmod n,\ k < n$	$O((\log_2 n)^3)$

Efficient calculation of $a^k \bmod n$ is essential in several cryptographic schemes. The calculation can be done naïvely by computing a^k and dividing by n or by computing $a^i \bmod n$, $1 \le i \le k$, by repeated multiplication; unfortunately, these calculations are inefficient in terms of storage or number of multiplications required. The method of repeated *square-and-multiply* provides an efficient calculation. The exponent is written in binary as $k = \sum_{i=0}^{t} k_i 2^i$, where $t = \lfloor \log_2 k \rfloor$, and then

$$a^k = \prod_{i=0}^{t} a^{k_i 2^i} = (a^{2^0})^{k_0} \cdots (a^{2^t})^{k_t} = \prod_{k_i=1} a^{2^i}.$$

Note that $a^{2^t} = (a^{2^{t-1}})^2$, and hence the value $a^k \bmod n$ can be calculated with t modular squarings and at most t modular multiplications. We present an algorithm for modular exponentiation which proceeds by calculating the partial products; other square-and-multiply algorithms may be found in [63]. Bit complexities for the basic operations in $\mathbb{Z}_n$ appear in Table 11.1.

Algorithm 11.1.7 (exponentiation by square-and-multiply) Input: $0 \neq a \in \mathbb{Z}_n$, and integer $0 \le k < n$ with binary representation $k = \sum_{i=0}^{t} k_i 2^i$. Output: $a^k \bmod n$.

1. Set $A \leftarrow a$ and $b \leftarrow 1$.
2. For i from 0 to t do the following:
   2.1 If $i > 0$ then set $A \leftarrow A^2 \bmod n$.
   2.2 If $k_i = 1$ then set $b \leftarrow bA \bmod n$.
3. Return (b).

Example 11.1.8 The algorithm is applied to $3^{26} \bmod 35$, i.e., $a = 3$, $k = 26 = \sum_{i=0}^{4} k_i 2^i = 11010_2$, and $n = 35$. The arithmetic can be collected in tabular form as follows:

i	0	1	2	3	4
k_i	0	1	0	1	1
A	3	$3^2 \bmod n = 9$	$9^2 \bmod n = 11$	$11^2 \bmod n = 16$	$16^2 \bmod n = 11$
b	1	$1 \cdot 9 \bmod n = 9$	9	$9 \cdot 16 \bmod n = 4$	$4 \cdot 11 \bmod n = 9$

and hence $3^{26} \bmod 35 = 9$. In this particular example, we may quickly verify by reducing the exponent modulo $\phi(n) = \phi(5 \cdot 7) = 24$, obtaining $3^k \bmod n = 3^2$.

Exercises

11.1.9 Verify the following properties of divisibility: (a) $a \mid a$; (b) if $a \mid b$ and $b \mid c$, then $a \mid c$; (c) if $a \mid b$ and $b \mid a$, then $a = \pm b$; (d) if $c \mid a$ and $c \mid b$, then $c \mid ax + by$ for all x, y.

11.1.10 Define the *least common multiple* $\text{lcm}(a,b)$ of positive integers a and b by $\text{lcm}(a,b) = ab/(a,b)$. Show that $\text{lcm}(a,b) \mid c$ whenever $a \mid c$ and $b \mid c$.

11.1.11 This question concerns the Euclidean algorithm 11.1.1.

(a) Show that the remainders satisfy $r_{i+2} < r_i/2$.

(b) Show that the algorithm returns (a,b).

11.1.12 This exercise examines elementary properties of $\mathbb{Z}_n$.

(a) Show that the operations of addition and multiplication on $\mathbb{Z}_n$ are well-defined in the sense described in the text.

(b) The set $\mathbb{Z}_n$ together with the defined addition and multiplication forms a ring, denoted $(\mathbb{Z}_n, +, \cdot)$. The ring properties follow directly from corresponding properties in $\mathbb{Z}$. Verify that multiplication distributes over addition; i.e., $([a]+[b])[c] = [a][c]+[b][c]$.

11.1.13 Use the Euclidean algorithm to find $d = (105, 180)$. Then find integers x and y such that $105x + 180y = d$.

11.1.14 Use the square-and-multiply algorithm to compute $47^{332} \bmod 576$.

11.1.15 The following statements are false in general. Give a counterexample to each statement.

(a) Let $a, b, n \in \mathbb{Z}$. If $n \mid ab$ then $n \mid a$ or $n \mid b$.

(b) Let p be a positive integer and $a \in \mathbb{Z}$. If $(a, p) = 1$ then $a^{p-1} \equiv 1 \pmod{p}$.

(c) If $a, b, c \in \mathbb{Z}$, then $(ab, c) = (a, c)(b, c)$.

11.1.16 Find the order of each element of $\mathbb{Z}_{11}^*$. Identify the generators of $\mathbb{Z}_{11}^*$.

11.1.17 Let $a \in \mathbb{Z}_n^*$. Prove that the elements $a^i \bmod n$, $0 \le i < \text{ord}(a)$, are pairwise distinct.

11.1.18 Verify the claim made in the paragraph following the Chinese remainder theorem 11.1.5 that $x = (sn_1a_2 + tn_2a_1) \bmod n$ (where $sn_1 + tn_2 = 1$) is the solution to the system of two congruences.

11.1.19 Determine if the pair of congruences

$$x \equiv 15 \pmod{70}$$
$$x \equiv 104 \pmod{151}$$

has a solution. If so, use the extended Euclidean algorithm to find all solutions.

11.1.20 Prove that the congruence $ax \equiv b \pmod{n}$ has a solution x if and only if $(a,n) \mid b$, in which case there are exactly (a,n) solutions.

11.1.21 Let $a \in \mathbb{Z}_n^*$. Prove the following claims:

(a) $a^x \equiv 1 \pmod{n}$ if and only if $\operatorname{ord}(a) \mid x$. In particular, $\operatorname{ord}(a) \mid \phi(n)$.

(b) $a^x \equiv a^y \pmod{n}$ if and only if $x \equiv y \pmod{\operatorname{ord}(a)}$.

(c) $a^x \bmod n = a^{x \bmod \operatorname{ord}(a)} \bmod n$.

11.1.22 Let p be prime and let $a \geq 1$ be an integer. Prove that the number of solutions in $\mathbb{Z}_p$ to $x^a \equiv 1 \pmod{p}$ is $(a, p-1)$.

11.1.23 If p is prime, then every nonzero element of $\mathbb{Z}_p$ has an inverse and $\mathbb{Z}_p$ is a field. Fermat's little theorem says that $a^{p-1} \equiv 1 \pmod{p}$ for $a \in \mathbb{Z}_p^*$. An elementary proof may be given as follows.

(a) Let $T = \{a, 2a, \ldots, (p-1)a\} \subseteq \mathbb{Z}_p$. Show that the elements of T are nonzero and pairwise distinct.

(b) Part (a) shows that $T = \mathbb{Z}_p^*$. Hence $1 \cdot 2 \cdots (p-1) \equiv a(2a) \cdots (p-1)a \pmod{p}$. Use division to complete the proof.

11.2 Quadratic residues

Let $a \in \mathbb{Z}_n^*$. Then a is a *quadratic residue* modulo n if there exists $x \in \mathbb{Z}_n^*$ with $x^2 \equiv a \pmod{n}$. In this case, x is a *square root* of a modulo n. Otherwise, a is a *quadratic nonresidue* modulo n.

The set of quadratic residues modulo n is denoted by Q_n; the nonresidues are $\overline{Q}_n$. Note that $\mathbb{Z}_n^* = Q_n \cup \overline{Q}_n$. There are elements $a \in \mathbb{Z}_n \setminus \mathbb{Z}_n^*$ for which $x^2 \equiv a \pmod{n}$ has a solution, but a is not a quadratic residue; for example, $4 \in \mathbb{Z}_6$ has $2^2 \equiv 4 \pmod{6}$ but $4 \notin Q_6$ (since $4 \notin \mathbb{Z}_6^*$).

Theorem 11.2.1 *Let $p > 2$ be prime and let α be a generator of $\mathbb{Z}_p^*$. Then $a \in \mathbb{Z}_p^*$ is a quadratic residue modulo p if and only if $a \equiv \alpha^{2i} \pmod{p}$ for some $i \in \mathbb{Z}$.*

Proof: If $a = \alpha^{2i} \bmod p$ for some i, then $x = \alpha^i$ satisfies $x^2 \equiv a \pmod{p}$ and a is a quadratic residue. Conversely, if $a \in Q_p$, then $x^2 \equiv a \pmod{p}$ has a solution $x \equiv \alpha^i \pmod{p}$ for some i, and $\alpha^{2i} \equiv a \pmod{p}$. □

Corollary 11.2.2 *Let $p > 2$ be prime and let α be a generator of $\mathbb{Z}_p^*$.*

1. *$Q_p = \{\alpha^i \bmod p \mid i$ even, $0 \leq i \leq p-2\}$, $\overline{Q}_p = \{\alpha^i \bmod p \mid i$ odd, $0 \leq i \leq p-2\}$.*
2. *$|Q_p| = |\overline{Q}_p| = \frac{p-1}{2}$.*
3. *If $a \in Q_p$, then $x^2 \equiv a \pmod{p}$ has exactly two solutions.*
4. *$\alpha^{\frac{p-1}{2}} \equiv -1 \pmod{p}$.*

Proof: The first two are immediate consequences of the theorem. The third follows since there are at least two solutions $\pm x$ by definition of a quadratic residue, and statement 2 of this corollary shows that there cannot be more than two solutions. For the fourth, note that $\alpha^{(p-1)/2}$ is a solution of $x^2 \equiv 1 \pmod{p}$ since the order of α is $p-1$. Necessarily, $\alpha^{(p-1)/2} \equiv \pm 1 \pmod{p}$, and only the congruence in 4 is compatible with the order of α. □

For a given $a \in \mathbb{Z}_p^*$, an exhaustive search through the elements $\{x^2 \bmod p \mid x \in \mathbb{Z}_p^*\}$ will, of course, determine if a is a quadratic residue. This is not efficient, requiring $O(p)$ modular multiplications in the worst case. The corollary can be used to develop a more efficient criterion. Define the *Legendre symbol* $\left(\frac{a}{p}\right)$ for prime $p > 2$ and integer a by

$$\left(\frac{a}{p}\right) = \begin{cases} 0, & p \mid a, \\ 1, & a \bmod p \in Q_p, \\ -1, & a \bmod p \in \overline{Q}_p. \end{cases}$$

Theorem 11.2.3 (*Euler's criterion*) *Let $p > 2$ be prime and $a \in \mathbb{Z}$. Then $\left(\frac{a}{p}\right) \equiv a^{\frac{p-1}{2}} \pmod{p}$.*

Proof: We consider the case that $a \in Q_p$; the cases $a \in \overline{Q}_p$ and $p \mid a$ are left as Exercise 11.2.15. Let α be a generator of $\mathbb{Z}_p^*$. Then there exists i such that $\alpha^{2i} \equiv a \pmod{p}$ by Theorem 11.2.1. By definition, $\left(\frac{a}{p}\right) = 1$, and $a^{(p-1)/2} \equiv (\alpha^{2i})^{(p-1)/2} \equiv (\alpha^{p-1})^i \equiv 1 \pmod{p}$. □

Euler's criterion suggests using $a^{\frac{p-1}{2}}$ to determine if a given a is a quadratic residue modulo the prime p. This can be done efficiently ($O(\log_2^3 p)$ bit operations) using a square-and-multiply approach. However, unlike exhaustive search, it will not exhibit a square root in the case $a \in Q_p$.

Example 11.2.4 Euler's criterion can be used to determine if 3 is in Q_p for $p = 23$. To calculate $3^{(p-1)/2} \bmod p$, write

$$\frac{p-1}{2} = 11 = 1011_2 = \sum_{i=0}^{3} k_i 2^i.$$

Following Algorithm 11.1.7, the table for the arithmetic is

i	0	1	2	3
k_i	1	1	0	1
A	3	$3^2 = 9$	$9^2 \bmod p = 12$	$12^2 \bmod p = 6$
b	3	$3 \cdot 9 \bmod p = 4$	4	$4 \cdot 6 \bmod p = 1$

and $\left(\frac{3}{p}\right) = 3^{\frac{p-1}{2}} \bmod p = 1$. This shows that $3 \in Q_{23}$, and hence there is an x with $x^2 \equiv 3 \pmod{23}$. Later, we will have an efficient algorithm for exhibiting such an x. In this toy example, it is easily verified that $7^2 \equiv 3 \pmod{23}$.

Properties of the Legendre symbol can be used to calculate $\left(\frac{a}{p}\right)$ more efficiently than the method suggested by the example. We shall return to this question after developing an extension of the Legendre symbol.

Let $n \geq 3$ be an odd integer with prime factorization $n = p_1^{e_1} \cdots p_k^{e_k}$, and let $a \in \mathbb{Z}$. The *Jacobi symbol* $\left(\frac{a}{n}\right)$ is defined in terms of the Legendre symbol by

$$\left(\frac{a}{n}\right) = \left(\frac{a}{p_1}\right)^{e_1} \cdots \left(\frac{a}{p_k}\right)^{e_k}.$$

Properties of the Jacobi symbol Let $m, n \geq 3$ be odd integers, and let $a, b \in \mathbb{Z}$.

1. $\left(\frac{a}{n}\right) \in \{-1, 0, 1\}$, and $\left(\frac{a}{n}\right) = 0$ if and only if $(a, n) \neq 1$.
2. $\left(\frac{ab}{n}\right) = \left(\frac{a}{n}\right)\left(\frac{b}{n}\right)$ and $\left(\frac{a}{mn}\right) = \left(\frac{a}{m}\right)\left(\frac{a}{n}\right)$.
3. If $a \equiv b \pmod{n}$ then $\left(\frac{a}{n}\right) = \left(\frac{b}{n}\right)$.
4. $\left(\frac{1}{n}\right) = 1$ and $\left(\frac{-1}{n}\right) = (-1)^{\frac{n-1}{2}} = \begin{cases} 1, & n \equiv 1 \pmod{4}, \\ -1, & n \equiv 3 \pmod{4}. \end{cases}$
5. $\left(\frac{2}{n}\right) = (-1)^{\frac{n^2-1}{8}} = \begin{cases} 1, & n \equiv \pm 1 \pmod{8}, \\ -1, & n \equiv \pm 3 \pmod{8}. \end{cases}$
6. (law of quadratic reciprocity) $\left(\frac{m}{n}\right) = \left(\frac{n}{m}\right)(-1)^{\frac{m-1}{2}\frac{n-1}{2}}$.

Applying these properties to the calculation of $\left(\frac{3}{23}\right)$ in Example 11.2.4, we obtain

$$\left(\frac{3}{23}\right) = \left(\frac{23}{3}\right)(-1)^{\frac{3-1}{2}\frac{23-1}{2}} = \left(\frac{2}{3}\right)(-1)^{1\cdot 11} = -\left(\frac{2}{3}\right) = -(-1) = 1.$$

Since 23 is prime, this establishes that $3 \in Q_{23}$, as seen earlier using Euler's criterion.

The definition of the Jacobi symbol $\left(\frac{a}{n}\right)$ suggests that n must be factored, which is believed to be a hard problem. However, the properties can be used to evaluate the symbol without factoring.

Example 11.2.5 Properties of the Jacobi symbol may be used to evaluate $\left(\frac{28}{55}\right)$ as follows:

$$\begin{aligned} \left(\frac{28}{55}\right) &= \left(\frac{2}{55}\right)^2\left(\frac{7}{55}\right) && \text{(property 2)} \\ &= \left(\frac{55}{7}\right)(-1)^{\frac{55-1}{2}\frac{7-1}{2}} && \text{(property 6)} \\ &= -\left(\frac{55}{7}\right) = -\left(\frac{6}{7}\right) && \text{(property 3)} \\ &= -\left(\frac{-1}{7}\right) = -(-1)^{\frac{7-1}{2}} = 1 && \text{(property 4)} \end{aligned}$$

Although the Jacobi symbol is 1, we cannot conclude that 28 is a quadratic residue modulo 55 (in fact, it isn't). Note that $28^{(55-1)/2} \equiv 52 \pmod{55}$, illustrating that

Euler's criterion need not hold for composites. Finally, recall that a quadratic residue modulo a prime has exactly two square roots. Here, $n = 55$ is not prime, and, for example, 1 has square roots 1 and $55 - 1$ and also 21 and $55 - 21$. (Roots are discussed in Section 11.4.)

As the example shows, the condition $\left(\frac{a}{n}\right) = 1$ does not distinguish quadratic residues from nonresidues in the case of composite n. However, if $a \in Q_n$, then there exists $x \in \mathbb{Z}_n^*$ such that $x^2 \equiv a \pmod{n}$ and hence $\left(\frac{a}{n}\right) = \left(\frac{x^2}{n}\right) = \left(\frac{x}{n}\right)^2 = 1$. Stated in the contrapositive, this says that $\left(\frac{a}{n}\right) = -1$ implies that a is a quadratic nonresidue. For odd integers $n \geq 3$ we define

$$J_n = \{a \in \mathbb{Z}_n^* \mid \left(\frac{a}{n}\right) = 1\}.$$

The elements of $\tilde{Q}_n = J_n \setminus Q_n$ are called *pseudosquares* modulo n. Note that $Q_n \subseteq J_n$, and $J_n = Q_n$ in the case that n is prime.

Example 11.2.6 The quadratic residues and pseudosquares for $n = 15$ are obtained. Note that $\left(\frac{a}{15}\right) = \left(\frac{a}{3}\right)\left(\frac{a}{5}\right)$ and

$$\left(\frac{a}{3}\right) = \begin{cases} 1, & a \equiv 1 \pmod{3}, \\ -1, & a \equiv 2 \pmod{3}, \end{cases} \qquad \left(\frac{a}{5}\right) = \begin{cases} 1, & a \equiv \pm 1 \pmod{5}, \\ -1, & a \equiv \pm 2 \pmod{5}. \end{cases}$$

The Jacobi symbols $\left(\frac{a}{n}\right)$ are calculated in the following table:

$a \in \mathbb{Z}_{15}^*$	1	2	4	7	8	11	13	14
$\left(\frac{a}{3}\right)$	1	-1	1	1	-1	-1	1	-1
$\left(\frac{a}{5}\right)$	1	-1	1	-1	-1	1	-1	1
$\left(\frac{a}{15}\right)$	1	1	1	-1	1	-1	-1	-1

Hence, $J_{15} = \{1, 2, 4, 8\}$. It can be verified that $Q_{15} = \{1, 4\}$, and then the pseudosquares are given by $\tilde{Q}_{15} = J_{15} \setminus Q_{15} = \{2, 8\}$.

Determining if a given $a \in J_n$ is a quadratic residue or pseudosquare modulo n is known as the *quadratic residuosity problem* (QRP). Consider the special case $n = pq$ for distinct odd primes p and q. It is shown in the exercises that $a \in J_{pq}$ is a quadratic residue if and only if $a \in Q_p$, and that $|Q_{pq}| = |\tilde{Q}_{pq}| = (p-1)(q-1)/4$. Applied to Example 11.2.6, $\left(\frac{a}{3}\right) = 1 = \left(\frac{a}{5}\right)$ if and only if $a \in \{1, 4\}$; necessarily, $Q_{15} = \{1, 4\}$ and $|Q_{15}| = 2 = (3-1)(5-1)/4$.

Exercises

11.2.7 Find Q_{30} and $\overline{Q}_{30}$.

11.2.8 Evaluate the Jacobi symbols $\left(\frac{156}{235}\right)$ and $\left(\frac{1833}{587}\right)$. Is $156 \in Q_{235}$?

11.2.9 Find the quadratic residues and pseudosquares for $n = 21$.

11.2.10 A careless colleague remarks "36 is a quadratic residue modulo n for any $n > 36$ since $6^2 = 36$." Correct the statement, and then determine if 36 is in Q_{745}.

11.2.11 Assume that the following properties of Legendre symbol are known:

- $\left(\frac{-1}{p}\right) = (-1)^{(p-1)/2}$ and $\left(\frac{2}{p}\right) = (-1)^{(p^2-1)/8}$ for odd primes p.
- If p and q are odd primes, then $\left(\frac{p}{q}\right) = \left(\frac{q}{p}\right)(-1)^{(p-1)(q-1)/4}$.

Let $n \geq 3$ be an odd integer. Prove the following facts about the Jacobi symbol.

(a) Show that if n_1 and n_2 are odd integers, then $\frac{n_1 n_2 - 1}{2} \equiv \frac{n_1-1}{2} + \frac{n_2-1}{2} \pmod 2$. Hence prove that $\left(\frac{-1}{n}\right) = (-1)^{(n-1)/2}$.

(b) Show that if n_1 and n_2 are odd integers, then $\frac{n_1^2 n_2^2 - 1}{8} \equiv \frac{n_1^2-1}{8} + \frac{n_2^2-1}{8} \pmod 2$. Hence prove that $\left(\frac{2}{n}\right) = (-1)^{(n^2-1)/8}$.

(c) Prove that if $a \geq 3$ is an odd integer, then $\left(\frac{a}{n}\right) = \left(\frac{n}{a}\right)(-1)^{(a-1)(n-1)/4}$.

11.2.12 Let p be an odd prime. Prove that $-3 \in Q_p$ if and only if $p \equiv 1 \pmod 3$.

11.2.13 Prove that a quadratic residue can never be a generator of $\mathbb{Z}_p^*$.

11.2.14 Let $n = pq$ for distinct odd primes p and q.

(a) Show that $a \in Q_n$ iff $\left(\frac{a}{p}\right) = 1 = \left(\frac{a}{q}\right)$.

(b) Show that $|Q_n| = \frac{(p-1)(q-1)}{4}$. Suggestion: show that the map $f : Q_n \to Q_p \times Q_q$ defined by $f(a) = (a \bmod p, a \bmod q)$ is a bijection.

11.2.15 Complete the proof of Euler's criterion (Theorem 11.2.3).

11.3 Primality testing

The generation of (large) prime numbers is a basic requirement in several public-key schemes. Determining if a given integer $n > 2$ is prime or composite is a sub-problem. Trial division by all integers (or all primes) between 2 and $\sqrt{n}$ will, of course, determine if n is prime. It also has the pleasant feature of exhibiting a nontrivial factor in the case that n is composite; unfortunately, trial division requires $O(\sqrt{n})$ divisions.

In this section we consider two probabilistic primality tests, Solovay-Strassen and Miller-Rabin. They are probabilistic in the sense that the test concludes either "composite" (in which case n is certainly composite) or "probably prime" (in which case n may actually be composite). For this reason, the tests are more accurately called tests for compositeness.

Solovay-Strassen is built on Euler's criterion (Theorem 11.2.3): if n is prime, then $a^{(n-1)/2} \equiv \left(\frac{a}{n}\right) \pmod n$. This motivates the following definition.

Definition 11.3.1 Let n be an odd composite integer and $1 \leq a < n$. If $(a,n) \neq 1$ or $a^{(n-1)/2} \not\equiv \left(\frac{a}{n}\right) \pmod n$ then a is an *Euler witness* (to compositeness) for n.

Theorem 11.3.2 *Let n be an odd composite integer and let $a \in \mathbb{Z}_n^*$ be an Euler witness for n. Then at least half of all elements in $\mathbb{Z}_n^*$ are Euler witnesses for n.*

Proof: The set $G = \{x \in \mathbb{Z}_n^* \mid x^{(n-1)/2} \equiv \left(\frac{x}{n}\right) \pmod{n}\}$ of non-witnesses is closed under the product in the finite group $\mathbb{Z}_n^*$, and hence G is a subgroup. By Lagrange's theorem, $|G|$ is a divisor of $|\mathbb{Z}_n^*|$. Since $a \in \mathbb{Z}_n^* \setminus G$, it follows that $|G| \leq |\mathbb{Z}_n^*|/2$.

As an alternative argument, verify directly that ab is an Euler witness for n whenever $b \in \mathbb{Z}_n^*$ is not a witness. Necessarily, the number of non-witnesses in $\mathbb{Z}_n^*$ is at most $|\mathbb{Z}_n^*|/2$. □

Theorem 11.3.3 *Let n be an odd composite integer. Then there exists an Euler witness for n in $\mathbb{Z}_n^*$.*

Proof: First, suppose that n is not square-free, i.e., $p^2 \mid n$ for some prime p. Let $a = 1 + n/p$. Then

$$\left(\frac{a}{n}\right) = \left(\frac{1+n/p}{(n/p)p}\right) = \left(\frac{1+n/p}{n/p}\right)\left(\frac{1+n/p}{p}\right) = \left(\frac{1}{n/p}\right)\left(\frac{1}{p}\right) = 1$$

and, in particular, $a \in \mathbb{Z}_n^*$. Also

$$a^p \equiv (1+n/p)^p \equiv 1 + \sum_{i=1}^{p} \tbinom{p}{i}(n/p)^i \equiv 1 \pmod{n}.$$

Hence $\operatorname{ord}(a) = p$ since $a \not\equiv 1 \pmod{n}$. Since $p \nmid n-1$, it follows that $a^{(n-1)/2} \not\equiv 1 \pmod{n}$, and a is an Euler witness.

Now consider the case that n is the product of distinct primes. Let p be a prime factor of n, and let b be a quadratic nonresidue modulo p. By the Chinese remainder theorem, there exists an a satisfying

$$\begin{aligned} a &\equiv b \pmod{p}, \\ a &\equiv 1 \pmod{n/p}. \end{aligned}$$

By properties of the Jacobi symbol,

$$\left(\frac{a}{n}\right) = \left(\frac{a}{p(n/p)}\right) = \left(\frac{a}{p}\right)\left(\frac{a}{n/p}\right) = \left(\frac{b}{p}\right)\left(\frac{1}{n/p}\right) = -1$$

(in particular, $a \in \mathbb{Z}_n^*$). The definition of a implies that $a^{(n-1)/2} \equiv 1 \pmod{n/p}$, and hence $a^{(n-1)/2} \not\equiv -1 \pmod{n/p}$. It follows that $a^{(n-1)/2} \not\equiv -1 \pmod{n}$, and a is an Euler witness. □

Roughly speaking, the Solovay-Strassen test looks for Euler witnesses for a given n, and, if none are found, concludes that n is probably prime. The number of Euler witnesses for a composite n is used to give an error bound.

Algorithm 11.3.4 (Solovay-Strassen) Input: an odd integer $n > 2$ and security parameter $t \geq 1$. Output: an answer of "composite" or "probably prime."

1. Do the following (at most) t times:
   1.1 Select a random integer a, $1 < a < n$.
   1.2 If $(a, n) \neq 1$, then return ("composite").
   1.3 If $a^{(n-1)/2} \not\equiv \left(\frac{a}{n}\right) \pmod{n}$, then return ("composite").
2. Return ("probably prime").

The running time for the inner loop is $O(\log_2^3 n)$ bit operations. The algorithm has been written for clarity; however, note that step 1.2 may be replaced by a comparison on $a^{(n-1)/2} \bmod n$, terminating with "composite" if the value is not 1 or $n-1$.

If the test outputs "composite," then a *certificate* is provided which allows efficient verification that n is indeed composite. For Solovay-Strassen, the certificate is an Euler witness for n, and the verification algorithm checks that $(a, n) \neq 1$ or that $a^{(n-1)/2} \not\equiv \left(\frac{a}{n}\right) \pmod{n}$. The probability that the test outputs "probably prime" when n is composite is at most 2^{-t}.

Tests such as Solovay-Strassen (and Miller-Rabin, discussed in the exercises) can be used to generate large random probable primes: choose random n of the desired size until the test declares n to be "probably prime." In practice, n may first be subjected to divisibility tests by small primes, and there may be additional constraints depending on the application.

Exercises

11.3.5 Let n be an odd composite integer and let $1 \leq a < n$. If $a^{n-1} \not\equiv 1 \pmod{n}$, then a is said to be a *Fermat witness* (to compositeness) for n. Prove that if a is a Fermat witness for n, then a is also an Euler witness for n.

11.3.6 Perform the Solovay-Strassen test on $n = 91$. Choose $a = 74$ as your first "random" a. Unless you are rather unlucky, your second random a should determine that n is composite.

11.3.7 (Miller-Rabin probabilistic primality test) Let n be an odd integer, and let $n - 1 = 2^s r$ where r is odd. Let $a \in \mathbb{Z}_n^*$.

Fact. If n is prime, then either $a^r \equiv 1 \pmod{n}$ or $a^{2^j r} \equiv -1 \pmod{n}$ for some $j, 0 \leq j < s$.

Definition. Suppose that n is composite. If $a^r \not\equiv 1 \pmod{n}$ and if $a^{2^j r} \not\equiv -1 \pmod{n}$ for all $j, 0 \leq j < s$, then a is called a *strong witness* for n.

Fact. If $n \neq 9$ is an odd composite integer, then at least three-quarter of all $a \in \mathbb{Z}_n^*$ are strong witnesses for n.

(a) Using the above concepts and facts, devise a test for determining the primality of an integer n.

(b) What is the running time (number of bit operations) of your test?

(c) Discuss the correctness of the results provided by this primality test.

11.4 Factoring and square roots

The problem of resolving a composite integer n into its prime factors is of more than academic interest. Some widely-used cryptographic schemes (such as RSA, discussed in Chapter 12) depend completely on the intractibility of factoring carefully chosen composite n. Factoring such an n can bring a measure of fame: the New York Times devoted front page coverage in 1988 to the factoring of a 100-digit integer by the quadratic sieve (discussed in Section 11.4.2) with a distributed network of 400 computers.[1]

No efficient method for factoring general n is known. A special-purpose algorithm can be effective when n is of certain form; for example, simple trial division can be used to find small factors, and Pollard's rho (discussed below) may efficiently find relatively small factors of n. The factoring challenge discussed in the New York Times article concerned $n = pq$ for primes p and q of 41 and 60 decimal digits, respectively, specifically chosen to defeat certain special-purpose algorithms. For such cases, a general-purpose algorithm from the random squares family has been the method of choice.

For some material which follows, there is an implicit assumption that n has at least two distinct prime divisors. An integer which is a perfect power (i.e., of the form x^k for some integers x and $k > 1$) is easily detected and, moreover, nontrivial factors are easily obtained (Exercise 11.4.9).

11.4.1 Pollard's rho

Consider the following problem. Let X be a finite set, let $f : X \to X$, and let $x_0 \in X$. We can define a sequence $(x_i) \subseteq X$ as follows: $x_1 = f(x_0)$, $x_2 = f(x_1)$, and, in general, $x_i = f(x_{i-1})$ for each positive integer i. Since X is finite, this sequence must eventually start repeating. In particular, for some $i < j$, we must have $x_i = x_j$. The problem is to find such a pair (i, j).

[1] Malcolm W. Browne, "A Most Ferocious Math Problem Tamed," 12 October 1988. Apparently, the title was insufficiently dramatic for the factoring enthusiast among the NYT editorial staff who inserted the heading "World's Fiercest Math Problem Is Tamed by Hundreds of Computers."

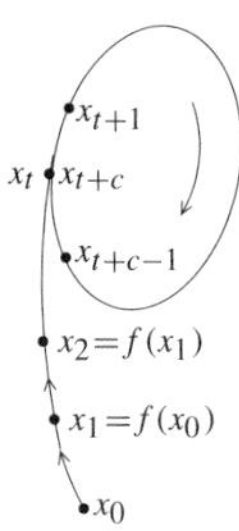

To help visualize this problem, we can construct the *rho-diagram* of f at the *seed* x_0. It has a vertex for each different x_i, and an arc from each x_i to $x_{i+1} = f(x_i)$. A typical rho-diagram may resemble the Greek letter ρ. We denote by c the number of arcs in the cycle of the diagram, and by t the number of arcs in the tail. Then the entire diagram has $k = t+c$ arcs, and k vertices. The point where the tail meets the cycle is $x_t = x_{t+c}$. Note that if i and j are non-negative integers, then $x_i = x_j$ if and only if either $i = j$, or $t \le i, j$ and $i \equiv j \pmod{c}$.

One way to solve our problem would be to successively compute and store x_i, comparing each new x_i to all the previously stored values, until a match is found. Unfortunately, this necessitates storing all k of the x_i in the rho diagram, and k is typically huge. Instead, Pollard's rho method stores only two variables, x and y. Begin with $x = x_0$ and $y = x_0$. The calculations

$$x \leftarrow f(x) \quad \text{and} \quad y \leftarrow f(f(y))$$

(that is, $f(x)$ replaces x and $f(f(y))$ replaces y) are repeated until $x = y$. After i repetitions, we'll have $x = x_i$ and $y = x_{2i}$. If the method stops after m steps with $x_m = x = y = x_{2m}$, then $(m, 2m)$ will be the required pair solving our problem.

It is easy to show that m will be the smallest positive integer with $m \ge t$ and $c \mid m$. The method will terminate after $m < k$ steps, using $3m < 3k$ applications of the function f. It can be shown that, for a random function f, if $|X| = n$ is large, we can expect both t and c to be about $\sqrt{\pi n/8}$, so that $k = c+t$ is about $\sqrt{\pi n/2}$, or approximately $1.253\sqrt{n}$.[2]

We now turn to the problem of factoring a given composite integer n, and suppose $p \le \sqrt{n}$ is an (unknown) prime divisor of n. Our goal is to find integers x, y with $x \not\equiv y \pmod{n}$, but $x \equiv y \pmod{p}$. Then $d = (x-y, n)$ will be not only a multiple of p, but also a nontrivial divisor of n. The process may be repeated on the factor d or n/d if detected as composite (perhaps by one of the tests in Section 11.3).

The idea is to run the rho method with some function f on $\mathbb{Z}_n$, but pretend it's really running on $\mathbb{Z}_p$, even though p is unknown. To get away with this pretension, f must have the property that for all $a, b \in \mathbb{Z}_n$, if $a \equiv b \pmod{p}$, then $f(a) \equiv f(b) \pmod{p}$. Polynomials have this property, so f is typically chosen to be a polynomial. It is desirable that f resemble a "random" function on $\mathbb{Z}_p$ to improve our chances of success. A typical choice of f is $f(x) = x^2+1$, with a seed $x_0 = 2$, though other choices can be used (a first degree polynomial would definitely be bad).

[2] The estimate on k is related to the *birthday paradox*: in a group of 23 people, the probability that at least two celebrate a birthday on the same day of the year is just over $1/2$ [63, 86]. Such considerations are common in schemes designed to thwart attacks based on finding collisions by random search (known as *birthday attacks*), leading to "square root" lower bounds on sizes for certain sets.

Here are the details, for our polynomial f with integer coefficients, and any $x_0 \in \mathbb{Z}_n$. Begin with $x = x_0$ and $y = x_0$. Repeat the two calculations

$$x \leftarrow f(x) \bmod n \quad \text{and} \quad y \leftarrow f(f(y)) \bmod n$$

until $d = (x - y, n) > 1$. If $d < n$, we have succeeded. If $d = n$, the method failed. We could try again, with a different f or a different x_0.

We expect this method to use the function f at most $3\sqrt{\pi p/2} = O(\sqrt{p}) = O(n^{1/4})$ times, since $p \le \sqrt{n}$. This is still not theoretically efficient, but it's better than the simple-minded method of trying all d, $1 < d \le \sqrt{n}$, checking if $d \mid n$, which could take $O(n^{1/2})$ divisions.

As an example, let's factor $n = 551$ by this method, with $f(x) = x^2 + 1 \bmod 551$ and $x_0 = 2$. Here are successive values of x, y, and $d = (x - y, n)$:

$x \leftarrow f(x)$	$y \leftarrow f(f(y))$	$d = (x - y, 551)$
5	26	1
26	449	1
126	240	19

Note that 19 and $551/19 = 29$ are both prime, so we've factored $551 = 19 \cdot 29$.

11.4.2 Random squares

Among general-purpose factoring methods, the most powerful have been those in the random squares family. The quadratic sieve variant was used to factor integers with 100–129 decimal digits by 1994. A more complicated variant known as the number field sieve factored well-known challenges from RSA Laboratories of 130 digits in 1996 and 140 and 155 digits in 1999. (The 155-digit result in August 1999 was somewhat of a milestone due to the implications for applications relying on the intractability of factoring 512-bit numbers.)

Given composite n, the idea is to locate $x, y \in \mathbb{Z}_n$ with $x^2 \equiv y^2 \pmod{n}$; if $x \not\equiv \pm y \pmod{n}$, then $(x + y, n)$ is a nontrivial factor of n since n divides $x^2 - y^2 = (x + y)(x - y)$ but does not divide either of the factors. As a special case, if $n = pq$ for distinct primes p and q, then $x^2 \equiv a^2 \pmod{n}$ for given $a \in \mathbb{Z}_n^*$ has exactly four solutions, as can be seen by the Chinese remainder theorem. If $n = 15$, for example, and we manage to stumble upon $x = 2$ and $y = 7$ satisfying $x^2 \equiv y^2 \pmod{15}$, then $(x + y, n) = (9, 15) = 3$, a nontrivial factor of n.

One method for finding appropriate x and y is to collect pairs $(a_i, b_i = a_i^2 \bmod n)$ for random a_i, seeking a subcollection S for which $\prod_{i \in S} b_i$ is a perfect square. In this case, $x = \prod_{i \in S} a_i$ and the square root y of $\prod_{i \in S} b_i$ satisfy $x^2 \equiv y^2 \pmod{n}$. If, in addition, $x \not\equiv \pm y \pmod{n}$, then the method has been successful; otherwise a different S can be selected (perhaps requiring the generation of more pairs (a_i, b_i)).

To be more precise, a *factor base* $B = \{p_1, \ldots, p_t\}$ consisting of the first t primes is selected. Pairs $(a, b = a^2 \bmod n)$ are retained if b factors over B; such a value b is said to be p_t*-smooth*. Suppose $t+1$ such pairs (a_i, b_i) are obtained, where the factorizations are given by $b_i = \prod_{j=1}^{t} p_j^{e_{ij}}$, $1 \le i \le t+1$. A set S is to be selected so that $\prod_{i \in S} b_i$ has only even powers of primes appearing. Note that the $t+1$ vectors $e_i = (e_{i1}, \ldots, e_{it}) \bmod 2$ are necessarily linearly dependent over $\mathbb{Z}_2$, and there exists S so that $\sum_{i \in S} e_i$ is the zero vector. The corresponding $\prod_{i \in S} b_i$ is then of the desired form.

Example 11.4.1 The method is applied to factor $n = 10057$. Suppose $t = 5$ so that the factor base $B = \{2, 3, 5, 7, 11\}$ is selected. The following table lists the a_i selected, retaining only those for which $b_i = a_i^2 \bmod n$ factors over the factor base.

i	a_i	$b_i = a_i^2 \bmod n$	factorization
1	7231	1018	$2 \cdot 509$
1	105	968	$2^3 \cdot 11^2$
2	115	3168	$2^5 \cdot 3^2 \cdot 11$
3	1006	6336	$2^6 \cdot 3^2 \cdot 11$
4	3010	8800	$2^5 \cdot 5^2 \cdot 11$
5	4014	882	$2 \cdot 3^2 \cdot 7^2$
6	4023	2816	$2^8 \cdot 11$

The choice $a = 7231$ is discarded since $a^2 \bmod n$ does not factor over the factor base. In such cases, the last column may be only a partial factorization.

There are $t + 1 = 6$ valid pairs (a_i, b_i). Necessarily, there must be some S so that $\prod_{i \in S} b_i$ is a perfect square. By inspection, $S = \{4, 5, 6\}$ gives $x^2 \equiv y^2 \pmod{n}$ for $x = 3010 \cdot 4014 \cdot 4023 \bmod n = 2748$ and $y = 2^7 \cdot 3 \cdot 5 \cdot 7 \cdot 11 \bmod n = 7042$. Since $x \not\equiv \pm y \pmod{n}$, we obtain a nontrivial factor $(x + y, n) = 89$, and $10057 = 89 \cdot 113$.

A perfect square is also obtained for $S = \{1, 5\}$. The corresponding values are $x = 105 \cdot 4014 \bmod n = 9133$ and $y = 2^2 \cdot 3 \cdot 7 \cdot 11 = 924$. Unfortunately, $x \equiv -y \pmod{n}$, and no useful information is obtained.

Choosing a larger factor base increases the chances that a given b_i will be p_t-smooth at the cost of requiring more relations. For a given t, one strategy to improve the chances of obtaining p_t-smooth numbers is to select a so that $b \equiv a^2 \pmod{n}$ is relatively small. The quadratic sieve is a famous example of such a method.

Let n be given and define $m = \lfloor \sqrt{n} \rfloor$. Define $q : \mathbb{Z} \to \mathbb{Z}$ by $q(z) = (z+m)^2 - n$. Note that $q(z) \approx z^2 + 2zm$ and $|q(z)|$ is small relative to n if $|z|$ is small. The quadratic sieve algorithm takes $a = z + m$ and $b = q(z) = a^2 - n$ for $z = 0, \pm 1, \cdots$. Since b can be negative, -1 is added to the factor base. In addition, note that if a prime p divides b, then $a^2 \equiv n \pmod{p}$ and n is a quadratic residue modulo p

(unless $p \mid n$). Hence, the factor base need only contain those primes p for which $\left(\frac{n}{p}\right) = 1$.

Example 11.4.2 The value $n = 10057$ from the last example is factored. Define $m = \lfloor\sqrt{n}\rfloor = 100$ and $q(z) = (z + 100)^2 - 10057$. For a factor base, suppose $B = \{2, 3, 11, 19\} \cup \{-1\}$ is selected (which includes those primes $p \le 19$ such that $\left(\frac{n}{p}\right) = 1$). The first few z for which $q(z)$ factors over the factor base are listed in the following table.

z	$a = z + m$	$b = q(z)$	factorization
0	100	−57	$-3 \cdot 19$
−1	99	−256	-2^8
1	101	144	$2^4 \cdot 3^2$
−3	97	−648	$-2^3 \cdot 3^4$
5	105	968	$2^3 \cdot 11^2$

The relations for $z \in \{-1, -3, 5\}$ give $x^2 \equiv y^2 \pmod{n}$ for $x = 99 \cdot 97 \cdot 105$ and $y = 2^7 \cdot 3^2 \cdot 11$. Unfortunately, $x \equiv y \pmod{n}$ and no useful information is obtained.

The line corresponding to $z = 1$ gives $101^2 \equiv 2^4 \cdot 3^2$. Note that $x = 101$ and $y = 2^2 \cdot 3$ satisfy $x \not\equiv \pm y \pmod{n}$, and hence a nontrivial factor $(x + y, n) = 113$ of 10057 has been obtained.

Collecting appropriate (a, b) pairs can be a distributed effort, and trial division is replaced by a more efficient sieving process to test smoothness. The 1994 factoring of a well-known 129-digit challenge involved 600 people and 1600 machines collecting more than 8 million relations over seven months, with a factor base of size 524339 [1]. However, as of 1999, factoring appropriately-chosen n with at least 1024 bits (308 decimal digits) appears to be well out of reach of even the more advanced number field sieve.

11.4.3 Square roots

The previous section suggests a relationship between the problems of factoring and extracting square roots. In fact, the problems are equivalent in a certain precise sense to be discussed in this section.

Recall that a random square factoring method attempts to construct x and y with $x^2 \equiv y^2 \pmod{n}$; if $x \not\equiv \pm y$, then a nontrivial factor $(x + y, n)$ of n has been obtained. Clearly, if it was possible to extract all of the square roots for some quadratic residue x^2 in $\mathbb{Z}_n^*$, then a nontrivial factor of n can be found. No efficient method in general for uncovering roots is known; however, we wish to consider the implications of such an algorithm.

To be specific, we will consider the case that $n = pq$ for distinct odd primes p and q, although the discussion extends to the general case. By Corollary 11.2.2, given a quadratic residue modulo a prime, there are exactly two square roots; the Chinese remainder theorem can be used to show that $x^2 \equiv a \pmod{pq}$ for $a \in Q_{pq}$ has exactly 4 solutions.

We suppose there exists an *oracle* for SQROOT; that is, we assume there is an algorithm returning a square root when presented with a quadratic residue. A factoring attack can then be constructed by selecting random $x \in \mathbb{Z}_n^*$ and passing $x^2 \bmod n$ to the oracle. For each such x, the root y returned by the oracle satisfies $y \not\equiv \pm x$ with probabilty $1/2$; a nontrivial factor $(x+y, n)$ of n is expected in two trials.

The problem of factoring n is said to *reduce* to the problem of finding square roots. More precisely, given computational problems A and B, we write $A \leq B$ if A can be solved in polynomial time (in terms of the size of the input) given a polynomial-time algorithm for B. Informally, $A \leq B$ says that A is no harder than B. The problems are computationally equivalent if $A \leq B$ and $B \leq A$. The same notation will be used in the case that the algorithm involves randomization and has expected running time which is polynomial in the size of the input. In particular, FACTOR $\leq$ SQROOT.

Now consider the problem of finding square roots of a quadratic residue $a \in Q_n$ given the factors of n. If roots modulo a prime can be extracted, then the 4 roots of a modulo $n = pq$ can be obtained by finding x and y satisfying the congruences

$$\begin{aligned} x &\equiv a_p \pmod{p} \\ x &\equiv a_q \pmod{q} \end{aligned} \quad \text{and} \quad \begin{aligned} y &\equiv -a_p \pmod{p} \\ y &\equiv a_q \pmod{q} \end{aligned}$$

where a_r denotes a square root of a modulo r; the roots are then $\pm x, \pm y$. Hence, we obtain an efficient algorithm for SQROOT if there is an efficient algorithm for extracting roots modulo a prime.

Consider first the case of a prime $p \equiv 3 \pmod{4}$. If $a \in Q_p$, then $a^{(p-1)/2} \equiv 1 \pmod{p}$ by Euler's criterion, and $(a^{(p+1)/4})^2 \equiv a^{(p+1)/2} \equiv a^{(p-1)/2}a \equiv a \pmod{p}$. Hence, the two square roots of a modulo p are $\pm a^{(p+1)/4}$. If both p and q are of this form (in which case $n = pq$ is known as a *Blum integer*), then we have an efficient deterministic algorithm for finding roots of a modulo n.

It turns out that there is a relatively simple algorithm for extracting roots modulo a prime provided that a quadratic nonresidue is known (in particular, if $p \equiv 5 \pmod{8}$ since $2 \in \overline{Q}_p$ in this case; see [63]). However, there is no known efficient deterministic algorithm for finding quadratic nonresidues modulo a prime. Since half of the elements of $\mathbb{Z}_p^*$ are quadratic nonresidues, an efficient probabilistic procedure for finding roots modulo a prime can be developed by selecting elements x at random until one is found with $\left(\frac{x}{p}\right) = -1$.

In short, there are efficient methods for extracting roots modulo a prime. It follows that SQROOT $\leq$ FACTOR and hence the two problems are computationally equivalent. The result is discussed again in Section 12.3 in connection with provable security.

Exercises

11.4.3 This exercise illustrates Pollard's rho factoring algorithm on the toy example $n = 391 = 17 \cdot 23$.

(a) Perform Pollard's rho with $x_0 = 2$ and $x_{i+1} = f(x_i) = x_i^2 + 1 \bmod n$. (Recall that the process terminates if $1 < (x_{2i} - x_i, n) < n$. A nontrivial factor is obtained for $i = 4$.)

(b) Complete the following table:

i	0	1	2	3	4	5	6	7	8
$x_i \bmod 17$	2	5	9	14	10	16	2		
$x_i \bmod 23$	2								

Sketch a rho-diagram for each row of the table, identifying the tail and the cycle.

(c) How should a composite n be chosen to defeat a factoring attack based on Pollard's rho?

11.4.4 Factor $n = 5141$ using Pollard's rho algorithm, with $x_0 = 1$ and $x_{i+1} = x_i^2 + 2 \bmod n$ for $i \geq 0$.

11.4.5 Apply the quadratic sieve (as in Example 11.4.2) to factor $n = 1081$ using an appropriate factor base consisting of integers ≤ 11.

11.4.6 Apply the quadratic sieve (as in Example 11.4.2) to factor $n = 24961$ using an appropriate factor base consisting of integers ≤ 23.

11.4.7 If $n = ab$ with $|a - b|$ relatively small, then *Fermat factorization* efficiently recovers nontrivial factors.

- Assume that n is odd. There is a 1–1 correspondence between the factorizations of n in the form $n = ab$, where $0 < a \leq b$, and the representations $n = t^2 - s^2$, where t and s are nonnegative. The correspondence is given by $ab = t^2 - s^2 = (t-s)(t+s)$, $t = (a+b)/2$, and $s = (b-a)/2$.
- If a and b are close together, then $s = (b-a)/2$ is small and $t \approx \sqrt{n}$. To factor n, test consecutive values for t starting with $\lceil \sqrt{n} \rceil$ until $t^2 - n$ is a perfect square.

Illustrate the method on $n = 2881$. Fermat factorization is discussed in [50, 74].

11.4.8 Illustrate the procedure for finding square roots of 179 in $\mathbb{Z}_{187}$ using the factorization $187 = 11 \cdot 17$.

11.4.9 Devise an efficient test which determines if n is a perfect power (i.e., $n = x^k$ for some integers x and $k > 1$) and, if n is such an integer, finds a partial factorization.

11.4.10 Let $n = pq$ for primes $p \neq q$, and let $\phi = \phi(n) = (p-1)(q-1)$. Let COMPUTE-$\phi$ denote the problem of finding ϕ given n. Describe an efficient algorithm for FACTOR which uses an oracle for COMPUTE-ϕ.

11.5 Discrete logarithms

Let p be an odd prime and α a generator of $\mathbb{Z}_p^*$. Given $\beta \in \mathbb{Z}_p^*$, the *discrete logarithm of* β *to the base* α, written $\log_\alpha \beta$, is the unique integer x, $0 \le x \le p-2$, such that $\beta \equiv \alpha^x \pmod{p}$. For example, $\alpha = 3$ is a generator of $\mathbb{Z}_5^*$ and $\log_3 4 = 2$ since $4 \equiv 3^2 \pmod{5}$.

Finding x given (p, α, β) is known as the *discrete logarithm problem* (DLP). As with integer factorization, it is of course a trivial problem in theory since we may calculate α^x for $x \ge 0$ until β is found. This is not efficient, requiring $O(p)$ modular multiplications. No efficient algorithm is known, and several cryptographic schemes rely for security on the supposed intractability of DLP. We shall consider two algorithms which, while not polytime, are more efficient than exhaustive search.

11.5.1 Baby-step giant-step

The baby-step giant-step algorithm is roughly similar to the meet-in-the-middle attack on double-DES, reducing the number of modular multiplications in exhaustive search at the cost of significant storage requirements.

Let $m = \left\lceil \sqrt{p-1} \right\rceil$. If $\beta \equiv \alpha^x \pmod{p}$, then we may write $x = im + j$ for $0 \le i, j < m$ and $\beta \equiv \alpha^x \equiv \alpha^{im}\alpha^j$, or $\beta\alpha^{-im} \equiv \alpha^j$. Form a table with entries $(j, \alpha^j \bmod p)$, $0 \le j < m$. For each i, $0 \le i < m$, calculate $\beta\alpha^{-im} \bmod p$ and check for a match in the table. On a match, we have $\beta\alpha^{-im} \equiv \alpha^j \pmod{p}$ and $\log_\alpha \beta = im + j$.

Example 11.5.1 The method is applied to find $\log_6 2$ in $\mathbb{Z}_{41}$ (i.e., $p = 41$, $\alpha = 6$, and $\beta = 2$). Let $m = \left\lceil \sqrt{40} \right\rceil = 7$ and form a table with entries (j, α^j) for $0 \le j < 7$:

j	0	1	2	3	4	5	6
$\alpha^j \bmod p$	1	6	36	11	25	27	39

We find $\alpha^{-1} \equiv 7 \pmod{p}$ and $\alpha^{-m} \equiv 7^7 \equiv 17 \pmod{41}$. It is now a matter of calculating $\beta(\alpha^{-m})^i \bmod p$ until a table entry is found:

$$\begin{aligned}
i = 0: &\quad \beta(\alpha^{-m})^0 \equiv \beta \equiv 2 \\
i = 1: &\quad \beta(\alpha^{-m})^1 \equiv 2 \cdot 17 \equiv 34 \\
i = 2: &\quad \beta(\alpha^{-m})^2 \equiv 34 \cdot 17 \equiv 4 \\
i = 3: &\quad \beta(\alpha^{-m})^3 \equiv 4 \cdot 17 \equiv 27
\end{aligned}$$

A match has been found for $i = 3$ and $j = 5$, giving $\beta\alpha^{-3m} \equiv \alpha^5$ and $\beta \equiv \alpha^{21+5} \pmod{p}$. Hence, $\log_6 2 = 26$ in $\mathbb{Z}_{41}$.

The table requires space for m group elements, built with $m - 1$ modular multiplications. The giant steps require an inversion and $O(m)$ modular multiplications, so the running time of the algorithm is $O(\sqrt{p-1})$ modular multiplications. This is better than exhaustive search, but much worse than polynomial time.

11.5.2 Index calculus

The most powerful methods for finding discrete logarithms are variants of the index calculus algorithm, portions of which resemble random squares algorithms for factoring. A computationally-expensive first stage determines logarithms for elements of a selected *factor base* B (which need not depend on the specific β for which $\log_\alpha \beta$ is desired). The second stage attempts to find an integer k so that $\alpha^k \beta$ factors over B; if successful, then $\log_\alpha \beta$ is easily obtained.

For $\mathbb{Z}_p$, the factor base $B = \{p_1, \dots, p_t\}$ consisting of the first t prime numbers may be selected. In the first stage, random k are selected in an attempt to find values $\alpha^k \bmod p$ which factor over the factor base. For such a k, $\alpha^k \bmod p = p_1^{e_1} \cdots p_t^{e_t}$ for some $e_i \geq 0$ and hence

$$k \equiv e_1 \log_\alpha p_1 + \cdots + e_t \log_\alpha p_t \pmod{p-1}.$$

Somewhat more than t such congruences are obtained, in the hope that the resulting linear system in the unknowns $\log_\alpha p_i$ has a unique solution.

In the second stage, we seek a value of k for which $\alpha^k \beta \bmod p$ factors over B. If successful, then $\alpha^k \beta \bmod p = p_1^{e_1} \cdots p_t^{e_t}$ for some $e_i \geq 0$, which implies

$$k + \log_\alpha \beta \equiv e_1 \log_\alpha p_1 + \cdots + e_t \log_\alpha p_t \pmod{p-1}$$

and $\log_\alpha \beta = (e_1 \log_\alpha p_1 + \cdots + e_t \log_\alpha p_t - k) \bmod (p-1)$.

Example 11.5.2 The method is illustrated for $p = 19$ and $\alpha = 2$, finding $\log_\alpha 17$. Suppose the factor base $B = \{2, 3, 5\}$ is selected. In this particular example, $\alpha \in B$ and $\log_\alpha 2 = 1$ is obtained directly. To determine the logs of the remaining two elements of B, we calculate $\alpha^k \bmod p$ for random k, seeking at least two values which factor over the factor base:

$$\begin{aligned} 2^9 \bmod p &= 2 \cdot 3^2 \\ 2^7 \bmod p &= 14 \\ 2^{11} \bmod p &= 3 \cdot 5 \end{aligned}$$

The second line is dropped since 14 does not factor over B. This gives the following system of congruences

$$\begin{aligned} 9 &\equiv \log_\alpha 2 + 2\log_\alpha 3 \pmod{p-1} \\ 11 &\equiv \log_\alpha 3 + \log_\alpha 5 \pmod{p-1} \end{aligned}$$

for the unknowns $\log_\alpha 3$ and $\log_\alpha 5$. However, these congruences do not determine a unique pair, giving candidates such as the incorrect solution ($\log_\alpha 3 = 4, \log_\alpha 5 = 7$). If the relation $\alpha^{14} \bmod p = 6$ is added, then the new system with the additional congruence $14 \equiv \log_\alpha 2 + \log_\alpha 3 \pmod{p-1}$ has a unique solution $\log_\alpha 3 = 13$ and $\log_\alpha 5 = 16$.

To find $\log_\alpha 17$, we seek k such that $\alpha^k \cdot 17 \bmod p$ factors over B. If $k = 5$, for example, then $\alpha^5 \cdot 17 \bmod p = 2^2 \cdot 3$ and $\log_\alpha 17 = (2\log_\alpha 2 + \log_\alpha 3 - 5) \bmod (p-1) = 10$.

The precomputation of logarithms of elements in the factor base is expensive, although collecting suitable relations can be a distributed effort. The first-stage results can be used to find the logarithm of any given β provided that a value of k can be found for which $\alpha^k\beta$ factors over the factor base. Choosing a larger factor base allows more elements of $\mathbb{Z}_p^*$ to be represented as products of elements of B at the cost of a larger system of congruences to be solved.

Sophisticated enhancements of the basic method were used in the 1990s to calculate logs modulo primes of 50–100 decimal digits. As an example, LaMacchia and Odlyzko [54] demonstrated in 1990 that calculation of logs modulo a certain 192-bit (58 decimal digit) prime was quite feasible using an index-calculus variant known as the Gaussian integer method. A system of 288017 relations with 96321 unknowns was reduced to one with 7262 equations and 6006 unknowns and then solved. The database could then be used to obtain individual logarithms with relatively little effort. The problem was of practical interest, since the security in a widely-used identification scheme proposed by Sun Microsystems depended, in part, on the difficulty of extracting logarithms modulo the prime [88].

In 1998, Joux and Lercier calculated discrete logarithms in $\mathbb{Z}_p^*$ where p was a 90 digit prime, using a Gaussian integer method. A network of 4 machines (each based on a 180 MHz Pentium Pro, a relatively inexpensive processor) collected 6.7 million equations over a month, obtaining 976062 equations for which every variable appeared at least twice. The linear system was reduced and then solved in 3 weeks. Selected logarithms required an average of 9 hours each on a single machine.

The number field sieve for factoring integers has been adapted for the log problem. Joux and Lercier used a sieve variant in 1999 to compute logarithms in $\mathbb{Z}_p^*$ with p having 100 digits. A machine based on a 450 MHz Pentium II collected 2.9 million equations over 8 months, passing the results to a 4-processor (DEC Alpha 500 MHz) computer which solved the linear system in 3 weeks. Individual logarithms were calculated in a day. They concluded that the number field sieve "seems to be better than the Gaussian integer method for computing discrete logarithms modulo primes over 100 digits" [46].

Exercises

11.5.3 Given that $\alpha = 5$ is a generator of $\mathbb{Z}_{97}^*$, illustrate baby-step giant-step on $\log_5 4$ in $\mathbb{Z}_{97}$.

11.5.4 Let $p = 41$ and $\alpha = 6$ (a generator of $\mathbb{Z}_p^*$). Illustrate the index calculus method on $\log_6 13$ by completing the following outline.

(a) Choose factor base $B = \{2, 3, 5\}$. Suppose that $\alpha^k \bmod p$ has been calculated for $k \in \{8, 20, 16\}$ giving

$$\begin{aligned}
\alpha^8 \bmod p = 10 &\implies 8 \equiv \log_\alpha 2 + \log_\alpha 5 \pmod{p-1} \\
\alpha^{20} \bmod p = 40 &\implies 20 \equiv 3\log_\alpha 2 + \log_\alpha 5 \pmod{p-1} \\
\alpha^{16} \bmod p = 18 &\implies 16 \equiv \log_\alpha 2 + 2\log_\alpha 3 \pmod{p-1}
\end{aligned}$$

Verify that the system of congruences does not determine a unique solution $(\log_\alpha 2, \log_\alpha 3, \log_\alpha 5)$.

(b) Add the congruence obtained from $\alpha^1 \bmod p = 2 \cdot 3$, and then solve. (The value of $\log_\alpha 2$ should match that found in Example 11.5.1.)

(c) Find $\log_\alpha 13$ by applying (b) to $\alpha^k \cdot 13 \bmod p$ for $k = 11$.

11.5.5 Let p be prime and α a generator of $\mathbb{Z}_p^*$. Show that the least significant bit of x can be efficiently determined from $\alpha^x \bmod p$.

11.5.6 Bach [2] discusses relationships between factoring and finding logarithms. In particular, this exercise shows that an oracle giving x for $a^x \equiv b \pmod{n}$ can be used in a probabilistic factoring attack on composite n.

Consider the case $n = pq$ for odd primes $p \neq q$. Let $\lambda = \operatorname{lcm}(\phi(p), \phi(q))$.

(a) Show that $K = \{z \in \mathbb{Z}_n^* \mid z^{\lambda/2} \equiv \pm 1 \pmod{n}\}$ is a proper subgroup of $\mathbb{Z}_n^*$. Hence, at least half the elements of $\mathbb{Z}_n^*$ are outside K.

(b) Let $a \in \mathbb{Z}_n^* \setminus K$, and suppose that $a^x \equiv 1 \pmod{n}$ for some $0 \neq x$ (known as an *exponent* for a). Show that there exists $0 < k < \log_2 x$ such that $a^{x/2^k}$ is a nontrivial square root of 1 (that is, $a^{x/2^k} \not\equiv \pm 1$ and $(a^{x/2^k})^2 \equiv 1$).

(c) Conclude that $(a^{x/2^k} + 1, n)$ is a nontrivial factor of n.

A factoring attack uses the oracle for $a^x \equiv b \pmod{n}$ to find an exponent for a. Although $\phi(n)$ is unknown, there must be some r among the first $\log_2 n$ primes such that $(r, \phi(n)) = 1$. For such an r, the oracle returns a solution y of $(a^r)^y \equiv a \pmod{n}$, and $x = ry - 1$ is an exponent for a.

11.6 Notes

Much of the material in this chapter is classical, for which many good introductory books exist, e.g., Rosen [74] and Koblitz [50]. Chapters 2 and 3 of Menezes, van Oorshot, and Vanstone [63] concisely covers some of the relevant material, and includes many references. Koblitz includes several examples of calculating time estimates (in terms of bit operations) for arithmetic, a topic which is less-commonly covered in number theory books.

Chapter 12

Public-key Cryptography

The fundamental feature which distinguishes public-key from symmetric-key schemes is the separation of encryption and decryption capabilities. To be slightly more precise, the key k in a public-key scheme is written as a key-pair $k = (e, d)$, where e is used for encryption and d is used for decryption. In this context, e is the *public key* and need not be secret; d is the *private key*, and is held only by those needing to decrypt messages. To be useful as an encryption scheme, it must be computationally infeasible for an adversary in possession of e and ciphertext c to find m so that $E_e(m) = c$.

The idea of public-key schemes was introduced by Diffie and Hellman in 1976 to exchange keys over an unsecured but authenticated channel. In the context of Figure 10.1, the understanding is that Alice and Bob are certain of the origin and integrity of communication over the unsecured channel, but there may be eavesdropping (passive attacks) by an adversary Eve. The problem is to maintain secrecy (even though Eve sees the entire conversation) without relying on the secure channel portion of the figure to transfer keys or other information.

The following *key agreement* is proposed: Alice and Bob choose a prime p and a generator α of $\mathbb{Z}_p^*$; p and α may be public. In private, Alice chooses a random a, $1 \le a < p$, and transmits α^a to Bob (in full view of Eve).[1] Similarly, Bob chooses a random b, $1 \le b < p$, and sends α^b to Alice. Alice and Bob may efficiently calculate $(\alpha^b)^a \bmod p$ and $(\alpha^a)^b \bmod p$, respectively, arriving at the shared secret $k = \alpha^{ab} \bmod p$ from which a common key may be derived for subsequent use in a symmetric-key scheme such as DES to achieve confidentiality.

Eve, of course, would also like to have the shared secret k. Her quest is known as the *Diffie-Hellman problem* (DHP), related to the discrete log problem (DLP):

DHP: Given prime p, generator α of $\mathbb{Z}_p^*$, α^a, and α^b, find α^{ab}.
DLP: Given prime p, generator α of $\mathbb{Z}_p^*$, and α^x, find x.

[1] For brevity, the operator "mod p" will often be omitted if the meaning is clear from context. Here, for example, we mean that $\alpha^a \bmod p$ is transmitted.

It is clear that DHP $\leq$ DLP; that is, DHP can be solved in polynomial time given a polytime oracle for DLP. In some special cases, it is known that DLP $\leq$ DHP, but the general case remains an open question [63]. The presumed intractability of DHP is the basis for the security of the Diffie-Hellman key agreement.

Public-key schemes can be used to address some difficulties inherent in symmetric-key schemes. The Diffie-Hellman key agreement suggests that secrecy can be maintained even without a secure channel for exchanging keys. (It is important to note the assumption of an authenticated channel—the agreement is not secure against an active adversary, as illustrated in Section 12.5.) Provided that the public keys can be authenticated, *key distribution* does not require a trusted courier. Since secrecy of the public key is not required, authentication is presumably easier than exchanging symmetric keys.

Public-key reduces the *key management* problem. If there are n users of a cryptosystem, then $\binom{n}{2}$ keys are required in a symmetric-key scheme compared with $2n$ in a public-key scheme, a significant difference if n is large.

Digital signatures (discussed in the following sections) are another area where public-key schemes are attractive. Alice should be able to sign a message in such a way that not only is Bob convinced that the message originated from Alice, but Bob can convince a third party of the same. The basic problem with using symmetric-key schemes for signatures is that Bob and Alice have the same capabilities. A trusted third party can be used to enable signatures, but public-key schemes provide a more mathematically elegant and practical solution.

12.1 One-way and hash functions

Two cryptographic primitives are examined in this section, trapdoor one-way functions (the fundamental notion in public-key schemes), and cryptographic hash functions (commonly used in signature schemes).

One-way functions

Informally, a function $f : \mathcal{M} \to \mathcal{C}$ is *one-way* if $f(m)$ is easy to compute for all $m \in \mathcal{M}$, and for essentially all $c \in \mathcal{C}$ it is computationally infeasible to find m so that $f(m) = c$. The function described in Section 10.3.2 for Unix passwords is believed to be one-way (under some ceiling on computational ability), storing $f(userid, password)$ rather than the password itself.[2] Another candidate is discrete exponentiation. Let p be prime and α a generator of $\mathbb{Z}_p^*$. The function $f : \mathbb{Z}_p^* \to \mathbb{Z}_p^*$ defined by $f(a) = \alpha^a \bmod p$ is believed to be one-way.

[2] There was sufficient confidence in the scheme that the stored values were visible to all the users of the system, inviting password-cracking analysis. Needless to say, this turned out to be a bad idea, since users often select predictable passwords. Modern systems tend to demand better passwords and have made the stored values private.

It is not known if one-way functions exist. Public-key schemes certainly assume that various functions, if not one-way, will be effectively one-way for the life of the specific security objective. A number of candidates for use in public-key schemes are discussed in the following sections.

A one-way function is *trapdoor* if it has the property that given some extra information, it becomes feasible to find m so that $f(m) = c$ for any given c. The trapdoor one-way function is the basic tool in public-key cryptography.

Example 12.1.1 (applications of trapdoor functions) *Confidentiality*. Each user A picks their own trapdoor one-way function f_A and makes it public. To transmit a confidential message m to A, the sender forwards $c = f_A(m)$. Only A has the trapdoor information allowing f to be inverted—even the sender cannot recover m from c. No secret information needs to be shared in advance, although it is necessary for the sender to have a means of authenticating the public key.

Non-repudiation. The analogue of a hand-written signature is desired: a message m from Alice is to be signed in such a way that Bob can convince any third party that m originated with Alice. Assume that m has some prescribed degree of redundancy. If Alice's trapdoor one-way function is $f_A : \mathcal{M} \to \mathcal{M}$, then Alice sends $s = f_A^{-1}(m)$. Bob computes $m = f_A(s)$ and (m, s) is the signed message. Although an adversary can calculate $m = f_A(s)$ for chosen s, forgeries are thwarted by the assumed redundancy in m. If secrecy is desired, Alice could send $c = f_B(s)$ rather than s directly, where f_B is Bob's trapdoor one-way function.

Cryptographic hash functions

A mapping $H : X \to Y$ which is not one-to-one is known as a hash function. For a given $x \in X$, the value $H(x)$ is called a *hash*, and serves as an "identifier" for x. By definition, there are necessarily collisions—values $x_1 \neq x_2$ with the same hash. Typical design goals for a hash function include spreading conditions on the collisions and efficient calculation of the hash values.

Public-key cryptosystems tend to be relatively computationally intensive, and signing long messages is a slow procedure. In practice, a hash function is used to create a *message digest* of the message, and it is the digest that is signed. In order for this to be secure, additional features of the hash function are needed.

Definition 12.1.2 A *cryptographic hash function* is a mapping $H : \{0, 1\}^* \to \{0, 1\}^n$ such that:

1. H can be efficiently computed;
2. (preimage resistance) for essentially all $y \in \{0, 1\}^n$, it is computationally infeasible to find $x \in \{0, 1\}^*$ such that $H(x) = y$;
3. (collision resistance) it is computationally infeasible to find $x_1 \neq x_2 \in \{0, 1\}^*$ such that $H(x_1) = H(x_2)$.

It is not known if cryptographic hash functions exist (since 1 and 2 imply that such a function is one-way); however, there are a number of candidates used for data integrity and signature schemes.

Example 12.1.3 (application to signatures) To sign a message m, Alice computes and signs the hash $H(m)$. The message m and the signature on $H(m)$ are sent to Bob, who computes $H(m)$ and verifies the signature. A scheme where the message itself is required in the verification process is known as a *digital signature scheme with appendix.*

If the hash function H is not preimage resistant, then an adversary (perhaps Bob) given a valid signature for $H(m)$ can forge Alice's signature by finding a message m' with $H(m') = H(m)$, obtaining a valid signature for m'.

If $m \neq m'$ giving collisions can be found, then Alice can cheat by signing m and later claiming to have signed m'. A variation on this occurs if an adversary finds such a collision and convinces Alice to sign one of the messages.

In the example, the signature presumably protects the integrity of the hash computed by Alice. In general, if the hash value can be protected by some mechanism, then a hash function can be used to verify that the corresponding data has not been modified. In this context, an unkeyed hash function is called a *modification detection code* (MDC). A keyed hash function providing data origin authentication using a secret key is called a *message authentication code* (MAC); the CBC-MAC described in Section 10.3.2 is an example.

Several hash functions have been proposed which are built on block ciphers. As noted, CBC-MAC is a keyed hash function, while the following two examples are unkeyed.

Example 12.1.4 (Matyas-Meyer-Oseas hash) Let E be a block cipher, $E_k : \{0,1\}^n \to \{0,1\}^n$, with keyspace $\mathcal{K}$. Let $g : \{0,1\}^n \to \mathcal{K}$ be a (non-secret) function, and let H_0 be a (non-secret) initial value in $\{0,1\}^n$. The mapping $H : \{0,1\}^* \to \{0,1\}^n$ is defined as follows:

1. Break x into n-bit blocks, say $x = x_1 \cdots x_t$.
2. Let $H_i = E_{g(H_{i-1})}(x_i) \oplus x_i$, $1 \le i \le t$. Then $H(x) = H_t$.

A schematic appears in Figure 12.1(a).

Roughly speaking, if the roles of the x_i and H_{i-1} are interchanged, then the following proposed hash function is obtained. Note however, that the splitting of x differs.

Example 12.1.5 (Davies-Meyer hash) Let E be an n-bit block cipher using k-bit keys. Let H_0 be a (non-secret) initial value in $\{0,1\}^n$. The mapping $H : \{0,1\}^* \to \{0,1\}^n$ is defined as follows:

1. Break x into k-bit blocks, say $x = x_1 \cdots x_t$.
2. Let $H_i = E_{x_i}(H_{i-1}) \oplus H_{i-1}$, $1 \le i \le t$. Then $H(x) = H_t$.

A schematic appears in Figure 12.1(b).

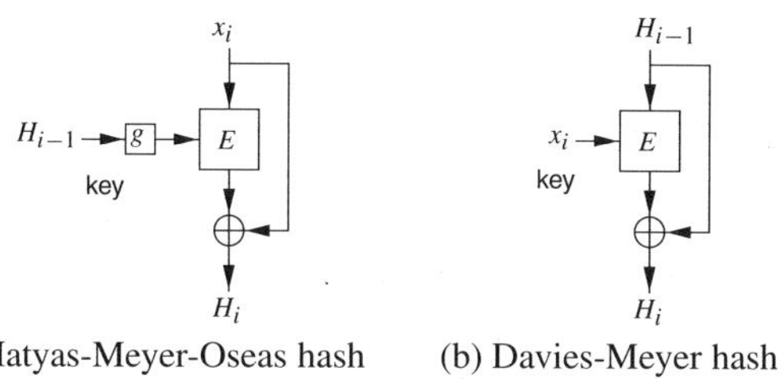

(a) Matyas-Meyer-Oseas hash (b) Davies-Meyer hash

Figure 12.1: *Unkeyed hash functions based on block cipher E.*

The message digest produced by an unkeyed hash function must be of sufficient length to prevent birthday attacks (random searches for collisions). For n-bit hash functions, it is expected that collisions can be found in at most $2^{n/2}$ operations. In particular, neither of the hash functions in Figure 12.1 is collision-resistant if $E = \text{DES}$. Two well-known hash functions, the Secure Hash Algorithm (SHA-1) and MD5 (both based on MD4, number 4 in a series of Message Digest algorithms from Rivest) have digest bitlength 160 and 128, respectively.

Exercises

12.1.6 Suppose $g : \{0,1\}^* \to \{0,1\}^n$ is a collision-resistant hash function. Let h be defined by

$$h(x) = \begin{cases} 1 \,\|\, x, & \text{if } x \text{ has bitlength } n, \\ 0 \,\|\, g(x), & \text{otherwise,} \end{cases}$$

where '‖' denotes concatenation. Give an informal argument to show that h is an $(n+1)$-bit hash function which is collision resistant but not preimage resistant. (The example is from [63, Note 9.20].)

12.1.7 This exercise is adapted from [63, Example 9.64], illustrating that some care must be taken when constructing a MAC from an MDC.

Suppose that h is an MDC defined in an iterated fashion on message $x = x_1 \cdots x_t$ by $H_i = f(H_{i-1}, x_i)$, $h(x) = H_t$, where H_0 is a given initial value. It is proposed that h can be converted into a MAC by prepending a secret key k so that the MAC on a message x is $M = h(kx)$. Show that knowledge of an (M, x) pair can be used to forge a MAC on xy, even though k is unknown.

12.1.8 Suppose p and q are primes such that $p' = 2p+1$ and $q' = 2q+1$ are also prime, and let $n = p'q'$. Suppose α is an element of order $2pq$ in $\mathbb{Z}_n^*$, and let $h : \mathbb{Z} \to \mathbb{Z}_n^*$ be defined by $h(x) = \alpha^x \bmod n$. If $h(x_1) = h(x_2) = h(x_3)$, show that n can be efficiently factored under suitable conditions on the collisions x_i.

Illustrate the process with the toy modulus $n = 77$ and $\alpha = 2$, where $h(9) = h(69) = h(129)$. (This exercise is adapted from [86, Exercise 7.4].)

12.2 RSA

Proposed in 1977 by Rivest, Shamir, and Adleman, the RSA cryptosystem is widely-used for encryption and signature schemes, with security based on the presumed intractability of the integer factorization problem. The RSA function itself is defined as follows.

1. Let $p \neq q$ be large primes, and define $n = pq$ and $\phi = (p-1)(q-1)$.
2. Choose random *encryption exponent* e, $1 < e < \phi$, so that $(e, \phi) = 1$.
3. Use the Euclidean algorithm to find *decryption exponent* d, $1 < d < \phi$, so that $ed \equiv 1 \pmod{\phi}$.
4. Define $f : \mathbb{Z}_n \to \mathbb{Z}_n$ by $f(m) = m^e \bmod n$.

The RSA function f is believed to be one-way with trapdoor d. Given d, recovery of m from $c = f(m)$ can be done efficiently using the property $ed \equiv 1 \pmod{\phi}$. To see this, first suppose that $p \nmid m$. Note that $ed = 1 + k\phi = 1 + k(p-1)(q-1)$ for some k, and by Fermat's theorem $m^{p-1} \equiv 1 \pmod{p}$ so that $m^{1+k(p-1)(q-1)} \equiv m \pmod{p}$. If $p \mid m$, then the last congruence holds trivially. This shows that

$$m^{1+k(p-1)(q-1)} \equiv m^{ed} \equiv m \pmod{p}.$$

By a similar argument $m^{ed} \equiv m \pmod{q}$, and hence $m^{ed} \equiv m \pmod{n}$ since p and q are distinct primes. It follows that

$$c^d \equiv (m^e)^d \equiv m \pmod{n},$$

efficiently recovering m from c by modular exponentiation.

Inverting f without possessing d is the *RSA problem*: given a product $n = pq$ of distinct primes, a positive integer e relatively prime to $(p-1)(q-1)$, and an integer c, find m such that $m^e \equiv c \pmod{n}$. If n can be factored, then d may be computed and m obtained efficiently. However, factoring n for appropriately chosen p and q is believed to be a hard problem.

Exercise 12.2.12 shows that an efficient method to factor n is obtained if d can be computed. Hence, the problem of factoring n and the problem of computing d from n and e are computationally equivalent. The equivalence provides some evidence that the RSA problem may be as hard as factoring, but this remains an open question.[3]

In the RSA cryptosystem, (n, e) is the public key and d is the private key. Encryption of $m \in [0, n-1]$ gives $c = m^e \bmod n$; decryption is $m = c^d \bmod n$.

Example 12.2.1 (RSA with toy parameters) Suppose $p = 7$ and $q = 13$ are used in RSA key generation. Then $\phi = (p-1)(q-1) = 72$, and we may choose encryption exponent $e = 5$. The condition $ed \equiv 1 \pmod{\phi}$ gives decryption exponent

[3] Boneh and Venkatesan [15] provide evidence that breaking low-exponent RSA (that is, RSA with small encryption exponent e) cannot be equivalent to factoring.

$d = 29$. The public key is $(n = 91, e = 5)$ and the private key is $d = 29$. Messages m consist of integers in $[0, 91)$. If $m = 23$, then $c = m^e = 23^5 \bmod 91 = 4$ and $c^d \bmod n = 4^{29} \bmod 91 = 23$ can be verified using repeated squaring.

An RSA encryption scheme passes some messages *unconcealed*; that is, there are messages m with $c = m^e \bmod n = m$. The messages $m \in \{0, 1, n-1\}$ are always unconcealed. Note that $m^e \equiv m \pmod{n}$ if and only if $m^e \equiv m \pmod{p}$ and $m^e \equiv m \pmod{q}$. Solutions of $m^e \equiv m \pmod{p}$ satisfy $m \equiv 0 \pmod{p}$ or $m^{e-1} \equiv 1 \pmod{p}$; there are $1 + (e-1, p-1)$ such solutions (Exercise 11.1.22). The Chinese remainder theorem can be applied to show that the number of unconcealed messages is $(1 + (e-1, p-1))(1 + (e-1, q-1))$. In particular, there are always at least 9 unconcealed messages since e, p, and q are odd. Example 12.2.1 has 15 unconcealed messages; $m = 8$ is one such message. Exercise 12.2.3 illustrates the extreme case where every message is unconcealed.

Although known- and chosen-plaintext attacks generally do not apply to public-key encryption, there are scenarios where a chosen-ciphertext attack is a concern. Let c_1 and c_2 be RSA encryptions of m_1 and m_2, respectively. Then $(m_1 m_2)^e \equiv m_1^e m_2^e \equiv c_1 c_2 \pmod{n}$, giving $c = c_1 c_2 \bmod n$ as the ciphertext corresponding to $m = m_1 m_2 \bmod n$. An adversary Eve may be able to exploit this multiplicative property by concealing the target ciphertext c in $\bar{c}$ and convincing the private-key holder Alice to provide decryption of $\bar{c}$. Eve chooses $x \in \mathbb{Z}_n^*$ and passes $\bar{c} = cx^e$ to Alice for decryption, obtaining $\bar{m} = \bar{c}^d \bmod n$. Since $\bar{c}^d \equiv c^d x^{ed} \equiv mx \pmod{n}$, Eve recovers $m = \bar{m}x^{-1} \bmod n$. Structural requirements on plaintext messages may defeat the attack.

The modulus selected during key generation must be sufficiently large to circumvent factoring attacks. In 1996, Menezes et al. [63] recommended a 768-bit or larger modulus, with 1024-bit moduli for long-term security. Lenstra and Verheul presented an argument for longer moduli in 1999, concluding that "768-bit RSA keys will soon no longer offer security comparable to the security of the DES in 1982" [55]. Additional restrictions on the factors may be imposed due to various factoring attacks; for example, p and q should be roughly the same bitlength but not so that $|p - q|$ is particularly small.

RSA signature scheme (with message recovery)

RSA may be used in digital signatures, interchanging the functions of encryption and decryption as outlined in Example 12.1.1. Alice's signature on m is $s = m^d \bmod n$, where d is Alice's private key. On receiving s, Bob computes $s^e \bmod n = m$ using Alice's public key (n, e), obtaining signed message (m, s).

In order to provide a mechanism to detect invalid messages, structural requirements are placed on messages m. A forger can choose s (and obtain corresponding $m = s^e \bmod n$ using Alice's public key), but has little control over the structure of the message m. Bob accepts signed message (m,s) only if the prescribed structure of m is present.

To reduce signature-verification or encryption times, it is desirable to choose a small exponent e, although exercises 12.2.4 and 12.2.5 illustrate some concerns with such a choice. Similarly, a private exponent d which is relatively small would improve decryption and signature-generation times, but the concern is that the key itself may be leaked. Under fairly general conditions, Wiener [95] showed that the private key can be recovered if d is small relative to n, using a continued-fractions method (see Exercise 12.2.7).

In practice, a scheme based on RSA would be implemented in a more sophisticated fashion than the basic versions described here. Padding of the message before encryption is commonly used to defeat chosen-ciphertext and other attacks; at a minimum, padding with some randomness has the advantage that repeated encryptions of a fixed message will likely give different ciphertexts [4]. Boneh [12] surveys two decades of attacks, noting that "none of them is devastating. They mostly illustrate the dangers of improper use of RSA. Indeed, securely implementing RSA is a nontrivial task."

Exercises

12.2.2 Alice chooses $p=31, q=47$, and $e=77$ for use in RSA.

(a) What is Alice's private key?

(b) Encrypt the message $m=3$ using Alice's public key.

(c) Verify your answer to (b) by decrypting the ciphertext to recover m.

12.2.3 Show that every message is unconcealed if $p=5$, $q=17$, and $e=33$ are chosen in RSA.

12.2.4 A small encryption exponent in RSA is desirable for encryption efficiency. Suppose three users have $e=3$ and RSA moduli n_1, n_2, and n_3, resp. An adversary intercepts ciphertext $c_i = m^e \bmod n_i$, $1 \le i \le 3$, from the common message m. If the moduli are pairwise relatively prime, show how Gauss' algorithm can be used to recover the message m.

This is an example of a *protocol failure* in RSA. A larger exponent (such as $e = 2^{16}+1$ with only a few 1s in its binary representation to maintain efficiency) is one countermeasure; generating a random bitstring and appending to the message for each encryption, known as *salting*, is another.

12.2.5 (Related messages and RSA) Coppersmith et al. [24] describe an effective attack against low-exponent RSA in the case that the underlying plaintext messages satisfy a known linear relationship. Consider the case that the encryption exponent is $e=3$ and that ciphertexts c_1 and c_2 correspond to messages m and $m+1$ for some (unknown) m; i.e., $c_1 = m^3 \bmod n$ and $c_2 = (m+1)^3 \bmod n$.

(a) Verify that m can be recovered from the ciphertexts by

$$\frac{c_2+2c_1-1}{c_2-c_1+2} \equiv m \pmod{n}.$$

(b) Note that $x-m$ is a common factor of x^3-c_1 and $(x+1)^3-c_2$. Establish the formula in (a) by adapting the Euclidean algorithm to find $((x+1)^3-c_2, x^3-c_1)$. Verify that the algorithm will indeed return a linear polynomial.

12.2.6 (Partial key-exposure) Let $n = pq$ where p and q are primes with $5 \le p < q < 2p$. Let integers e and d satisfy $1 < e, d < \phi(n)$ and $ed \equiv 1 \pmod{\phi(n)}$.

(a) Since $ed \equiv 1 \pmod{\phi(n)}$, there exists an integer k with $ed - k\phi(n) = 1$. Prove that $1 \le k < e$.

(b) Let $\hat{d} = \lfloor \frac{kn+1}{e} \rfloor$. Prove that $|\hat{d} - d| < 3\sqrt{n}$.

(c) If $e = 3$, then prove that $k = 2$.

(d) Devise an efficient algorithm for computing the leftmost-half bits of d, given only n and $e = 3$. (More precisely, the algorithm should narrow the possible values to one or two.)

The exercise is adapted from [12].

12.2.7 (Small decryption exponent) Let $n = pq$ for odd primes p and q satisfying $p < q < 2p$. Let integers e and d satisfy $1 < e, d < \phi(n)$ and $ed \equiv 1 \pmod{\phi(n)}$. Suppose that $d < \frac{1}{3}n^{1/4}$, and let k be such that $ed - k\phi(n) = 1$.

(a) Prove that $n - \phi(n) < 3\sqrt{n}$; that is, n is a good approximation of $\phi(n)$.

(b) Prove that $\frac{e}{n}$ is a good approximation of $\frac{k}{d}$. More precisely, prove that $|\frac{e}{n} - \frac{k}{d}| < \frac{1}{2d^2}$.

(c) Using the fact below, devise an efficient algorithm for computing d, given only n and e.

Fact. Let $1 \le x_0 < y_0$ for integers x_0 and y_0. The number of pairs (x, y) with $1 \le y < y_0$ such that $|\frac{x_0}{y_0} - \frac{x}{y}| < \frac{1}{2y^2}$ is bounded by $2\log_2 y_0$. Moreover, all such pairs can be found efficiently (as convergents of the continued fraction expansion of $\frac{x_0}{y_0}$; see Hardy and Wright [42]).

The attack is discussed in [12, 14] and is due to Wiener [95].

12.2.8 (Fault analysis attack [13, 47]) Suppose that a smartcard is using the Chinese remainder theorem for RSA decryption; that is, decryption of ciphertext c is performed by computing $m_p = c^{d \bmod (p-1)} \bmod p$ and $m_q = c^{d \bmod (q-1)} \bmod q$, and then finding m, $0 \le m < n$, such that $m \equiv m_p \pmod{p}$ and $m \equiv m_q \pmod{q}$.

(a) Prove that the process provides the correct decryption (i.e., $m = c^d \bmod n$).

(b) Suppose that the smartcard can be induced to compute m_p incorrectly (and m_q correctly). Let m' be the resulting (incorrect) decryption of c. Show how this information can be used to factor n.

12.2.9 A *cycling attack* against RSA finds the first positive integer k such that $c^{e^k} \equiv c \pmod{n}$.

(a) Show that such an integer k exists. Then show that an adversary recovers the message with $c^{e^{k-1}} \equiv m \pmod{n}$.

(b) The attack can be generalized. Let u be the smallest positive integer such that $(c^{e^u} - c, n) > 1$. Show that either a nontrivial factor of n has been obtained or the method has reduced to the basic cycling attack (i.e., $u = k$).

Cycling attacks are not likely to succeed for $n = pq$ if $p-1$ and $q-1$ have large prime factors [63]. The generalized attack is expected to terminate before the basic cycling, and can be viewed as a factoring attack (and so not likely to be successful if factoring is intractable).

12.2.10 Verify that RSA key generation could use the *universal exponent* $\lambda(pq) = \operatorname{lcm}(p-1, q-1)$ in place of $\phi(n)$. Using λ may result in a smaller decryption exponent d.

12.2.11 RSA key generation requires large primes p and q. Suppose, in fact, that a probabilistic primality test produced a "probably prime" p that was actually composite. Consider the case that $p = p_1 p_2$ where $p_1 \neq p_2$ are primes distinct from q. Key generation will obtain e and d from $\phi(p,q) = (p-1)(q-1)$ rather than $\phi(n) = (p_1 - 1)(p_2 - 1)(q-1)$.

(a) Note that $\lambda = \operatorname{lcm}(p_1 - 1, p_2 - 1, q-1) \mid \phi(n)$. Show that if $\lambda \mid \phi(p,q)$ then encryption and decryption will succeed.

(b) Illustrate (a) with $p = 15$ and $q = 7$, finding λ, $\phi(n)$, and $\phi(p,q)$.

(c) Suppose $p = 21$ and $q = 5$. Show that $\lambda \nmid \phi(p,q)$. Find d for encryption exponent $e = 3$, and exhibit a message m with $c^d \bmod n \neq m$ where $c = m^e \bmod n$.

12.2.12 This exercise shows that possession of the decryption exponent d in RSA allows n to be factored efficiently. The main idea is that nontrivial square roots modulo n of 1 can be found.

Since $ed \equiv 1 \pmod{\phi}$, it follows that $m^{ed-1} \equiv 1 \pmod{n}$ for all $m \in \mathbb{Z}_n^*$. Write $ed - 1 = 2^s t$ where t is odd. The proof consists of showing that, for at least half of all $m \in \mathbb{Z}_n^*$, there exists $r \in [1, s]$ such that $m^{2^{r-1}t} \not\equiv \pm 1 \pmod{n}$ and $m^{2^r t} \equiv 1 \pmod{n}$; for such an m, $(m^{2^{r-1}t} - 1, n)$ is a nontrivial factor of n.

An $m \in \mathbb{Z}_n^*$ fails to lead to a factor if

$$m^t \equiv 1 \pmod{n} \quad \text{or} \quad m^{2^r t} \equiv -1 \pmod{n} \text{ for some } 0 \leq r < s.$$

Determining the number solutions to these congruences is the main work. Let $p - 1 = 2^i p'$ and $q - 1 = 2^j q'$ for p' and q' odd. Recall that $ax \equiv b \pmod{n}$ has a solution x iff $(a,n) \mid b$ in which case there are exactly (a,n) solutions (Exercise 11.1.20).

Case $m^t \equiv 1 \pmod{n}$. First consider the congruence modulo p. Let α be a generator of $\mathbb{Z}_p^*$. We seek the number of solutions x of $(\alpha^x)^t \equiv 1 \pmod{p}$.

(a) Show that p' divides t.

(b) Note that $\alpha^{xt} \equiv 1 \pmod{p}$ iff $xt \equiv 0 \pmod{p-1}$. Show that there are exactly p' solutions.

(c) Similarly, the number of solutions of $m^t \equiv 1 \pmod{q}$ is q'. Use the Chinese remainder theorem to show that the number of solutions of $m^t \equiv 1 \pmod{n}$ is $p'q'$.

Case $m^{2^r t} \equiv -1 \pmod{n}$. As above, the congruence is first is examined modulo p and then modulo q. We seek the number of solutions x of $(\alpha^x)^{2^r t} \equiv -1 \pmod{p}$.

(d) Note that $\alpha^{(p-1)/2} \equiv -1 \pmod{p}$ so that $(\alpha^x)^{2^r t} \equiv -1 \pmod{p}$ iff $x2^r t \equiv (p-1)/2 \pmod{p-1}$. Show that there are solutions iff $r < i$, in which case there are exactly $2^r p'$ solutions

We may assume without loss of generality that $i \leq j$. The Chinese remainder theorem may be applied, showing that the number of solutions to $m^{2^r t} \equiv -1 \pmod{n}$ is $2^{2r} p'q'$ if $r < i$ and 0 otherwise.

An upper bound on the number of $m \in \mathbb{Z}_n^*$ satisfying $m^{2^r t} \equiv -1 \pmod{n}$ for some $0 \leq r < s$ is then $\sum_{r=0}^{i-1} 2^{2r} p'q' = p'q'(2^{2i} - 1)/3$. Necessarily, an upper bound on the number of $m \in \mathbb{Z}_n^*$ which fail to lead to a factorization of n is then

$$p'q'(1 + \frac{2^{2i} - 1}{3}) = p'q'(\frac{2}{3} + \frac{2^{2i}}{3}).$$

Since $2^{2i} p'q' \leq 2^i p' 2^j q' = (p-1)(q-1) = \phi(n)$, it follows that

$$p'q'(\frac{2}{3} + \frac{2^{2i}}{3}) \leq \frac{\phi(n)}{6} + \frac{\phi(n)}{3} = \frac{\phi(n)}{2}.$$

Necessarily, for at least half the elements $m \in \mathbb{Z}_n^*$ there exists $1 \leq r \leq s$ such that $m^{2^{r-1} t} \not\equiv \pm 1 \pmod{n}$ and $m^{2^r t} \equiv 1 \pmod{n}$. To factor n, select random $m \in \mathbb{Z}_n^*$ and determine if r exists; if so, calculate $(m^{2^{r-1} t} - 1, n)$. A nontrivial factor of n is expected in two trials.

12.2.13 If it is known that ciphertext $c = m^e \bmod pq$ was obtained for $m \in [0, p)$, then decryption can be done in $\mathbb{Z}_p$, recovering the message as $m = c^d \bmod n = c^{d \bmod p-1} \bmod p$. Shamir [78] proposed an unbalanced RSA which selects primes $p < q$ of very different sizes, say 500 and 4500 bits, respectively, with plaintext messages restricted to the interval $[0, p)$. Factoring attacks on $n = pq$ are defeated, but decryption is as fast as RSA with a 500-bit modulus.

Show that unbalanced RSA is subject to a complete break by a chosen-ciphertext attack.

12.2.14 A "dark side" of black-box cryptography is examined in CRYPTO '96 [102]. The black-box is contaminated with a mechanism that allows the manufacturer to extract secrets, but protects against detection and attacks by others. The mechanism is known as a Secretly Embedded Trapdoor with Universal Protection (SETUP).

The authors' most straightforward SETUP concerns RSA. The idea is to hide enough information in an RSA public exponent e so that the attacker can factor n. The black-box normally selects primes $p \neq q$ and then produces an RSA key $(n = pq, e, d)$. The process is contaminated using an attacker's key (n', e'), attempting to select a prime p for which $e = p^{e'} \bmod n'$ satisfies $(e, \phi(n)) = 1$.

(a) The authors of [102] left a few details to the reader. How does the attacker factor n from the public key (n, e), and what assumptions have been made?

(b) Speculate on the likeliness that the SETUP will be discovered, perhaps based on key-generation times or the form of the keys produced.

The SETUP described will not be effective in cases where a small e is required. The authors give a "Pretty Awful Privacy" SETUP which is similar to PGP (Pretty Good Privacy [37, 104]), but hides information about p in the modulus n. See also [103] and Exercise 12.5.6.

12.3 Provable security

The security in RSA is said to be *based* on the presumed intractability of factoring; however, systematic recovery of plaintext from ciphertext in RSA is not *known* to be as difficult as factoring. It is possible that the integer factorization problem may be intractable but breaking RSA is easy.

In 1979, Rabin [69] introduced a scheme which is provably secure in the sense that recovery of plaintext from some given ciphertext is as difficult as solving a computational problem believed to be intractable. Provable security clarifies and minimizes assumptions, and allows a more precise definition of security. It should be emphasized that the proof is relative to the assumptions about the related computational problem—there may be considerable evidence that problems such as factoring and discrete logs are hard, but none are proven computationally infeasible.

The Rabin scheme is similar to RSA in that the encryption function in both is of the form $f(m) = m^e \bmod pq$. In RSA, the operation is invertible; however, Rabin uses $e = 2$ and computation of square roots recovers the possible choices for m. To be precise, the Rabin scheme chooses primes $p \neq q$, forming public key $n = pq$ and private key (p, q). The encryption function $f : \mathbb{Z}_n \to \mathbb{Z}_n$ is given by $f(m) = m^2 \bmod n$. Given ciphertext c, decryption proceeds by solving $c = m^2 \bmod n$ for the four possible roots using the techniques described in Section 11.4.

Example 12.3.1 Consider the Rabin scheme with toy parameters $p = 31$ and $q = 41$. The message $m = 814$ is encrypted with the public key $n = pq = 1271$, obtaining $c = f(m) = m^2 \bmod n = 814^2 \bmod 1271 = 405$. To decrypt, the private key $(p = 31, q = 41)$ is used to extract square roots, solving the congruences

$$m^2 \equiv 405 \equiv 2 \pmod{31}$$
$$m^2 \equiv 405 \equiv 36 \pmod{41}$$

for m. Section 11.4 shows that this can be done efficiently. In this toy problem, $p \equiv 3 \pmod 4$ so that the roots modulo p are given by $m \equiv \pm 2^{(p+1)/4} \equiv \pm 8 \pmod{31}$; the second congruence gives $m \equiv \pm 6 \pmod{41}$ by inspection. Gauss' algorithm 11.1.6 may be applied, obtaining (at most) four possibilities for m:

$m \equiv 8 \pmod{31}$	$m \equiv -8 \pmod{31}$	$m \equiv 8 \pmod{31}$	$m \equiv -8 \pmod{31}$
$m \equiv 6 \pmod{41}$	$m \equiv 6 \pmod{41}$	$m \equiv -6 \pmod{41}$	$m \equiv -6 \pmod{41}$
$m_1 = -240$	$m_2 = 457$	$m_3 = -457$	$m_4 = 240$

(Note that only the first two need to be solved; the roots are then $\pm m_1, \pm m_2$.) Four distinct candidates m_i are obtained for m. Unless structural requirements are placed on messages, the receiver is unable to determine that $m_3 \bmod n = 814$ is the original message.

To understand the security of the scheme, consider the problem of interest to an adversary:

RABIN: Given $n = pq$ and $c = m^2 \bmod n$, find x so that $c \equiv x^2 \pmod n$.

This is the square root problem discussed in Section 11.4. If $p \equiv q \equiv 3 \pmod 4$, then $n = pq$ is a *Blum integer* and square roots can be extracted in polynomial time. In the example, $q \equiv 1 \pmod 8$, and n is not of the special form. There is no known polynomial-time deterministic algorithm for solving $x^2 \equiv c \pmod q$ when $q \equiv 1 \pmod 8$; there is, however, the randomized method discussed in Section 11.4 which runs in expected polynomial time. Hence, RABIN $\leq$ FACTOR; that is, given an oracle for FACTOR that runs in expected polynomial time, then we may solve RABIN in expected polynomial time.

To see that FACTOR $\leq$ RABIN, recall that if $x^2 \equiv y^2 \pmod n$ and $x \not\equiv \pm y \pmod n$, then $(x + y, n)$ is a nontrivial factor of n. Choose $x \in \mathbb{Z}_n^*$ at random, and compute $c = x^2 \bmod n$. The oracle for RABIN is queried, and a square root y of c is returned in expected polynomial time. With probability $1/2$, the root y satisfies $y \not\equiv \pm x$; in this case, $(x + y, n)$ is one of the prime factors of n.

Hence, breaking the Rabin system is equivalent to factoring n. Note, however, the argument also shows that the scheme is not secure against a chosen-ciphertext attack. In addition, a protocol failure of the type discussed in Exercise 12.2.4 applies to Rabin.

A difficulty in Rabin decryption is that the correct plaintext must be identified from four candidates. One practical solution is to add structural requirements (e.g., replicated bits) to the messages in such a way that it is unlikely that more than one of the roots will possess the proper structure. This also thwarts the chosen-ciphertext attack to recover roots (since the oracle returns no useful information to the attacker in this case). However, the proof of equivalence to the factoring problem no longer holds for this modified scheme. Exercise 12.3.3 examines a Rabin-like scheme (on Blum integers n) that permits identification of the actual message.

Exercises

12.3.2 Let $n = 551$ in a (toy) Rabin encryption scheme.

(a) Encrypt the message $m = 53$, obtaining ciphertext $c = m^2 \bmod n$.

(b) Show the procedure for decrypting c, obtaining four candidates for m.

(c) Illustrate a chosen-ciphertext attack to factor n as follows. A random $x \in \mathbb{Z}_{551}^*$ is selected, say $x = 53$. The value $c = x^2 \bmod n$ is passed to the oracle for RABIN. What happens if the oracle returns 498? If the oracle returns 517, show that n can be factored.

12.3.3 This exercise outlines a scheme proposed by Williams [96, 97] for certain composite n which is similar to that of Rabin. Recovering plaintext from ciphertext is equivalent to factoring n, but the ambiguity in selecting the proper root is eliminated.

Let $n = pq$ with $p \equiv q \equiv 3 \pmod 4$, and define $d = ((p-1)(q-1)/4+1)/2$. Choose s so that $\left(\frac{s}{n}\right) = -1$. The public key is (n, s) and d is the private key.

Encryption: Given message m with $(m, n) = 1$, calculate $b_1 \in \{0, 1\}$ so that $\left(\frac{m}{n}\right) = (-1)^{b_1}$ and calculate $m_0 = s^{b_1} m \bmod n$. The triple $(c = m_0^2 \bmod n, b_1, b_2 = m_0 \bmod 2)$ is sent.

Decryption: Given the triple (c, b_1, b_2), calculate $m_0 = \pm c^d \bmod n$, where the sign is chosen so that $m_0 \equiv (-1)^{b_2} \pmod 2$. Then $m = s^{-b_1} m_0 \bmod n$ is the recovered text.

(a) If $\left(\frac{x}{n}\right) = 1$ and $c = x^2 \bmod n$, show that $c^d \equiv \pm x \pmod n$.

(b) Verify that the decryption procedure recovers m.

(c) Let $p = 7$, $q = 11$, and $n = pq$. Note that $p \equiv q \equiv 3 \pmod 4$. Verify that $s = 2$ satisfies $\left(\frac{s}{n}\right) = -1$. Illustrate the encryption and decryption steps for the message $m = 31$.

The basic idea used in this scheme is that a distinguished square root (among the 4 possible) can be found in the case that $n = pq$ with $p \equiv q \equiv 3 \pmod 4$. Following the notation in Williams' paper, let $[a, b]$ denote the residue class modulo n such that if $y \in [a, b]$ then $y \equiv a \pmod p$ and $y \equiv b \pmod q$.

(d) Show that $\left(\frac{-1}{p}\right) = -1$. Hence, if $(c, p) = 1$ then exactly one of $\pm c$ is a quadratic residue modulo p.

(e) If $(y, n) = 1$, show that the square roots of y^2 in $\mathbb{Z}_n$ can be written $[a, b]$, $[-a, -b]$, $[-a, b]$, and $[a, -b]$, where $a \in Q_p$ and $b \in Q_q$.

(f) If $y \in [a, b]$ or $y \in [-a, -b]$, then y is said to be a type 1 root of y^2; the other roots are said to be of type 2. Show that y is type 1 iff $\left(\frac{y}{n}\right) = 1$; hence factoring is not necessary to determine type.

(g) If y_1 and y_2 are the distinct type 1 roots, then $y_1 \equiv -y_2 \pmod{n}$ and exactly one of these roots is even.

An adversary with the ability to decrypt obtains a type 1 and a type 2 root of some number, and is then able to factor n.

(h) The adversary seeks an x with $\left(\frac{x}{n}\right) = -1$ and for which the decryption procedure can be applied to x^2. If every valid ciphertext can be decrypted, then $x = s$ may be selected. The adversary decrypts $(x^2, 0, 0)$, obtaining a type 1 root y. Verify that $(y - x, n)$ is a nontrivial factor of n.

12.4 ElGamal

The presumed intractability of the discrete logarithm problem is the basis for encryption and signature schemes proposed by ElGamal in 1985 [29]. The first recognized digital signature algorithm, adopted by the US Government in 1994 as the Digital Signature Standard (DSS), is a variant of the ElGamal signature scheme.

ElGamal encryption requires a prime p and a generator α of $\mathbb{Z}_p^*$. Each user selects a random a, $1 \le a \le p-2$, as a private key, and the corresponding public key is $(p, \alpha, \alpha^a \bmod p)$. To send a message m, $0 \le m < p$, using the public key, a random k, $1 \le k < p$, is selected, and the pair $(\alpha^k, m(\alpha^a)^k) \bmod p$ is delivered. Possession of the private key a allows recovery of m, since α^{-ak} can be computed and then $m(\alpha^a)^k \alpha^{-ak} \bmod p = m$.

Example 12.4.1 (ElGamal encryption with toy parameters) Consider the case $p = 13$. We may select generator $\alpha = 2$ of $\mathbb{Z}_{13}^*$. For the private key a, $1 \le a \le 13-2$, suppose Alice chooses $a = 6$. Alice calculates $\alpha^a \bmod p = 2^6 \bmod 13 = 12$, and publishes $(p, \alpha, \alpha^a \bmod p) = (13, 2, 12)$ as her public key.

To send a message $m = 9$, Bob selects a random k, $1 \le k < p$, perhaps $k = 3$. Using the public key, Bob delivers

$$(\gamma, \delta) = (\alpha^k, m(\alpha^a)^k) \bmod p = (2^3, 9(12)^3) \bmod 13 = (8, 4)$$

to Alice. On receipt, Alice may recover the message with her private key $a = 6$ by calculating

$$(\alpha^k)^{-a} \equiv \gamma^{-a} \equiv \gamma^{p-1-a} \equiv 8^{13-1-6} \equiv 12 \pmod{p},$$

and then $m = \delta\alpha^{-ak} \bmod p = 4 \cdot 12 \bmod 13 = 9$. Note that key-generation in this example has given $\alpha^a \equiv -1 \pmod{p}$, which is probably undesirable (see Exercise 12.4.5).

ElGamal has explicit randomization in its encryption, and a message m will map to different ciphertexts depending on the choice of the random k. This may be a desirable feature, making some attacks less feasible. Randomization added to the message in an RSA-based scheme has similar advantages. On the downside, ElGamal suffers from message expansion (since ciphertext consists of pairs of integers each as large as the message itself).

Consider the problem of interest to an adversary:

ELGAMAL: Given prime p, generator α of $\mathbb{Z}_p^*$, α^a, α^k, and $m(\alpha^a)^k$, find m.

Clearly, if there is a polynomial-time algorithm for the discrete log problem, then ELGAMAL may be solved efficiently; that is ELGAMAL $\leq$ DLP. The security is said to be based on discrete logs, although it is unknown if ELGAMAL is equivalent to DLP.

Note that the exchange of α^a and α^k is part of a Diffie-Hellman key agreement to obtain a session key α^{ak}; ElGamal then uses the session key to encrypt the message m by multiplication. An algorithm for the Diffie-Hellman problem (DHP) immediately solves the ElGamal problem. To see that DHP $\leq$ ELGAMAL, suppose we have a polynomial-time oracle for the ElGamal problem; that is, given an instance $(p, \alpha, \alpha^a, \alpha^k, m\alpha^{ak})$, the oracle returns m in polynomial time. In the Diffie-Hellman problem, we seek α^{ak} from $(p, \alpha, \alpha^a, \alpha^k)$. The oracle for ELGAMAL is given $(p, \alpha, \alpha^a, \alpha^k, 1)$, and $m = \alpha^{-ak}$ is returned; inverting can be done in polynomial time, giving α^{ak}.

Signatures

The ElGamal signature scheme uses a hash function to map a message m of arbitrary length to a message digest x, which is then signed. Verification requires the message m as part of the process, and hence ElGamal is an example of a signature scheme with appendix.

Key generation for signatures is the same as for encryption. Suppose $m \in \{0, 1\}^*$ is to be signed. A known hash function $H : \{0, 1\}^* \to \{0, \ldots, p-1\}$ is used to obtain a message digest $x = H(m)$. A random k, $1 \leq k < p$, is selected with $(k, p-1) = 1$, and then $r = \alpha^k \bmod p$ is calculated. The congruence $x \equiv ar + ks \pmod{p-1}$ is solved for s (using the private key a), and the pair (r, s) is the signature on m.

Verification from the public key uses the fact that $\alpha^x \equiv \alpha^{ar+ks} \equiv (\alpha^a)^r(\alpha^k)^s \pmod{p}$ for a valid signature. Given a purported signature (r, s) on m, $x = H(m)$ is obtained from the known hash function. The signature is accepted if $1 \leq r < p$

and the values of α^x and $(\alpha^a)^r(\alpha^k)^s$ agree (see Exercise 12.4.3 concerning the first condition).

An adversary wishing to forge a signature on a message m may calculate $x = H(m)$ and $r = \alpha^k$ for any k, but the congruence $x \equiv ar + ks \pmod{p-1}$ has unknowns a and s. However, it is possible to construct an x and signature (r,s) for which the verification condition $\alpha^x \equiv (\alpha^a)^r(\alpha^k)^s$ holds. Choose integers j,k with $1 \le k < p$ and $(k, p-1) = 1$, and let

$$
\begin{aligned}
r &= \alpha^j(\alpha^a)^k \bmod p,\\
s &= -rk^{-1} \bmod (p-1), \text{ and}\\
x &= sj \bmod (p-1).
\end{aligned}
$$

To see that (r,s) is a valid signature on x, note that $(\alpha^a)^r r^s \equiv \alpha^{ar}\alpha^{js}\alpha^{aks} \equiv \alpha^{js} \equiv \alpha^x \pmod{p}$. The signature would be accepted if a message m which hashes to x can be found. In this case, the deception is known as an *existential forgery*, since the adversary has little control over the content of m.

A more interesting break of the ElGamal signature scheme would occur if an adversary could solve $\alpha^x \equiv (\alpha^a)^r r^s \pmod{p}$ for the signature (r,s). Of course, if the private key a could be recovered (perhaps from a known signature), then the scheme is completely broken; however, recovering a from public information appears to be the discrete log problem. Solving for s in terms of r is also a discrete log problem, and solving for r in terms of s leads to a mixed exponential congruence in r for which no efficient method of solution is known.

For security, the modulus p must be sufficiently large so that the discrete log problem in $\mathbb{Z}_p^*$ is infeasible. In 1996, Menezes et al. [63] noted that "a 512 bit modulus p provides only marginal safety from concerted attack." A modulus of at least 768 bits was recommended, and 1024 bits or more should be used for long-term security. Unfortunately, the signatures are twice as long as the modulus, which may be of concern in applications such as smartcards.

The Digital Signature Standard (DSS), adopted in 1994, uses a variant of the ElGamal scheme. Although the modulus p is 512–1024 bits, a 320-bit signature is obtained on a 160-bit hash by working in a subgroup of $\mathbb{Z}_p^*$. A brief summary follows; see [63] for details on the Digital Signature Algorithm (DSA) and the Secure Hash Algorithm (SHA-1) used as the hashing function.

Key generation in DSA chooses a 160-bit prime q and a prime number p so that $q \mid p-1$ and so that p has $512 + 64t$ bits for some $0 \le t \le 8$ (for a ceiling of 1024 bits). Let β be a generator of the cyclic subgroup of order q in $\mathbb{Z}_p^*$ (see Exercise 12.4.4). A private key a, $1 \le a < q$, is randomly selected; the corresponding public key is $(p, q, \beta, \beta^a \bmod p)$.

To sign a message m, the 160-bit hash x for m is obtained. A random k, $1 \le k < q$, is selected, and then the signature (r,s) is calculated by $r = (\beta^k \bmod$

p) mod q and $s = (x + ar)k^{-1}$ mod q. Verification accepts (r,s) as a valid signature on m if the condition

$$(\beta^{xs^{-1} \bmod q}(\beta^a)^{rs^{-1} \bmod q} \bmod p) \bmod q = r$$

holds (see Exercise 12.4.4).

Exercises

12.4.2 Illustrate the ElGamal signature scheme in this toy example. Suppose Alice chooses $p = 17$, generator $\alpha = 3$ of $\mathbb{Z}_{17}^*$, and private key $a = 6$; the corresponding public key is then $(p, \alpha, \alpha^a \bmod p) = (17, 3, 15)$. The (toy) hash function H is given by $H(m) = m \bmod p$.

(a) Find the hash value x and signature (r,s) on the message $m = 26$, assuming that Alice chooses $k = 11$ (so that $(k, p-1) = 1$ is satisfied).

(b) Show the details of the verification of (r,s) on m. (Show clearly that the process does not require knowledge of the private key a.)

12.4.3 If the condition $1 \le r < p$ is not checked in the verification of an ElGamal signature, then a signature on a given message m' can be forged provided a valid signature (r,s) on some digest x with $(x, p-1) = 1$ is known. In this case, let $x' = H(m')$ and $u = x'x^{-1} \bmod (p-1)$. Define $s' = su \bmod (p-1)$ and note that the system

$$\begin{aligned} r' &\equiv ru \pmod{p-1} \\ r' &\equiv r \pmod{p} \end{aligned}$$

has a solution r' by the Chinese remainder theorem. Verify that (r', s') is a signature on m' which will be accepted if the requirement that $1 \le r' < p$ is omitted. (This exercise is adapted from [10]; see also [63, Note 11.66].)

12.4.4 This exercise examines two details in the Digital Signature Algorithm.

(a) Suppose that $g \in \mathbb{Z}_p^*$ satisfies $\beta = g^{(p-1)/q} \bmod p \ne 1$. Show that β has order q.

(b) If $s \ne 0$, show that the verification condition holds.

12.4.5 In Example 12.4.1, key-generation yielded $\alpha^a \equiv -1 \pmod{p}$. Why is this a bad choice? (Hint: what is $m(\alpha^a)^k$ for each choice of k?)

12.4.6 (Weak generators) Suppose $p \equiv 1 \pmod 4$ and the generator α of $\mathbb{Z}_p^*$ satisfies $\alpha \mid p-1$. If computing logarithms in the subgroup G of order α in $\mathbb{Z}_p^*$ is feasible, then an adversary can construct a signature (r,s) on a given message m as follows.

Let α^a be Alice's public key, and let r be defined by $p - 1 = \alpha r$.

(a) Verify that α^r is a generator of G. Hence, it is feasible to find z such that $\alpha^{rz} \equiv (\alpha^a)^r \pmod{p}$

(b) Show that $r^{(p-1)/2} \equiv -1 \pmod{p}$.

(c) Let $s = \frac{p-3}{2}(H(m) - rz) \bmod (p-1)$. Verify that (r, s) will be accepted as a signature on m.

This exercise is adapted from [10]; see also [63, Note 11.67].

12.4.7 Re-use of the random k in ElGamal could be disastrous.

(a) Suppose that the same k is used for encrypting messages m_1 and m_2. Show that an adversary in possession of the ciphertexts and $m_1 \neq 0$ can efficiently recover m_2.

(b) Suppose that messages m_1 and m_2 are signed using the same k. Show that an adversary is likely to recover the private key.

12.5 Cryptographic protocols

A framework of procedures in which cryptographic primitives are applied is known as a *protocol*, defined informally in [25] as "an algorithm for implementing a class of transactions (logical units of communication activity)." This short section introduces several protocol-related topics. Two "classical" problems are discussed: in the coin-tossing protocol, two parties (who do not trust each other) wish to flip a coin by telephone to resolve a dispute; the idea in zero-knowledge is to provide proof of possession of a secret without revealing anything about the secret itself. The need to clearly identify the assumptions in the protocol is illustrated by an active attack on the Diffie-Hellman key exchange. Even when the assumptions are clear, it may be unknown if they are in fact met in a specific case; an example of this type is given by the mental poker protocol (a fair game of poker without cards) of Shamir, Rivest, and Adleman [79], which was later shown to leak enough information to (partially) mark the cards.

When a security weakness is discovered, it is not always clear if the protocol or an underlying cryptographic function deserves the blame. Moore [64] writes: "The distinction seems to be that when a weakness is reported in a cryptosystem, the effect of which is to merely limit the scope of application or more clearly define the range of parameters that should be used for the algorithm, then the flaw discovered probably represents a protocol failure. However, if the effect is to leave the cryptosystem useless in any setting or to so severely restrict the possible range of parameters that the definition of a strong cryptofunction is infeasible, then the cryptosystem is actually 'broken'." Hence, the weakness in Exercise 12.2.4 is a protocol failure according to Moore. In Exercise 10.3.8, two apparently secure schemes were combined in such a way that encryption compromised authentication. It can be argued that this is a kind of protocol failure, although Moore's distinction would label this a broken (by design, actually) cryptosystem.

Shamir's 3-pass protocol The difference between a protocol and a cryptographic function is illustrated by Shamir's 3-pass protocol, designed to achieve confidentiality with no advance exchange of keys. A symmetric-key encryption scheme is selected with the property that $E_{k_1} E_{k_2} = E_{k_2} E_{k_1}$ for all keys k_1, k_2. Encryption can be viewed as adding a "lock" to the envelope containing the message. The following protocol delivers a message m from A to B.

1. A and B pick random private keys k_A and k_B, respectively.
2. A adds her lock to the message, sending $c_1 = E_{k_A}(m)$ to B.
3. B adds his lock, returning $c_2 = E_{k_B}(c_1) = E_{k_B} E_{k_A}(m)$ to A.
4. A removes her lock, sending $c_3 = D_{k_A}(c_2)$ to B. B decrypts c_3 to recover m.

Under suitable complexity assumptions on E, it appears that the isolated exchanges are secure from passive attacks. However, the protocol places additional (implicit) assumptions on the cipher. Consider the case that the cipher is the one-time pad, $E_k(m) = k \oplus m$. A passive adversary obtains $c_1 = k_A \oplus m$, $c_2 = k_B \oplus c_1$, and $c_3 = k_B \oplus m$. Since $c_1 \oplus c_2 \oplus c_3 = m$, the transfer is totally insecure, even though an unconditionally secure cipher was employed. Exercise 12.5.1 suggests an alternative cipher for use in this protocol.

12.5.1 Diffie-Hellman key agreement

In the key agreement described on page 279, Alice and Bob exchange $\alpha^a \bmod p$ and $\alpha^b \bmod p$ over an unsecured channel, arriving at the shared secret α^{ab}. The scheme is secure against passive attacks, but not against active attacks.

If the keys are not authenticated, then in addition to impersonation, an active adversary may mount an intruder-in-the-middle attack which will go undetected by Alice and Bob. The adversary Eve shares the secret $\alpha^{ab'}$ with Alice and $\alpha^{a'b}$ with Bob, where Eve has selected a' and b'. If Alice sends a message encrypted with a key derived from $\alpha^{ab'}$, then Eve intercepts the message, decrypts it, re-encrypts with a key derived from $\alpha^{a'b}$, and passes it on to Bob. In this fashion, Eve obtains the entire plaintext correspondence.[4]

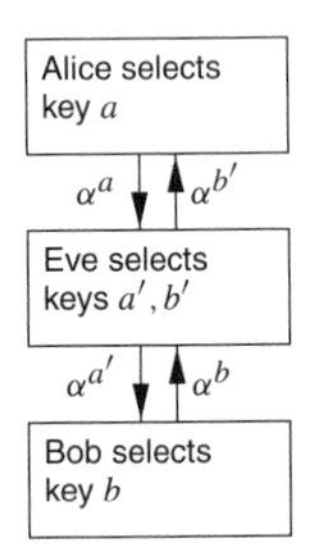

Intruder-in-the-middle

A trusted party or *Certification Authority* (CA) is sometimes used to provide authentication. After verifying the identity of an entity A, the CA forms a message containing identifying information (name, address, etc.), along with A's public key (perhaps α^a in the present context). The message is signed by the CA, forming a "certificate" C_A binding A's identity to her public key. Alice and Bob exchange

[4] See also Exercise 12.5.5 for a suggested protocol to force Eve to act nontransparently.

their certificates C_A and C_B, which include α^a and α^b, respectively. On receipt of C_A, Bob verifies the CA's signature, and is thus convinced that Alice's public key is α^a. Similarly, Alice is convinced that Bob's public key is α^b. Impersonation is still possible in the sense that an intruder may forward a certificate belonging to, say, Alice, but will not be able to form the shared secret α^{ab}.

Use of a CA in this fashion requires an expensive one-time creation of the certificate for each entity, but the verification of signatures does not require on-line support from the CA. The CA's public key must be authenticated, but secrecy is not required. On the downside, a CA providing services to a large number of clients becomes a very attractive target, and compromise of the CA may be catastrophic. Also, procedures are needed to distribute revocation information in the case that individual certificates or CA signatures become invalid.

Certificates are commonly used in secure purchases via internet. The authentication is typically one-way (the merchant delivers a certificate to the client), since client-side certificates are rare in this context. The client, perhaps using a web browser such as Netscape, maintains a list of Certification Authorities from which signatures will be accepted. There is a rather optimistic protocol assumption that the person on the client-side will actually examine the certificate. A valid certificate from http://www.delta.com offers convincing evidence that the public key for www.delta.com has been obtained; however, the person expecting to purchase plane tickets may be surprised to learn that Delta Air Lines is at the address www.delta-air.com.[5]

12.5.2 Zero-knowledge proofs

Alice (the *prover*) wishes to convince Bob (the *verifier*) that she possesses a secret s. One option open to Alice is to simply reveal the secret—of course, it is then no longer her secret. In the context of the password authentication scheme discussed in Section 10.3.2, an adversary obtains Alice's password, and can then impersonate Alice. Zero-knowledge protocols are designed to allow the prover to provide convincing evidence that she possesses the secret, without revealing anything that could be used by the verifier in subsequent demonstrations.

A rigorous discussion of zero-knowledge in interactive protocols involves non-trivial and somewhat subtle concepts. Readers interested in more formal or extensive treatments than presented in this brief overview should consult the references mentioned in Section 12.6 (where two non-mathematical introductions to zero-knowledge concepts are also noted).

As an illustration of (not necessarily zero-knowledge) proof systems, consider the problem of proving that a given $v \in J_n$ is a quadratic nonresidue, where n is a product of large and secret primes. A prover in possession of the factorization of

[5] deltaComm remarks that 8000 visitors per day access www.delta.com looking for Delta Air. In 1999, modifications in their web pages were made to minimize the data-transfer cost of the unwelcomed accesses.

n could offer irrefutable proof that $v \in \overline{Q}_n$ by exhibiting the factors. Considerably more than simply "v is indeed a quadratic nonresidue" has been revealed to the verifier, however.

A more interesting proof system for the problem is given in [40]. In this context, "proof" is understood to mean "convincing evidence" rather than certainty.

1. The verifier B chooses a security parameter $t > 0$, and random $b_i \in \{0, 1\}$ and $z_i \in \mathbb{Z}_n^*$, $1 \leq i \leq t$. B then challenges the prover A with the values $w_i = z_i^2 v^{b_i} \bmod n$, $1 \leq i \leq t$.
2. A determines (somehow) if each w_i is a quadratic residue, and gives the response $c_i = 0$ if w_i is a quadratic residue and $c_i = 1$ otherwise, $1 \leq i \leq t$.
3. B checks if $b_i = c_i$ for every i; if so, B accepts the proof (that v is a quadratic nonresidue).

If v is a quadratic nonresidue, then the challenge w_i is a quadratic residue if and only if $b_i = 0$. If t is sufficiently large, and both parties follow the protocol, then B will be convinced that v is a quadratic nonresidue. On the other hand, if v is in fact a quadratic residue, then every w_i is a quadratic residue and the probability that $b_i = c_i$ for every i is apparently 2^{-t}, making it unlikely that B will accept a claim that $v \in \overline{Q}_n$.

If both parties follow the protocol, then B learns nothing beyond what he could have calculated without A (other than the fact that prover is indeed able to respond successfully to the challenges). The protocol is not zero-knowledge, however. The verifier is not forced to follow the protocol, and may obtain responses for w_i of his choice; that is, the verifier is able to use the prover (provided the prover is not also cheating) to determine if elements of his choice (and not necessarily of the form in the protocol) are quadratic residues. A zero-knowledge version of this protocol in [40] essentially forces the verifier to play fair.

As mentioned above, one application of zero-knowledge concepts is in identification. The following protocol is built on a zero-knowledge proof that a known value v is a quadratic residue modulo n.

Protocol (Fiat-Shamir identification) A trusted center chooses an RSA-like modulus $n = pq$, keeping the factors private. The prover A obtains a secret $s \in \mathbb{Z}_n^*$ from the trusted center; $v = s^2 \bmod n$ is A's public key. The prover convinces the verifier B of her possession of s by successfully completing the following 3-pass protocol t times, where $t > 0$ is a security parameter.

1. A chooses a random *commitment* r, $1 \leq r < n$, and sends the *witness* $x = r^2 \bmod n$ to B.
2. B replies with a random *challenge* $e \in \{0, 1\}$.
3. A's *response* is $y = rs^e \bmod n$.
4. B verifies that $y \neq 0$ and $y^2 \equiv xv^e \pmod{n}$.

B accepts the proof if all t rounds succeed.

The verifier learns nothing about s: the response $y = r$ is independent of s, and the random r in the response $y = rs$ is unknown to B. In each round, an adversary impersonating A can cheat successfully if the challenge can be predicted: if $e = 0$ is expected, the witness and response are unchanged; if $e = 1$ is expected, then $x = r^2 v^{-1}$ is selected as the witness and $y = r$ as the response. Since the challenges are selected at random, the probability of a successful prediction is only $1/2$ for each round. Exercise 12.5.2 shows that such an imposter is likely to be detected. This inability to predict the challenges also thwarts a replay attack from an adversary in possession of a transcript from a valid protocol session.

12.5.3 Coin-tossing and mental poker

Two additional cryptographic protocols are considered in this section, giving a glimpse of the wide range of applications addressed by such protocols, and further emphasizing the need to identify protocol assumptions and verify that these requirements are met. Section 12.6 contains references to many other applications and attacks on such protocols.

Coin-tossing by telephone was suggested by Blum [11]. Alice and Bob have experienced a messy divorce, and wish to flip a coin by telephone to see who gets the kids. The predicament seems to be that neither party is willing to go first in declaring their call or in announcing the result of the toss. The basic idea in the following protocol is that Alice commits to "heads" or "tails" and announces the commitment in a way that conceals the choice but binds her to the selection. Bob makes his guess at her choice, and then Alice reveals information which makes the commitment public. The security depends on the intractability of the quadratic residuosity problem.

Protocol (coin-tossing)

1. Alice selects $n = pq$ for odd primes $p \neq q$ and a random $x \in J_n$, and announces n and x to Bob.
2. Bob responds with either "$x \in Q_n$" or "$x \in \tilde{Q}_n$" (with 50% chance of being correct, assuming QRP is hard).
3. Alice reveals p and q. Bob verifies that p and q are indeed prime (and that $x \in J_n$); the correctness of Bob's response is determined by $\left(\frac{x}{p}\right)$.

If Bob fails to verify that p and q are prime, then Alice can cheat by forming $n = p_1 p_2 p_3$ for primes p_i, and choosing x with $\left(\frac{x}{p_1}\right) = \left(\frac{x}{p_2}\right) = -1$ and $\left(\frac{x}{p_3}\right) = 1$ (so that $\left(\frac{x}{n}\right) = 1$). Once Bob announces his guess, then Alice reveals the pair $(p = p_1 p_2, q = p_3)$ or $(p = p_1, q = p_2 p_3)$, depending on the outcome she desires (e.g., if she wants Bob to think that x is a quadratic residue, then she reveals the former).

Mental poker Cryptographers are apparently quite interested in a fair game of poker without cards. In 1979, Shamir, Rivest, and Adleman suggested a protocol for dealing, published in *The Mathematical Gardner* in 1981. The basic idea is to use Shamir's 3-pass protocol. Alice and Bob agree on a set of messages m_i, $1 \le i \le 52$, identifying the 52 cards. Alice encrypts these messages, sending $E_{k_A}(m_i)$, $1 \le i \le 52$, in random order. Bob selects five ciphertexts as Alice's hand, and returns them to her. He encrypts an additional five ciphertexts with E_{k_B}, sends these to Alice, who removes her locks with D_{k_A} and returns the results as Bob's hand.

Encryption with RSA-like key-generation was suggested. Alice and Bob agree on a modulus n (prime or a product of distinct odd primes), and each selects a secret key-pair $k = (e,d)$ with $(e,\phi(n)) = 1$ and $ed \equiv 1 \pmod{\phi(n)}$, and then $E_k(m) = m^e \bmod n$ and $D_k(c) = c^d \bmod n$. The key-pairs are revealed at the end of the game.

Unfortunately, shortly after the scheme was proposed, Lipton showed that the suggested function fails to meet an implicit assumption in the protocol, that the cards cannot be marked [25]. The Jacobi symbol can be efficiently calculated, and the value is preserved by encryption; i.e., $\left(\frac{m}{n}\right) = \left(\frac{m}{n}\right)^e = \left(\frac{m^e}{n}\right)$. Unless the Jacobi symbol gives the same result for every m_i, Bob can select cards with a specific Jacobi symbol to return to Alice, possibly offering an advantage. This particular attack may be defeated by choosing encodings m_i which are all quadratic residues. The interested poker player may find references in Section 12.6 for suggested protocols and ways to cheat.

Exercises

12.5.1 In Shamir's 3-pass protocol, suppose that $E_k(m) = m^k \bmod p$ for suitable prime p.

(a) Verify that the encryption scheme meets the commutativity requirement for use in the protocol.

(b) How will k_A and k_B be selected? Find c_1, c_2, and c_3 in the exchange.

(c) Discuss the security.

12.5.2 This exercise concerns the Fiat-Shamir identification protocol.

(a) Show that if an impersonator successfully predicts a challenge e, then the witness x and response y will be accepted by the verification step.

(b) If the prediction turns out to be incorrect, explain why the impersonator is likely to be discovered.

12.5.3 (Proof of possession of a discrete log [20, 19]) Let p be prime and g an element of prime order q in $\mathbb{Z}_p^*$. Entity A has private key s, $1 \le s < q$, and public key $S = g^s \bmod p$. A proves knowledge of s to B in $t > 0$ rounds.

1. A chooses random commitment x, $1 \le x < q$, and sends the witness $X = g^x \bmod p$ to B.
2. B replies with a random challenge $e \in \{0, 1\}$.
3. A's response is $y = x$ if $e = 0$, or $y = sx^{-1} \bmod q$ if $e = 1$.
4. B checks that $X = g^y \bmod p$ if $e = 0$, or that $S = X^y \bmod p$ if $e = 1$.

B accepts the proof if all t rounds succeed.

(a) If both parties follow the protocol, verify that B will accept.

(b) Indicate how an imposter can cheat, assuming that the challenges can be predicted (but s is unknown).

(c) Discuss the dilemma faced by an adversary in the case that a prediction turns out to be incorrect.

12.5.4 Consider the following proposed identification scheme. A certification authority binds Alice's identity to $n = pq$, where n is public and the primes $p \ne q$ are Alice's secret.

1. Bob challenges Alice with x, a random quadratic residue modulo n.
2. Alice's response is a square root y of x.
3. Bob verifies that $y^2 \equiv x \pmod{n}$.

If several rounds are performed successfully, will Bob be convinced that Alice possesses the secret? Explain why this scheme is seriously flawed.

12.5.5 (Key agreement in the presence of active adversaries) Suppose that Alice and Bob can rely on voice recognition during key agreement. Rather than using the Diffie-Hellman shared secret α^{ab} directly, Alice and Bob establish a voice connection, and each reads a portion of α^{ab}. After verifying these pieces of α^{ab}, the remaining portion becomes the shared secret k.

(a) Assume that the adversary cannot efficiently recover k from α^a, α^b, and the leaked portions of α^{ab}. Will Alice and Bob be convinced that the adversary does not know k?

Rivest and Shamir [72] suggest a protocol change which forces an intruder-in-the-middle to act non-transparently (and thus possibly revealing her presence). Alice is to select a message m and send half of $E_k(m)$, where k is the key that she has calculated (possibly shared with the intruder rather than with Bob); Bob will reply with half of the ciphertext for his selected message. Alice then transmits the remaining part of $E_k(m)$, and Bob responds similarly.

(b) Assume that fragments of plaintext cannot be discovered from possession of only half of $E_k(m)$. Discuss the options open to the adversary (in particular, describe what happens if she simply forwards the half of $E_k(m)$ from Alice's first transmission).

12.5.6 (Subliminal channel) Authentication schemes may permit an undetectable covert channel between parties. Simmons [82, 83] suggests the following scenario.

> *Prisoners' problem.* Two accomplices in a crime have been arrested and are about to be locked in widely separated cells. Their only means of communication after they are locked up will be by way of messages conveyed for them by trustees—who are known to be agents of the warden. The warden is willing to allow the prisoners to exchange messages in the hope that he can deceive at least one of them into accepting as a genuine communication from the other either a fraudulent message created by the warden himself or else a modification by him of a genuine message. However, since he has every reason to suspect that the prisoners want to coordinate an escape plain, the warden will only permit the exchanges to occur if the information contained in the messages is completely open to him—and presumably innocuous. The prisoners, on the other hand, are willing to accept these conditions, i.e., to accept some risk of deception in order to be able to communicate at all, since they need to coordinate their plans. To do this they will have to deceive the warden by finding a way of communicating secretly in the exchanges, i.e., of establishing a "subliminal channel" between them in full view of the warden, even though the messages themselves contain no secret (to the warden) information. Since they anticipate that the warden will try to deceive them by introducing fraudulent messages, they will only exchange messages if they are permitted to authenticate them.

The ElGamal signature scheme allows such a subliminal channel to be established between prisoners Alice and Bob. Key-generation for Alice remains unchanged: Alice chooses prime p, generator α of $\mathbb{Z}_p^*$, and a private a, $1 \leq a \leq p-2$; her public key is $(p, \alpha, \alpha^a \bmod p)$.

Normally, Alice signs a message m by selecting a random $k < p$ with $(k, p-1) = 1$ and computing (r, s), where $r = \alpha^k \bmod p$ and s is obtained from $H(m) \equiv ar + ks \pmod{p-1}$; then (m, r, s) is delivered to Bob through the warden. However, if Alice can arrange to share the secret a with Bob, then k may be used to transport the hidden message.[6]

(a) If Alice and Bob share a, identify conditions on s which will allow Bob to efficiently recover the subliminal message k from (m, r, s).

Given her current predicament, Alice may be willing to share her secret a with Bob (even though it means that Bob will be able to forge her signature), although

[6] Although an ElGamal signature (r, s) may require $2\log_2 p$ bits, there are only $\log_2 p$ bits of security; the remaining bits are available for the subliminal channel. However, since k is relatively prime to $p-1$, only $\phi(p-1)$ distinct messages k may be sent, and it may be infeasible to recover those for which $xs \equiv H(m) - ar \pmod{p-1}$ has many solutions x. Simmons [85, 84] observes that these "shortcomings" are avoided in the DSA, the "most hospitable setting for subliminal communications discovered to date."

a method of securely delivering a is required. Young and Yung describe a SETUP (see Exercise 12.2.14) which may allow Alice to leak her private key to Bob, provided that Bob has a public key $(p, \alpha, \alpha^b \bmod p)$ known to Alice. Alice contaminates her signing process, producing (m_1, r_1, s_1) and (m_2, r_2, s_2) in such a way that possession of b permits recovery of a.

To leak a, Alice attempts to select a random k_1 with k_1, $\beta = (\alpha^b)^{k_1} \bmod p$, and $\alpha^{\beta^{-1}} \bmod p$ relatively prime to $p-1$, where β^{-1} satisfies $\beta\beta^{-1} \equiv 1 \pmod{p-1}$. Rather than choosing k_2 at random, Alice selects $k_2 = \beta^{-1}$. Finally, let $r_i = \alpha^{k_i} \bmod p$ and $s_i = (H(m_i) - ar_i)k_i^{-1} \bmod (p-1)$, $i \in \{1, 2\}$, as usual.

(b) Show that Bob can recover a by calculating $r_2^{-1}(H(m_2) - s_2/(r_1^b \bmod p)) \bmod (p-1)$.

(c) As an illustration, consider the toy example with $p = 13$ and $\alpha = 2$. Verify that β and $\alpha^{\beta^{-1}} \bmod p$ are relatively prime to $p-1$ if $b = 5$ and $k_1 = 7$. If $b = 3$, then show that Alice is unable to find k_1 satisfying the desired properties.

12.6 Notes

In addition to the schemes covered here, cryptographic methods based on elliptic curves have attracted considerable interest, in part because security is apparently maintained with shorter keys when compared with, say, RSA. The Elliptic Curve Digital Signature Algorithm (ECDSA, an elliptic curve analogue of the Digital Signature Algorithm) was accepted by the American National Standards Institute in 1999 (ANSI X9.62). Johnson and Menezes [44] discuss design decisions and related security, implementation, and interoperability issues for ECDSA; their paper also includes a short primer on elliptic curves. Koblitz [50] and Stinson [86] contain introductions to elliptic curves and applications to cryptography; more advanced texts on elliptic curve methods include Blake, Seroussi, and Smart [8] and Menezes [62].

Public-key methods were known to British cryptographers in the early 1970s, according to technical reports released by the Communications-Electronics Security Group (CESG) in December 1997 [31]. Known as "non-secret encryption" within CESG [30], an RSA-like scheme appears in Cocks [21] and the ideas of the Diffie-Hellman key agreement are given in Williamson [100].[7]

[7] CESG remarks "It is interesting to note that although many different ideas for public-key systems have been proposed, the two which have stood the test of time were the first two to be discovered. It is also interesting that the order of discovery in academia was the opposite to the order of discovery at CESG." Williamson [100] offers a few cautionary words in his introduction: "One of the reasons for the delay in writing this is that I find myself in an embarrassing position; having written [99], I have come to doubt the whole theory of non-secret encryption. The trouble is that I have no proof that the method of [99] is genuinely secure, in other words that it has a guaranteed work-factor involved in breaking it."

Well-known applications that combine public-key and symmetric-key methods to provide authentication and confidentiality include Pretty Good Privacy (PGP) [37, 104] and (at the systems level) Sun Microsystems' remote procedure call (RPC) mechanism [88, 70]. It is interesting to note that a portion of the security in Sun's scheme rested on exponentiation modulo a 192-bit prime, considered insecure even in 1991 [54]. Vulnerability assessments must consider the larger framework of network security, which involves much more than cryptographic primitives. Indeed, security problems often do not directly involve cryptography. The 1990s saw a flood of security alerts and system compromises due to buffer overruns (caused by contrived messages which exceed implicit length assumptions) and shell escapes (privileged processing triggered by messages containing unexpected characters), some of which were in the very programs implementing security mechanisms.

The material on zero-knowledge is adapted from Goldwasser, Micali, and Rackoff [40] and Menezes, van Oorshot, and Vanstone [63]; see also Chapter 13 of Stinson [86]. Brassard and Crépeau [18] sort out various notions of zero-knowledge.

Interesting (or at least amusing) non-mathematical introductions to zero-knowledge have been presented at CRYPTO rump sessions. Quisquater, Guillou, and Berson [68] explore "The Strange Cave of Ali Baba," which has an entry forking to passages with apparent dead ends. An interactive test is devised so that a claimant can provide convincing proof of possession of magic words which open a corridor between the dead ends, without revealing the secret itself. The claimant, who has entered the cave alone some time earlier, is asked to return using a passage selected by a witness placed at the fork. The process is repeated until the witness is convinced that the claimant possesses the magic words.[8]

In the CRYPTO '98 rump session [65], zero-knowledge was introduced with the help of *Where's Waldo* [41], a game where a certain figure (Waldo) is to be located within a complicated illustration. Alice wishes to prove to Bob that she has found Waldo, but does not want to reveal the solution. She could use her scissors to carefully remove Waldo from the background, but perhaps Bob will not be convinced, accusing her of using an image from some other source. Alice's solution is to use an opaque sheet of paper, twice the size of the illustration, with a small window in which to isolate Waldo.

Overviews on protocols (and attacks) for applications ranging from secret sharing and subliminal channels to anonymous digital cash and voting schemes appear in Salomaa [75], Seberry and Pieprzyk [77], and Schneier [76]. Simmons [84] gives a survey of subliminal channels, beginning with a historical introduction concerning verification proposals for the Strategic Arms Limitation Treaty (SALT II). Suggested protocols and ways to cheat at mental poker may be found in Fortune and Merritt [33] and Coppersmith [22] and the references therein.

[8] The proof could have been provided in one step by asking the claimant to complete the loop beginning at the fork, rather spoiling the story (and the analogy with mathematical zero-knowledge).

Appendix A

The Euclidean Algorithm

The greatest common divisor (or gcd) of two polynomials $f(x), g(x) \in K[x]$ is the polynomial $d(x) \in K[x]$ of largest degree such that $f(x) = q_1(x)d(x)$ and $g(x) = q_2(x)d(x)$; we will denote this by $\gcd(f(x), g(x)) = d(x)$.

Example A.1 We find the greatest common divisor of $f(x)$ and $g(x)$ assuming that we know the factorization of $f(x)$ and $g(x))$ into irreducible polynomials where $f(x) = 1+x^2+x^3+x^6+x^7+x^8 = (1+x)(1+x+x^3)(1+x^4)$ and $g(x) = 1+x^3+x^5+x^6 = (1+x)(1+x^2)(1+x+x^3)$. The polynomial of highest degree which is a common factor of both $f(x)$ and $g(x)$ is $1+x+x^3$. Thus

$$\gcd(f(x), g(x)) = 1+x+x^3.$$

Factoring $f(x)$ and $g(x)$, then hunting for the common factor of highest degree, is not an efficient way to find the greatest common divisor. Below we give a famous algorithm for accomplishing this task more readily.

Euclidean Algorithm Given $f(x), g(x) \in K[x]$ with degree $f(x) \geq$ degree $g(x)$ and $g(x) \neq 0$

1. (Initialize) $r_0(x) = f(x), r_1(x) = g(x), i = 1$.
2. While $r_i(x) > 0$, divide $r_i(x)$ into $r_{i-1}(x)$ and let $r_{i+1}(x)$ be the remainder. That is $r_{i+1}(x) = r_{i-1}(x) \bmod r_i(x)$. Increment i and repeat.
3. $r_i(x) = 0$. Then $\gcd(f(x), g(x)) = r_{i-1}(x)$.

Note that this algorithm must stop, after a finite number of steps, since for each $i > 1$, the degree of the remainder $r_{i+1}(x)$ is less than the degree of the remainder $r_i(x)$.

We can modify this algorithm to produce polynomial $t_i(x), s_i(x) \in K[x]$ such that

$$t_i(x)f(x) + s_i(x)g(x) = r_i(x) \text{ for } i = 0, 1, \ldots$$

Define

$$t_0(x) = 1 \qquad t_1(x) = 0$$
$$s_0(x) = 0 \qquad s_1(x) = 1$$

Assuming that $r_{i-1}(x) = q_i(x)r_i(x) + r_{i+1}(x)$ (using the Division Algorithm) define

$$t_i(x) = q_{i-1}(x)t_{i-1}(x) + t_{i-2}(x)$$
$$s_i(x) = q_{i-1}(x)s_{i-1}(x) + s_{i-2}(x) \quad \text{for } i = 2, \ldots.$$

Then

$$r_j(x) = (-1)^j[-t_j(x)r_0(x) + s_j(x)r_i(x)]$$
$$= t_j(x)r_0(x) + s_j(x)r_1(x).$$

Since we are working over the binary field we can ignore the minus signs.

Example A.2 We use the Euclidean Algorithm to find the greatest common divisor of the polynomials

$$f(x) = x^2 + x^3 + x^6 + x^7$$
$$g(x) = 1 + x^3 + x^4 + x^5.$$

The computations proceed as follows. Set $i = 0, r_0(x) = f(x)$ and $r_1(x) = g(x)$. Dividing $r_1(x)$ into $r_0(x)$ yields

$$x^2 + x^3 + x^6 + x^7 = (1 + x^3 + x^4 + x^5)(1 + x^2) + (1 + x^4).$$

Thus $r_2(x) = 1 + x^4$ and $q_2(x) = 1 + x^2$. Dividing $r_2(x)$ into $r_1(x)$ yields

$$1 + x^3 + x^4 + x^5 = (1 + x^4)(1 + x) + (x + x^3).$$

Thus $r_3(x) = x + x^3$ and $q_3(x) = 1 + x$. Next,

$$1 + x^4 = (x + x^3)(x) + (1 + x^2).$$

Thus $r_4(x) = 1 + x^2$ and $q_4(x) = x$. Next

$$x + x^3 = (1 + x^2)(x) + 0,$$

so $r_5(x) = 0$. Since the last nonzero remainder is $r_4(x) = 1 + x^2$, $r_4(x)$ is the required common divisor of $f(x)$ and $g(x)$:

$$1 + x^2 = \gcd(1 + x^3 + x^4 + x^5, x^2 + x^6 + x^7).$$

In this example, we could also compute $t_i(x)$ and $s_i(x)$ using the quotients $q_i(x)$ computed in each iteration of (see table below). We claim that for each $i, i = 0, 1, 2, 3, 4$

$$r_i(x) = t_i(x)f(x) + s_i(x)g(x).$$

It is obviously true for $i = 0, 1$, and $i = 2$ since $r_0(x) + q_1(x)r_1(x) = r_2(x)$. For $i = 3$ we have

$$\begin{aligned} r_3(x) = x + x^3 &= (1+x)f(x) + (x + x^2 + x^3)g(x) \\ &= (1+x)(x^2 + x^3 + x^6 + x^7) \\ &\quad + (x + x^2 + x^3)(1 + x^3 + x^4 + x^5), \end{aligned}$$
$$\text{and } r_4(x) = 1 + x^2 = (1 + x + x^2)f(x) + (1 + x^3 + x^4)g(x).$$

Summarizing, we get:

i	$t_i(x)$	$s_i(x)$	$r_i(x)$
0	1	0	$f(x)$
1	0	1	$g(x)$
2	1	$1+x^2$	$1+x^4$
3	$1+x$	$x+x^2+x^3$	$x+x^3$
4	$1+x+x^2$	$1+x^3+x^4$	$1+x^2$
	–	–	0

Using induction one can prove the following.

Theorem A.3 *If* $\gcd(f(x), g(x)) = d(x)$ *then there exist polynomials* $t(x)$ *and* $s(x)$ *in* $K[x]$ *such that*

$$t(x)f(x) + s(x)g(x) = d(x).$$

Exercises

A.4 Find the greatest common divisor of each of the following pairs of polynomials.

(a) $f(x) = 1 + x + x^5 + x^6 + x^7, g(x) = 1 + x + x^3 + x^5$

(b) $f(x) = 1 + x^2 + x^3 + x^7, g(x) = 1 + x + x^3$

(c) $f(x) = 1 + x + x^4 + x^5 + x^8 + x^9, g(x) = 1 + x^2 + x^3 + x^7$

(d) $f(x) = 1 + x + x^2 + x^3 + x^4, g(x) = x + x^3 + x^4$

A.5 Find $\gcd(f(x), g(x))$ for $f(x) = 1 + x^9$ and $g(x)$ as given in each part.

(a) $g(x) = x + x^2 + x^4 + x^5 + x^7 + x^8$

(b) $g(x) = x^3 + x^6$

(c) $g(x) = 1 + x + x^2 + x^4 + x^5 + x^7 + x^8$

(d) $g(x) = 1 + x^3 + x^6$
(e) $g(x) = x + x^2 + x^3 + x^4 + x^5 + x^6 + x^7 + x^8$

A.6 Find $\gcd(f(x), g(x))$ for $f(x) = 1 + x^{15}$ and $g(x) = x + x^2 + x^4 + x^8$.

A.7 Find $\gcd(f(x), g(x))$ for $f(x) = 1 + x^{23}$ and

$$g(x) = x + x^2 + x^3 + x^4 + x^6 + x^8 + x^9 + x^{12} + x^{13} + x^{16} + x^{18}.$$

Appendix B

Factorization of $1+x^n$

The factorization of $1+x^n$ into irreducible polynomials for $1 \leq n \leq 31$, n odd.

n	Factorization
1	$1+x$
3	$(1+x)(1+x+x^2)$
5	$(1+x)(1+x+x^2+x^3+x^4)$
7	$(1+x)(1+x+x^3)(1+x^2+x^3)$
9	$(1+x)(1+x+x^2)(1+x^3+x^6)$
11	$(1+x)(1+x+\cdots+x^{10})$
13	$(1+x)(1+x+\cdots+x^{12})$
15	$(1+x)(1+x+x^2)(1+x+x^2+x^3+x^4)(1+x+x^4)(1+x^3+x^4)$
17	$(1+x)(1+x+x^2+x^4+x^6+x^7+x^8)(1+x^3+x^4+x^5+x^8)$
19	$(1+x)(1+x+x^2+\cdots+x^{18})$
21	$(1+x)(1+x+x^2)(1+x^2+x^3)(1+x+x^3)$ $(1+x^2+x^4+x^5+x^6)(1+x+x^2+x^4+x^6)$
23	$(1+x)(1+x+x^5+x^6+x^7+x^9+x^{11})$ $(1+x^2+x^4+x^5+x^6+x^{10}+x^{11})$
25	$(1+x)(1+x+x^2+x^3+x^4)(1+x^5+x^{10}+x^{15}+x^{20})$
27	$(1+x)(1+x+x^2)(1+x^3+x^6)(1+x^9+x^{18})$
29	$(1+x)(1+x+\cdots+x^{28})$
31	$(1+x)(1+x^2+x^5)(1+x^3+x^5)(1+x+x^2+x^3+x^5)$ $(1+x+x^2+x^4+x^5)(1+x+x^3+x^4+x^5)(1+x^2+x^3+x^4+x^5)$

Appendix C

Example of Compact Disc Encoding

Since it would take too much space and time to do an example of Compact Disc encoding (see section 7.3), let us scale it down to something reasonable to do by hand. Consider the Reed-Solomon code C over $GF(2^4)$ with generator $g(x) = (1+x)(\beta+x)(\beta^2+x)(\beta^3+x) = \beta^6 + \beta^0 x + \beta^4 x^2 + \beta^{12} x^3 + x^4$. This is a $(15, 11, 5)$ code, which we could shorten to an $(8, 4, 5)$ code C_1 or a $(12, 8, 5)$ code C_2. These could be delay interleaved by two columns and to a depth of 8.

A message stream such as m would first be encoded to a codeword c in the code C_1 by using some generating matrix (see Table C.1).

$$
m = \begin{array}{cccc}
\beta^4 & 0 & 0 & \beta^3 \\
\beta^1 & \beta^{12} & \beta^3 & 0 \\
0 & 0 & \beta^2 & \beta^4 \\
0 & 0 & 0 & \beta^{13} \\
\beta^1 & 0 & 0 & 0 \\
0 & \beta^3 & \beta^2 & 0 \\
0 & 0 & 0 & 0 \\
\beta^4 & \beta^4 & 0 & \beta^1 \\
0 & 0 & 0 & 0 \\
0 & 0 & 0 & 0 \\
\beta^1 & 0 & 0 & 0 \\
0 & 0 & 0 & 0 \\
0 & 0 & 0 & 0 \\
0 & 0 & 0 & 0 \\
0 & 0 & 0 & 0
\end{array}
\rightarrow c = \begin{array}{cccccccc}
\beta^{10} & \beta^4 & \beta^8 & \beta^3 & \beta^7 & \beta^7 & \beta^0 & \beta^3 \\
\beta^7 & \beta^9 & \beta^4 & \beta^{10} & \beta^4 & \beta^{11} & \beta^3 & 0 \\
0 & 0 & \beta^8 & \beta^4 & \beta^{12} & \beta^6 & \beta^5 & \beta^4 \\
0 & 0 & 0 & \beta^4 & \beta^{13} & \beta^2 & \beta^{10} & \beta^{13} \\
\beta^7 & \beta^1 & \beta^5 & \beta^{13} & \beta^1 & 0 & 0 & 0 \\
0 & \beta^9 & \beta^{13} & \beta^{12} & \beta^{13} & \beta^0 & \beta^2 & 0 \\
0 & 0 & 0 & 0 & 0 & 0 & 0 & 0 \\
\beta^{10} & \beta^2 & \beta^5 & \beta^6 & \beta^4 & \beta^8 & \beta^{13} & \beta^1 \\
0 & 0 & 0 & 0 & 0 & 0 & 0 & 0 \\
0 & 0 & 0 & 0 & 0 & 0 & 0 & 0 \\
\beta^7 & \beta^1 & \beta^5 & \beta^{13} & \beta^1 & 0 & 0 & 0 \\
0 & 0 & 0 & \beta^6 & \beta^0 & \beta^4 & \beta^{12} & \beta^0 \\
0 & 0 & 0 & 0 & 0 & 0 & 0 & 0 \\
0 & 0 & 0 & 0 & 0 & 0 & 0 & 0 \\
0 & 0 & 0 & 0 & 0 & 0 & 0 & 0\ldots
\end{array}
$$

Table C.1: *Message stream and first encoding.*

To delay interleave these codewords in C_1, they should be viewed as

$$
\begin{array}{ccccccccccccccccccc}
\beta^{10} & \beta^{7} & 0 & 0 & \beta^{7} & 0 & 0 & \beta^{10} & 0 & 0 & \beta^{7} & 0 & 0 & 0 & 0 & \ldots & & & \\
 & & \beta^{4} & \beta^{9} & 0 & 0 & \beta^{1} & \beta^{9} & 0 & \beta^{2} & 0 & 0 & \beta^{1} & 0 & 0 & 0 & 0 & \ldots & \\
 & & & & \beta^{8} & \beta^{4} & \beta^{8} & 0 & \beta^{5} & \beta^{13} & 0 & \beta^{5} & 0 & 0 & \beta^{5} & 0 & 0 & 0 & 0 \\
 & & & & & & \beta^{3} & \beta^{10} & \beta^{4} & \beta^{4} & \beta^{13} & \beta^{12} & 0 & \beta^{6} & 0 & 0 & \beta^{13} & \beta^{6} & 0 \\
 & & & & & & & & \beta^{7} & \beta^{4} & \beta^{12} & \beta^{13} & \beta^{1} & \beta^{13} & 0 & \beta^{4} & 0 & 0 & \beta^{1} \\
 & & & & & & & & & & \beta^{7} & \beta^{11} & \beta^{6} & \beta^{2} & 0 & \beta^{0} & 0 & \beta^{8} & 0 \\
 & & & & & & & & & & & & \beta^{0} & \beta^{3} & \beta^{5} & \beta^{10} & 0 & \beta^{2} & 0 \\
 & & & & & & & & & & & & & & \beta^{3} & 0 & \beta^{4} & \beta^{13} & 0
\end{array}
$$

The columns of this array are then viewed as messages and encoded to codewords in C_2 with each row of the following array a codeword:

$$
\begin{array}{cccccccccccc}
\beta^{1} & \beta^{10} & \beta^{14} & \beta^{7} & \beta^{10} & 0 & 0 & 0 & 0 & 0 & 0 & 0 \\
\beta^{13} & \beta^{7} & \beta^{11} & \beta^{4} & \beta^{7} & 0 & 0 & 0 & 0 & 0 & 0 & 0 \\
0 & \beta^{10} & \beta^{4} & \beta^{8} & \beta^{1} & \beta^{4} & 0 & 0 & 0 & 0 & 0 & 0 \\
0 & \beta^{0} & \beta^{9} & \beta^{13} & \beta^{6} & \beta^{9} & 0 & 0 & 0 & 0 & 0 & 0 \\
\beta^{13} & \beta^{7} & \beta^{10} & \beta^{5} & \beta^{2} & \beta^{5} & \beta^{8} & 0 & 0 & 0 & 0 & 0 \\
0 & 0 & \beta^{10} & \beta^{4} & \beta^{8} & \beta^{1} & \beta^{4} & 0 & 0 & 0 & 0 & 0 \\
0 & \beta^{7} & \beta^{7} & \beta^{14} & \beta^{9} & \beta^{12} & \beta^{2} & \beta^{3} & 0 & 0 & 0 & 0 \\
\beta^{1} & \beta^{5} & \beta^{4} & \beta^{2} & \beta^{6} & \beta^{4} & \beta^{7} & \beta^{10} & 0 & 0 & 0 & 0 \\
0 & 0 & \beta^{11} & \beta^{0} & \beta^{2} & \beta^{9} & \beta^{9} & 0 & \beta^{7} & 0 & 0 & 0 \\
0 & \beta^{8} & \beta^{10} & \beta^{5} & \beta^{14} & \beta^{8} & \beta^{9} & \beta^{0} & \beta^{4} & 0 & 0 & 0 \\
\beta^{13} & \beta^{7} & \beta^{11} & 0 & \beta^{11} & \beta^{5} & \beta^{11} & \beta^{14} & \beta^{6} & \beta^{7} & 0 & 0 \\
0 & 0 & \beta^{11} & \beta^{11} & \beta^{5} & \beta^{11} & \beta^{5} & \beta^{14} & \beta^{3} & \beta^{11} & 0 & 0 \\
0 & \beta^{7} & \beta^{1} & \beta^{5} & \beta^{5} & \beta^{12} & \beta^{5} & \beta^{7} & \beta^{14} & \beta^{4} & \beta^{0} & 0 \\
0 & 0 & 0 & \beta^{12} & \beta^{12} & \beta^{12} & \beta^{1} & \beta^{12} & \beta^{12} & \beta^{8} & \beta^{3} & 0 \\
0 & 0 & \beta^{11} & \beta^{5} & \beta^{9} & \beta^{2} & \beta^{3} & \beta^{6} & \beta^{1} & \beta^{12} & \beta^{10} & \beta^{3} \\
0 & 0 & 0 & 0 & \beta^{10} & \beta^{12} & \beta^{5} & \beta^{5} & \beta^{8} & \beta^{9} & \beta^{10} & 0 \\
0 & 0 & 0 & \beta^{4} & \beta^{13} & \beta^{2} & \beta^{10} & \beta^{9} & \beta^{4} & \beta^{8} & \beta^{1} & \beta^{4} \\
0 & 0 & 0 & \beta^{12} & \beta^{6} & \beta^{11} & \beta^{3} & \beta^{2} & \beta^{10} & \beta^{3} & \beta^{4} & \beta^{13} \\
0 & 0 & 0 & 0 & \beta^{7} & \beta^{1} & \beta^{5} & \beta^{13} & \beta^{1} & 0 & 0 & 0\ldots
\end{array}
$$

In binary, these codewords would be:

0100 1110 1001 1101 1110 0000 0000 0000 0000 0000 0000 0000
1011 1101 0111 1100 1101 0000 0000 0000 0000 0000 0000 0000
0000 1110 1100 1010 0100 1100 0000 0000 0000 0000 0000 0000
0000 1000 0101 1011 0011 0101 0000 0000 0000 0000 0000 0000
1011 1101 1110 0110 0010 0110 1010 0000 0000 0000 0000 0000
0000 0000 1110 1100 1010 0100 1100 0000 0000 0000 0000 0000
0000 1101 1101 1001 0101 1111 0010 0001 0000 0000 0000 0000
0100 0110 1100 0010 0011 1100 1101 1110 0000 0000 0000 0000
0000 0000 0111 1000 0010 0101 0101 0000 1101 0000 0000 0000
0000 1010 1110 0110 1001 1010 0101 1000 1100 0000 0000 0000
1011 1101 0111 0000 0111 0110 0111 1001 0011 1101 0000 0000
0000 0000 0111 0111 0110 0111 0110 1001 0001 0111 0000 0000
0000 1101 0100 0110 0110 1111 0110 1101 1001 1100 1000 0000
0000 0000 1111 1111 1111 0100 1111 1111 1010 0001 0000 0000
0000 0000 0111 0110 0101 0010 0001 0011 0100 1111 1110 0001
0000 0000 0000 0000 1110 1111 0110 0110 1010 0101 1110 0000
0000 0000 0000 1100 1011 0010 1110 0101 1100 1010 0100 1100
0000 0000 0000 1111 0011 0111 0001 0010 1110 0001 1100 1011
0000 0000 0000 0000 1101 0100 0110 1011 0100 0000 0000 0000...

This could be modulated from 4-bit strings to 6-bit strings (say, having the property that at least 1 and at most 4 zeros occur between ones) by using the following table look-up:

0000	000100	0001	010001
1000	000101	1001	101000
0100	001010	0101	101001
1100	001001	1101	101010
0010	001000	0011	100100
1010	010100	1011	100101
0110	010101	0111	100010
1110	010010	1111	100001

Between 6-bit words, a bit is added (the nor of the two neighboring end bits) to maintain this property. The original message stream m (see Table C.1) would then finally appear as:

001010 1 010010 0 101000 0 101010 1 010010 1 000100 1
000100 1 000100 1 000100 1 000100 1 000100 1 000100 0–
100101 0 101010 0 100010 1 001001 0 101010 1 000100 1
000100 1 000100 1 000100 1 000100 1 000100 1 000100 1–
000100 1 010010 1 001001 0 010100 1 001010 1 001001 0
000100 1 000100 1 000100 1 000100 1 000100 1 000100 1–
000100 1 000101 0 101001 0 100101 0 100100 0 101001 0

000100 1 000100 1 000100 1 000100 1 000100 1 000100 0–
100101 0 101010 1 010010 1 010101 0 001000 1 010101 0
010100 1 000100 1 000100 1 000100 1 000100 1 000100 1–
000100 1 000100 1 010010 1 001001 0 010100 1 001010 1
001001 0 000100 1 000100 1 000100 1 000100 1 000100 1–
000100 0 101010 0 101010 0 101000 0 101001 0 100001 0
001000 0 010001 0 000100 1 000100 1 000100 1 000100 1–
001010 1 010101 0 001001 0 001000 0 100100 1 001001 0
101010 1 010010 1 000100 1 000100 1 000100 1 000100 1–
000100 1 000100 0 100010 1 000100 1 000100 0 101001 0
101001 0 000100 0 101010 1 000100 1 000100 1 000100 1–
000100 1 010100 1 010010 1 010101 0 101000 1 010100 0
101001 0 000101 0 001001 0 000100 1 000100 1 000100 0–
100101 0 101010 0 100010 1 000100 0 100010 1 010101 0
000100 0 101000 0 100100 0 101010 1 000100 1 000100 1–
000100 1 000100 0 100010 0 100010 1 010101 0 100010 0
010101 0 101000 1 010001 0 100010 1 000100 1 000100 1–
000100 0 101010 1 001010 1 010101 0 010101 0 100001 0
010101 0 101010 0 101000 1 001001 0 000101 0 000100 1–
000100 1 000100 0 100001 0 100001 0 100001 0 001010 0
100001 0 100001 0 010100 1 010001 0 000100 1 000100 1–
000100 1 000100 0 100010 1 010101 0 101001 0 001000 1
010001 0 100100 1 001010 0 100001 0 010010 1 010001 0–
000100 1 000100 1 000100 1 000100 1 010010 0 100001 0
010101 0 010101 0 010100 0 101001 0 010010 1 000100 1–
000100 1 000100 1 000100 1 001001 0 100101 0 001000 1
010010 0 101001 0 001001 0 010100 1 001010 1 001001 0–
000100 1 000100 1 000100 0 100001 0 100100 0 100010 1
010001 0 001000 1 010010 1 010001 0 001001 0 100101 0–
000100 1 000100 1 000100 1 000100 0 101010 1 001010 1
010101 0 100101 0 001010 1 000100 1 000100 1 000100 ?–

Appendix D

Solutions to Selected Exercises

1 Introduction to Coding Theory

1.2.1 (a) 000, 010, 100, 110, 001, 011, 101, 111 (b) 0000, 0100, 1000, 1100, 0001, 0101, 1001, 1101 0010, 0110, 1010, 1110, 0011, 0111, 1011, 1111

1.2.2 2^n

1.2.4 Such a channel can be converted into a perfect channel by replacing each 1 with a 0 and each 0 with a 1.

1.2.5 Replace each 0 with a 1 and each 1 with a 0.

1.2.6 Nothing can be deduced about the codeword sent from the word received.

1.3.4 001

1.3.5 $C = \{0000, 0011, 0101, 0110, 1001, 1010, 1100, 1111\}$ (a) Yes. (b) 0101, 1001, 1100, 1111. (c) No. Each word of length 4 which does not belong to C has 4 different closest codewords.

1.3.7 8 **1.3.8** 16, 32, 2^{n-1} **1.4.1** 1, 3/4, 1/3

1.6.2 (a) $p^3(1-p)^5 = 2 \cdot 2 \times 10^{-8}$, (b) $p^7 = .81$, (c) $(1-p)^5 = 2 \cdot 4 \times 10^{-8}$, (d) $p^5 = .86$, (e) $p^4(1-p)^3 = 2 \cdot 4 \times 10^{-5}$, (f) $(1-p)^5 = 2 \cdot 4 \times 10^{-8}$, (g) $(1-p)^6 = 7 \cdot 3 \times 10^{-10}$

1.6.5 0001110 **1.6.6** 101101101 **1.6.7** 00011 **1.6.8** 100110 **1.6.9** 110101 or 101000

1.6.10 (a) $\phi_p(v_1, w) \le \phi_p(v_2, w)$ iff $d_1 \le d_2$
(b) $\phi_p(v, w) = (1/2)^n$ for any w and any v.

1.9.5 If 000, 001, 010, or 011 is received then IMLD decides that 001 was sent. In all other cases IMLD incorrectly decides that 101 was sent.

1.9.6 000 is decoded as 000. 001, 011 and 101 are decoded as 001. 110 and 111 are decoded as 110. 010 and 100 require retransmission.

1.9.7 $*$ in the following table indicates that retransmission is required.

(a)

Received Word	Decoded to
000	*
001	*
010	011
011	011
100	101
101	101
110	111
111	111

(b)

Received Word	Decoded to
000	000
001	001
010	010
011	011
100	000
101	001
110	010
111	011

1.10.2 (a) $L(001) = \{000, 001, 010, 011\}$. Therefore $\theta_p(C, 001) = p^3 + 2p^2(1-p) + p(1-p)^2$. (b) $L(101) = \{100, 101, 110, 111\}$. Therefore $\theta_p(C, 101) = p^3 + 2p^2(1-p) + p(1-p)^2$

1.10.4 (a) $\theta_p(C, 110) = p^3 + p^2(1-p)$ (b) To decode to 000 only 000 can be received, so $\theta_p(110, 000) = p(1-p)^2$.

1.10.5 (a) $\theta_p(C, 101) = p^3 + p^2(1-p)$ for all $v \in C$. (b) $\theta_p(C, v) = p^3 + p^2(1-p)$ for all $v \in C$. (c) $\theta_p(C, 0000) = p^4 + 3p^3(1-p), \theta_p(C, 0001) = p^4 + 3p^3(1-p)$ and $\theta_p(C, 1110) = p^4 + 4p^3(1-p)$. (e) $\theta_p(C, 00000) = \theta_p(C, 11111) = p^5 + 5p^4(1-p) + 10p^3(1-p)^2$. (g) $\theta_p(C, v) = p^5 + 3p^4(1-p)$ for all $v \in C$. (h) $\theta_p(C, v) = p^6 + 6p^5(1-p) + 9p^4(1-p)^2$ for all $v \in C$.

1.11.2 (a) No (b) Yes (c) No

1.11.3 (a) (i) No (ii) Yes (iii) No (b) (i) Yes (ii) Yes (iii) No **1.11.4** None

1.11.7 (a) 001, 011, 101, 111 (c) $K^4 \backslash \{0000, 0001, 1110, 1111\}$ (e) $K^5 \backslash \{00000, 11111\}$ (h) $K^6 \backslash \{000000, 101010, 010101, 111111\}$

1.11.12 (a) 1 (b) 1 (c) 1 (d) 2 (e) 5 (f) 3 (g) 2 (h) 3

1.11.13 2 **1.11.18** $K^3 \backslash \{000, 011, 101, 110\}$

1.11.19 (a) None (d) 1000, 0100, 0010 and 0001 (e) all error patterns of weight 1, 2, 3 or 4 (h) all error patterns of weight 1 or 2

1.12.12 (a) (i) 000, 001 (ii) 000 (c) (i) 0000, 0010, 0100, 1000 (ii) 0000 (f) (i) 00000, 10000, 01000, 00100, 00010, 00001 (ii) 00000, 10000, 01000, 00100, 00010, 00001 (g) (i) 00000, 01000, 00100, 00010 (ii) 00000

2 Linear Codes

2.1.1 (a) and (c) are not linear codes; the rest are linear codes.

2.2.3 (a) $\langle S \rangle = \{000, 010, 011, 111, 001, 101, 100, 110\}$ (b) $\langle S \rangle = \{0000, 1010, 0101, 1111\}$ (d) $\langle S \rangle = K^4$

2.2.7 (a) $C^\perp = \{000\}$ (b) $C^\perp = \{0000, 1010, 0101, 1111\}$

(c) $C^\perp = \{0000, 1111\}$

2.3.4 (a) linearly independent (b) $\{101, 011, 010\}$ (e) linearly independent (f) $\{1100, 1010, 1001\}$ (i) $\{10101010, 01010101\}$

2.3.7 (a) $B = \{100, 010, 001\}$, $B^\perp = \emptyset$ (b) $B = \{1010, 0101\}$, $B^\perp = B$ (c) $B = \{0101, 1010, 1100\}$, $B^\perp = \{1111\}$
(e) $B = \{11000, 01111, 11110, 01010\}$, $B^\perp = \{11111\}$

2.3.8 (a) $\dim C = 3$, $\dim C^\perp = 0$ (b) $\dim C = 2$, $\dim C^\perp = 2$ (c) $\dim C = 3$, $\dim C^\perp = 1$ (e) $\dim C = 4$, $\dim C^\perp = 1$ (f) $\dim C = 3$, $\dim C^\perp = 2$

2.3.16 (a) $\dim C = 4$ (b) $|C| = 16$ **2.3.17** $|C| = 32$

2.4.1 $BC = \begin{bmatrix} 110000 \\ 011101 \\ 101101 \end{bmatrix}$ $BD = \begin{bmatrix} 1000 \\ 0010 \\ 1010 \end{bmatrix}$ $DC = \begin{bmatrix} 101011 \\ 110000 \\ 011011 \\ 000110 \end{bmatrix}$

2.4.6 $A \leftrightarrow \begin{bmatrix} 11011 \\ 00101 \\ 00000 \end{bmatrix}$ $B \leftrightarrow \begin{bmatrix} 1001 \\ 0101 \\ 0000 \end{bmatrix}$ $C \leftrightarrow \begin{bmatrix} 101011 \\ 011011 \\ 000110 \\ 000000 \end{bmatrix}$ $D \leftrightarrow \begin{bmatrix} 1000 \\ 0101 \\ 0010 \\ 0000 \end{bmatrix}$

2.5.3 (a) $\{100, 010, 001\}$ (c) $\{1001, 0101, 0011\}$
(e) $\{100001, 01001, 00101, 00011\}$ (g) $\{101, 0101, 0011\}$

2.5.6 (a) $\{010, 011, 111\}$ (c) $\{0101, 1010, 1100\}$
(e) $\{11000, 01111, 11110, 01010\}$ (g) $\{0110, 1010, 0011\}$

2.5.10 (a) $\emptyset$ (b) $\{1010, 0101\}$ (e) $\{11111\}$ (h) $\{101000, 110110, 000101\}$

2.5.12 (a) $B = \{111000, 000111\}$
(b) $B = \{1000110, 0100011, 0010111, 0001101\}$
(c) $B = \{1000001, 0100001, 0010001, 0001001, 0000101, 0000011\}$
(f) $B = \{001000, 000100, 000010, 000001\}$

2.6.4 (i) Yes (ii) No **2.6.5** (a) $\begin{bmatrix} 010 \\ 001 \end{bmatrix}$ (b) $\begin{bmatrix} 1001 \\ 0110 \end{bmatrix}$ (d) $\begin{bmatrix} 11011 \\ 00111 \end{bmatrix}$

2.6.6 (a) $\begin{bmatrix} 100110 \\ 010101 \\ 001011 \end{bmatrix}$, $\dim C = 3$.

2.6.7 (a) $\begin{bmatrix} 10010110 \\ 01010101 \\ 00110011 \\ 00001111 \end{bmatrix}$, $(8, 4, 4)$ (c) $\begin{bmatrix} 100100100 \\ 010010010 \\ 001001001 \end{bmatrix}$, $(9, 3, 3)$

(f) $\begin{bmatrix} 101010 \\ 011010 \\ 000111 \end{bmatrix}$, $(6, 3, 2)$ (g) $\begin{bmatrix} 1001011 \\ 0101010 \\ 0011001 \\ 0000111 \end{bmatrix}$, $(7, 4, 3)$

2.6.10 (a) (i) 10011 (ii) 01010 (iii) 11100

2.6.11 10110, 01011, 01110, 00101, 01011, 10011, 01011

2.6.12 (a) 1001100, 0001011, 1110100, 1111111
(b) 0001100, 0001011, 1110101, 1111001

2.6.13 (2.6.6) (a) $|C| = 8$, $R = 1/2$ (b) $|C| = 8$, $R = 1/3$ (c) $|C| = 4$, $R = 1/5$ (2.6.7) (a) $|C| = 16$, $R = 1/2$ (b) $|C| = 16$, $R = 1/2$ (c) $|C| = 8$, $R = 1/3$ (d) $|C| = 8$, $R = 3/5$ (f) $|C| = 8$, $R = 1/3$ (g) $|C| = 16$, $R = 4/7$

2.7.4 (a) $\begin{bmatrix} 1 \\ 0 \\ 0 \end{bmatrix}$ (b) $\begin{bmatrix} 01 \\ 10 \\ 10 \\ 01 \end{bmatrix}$ (e) $\begin{bmatrix} 001 \\ 111 \\ 100 \\ 010 \\ 001 \end{bmatrix}$

2.7.5 (a) $\begin{bmatrix} 110 \\ 101 \\ 011 \\ 100 \\ 010 \\ 001 \end{bmatrix}$ (b) $\begin{bmatrix} 10010 \\ 01010 \\ 00101 \\ 10000 \\ 01000 \\ 00100 \\ 00010\ 00001 \end{bmatrix}$ (e) $\begin{bmatrix} 1000 \\ 1000 \\ 0010 \\ 0010 \\ 0100 \\ 0100 \\ 0001 \\ 0001 \end{bmatrix}$ (g) $\begin{bmatrix} 11 \\ 01 \\ 10 \\ 01 \\ 01 \end{bmatrix}$ (j) $\begin{bmatrix} 111 \\ 110 \\ 101 \\ 100 \\ 011 \\ 010 \\ 001 \end{bmatrix}$

2.7.9 (a) $G(G^{\perp}) = G(C) = \begin{bmatrix} 110000 \\ 001010 \\ 000101 \end{bmatrix}$

2.7.10 $C^{\perp}$ consists of the 16 words of even weight in K^5.

2.7.11 (a) $\dim C = t$, $\dim C^{\perp} = 2^t - t - 1$, $|C| = 2^t$, $|C^{\perp}| = 2^{2^t - t - 1}$, $R = t/(2^t - 1)$ (b) $\dim C = 11$, $\dim C^{\perp} = 12$, $|C| = 2^{11} = 2048$, $|C^{\perp}| = 2^{12} = 4096$, $R = 11/23$ (c) $\dim C = 8$, $\dim C^{\perp} = 7$, $|C| = 2^8 = 256$, $|C^{\perp}| = 2^7 = 128$, $R = 8/15$

2.8.4 (a) 1111100 (b) 1011000

2.8.10 (a) $C' = \{00000, 11100, 10101, 01001\}$

2.8.11 (a) $G' = \begin{bmatrix} 100011 \\ 010010 \\ 001001 \\ 000100 \end{bmatrix}$ **2.8.12** (a) $G' = \begin{bmatrix} 10110 \\ 01011 \end{bmatrix}$

2.8.14 (a) Yes (b) Yes (c) No **2.9.4** (a) 4 (b) 4 (c) 4

2.10.6 (a) $C, C+1000, C+0010, C+0011$ (b) $C, C+1000, C+0100, C+0001$

2.10.7 (a) C, $C+100000$, $C+010000$, $C+001000$, $C+000100$, $C+000010$, $C+000001$, $C+001001$ (d) C, $C+100000$ (f) C, $C+1000$, $C+0100$, $C+0010$, $C+0001$, $C+1100$, $C+1010$, $C+1001$

2.10.8 (a) C, $C+1000$, $C+0100$, $C+0001$ (b) C, $C+1000000$, $C+0100000$,

$C+0010000$, $C+0001000$, $C+0000100$, $C+0000010$, $C+0000001$ (c) C, $C+000100$, $C+010000$, $C+001100$, $C+100000$, $C+100100$, $C+110000$, $C+110100$

2.11.2 (a) 010011 (b) 101001 (c) 001111 (d) 010011 (e) 110101 (f) 001111.

2.11.8 (a)

Error Pattern	Syndrome
*	11
0000	00
*	01
0010	10

$$H = \begin{bmatrix} 01 \\ 01 \\ 10 \\ 01 \end{bmatrix}$$

2.11.9 (a)

Error Pattern	Syndrome
000000	000
000001	001
000010	010
100000	011
000100	100
010000	101
001000	110
*	111

$$H = \begin{bmatrix} 011 \\ 101 \\ 110 \\ 100 \\ 010 \\ 001 \end{bmatrix}$$

2.11.10 (b)

Error Pattern	Syndrome
0000000	000
0000001	001
0000010	010
0001000	011
0000100	100
0010000	101
0100000	110
1000000	111

2.11.19 (a) (i) 1100 (ii) 1001 (iii) 0101 (c) (i) 001110 (ii) 001110 (iii) 011011

2.11.21 (a)

Error Pattern	Syndrome
0000000	000
0000001	001
0000010	010
0001000	011
0000100	100
0010000	101
0100000	110
1000000	111

2.12.2 (2.10.6) (a) $\theta_p(C) = p^4 + p^3(1-p)$ (c) $\theta_p(C) = p^5 + 3p^4(1-p)$ (2.10.7) (a) $\theta_p(C) = p^6 + 6p^5(1-p)$ (b) $\theta_p(C) = p^6 + 6p^5(1-p) + 9p^4(1-p)^2$ (2.10.8) (a) $\theta_p(C) = p^4 + 2p^3(1-p)$ (b) $\theta_p(C) = p^7 + 7p^6(1-p)$

3 Perfect and Related Codes

3.1.5 (a) 2^4 (b) 2^4 (c) 2^4 (e) 2^8 (f) 4096

3.1.18 (a) (8, 6, 3), No $16 \le |C| \le 16$ (d) (15, 6, 3), Yes 2048

3.1.19 (a) $64 \le |C| \le 256$ (b) $2048 \le |C| \le 2048$ (c) $128 \le |C| \le 128$ (d) $256 \le |C| \le 256$ (e) $32 \le |C \le 256$ (f) $16 \le |C| \le 32$

3.1.20 No

3.3.4

Error Pattern	Syndrome
0000000	000
1000000	111
0100000	110
0010000	101
0001000	011
0000100	100
0000010	010
0000001	001

$$H = \begin{bmatrix} 111 \\ 110 \\ 101 \\ 011 \\ 100 \\ 010 \\ 001 \end{bmatrix}$$

(a) 0101011 (c) 0011110

3.4.7 (a) 696 (b) 17 (c) 17

3.6.5 (a) 100000001001, 000000000000 (b) 000000100000, 001000010000 (c) 000000100000, 000000010000 (d) ask for retransmission (e) 011000000000, 00000000100 (g) 000000000000, 001010000000

3.6.6 (a) 010010000000, 000000000000 (b) 000000000000, 001000110000 (c) 001000000000, 100000000000 (d) 000000000101, 000000000001 (e) 000100000000, 000110000000 (f) 000001000000, 000000001000

3.7.3 (a) 111111100000, 10101111011 (b) 100000000000, 11011100010 (c) 000101011001, 11100000000 (d) 011000001001, 011011011011

3.7.7 253

3.8.5

$$\begin{bmatrix} 1111 & 1111 \\ 0101 & 0101 \\ 0011 & 0011 \\ 0001 & 0001 \\ 0000 & 1111 \\ 0000 & 0101 \\ 0000 & 0011 \end{bmatrix}$$

3.8.10 (a) 0101 1010 (b) 0110 0110 (c) ask to retransmit (d) 1100 1100

3.9.6

(a) $w_3 = (2, -2, 2, -2, -2, -6, -2, 2)$ $m = (0101)$

(b) $w_3 = (2, -2, -2, -6, -2, 2, 2, 2)$ $m = (0110)$

(c) $w_3 = (-4, -4, 0, 0, 0, 0, -4, 4)$ $m = ?$

(d) $w_3 = (2, 2, 6, -2, -2, -2, 2, 2)$ $m = (1010)$

Too Bad Getting In Isn't This Easy!
www.GradSchools.com

3.1.6a)
3.1.19a)
3.1.22
3.3.3
3.3.4
3.4.3
3.6.5a) c)
3.7.3a)
3.8.10 a)
3.9.6

4 Cyclic Linear Codes

4.1.10 (a) $q(x) = x^3, r(x) = x^3$

4.1.13 (a) $\{0 + x^2, x, x + x^2\}$ (c) $\{0, x^3, 1 + x + x^2\}$

4.2.22 (a) $g(x) = 1$ (e) $g(x) = 1 + x$

4.3.5 (a) $\begin{bmatrix} 1011000 \\ 0101100 \\ 0010110 \\ 0001011 \end{bmatrix}$ **4.3.6** (b) $g(x) = 1 + x^2 + x^4 \begin{bmatrix} 101010 \\ 010101 \end{bmatrix}$

5 BCH Codes

5.1.15 (a) $\begin{bmatrix} 00 & 0 \\ 10 & \beta^0 \\ 01 & \beta \\ 11 & \beta^2 \end{bmatrix}$ (b) $\begin{bmatrix} 000 & 0 \\ 100 & \beta^0 \\ 010 & \beta \\ 001 & \beta^2 \\ 101 & \beta^3 \\ 111 & \beta^4 \\ 110 & \beta^5 \\ 011 & \beta^6 \end{bmatrix}$

5.1.17 $\beta, \beta^2, \beta^4, \beta^7, \beta^8, \beta^{11}, \beta^{13}, \beta^{14}$

5.2.7

element	minimal polynomial
0	x
1	$1+x$
β, β^2, β^4	$1+x+x^3$
β, β^6, β^5	$1+x^2+x^3$

5.2.8

element	minimal polynomial
0	x
1	$1+x$
β^5, β^{10}	$1+x+x^2$
$\beta^7, \beta^{14}, \beta^{13}, \beta^{11}$	$1+x+x^4$
$\beta, \beta^2, \beta^4, \beta^8$	$1+x^3+x^4$
$\beta^3, \beta^6, \beta^9, \beta^{12}$	$1+x+x^2+x^3+x^4$

5.5.9 (a) Ask for retransmission (b) 10 (c) 5 and 8 (d) 6 and 11 (e) Ask for retransmission (f) Ask for retransmission (g) 0 and 13 (h) Codeword

6 Reed-Solomon Codes

6.1.6 (a) 2^{15} (b) $g(x) = \beta + \beta^3 x + x^2$ (c) (i) $\beta\beta\beta^6\beta^6 000$ (d) $g_k(x) = (1 + x)(\beta + x)(\beta^2 + x)(\beta^4 + x)$

6.1.7 (a) 2^{44} (b) $g(x) = \beta^{10} + \beta^3 x + \beta^6 x^2 + \beta^{13} x^3 + x^4$
(c) (i) $\beta^{10}\beta^3\beta^6\beta^{13}100000\beta^2\beta^{10}\beta^{13}\beta^5\beta^7$
(d) $g_k = (\beta^8 + x)(\beta^6 + x)(\beta^{12} + x)(\beta^9 + x)g(x)$

6.2.3 (a) β^2 (b) β^5 (c) β^4

6.2.7 (a) $n=3, k=1, d=3$ and $|C|=4$ (b) $G=[\beta\beta^2 1]$

(c)

message	codeword c	$f(c)$
0	0 0 0	0 0 0 0 0 0
1	$\beta\ \beta^2\ 1$	0 1 1 1 1 0
β	$\beta^2\ 1\ \beta$	1 1 1 0 0 1
β^2	$1\ \beta\ \beta^2$	1 0 0 1 1 1

6.2.8 (a) $n=7, k=3, d=5$ and $|C|=8^3=512$ (b) $g(x)=\beta^6+\beta^5x+\beta^5x^2+\beta^2x^3+x^4$

6.2.9 (a) $\beta+\beta^2x+x^2=(\beta^3+x)(\beta^4+x)=(1+x)(\beta+x)$ (b) $1+\beta^6x+x^2=(\beta^3+x)(\beta^4+x)$ (c) $\beta^3+\beta x+x^2+\beta^3x^3+x^4=(\beta+x)(\beta^2+x)(\beta^3+x)(\beta^4+x)$ (d) $\beta^{10}+\beta^3x+\beta^6x^2+\beta^3x^3+x^4=(\beta+x)(\beta^2+x)(\beta^3+x)(\beta^4+x)$ (e) $\beta^{21}+\beta^{24}x+\beta^{16}x^2+\beta^{24}x^3+\beta^9x^4+\beta^{10}x^5+x^6=(\beta+x)(\beta^2+x)\dots(\beta^6+x)$

6.3.5 (a) $00\beta\beta^5\beta^3\beta^2\beta^{13}\beta^{10}\beta000000$ (b) $1\beta^4\beta^2\beta\beta^{12}\beta^9 10\beta\beta^5\beta^3\beta^2\beta^{13}\beta^{10}\beta$ (c) $\beta\beta^{10}\beta^7 0\beta^{12}\beta^3\beta^3 10000000$

6.3.6 (a) $001\beta^8\beta^{11}\beta^3\beta^5 00000000$ (b) $0\beta^{10}\beta^3\beta^6\beta^{13}0\beta^8\beta^{11}\beta^3\beta^5 00000$ (c) $\beta^4\beta^{12}1\beta^7 0\beta^2\beta^5\beta^{12}\beta^{14}000000$

6.3.8 (a) $0\beta^2 0000000000000$ (b) $00\beta00\beta^3 000000000$ (c) 100000000000000 (d) $\beta^5 11100000000000$ (e) $\beta^{10}\beta^3 0001000010000$ (f) $\beta^2 0000\beta^2 0000\beta^2 0000$

6.5.4 (a) $(\beta+x)$ (b) $(\beta^2+x)(\beta^5+x)$ (c) $(\beta^5+x)(\beta^{10}+x)$
(d) $(1+x)(\beta+x)(\beta^2+x)(\beta^3+x)$ (e) $(1+x)(\beta+x)(\beta^5+x)(\beta^{10}+x)$
(f) $(1+x)(\beta^5+x)(\beta^{10}+x)$

In the following tables, for p_i and q_i the symbol $*$ represents the zero field element and i represents β^i.

(a)

−1	0	2	3	4	5	6	7	8	9				0	−1	$-\infty$
0	2	3	4	5	6	7	8	9				0	*	0	−1
1	7	8	9	10	11	12	13				0	2	*	1	0
2	*	*	*	*	*	*				0	1	*	*	2	1
3	*	*	*	*	*				0	1	*	*	*	4	1
4	*	*	*	*				0	1	*	*	*		6	1
5	*	*	*				0	1	*	*	*			8	1
6	*	*				0	1	*	*	*				10	1
7	*				0	1	*	*	*					12	1
8				0	1	*	*	*						(14)	(1)

$$\sigma(x)=x+\beta^1$$

(b)

−1	0	9	13	7	4	12	4	8	2				0	-1	$-\infty$
0	9	13	7	4	12	4	8	2				0	*	0	−1
1	8	*	0	1	12	3	*				0	9	*	1	0
2	12	13	9	0	*	7				0	4	*	*	2	1
3	13	14	10	1	*				0	*	13	*	*	3	2
4	*	*	*	*				0	1	7	*	*		4	3
5	*	*	*				0	1	7	*	*			6	3
6	*	*				0	1	7	*	*				8	3
7	*				0	1	7	*	*					10	3
8				0	1	7	*	*						(12)	(3)

$$\sigma(x) = x^2 + \beta^1 x + \beta^7 = (x + \beta^2)(x + \beta^5)$$

(c)

−1	0	0	0	0	0	0	0	0	0					0	−1	$-\infty$
0	0	0	0	0	0	0	0	0					0	*	0	−1
1	*	*	*	*	*	*	*					0	0	*	1	0
2	*	*	*	*	*	*					0	0	*	*	3	0
3	*	*	*	*	*					0	0	*	*	*	5	0
4	*	*	*	*					0	0	*	*	*		7	0
5	*	*	*					0	0	*	*	*			9	0
6	*	*					0	0	*	*	*				11	0
7	*					0	0	*	*	*					13	0
8					0	0	*	*	*						(15)	(0)

$$\sigma(x) = x + \beta^0$$

(d)

−1	0	10	3	13	3	12	5	13	3				0	−1	$-\infty$
0	10	3	13	3	12	5	13	3				0	*	0	−1
1	11	*	13	1	13	6	13				0	10	*	1	0
2	4	2	0	*	*	2				0	8	*	*	2	1
3	2	13	9	6	13				0	*	3	*	*	3	2
4.	6	10	6	13				0	13	2	*	*		4	3
5	4	0	9				0	11	2	7	*			5	4
6	2	14				0	4	9	9	*				6	5
7	2				0	11	*	7	5					7	6
8				0	12	4	0	6						(8)	(7)

$$\sigma(x) = x^4 + \beta^{12}x^3 + \beta^4 x^2 + \beta^0 x + \beta^6$$
$$= (x + \beta^0)(x + \beta^1)(x + \beta^2)(x + \beta^3)$$

(e)

−1	0	12	8	*	7	13	4	13	0				0	−1	−∞
0	12	8	*	7	13	4	13	0				0	*	0	−1
1	12	5	7	11	2	12	5				0	12	*	1	0
2	4	7	8	14	6	7				0	11	*	*	2	1
3	2	6	0	5	3				0	8	4	*	*	3	2
4	9	13	14	7				0	3	14	*	*		4	3
5	*	1	2				0	4	3	11				5	4
6	1	2				0	4	3	11	*				7	4
7	1				0	4	4	14	6					6	6
8				0	1	*	0	1						(8)	(7)

$$\begin{aligned}\sigma(x) &= x^4+\beta^1x^3+\beta^0x+\beta^1\\ &= (x+\beta^1)(x+\beta^0)(x+\beta^5)(x+\beta^{10})\end{aligned}$$

(f)

−1	0	2	*	*	2	*	*	2	*				0	−1	−∞
0	2	*	*	2	*	*	2	*				0	*	0	−1
1	4	*	2	4	*	2	4				0	2	*	1	0
2	*	2	*	*	2	*				0	*	*	*	2	1
3	2	*	*	2	*				0	*	*	*	*	4	1
4	*	0	*	*				0	*	13	0	*		3	3
5	0	*	*				0	*	13	0	*			5	3
6	*	*				0	*	*	0	*				6	3
7	*				0	*	*	0	*					8	3
8				0	*	*	0	*						(10)	(3)

$$\sigma(x) = x^3+1 = (x+\beta^0)(x+\beta^5)(x+\beta^{10})$$

6.6.9 (a) 1010 1111 1111 0011 1001 0000 0000 (b) 1001 1010 0000 0011 1010 0011 1001 (c) 0101 1001 0000 1100 1001 1100 0101 (d) 0000 1010 1111 1111 0011 1001 0000

6.6.10 Decode $f(w)$ to $f(c)$, where c is: (a) $\beta^{10}\beta^{12}\beta^7\beta^3\beta^{12}\beta^8\beta^8\beta^2 0000000$ (b) $\beta^{10}0\beta\beta^7\beta^7 0\beta^0\beta^2 0000000$ (c) $0\beta^{12}\beta^{14}\beta^4\beta^2\beta^8\beta^2 00000000$

6.6.11 Decode $\overline{f}(w)$ to $\overline{f}(c)$ where $c = \beta^7\beta^7 1\beta^9\beta\beta^{10}\beta^8 10000000$.

7 Burst error-correcting codes

7.1.5 C is not a 2 error-correcting code since it has only 32 cosets.

7.1.6 C is not 3 error-correcting code since it has only 64 cosets.

7.1.13 (a) 101100000001000 (c) 100000101010011 (e) 000001111100100

7.1.14 (a) 010100000010010 (c) 001110000000100 (e) 000000011111010

7.2.4 (a) 1000110 0110110 1110000 0011100 0110110 0001111
(b) 10 01 01 00 11 11 00 10 10 11 01 01 00 00 00 10 10 01 11 11 01
(c) 101 011 011 000 110 110 000 000 010 110 101 111 011 001

7.2.8 (a) $1******00*****110****0110***00101**011011*$
(b) $1******0******10*****01*****010****001****$

7.2.9 The codewords are transmitted in order with no interleaving.

7.2.12 (a) 01 10 11 11 10 01 10 11 11 01 01 00 01 00 11 01 10 11 10 10 11 00 01 01 (b) 011 101 111 110 100 010 001 100 111 101 110 011

7.2.13 (a) $m_1 = 0000, m_2 = 0011, m_3 = 0000$ (b) $m_1 = 1000, m_2 = 0110, m_3 = 0011$.

8 Convolutional Codes

8.1.7 (a) 11101001... (b) 0010111...

8.1.12 (a) 000, 0010000 (b) 001, 1110000

8.1.14 (a) 000, 0010000 (b) 000, 100

8.2.2 (a) $c(x) = (1+x+x^4+x^6, 1+x+x^2+x^4+x^5+x^6, 1+x^2+x^5+x^6)$
(b) $c(x) = (1+x^2+x^6, 1+x^3+x^5+x^6, 1+x+x^2+x^3+x^4+x^5+x^6)$
(c) $c(x) = (1+\sum_{i=3}^{\infty} x^i, 1+x^2, 1+x+\sum_{i=3}^{\infty} x^i)$

8.2.3 (a) $c(x) = (1+x+x^2+x^3+x^6, 1+x^2+x^5+x^6)$ (b) $c(x) = (1+x+x^5+x^6+x^7, 1+x^7)$ (c) $c(x) = (1+x^2+\sum_{i=1}^{\infty} x^{2i+1}, 1+x+\sum_{i=3}^{\infty} x^i)$

8.2.6 The interleaved form of the codewords are as follows: (from 8.2.2) (a) 111 110 011 000 110 011 111 ... (b) 111 001 101 011 001 011 111 (c) 111 001 010 101 101 101 101 ... (from 8.2.3) (a) 11 10 11 10 00 01 11 ... (b) 11 10 00 00 00 10 10 11 ... (c) 11 01 10 11 01 11 01 11 01 ...

8.2.11 (a)

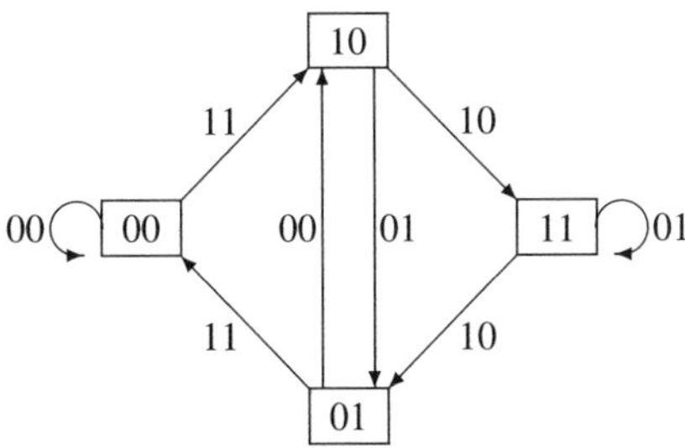

(b) (i) 11 01 00 01 11 00 00 ... (ii) 11 10 01 10 11 00 00 ...
(c) (i) 1 0 1 0 0 0 ... (d) (ii) 0 1 1 1 1 0 1 ...

8.2.12 (a)

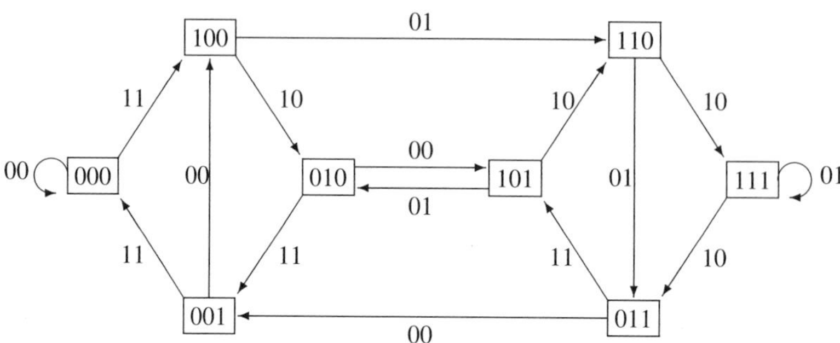

(b) (i) 11 10 11 00 10 11 11 00 00 ...
(ii) 11 01 01 11 01 11 11 00 00 ... (iii) 11 01 10 01 01 01 ...
(c) (i) 1 0 1 0 1 1 1 ... (ii) 0 1 1 1 1 0 0 ...

8.3.1 (a) $m = 1010101 \cdots = \sum_{i=0}^{\infty} x^{2i}$ (b) $1 * 1 * 1 * \ldots$ (c) $*000\ldots$

8.3.2 (a) gcd $= 1 + x$; the loop on state 111 is a zero weight cycle (b) gcd $= 1$; not catastrophic (c) gcd $= 1 + x + x^2$; $(0110, 1011, 1101)$ is a zero weight cycle.

8.3.3 (a) 5 (b) 6 (c) 7

8.3.6 (a) $\tau(a) = 2$, $\tau(2) = 6$ (b) $\tau(1) = 2$, $\tau(2) = 6$ (c) $\tau(1) = 2$, $\tau(2) = 9$, $\tau(3) = 13$

8.4.4

State s	$t = 8$	$t = 9$	$t = 10$	$t = 11$	$t = 12$
000	3,00000**	3,000000*	3,0000000	3,0000000	3,0000000
100	5,100****	3,1001001	5,100****	3,1001110	5,100****
010	4,0100100	4,0101001	4,0100100	4,0101110	4,0100111
110	4,1100100	4,1101001	4,1100100	4,1101110	4,1100111
001	3,0010011	5,001****	3,0011100	5,001***0	5,001*1*1
101	3,1010011	5,101****	3,1011100	5,101***0	5,101*1*1
011	4,011*0**	2,0111001	4,0111*0*	4,0111010	5,0111001
111	2,1110011	4,111*0**	4,1110100	4,1110010	4,1110111
Decode to:	1	1	0	0	0

8.4.5 (a) $m = 0\,0\,0$ (b) $m = 1\,0\,0$

8.4.14 (b)

State	Output										
s	$X_3=0$	$X_3=1$	$t=1$	2	3	4	5	6	7	8
000	00	11	∞	∞	∞	7	6	6	6	6
100	11	00	2	∞	∞	5	4	5	5	6
010	10	01	∞	3	∞	4	6	5	6	6
110	01	10	∞	3	∞	4	6	5	6	6
001	11	00	∞	∞	5	4	5	5	6	6
101	00	11	∞	∞	3	6	4	6	5	6
011	01	10	∞	∞	4	5	5	6	6	7
111	10	01	∞	∞	4	5	5	6	6	7

$$d=6,\ \tau(1)=2,\ \tau(2)=6.$$

9 Reed-Muller and Preparata Codes

9.1.3 (a) $f_I(x)=(x_0+1)(x_3+1)$ (b) $v_I=1000100000000000$, $f_I(x)=(x_0+1)(x_1+1)(x_3+1)$ (c) $f_I(x)=(x_1+1)$ (d) $v_I=1111000000000000$, $f_I(x)=(x_2+1)(x_3+1)$ (e) $v_I=1$, $f_I(x)=1$ (f) $100\ldots0$, $f_I(x)=\prod_{i=0}^{3}(x_i+1)$

9.1.4 (a) $f_I(x)=(x_0+1)(x_4+1)$ (c) $f_I(x)=(x_1+1)$ (d) $f_I(x)=(x_1+1)(x_2+1)(x_4+1)$ (e) $v_I=11\ldots1$, $f_I(x)=1$ (f) $v_I=100\ldots0$, $f_I(x)=\prod_{i=1}^{4}(x_i+1)$

9.1.5 There are $|I|$ coordinates which must be 0 and there are two choices for each of the other $m-|I|$ coordinates in H_I.

9.1.6 Since all v_I have even weight except for v_{I_m}, v will have even weight if and only if $v\in\langle v_{I_m}\rangle^{\perp}$.

9.1.9 (a)

$$\begin{bmatrix}11111111\\11110000\\11001100\\10101010\\11000000\\10100000\\10001000\end{bmatrix}\begin{matrix}v_{\emptyset}\\v_2\\v_1\\v_0\\v_{1,2}\\v_{0,2}\\v_{0,1}\end{matrix}$$

9.1.12 (a) $c=v_2+v_0=0101\ 1010\ 0101\ 1010$
(b) $c=v_{0,1}=1000\ 1000\ 1000\ 1000$ (c) $c=v_2+v_{0,3}=0101\ 1010\ 1111\ 0000$

9.2.7 (a) 0 1000 000001 (b) 0 0000 0 11000 (c) 1 1001 100000 (d) 1 1111 111111 (e) 0 0100 000100 (f) 0 0101 010000 (g) 0 0000 000010 (h) 0 0110 00000 (i) 1 0001 000101

9.2.8 (a) 0 00000 0000000100 (b) 0 00100 1000100001 (c) 1 00000 0000010000 (d) 1 00100 1100000000 (e) 0 01001 0000000100 (f) 0 10010 0000000000 (g) ask for retransmission

9.3.10 (a) (ii) 10011010 11110011 (iii) 01100101 11110011 (c) (ii) 11000110 10101111 (iii) 11001001 11100111

9.1.11 (a) If $\alpha = 0$ then $\alpha U = \{0\}$, so $|\alpha U|$ is odd, so $[\chi(U), \chi(V)]$ does not satisfy (i) of Definition 9.3.3.

9.3.17 (a) 01000001 01110100 (b) 00001001 01001110 (c) 00000011 11010010

9.4.6 (a) 10101001 11011011 (b) 10101001 00100100 (c) 11111111 11111111 (d) 11111111 00000000 (e) 00000000 11111111

9.4.7 (a) 10100...0 00000100010...0 (b) 10100...0 00 ... 0

9.4.8 (a) 31 (b) 21

9.5.3 (a) 10000001 11101000 (b) 00011110 01000010 (c) 00000101 10100110 (d) 01000010 00011110 (e) 11101000 10000001 (f) 10011001 01111101 (g) Ask for retransmission (h) 10100101 10010000 (i) 11101101 01010101 (j) 10111011 01101010 (k) 01010101 11101101 (n) 01101010 10111011 (o) 10100101 10010000

9.5.4 (a) 11000 11000 10000 00000 00000 10000 11 00011 11000 00000 01000 00011 00100 00 (b) 10100 00000 00000 00000 00000 00000 00 00000 10001 00000 00000 01010 10111 00

9.5.5 No

10 Classical Cryptography

10.2.5 The '`VHV`' fragments suggest a keylength dividing 16. Since plaintext '`an`' maps to ciphertext '`AE`', it follows that the key contains '`AR`'. After showing that the keylength must be greater than 2, consider the case that the length is 4. The information concerning the '`AE`' fragment gives key '`?AR?`', where the question-mark denotes an unknown character. Now use the information concerning the pair of common three-letter words to make an educated guess at the key.

10.2.8 There are scenarios where compression followed by encryption could aid cryptanalysis (for example, if compression places a known header on the output, then a known-plaintext attack may be possible, depending on the encryption method). However, the general recommendation is for compression first. Compression may be more effective on plaintext than ciphertext. If encryption or transmission is time-expensive, then compressing first may improve throughput. Attacks based on source redundancy may be frustrated by compression before encryption. See Boyd [16] and the references therein.

10.3.1 $m = (m_0, m_1) = (1110, 0000)$ **10.3.3** $m_1 = m_3 \oplus f_{k_2}(m_2) = 1010 \oplus f_1(1011) = 0000$ and $m = (m_0, m_1) = (1110, 0000)$.

10.3.4 (a) In CBC, decryption is $m_i = \mathrm{DES}_k^{-1}(c_i) \oplus c_{i-1}$. Only m_j and m_{j+1} depend on c_j.

10.3.5 (a) Note that $k_2 = \mathrm{DES}_{k_1}(m) \oplus E_k(m)$. For each $0 \le i < 2^{56}$, set $j = \mathrm{DES}_i(m_1) \oplus c_1$. If $\mathrm{DES}_i(m_2) \oplus j = c_2$, then it is likely that $(i, j) = (k_1, k_2)$. At most 2^{57} DES operations are required to find a candidate.

10.3.7 It is not known if the complementation property can be used to improve exhaustive key search under a known-plaintext attack. For a chosen-plaintext attack, obtain pairs (m, c_1) and $(\overline{m}, c_2)$ and use the complementation property to eliminate two candidate keys with each DES operation.

11 Topics in Algebra and Number Theory

11.1.14 Algorithm 11.1.7 with $n = 576$ gives:

i	0	1	2	$\cdots$	8
k_i	0	0	1	$\cdots$	1
A	47	$47^2 \bmod n = 481$	$481^2 \bmod n = 385$	$\cdots$	$193^2 \bmod n = 385$
b	1	1	$1 \cdot 385 \bmod n = 385$	$\cdots$	$385 \cdot 385 \bmod n = 193$

and $47^{332} \bmod 576 = 193$.

11.1.16 The set $\{2, 6, 7, 8\}$ of generators can be found by exhaustive calculation; e.g., $2^2 \equiv 4$, $2^4 \equiv 4 \cdot 4 \equiv 5$, and $2^5 \not\equiv 1$, so 2 has order 10 since the order of an element must divide $\phi(11) = 10$. If $\mathbb{Z}_n^*$ has a generator α, then it can be shown that α^i is a generator iff $(i, \phi(n)) = 1$. It follows that if $\mathbb{Z}_n^*$ is cyclic, then there are $\phi(\phi(n))$ generators. In this exercise, there are $\phi(\phi(11)) = \phi(10) = 4$ generators, given by 2^i for $i \in \{1, 3, 7, 9\}$.

11.1.21 (a) Use the division algorithm to write $x = q \cdot \mathrm{ord}(a) + r$, $0 \le r < \mathrm{ord}(a)$. Suppose $a^x \equiv 1 \pmod{n}$. Then $1 \equiv a^{q \cdot \mathrm{ord}(a) + r} \equiv a^r \pmod{n}$. Since $r < \mathrm{ord}(a)$, it follows (from the definition of order) that $r = 0$ and hence $\mathrm{ord}(a) \mid x$.

11.1.22 Use the fact that $\mathbb{Z}_p^*$ has a generator and apply Exercise 11.1.20.

11.2.7 Calculate $x^2 \bmod 30$ for each $x \in \mathbb{Z}_{30}^* = \{1, 7, 11, 13, 17, 19, 23, 29\}$ to obtain $Q_{30} = \{1, 19\}$. (It suffices to consider $x < 30/2$ since $n - x \equiv -x \pmod{n}$.)

11.2.8 $\left(\frac{156}{235}\right) = -1$, $\left(\frac{1833}{587}\right) = \left(\frac{72}{587}\right) = \left(\frac{2^3 3^2}{587}\right) = \left(\frac{2}{587}\right)^3 \left(\frac{3}{587}\right)^2 = -1$.

11.2.13 Apply Euler's criterion.

11.3.5 If a is not an Euler witness, then $(a, n) = 1$ and $a^{(n-1)/2} \equiv \left(\frac{a}{n}\right) \pmod{n}$. Consider the square of each quantity in the congruence.

A test for compositeness which searches for Fermat witnesses can be constructed; however, there are composite n (known as Carmichael numbers) for which there are no Fermat witnesses in $\mathbb{Z}_n^*$.

11.4.5 $m = \lfloor\sqrt{n}\rfloor = 32$ and $q(z) = (z+32)^2 - 1081$. The factor base is $B = \{-1, 2, 3, 5, 11\}$ since $\left(\frac{n}{7}\right) = -1$. The first few values of z for which $q(z)$ factors over B are given in the following table.

z	$a = z+m$	$b = q(z)$	factorization
-1	31	-120	$-2^3 \cdot 3 \cdot 5$
1	33	8	2^3
2	34	75	$3 \cdot 5^2$
-3	29	-240	$-2^4 \cdot 3 \cdot 5$

The relations for $z \in \{-1, 1, -3\}$ give $x^2 \equiv y^2 \pmod{n}$ for $x = 31 \cdot 33 \cdot 29$ and $y = 2^5 \cdot 3 \cdot 5$; unfortunately, $x \equiv 480 \equiv y \pmod{n}$. No other combination produces a perfect square, so more entries must be generated.

11.4.6 This problem appears in [63]. Values x and y satisfying $x^2 \equiv y^2$ are found corresponding to $z \in \{0, 1, -2\}$ and to $z \in \{-1, 4, -6\}$; the first of these gives $x \equiv -y$.

11.4.8 Note that $179 \equiv 3 \pmod{11}$ and $179 \equiv 9 \pmod{17}$. The congruence $x^2 \equiv 3 \pmod{11}$ has solutions $x = \pm 3^{(11+1)/4}$ since $11 \equiv 3 \pmod{4}$. Although we have not described an algorithm for solving $x^2 \equiv 9 \pmod{17}$, the congruence can easily be solved by inspection. Gauss' algorithm gives 71 as one of the roots of 179.

11.4.10 The value $p+q$ can be calculated from n and ϕ. Consider the equation $(x-p)(x-q) = 0$.

11.5.3 The table of (j, α^j) pairs is:

j	0	1	2	3	4	5	6	7	8	9
$\alpha^j \bmod p$	1	5	25	28	43	21	8	40	6	30

Calculate $\beta\alpha^{-im} \bmod p$ until a match is found:

$$\begin{aligned}
i = 0: &\quad \beta(\alpha^{-m})^0 \equiv \beta \equiv 4 \\
i = 1: &\quad \beta(\alpha^{-m})^1 \equiv 4 \cdot 11 \equiv 44 \\
i = 2: &\quad \beta(\alpha^{-m})^2 \equiv 44 \cdot 11 \equiv 96 \\
i = 3: &\quad \beta(\alpha^{-m})^3 \equiv 96 \cdot 11 \equiv 86 \\
i = 4: &\quad \beta(\alpha^{-m})^4 \equiv 86 \cdot 11 \equiv 73 \\
i = 5: &\quad \beta(\alpha^{-m})^5 \equiv 73 \cdot 11 \equiv 27 \\
i = 6: &\quad \beta(\alpha^{-m})^6 \equiv 27 \cdot 11 \equiv 6
\end{aligned}$$

Hence, $\beta\alpha^{-im} \equiv \alpha^j$ for $i = 6$ and $j = 8$, giving $\log_5 4 = 68$ in $\mathbb{Z}_{97}$.

11.5.6 (a) If $\lambda = 2^i\lambda'$ with λ' odd, then we may assume without loss of generality that $2^i \mid \phi(p)$. Consider an element $a \in \mathbb{Z}_n^*$ with order $\phi(p)$ as an element of $\mathbb{Z}_p^*$ and order $\phi(q)/2$ as an element of $\mathbb{Z}_q^*$.

(b) Show that $\lambda = \text{ord}(a)\lambda'$ and $x = 2^i \text{ord}(a)x'$ for some $i \geq 0$ and odd λ' and x'. Then $a^{\lambda/2} \equiv a^{\text{ord}(a)\lambda'/2} \equiv a^{\text{ord}(a)/2} \equiv a^{x/2^{i+1}} \pmod{n}$.

12 Public-key Cryptography

12.1.7 The adversary may calculate $h(kxy) = f(M, y)$ for any single block y.

12.1.8 Note that $2pq \mid x_i - x_j$. If, for example, $d = (x_1 - x_2, x_1 - x_3) < n$, then either $2pq$ or $4pq$ has been recovered. Since $n = (2p+1)(2q+1)$, it is then possible to efficiently recover p and q from n and d.

12.2.2 (a) The Euclidean algorithm gives $d = 233$. (b) Algorithm 11.1.7 can be used to show $c = m^e \bmod pq = 921$.

12.2.3 The question may be answered directly by checking the formula for the number of unconcealed messages. More generally, for any RSA modulus $n = pq$, it is easy to show that there is an exponent e with $1 < e < \phi(n)$, $(e, \phi(n)) = 1$, and $m^e \equiv m \pmod{n}$ for all m. Consider $e = 1 + j\phi(n)/(p-1, q-1)$ for some $1 \leq j < (p-1, q-1)$. The exercise is the case $j = (p-1, q-1)/2$.

12.2.4 The system of congruences $x \equiv c_i \pmod{n_i}$ has a solution $x < n_1 n_2 n_3$. Since $m < n_i$, it follows that $x = m^3$. The (integer) cube root of x can be recovered efficiently, giving m. (In the unlikely event that the moduli n_i are not pairwise relatively prime, then a modulus can be factored.)

12.2.6 (a) If $k < 1$, then $1 = ed - k\phi(n) \geq ed$, a contradiction. Since $d < \phi(n)$, it follows that $1 = ed - k\phi(n) < (e-k)\phi(n)$ and $k < e$. (b) $1 = ed - k\phi(n) = ed - k(n-p-q+1)$, so $\frac{kn+1}{e} - d = \frac{k}{e}(p+q-1) < p+q$.

12.2.7 (a) $n - \phi(n) = n - (n-p-q+1) < p+q < 3\sqrt{n}$. (b) $|\frac{e}{n} - \frac{k}{d}| = |\frac{ed-kn}{dn}| < \frac{k(n-\phi(n))}{dn} < \frac{3k}{d\sqrt{n}} < \frac{1}{3d^2}$. (c) Compute the close approximations $\frac{k'}{d'}$ to $\frac{e}{n}$. The candidate d' can be checked by finding ϕ' from $ed' - k'\phi' = 1$ and (if $\phi' \in \mathbb{Z}$) attempting to factor n using Exercise 11.4.10.

12.2.10 If $ed \equiv 1 \pmod{\lambda}$, then $ed \equiv 1 \pmod{p-1}$ and $m^{ed} \equiv m \pmod{p}$. Similarly, $m^{ed} \equiv m \pmod{q}$ and hence $m^{ed} \equiv m \pmod{n}$. Note that $\lambda \mid \phi(n)$, so using λ may result in a smaller d; however, if p and q are chosen at random, then $(p-1, q-1)$ is expected to be small.

12.2.11 (a) The argument is essentially that in 12.2.10. (b) $\lambda = 12$, $\phi(n) = 48$, $\phi(p,q) = 84$, and $\lambda \mid \phi(p,q)$.

12.2.13 Select a message $m > p$ and calculate $c = m^e \bmod n$ as the chosen-ciphertext.

12.4.2 (a) $x = 9$ and $(r, s) = (7, 13)$.

12.5.3 (b) If $e = 1$ is expected, then the choice $X = S$ and $y = 1$ would satisfy the corresponding verification condition, although a transcript from such a session would not look genuine. Instead, consider the case that $X = S^x$ is selected.

12.5.5 (a) Consider the scenario where the adversary intercepts α^a and α^b, replacing each by the value 1.

Bibliography

[1] Derek Atkins, Michael Graff, Arjen K. Lenstra, and Paul C. Leyland. The magic words are squeamish ossifrage. In Josef Pieprzyk and Reihanah Safavi-Naini, editors, *Advances in Cryptology – ASIACRYPT '94*, volume 917 of *Lecture Notes in Computer Science*, pages 263–277. Springer-Verlag, 1995.

[2] Eric Bach. Discrete logarithms and factoring. Technical Report UCB/CSD 84/186, University of California Berkeley, Computer Science Division, June 1984.

[3] Henry Beker and Fred Piper. *Cipher Systems: The Protection of Communication.* J. Wiley & Sons, New York, 1982.

[4] Mihir Bellare and Phillip Rogaway. Optimal asymmetric encryption. In Alfredo De Santis, editor, *Advances in Cryptology – EUROCRYPT '94*, volume 950 of *Lecture Notes in Computer Science*, pages 92–111. Springer-Verlag, 1995. A revised version is available via http://www-cse.ucsd.edu/users/mihir/.

[5] E. R. Berlekamp. *Algebraic Coding Theory*. McGraw-Hill, 1968.

[6] R. E. Blahut. *Theory and Practice of Error Control Codes.* Addison-Wesley, 1983.

[7] I. F. Blake and R. C. Mullin. *An Introduction to Algebraic and Combinatorial Coding Theory*. Academic Press, 1976.

[8] Ian F. Blake, G. Seroussi, and Nigel P. Smart. *Elliptic Curves in Cryptography*, volume 265 of *London Mathematical Society Lecture Note Series*. Cambridge University Press, 1999.

[9] Matt Blaze, Whitfield Diffie, Ronald L. Rivest, Bruce Schneier, Tsutomu Shimomura, Eric Thompson, and Michael Wiener. Minimal key lengths for symmetric ciphers to provide adequate commercial security: A report by an ad hoc group of cryptographers and computer scientists. Available through http://www.bsa.org/, January 1996.

[10] Daniel Bleichenbacher. Generating ElGamal signatures without knowing the secret key. In Maurer [59], pages 10–18. A revised version correct-

ing Corollary 2 is available from the Information Security and Cryptology Research Group, ETH-Zurich, ftp://ftp.inf.ethz.ch.

[11] M. Blum. Coin flipping by telephone: a protocol for solving impossible problems. In *Proceedings of the 24th IEEE Computer Conference (CompCon)*, pages 133–137, 1982.

[12] Dan Boneh. Twenty years of attacks on the RSA cryptosystem. *Notices of the AMS*, 46(2):203–213, February 1999. Available via http://theory.stanford.edu/~dabo/.

[13] Dan Boneh, Richard A. DeMillo, and Richard J. Lipton. On the importance of checking cryptographic protocols for faults. In Fumy [35], pages 37–51. The extended abstract is expanded in "On the importance of eliminating errors in cryptographic computations," available via http://theory.stanford.edu/~dabo/.

[14] Dan Boneh and Glenn Durfee. New results on the cryptanalysis of low exponent RSA. In J. Stern, editor, *Advances in Cryptology – EUROCRYPT '99*, volume 1592 of *Lecture Notes in Computer Science*, pages 1–11. Springer-Verlag, 1999. Available via http://theory.stanford.edu/~dabo/.

[15] Dan Boneh and Ramarathnam Venkatesan. Breaking RSA may be easier than factoring. In K. Nyberg, editor, *Advances in Cryptology – EUROCRYPT '98*, volume 1403 of *Lecture Notes in Computer Science*, pages 59–71. Springer-Verlag, 1998. Available via http://theory.stanford.edu/~dabo/.

[16] Colin Boyd. Enhancing security by data compression: theoretical and practical aspects. In D. W. Davies, editor, *Advances in Cryptology – EUROCRYPT '91*, pages 267–280. Springer-Verlag, 1991.

[17] Gilles Brassard, editor. *Advances in Cryptology – CRYPTO '89*, volume 435 of *Lecture Notes in Computer Science*. Springer-Verlag, 1989.

[18] Gilles Brassard and Claude Crépeau. Sorting out zero-knowledge. In J.-J. Quisquater and J. Vandewalle, editors, *Advances in Cryptology – EUROCRYPT '89*, volume 434 of *Lecture Notes in Computer Science*, pages 181–191. Springer-Verlag, 1990.

[19] David Chaum, Jan-Hendrik Evertse, and Jeroen van de Graaf. An improved protocol for demonstrating possession of discrete logarithms and some generalizations. In David Chaum and Wyn L. Price, editors, *Advances in Cryptology – EUROCRYPT '87*, volume 304 of *Lecture Notes in Computer Science*, pages 127–141. Springer-Verlag, 1988.

[20] David Chaum, Jan-Hendrik Evertse, Jeroen van de Graaf, and René Peralta. Demonstrating possession of a discrete logarithm without revealing it. In Andrew M. Odlyzko, editor, *Advances in Cryptology – CRYPTO*

'86, volume 263 of *Lecture Notes in Computer Science*, pages 200–212. Springer-Verlag, 1987.

[21] Clifford C. Cocks. A note on 'non-secret encryption'. Technical report, Communications Electronics Security Group (CESG), November 1973. Available via http://www.cesg.gov.uk.

[22] Don Coppersmith. Cheating at mental poker. In Williams [98], pages 104–107.

[23] Don Coppersmith. The Data Encryption Standard (DES) and its strength against attacks. *IBM Journal of Research and Development*, 38(3):243–250, May 1994.

[24] Don Coppersmith, Matthew Franklin, Jacques Patarin, and Michael Reiter. Low-exponent RSA with related messages. In Maurer [59], pages 1–9.

[25] Richard A. DeMillo, Georgie I. Davida, David P. Dobkin, Michael A. Harrison, and Richard J. Lipton. *Applied Cryptology, Cryptographic Protocols, and Computer Security Models.* Proceedings of Symposia in Applied Mathematics. American Mathematical Society, Providence, 1983. Lecture notes for the AMS short course *Cryptology in Revolution: Mathematics and Models*, San Francisco, 1981.

[26] Whitfield Diffie. The first ten years of public key cryptography. In Simmons [81], chapter 3, pages 135–175.

[27] Whitfield Diffie and Martin E. Hellman. New directions in cryptography. *IEEE Transactions on Information Theory*, 22(6):644–654, 1976.

[28] Whitfield Diffie and Martin E. Hellman. Exhaustive cryptanalysis of the NBS Data Encryption Standard. *Computer*, 10(6):74–84, June 1977.

[29] Taher ElGamal. A public key cryptosystem and a signature scheme based on discrete logarithms. *IEEE Transactions on Information Theory*, 31(4):469–472, July 1985.

[30] J. H. Ellis. The possibility of secure non-secret digital encryption. Technical report, Communications Electronics Security Group (CESG), January 1970. Available via http://www.cesg.gov.uk.

[31] J. H. Ellis. The history of non-secret encryption. Technical report, Communications Electronics Security Group (CESG), December 1997. Available via http://www.cesg.gov.uk.

[32] David C. Feldmeier and Philip R. Karn. Unix password security—ten years later. In Brassard [17], pages 44–63.

[33] Steven Fortune and Michael Merritt. Poker protocols. In G. R. Blakley and David Chaum, editors, *Advances in Cryptology – CRYPTO '84*, volume 196

of *Lecture Notes in Computer Science*, pages 454–464. Springer-Verlag, 1985.

[34] Electronic Frontier Foundation. *Cracking DES: Secrets of Encryption Research, Wiretap Politics, and Chip Design*. Distributed by O'Reilly and Associates, 1998.

[35] Walter Fumy, editor. *Advances in Cryptology – EUROCRYPT '97*, volume 1233 of *Lecture Notes in Computer Science*. Springer-Verlag, 1997.

[36] R. G. Gallager. *Information Theory and Reliable Communication*. John Wiley and Sons, 1968.

[37] Simson Garfinkel. *PGP: Pretty Good Privacy*. O'Reilly & Associates, 1995.

[38] W. J. Gilbert. *Modern Algebra with Applications*. Wiley, 1976.

[39] Ian Goldberg and David Wagner. Randomness and the Netscape browser. *Dr. Dobb's Journal*, pages 66–70, January 1996.

[40] Shafi Goldwasser, Silvio Micali, and Charles Rackoff. The knowledge complexity of interactive proof systems. *SIAM Journal on Computing*, 18(1):186–208, February 1989.

[41] Martin Handford. *Where's Waldo?* Little, Brown, Boston, 1987.

[42] G. H. Hardy and E. M. Wright. *An Introduction to the Theory of Numbers*. Oxford Clarendon Press, second edition, 1945.

[43] R. Hill. *A First Course in Coding Theory*. Oxford University Press, 1986.

[44] Don Johnson and Alfred Menezes. The Elliptic Curve Digital Signature Algorithm (ECDSA). CORR 99-34, University of Waterloo, Canada, August 1999. Available from http://www.cacr.math.uwaterloo.ca.

[45] D. S. Jones. *Elementary Information Theory*. Oxford University Press, 1979.

[46] Antoine Joux and Reynald Lercier. State-of-the-art in implementing algorithms for the (ordinary) discrete logarithm problem. The 3rd workshop on Elliptic Curve Cryptography (ECC '99), University of Waterloo, http://www.cacr.math.uwaterloo.ca, November 1–3 1999.

[47] Marc Joye, Arjen K. Lenstra, and Jean-Jacques Quisquater. Chinese remaindering based cryptosystems in the presence of faults. *Journal of Cryptology*, 12(4):241–245, Autumn 1999.

[48] David Kahn. *The Codebreakers: The Story of Secret Writing*. Scribner, New York, revised edition, 1996.

[49] Joe Kilian and Phillip Rogaway. How to protect DES against exhaustive key search. In Koblitz [51], pages 252–267. Available via http://www.cs.ucdavis.edu/~rogaway/; a summary appears in [73].

[50] Neal Koblitz. *A Course in Number Theory and Cryptography*. Springer, second edition, 1994.

[51] Neal Koblitz, editor. *Advances in Cryptology – CRYPTO '96*, volume 1109 of *Lecture Notes in Computer Science*. Springer-Verlag, 1996.

[52] Paul Kocher, Joshua Jaffe, and Benjamin Jun. Differential power analysis. In Michael Wiener, editor, *Advances in Cryptology – CRYPTO '99*, volume 1666 of *Lecture Notes in Computer Science*, pages 388–397. Springer-Verlag, 1999.

[53] Paul C. Kocher. Timing attacks on implementations of Diffie-Hellman, RSA, DSS, and other systems. In Koblitz [51], pages 105–113.

[54] B. A. LaMacchia and A. M. Odlyzko. Computation of discrete logarithms in prime fields. *Designs, Codes and Cryptography*, 1(1):47–62, May 1991.

[55] Arjen K. Lenstra and Eric R. Verheul. Selecting cryptographic key sizes. The 3rd workshop on Elliptic Curve Cryptography (ECC '99), University of Waterloo, http://www.cacr.math.uwaterloo.ca, November 1–3 1999.

[56] R. Lidl and H. Neiderreiter. *Finite Fields*. Cambridge University Press, 1984.

[57] S. Lin and D. J. Costello, Jr. *Error Control Coding: Fundamentals and Applications*. Prentice-Hall, 1983.

[58] F. J. MacWilliams and J. J. A. Sloane. *The Theory of Error-Correcting Codes*. North-Holland, 1977.

[59] Ueli Maurer, editor. *Advances in Cryptology – EUROCRYPT '96*, volume 1070 of *Lecture Notes in Computer Science*. Springer-Verlag, 1996.

[60] R. J. McEliece. *The Theory of Information and Coding*. Addison-Wesley, 1977.

[61] R. J. McEliece. *Finite Fields for Computer Scientists and Engineers*. Kluwer Academic Publishers, 1987.

[62] Alfred J. Menezes. *Elliptic Curve Public Key Cryptosystems*, volume 234 of *Kluwer international series in engineering and computer science*. Kluwer Academic Publishers, 1993.

[63] Alfred J. Menezes, Paul C. van Oorschot, and Scott A. Vanstone. *Handbook of Applied Cryptography*. CRC Press, Boca Raton, 1996. Errata and a complete on-line copy of the book are available on http://www.cacr.math.uwaterloo.ca/hac/.

[64] J. H. Moore. Protocol failures in cryptosystems. In Simmons [81], chapter 11, pages 541–558.

[65] Moni Naor, Yael Naor, and Omer Reingold. Applied kid cryptography, or how to convince your children that you are not cheating. CRYPTO '98 rump session, August 1998.

[66] W. W. Peterson and E. J. Weldon, Jr. *Error-Correcting Codes*. MIT Press, 1972.

[67] V. Pless. *Introduction to the Theory of Error-Correcting Codes*. Wiley, 1982.

[68] Jean-Jacques Quisquater, Louis Guillou, and Tom Berson. How to explain zero-knowledge protocols to your children. In Brassard [17], pages 628–631.

[69] M. O. Rabin. Digitalized signatures and public-key functions as intractable as factorization. Technical Report 212, MIT Laboratory for Computer Science, 1979.

[70] Rick Ramsey. *All About Administering NIS+*. SunSoft, second edition, 1994.

[71] Ronald L. Rivest. Cryptography. In van Leeuwen [91], pages 719–755.

[72] Ronald L. Rivest and Adi Shamir. How to expose an eavesdropper. *Communications of the ACM*, 27(4):393–395, April 1984.

[73] Phillip Rogaway. The security of DESX. *CryptoBytes*, 2(2):8–11, Summer 1996. RSA Laboratories newsletter, http://www.rsa.com. The article is a summary of [49].

[74] Kenneth H. Rosen. *Elementary Number Theory and its Applications*. Addison-Wesley, third edition, 1993.

[75] Arto Salomaa. *Public-Key Cryptography*. Texts in theoretical computer science. Springer-Verlag, second edition, 1996.

[76] Bruce Schneier. *Applied Cryptography: protocols, algorithms, and source code in C*. John Wiley & Sons, Inc., second edition, 1996.

[77] Jennifer Seberry and Josef Pieprzyk. *Cryptography: an introduction to computer security*. Prentice Hall, 1989.

[78] Adi Shamir. RSA for paranoids. *CryptoBytes*, 1(3):1–4, Autumn 1995. RSA Laboratories newsletter, http://www.rsa.com.

[79] Adi Shamir, Ronald L. Rivest, and Leonard M. Adleman. Mental poker. In David A. Klarner, editor, *The Mathematical Gardner*, pages 37–43. Prindle, Weber, and Schmidt, Boston, 1981.

[80] C. E. Shannon. A mathematical theory of communication. *Bell System Technical Journal*, 27:379–423 and 623–56, 1948.

[81] G.J. Simmons, editor. *Contemporary Cryptology: the science of information integrity*. IEEE Press, 1992.

[82] Gustavus J. Simmons. The prisoners' problem and the subliminal channel. In David Chaum, editor, *Advances in Cryptology – CRYPTO '83*, pages 51–67, New York, 1984. Plenum Press.

[83] Gustavus J. Simmons. The subliminal channel and digital signatures. In Thomas Beth, Norbert Cot, and Ingemar Ingemarsson, editors, *Advances in Cryptology – EUROCRYPT '84*, volume 209 of *Lecture Notes in Computer Science*, pages 364–378. Springer-Verlag, 1985.

[84] Gustavus J. Simmons. Subliminal channels; past and present. *European Transactions on Telecommunications*, 5(4):459–473, July-August 1994.

[85] Gustavus J. Simmons. Subliminal communication is easy using the DSA. In Tor Helleseth, editor, *Advances in Cryptology – EUROCRYPT '93*, volume 765 of *Lecture Notes in Computer Science*, pages 218–232. Springer-Verlag, 1994.

[86] Douglas R. Stinson. *Cryptography: Theory and Practice*. CRC Press, Boca Raton, Florida, 1995.

[87] Robert Sugarman. On foiling computer crime. *IEEE Spectrum*, 16(7):31–32, July 1979. This is the first of a series of articles: Martin E. Hellman, DES will be totally insecure within ten years, 32–39; Security Agency denies tampering with DES, National Security Agency, 39; George I. Davida, Hellman's scheme breaks DES in its basic form, National Science Foundation, 39; Walter Tuchman, Hellman presents no shortcut solutions to the DES, 40–41; Dennis Branstad, Hellman's data does not support his conclusion, National Bureau of Standards, 41.

[88] Bradley Taylor and David Goldberg. Secure networking in the Sun environment. Technical Report 905, Sun Microsystems, January 1991.

[89] A. Tietäväinen. On the nonexistence of perfect codes over finite fields. *SIAM Journal on Applied Mathematics*, 24:88–96, 1973.

[90] Malcolm Turnbull. *The Spycatcher Trial: the scandal behind the #1 best seller*. Salem House Publishers, 1989. See [101].

[91] J. van Leeuwen, editor. *Handbook of Theoretical Computer Science*. Elsevier Science Publishers, 1990.

[92] J. H. van Lint. *Introduction to Coding Theory*. Springer-Verlag, 1982.

[93] Michael Wiener. Efficient DES key search. In W. Stallings, editor, *Practical Cryptography for Data Internetworks*, pages 31–79. IEEE Computer Society Press, 1996. Reprinted from Crypto 93 rump session.

[94] Michael Wiener. Efficient DES key search—an update. In *Cracking DES* [34], chapter 11, pages 1–4.

[95] Michael J. Wiener. Cryptanalysis of short RSA secret exponents. *IEEE Transactions on Information Theory*, 36(3):553–558, May 1990.

[96] H. C. Williams. A modification of the RSA public-key encryption procedure. *IEEE Transactions on Information Theory*, 26(6):726–729, November 1980.

[97] H. C. Williams. An M^3 public-key encryption scheme. In Williams [98], pages 358–368.

[98] Hugh C. Williams, editor. *Advances in Cryptology – CRYPTO '85*, volume 218 of *Lecture Notes in Computer Science*. Springer-Verlag, 1985.

[99] Malcolm J. Williamson. Non-secret encryption using a finite field. Technical report, Communications Electronics Security Group (CESG), January 1974. Available via http://www.cesg.gov.uk.

[100] Malcolm J. Williamson. Thoughts on cheaper non-secret encryption. Technical report, Communications Electronics Security Group (CESG), August 1976. Available via http://www.cesg.gov.uk.

[101] Peter Wright. *Spycatcher: the candid autobiography of a senior intelligence officer*. Viking, New York, 1987. See also [90].

[102] Adam Young and Moti Yung. The dark side of "black-box" cryptography, or: should we trust Capstone. In Koblitz [51], pages 89–103.

[103] Adam Young and Moti Yung. Kleptography: using cryptography against cryptography. In Fumy [35], pages 62–74.

[104] Philip R. Zimmermann. *The Official PGP User's Guide*. MIT Press, Cambridge, Massachusetts, 1995.

[105] V. Zinoviev and V. Leontiev. The nonexistence of perfect codes over Galois fields. *Problems of Control and Information Theory*, 2(2):16–24, 1973.

Index